GW00762039

THE
ANTI-IMPERIALIST
READER

THE
ANTI-IMPERIALIST
READER

A Documentary History
of Anti-Imperialism
in the United States

VOLUME II
The Literary
Anti-Imperialists

EDITED BY
Philip S. Foner

HM

HOLMES & MEIER PUBLISHERS, INC.
New York • London

"Harry Wilmans," from Edgar Lee Masters, *Spoon River Anthology* (New York: Macmillan, 1916) quoted by permission of Ellen C. Masters.

"The Quarry" appeared in William Vaughn Moody, *Poems* (Boston: Houghton Mifflin, 1901).

First published in the United States of America 1986 by
Holmes & Meier Publishers, Inc.
30 Irving Place
New York, N.Y. 10003

Great Britain:
Holmes & Meier Publishers Ltd.
Pindar Road
Hoddesdon, Hertfordshire EN 11 OHF

Copyright © 1986 by Phillip S. Foner
All rights reserved

Library of Congress Cataloging-in-Publication Data
(Revised for vol. 2)
Main entry under title:

The Anti-imperialist reader.

    Includes bibliographical references and indexes.
    Contents: v. 1. From the Mexican War to the election of 1900. — v. 2. The literary anti-imperialists.
    1. Anti-imperialist movements—United States—History—Sources.   2. United States—Territorial expansion—Sources.   3. United States—Foreign relations— · Sources.   I. Foner, Philip Sheldon, 1910– II. Winchester, Richard C.
E179.5.A57   1984   973   327.73   83-10854
ISBN   0-8419-0768-4 (v. 1)
ISBN   0-8419-0769-2 (v. 2)

Manufactured in the United States of America

The Anti-imperialist reader.

To Elizabeth, Laura, Kim, and Steven

TABLE OF CONTENTS

PREFACE

Historians have recently published more books and articles than ever before about the anti-imperialist crusade that accompanied and followed the war between the United States and Spain in 1898.[1] In all these works, however, the authors have slighted the significant issue of the role played by and contributed to the American anti-imperialist movement by the leading literary figures of the period. Indeed, apart from a handful of books, scholarly articles, and three unpublished dissertations, this aspect of American anti-imperialism has been totally neglected.[2]

It is the purpose of the present volume to restore the literary anti-imperialists to the place in our history and literature that they deserve, and, at the same time, make available the major portion of their literary contributions in a single volume.

Certain derogatory references to blacks by anti-imperialist writers have been included because they are usually put into the mouths of the champions of imperialism, and reflect the racism of the period.

The present volume is the second in the series, The Anti-Imperialist Reader" A Documentary History of Anti-Imperialism in the United States. Originally scheduled to be volume III in the series, it has been advanced to volume II because it adds substantially to the material already published in the first volume.

A large number of institutions gave me considerable assistance by enabling me to use their facilities. I wish to thank the staffs of the Library of Congress; National Archives; Bancroft Library, University of California, Berkeley; University of Chicago; University of California, Los Angeles; University of Pittsburg; New York University; University of Pennsylvania; Historical Society of Pennsylvania; Harvard University; Boston Public Library; New York Public Library; Columbia University; Library Company of Philadelphia; Lincoln University, Pennsylvania; and University of Maine, Farmington.

I wish to thank Professor Richard C. Winchester, my excellent collaborator on The American Anti-Imperialist Reader: A Documentary History of Anti-Imperialism in the United States for reading the manuscript and making valuable suggestions.

Philip S. Foner

Professor Emeritus of History
Lincoln University, Pennsylvania

June, 1985

ix

1. The books include: Robert L. Beisner, Twelve against
Empire: The Anti-Imperialists, 1898-1900 (New York, 1968);
Daniel B. Schirmer, Republic or Empire: American Resistance to
the Philippine War (Morristown, N.J., 1972); E. Berkeley
Tompkins, Anti-Imperialism in the United States: The Great
Debate, 1899-1920 (Philadelphia, 1970); I. Dementyev, USA:
Imperialists and Anti-Imperialists: The Great Debate at the Turn
of the Century (Moscow, 1979); Richard E. Welch, Jr., Response to
Imperialism: The United States and the Philippine-American War,
1899-1902 (Chapel Hill, North Carolina, 1979).
    The articles include: Richard E. Welch, Jr., "Motives and
Policy Objectives of Anti-Imperialists, 1898," Mid-America
51(1969): 119-29; John M. Gates, "Philippine Guerrillas, American
Anti-Imperialists and the Election of 1900," Pacific Historical
Review 46(February, 1977): 51-64; Willard B. Gatwood, Jr., "Black
Americans and the Quest for Empire, 1898-1903," Journal of
Southern History 38(1972): 545-66.

2. The books are: Philip S. Foner, Mark Twain: Social
Critic (New York, 1958), and Roger J. Bresnahan, compiler, In
Time of Hesitation: American Anti-Imperialists and the Philippine-
American War (Quezon City, Philippines, 1981); the articles are:
Fred Harvey Harrington, "Literary Aspects of American
Anti-Imperialism, 1898-1902," New England Quarterly 10(1937):
640-56; Thomas Arthur Gullason, "Stephen Crane:
Anti-Imperialist," American Literature 30(May, 1958): 235-32;
William M. Gibson, "Mark Twain and Howells: Anti-Imperialists,"
New England Quarterly 20(December, 1977): 430-49; Perry E.
Gianakos, "Ernest Howard Crosby: A Forgotten Tolstoyan
Antimilitarist and Anti-imperialist," in Charles Chatfield,
editor, Peace Movements in America (New York, 1978), pp. 1-19;
Perry E. Gianakos, "The Spanish-American War and the Double
Paradox of the Negro American," Phylon 12(Spring, 1965): 32-49;
Perry E. Gianakos, "George Ade's Critique of Benevolent
Assimilation," Diplomatic History 7(Summer, 1983): 223-38; Hunt
Hawkins, "Mark Twain's Involvement with the Congo Reform
Movement: 'A Fury of Generous Indignation,'" New England
Quarterly 51(June, 1978): 147-75; Heimbrecht Breinig, "Mark
Twain-Anti-Imperialist?" Gulliver (Deutsch-Englische Jahrbucher)
9(1981): 178-98. The unpublished dissertations are: William M.
Gibson, "Mark Twain and William Dean Howells, Anti-Imperialists,"
Unpublished Ph.D. dissertation, University of Chicago, 1940;
Perry E. Gianakos, "The Yanko-Spanko War: Our War with Spain in
American Fiction," Unpublished Ph.D. dissertation, New York
University, 1961; and Howard Spierer, "Mark Twain and
Anti-Imperialism," Unpublished M.A. thesis, Columbia University,
1968; Rober J. Bresnahan, "The Literature of the Spanish-American
War: An Anti-Imperialist Anthology," Unpublished Ph.D.
dissertation, University of Massachusetts, 1974.

INTRODUCTION

By Philip S. Foner

INTRODUCTION

On February 4, 1899, shots were exchanged between American and Filipino patrols on the outskirts of Manila, and the war for the conquest of the Philippines was on. This "war of conquest," as Walter Millis wrote, "was to flicker on for several years, which was to cost us as much in life and effort as the whole of the war with Spain, and which was to repeat in a kind of grotesque analogy almost everything which we had charged against the Spaniards since the 1895 outbreak in Cuba." The reference was to the brutality of American military forces in the Philippines. Reports from the islands, including letters from American soldiers, told of the Filipinos being rounded up and placed in concentration camps, of whole villages being wiped out, of prisoners of war being subjected to the "water cure" or shot down in cold blood, and of other tactics which made the charges of the United States against Spain's policy in Cuba seem mild indeed. And all this was supposedly for the purpose "of extending Christian civilization to the Filipinos." The nature of this "civilizing" was reflected in an American Army ballad which went:

> Damn, damn the Filipinos
> Cross-eyed Kakiack ladrones
> Underneath our starry flag, civilize 'em with a Krag,
> And return us to our beloved homes.

The "war of conquest" took 41 months. Before it was over, 126,500 Americans saw service in the Philippines, and their army suffered battle losses of over 4,200 men killed and over 2,600 wounded. The Filipinos suffered battle losses of 16,000 to 20,000 men killed, while famine and disease accounted for the death of as many as 200,000 Filipino civilians.

Despite the length and cost of this war of imperial conquest, it had received comparatively little attention from American historians. Usually labeled "the Philippine Insurrection,"[1] it is characterized in most textbooks as an unfortunate epilogue to the Spanish-American War, a minor incident in America's assumption of world power. Little attention has been paid to the opposition that emerged in the United States to the military subjugation of the Filipinos, and even less has been paid to the literary expression of this opposition.

With rare exceptions, the writers whose works are studied and presented in the present collection, had at first accepted the war with Spain as a crusade for liberation, and many had favored that the United States should use force to free Cuba. That their country would betray this mission and embark on an imperialist career was unthinkable. (Most had evidently learned little about the Mexican War of 1846-48.) So when McKinley made clear the imperialist course the United States would follow, they were shocked and bitter. Many decided to toss aside their usual reliance on gentility and pour out their hatred of the betrayal in bitter poetry, sardonic satire, and, in a few instances, sharply-worded fiction.

In Gertrude Atherton's 1900 novel, Senator North, the anti-war heroine Betty Madison states that "so false is the sentiment (of the war against Spain) that it will not inspire one great patriotic poem, nor even one of merit. . . ." William Dean Howells, America's leading man of letters, agreed. "No good can come from war," he wrote in May, 1899. "It can inspire nothing that is worthy in war or literature."[2]

In actuality, there did emerge an important body of literature after the war with Spain. For from the first, the anti-imperialist movement attracted the leading men of letters in the United States, including at least twenty men of national reputation: Charles Francis Adams, George Ade, Thomas Bailey Aldrich, Ambrose Bierce, Gamaliel Bradford, Hezekah Butterworth, George W. Cable, John White Chadwick, John Jay Chapman, Stephen Crane, Ernest Howard Crosby, Finley Peter Dunne, Henry Blake Fuller, Hamlin Garland, William Lloyd Garrison, E. L. Godkin, Thomas Wentworth Higginson, William Dean Howells, Edgar Lee Masters, Joaquin Miller, William Vaughn Moody, Charles Eliot Norton, Bliss Perry, Edgar Arlington Robinson, Lincoln Steffens, Mark Twain, Charles Dudley Warner.[3] Among the supporters of American imperialism were only a half-dozen poets and authors of note: Julia Ward Howe, Bliss Carman, Richard Hovey, Gertrude Atherton (anti-war in her novel Senator North, but later an imperialist), Brooks Adams, Julian Hawthorne. These six writers offered some poetry and prose in behalf of American imperialism. The anti-imperialist writers, on the other hand, were both numerous and prolific. One scholar views it "as significant and a little surprising that with so few exceptions American poets and novelists sided with the anti-imperialists, and that many of them were active members of the Anti-Imperialist Leagues in Boston, New York, Washington, Chicago, and other American cities."[4]

The nature of the involvement of these writers in the anti-imperialist movement varied. Some were vigorous proponents of the cause: Hamlin Garland was active in the Chicago branch of the American Anti-Imperialist League; William Dean Howells and Mark Twain were honorary vice-presidents of the New York Anti-Imperialist League, and Ernest Howard Crosby was its president. John Chadwick was also one of the vice-presidents of the New York league. Some American authors, Thomas Aldrich, to name one, were anti-imperialists, but wrote nothing to denounce imperialism. Some scholars have attributed this small literary activity on the part of several anti-imperialist writers to the difficulties of getting such literary output published. As a rule, the leading literary-political journals--Harper's Magazine, Century Magazine, Atlantic Monthly, and the North American Review--did not open their columns to articles attacking U.S. foreign policy unless the author was too important to be ignored. Anti-imperialist writings appeared usually in relatively small journals like the Arena, the Dial, City and State, and The Nation, and in the general newspapers which opposed imperialism, especially the Springfield Republican.[5]

Anti-imperialist poets served as their own publishers, and saw their verses distributed as addenda to tracts of the Anti-Imperialist League, but a few published their poems in contemporary newspapers and magazines. The Springfield Republican observed that "as the anti-slavery poets had but few outlets in the press, so it has been with the anti-imperialist poets, who are in the same line of the inspiration of God against the devils of greed and oppression."[6] This was written to hail the appearance of the Liberty Poems Inspired by the Crisis of 1898-1900, the anthology of anti-imperialist verse published by the New England Anti-Imperialist League. The volume included 75 poems by 50 poets from all parts of the United States plus two or three poems by English poets whose poems fitted the American anti-imperialist cause. Several poems were unsigned or signed only by initials. The thirteen sonnets of William Lloyd Garrison was the largest selection representing a single poet.

On August 13, 1898, Samuel Gompers, president of the American Federation of Labor, wrote to Ed O'Donnell of Boston:

> . . . I am neither a poet nor a rhymster, but the thought occurred to me that there is a subject now for a pretty good labor poem. As a result of the present war with Spain, Hawaii has been annexed, Porto Rico will be ceded and the Philippines are hanging in the balance. . . .
> When in some leisure hour, you are courting the muse, why not dash off some lines upon it.[7]

While there is no labor poet who was part of the literary anti-imperialist movement, the labor press did occasionally publish anti-imperialist poetry. The poem "Aguinaldo," by Thomas Fleming Day, in praise of the Filipino patriot leader was written especially for the Coast Seamen's Journal, the official organ of the Sailor's Union of the Pacific, and published in its issue of May 14, 1899. The following poem by the popular poet Ella Wheeler Wilcox, directed against the seizure of the Philippines, was featured in the Journal of the Metal Polishers and Buffers:

> Goddess of Liberty, answer!
> How can the slaves of Spain
> Find freedom under your banner
> While your own still wear the chain?

> Loud is the screech of your eagle
> And boastful the voice of your drums,
> But they do not silence the will of despair
> That rise out of your slums.
> What will you do with your conquest,
>   And how shall your hosts be fed,
> While your streets are filled with desperate throngs
>   Crying for work or bread?[8]

On the other hand, there were few Socialists among the literary anti-imperialists. The Socialists saw the dispute between the imperialists and anti-imperialists as a struggle between small and large business groups, between half-bankrupt capitalists and trusts, "a dispute in which the Socialists had no stake." In the presidential election of 1900, the Socialists insisted that "from the point of view of the working class, expansion is not worth talking about." Hence neither the Socialist Labor Party nor the Social Democratic Party had a foreign policy platform. "What is the paramount issue of the campaign?" asked the Workers' Call on behalf of the SLP? It answered: "McKinley says: Sound money, expansion, and prosperity. Bryan says: Imperialism. The Socialist says, as working men that it is whether they shall continue to be wage slaves."[9] Eugene V. Debs, the Social Democratic Party's presidential candidate, virtually ignored the Philippines during the campaign, and insisted that such issues as "imperialism" and "expansion" "do not concern the working class."[10]

This attitude continued after the 1900 campaign. When Debs ran for president in 1904, this time as the candidate of the Socialist Party of America, he asserted that the issue of imperialism and anti-imperialism concerned only the capitalists. "They [the workingmen] know by experience and observation that . . . imperialism and anti-imperialism, mean capitalist rule and wage-slavery."[11] Most Socialists viewed the anti-imperialist crusade as merely a side show to the class struggle at home. Hence while we do find an occasional anti-imperialist poem such as "Imperialist Hymn," in the Socialist Appeal to Reason,[12] it amounted to very little in the output of anti-imperialist poetry.

Many of the anti-imperialist poems have been called "more effective as propaganda than as poetry,"[13] but even these critics acknowledged that several demonstrated an aptitude for imagery as well as anger, and two works of William Vaughn Moody are considered to be "among the finest narrative poems in American literature."[14] Moody's "An Ode in Time of Hesitation" was composed in Boston during the winter of 1899-1900. "The 'ode,'" writes Martin Halpern, "is simultaneously a poem of protest and a celebration. What it protests against is the corruption of America's national ideals; what it celebrates is those ideals themselves as symbolized chiefly by the Civil War hero Robert Gould Shaw, the young and high-born New England colonel who had died while leading the first Negro regiment of the Union army in an attack on Fort Wagner in July 1863, and had been buried in a common grave with the former slaves whom he commanded."[15]

Moody himself explained that the ode was written "after seeing at Boston the statue of Robert Gould Shaw, killed while storming Fort Wagner . . . at the head of the first enlisted Negro regiment, the 54th Massachusetts." The Ode begins with a reference to the "glories" of the Civil War and a laudatory picture of the continental United States. The purpose was to set forth a comparison between a war of liberation and a war of subjugation such as that against the Filipinos, who oppose U.S. annexation. Moody does this effectively by using the record of the famous 54th Massachusetts black regiment. Turning to the Philippines, Moody acknowledges his sense of shame, his incredulity at the thought of the United States crushing the revolt of a people desiring the very liberty and self-government Americans had long treasured as the "loftiest heritage."

> Alas! what sounds are these that come
> Sullenly over the Pacific Seas,--
> Sounds of ignoble battle, striking dumb
> The season's half-awakened ecstacies?. . . .

> Lies! lies! It cannot be! The wars we wage
> Are noble, and our battles still are won
> By justice for us, ere we lift the gage.
> We have not sold our loftiest heritage
> The proud republic hath not stooped to cheat
> And scramble in the market place of war;
> Her forehead weareth yet its solemn star.

> Ah no!
> We have not fallen so.
> We are our father's sons: let those who lead us know
> 'Twas only yesterday sick Cuba's cry
> Came up the tropic wind, 'now help us for we die!'

Still expressing his amazement, Moody refers with scorn to the imperialists, "our fluent men of place and consequence," with "their dull commercial liturgies." Then, following an eloquent lament for the "eager boys" who gave their lives for the sake of Cuban freedom, he points to the glorious example of Shaw and his black regiment. Moody concludes with a note of warning for the McKinley Administration. "For," he thunders, "save we let the island men go free."

> Then on your guiltier head
> Shall our intolerable self-disdain
> Wreak suddenly its anger and its pain:
> For manifest in that disastrous light
> We shall discern the right
> And do it tardily,--O ye who lead,
> Take heed!
> Blindness we may forgive, but baseness we will smite.[16]

Moody's "ode" appeared in the Atlantic Monthly in May, 1900. Bliss Perry, editor of the Atlantic, had been hesitant about publishing the poem because of its sharp attack on McKinley's foreign policy, but he was finally convinced by the quality of the ode, which he felt was "the finest American political poem of thirty years." The ode was joyously received in anti-imperialist circles, and Oswald Garrison Villard, editor of the New York Evening Post and the Nation, later recalled the "sensation it created around the country." Senator Hoar introduced many of his anti-imperialist speeches with extracts from the ode, declaring it "the strongest utterance since Lowell's 'Ode to Freedom.'" In the summer of 1900, Moody's ode occupied a prominent place in the Liberty Poems, and Edmund Stedman in the process of completing his An American Anthology, decided to include a large portion of the ode in the section devoted to the works of America's new, young writers.[17]

Less than a year later, Moody published what was the most elegaic of all the anti-imperialist poems. A number of authors had sought to distinguish between the organizers of the Philippine policy and their soldier instruments, but none did it so effectively as Moody in his poem "On a Soldier Fallen in the Philippines." A soldier has been killed in Luzon while acting under orders to shoot down the Filipino guerrillas, and destroy their hopes of self-government. Moody advised America to honor the soldier killed fighting the Filipino insurgents, even though they died taking away a people's liberty, and, by doing so, endangered the future of American institutions:

Toll! let him never guess
What work we set him to.
Laurel, laurel, yes;
He did what we bade him to.
Praise, and never a whispered hint but the
fight he fought was good;
Never a work that the blood on his sword was his country's
own hearts'--blood.[18]

In "The Quarry" on the other hand, Moody turns from a poem of protest against the imperialist policy of the McKinley Adminitration to a poem of praise for what he naively believes is the anti-imperialism of Secretary of State John Hay's "Open Door Policy" in the Chinese crisis of 1899 and 1900. The crisis arose when the "Boxers" rose up in China against the territorial encroachments upon their country by foreign imperialists, and the division of the thirteen richest, most populous, and most desirable of the eighteen Chinese provinces into "spheres of influence." War was the imperialists' answer to the attempt of the Chinese people to keep their country for themselves. In June, 1900, an international fleet bombarded and captured the Taku forts, which commanded the approach to Peking, and the American Admiral Kempff cooperated in the attack. Some 18,000 international troops of eight powers, including 2,000 American soldiers, attacked China, plundering the country, executed leaders of the anti-imperialist movement, and imposed a humiliating treaty of peace. The dismemberment of China continued. France took Annam and Tonkin, later to be called French Indochina; Britain took Burma; Russia took Port Arthur; Japan took Korea; and Germany reserved Shantung province as its "sphere of influence," and took twelve miles of territory. Although the United States took no territory, American imperialism gained control of important sections of China's economic resources through numerous consortiums, or loans under usurious conditions, forced upon China by international bankers, among whom those from the United States were most prominent.[19]

In his "open door" statement, U.S. Secretary of State John Hay urged the adherence of all powers with interests in China to a doctrine of equal economic access to all Chinese areas. The statement was clearly economically self-serving, especially when one considers that Hay was, to a degree, prompted by visions of economic expansion stimulated by the recent conquest of the Philippines. But as Moody saw it, Hay had prevented the imperialist governments of England, France, Russia, Germany, and Japan from totally dividing up China while the United States had made it possible for the Chinese to build a society based on modern economic and political reforms. Hay had thus redeemed to no small extent the evil of U.S. imperialism elsewhere in the Far East.[20]

Moody portrays this in "The Quarry" by the use of an allegorical animal fable in which an elephant, representing China, is about to be attacked by a group of rapacious "birds of prey," the imperialist powers, when they are suddenly repulsed by an eagle--the United States. That the eagle plays this anti-imperialist role comes as a surprise to Moody. For when it first flies above the elephant as it is surrounded by the imperialist beasts ready for the kill, he fears it will repeat its role in the Philippines and join the murderous crew:

Just as they gathered stomach for the leap,
The sun was darkened, and wide-balanced wings
Beat downward on the trade-wind from the sea.
A wheel of shadow sped along the fields
And o'er the dreaming cities. Suddenly
My heart misgave me, and I cried aloud,
"Alas! What dost thou here? What dost thou here?"[21]

But to his surprise and joy, the eagle drives off the attackers and proves that the "trade winds" that bore the bird from the United States, in the case of China, bring freedom and not domination. The poem ends with the eagle flying off "Crying a word I could not understand." Clearly there was much about American imperialism Moody did not understand. Like many honest anti-imperialists, he did not fully grasp the underlying economic and materialist forces in the policy of the "New American Empire."[22]

No such confusion is present in Henry Blake Fuller. Furious at President McKinley's imperialistic policy and unwilling to be dazzled by the seemingly benevolent outer sheen of the "Open Door Policy," Fuller issued The New Flag: Satires, a pamphlet of sixty pages. So savage was the satire that even though Fuller had already published four novels in Chicago, and was viewed as an outstanding literary figure in America's Midwest, no publisher would touch The New Flag, and he was forced to finance its publication.[23]

The poem opens with a quotation from Abraham Lincoln asserting that no man may rightfully govern another without his consent. This is followed by a prose introduction which sets the temper of the satire:

> "Who will haul down the flag?" McKinley says, and in the pose of a righteous defender of our glorious banner, glorious still in spite of him, he waits for Congress to make reply. More properly he should have said, Who has hauled down the flag, the American flag, and put up the Pirates' in its stead?
>
> "And if we were to answer the question rightly, we should say, You have, William McKinley, You hauled down our flag when you hauled down our principles."

The flag has become a pirate's flag, continues Fuller, because "you have embraced a pirate's principles. . . . And the sooner you haul it down the better for you."

In the same prose introduction, the imperialists are pictured as hogs:

> This is not the age of romance, of the lofty but illogical lion, but of the practical hog . . . . A lion eats when he is hungry and so far as he is a good Imperialist; but he stops there. When a hog satisfies his hunger he has only begun. After the needs of nature becomes Benevolent Assimilation--duty seconds appetite--his higher nature comes in (or rather out). He considers what he owes to the world and so he goes right on eating and so does the Imperialist.[24]

Fuller assailed the imperialists by name. He reserved his special venom for men like Mark Hanna and William McKinley. Here is what he writes about Hanna, the Cleveland traction magnate, who, with the ample assistance of monopoly capitalists, put McKinley into the presidency in 1896:

> Him the plutocrat, behold,
> Panoplied in glittering gold,
> Man in form, in soul a beast,
> Hyena-headed, Hanna faced,
> On an elephant raised high
> Sharp against the coal black sky.
>
> Grinning, coarsely fleshed and gross
> Following a mighty cross,
> Nailed upon whose either side

Hangs a Malay crucified--
Which some Christians, over-civil
Carry to oblige the Devil.

Next, to pulsing pipes and drums
See the toad-shaped Idol comes;
Of Destiny the second son,
A sorry shade of number one . . .
This servile Caliban of Fate
Rides throned upon the Ship of State,
(Monopoly's expensive float,
Modeled on the Federal boat) . . .

Hail! Jove with all the coward thunder!
Last in the fight but first to plunder!
Thou sutler in the place of chief!
Thou magic word twixt thief and thief! . . .[25]

Here is what he said of President McKinley:

Thou sweating chattel slave to swine!
Who dost befoul the holy shrine
Of liberty with murder!
What canting lines can save thee now,
Red-handed as thou are, thy knife
Drinking the struggling patriots' life!
What shame can reach thy soddened heart
In shame, blood scarlet as thou art!
Who for coral bead or rattle
'Gainst unarmed babes doth march to battle!
Calling with sanctimonious face
On Gold to sanction thy disgrace!
May he inflict on thee again
The curse of thine own brother Cain.[26]

The reference to "calling with sanctimonious face on God" is
to the well-publicized statement by McKinley to a group of
ministers that at first he had thought of retaining only Manila
in the Philippines for the United States, then Luzon. After much
prayer, God helped him to reach a correct decision. He could not
turn the Philippines over to another power--"that would be bad
business and discreditable;" he could not leave them to
themselves, for they were unfit for self-rule. "There was
nothing left for us to do but to take them all, and to educate
the Filipinos and uplift and civilize and Christianize them."
Then he thanked God, went to sleep, and slept soundly.[27]

In his complete "Administration Alphabet," Fuller again
refers sardonically to McKinley's relation to the Almighty in the
interest of imperialism:

G is for Guns that McKinly has sent
To teach Filipinos what Jesus Christ meant.
G--Gospel of Guns.[28]

Fuller described Theodore Roosevelt, the "Rough Rider" and ardent imperialist as follows:

I'm a cut and thrusting bronco-busting
Megaphone of Mars.
And it's fire I breathe and I cut my teeth
On nails and wrought-iron bars.

Of General E.S. Otis, in command at Manila, Fuller wrote bitterly:

'Tis Butcher Otis and his men,
Fresh from the Philippine slaughter pen.
Our Weyler who out-Weylers Weyler
And viler, if there is a viler.
Whose coward warfare naught respects
Nor prisoners nor the female sex.[29]

All of Fuller's readers knew that the reference to Weyler was to Valierono Weyler, whose "Reconcentrado" policies in Cuba had been denounced in the American press and on the floors of Congress as particularly inhuman and atrocious. With reports from the Philippines of even worse concentration camps set up by American military commanders, Fuller decided to give vent to his rage in describing Otis.

Evidently the anti-imperialists felt squeamish about Fuller's bitter attacks. In the Liberty Poems, published by the New England Anti-Imperialist League, there are no excerpts from Fuller's The New Flag. This attitude has persisted to the present day with rarely an exception. In his New England Quarterly article of 1937, "Literary Aspects of American Anti-Imperialism, 1898-1902," Fred Harvey Harrington cannot contain his anger at Fuller. He calls The New Flag "doggerel," as "dished out" rather than written, and speaks only of its "mediocrity."[30] One of Fuller's biographers dismisses The New Flag as "very bad verse,"[31] another as "very bad indeed,"[32] and still another considers that it was fortunate for Fuller that "the work passed almost unnoticed in the newspapers and magazines," and that, in all, it was "an inferior piece of work."[33] However, Robert Morss Lovett, writing in 1929, while noting that Fuller was "not a natural satirist," does concede the great power of The New Flag.[34] In any event, as one of Fuller's biographers points out, "it is today practically impossible to secure a copy [of The New Flag]."[35] Now that a major portion of the work is presented in the present collection, readers will be able to see that many of the extremely critical judgments are based on a dislike of Fuller's tendency to tell it like it is, and a respect for gentility rather than for ability.

The fact that Fuller began his satire with a quotation from Abraham Lincoln is hardly suprising. References to Lincoln were common in anti-imperialist literature, the implication always being that imperialism and the ideal of self-government for which Lincoln stood are incompatible. One poet asked "What Would Lincoln Say?"

> What would he say of men who spurn aside
>   The high ideal on which our sires were bent,
> The great seed-fact for which they fought and died,
>   A government derived from free consent?
> What would he say when all our strength and skill
>   Are mustered forth to crush and shoot away
> The self-same cause that hallowed Bunker Hill
>   What would the freedom-loving Lincoln say?[36]

In 1899 Rudyard Kipling wrote his "Take up the White Man's Burden." Addressed to Americans, Kipling told them to "Send forth the best ye breed"

> To wait in heavy harness,
> On fluttered folk and wild--
> Your new-caught, sullen
>   peoples,
> Half-devil and half child.
>
> Take up the White Man's burden
> The savage wars of peace--
> Fill full the mouth of Famine
> And bid the sickness cease;
>   . . .
> Take up the White Man's
>   burden--
> Ye dare not stoop to less.

The advice, published in a two-page spread by McClure's Magazine, was quoted across the country within a week, and helped the McKinley Administration to win support among Americans for the expenditure of bullets, brutality, and hypocrisy to carry out is program.[37] Kipling's poem also spawned a host of parodies. Instead of civilizing others, said John White Chadwick, Americans should

> Take up the black man's burden!
>   Not his across the seas,
> But his who grows your cotton,
>   And sets your heart at ease.[38]

The most bitter was Ernest Howard Crosby's parody, "The Real 'White Man's Burden'" published as a letter to the Editor of the New York Times, with the usual "Apologies to Rudyard Kipling." The first and last verses went:

Take up the White Man's Burden;
Send forth your sturdy sons.
And load them down with whisky
  And Testament and guns.
Throw in a few diseases
  To spread in tropic climes.
For there the healthy niggers
  Are quite behind the times . . . .

Take up the White Man's Burden,
  And if you write in verse.
Flatter your Nation's vices
  And strive to make them worse.
Then learn that if with pious words
  You ornament each phrase.
In a world of canting hypocrites
  That kind of business pays.[39]

The most prolific anti-imperialist poet, Ernest Howard
Crosby, combined his attacks on imperialism with diatribes
against the evils of industrial society. A Single Taxer,
Tolstoyan Pacifist, and Christian Socialist, Crosby attacked
militarism, capitalism, the trusts, the profit motive, machines,
slum conditions, low wages, and championed organized labor. He
is also almost completely neglected in works dealing with the
emergence of American imperialism.[40]

Born into a patrician New York family in 1885, Crosby was
educated in New York City at New York University and Columbia Law
School, graduating in 1878. After a brief career as a practicing
lawyer, he was elected to the New York legislature in 1887,
succeeding his friend Theodore Roosevelt. Two years later, he
was nominated by President Benjamin Harrison to sit as a judge on
the International Court in Egypt, an appointment approved by the
Khedive. Although this was a lifetime appointment, Crosby
remained in Egypt for only four years. But long enough to see
for himself the imperialist arrogance and resulting economic
injustice imposed upon Egypt by the European powers.

After reading Count Leo Tolstoy's Life, Crosby was converted
to the Tolstoyan philosophy of love. He thereupon resigned his
post and returned to the United States, but not before meeting
Count Tolstoy in Russia, a meeting which confirmed and
strengthened his Tolstoyan beliefs. When he arrived in the
United States, Crosby became the leading Tolstoyan in this
country. When Crosby died suddenly in 1907, Tolstoy wrote: I
hope that Ernest Crosby did not estimate me more than I loved and
estimated him."[41]

On his return to the United States from his years in Egypt,
Crosby told a reporter for the New York Times: "It seems to me
the labor question is the question of the day throughout the
civilized world," and that "the present attitude of our
capitalists and of the Government makes a practical solution of
the labor question impossible."[42] To aid in the "practical
solution," Crosby joined the single tax movement headed by Henry

George, and publicly supported the trade union movement. He became involved in child labor reform, settlement house work among immigrants, support of labor's right to unionize and to strike, and civil liberties, writing in support of aliens arbitrarily detained for alleged anarchist beliefs.

In 1895 Crosby pubished an article in the American Federationist, official organ of the American Federation of Labor, in which he urged "the wage-earners of the civilized world" to say with one voice:

> Suppose we stop making war. It is we who do the fighting, who get killed and wounded, who pay the war taxes by our labor, whose wives and children are left to hunger and thirst, whose just cause is lost sight of in foreign quarrels and over whom the army, ostensibly raised for another foe, will be held as a continual menace. It is to others that go the military and political glory, the advancement and promotion and the profits of speculation, and it is their privileges which will be maintained by an enlarged military establishment. We, wage-earners of the world, have no quarrel with each other. We have only one common foe--the monster of social injustice--and we shall not allow anything to divert our attention from him.[43]

Such radical views naturally caused Crosby to be ostracized by his former friends who now considered him as a "traitor to his class." This was even before he became deeply involved in the anti-imperialist movement. It is hardly surprising that more than any other literary figure in the movement, Crosby's anti-imperialist writings connected anti-imperialism with the drive for world peace and social reform. For example, Crosby pointed out in detail how military force, instead of being used for the legitimate defense of the United States, was being utilized to crush organized labor both in the territories acquired from Spain and in this country.[44]

At the same time, however, that Crosby linked imperialism to the injustices of American society, he emphasized that imperialism and militarism were new policies for the United States and, therefore, represented a departure from our past. He could not quite understand the reasons for the sudden change:

> What hell-born curse
> Has stirred these gentle hearts to strike?
> What anti-natural taint
> Makes devil and saint
> In hate and cruelty alike.

In answer to the argument that the United States had a moral obligation to "civilize" the Filipinos, Crosby, like nearly all of the anti-imperialist writers, maintained that our mission lay in adherence to our past ideals. Clearly, the imperialists were operating under a mistaken assumption:

xxv

Think you to lead again by dint of armies
and navies and coast defenses?
Not so is the world mastered.
Speed your frontiers, take Cuba and Hawaii,
bring in Canada if you can, push on over
the great Southern Hemisphere;
Will these lands be yours?
There is only one possession in them worth
the capturing, and that is the hearts of
men;
And these hearts can never be won by a nation
of slaves.
Be free, and all mankind will flock to your
standard.[45]

Crosby's first book of poems, Plain Talk in Psalm and
Parable, was published in London in 1898 and in the United States
a year later. It consists largely of rhymeless verse in the form
made familiar by Walt Whitman, arraigning the injustices of
society, and prophesying an era of peace and fellowship. Two
collections of the same type succeeded Plain Talk, namely Swords
and Ploughshares, first published in 1902, and Broad-Cast,
published in 1905. (Both books were brought out simultaneously
in Great Britain and the United States.) Swords and Ploughshares
is devoted in large part to denunciations of war and the war
spirit, including even the Civil War which Crosby, as a pacifist,
viewed as a mistake, "a pitiable error." Broad-Cast was made up
of new chants and songs of labor, together with a denunciation of
war.
    All of Crosby's poetry reflected his concern with the
burning issues of the day, especially as they affected the common
people. For the writers and artists who cut themselves off from
the common people, Crosby had only pity. As he expressed it:

Pity our dilettante literary men and artists,
Cut off from their base of supplies, the common people,
Starving, as it were, in a foreign land;
Uttering trim fatalities for each other's edification,
Their prophetic function all forgotten.

Such were not the men of old--
Sophocles and Euripedes, when all Athens watched from
    sunrise to sunset
    the destiny of Oedipus or Orestes;
And Cimbaue, when the populace of Florence bore his
    Madonna of the
    Dawn in triumph from his studio to the Altar.
Such were not the great musical composers of our own
    time, for they too
    spake for the masses;
And to-day, where German workmen meet together, you may
    hear sung
    the noblest chorals,

xxvi

And the forlornest Italian village can appreciate Verdi
            and Mascagni.
The artist must embrace his lowliest fellow men; in vain
            will he seek for
            inspiration elsewhere.
The bard and painter should be the head and right arm of
            the people;
What can we expect from Art when we lop these from the
            trunk?[46]

By far the most effective of the anti-imperialist prose
writers were the satirists--George Ade, Finley Peter Dunne,
Ambrose Bierce, and Mark Twain being the leading examples. It is
impossible to recreate orally the brilliant satire of "Mr.
Dooley," Finley Peter Dunne's philosophical Irish-American saloon
keeper, who defined the policy of "benevolent assimilation" as a
belief that "twud be a disgrace f'r to lave befure we've pounded
these friendless an' ongrateful people into insensibility."
Dunne rendered the anti-imperialist cause great service by openly
sympathizing with the Filipinos, by making fun of the jingoistic,
over-enthusiastic expansionists, and by attacking the racism of
imperialism. His most celebrated sayings, his suggestion that
Theodore Roosevelt name his book of war reminiscences, "Alone in
Cuba," and "no matter, whether the constitution follows the flag
or not, th' supreme court follows th' lict'on returns," came out
of the struggle against imperialism. His articles are full of
allusions to the Filipino insurrection, and to his sympathy for
the insurrectionists.
       Ambrose Bierce, who became known as "Bitter Bierce" for his
vitriolic wit, published a series of short pieces indicting
imperialism in general and that of the United States in
particular. In "Warlike America," Bierce quoted from a speech
delivered by President McKinley at Huntsville, Alabama, in which
McKinley asserted that the United States "have never gone to war
for conquest, for territory, but always for liberty and humanity,
and in our recent war with Spain the people of the whole United
States as one man marched with the flag for the honor of the
nation, to relieve the oppressed people of Cuba." Bierce's
comment is a good example of his satire:

       It seems that "we have never gone to war for conquest,
       for exploitation, nor for territory;" we have the word of a
       president for that. Observe now, how Providence overrules
       the intentions of the truly good for their advantage. We
       went to war with Mexico for peace, humanity and honor, yet
       emerged from the contest with an extension of territory
       beyond the dreams of political avarice. We went to war with
       Spain for relief of an oppressed people, and at the close
       found ourselves in possession of vast and rich insular
       dependencies and with a pretty tight grasp upon the country
       for relief of whose oppressed people we took up arms. We
       could hardly have profited more had "territorial

aggrandizement" been the spirit of our purpose and the heart of our hope.[47]

In a brilliantly amusing series of stories which appeared in the Chicago Record during the summer and fall of 1899, George Ade, the Hoosier satirist, attacked American imperialism, cleverly dissecting the Administration's program of "benevolent assimilation" for the Tagalos (Ade's name for the Filipinos). The sixteen weekly stories follow the activities of Washington Conner, the official representative to the Philippines of the "Bureau of Benevolent Assimilation," as he tries to convert a single Tagalo (Filipino) family to the American way of life. While Ade does not have the passion of Mark Twain,[48] his attacks effectively demolish American claims to moral, cultural, and political superiority. Early in the series, Conner explains to the Kakyak family that his aim is to achieve their "benevolent assimilation." When the father replies that he does not want to be assimilated, Conner replies: "Those who don't want to be assimilated had better take to the jungle. This isn't the first time that we've tried this benevolent assimilation. We've assimilated Indians, Mexicans, and Chinamen, to say nothing of several million of negroes, and when any one of them hung back, I'll tell you, it went hard with him."

Later in the series, Conner reveals the extent to which Americans plan to "assimilate" Negroes:

"We may borrow our popular songs from the negro, but in the important matter of handling the dollars we are still on the top, and will continue to remain there."
"Even when the negro has become assimilated," asked Mr. Kakyak.
"Well, we are not going to assimilate him to that extent."

In the following excerpt, the whole commercial scheme of exploitation behind the program of "benevolent assimilation" is laid bare. Conner tells Eulalie Kakyak, the young Filipino, that the United States prized the island of Luzon very highly because of the hardwoods, which in due time were to be made into furniture for the American market.

"Eulalie, you won't recognize this valley after we've had it for a few years," he said to her one day. "We will have a railway line through here, saw-mills all along the river and probably a new town with trolley cars and a ball park."
"Oh, I hope not," said Eulalie. "It might help your countrymen to make money, but what would become of us?"
"Your family would become assimilated and work in one of our factories."
"I think we would be happier in our present condition."
"The object of modern civilization is not to make people happy, but to make them useful," replied Conner. "Of course, if people can be reasonably happy at the same time

that they are making themselves useful, so much the better for them."

"But surely your countrymen will not cut down all these beautiful trees and leave this hillside covered with ugly stumps and tangled bush?" she asked.

The missionary explained to her that a mere sentimental preference for shade and foliage, or what some people termed the aesthetic conscience, must never stand in the way of a manufacturing enterprise. The reason for this was that a manufacturing enterprise gave employment to many people and made them busier than they could possibly be while living in an environment of unbroken fields and uncleared forests.

"He said that a hustling American didn't permit his regard for scenery to interfere with plans for money-making. For instance, the landscapes throughout America were checkered with flamboyant bill-boards, advertising patent medicines, bicycles and various makes of beer. And this was true beauty which Eulalie's people could now share."

Washington Conner finds the poor, benighted Tagalos unable to understand the complexities of American business. He has made the mistake of giving Mr. Kakyak a book of American history to read. Kakyak has given a great deal of attention to the Declaration of Independence, and has a number of embarrassing questions to ask Conner. When Kakyak presses him on Filipino independence, Conner loses his temper.

"Did you expect us to come over here and destroy the Spanish fleet and afterward pay out $20,000,000 for the mere satisfaction of permitting you people to govern yourselves?"
"If you do," Conner adds, "Then you have a very elementary notion of business."[49]

"I am an anti-imperialist. I am opposed to having the eagle put its talons on any other land." So Mark Twain told the press on the day of his return to the United States in the autumn of 1900, after a nine-year absence. He added that he had not always taken this position; indeed, at one time he had even been a "red-hot imperialist." But he had soon learned better and changed his mind.[50]

Unlike William Dean Howells, Henry James, William James, Charles Eliot Norton, Ambrose Bierce, Finley Peter Dunne, and other American men of letters who could see no good in fighting Spain, Mark Twain looked upon the war as a "just and righteous one," to liberate Cuba from a tyrannical Spain and deliver it into the arms of independence and liberty. Consumed by his passion for liberty, Twain at the outset wholeheartedly supported the war. To Joseph Twichell, whose son had enlisted in the war, he wrote:

"I have never enjoyed a war--even in written history-- as I am enjoying this one. For this is the worthiest one that was ever fought, so far as my knowledge goes. It is a worthy thing to fight for one's freedom; it is another sight finer to fight for another man's. And I think this is the first time it has been done.[51]

The phrase in this letter, "so far as my knowledge goes," provides the key to Twain's uncritical support of the war. Far removed from the sources of information, he could not see through the fog of propaganda. He was convinced that the purpose of American intervention as stated, was to free Cuba, and he was satisfied that a war to aid an oppressed people in their revolt for freedom was a just one. When he was asked to speak at the Decoration Day banquet in Paris, he declared that he would take the opportunity to praise the United States soldiers whom, he hoped, would "make short and decisive work of it [the war] and leave Cuba free and fed when they face for home again."[52]

Soon, however, Twain received news of the United States annexation of the Philippines, and he began to distinguish between the Cuban and the Philippine wars:

When the United States sent word that the Cuban atrocities must end, she occupied the highest moral position ever taken by a nation since the Almighty made the Earth. But when she snatched the Philippines and butchered a poverty-stricken priest-ridden nation of children, she stained the flag. That's what we have today--a stained flag.[53]

Twain left London on October 6, 1900, and arrived in New York nine days later. Interviewed by reporters, he made it clear that he viewed United States activity in the Philippines as a betrayal of American ideals. At a dinner in his honor at the Lotos Club on November 10, he reiterated his belief that the war with Spain had been "a righteous war"--but "why, why, why that most righteous purpose of ours has apparently miscarried I suppose I never shall know."[54] Two weeks later, addressing the Public Education Association, he publicly announced, "I am a Boxer"; adding: "The Boxer is a patriot; he is the only patriot China has, and I wish him success." Since the imperialist powers, including the United States, would reject foreign control of their territory, common decency dictated that they grant the same privilege to China, the Philippines, and to the Africans.[55]

Twain sought to compensate for his delayed conversion to anti-imperialism with a tremendous burst of energy on behalf of the cause. Moreover, unlike many anti-imperialists, Twain did not despair after McKinley's victory over William Jennings Bryan in the presidential election of 1900. He hoped the administration's policy could still be reversed. On December 3, he requested of a close friend that he ask Grover Cleveland if and how it was possible to bring the Treaty of Paris before the Supreme Court to test its constitutionality.[56] Meanwhile, he continued to publicize the anti-imperialist cause in speeches and articles. Between December, 1900 and April, 1902, there was seldom a month that did not see an interview, essay, or public letter from Mark Twain, in which he mocked the hypocrisy of American imperialist policy and decried the brutality and destruction that marked the war in the Philippines.[57]

Although there has been some tendency recently to denigrate Twain's contributions to the anti-imperialist movement,[58] the fact is that he was the most outspoken and influential of the anti-imperialists. On December 30, he published in the New York Herald his personal greetings to the twentieth century. It was a short, but effective attack on world imperialism, including that of his own country:

> I bring you the stately matron named Christendom, returning bedraggled, besmirched and dishonored from pirate raids in Kiao-Chow, Manchuria, South Africa and the Philippines, with her soul full of meanness her pocket full of boodle, and her mouth full of pious hypocrisies. Give her soap and towel, but hide the looking-glass.[59]

The "Greeting" was widely reprinted, especially in the anti-imperialists press. In addition, it was printed on small cards and distributed throughout the nation by the branches of the American Anti-Imperialist League. The cards contained two additional lines probably written by Twain. Following the final sentence, "Give her soap and a towel, but hide the looking-glass," there was the couplet:

> Give her the glass; it may from error free her,
> When she shall see herself as others see her.[60]

"It is by the goodness of God," Twain wrote in Following the Equator, "that in our country we have those three precious things: freedom of speech, freedom of conscience--and the prudence never to practice any of them." It did not take him long after his return from Europe to see that the anti-imperialist movement did not attract prudent people. Anti-imperialist writers were denounced as "traitors" in the jingo press; they were threatened with physical violence, and their writings were barred from the mails.[61] But Twain was not at all frightened. He had made his position clear as far back as 1884 when his friends had asked him where he would stand if the United States went to war for an unjust cause with the approval of the great majority of the people. He replied:

> If I thought it an unrighteous war I would say so. If I were invited to shoulder a musket in that cause and march under that flag, I should decline . . . . If the country obliged me to shoulder the musket, I could not help myself, but I would never volunteer. To volunteer would be the act of a traitor to myself, and consequently traitor to my country. If I refused to volunteer, I should be called a traitor. The unanimous vote of the sixty millions could not

make me a traitor. I should still be a patriot, and in my opinion, the only one in the country.[62]

In 1901 Twain still adhered to this position. He refused, therefore, to heed the counsel of friends who advised caution. When Twichell warned him to avoid the subject of imperialism lest he damage the sale of his books and injure himself and his publisher, Twain was stirred to anger: "I can't understand it. You are a public guide and teacher, Joe, and you are under a heavy responsibility to men, young and old; if you teach your people--as you teach me--to hide their opinions when they believe the flag is being abused and dishonored, lest the utterance do them and a publisher a damage, how do you answer for it to your conscience? You are sorry for me; in the fair way of give and take, I am willing to be a little sorry for you.[63]

Most anti-imperialists felt that Twain's emergence as a vehement critic of American foreign policy was an invaluable asset to the cause. The Nation, praising Twain for his courage in risking popularity and income by making himself obnoxious "to the people [who] hold the purse strings," and this at a time when he had just finished paying off his creditors, observed: "He is a man to be reckoned with in this business . . . . Mark Twain comes home to tell our flaunting imperialists that he sees through his hypocrisies. Tell us what you think of him, champions of Imperialism . . . give us your honest opinion of this typical and whole-hearted American, who stepped from the pilot-house of a Mississippi steamboat into first a national and then a European fame, and now fearlessly sides with the Filipinos against the American oppressors."[64]

In a letter to the New York Times, Moncure Daniel Conway (himself a staunch anti-imperialist) welcomed Twain to the ranks of the anti-imperialist writers. The noted biographer of Thomas Paine pointed out that Twain was following in the path of American writers who, a half-century earlier, had opposed the war of aggression against Mexico and had spoken out for peace:

> The cause of peace has certainly declined in the past fifty years. The authors who gave America its literary fame in the middle of the last century, Emerson, Longfellow, Sparks, Hawthorne, Bryant, Holmes, Lowell, Whittier, Motley-- to name some--were celebrants of peace . . . .
> The nation has already heard the protests of some of its finest intellectuals . . . and it may now be hoped that the bugle call of Samuel Clemens will be the signal for an uprising of intellectual forces in America similar to that which in France (in the Dreyfus Case) has just laid low the militant dragon and plucked the spoil out of its teeth.[65]

The "bugle call" was already being prepared when Conway's letter was published in the Times on January 11, 1901. A week before, Twain had told a reporter for the New York Herald that he was writing "an article" on the subject of imperialism. It was

"To the Person Sitting in Darkness," Mark Twain's most important anti-imperialist writing.

"To the Person Sitting in Darkness" appeared in the North American Review in February, 1901. The title, derived from the Bible (Matt: 4: Verses 13-17) is a satirical use of the imperialist concept of the colonial peoples--the Chinese, the Boer, the African, the Filipino--to whom the imperialists claimed to be bringing the gospels of Christ and the benefits of civilization. The article is addressed to the "person" ostensibly to reconcile him to the receipt of the blessings bestowed upon him by imperialism.

The essay opens with two quotations which had appeared in the New York Sun. One described the terrible conditions in New York's East Side districts "where naked women dance by night in the streets . . . where the education of the infant begins with the knowledge of prostitution. . . where the children that have adult diseases are the chief patrons of the hospitals and dispensaries." The other, a letter from China, reported that the Rev. Mr. William Ament of the American Board of Foreign Missions had returned from a trip into the interior of China to collect indemnities for damages done by the Boxer uprising. The hundred Chinese Christians under the guardianship of the American Board had been killed, and Rev. Ament had collected 300 taels for each, had compelled full compensation for all property that had been destroyed, and had also assessed fines amounting to thirteen times the amount of the indemnity. This money, Rev. Ament announced, would be used for the propagation of the Gospel.

Justifying his actions, Ament stated that, compared to the Catholics, whose fee was 500 taels for each Catholic murdered as well as "head for head," the demands of the American Board of Foreign Missions were moderate. In addition, he criticized American missionaries for being too soft with the Chinese.[66] Twain ridiculed Ament's generosity and attitude, questioned his motives, and, in general, voiced his contempt for those missionaries who served as a front for imperialism. In their dealings with the Chinese, Twain asserted, they represented not only Christian charity and kindness, but, just as important, "the American spirit."[67] Behind their avowed purpose of converting souls was a lust for profits. As such, they could not be doing a better job of spreading American civilization.

Playing on the commercial spirit of the imperialists, Twain declared, sarcastically, that it was time to deal with imperialism as a real business, to take stock and see where we stand in our efforts to transmit the benefits of our civilization to the poor natives. What was imperialism anyway if not a gigantic "Blessings-of-Civilization Trust"? And so let us take inventory:

> Would it not be prudent to get our Civilization-tools together, and see how much stock is left on hand in the way of Glass Beads and theology, and Maxim Guns and Hymn Books, and Trade-Gin and Torches of Progress and Enlightenment

(patent adjustable ones, good to fire villages with, upon occasion), and balance the books, and arrive at the profit and loss, so that we may intelligently decide whether to continue the business or sell out the property and start a new Civilization Scheme on the proceeds?[68]

Upon investigation, Twain discovered that the trust was not being run efficiently. Instead of hiding their true motives and thus playing the game correctly, the imperial powers were so open in their robbery and murder that the colonials were begining to see the light. The result was that the sale of "Law and Order," "Liberty," "Christianity," and "Protection of the Weak" had fallen off. Business was poor because "our Mr. McKinley, and Mr. Chamberlain, and the Kaiser, and the Czar and the French have been exporting the actual thing with the outside cover left off. This is bad for the game. It shows that these new players of it are not sufficiently acquainted with it."[69] Indeed, what will the colonials say when they see Christian fighting Christian for the sake of gold in the Boer War? when they see the Kaiser demanding territory, money and a monument as indemnity for the lives of two missionaries; when they see the Czar looting Manchuria? In short, what will they see when they see each "Civilized Power with its banner of the Prince of Peace in one hand and its loot-basket and its butcher-knife in the other. Is there no salvation for us but to adopt Civilization and lift ourselves down to its level?"[70] Not to be outdone by the European nations, the United States enters the game and, by her very entrance, deals the business a devastating blow. For how will she explain to the person sitting in darkness the contrast between her policy of liberation in Cuba and her policy of conquest in the Philippines.

Clearly, Twain still clung to the idealistic interpretation of the origin of the war with Spain, and drew a picture of McKinley, acting in the best American tradition, leading the nation into a just war for Cuba's freedom. In Cuba he was playing the American game, but in the Philippines, McKinley began to play the European game. Twain, however, did voice his fear that the United States was trying to "slip out" of her promise to Cuba of independence, and was plotting to "give her something in place of it." That "something" proved to be the Platt Amendment forced on Cuba by the United States in 1902, and which reduced the island to the status of a semi-colony.

Twain compares America's loss in the Philippines of 268 killed and 750 wounded to the Filipino loss of 3,227 killed and 694 wounded, and follows this with the scorching indictment contained in a letter from an American soldier in the Philippines to his mother, describing the victorious finish to the battle: "We never left one alive, if one was wounded, we would run our bayonets through him."[71] Americans, however, were searching for a uniform and a flag suited to this type of warfare in the Philippines. Twain has a simple solution for this problem. The British imperialists used a "cloth . . . called khaki. We could adopt it. It is light,

comfortable, grotesque, and deceives the enemy, for he cannot
conceive of a soldier being concealed in it."

And as for a flag for the Philippine Province, it is
easily managed. We can have a special one--our States do
it, we can have just our usual flag, with the white stripes
painted black and the stars replaced by the skull and
cross-bones.

And Twain concludes his scathing satire: "By help of these
suggested amendments, Progress and Civilization in that country
can have a boom, and it will take in the Persons who are Sitting
in Darkness, and we can resume business at the old stand."[72]
    Leading anti-imperialist spokespersons hailed "To the Person
Sitting in Darkness" as a great contribution to the struggle.
Secretary of the New England Anti-Imperialist League, Erving
Winslow, welcomed Twain "into the front ranks of the leaders of
the anti-imperialist cause. Probably no one shot will tell with
such effect of yours and I much doubt if all of them put together
will do so." W. A. Croffut, Secretary of the Washington
Anti-Imperialist League, confessed to Twain that though "an old-
fashioned Republican I have been greatly dispirited since the
election. But your trumpet-blast sounds the pulse again and
sounds like the beginning of a new campaign."[73] By "a new
campaign," anti-imperialists meant Filipino independence and the
end of army brutality.
    Many newspapers and magazines reprinted Twain's article in
part, and most publications in the United States and England
commended it editorially. In London the Review of Reviews
editorialized: "This article is a masterpiece in its way, and as
a contribution to current political controversy there is nothing
like it printed in the English language. It is a thousand pities
that so admirable a contribution to the great controversy of the
day should not be reprinted and circulated by the million
throughout the United States and in the United Kingdom."[74]
    The article did receive a wide circulation after it was
published in pamphlet form by the New York Anti-Imperialist
League. One hundred and twenty-five thousand copies were
distributed, according to the League's Secretary, making it the
organization's most popular piece of literature.[75]
    "To the Person Sitting in Darkness" enraged the imperialists,
and even the charge of "treason" was hurled at Twain. "Mark
Twain a Traitor," read a headline in a pro-imperialist paper. A
clergyman agreed, and gave as further proof of Twain's "treason"
the fact that the humorist had not gone to fight in the
Philippines.[76]
    Twain replied in a speech before the Lotos Club, and accused
the clerical critic of confusing the issue. Acting when the
country's life was in danger was a different thing from
supporting a war of agression in an arena far removed from its
boundaries. As he pointed out several times during the winter
and spring of 1901, true patriotism consisted of opposing the
government sending "young fellows . . . to the Philippines on a

land-stealing and liberty-crucifying crusade." The men who were
being hailed as "patriots" by the imperialist press were simply
people who had "turned Traitor to keep from being called
Traitor." The real "patriot" was the Filipino who resisted the
invasion of his country by "bandits" in American uniforms. On
February 14, 1901, Twain inscribed the following in a book for a
friend:

> I have rearranged the "Battle Hymn of the Republic" this
> afternoon and brought it down to date--sample stanza:
> I have read this bandit gospel writ in burnished rows of
> steel,
> As ye deal with my pretentions, so with you my wrath
> shall deal,
> Let the faithless sons of freedom, crush the patriot
> with his heel
> Lo, Greed is marching on.

> The other stanzas read:

> Mine eyes have seen the orgy of the launching of the
> Sword;
> He is searching out the hoardings where the stranger's
> wealth is stored;
> He has loosed his fateful lighting, & with woe & death
> has scored;
> His lust is marching on.

> I have seen him in the watch-fires of a hundred circling
> camps;
> They have builded him an altar in the Eastern dews &
> damps;
> I have read his doomful mission by the dim & flaring
> lamps--
> His might is marching on.

> We have legalized the Strumpet & are guarding her
> retreat;
> Greed is seeking out commercial souls before his judgment
> seat;
> Or, be swift, ye clods, to answer him! be jubilant my
> feet!
> Our god is marching on!

> In a sordid slime harmonious, Greed was born in yonder
> ditch;
> With a longing in his bosom--for other's goods an itch;
> Christ died to make men holy, let men die to make us
> rich;
> Our god is marching on.[77]

"To the Person Sitting in Darkness" brought Mark Twain much
abuse, but it won countless supporters for the anti-imperialist

cause. Small wonder a leader of the Anti-Imperialist League exalted: "Peace to the Eternal! A voice has been found."[78]

The clergyman who called Mark Twain a "traitor" was only one of scores of ministers who attacked him following the publication of "To the Person Sitting in Darkness." What particularly rankled the clergy were his satirical thrusts at the missionaries' role in imperialism. In an open letter to Twain in the New York Daily Tribune, the Reverend Dr. Judson S. Smith, Secretary of the American Board of Commissioners for Foreign Missions, defended Reverend Ament's character and demanded an apology.[79] A few weeks later, he declared that the Reverend admitting fining the Chinese only one-third instead of thirteen times the indemnity. The "fines thirteen times the indemnity" was a cable error for "fines one third the indemnity." Again he demanded that Twain apologize.

This admission of guilt was all Twain needed. He answered Reverend Smith publicly in "To My Missionary Critics." Referring to the extra fine, albeit now only one-third the indemnity, as "tainted money," he arraigned Reverend Ament for making the innocent pay for the crimes of the guilty, and said that giving the money to widows and orphans still did not justify his actions.[80] Once again Twain's outspokenness received high praise in anti-imperialist quarters.[81]

About the same time, in the unpublished piece, "The United States of Lyncherdon," Twain urged the missionaries to leave China where they could do no good, and return to the United States to reform the mobs who were lynching Negroes. "O kind missionary, o compassionate missionary, leave China! come home and convert these Christians."[82]

Along with William Dean Howells, Twain was now an honorary vice-president of the American Anti-Imperialist League, and on July 4, 1901, they signed a manifesto, issued by the League, which called for Filipino independence. They also signed a petition presented, through Senator George F. Hoar of Massachusetts, to Congress in February, 1902, entitled "Petition from Sundry Citizens of the United States Favoring the Suspension of Hostilities in the Philippine Islands and a Discussion of the Situation between the Government and the Filipino leaders."[83] Congress took no action on the petition.

Twain's decision to affix his name to the petition came after a long and careful study of well-substantiated reports of outrages perpetrated upon the Filipinos by American troops. Enraged both by these reports and by the indifference of Congress to the petition, he expressed his fury in scores of anti-imperialist writings. Nearly all, however, remained unpublished, probably because of his wife's objections.[84]

One such unpublished sketch was "The Stupendous Procession," written on the anniversary of his "Twentieth-Century Greetings." Its basic theme was that imperialism made a mockery of Christian ideas, patriotism, and the concepts of freedom and equality. As usual, the imperialist powers were indicted together. England had her Boer War, Germany her Shantung incident, and the United States her Philippine War. While the names and places were different, the causes and characteristics of imperialism were the same. Each country was motivated by greed, by the twentieth-century motto, "Get What You Can, Keep What You Get."[85] Each country, in its individual conquests, used Christianity as a front for murder and land-grabbing. The hypocrisy of the Christian powers, the identification of Christianity with imperialism, was too much for Twain, and he described the appearance of Christendom as she paraded before the world:

A majestic matron in flowing robes drenched with blood. On her head a golden crown of thorns; impaled on its spine the bleeding heads of patriots who died for their country--Boers, Boxers, Filipinos; in one hand a slingshot in the other, a Bible, open at the text--"Do unto others," etc.[86]

The last of the powers to pass in review was the United States. Once a proud nation with a tradition of freedom and equality, the United States, due to her foreign policy, was reduced to a thief and a murderer. After reviewing the record in the Philippines, and how such a record debased the flag and produced a false sense of patriotism, Twain exposed the injustices in American life itself.

In "The Stupendous Procession," Twain, unlike most anti-imperialist writers apart from Ernest Howard Crosby, stresses the connection between oppression at home and imperialism abroad. Imperialist Russia exiles its own advocates of freedom for Russians; imperialist France frames Dreyfus and persecutes Zola and other friends of freedom; imperialist America deprives its own Negro population of the democratic rights promised to all in the Declaration of Independence and the Constitution. It follows logically that the friends of freedom in one's own country must support the struggle for freedom of the colonial people, for both struggles are intertwined.[87]

One of the things about the debate over imperialism which angered Twain most was that imperialists often branded their opponents traitors and thus denied them the right to dissent. Responsible for the capture of the Filipino leader Emilio Aguinaldo, Frederick Funston, Brigadier-General of Volunteers in the American Army, returned from the Philippines late in 1901 to be hailed as a hero in the imperialist press. At a Lotus Club dinner on March 8, 1902, he referred to the Filipinos as "a drunken, uncontrollable mob" unfit for self-government. He saved his real fire, however, for the anti-imperialists. "I say that I would rather see any of these men hanged--hanged for treason, hanged for giving aid and comfort to the enemy--than see the humblest soldier in the United States Army lying dead on the field of battle."[88] To Twain who thought the Filipino war unrighteous and who cherished independence of thought, Funston's remarks could not go unanswered. If expressing one's true convictions was treason, Twain wrote next to Funston's statement, "I would rather be a traitor than an archangel. On these terms I am quite willing to be called a traitor--quite willing to wear that honorable badge--and not willing to be affronted with the title of Patriot & be classified with the Funstons when so help me God I have not done anything to deserve it."[89]

Publicly, Twain used Funston as a point of departure for another attack on American imperialism. In "A Defense of General Funston," published in the North American Review of May, 1902, he blasted Funston and used him as a springboard for a general condemnation of imperialism in the Philippines. Imperialism condoned all acts of treachery in its behalf, hence Funston could consider it perfectly normal to accept food and guidance from Aguinaldo, when he and his party, eight miles from the rebel leader's camp, were unable to move from exhaustion, and then turn around and shoot down the Filipinos who saved them and capture Aguinaldo himself. This, Twain labels, "hospitality repaid in a brand-new, up-to-date, Modern Civilization fashion." Mixed with Twain's irony is his deep concern lest Funston's brand of patriotism might supersede Washington's and Lincoln's with the youth of America. Funston, "a weak-headed and weak-principled" officer, he warns, was already being hailed as a great American hero, and "there are now public-school teachers and superintendents who are holding up Funston as a model hero and a Patriot in the schools."

Compared to the "Funston Patriots," Twain admits that he and other anti-imperialists were "Traitors." But to be called "Traitors" by the "Funston Patriots" did not disturb him. "They are always doing us little compliments like that; they are just born flatterers, these boys." For what did Funstonism mean? It meant "the torturing of Filipinos by the awful 'water-cure'"; it means General Smith's notorious order to "kill and burn" and "make Samar a howling wilderness." If this was patriotism, then Twain was proud to be called a "traitor" by such "patriots."[90]

Following "In Defense of General Funston," Twain published nothing on imperialism for almost three years, although he continued to write much on the subject, which he withheld from publication.[91] His final anti-imperialist effort, published in 1905, was King Leopold's Soliloquy, his longest anti-imperialist work.

In 1876, Leopold II of Belgium organized and assumed the presidency of the International Association for the Exploration and Civilization of Central Africa. When the African explorer, Henry M. Stanley, failed to interest British capital or officialdom in the lower Congo, he turned to Leopold who sent him back to Africa to stake claims for the Association. The United States became the first to recognize Leopold's claim to the Congo, based on 450 treaties signed with local chiefs by his agent Henry Stanley, on April 22, 1884. The Berlin Conference of 1885, summoned to settle European conflicts in Africa, admitted Leopold's claims but called for free trade, the "moral well-being" of the native population, and suppression of the slave trade. King Leopold's "exclusive mission," it declared, was "to introduce civilization and trade into the center of Africa." The Congo Free State was established as a sovereign state under the personal suzerainty of Leopold. The Belgian parliament sanctioned Leopold's "exclusively" personal ownership of the Congo. Thus Leopold secured possession of one million miles of territory occupied by some twenty million Africans. The most brutal imperialist exploitation developed in the so-called Congo Free State. Leopold declared "all vacant lands" in this vast country state property (or his own personal property), likewise all the produce of these lands. The dispossessed people were driven into slave labor, to collect such "state property" as rubber and ivory. By 1904 Leopold's "exclusive mission" had cost between five and eight million lives. Others had survived only as cripples, for amputation of hands and feet as punishment for trifling offenses was the common practice of Leopold's agents.[92]

Protests were voiced during the 1890's and early 1900's by explorers, missionaries, and reformers. But the stories they told were so horrible that they were disbelieved. Then in February, 1904, the British Foreign Office released the report of Roger Casement, its consul at Boma, Belgian Congo. This fearful document revealed the fiendish exploitation of the African people. Casement described the forced labor--a virtual state of slavery--by which European fortunes were made. The Africans had to gather their quota of rubber from the wild vines or have their hands chopped off, their genitals severed, their villages burned down, their children mutilated and murdered. Bosses of labor gangs brought their superiors baskets full of hands; smoked to preserve them in the humid climate. African women were tortured, murdered, raped, and driven into brothels for King Leopold's soldiers or agents. The iniquitous tax system forced the African workers to return to Leopold the miserable pay they earned for their hard labor. Whole villages were wiped out, the land expropriated, and the communal society destroyed. Leopold's Congo rule, which had made him one of the richest men in the world, was revealed as imperialism at its worst.[93]

Casement's report specifying these atrocities led to the creation of the English Congo Reform Association by Edmund Dene Morel on March 23, 1904. Simultaneously, a protest movement was being organized in the United States, and in September, 1904, Morel sailed for the United States to help strengthen the American protest movement. Drawn to Twain because of his reputation as an anti-imperialist, Morel sought a meeting with the famous writer. They met at Twain's home in New York City on the evening of October 17, and Twain promised "to use his pen for the cause of the Congo natives." Before leaving the country, Morel sent Twain a "packet of Congo literature," and promised to send a copy of his recent book, King Leopold's Rule in Africa.[94]

During the winter of 1904-1905, Twain set to work on King Leopold's Soliloquy which he finished near the end of February, 1905. It proved to be "too strong a diet" for the North American Review which had published his other anti-imperialist articles, and they turned it down. Later Twain wrote angrily that it was likely "that Leopold had bought up the . . . silence, along with hundreds of other papers."[95]

xi

Following the rejection, the American Congo Reform Association published the Soliloquy, at Twain's request, as a pamphlet. Following Twain's suggestion, it contained several photographs of mutilated Congolese. The pamphlet sold for twenty-five cents, and Twain donated all proceeds to the CRA. The pamphlet was also issued in England, with Morel stating in the preface that Twain was donating all proceeds from the sales of the pamphlet to the relief of the Congolese.[96]

Probably because he was satisfied with "The Czar's Soliloquy," which he had just finished, Twain chose the same form for the Leopold pamphlet. It opens with a picture of Leopold deeply disturbed: "Throws down pamphlets which he has been reading. Excitedly combs his flowing spread of whiskers with his fingers; pounds the table with his fists, lets off brisk volleys of unsanctified language at brief intervals, repentantly drooping his head, between volleys, and kissing Louis II crucifix hanging from his neck, accompanying the kisses with mumbled apologies; presently rises, flushed and perspiring, and walks the floor, gesticulating."

Leopold is distressed because at last the truth of his exploitation of the Congo is being made public. "In these twenty years," he rages, "I have spent millions to keep the press of the two hemispheres quiet, and still these leaks keep on occurring. i have spent millions on religion and art, and what do I get for it? Nothing. Not a compliment. These generosities are studiedly ignored, in print. In print I get nothing but slanders--and slanders again--and still slanders, and slanders on top of slanders! . . . Miscreants they are telling everything!"[97]

As Leopold reads the gruesome reports of the savagery inflicted upon the Congo people, he remains undisturbed until he comes upon the statement: "The crucifying of sixty women!" Now he is upset.

How stupid, how tactless! Christendom's goose flesh will rise with horror at the news. "Profanation of the sacred emblem." That is what Christendom will shout. Yes, Christendom will buzz. It can hear me charged with half a million murders a year for twenty years and keep its composure, but to profane the Symbol is quite another matter. It will regard this as serious. It will wake up and want to look into my record. Buzz? Indeed it will; I seem to hear the distant hum already. . . . It was wrong to crucify the women, clearly wrong, manifestly wrong. I believe that it would have answered just as well to skin them . . . (With a sigh). But none of us thought of that; one cannot think of everything; and after all it is but human to err.

Leopold consoles himself with the knowledge that, regardless of the reports, his tenure is secure. He congratulates himself for having the United States behind him, it having been the first nation to grant him the wardenship of the Congo Free State. He observes gleefully that the self-appointed Champion and Promoter

of Liberties of the World, is the only democracy in history that
has lent its power and influence to the establishing of an
absolute monarch." Since the other nations also sanctioned the
grant, Leopold feels secure, because "neither nations nor
governments can afford to confess a blunder."[98]
     From England Twain received the heart-felt thanks of the
Congo Reformers. "I thank you most deeply for having written
it," wrote E. D. Morel, "and for placing it so generously at the
disposal of the American Congo Reform Association." The British
press was almost unanimous in its praise. The Atheneaum hailed
it as "a trenchant satire," and praised Twain as "a serious
writer of remarkable courage as well as a humorist." "We are
glad to see Mark Twain taking part in a campaign against the
owner of the Congo Free State," declared Punch. The Bookman
called the Soliloquy a "remarkable book" and concluded its
review: "There has not in our time been a fiercer satire or a
finer instance of the value of humour as an instrument of
reform. The book is a terrible indictment . . . ."
     In the United States, readers of the Soliloquy also
expressed their gradditude to the author. A typical letter was
from W. W. Morrison of Lexington, Kentucky, which read: "I am
writing, not only in my own name, but I venture to assert also in
the names of the millions in the Congo Free State, to thank you
for your little book, 'King Leopold's Soliloquy'! I believe it
has done and will do more good than anything that has yet been
written on this gruesome theme. People are reading it and they
are talking."
     They were doing more than "talking." In December, 1905,
Henry I. Kowalksy, an agent employed by the Belgian government,
frantically notified King Leopold that as a result of Twain's
pamphlet, a strong anti-Leopold movement was developing in the
United States. "The fight here has been organized as it has
never been before. Monster petitions have been circulated and
signed; the industry of the opposition is very manifest, and I
can assure you that you cannot afford to turn a deaf ear to what
I am saying."[99]
     Mark Twain's final anti-imperialist writing played a major
role in arousing the public indignation that helped eventually to
bring about reform in the Congo.[100]
     When Mark Twain died in 1910, the Executive Committee of the
American Anti-Imperialist League noted the event in the following
statement:

          In the death of Samuel Langhorne Clemens, an honored
     Vice-President of the League, the loss to the nation's
     gayety is even less than the loss to mankind of one who
     zealously advocated justice and liberty and from whom public
     and private wrong met stern rebuke.
          The basis of Mr. Clemens' humor and the sport of his
     lighter vein were that sense of proportion which enabled him
     to see clearly and to expose with force and vigor all such
     violations of it as that which the League strives to
     amend--the subjugation by a democratic Republic of an alien

people. He made exceedingly valuable contributions to the cause, and some of the most pungent and convincing words in its behalf were those written for the enlightment of "the person sitting in darkness" upon the gratuitous inconsistency of our seizure of the Philippines.[101]

Mark Twain produced no works of fiction about the war with Spain or the Filipinos. Not that there was a lack of stories and novels about these wars. In fact, the wars produced a flood of short stories and novels. From 1897 to 1907 more than 48 novels were published, and in the same period, an even greater number of nickle and dime novels were brought out. Serialized novels were published in some popular periodicals, and other magazines produced complete novels. While the Cuban campaign produced most of these works of fiction, twenty-two novels deal exclusively with the war in the Philippines.[102]

In keeping with the trend of literature at the turn of the century, romantic war fiction reigned supreme. The novels and stories, including nickel and dime novels, stressed the "glory" of war and patriotism. Richard Harding Davis, Frederic Remington, and Charles King produced romantic stories and novels which were published in the most popular magazines, while Upton Sinclair published at least 64 nickel and dime novels, which, without exception, celebrated aspects of the war against Spain.[103] A typical novel of the period dealing with war is Israel Putnam's Daniel Everton, Volunteer-Regular, sub-titled A Romance of the Philippines, published in 1902.

The only story produced by one of the great authors of serious literature of the period dealing with war and imperialism was by William Dean Howells. Unlike his friend Mark Twain, Howells had disapproved of the war with Spain, and when he learned that the McKinley Administration intended to annex the Philippines, he was furious but not surprised. "Our war for humanity has unmasked itself as a war for coaling stations," he wrote to Henry James in July, 1898, "and we are going to keep our booty to punish Spain for putting us to the trouble of using violence in robbing her."[104]

Howells became a vice-president of the New York Anti-Imperialist League. While he did not write an anti-war or anti-imperialist novel, he did produce a short story "Editha" which vividly portrays and bitterly indicts the romantic view of war. Published in Harper's Monthly in 1905 and reprinted two years later in the collection Between the Dark and the Daylight, Romances, it is a devastating attack on the female jingo who looks upon war as something "glorious" and views the war against the Filipinos as a "sacred war for liberty and humanity."

When her fiancé, George Gearson, a former divinity student who is now studying law and is a Tolstoyan opposed to war, asks Editha Balcom about the war, she, who believes the war is "glorious," is puzzled by George's feeling against it. It seemed to her that there is "a want of earnestness at the core of his being," for George tells her that it is not "glorious to break the peace." But to George's talk of peace, Edith parrots the jingo press: "That ignoble peace! It was no peace at all, with that crime and shame at our very gates." It is not a question of wrong to Editha, for she is convinced that it is a "sacred war for liberty and humanity." Because George is so much in love with Editha and because she is so insistent, he becomes less sure of himself and of his ideas. "Why shouldn't this thing have been settled reasonably?" he asks her. But Editha answers triumphantly: "Because, God meant it to be a war."

Still unconvinced, George leaves her, promising to think it over. He is well aware of his mother's wish that he not volunteer for service. And Editha's demand, of course, presents him with a dilemma. Editha, by now so carried away by her exaggerated feelings of patriotism, retires to her room and writes George a letter. If they cannot be one in this, she writes, they never can be one. She plans to return his things and promises not to marry: "But the man I marry must love his country first of all, and be able to say to me,

> 'I could not love thee, dear so much
> Love I not honor more.'"

And continuing, she reminds him that there is no honor above America: "In this great hour there is no other honor." By this act, Editha adheres to the pattern already noted in much of the fiction--she "threatens" her sweetheart with the loss of her love if he does not volunteer.

Editha does not mail the letter but gives it to George when he returns the next day to tell her that he has enlisted--asking him to read it only when "he has a doubt." The demands of Editha's "high ideals" have triumphed over George's own ethical scruples and he has volunteered for the war, the "big war, the glorious war, the holy war ordained by the pocket Providence that blesses butchery." And in an obvious thrust at the specious reasoning so many people indulged in about the war, George continues:

> "It's astonishing . . . how well the worse reason looks when you try to make it appear the better. Why, I believe I was the first convert to the war in that crowd to-night! I never thought I should like to kill a man; but now I shouldn't care; and the smokeless powder lets you see the man drop that you kill. It's all for the country. What a thing it is to have a country that can't be wrong, but if it is, is right, anyway."

Editha's "high ideals" allow her to overlook the killing that results from war, but not to compromise with the evils of drink. George had returned the following day feeling un-well (hung-over), having, as he says, "consecrated himself to her god of Battles . . . by pouring too many libations to him down his throat." "Promise me," Editha commanded, "that you'll never touch it again." And in another ironic passage, Howells tells us that George promised, for he did not belong to himself now--he

belongs to Editha and to his country, and he had a sacred charge
to keep himself strong and well for his country's sake.

George had been taught by his mother that war was a "fool
thing," for she had seen his father come back from the Civil War
with one arm missing. And remembering his mother's feelings, he
asks his sweetheart to visit her in Iowa if he should not
return. He knows that it will be a blow to his mother when she
discovers that he has volunteered. But Editha's pride is such
that she writes to the old lady and glorifies George as a hero.
However, George's mother never answers her letters. Instead
Editha hears from a neighbor of the old lady who informs her that
Mrs. Gearson is confined to a wheel chair.

Editha is prostrated at George's death and takes to her bed.
When she is sufficiently recovered, she drapes herself in black,
and she and her father make the solemn trip to see George's
mother. Mrs. Gearson's greeting when Editha enters on the arm of
her father indicates immediately that she is no sentimentalist
about war; for she bluntly asks Editha what she came for. Poor,
distraught Editha tries to stammer an answer. Although her son
had written to tell her that she could expect a visit from
Editha, she is obviously disgusted with the girl. She taunts
Editha when she asks: "You didn't expect him to be killed when
you sent him, did you?" Editha protested that she would rather
die than have done that, for she had, she said, "tried to leave
him free." Mrs. Gearson storms back, "Yes, that letter of yours,
that come back with his other things left him free." And
continuing, she taunts Editha about her delicate health.
Mr. Balcom, who has remained silent all this time and who
apparently shares the beliefs of his daughter, replies that
Editha's life had been despaired of. To which the old lady says
that Editha should have been "glad to die" since she was such a
"brave person." Her son, she reminds them, was not glad to die.
The old lady also reminds the company that she has been through
one war; and that, when girls send their men off to war, they
always think they'll come marching back as gay as they went, that
if they come back with empty sleeves, it's all the more glory and
they are proud of them. At this, Editha bursts into tears.
Mrs. Gearson, who has clearly shown that she has no sympathy for
Editha or for women like her, concedes that Editha did not expect
George to be killed; but, she says, Editha expected him to kill
some other mother's son--some poor conscript. She thanks God
that he didn't live to do it. And then turning to Editha, who
stands before her the epitome of everything she hates, she asks
why she is draped in black: "Take it off, take it off, before I
tear it off your back!"

Howells make it clear that he does not think the experience
had taught Editha very much. Back home, Editha is temporarily
distraught, but when a consoling woman friend agrees with her
father that the "old lady" was not in her "right mind" and
further adds that what she said to Editha was "dreadful" and
"vulgar," Editha is shocked out of her "grovelling in shame and
self-pity." She began, Howells concludes in a final ironic
thrust, "to live again in the ideal."[105]

xlv

Howells portrait of the female jingo is confirmed in Edith
Elmer Wood's The Spirit of the Service. In this novel, published
in 1903, the wife of Captain Cartwright is described as a
"fighting patriot to the core," and likened to a "Roman matron"
sending her son to battle. The author's admiration for the
female jingo is unbounded:

> There were many like her, but of course, there were
> other types too,--the timid, weeping, clinging kind whose
> love of their husbands would not rise above solicitude for
> their personal safety, who hoped and prayed that they might
> be kept at the navy yards or attached to ships not likely to
> meet the enemy.
> Mrs. Cartwright was so cheerful, so optimistic, so
> positively eager for the fray, that in some quarters she was
> freely accused of heartlessness. Yet no one who understood
> her devotion to her husband could doubt that if she was
> willing to expose him to Spanish bullets, it was the
> supremest proof he could give of her patriotism, and that
> she would have exposed herself to them with far greater
> cheerfulness.[106]

In contrast to the admirable and praiseworthy patriotism of
Mrs. Cartwright is Barbara Thornhill whom the author barely
avoids labelling a traitor:

> Barbara was one of those who felt that the coming war
> was a thing of unmixed evil. She had been brought up to a
> warm admiration for Spain, not only as the most faithful of
> nations in a degenerate age, from the standpoint of
> Catholicism, but on account of its great historical
> achievements. She was rankly incredulous, not only of the
> outside destruction of the Maine, but of the cruelties and
> atrocities reported in the newspapers as practiced on the
> Cubans. Even the senatorial and consular reports on the
> reconcentration camps could not shake her faith in Spanish
> humanity.[107]

A third character in the novel, Sue Ballinger, becomes
converted to the female jingo viewpoint:

> And little by little, she found the virile blood of her
> pioneer forbears asserting itself against the acquired
> doctrines of the barbarism of war and the unworthiness of
> revenge, until she was passionately convinced that peace
> could be bought only at the price of national dishonor, and
> that war hideous as it was, was the lesser evil of the
> two.[108]

It was this theme, and not the slashing attack on it by
Howells in "Editha," that dominated the fiction of the era.
The period of the birth of American imperialism saw the
publication of two distinctly anti-imperialist and

anti-militarist novels: Ernest Howard Crosby's Captain Jinks, Hero and Raymond Landon Bridgman's Loyal Traitors. There were, however, other novels published which contained elements of both characteristics. Gertrude Atherton's Senator North (New York, 1900) is anti-war in opposing the war with Spain supposedly to free Cuba, but it uses racism freely and the alleged inferiority of Black Americans to oppose the war. (Later, as we have noted, the author became a fervent imperialist.) On the other hand, Edward Stratemeyer's Fighting in Cuban Waters (Boston, 1899) fully supports the war in Cuba, but uses it to condemn Southern Jim Crow laws and to praise Negro fighters.[109]

It is in the two explicitly anti-imperialist novels that these contradictions disappear.

In speeches and in a poem, Ernest Howard Crosby had called for a new Cervantes to "prick this bubble of militarism" with a new Don Quixote that would "make the profession of war impossible by opening our eyes to the irresistible comicality of it." He suggested that "perhaps Mr. Dooley or Mark Twain might do the job."

> Will not one of these gentlemen, or some other genius yet to be discovered turn his winged shafts squarely against war and the warmaker? When another Cervantes shall have decked out another soldier Don Quixote in his true colors,-- when he shall have laid bare the childishness of the paint and tinsel that have so long held us under their spell,--then indeed the twentieth century will be able to boast of a greater start in the literature than has yet appeared, and bold indeed will be the "hero" who will thereafter select war as a career. Such a book would ring down the curtain upon the profession of the soldier.[110]

When no other "genius" was ready to write such a novel, Crosby decided to do the job himself. The result was Captain Jinks, Hero. The novel, like Don Quixote, followed a picaresque form. (So much so, in fact, that one reader addressed Crosby by mail as "The American Cervantes."[111]) It satirizes the idea of the hero and tells its story through a series of adventures in which the hero (Captain Sam Jinks) is accompanied by his trusty companion, Cleary.

Like all picaresque novels, the plot of Captain Jinks, Hero is quite simple. It opens with young Sam Jinks, a good, happy farmer's boy, "who looked at the horses and cows as fellows," introduced to the idea of militarism and the concept of the "hero" through a gift of some lead soldiers from his father. Determined to become a "hero," Sam joins the "John Wesley Boys Brigade," whose marching song, with words adapted by the local Methodist pastor, is sung to the tune of "Onward Christian Soldiers":

> Onward Christian soldiers
> 'Gainst the heathen crew!

In the name of Jesus
Let us run them through! [112]

Sam and his friend Cleary obtain appointments to "East
Point," the army academy. Here Sam wins high honors in sadistic
practical joking, cringing submission to authority, and outspoken
contempt for such weakening civilian virtues as charity,
tolerance, and love. Crosby uses his "hero" to protest against
the practice of hazing. He has Sam willingly submit to two
brutal hazings which put him into the hospital for three weeks,
because he is told that all military "greats" who had preceded
him at the "Point" underwent the same experience. Therefore Sam
tells his friend Cleary: "I wouldn't miss it for anything. It
has always been done and by the greatest men, and it must be the
right thing to do." [113]
While they are at the "Point" war has broken out on the
island of "Cubapines" (a thinly disguised name for Cuba and the
Philippines). Both Sam and Cleary resign from the "Point" so
they can get into the war, Sam as a Captain of the Volunteers and
Cleary as correspondent for the Daily Lyre, a yellow journal that
is said to be "largely responsible for the war," an obvious
thrust at William Randolph Hearst's New York Journal and Joseph
Pulitzer's New York World.
Sam's sweetheart, Marian Hunter, is another prototype for
Howell's Editha, for Crosby tells us she was "possessed of an
uncontrollable passion for things military. Manhood and brass
buttons were with her incontrovertible terms and the idea of
uniting her young life to a plain civilian seemed to her nothing
less than shocking." When Sam reveals his plan to resign from
the "Point" and enlist as a volunteer for service in the
Cubapines, Marian is overjoyed:

"Just think of it! You'll come back a hero and a
general, and I don't know what not, and we'll get married,
and the President will come to the wedding; and then we'll
have our wedding tour up here, and the corps will turn out
and fire a salute, and we'll be the biggest people at East
Point. Won't it be splendid."

At Sam's suggestion that he might be killed in the war,
Marian is even more ecstatic:

"Oh, Sam! If you did, how proud I'd be of it. I'd wear
black for a whole year, and they'd put up a monument to you
over there in the cemetery and have a grand funeral and I'd
be in the first carriage, and the flag would be draped, and
the band would play the funeral march. Oh, dear! How grand
it would be, and how all the girls would envy me!" [114]

Before leaving for the Cubapines, Sam and Cleary are
relaxing reading newspapers when suddenly Sam tells his friend:

xlviii

"Even if I don't do anything wonderful, . . . and I hope
I shall, I shall be taking part in a great work, and doing
my share of civilizing and Christianizing a barbarous
country. They have no conception of our civilized and
refined manners, of the sway of law and order, of all our
civilized customs, the result of centuries of improvement
and effort."

Cleary agrees, and both return to reading their newspapers.
Suddenly Sam asks, "What's that other newspaper lying there?" and
Cleary replies: "That's the Evening Star; do you want it?" He
hands Sam the paper, and as he opens the paper, Cleary exclaims,
"Good Lord! what's that frightful picture?" Sam replies rather
casually.

"Oh, I see; it's that lynching yesterday. Why, it's
from a snapshot; that's what I call enterprise! There's
that darkey tied to the stake, and the flames are just up to
his waist. My! how he squirms. It's fearful, isn't it?
And look at the crowd! There are small boys bringing wood,
and women and girls looking on, and upon my word, a baby in
arms, too! I know that square very well. I've often been
there. That's the First Presbyterian Church there behind
the stake. Rather a handsome building."

Crosby continues: "Cleary turned back to his own paper,
while Sam settled down in his corner to read how the leading
citizens gathered bones and charred flesh as mementoes and took
them home to their children. No one could have guessed what he
was reading from his expression, for his face spoke of nothing
but a guileless conscience and a contented heart."[115]
Later in the novel, after they have reached the "Cubapines,"
and Sam has been promoted to Major, he meets the white commanding
Colonel of a Negro regiment. Sam is curious about the fighting
quality of the black soldiers, and learns that they make much
better soldiers than white men. When Sam asks why this is so,
the Colonel replies:

"Well, they're more impressible, for one thing. You can
work them up into any kind of passion you want to. Then
they're more submissive to discipline; they're used to being
ordered about and kicked and cuffed, and they don't mind
it. Besides, they're accustomed from their low social
position to be subordinate to superiors, and rather expect
it than not. They are all poor, too, and used to poor food
and ragged clothes, and no comforts, and of course they
don't complain of what they get from us.[116]

"The colonel's explanation," Perry E. Gianakos comments, "is
a damning illustration of the white American's inhumanity to
Negroes. To Crosby, a disciple of Tolstoy, it was also damning
proof of what militarism does to human beings."[117]

xlix

The novel follows Sam and Cleary through the campaign in Cuba, into the war in the Philippines, and the seige of Peking. As it proceeds it reveals the role played by the trusts and monopolies which profit from imperialism and the willingness of the press and the clergy to aid them in accumulating profits at the expense of the people in the conquered lands. Sam, now Colonel Sam Jinks, is introduced to Canon Gleeb, a missionary, while he is stationed in Porsslania (China):

> "These are great days, Colonel Jinks," he said. "Great Days, indeed, for foreign missions. What would St. John have said on the island of Patmos if he could have cabled for half-dozen armies and half-a-dozen fleets, and got them too? He would have made short work of his jailers. As he looks down upon us to-night, how his soul must rejoice? The Master told us to go into all nations, and we are going to go if it takes a million troops to send us and keep us there."[118]

As he moves from one scene of battle to another, the young "hero" encounters repeated examples of savagery, profiteering, and lying which disillusion his companion Cleary but have no effect on Sam. The "hero" remains true to his beliefs--if such things occur in war, they must have a good reason and be part of the natural scheme of things. In any case, his duty is clear. As he replies when the Tutonian Emperor asks him what he thinks of expansion, "I beg Your Majesty's pardon . . . but I do not think. I obey orders."[119] With such an attitude it is not surprising that Sam rises quickly in his profession.

Sam's secret ambition is not merely to be a good soldier, but to become The Perfect Soldier. He almost succeeds, but in the end is brought down by a tragic flaw. In his leisure time, Sam has trained himself to perform "spiritual exercises." He would ask himself "If I were ordered to do thus and such, would I obey?" Whatever the deed posed, no matter how dreadful, his answer invariably is "Yes." But one fatal day, the question posed is if he would execute his sweetheart if ordered to do so by the Commanding Officer. To his horror, he finds he cannot say "Yes." He is brought crashing down, unable to achieve his goal as The Perfect Soldier.

After receiving an injury in combat, Sam is furloughed home. Now a Brigadier, he is hailed in the United States, thanks to the press agentry of his constant companion, Cleary, as the great "hero." Women rush to embrace him with kisses, a process that is repeated in every town he visits. At the same time, a popular new song sweeps the land:

> I am Captain Jinks of the Cubapines,
> The pink of human war-machines,
> Who teaches emperors, kings and queens
> The way to run an army.

1

In order to stop the constant kissing of her "hero," Sam's sweetheart insists on an instant marriage. This turns the public against him. Sam, who has already been somewhat shattered by his failure to become The Perfect Soldier, is completely broken by the new shock. He is shipped off to an insane asylum, and ends his days in the madhouse, sitting for hours playing with toy soldiers and sending the lead soldiers out to die. "Harmless, perfectly harmless," says the keeper to Cleary, who goes to visit Sam. "Perfectly harmless," Cleary repeats to himself as he gets into his carriage. "What an idea! A perfectly harmless soldier!"[120] In fact, the world's only harmless soldier.

When it was published in 1902 by Funk & Wagnalls Company, with illustrations by Dan Beard, a number of reviewers pointed out that since Crosby had satirized many events which were widely reported in the press, the readers would need no further elaboration to get the point.[121] As for the quality of the novel, the Literary Digest, by no means an anti-imperialist journal, expressed the common view when it called Captain Jinks, Hero "a vigorous and varied protest against militarism in America, and belongs in a class with the 'Bigelow Papers.'"[122] Since James Russell Lowell's 1848 satiric, trenchant criticism of the government of the United States in its conduct of the Mexican War, especially in relation to the expansion of slavery, is considered a masterpiece of American Literature, this was a high compliment indeed. City and State saw a special virtue in Crosby's effective use of humor. "War is hell in the dictum of General Sherman," it noted in its review of Captain Jinks, Hero, "but the reading world has reason to thank Ernest Crosby for compelling it to see what an unmitigatedly fool-thing it is."[123]

The compliments were well deserved. Crosby united a sustained humor with a devastating attack on imperialism and militarism. One scholar notes that "Crosby, with Voltarian wit and understatement, shows the complex relationship that bound trusts, armies, venal journalists, and cynical, expansionist governments into an unholy alliance dedicated to devastation, misery, and mutual profit."[124] Although Captain Jinks, Hero deals with the era of William McKinley and Theodore Roosevelt, it is replete with meaning for today. Another scholar has pointed out that Captain Jinks, Hero is "still effective as an antiwar document."[125]

The other explicitly anti-imperialist novel, Raymond Bridgman's Loyal Traitors, published in 1903, is more often a tract against imperialism than a novel. Bridgman, a newspaper man who had previously written several historical monographs and was to write a popular work on international peace, presented a heavy-handed work, lacking the humor that made Captain Jinks, Hero such a delight to read. But Bridgman did include all of the main arguments against America's imperialist policies.

The novel has three heroes, and one heroine, all anti-imperialists. Two of the heroes are white--George Brown, and Alfred Wheelwright, and one is black, Washington Douglass, son of a freed Negro slave. The heroine is Faith Fessenden. George Brown is a dedicated Boston anti-imperialist, and early in the

novel, he engages in the argument with his imperialist friend,
Morgan Rich. The latter has just bought a steamer which he is
outfitting for the new Philippine trade. He plans to transport
"whiskey, beer and that sort of goods" in exchange for hemp and
other Philippine products. "I believe," says Rich, "there is a
mint of money in it for the man who jumps in first. I tell you,
McKinley is a great President. We Americans have got to
expand." As for the arguments of the anti-imperialists, he
dismisses them as inconsequential: ". . . if there is anything
contemptible it is these little Americans who are talking about
the rights of those niggers out there. We have bought them and
paid for them. Now we will make money out of them."[126]

When Brown reminds Rich that he is one of those Americans
who believe the Filipinos are right; that they have the spirit of
Patrick Henry, and deserve to win, his imperialist friend replies
that he doesn't recognize the name. "I don't recollect," he
says, "seeing his name lately on the list of Dun and Company's
agency. What is his rating?" He dismisses all further appeals
in the name of American patriots with the comment: "Oh, bosh, I
let those run to politics who want office. They want office, I
want money. We both get what we want, and I don't complain."[127]

The Filipinos, Rich declares, are foolish to resist the
Americans. Instead of hampering trade, they could be making
fortunes. "They might be well-dressed niggers above ground
instead of a heap of rotting bones below." And to Brown's
suggestion that the Americans should promise the Filipinos
independence, the answer is an unequivocal: "Bosh! We shall
never do anything of the sort. We're in the island to stay, and
they might as well accept the fact. We will do the right thing
by them if they submit, but, if they won't submit, we shall have
to compel them. We won't stand any nonsense from those niggers.
We bought their country and paid for it, and it is ours." When
Brown warns that the Filipinos might win, a businessman replies:
"I'll run my chances on that with the army of the United States
behind my investment."[128]

Other anti-imperialists appear in the novel, and they charge
that the talk of duty and destiny that the expansionists use is
all a "matter of dollars." It is the "cursed love of the
almighty dollar on the part of our businessmen" who have gotten
us into this disgraceful war. Pastor Ansel Robinson, a man who
has lost his church because of his anti-imperialist beliefs,
recognizes "fully the commercial spirit which was at the bottom
of the imperialist propaganda, as well as the religious blindness
which took advantage of it."[129]

The anti-imperialists in the novel see the Filipinos as the
victim of a "commercialism" that was rampant, strangling Cuba,
and plundering the masses of the people of the United States
through "trust privileges." When the imperialists cite the
example of England, the anti-imperialists reply: "Yes, look at
England in India! See the land drained of its resources to the
amount of hundreds of millions of dollars in order to enrich the
capitalists of England!"[130]

lii

Faith Fessenden, the heroine of the novel, sees the jingo females as even more imperialistic than the capitalists. They, in turn, are the products of the flood of romantic novels and stories emphasizing the beauty of war and violence:

Look at the books-shop windows. Note what are the most popular books. See what a rage there is now for the "historical" novels. Enlarged drawings of the pictures are put in the windows; what do they set forth? Violence,-- shootings, rapier-thrusts, fires, runaway horses, ship wrecks, assassinations, anything sensational in a grossly material way . . . .
Women are the greatest readers, and the nation which has taste for such matters will in time show its character in its actions.

All this, she continues, reflects the nation's enthusiasms: "Speculative enterprise, invention, expansion, wealth, display, mastery of material things, Greece had its enthusiasms for philosophy, poetry, the drama, sculpture, and architecture, and she has ever since been a prodigious force for civilization." And what of the United States? "Our one great contribution to the world was a political principle, and the present Administration and many people are to-day false to that. If that is betrayed, we are a national failure and the nation will perish."[131] Thus she concludes her assessment with a typical anti-imperialist argument.
A number of the anti-imperialists in the novel feel that the national betrayal has already advanced to the point where little can be done to save the nation. "I can't bear the sight of the United States flag," one of them cries. "It is a floating lie. It stands for deceit, for hypocrisy, for trampling on the rights of man, for robbery, murder, and oppression in the name of liberty." But Pastor Robinson refuses to abandon hope for the nation. "Times will become better," he assures those who are rapidly losing hope. "Brotherhood is our true motto, not expansion for expansion is nothing but selfishness. Expansion is always selfish--looking out for its own good." Then he turns to the supporters of imperialism and tells them: "You don't agree with me now, I can't convince you now; but I stand my ground and appeal to the future."[132]
All this by 1903 when the novel was published had been said many times before in anti-imperialist literature. What is new and different about Bridgman's novel is the title, Loyal Traitors, and the subtitle which read: "A Story of Friendship for the Filipinos." For that friendship took the most advanced form of anti-imperialist activity. Ernest Howard Crosby dedicated his collection of poems Swords and Ploughshares "To the Noble Army of Traitors and Heretics," and he broke with Tolstoyan pacifism in the poem "Rebels" in that collection when he wrote:

Or if you will persist to fight
With all a soldier's pride,

Why, then be rebels for the right
by Aguinaldo's side

While anti-imperialists in the United States engaged in a
variety of activities in an attempt to end American imperialist
expansion and the war it had spawned in the Philippines,
including even, as documents captured by the U.S. Army showed,
communicating directly with the Philippine revolutionaries,[133]
few actually fought with the Filipinos. But, a handful of
American Negro soldiers defected from the U.S. Army and fought as
officers in Emilio Aguinaldo's irregular army. Corporal David
Fagen, the most celebrated of these rebels, led insurrecto troops
against the American army for two years as a guerrilla officer.
In the fall of 1900, details of Fagen's activities as well
as accounts of other black defectors who went over to the
Filipinos, began to appear in the American press. While it was
later reported that Fagen was killed, the activities of the
defectors on behalf of the Filipinos attested to the intensity of
black hostility to American imperialism.[134]
Whether or not Bridgman obtained the idea for his novel from
blacks who fought with the Filipinos there is no way of knowing.
But three of his main characters, George Brown, Alfred
Wheelwright, and Washington Douglass, leave for the Philippines
to give more than moral support to the Filipino cause. In
support of their beliefs, they volunteer to fight with the
Filipino forces resisting the Americans. They are loyal to
American ideals but technically they are traitors in the eyes of
the imperialist- dominated government.
Fighting for the Filipinos is the idea of Washington
Douglass, and he convinces the two white anti-imperialists to
join him in this fight. Douglass, described by Bridgman, as "a
full-blooded Negro" of "manly bearing, genial disposition and
evident strength of character," convinces Brown and Wheelwright.
He first persuades Wheelwright with the argument that loyalty to
America requires that he obey a higher law than the one in
Washington. Then he points out:

My mother was a slave, and I know something of the
wrongs of our race . . . . I know what the Emancipation
Proclamation meant to the Negro race. I believe that I have
some idea of what freedom and liberty and duty mean. Now we
are trying to conquer the Filipinos. As nearly as I can
understand it, they have just as much right to their
liberty, if there is such a thing as human rights anyway, I
don't see why the Filipinos have not a right to themselves.
We can't get any right to them by buying them or by
conquering them. But I am ashamed to say that there are two
regiments of Negroes in the United Stated army who have gone
over to help the white man conquer these brown men, killing
them because they are fighting for their liberty and
independence. Perhaps I may be wrong, but I believe I am
right, and it seems to me that my duty calls me to go over

and fight with the Filipinos and help them to get their independence.[135]

Bridgman reports that in his talk with George Brown, Douglass "stated again his belief that his life ought to be spent in positive service to the cause of human liberty as a personal and race tribute and requital to the memory of Abraham Lincoln, whose Proclamation freed his mother, and to the spirit of human liberty which makes all men free under government of the people, by the people, and for the people; a government which cannot tolerate colonies, and in which there must be the harmonious assimilation of all the people who share the government."[136]

Douglass is now convinced "that duty to country may involve a higher standard than support of any Administration," that it may even demand "armed resistance" to the Administration so that the "true spirit and forms of liberty" may be preserved. He is further convinced that "the Filipinos were thoroughly right in their moral and political position," and the United States is "without legal or moral justification" in its war against them. Because Douglass has presented his arguments "intelligently and with enthusiasm," and made him see the justice of his decision to fight with the Filipino forces, George Brown agrees to go with Douglass and Wheelwright to the Philippines and join the Filipino armed forces.[137]

As the novel proceeds, all three go to the Philippines, where both Douglass and Wheelwright are killed in an engagement against the Americans, who are especially determined to kill the black who dared to fight on the side of the enemy. George Brown is the sole survivor, and his vow to continue the fight against the imperialists, begins, as Bridgman puts it, "another chapter in the history of the war."[138]

The war continued for several years, and it was 1905 before final skirmishes were over. By that time the work of the literary anti-imperialists had pretty well come to an end. They had not succeeded, of course, in preventing the American imperialists from establishing the "New American Empire." But they did help educate important sections of the American public to the true nature of American overseas expansion. Many in the United States refused to acknowledge that the subjugation of Puerto Rico and the Philippines was comparable to the imperialist exploits of monarchical European powers. American expansion, they believed, was different because our cherished political principles were different. American expansion, in the words of a Presbyterian minister, was "enthusiastic, optimistic and beneficial republicanism." If it was imperialism--and the word was rarely used among such Americans--it was of a special and salutary kind--"not for domination but for civilization, not for absolutism but for self-government."[139]

The literary anti-imperialists made an important and lasting contribution in exposing this self-deception and hypocrisy. In so doing, they left behind a tradition which is still very much alive in the United States.

NOTES TO INTRODUCTION

[1]In 1960, Carlos P. Romulo wrote that the "Philippine Insurrection" was not an "insurrection," and should be called the "Philippine-American War." (New York Times, November 19, 1960.) The editors of the New York Times agreed, entitling the editorial, "It Was a War." (Ibid., November 20, 1960).

[2]Gertrude Atherton, Senator North (New York, 1900), p. 259; William M. Gibson, "Mark Twain and William Dean Howells, Anti-Imperialists," Unpublished Ph.D. dissertation, University of Chicago, 1940, p. 62 n.19.

[3]Stephen Crane did not publish any stories associated with the war in the Philippines, but in "Stephen Crane: Anti-Imperialist," Thomas Arthur Gullason writes that of American writers "none was a more ardent anti-imperialist, a more serious, defiant, sincere humanitarian than Stephen Crane." (American Literature 30(May, 1958):237.) However, Crane did believe in the doctrine of "necessity," according to which doctrine American occupation of the Philippines was "necessary" in order to forestall annexation by some other power or powers. (See Stephen Crane, "The New America," The Outlook 3(February 4, 1899),p. 12.)
Edgar Lee Masters contributed little to the literature of anti-imperialism during the early 1900's. It was in 1915 in Spoon River Anthology that Masters voiced his despair and anger. He spoke through the voice of "Harry Wilmans" in the burial ground of Spoon River who talks of the "beastly acts" committed by American soldiers in the Philippines, and who was "shot through the guts." He ends:
Now there's a flag over me in Spoon River!
A flag! A flag!
(Edgar Lee Master, Spoon River Anthology (New York, 1915), pp. 185.
[4]William M. Gibson, "Mark Twain and Howells: Anti-Imperialists," New England Quarterly 20(December, 1977): 435-36.
[5]I. Dementyev, USA: Imperialists and Anti-Imperialists: The Great Foreign Policy Debate at the Turn of the Century (Moscow, 1979), pp. 220-21. For a different view, see Richard E. Welch, Jr., Response to Imperialism: The United States and the Philippine-American War, 1899-1902 (Chapel Hill, 1979, pp. 131-32.

[6]Springfield Republican, July 1, 1900.

[7]Samuel Gompers to Ed O'Donnell, August 13, 1898, Samuel Gompers Papers, AFL Archives, Manuscript Division, Library of Congress and reprinted in Philip S. Foner and Richard C. Winchester, editors, The American Anti-Imperialist Movement: A Documentary History (New York, 1983) volume I (From the Mexican War to the Election of 1900), p. 190.

[8]Journal of the Metal Polishers and Buffers, November 1, 1899, p. 321.
Ella Wheeler Wilcox (1850-1919), poet, novelist, was the author of some twenty volumes, for the most part poetry, which some critics charged was marked by platitudes and sentimentality, but which she defended as bringing poetry to the great masses of the American people.

[9]Worker's Call, May 13, 1899, September 22, October 3, 1900; H.L. Boothman, "Philosophy of Imperialism," International Socialist Review 1(1900):303; Kirk H. Porter, compiler, National Party Platforms (New York, 1924), pp. 239-42.

[10]International Socialist Review 1(September, 1900):132-33.

[11]Eugene V. Debs, "The Socialist Party and the Working Class," ibid 5(1904-05):130.

[12]Appeal to Reason, April 14, 1900; See also Daily People, February 12, 1902.

[13]Fred Harvey Harrington, "Literary Aspects of American Anti-Imperialism, 1898-1902," New England Quarterly 10(1937):651.

[14]Welch, op.cit., p. 127. See also Harrington, op.cit., p. 651.

[15]Martin Halpern, William Vaughn Moody, New York, 1964, p. 72.

[16]Atlantic Monthly 85(May, 1900):593-98.

[17]Wallace Ludwig Anderson, "Some Critical Attitudes Toward Poetry in America as Reflected in the Development of the Reputation of William Vaughn Moody as a Poet, 1900-1912," Unpublished Ph.D. dissertation, University of Chicago, 1948, p. 17; Maurice F. Brown, Estranging Dawn: The Life and Works of William Vaughn Moody, Carbondale, Ill., 1973, pp. 132-35.

[18]Atlantic Monthly 85(May, 1900):593-98.

[19]Victor Perlo, American Imperialism (New York, 1951), pp. 102-08; A. Whitney Griswold, The Far Eastern Policy of the United States (New York, 1941), pp. 468-70; Samuel Flagg Bemis, A Short History of American Foreign Policy and Diplomacy, (New York, 1959), pp. 349-50.

[20]Halpern, op.cit., pp. 80-82.

[21]Poems and Plays of William Vaughn Moody (Boston and New York, 1912), pp. 26-28.

[22]See Walter LaFeber, The New Empire, Ithaca, N.Y., 1963, and William Appleman Williams, The Roots of the Modern American Empire, New York, 1969.

[23]Robert Morss Lovett, "Fuller of Chicago," New Republic 60(August 21, 1929): 16.

[24]Henry B. Fuller, The New Flag (Chicago, 1899), p. 1. It is interesting that the symbol of the "pig" to represent the police and later extended to all elements of the capitalist power structure, was popularized by the Black Panthers in the 1960's, and later adopted by other radical groups including many student protesters against the war in Vietnam. They did not, however, know that in the anti-imperialist poem, The New Flag, Henry Blake Fuller depicted American imperialists as a hog. (See Philip S. Foner, editor, The Black Panthers Speak (New York, 1970), p. xx.

[25]Fuller, The New Flag, p. 9.

[26]Ibid., pp. 9-10.

[27]Christian Advocate, Jan. 22, 1903.

[28]Fuller, The New Flag, pp. 13-14.

[29]Ibid., pp. 15.

[30]Harrington, op.cit., p. 655.

[31]Bernard R. Bowron, Henry B. Fuller, of Chicago: The Ordeal of a Genteel Realist in Ungenteel America, Westport, Conn. 1974, p. 178.

[32]Constance M. Griffin, Henry Blake Fuller, Philadelphia, 1939, p. 53.

[33]John Pilkington, Jr., Henry Blake Fuller, New York, 1970, p. 128.

[34]Lovett, op.cit., pp. 16-18.

[35]Griffin, op.cit., p. 54.

[36]Howard S. Taylor, "What Would Lincoln Say?" Liberty Poems: Inspired by the Crisis of 1898-1900 (Boston, 1900), p. 98.

[37]Barbara W. Tuchman, "Can History Be Served Up Hot?" New York Times Book Review, March 8, 1964.

[38]John White Chadwick, Later Poems (Boston and New York, 1905), p. 115.

[39]New York Times, February 15, 1899 reprinted in Ernest Crosby, Swords and Ploughshares (New York, 1902), pp. 33-34.
       C. Berkeley Tompkins argues that Crosby and other parodists overlooked the fact that if Kipling's poem was an example of Anglo-Saxon racism and a bid for America to join the British in performing civilization's mission in foreign lands, it was also a warning that the path of duty would prove hard and difficult. (Anti-Imperialism in the United States, New York, 1978, pp. 236-39.)
       An interesting if unconscious irony on the "White Man's Burden," appeared in a report from Manila. When a reporter for the Army and Navy Journal encounters some black members of a Negro regiment, he asks one "tall negro giant": "'What do you think you're going to do over here!" The big Negro replied, 'Well, I doan know, but I ruther reckon we're sent over hah to take up de White Man's burden!'" (Army and Navy Journal 37[November 11, 1899]: 259.)

[40]Tompkins, op.cit., notes that Crosby was head of the New York Anti-Imperialist League and quotes some of his poetry, but Crosby is not mentioned in David Healy's United States Expansionism: The Imperialist Urge in the 1890's (Madison, 1970), or in Robert L. Beisner's Twelve Against the Empire: The Anti-Imperialists 1898-1900 (Boston, 1968) or in Frank Friedel, Dissent in Three American Wars (1970).

[41]"A Letter From Tolstoy on Crosby's Death," The Public, March 8, 1907, p. 1169.
       The only scholarly biographical treatment of Crosby is Perry E. Gianakos, "Ernest Howard Crosby: A Forgotten Tolstoyan Antimilitarist and Anti-Imperialist," in Charles Chatfield, editor, Peace Movements in America, (New York, 1978), pp. 1-19. Gianokos' discussion is the first to be based on the Ernest Howard Crosby papers in the Michigan State University Library. Gianakos is also the author of "The Yanko-Spanko War: Our War with Spain in American Fiction," Unpublished Ph.D. dissertation, New York University, 1961. In this study, the most detailed of any dealing with the subject, Gianakos examined around three hundred separate pieces of fiction.

[42]New York Times, July 13, 1894.

[43]American Federationist 1(December, 1895):221.

[44]For the use of U.S. troops to break strikes in Cuba, see Philip S. Foner, The Spanish-Cuban-American War and the Birth of American Imperialism 1895-1902 (New York, 1972)2:489-503.

45Ernest Crosby, Swords and Ploughshares (New York, 1902), p. 34; Ernest Crosby, Plain Talk in Psalm and Parable (Boston, 1899), pp. 58-59.

46Literary Digest 20(March 31, 1900):393.

47Finley Peter Dunne, Mr. Dooley in the Hearts of His Countrymen (New York, 1900), p. 6; Literary Digest, February 11, 1899, p. 155; Mr. Dooley in Peace and War (Boston, 1899); Observation of Mr. Dooley (New York, 1906); The Collected Works of Ambrose Bierce (New York and Washington, 1912) 11:94-95.

48Perry E. Gianakos tends to denigrate Ade's contributions to the anti-imperialist cause, and he does the same with those of Finley Peter Dunne. While noting that both Dunne and Ade "employed satirical styles that effectively juxtaposed American professions of altruism with contradictory actions, the effect they produced was neither so profound nor so unsettling as that produced by Crosby. That the image of the war still retains its opera buffa aspect is due in part to the writings of Dunne and Ade. For the impression of warfare and expansionism that emerges from their writing is a bloodless one, and in Ade's case, a passionless one. What is missing is Crosby's Tolstoyan abhorrence of war. Hence, both Dunne and Ade were tolerable to the expansionists." (op.cit., p. 15.)
It is true that Ade wrote two musicals satirizing the imperialists: The Sultan of Sulu (New York, 1903), and The Sho-Gun (New York, 1904). In the first place, Ade satirized McKinley's program of "Benevolent Assimilation," and in the second, he modeled the leading character, an expansionist, after Theodore Roosevelt. It is also true that Theodore Roosevelt found some of Dunne's anti-imperialist satire "delicious." But it is hardly necessary to diminish the contributions of Ade and Dunne to point up those of Crosby. For one thing, the anti-imperialists could have said of both Ade and Dunne as Frederick Douglass replied when told that many white Abolitionists were not sufficiently active in the struggle against racism, "I wish there were more of them." For another, both Ade and Dunne reached a much wider audience than did Crosby and their influence was much greater, no small fact when one considers the difficulty anti-imperialist writers had in reaching any audience at all through the newspapers and magazines. For Roosevelt's comment, see Elmer Ellis, Mr. Dooley's America: A Life of Finley Peter Dunne (New York, 1941), pp. 117, 147.
Fred C. Kelly in his biography of George Ade, devotes a good deal of attention to Ade's anti-imperialist musical play The Sultan of Sulu, but ignores the series in the Chicago Record, mentioning only that Ade had written a series of stories "spoofing our new imperialistic policies." (Fred C. Kelly, George Ade, Warmhearted Satirist (Indianapolis, 1947), p. 163.) Of course, Ade's stories do much more than just "spoof" these policies. None other than Perry E. Gianakos put it well when he wrote: "These stories constitute a penetrating analysis of turn-

lx

of-the-century American civilization, for Ade effectively demolishes American claims to moral, cultural, racial, and political superiority. In several of the stories, the attack on American racist ideas is specific." ("The Spanish-American War and the Double Paradox of the Negro American," Phylon (Spring, 1965):45.)

[49]Chicago Record, July 15, August 12, 26, September 2, 1899.

[50]Philip S. Foner, Mark Twain: Social Critic (New York, 1958), p. 239.

[51]Ibid., p. 256.

[52]Howard Spierer, "Mark Twain and Anti-Imperialism," unpublished M.A. thesis, Columbia University, 1968, p. 96.

[53]Foner, Mark Twain: Social Critic, p. 255.

[54]Spierer, op.cit., p. 98; Albert Bigelow Paine, editor, Mark Twain's Speeches (New York, 1923), p. 200.

[55]Mark Twain's Speeches, p. 212; Spierer, op.cit., p. 99.

[56]Foner, Mark Twain: Social Critic, p. 263.

[57]Spierer, op.cit., pp. 99-100.

[58]Heimbrecht Breinig argues that while Mark Twain's reputation as an anti-imperialist "is well-deserved," it has been "exaggerated seen in the context of his lifelong endeavor to formulate his attitude with respect to such related concepts as savagism and civilization, primitivism and progressivism, Manifest Destiny, and imperialism in an extended sense." ("Mark Twain--Anti-Imperialist?" Gulliver (Deutsch-Englische Jahrbucher) 9(1981):178-98). One wonders why if Twain's reputation as an anti-imperialist "is well-deserved," the title of the article questions his being an anti-imperialist. As for the fact that he came to anti-imperialism late, that is true, but does not negate the contributions he made once he reached that stage. To argue that Mark Twain had backward opinions on these issues at various stages in his life, is merely to state the obvious. Since all this is made clear by students of Twain's anti-imperialism, including myself, one wonders what the fuss is all about.

[59]"New Century Greeting Which Twain Recalled," New York Herald, December 30, 1900.

[60]Foner, Mark Twain: Social Critic, p. 266.

[61]Even a conservative scholar like Charles Eliot Norton of Harvard, translator of Dante and a leading art historian, was

subjected to a campaign of vilification for daring to call for peace. In his lecture on "True Patriotism," Norton had upheld the duty of opposing an unjust war, like that being waged in the Philippines. He wrote his friend Leslie Stephens in England: "My mail (after the lecture) was loaded down with letters and post cards full of abuse, mostly anonymous, some of them going so far as to bid me to look for a stray bullet." (Foner, Mark Twain: Social Critic, p. 267.)

[62]Ibid.

[63]Ibid.

[64]"Mark Twain, American Citizen," Nation 81(November 29, 1900):419.

[65]Moncure Daniel Conway, "Mark Twain, Literature and War," New York Times, January 11, 1901.

[66]Mark Twain, "To the Person Sitting in Darkness," North American Review, 72(February, 1901):162.

[67]Ibid., p. 163.

[68]Ibid., pp. 164-65.

[69]Ibid., p. 166.

[70]Ibid., p. 169.

[71]Ibid., p. 175-76.
For the Platt Amendment, see Philip S. Foner, The Spanish-Cuban-American War and the Birth of American Imperialism, 1895-1902 (New York, 1972) 2:560-633, 668-69.

[72]"To the Person Sitting in Darkness," pp. 181-82.

[73]Foner, Mark Twain: Social Critic, p. 275.
Fred Harvey Harrington calls "To the Person Sitting in Darkness" "disappointing," and Richard E. Welch, Jr. writes: "Read today its irony seems rather labored and heavy-handed . . . ." (Harrington, op.cit., p. 661; Welch, Jr., op.cit., p. 125.) But these are distinctly minority views.

[74]Foner, Mark Twain: Social Critic, p. 276.

[75]Ibid.

[76]Ibid.

[77]Ibid., pp. 277-78.

[78]Ibid., p. 279.

[79]New York Daily Tribune, February 15, 1901.

[80]Mark Twain, "To My Missionary Critics," North American Review, 172(April, 1901):528-29.

[81]Foner, Mark Twain: Social Critic, pp. 281-82.

[82]Ibid., p. 282.

[83]Ibid., pp. 282-83.

[84]Ibid., p. 284.

[85]Ibid., pp. 284-86.

[86]Ibid., p. 287.

[87]Ibid., p. 289.

[88]New York Sun, March 9, 1902.

[89]Foner, Mark Twain: Social Critic, pp. 291-92.

[90]Mark Twain, "In Defence of General Funston," North American Review, 174(May, 1902):613.

[91]Perhaps the most bitter was "The War Prayer," a condemnation of war and the war makers in The Mysterious Stranger. Never has the process by which a nation may be seduced into supporting an unjust war been more brilliantly described. It was published after Twain's death in Harper's Monthly of November, 1916.

[92]Parker Thomas Moon, Imperialism and World Politics (New York, 1963), pp. 86-87; Ruth Slade, King Leopold's Congo (London, 1962), pp. 22-144.

[93]Neal Ascherson, "The King Incorporated: Leopold II in the Age of Trusts (London, 1963), pp. 84-88.

[94]Hunt Hawkins, "Mark Twain's Involvement with the Congo Reform Movement: 'A Fury of Generous Indignation,'" New England Quarterly 51(June, 1978):152-54.

[95]Ibid., p. 156.

[96]Foner, Mark Twain: Social Critic, pp. 297-98; Robert Wuliger, "Mark Twain on King Leopold's Soliloquy," American Literature 25(1953):234-37.

[97]Mark Twain, King Leopold's Soliloquy: A Defense of His Rule (Boston, 1905):6.

98Ibid., pp. 23-26.
Twain erred in writing that the United States was one of the powers that had signed the Berlin Act. "America and thirteen great European states wept in sympathy with me," he has Leopold say, ". . . their representatives met in convention in Berlin and made me Head Foreman and Superintendent of the Congo State." (Ibid., p. 6.) While the United States had been part of the group drawing up the Act, President Grover Cleveland had withheld it from Senate ratification. (Hawkins, op.cit., p. 133.)

99Foner, Mark Twain: Social Critic, pp. 300-01.
Pressure to prevent reviews of Twain's Soliloquy in the United States came from business interests in this country, headed by J.P. Morgan, John D. Rockefeller, Thomas Fortune Ryan, and Daniel Guggenheim, who shared in the profits from the Congo. The New York American revealed that these finance capitalists and Leopold's agents in the United States spent money lavishly to prevent wide-spread notice of Twain's pamphlet. They also financed the wide circulation of a pamphlet entitled, An Answer to Mark Twain, which accused the author of King Leopold's Soliloquy of "an infamous libel against the Congo State" and of having lent his name to a "filthy work." (Paul McStallworth, "The United States and the Congo Question, 1884-1914," Unpublished Ph.D. dissertation, Ohio State University, 1954, pp. 134-36.)

100Stanley Shaloff, Reform in Leopold's Congo (Richmond, Va., 1970), pp. 188-90.

101The Public, May 13, 1910, p. 443.

102Perry E. Gianakos, "The Yanko-Spanko War: Our War with Spain in American Fiction," Unpublished Ph.D. dissertation, New York Univesity, 1961, pp. 141-48.

103Gianakos, "Ernest Howard Crosby," op.cit., pp. 5, 17.
Upton Sinclair, then a young writer at Columbia University struggling to earn a living, wrote at least 29 nickel novels for Street & Smith's "True Blue" series under the pseudonym of "Ensign Clarke Fitch"; at least 18 nickel novels for Street & Smith's "Starry Flag" series under the pseudonym of "Douglas Wells"; and at least 17 dime novels for Street & Smith's "Columbia Library" series in which he used both pseudonyms.

104William M. Gibson, "Mark Twain and William Dean Howells, Anti-Imperialists," Unpublished Ph.D. dissertation, University of Chicago, 1940, pp. 122-23 and William M. Gibson, "Mark Twain and Howells: Anti-Imperialists," New England Quarterly 20(December, 1947):437.
In August, 1898, Howells published in Harper's Weekly his first anti-imperialist article, "Our Spanish Prisoners at Portsmouth" in which he held the United States responsible for the war.

[105]William Dean Howells, "Editha," Harper's Monthly 110(January, 1905):214-25, and reprinted in Between the Dark and the Daylight, Romances (New York, 1907), pp. 127-43.

[106]Edith Elmer Wood, The Spirit of the Service (New York, 1903), pp. 203-04.

[107]Ibid., pp. 237-38.

[108]Ibid., pp. 236-37.

[109]Perry E. Gianakos, "The Spanish-American War and the Double Paradox of the Negro American," Phylon (Spring, 1965):37, 39-40.
In Stratemeyer's novel, Walter Russell and Si Doring, two of the leading characters, encounter Jim Crow practices for the first time when they journey by train from Washington to Fort Monroe, Virginia. Walter observes that "it is odd . . . to see separate cars for negroes and whites [for] we don't have any such thing up North." The incident ends when Si draws Walter's attention to a newspaper story: "By the way, I see in the newspaper that among the first troops to be sent to Cuba will be two regiments of negroes. Harrah for those boys, say I." Earlier in the novel, Antonio Maceo, the great Cuban guerrilla leader, is referred to as "one of the best negro patriots that ever existed." (Edward Stratemeyer, Fighting in Cuban Waters; or, Under Schley on the Brooklyn (Boston, 1899), pp. 87, 57. For Maceo, see Philip S. Foner, Antonio Maceo: The "Bronze Titan" of Cuba's Struggle for Independence (New York, 1978).

[110]Gianakos, "Ernest Howard Crosby," p. 15.
City and State, a leading anti-imperialist weekly published in Philadelphia, reported that when Crosby made this appeal at a public meeting in Boston, members of the audience came up to him after his talk, and urged him "to do that very thing himself," (April 3, 1902.)

[111]Gianakos, "Ernest Howard Crosby," p. 18.

[112]Ernest Crosby, Captain Jinks, Hero (New York, 1902), p. 12.

[113]Ibid., p. 24.

[114]Ibid., pp. 71-72.

[115]Ibid., pp. 121-22.

[116]Ibid., pp. 190-91.

[117]Gianakos, "Ernest Howard Crosby," p. 8; Gianakos, "The Spanish-American War," p. 48.

[118]Ernest Crosby, Captain Jinks, Hero, p. 270-71.

[119]Ibid., p. 323.

[120]Ibid., pp. 361, 393.

[121]Perry E. Gianakos points to several specific instances
in which Crosby satirized events well-known to readers of the
novel. For example, he notes that the kissing of Sam by the young
ladies on his return home was based on the real event known as the
"Kissing Hobson." Lt. Richmond Pearson Hobson was taken prisoner
by the Spaniards after his attempt to trap Cervera's fleet inside
Santiago harbor failed. But his action was made an heroic episode
of the war in the press, and when he appeared in the United
States after the war, he was kissed by a number of women. From
then on, wherever he went, he was mobbed by young women anxious
to kiss Hobson. (Gianakos, "Ernest Howard Crosby," p. 18.)

[122]Literary Digest, March 29, 1902, p. 441.

[123]W.J.S. in City and State, April 3, 1902.

[124]F.C.S. in preface to Ernest Crosby, Captain Jinks, Hero,
(Upper Saddle River, N.J., 1968). This facsimile reprint of the
1902 edition is part of the series of "American Novels of
Muckraking, Propaganda, and Social Protest."

[125]Gianakos, "Ernest Howard Crosby," p. 4.
However, Fred H. Harrington's essay, "The Literary Aspects
of Anti-Imperialism," published in the New England Quarterly for
1937, devoted only one paragraph to a description and discussion
of Captain Jinks, Hero.

[126]Raymond Landon Bridgman, Loyal Traitors: A Story of
Friendship for the Filipinos, Boston, 1903, pp. 23-24.

[127]Ibid., pp. 217-20.

[128]Ibid., pp. 54-56.

[129]Ibid., pp. 35-37, 89, 306-07.

[130]Ibid., pp. 12-16.

[131]Ibid., pp. 67-68.

[132]Ibid., pp. 48-52.

[133]Ernest Howard Crosby, Swords and Ploughshares (New York
and London, 1906), p. 26; John M. Gates, "Philippine Guerrillas,
American Anti-Imperialists, and the Election of 1900," Pacific
Historical Review 46(September, 1977):53-54; New York Times,
October 1, 1900.

[134]Michael C. Robinson and Frank N. Schubert, "David Fagen: An Afro-American Rebel in the Philippines, 1899-1901," Pacific Historical Review 44(February, 1975):68-83.

[135]Bridgman, Loyal Traitors, pp. 70, 95.
For discussions of the Negro soldiers in the war against the Filipinos, see Willard B. Gatewood, Jr., editor, "Smoked Yankees" and the Struggle for Empire: Letters from Negro Soldiers, 1898-1902 (Urbana, Ill., pp. 101-255; Willard B. Gatewood, Jr., "Black Americans and the Quest for Empire, 1898-1903," Journal of Southern History 38(1972):545-66.

[136]Bridgman, Loyal Traitors, p. 101.

[137]Ibid., pp. 217-18.

[138]Ibid., p. 310.

[139]This is not, however, the view of Fred Harvey Harrington who believes that the poor quality of the literary output of American anti-imperialism merits the oblivion it achieved. (op.cit., pp. 666-67.)

CHAPTER I

POETRY

1. WILLIAM VAUGHN MOODY

AN ODE IN TIME OF HESITATION

(After seeing at Boston the statue of Robert Gould Shaw, killed while storming Fort Wagner, July 18, 1863,[1] at the head of the first enlisted Negro regiment, the Fifty-fourth Massachusetts.)

I

Before the solemn bronze Saint Gaudens[2] made
To thrill the heedless passer's heart with awe,
And set here in the city's talk and trade
To the good memory of Robert Shaw,
This bright March morn I stand,
And hear the distant spring come up the land;
Knowing that what I hear is not unheard
Of this boy soldier and his negro band,
For all their gaze is fixed so stern ahead,
For all the fatal rhythm of their tread.
The land they died to save from death and shame
Trembles and waits, hearing the spring's great name,
And by her pangs these resolute ghosts are stirred.

II

Through street and mall the tides of people go
Heedless; the trees upon the Common show
No hint of green; but to my listening heart
The still earth doth impart
Assurance of her jubilant emprise,
And it is clear to my long-searching eyes
That love at last has might upon the skies.
The ice is runneled on the little pond;
A telltale patter drips from off the trees;
The air is touched with southland spiceries,

3

As if but yesterday it tossed the frond
Of pendant mosses where the live-oaks grow
Beyond Virginia and the Carolines,
Or had its will among the fruits and vines
Of aromatic isles asleep beyond
Florida and the Gulf of Mexico.

III

Soon shall the Cape Ann children shout in glee,
Spying the arbutus, spring's dear recluse;
Hill lads at dawn shall hearken the wild goose
Go honking northward over Tennessee;
West from Oswego to Sault Sainte-Marie,
And on to where the Pictured Rocks are hung,
And yonder where, gigantic, wilful, young,
Chicago sitteth at the northwest gates,
With restless violent hands and casual tongue
Moulding her might fates,
The Lakes shall robe them in etheral sheen;
And like a larger sea, the vital green
Of springing wheat shall vastly be outflung
Over Dakota and the prairie states.
By desert people immemorial
On Arizonan mesas shall be done
Dim rites unto the thunder and the sun;
Nor shall the primal gods lack sacrifice
More splendid, when the white Sierras call
Unto the Rockies straightway to arise
And dance before the unveiled ark of the year,
Sounding their windy cedars as for shawms,
Unrolling rivers clear
For flutter of broad phylacteries;
While Shasta signals to Alaskan seas
That watch old sluggish glaciers downward creep
To fling their icebergs thundering from the steep,
And Mariposa through the purple calms
Gazes at far Hawaii crowned with palms
Where East and West are met,--
A rich seal on the ocean's bosom set
To say that East and West are twain,
With different loss and gain:
The Lord hath sundered them; let them be sundered yet.

IV

Alas! what sounds are these that come
Sullenly over the Pacific seas,--
Sounds of ignoble battle, striking dumb
The season's half-awakened ecstasies?
Must I be humble, then,
Now when my heart hath need of pride?
Wild love falls on me from these sculptured men;

4

By loving much the land for which they died
I would be justified.
My spirit was away on pinions wide
To sooth in praise of her its passionate mood
And ease it of its ache of gratitude.
Too sorely heavy is the debt they lay
On me and the companions of my day.
I would remember now
My country's goodliness, make sweet her name.
Alas! what shade art thou
Of sorrow or of blame
Liftest the lyric leafage from her brow,
And pointest a slow finger at her shame?

V

Lies! lies! It cannot be! The wars we wage
Are noble, and our battles still are won
By justice for us, ere we lift the gage.
We have not sold our loftiest heritage.
The proud republic had not stooped to cheat
And scramble in the market-place of war;
Her forehead weareth yet its solemn star.
Here is her witness: this, her perfect son,
This delicate and proud New England soul
Who leads despisèd men, with just-unshackled feet,
Up the large ways where death and glory meet,
To show all peoples that our shame is done,
That once more we are clean and spirit-whole.

VI

Crouched in the sea fog on the moaning sand
All night he lay, speaking some simple word
From hour to hour to the slow minds that heard,
Holding each poor life gently in his hand
And breathing on the base rejected clay
Till each dark face shone mystical and grand
Against the breaking day;
And lo, the shard the potter cast away
Was grown a fiery chalice crystal-fine
Fulfilled of the divine
Great wine of battle wrath by God's ring-finger stirred.
Then upward, where the shadowy bastion loomed.
Huge on the mountain in the wet sea light,
Whence now, and now, infernal flowerage bloomed,
Bloomed, burst, and scattered down its deadly seed,--
They swept, and died like freemen on the height,
Like freemen, and like men of noble breed;
And when the battle fell away at night
By hasty and contemptuous hands were thrust
Obscurely in a common grave with him
The fair-haired keeper of their love and trust.

Now limb doth mingle with dissolvèd limb
In nature's busy old democracy
To flush the mountain laurel when she blows
Sweet by the southern sea,
And heart with crumbled heart climbs in the rose:--
The untaught hearts with the high heart that knew
This mountain fortress for no earthly hold
Of temporal quarrel, but the bastion old
Of spiritual wrong,
Built by an unjust nation sheer and strong,
Expugnable but by a nation's rue
And bowing down before that equal shrine
By all men held divine,
Whereof his band and he were the most holy sign.

VII

O bitter, bitter shade!
Wilt thou not put the scorn
And instant tragic question from thine eye?
Do thy dark brows yet crave
That swift and angry stave--
Unmeet for this desirous morn--
That I have striven, striven to evade?
Gazing on him, must I not deep they err
Whose careless lips in street and shop aver
As common tidings, deeds to make his cheek
Flush from the bronze, and his dead throat to speak?
Surely some elder singer would arise,
Whose harp hath leave to threaten and to mourn
Above this people when they go astray.
Is Whitman,[3] the strong spirit, overworn?
Has Whittier[4] put his yearning wrath away?
I will not and I dare not yet believe!
Though furtively the sunlight seems to grieve,
And the spring-laden breeze
Out of the gladdening west is sinister
With sounds of nameless battle overseas;
Though when we turn and question in suspense
If these things be indeed after these ways,
And what things are to follow after these,
Our fluent men of place and consequence
Fumble and fill their mouths with hollow phrase,
Or for the end-all of deep arguments
Intone their dull commercial liturgies--
I dare not yet believe! My ears are shut!
I will not hear the thin satiric praise
And muffled laughter of our enemies,
Bidding us never sheathe our valiant sword
Till we have changed our birthright for a gourd
Of wild pulse stolen from a barbarian's hut;
Showing how wise it is to cast away
The symbols of our spiritual sway,

6

That so our hands with better ease
May wield the driver's whip and grasp the jailer's keys.

VIII

Was it for this our fathers kept the law?
This crown shall crown their struggle and their ruth?
Are we the eagle nation Milton[5] saw
Mewing its mighty youth,
Soon to possess the mountain winds of truth,
And be a swift familiar of the sun
Where aye before God's face his trumpets run?
Or have we but the talons and the maw,
And for the abject likeness of our heart
Shall some less lordly bird be set apart?--
Some gross-billed wader where the swamps are fat?
Some gorger in the sun? Some prowler with the bat?

IX

Ah no!
We have not fallen so.
We are our fathers' sons: let those who lead us know!
'Twas only yesterday sick Cuba's cry
Came up the tropic wind, "Now help us, for we die!"
Then Alabama heard,
And rising, pale, to Maine and Idaho
Shouted a burning word.
Proud state with proud impassioned state conferred,
And at the lifting of a hand sprang forth,
East, west, and south, and north,
Beautiful armies. Oh, by the sweet blood and young
Shed on the awful hill slope at San Juan,[6]
By the unforgotten names of eager boys
Who might have tasted girls' love and been stung
With the old mystic joys
And starry griefs, now the spring nights come on,
But that the heart of youth is generous,--
We charge you, ye who lead us,
Breathe on their chivalry no hint of stain!
Turn not their new-world victories to gain!
One least leaf plucked for chaffer from the bays
Of their dear praise,
One jot of their pure conquest put to hire,
The implacable republic will require;
With clamor, in the glare and gase of noon,
Or subtly, coming as a thief at night,
But surely, very surely, slow or soon
That insult deep we deeply will requite.
Tempt not our weakness, our cupidity!
For save we let the island men go free,
Those baffled and dislaureled ghosts
Will curse us from the lamentable coasts

Where walk the frustrate dead.
The cup of trembling shall be drained quite,
Eaten the sour bread of astonishment,
With ashes of the hearth shall be made white
Our hair, and wailing shall be in the tent;
Then on your guiltier head
Shall our intolerable self-disdain
Wreak suddenly its anger and its pain;
For mainfest in that disastrous light
We shall discern the right
And do it, tardily.--O ye who lead,
Take heed!
Blindness we may forgive, but baseness we will smite.

Atlantic Monthly, vol LXXXV, May, 1900, pp. 593-98

ON A SOLDIER FALLEN IN THE PHILIPPINES

Streets of the roaring town,
Hush for him, hush, be still!
He comes, who was stricken down
Doing the word of our will.
Hush! Let him have his state,
Give him his soldier's crown.
The grists of trade can wait
Their grinding at the mill,
But he cannot wait for his honor, now the trumpet has
been blown;
Wreathe pride now for his granite brow, lay love on his
breast of stone.

Toll! Let the great bells toll
Till the clashing air is dim.
Did we wrong this parted soul?
We will make up it to him.
Toll! Let him never guess
What work we set him to.
Laurel, laurel, yes;
He did what we bade him do.
Praise, and never a whispered hint but the fight he
fought was good;
Never a word that the blood on his sword was his
country's own heart's-blood.

A flag for the soldier's bier
Who dies that his land may live;
O, banners, banners here,
That he doubt not nor misgive!
That he heed not from the tomb
The evil days draw near
When the nation, robed in gloom,
With its faithless past shall strive.

8

Let him never dream that his bullet's scream went wide
        of its island mark,
Home to the heart of his darling land where she stumbled
        and sinned in the dark.

Atlantic Monthly, vol LXXXV, May, 1900, pp. 593-98

THE QUARRY

Between the rice swamps and the fields of tea
I met a sacred elephant, snow-white.
Upon his back a huge pagoda towered
Full of brass gods and food of sacrifice.
Upon his forehead sat a golden throne,
The massy metal twisted into shapes
Grotesque, antediluvian, such as move
In mythe or have their broken images
Sealed in the stony middle of the hills.
A peacock spread his thousand dyes to screen
The yellow sunlight from the head of one
Who sat upon the throne, clad stiff with gems,
Heirlooms of dynasties of buried kings,--
Himself the likeness of a buried kind,
With frozen gesture and unfocused eyes.
The trappings of the beast were overscrawled
With broideries--sea-shapes and flying things,
Fan-trees and dwarfed nodosities of pine,
Mixed with old alphabets, and faded lore
Fallen from ecstatic mouths before the Flood,
Or gathered by the daughters when they walked
Eastward in Eden with the Sons of God
Whom love and the deep moon made garrulous.
Between the carven tusks his trunk hung dead;
Blind as the eyes of pearl in Buddha's brow
His beaded eyes stared thwart upon the road;
And feebler than the doting knees of eld,
His joints, of size to swing the builder's crane
Across the war-walls of the Anakim,
Made vain and shaken haste. Good need was his
To hasten: panting, foaming, on the slot
Came many brutes of prey, their several hates
Laid by until the sharing of the spoil.
Just as they gathered stomach for the leap,
The sun was darkened, and wide-balanced wings
Beat downward on the trade-wind from the sea.
A wheel of shadow sped along the fields
And o'er the dreaming cities. Suddenly
My heart misgave me, and I cried aloud,
"Alas! What dost thou here? What dost thou here?"
The great beasts and the little halted sharp,
Eyed the grand circler, doubting his intent.
Straightway the wind flawed and he came about,

9

Stooping to take the vanward of the pack;
Then turned, between the chasers and the chased,
Crying a word I could not understand,--
But stiller-tongued, with eyes somewhat askance,
They settled to the slot and disappeared.

Poems and Plays of William Vaughn Moody (Boston and New York,
1912), pp. 26-28

EXPLANATORY NOTES

[1]The Massachusetts all-Negro Fifty-Fourth Regiment, under the command of white Colonel Robert Gould Shaw, was ordered to storm Fort Wagner in South Carolina, even though the men were sick and exhausted from days of fighting and forced marches. A weary regiment led the ill-starred assault and suffered about 42 percent casualties. Colonel Shaw and many of his soldiers were killed, but the bravery of the Negro soldiers in one of the hardest-fought battles of the Civil War became famous throughout the North.

[2]The "Shaw Memorial" opposite the State House in Boston by the sculptor Augustus Saint-Gaudens (1848-1907), was unveiled in 1897.

[3]Walt Whitman (1819-1892), was one of the greatest literary figures in American history, and has often been identified with the American democratic tradition. His Leaves of Grass (1855) broke with conventional verse and conventional ideas, and his Democratic Vistas (1871) was a prose testimony of faith in democracy.

[4]John Greenleaf Whittier (1807-1892), militant Abolitionist poet, author of books of poetry including The Voices of Freedom (1846).

[5]John Milton (1608-1647), one of England's greatest poets, author of Paradise Lost (1667), and the sequel Paradise Regained (1671).

[6]The Battle of San Juan Hill was a famous battle of the war against Spain. It was fought on July 1, 1898 during the American advance on Santiago de Cuba. The Americans captured the hill. The American division included the "Rough Riders."

11

2. HENRY BLAKE FULLER

Selections from THE NEW FLAG: SATIRES

PICTURE OF THE GREAT EXPANSION ARGUMENT

The author is able to enrich his volume with an authentic
picture of the One Great Expansion Argument. All others spurious.
In doing so he would fain temper the shock to those pure souls
who still suppose it should look more like a lion; he cannot,
however, overlook his duty to the truth. This is not the age of
romance, of the lofty but illogical lion, but of the practical
hog. Contrast the two animals. A lion eats when he is hungry
and so far he is a good Imperialist; but he stops there. When a
hog satisfies his hunger he has only begun. After the needs of
nature comes Benevolent Assimilation--duty seconds appetite--his
higher nature comes in (or rather out). He considers what he
owes to the world and so he goes right on eating, and so does the
Imperialist.
A lion stays thin; he won't eat more than nature requires.
He'd call it Criminal Aggression to do so. He has certain
regulations you couldn't tempt him to violate with a can of
Administration beef. His food has to be game or he won't touch
it--no half eaten carcasses and left over dishes for your lion.

Thou shalt commit no murder. God (Moses' interpretation.)
That does not apply to the wholesale business. McKinley's
interpretation (after fasting and prayer).

But a hog isn't so "fussy;" neither is an Imperialist.
A useful hog, a pleasant Imperialist that would be to
question his victuals. All is grist to his mill. "Expansion" is
the word in his stye, and you never saw a hog or an Imperialist
go and hide when he saw the swill coming. He doesn't say "please
help the others," either.

The hog is up to date, not up to 1776 or
1863, but up to 1899; he knows when things are moving his way,
and he thinks there isn't a slice of the earth big enough to bust
his Constitution.

What's history to a hog, what's experience to a hog, what's
truth and reason to a hog, what's humanity to a hog--well, what
are those things to an Imperialist?

There are points of likeness between the two--they think
alike, they feel alike, they look alike, they talk alike, they
vote alike, and if they don't walk alike it is only because the
Imperialist is smarter than a hog. He goes on his hind legs so
he can feed himself with his front. No, the lion is decorative
but inefficient; he's old fogey, an "Auntie," a "little American."
He doesn't Improve like a hog. Why, I've seen a hog eat off a
plate, ride in horsecars, chew tobacco, pick his teeth in the
parlor, and go to the Senate. Altogether there are worse animals
than hogs.
Study Ohio politics for further information on this point.

14

Thou shalt not steal.   Moses
That would be criminal aggression.   McKinley
Nit--What has Moses got to say about it? McKinley (revised)

INVOCATION

Forever that ensanguined hour
Of dereliction without soul,
Unhallowed, when the carnate flower
Of Liberty cast by the stole
Of virgin pride: forever mate
That hour, O Time, with living hate!

When She the pure, ungirt and nude,
Apostatized from truth and right,
Yielded in concubinage lewd
To that old swollen Molochite,
That slavering Anti-Christ obscene,
The gray Imperial Libertine.

While he, the tentacle of wrong
Octopian, tool of sateless greed,
That Baal priest of corruption, strong
Only to purvey and feed
Lambs to the wolves, while he upstood
And sealed the impious bond in blood.

Upstood like Judas to betray
Our holiest to his master--Hell,--   DESTINY:
Of God unmindful so he may   See Mac's Home
To men the act dissemble well,   Market Club Speech.
As fruit of destiny true gotten,   He said: "Destiny led
Which they're to eat, albeit rotten. us into the East," Why
                isn't Destiny all right
The while--in Scripture guise again,-- for a scapegoat?
Like Pilate in the market place,

15

For this people's heart is waxed gross and their ears are
dull of hearing, and their eyes they have closed.

Matt. xiii. 15

He cleansed him of the filthy stain,
"Cold pot grease
of McKinley's
cant."
Prof James gave
us this pearl.
He found it in the
Home Market Speech
oyster shell.

He cleansed him of the filthy stain,
Besmearing o'er his foul disgrace
With cant's "cold pot grease," mixture,
  sooth,
He's used in lieu of soap from youth.

On him, the pustulated boil
On Mammon's nose, the noxious breath
From Typhon's maw, whose purple coil
Creeps upward in a winding wreath,
To wave defiance in Jove's eye,
And write McKinley o'er the mad'ning sky.

On him and on his parent tree,
Corruption's Upas, from whose crest
A leaf that veers incessantly
With winds that vary without rest,
He dangles: on the poisoned shoot
And poisoning stem from branch to root

Pour down thy Hell defeating wrath
Ye Heaven Born! let the fervid hour
Of quickened justice clear the path
Of duty with the old time power
That glowed in Garrison[1] and Brown;[2]
And turn the base Predestinators down!

That is the distinction of the gentleman, to defend the weak and redress the injured, as it is of the savage and the brutal to usurp and use others.   Emerson [3]

===

I HAD A DREAM THAT WAS NOT ALL A DREAM.
                              --Byron [4]

Reason falters near her noon
In a cataclysmal swoon,
And about the groping brain
Sudden chaos comes again,
Crowding back the angel light   Darkness which may be
With the ashen demon night,   felt. Ex. x. 21
Clouding o'er with shadows blind
All the temples of the mind--
While the beacons that have shone
Hope to man, fail one by one,
Till a fading spark alone
Tells the watcher where should be
The blazing Pharos of the Free.

Hark! upon the straining ear
Breaks the din the damned must hear,   POLITICIANS.
In Hell torment--all abroad   For wheresoever the
Belial's people push and crowd,   carcase is, there will
Sheltered by the drifting murk,   the eagles be gathered
Bent upon the Imperial work   together. Matt. xxiv.
Of the arch Expansionist,   28
Satan, foremost in the list
Of kings who rule by right divine,
And hold the faith of "Thine is mine."
Hark! They come, the crew accursed,
For murder ripe, for spoils athirst,
Clattering on cloven feet,
Laughing loud in goatish bleat;

17

THE AUNTIES' SCRAP-BOOK

Blessed are the peacemakers for they shall be called
children of God.   Matt. v. 9
You have heard that it was said by them of old time "thou
shalt not kill."   Matt. v. 21

In the viper's hiss they speak,
Vermin like they squall and squeak.

Lo! along the western flood
Dawns a lurid gleam of blood
Lighting dim the hither shore,
Where the waves of clotted gore
Softly lap--and traveling on
Through the shades of Phlegethon
Marks the Conquerer and his host
Marching onward to the coast,
Down the broad and easy way--
The frowsy horde in loose array.

And Satan came also.   Him, the plutocrat, behold,
Job i. 6   Panoplied in glittering gold,
                            Man in form, in soul a beast,
                            Hyene headed, Hanna⁵ faced,
                            On an elephant raised high
                            Sharp against the coal black sky,
                            Grinning, coarsely fleshed and gross
                            Following a mighty cross,
                            Nailed upon whose either side
                            Hangs a Malay crucified--
                            Which some Christians, over civil,
                            Carry to oblige the Devil.

Next, to pulsing pipes and drums,
See the toad shaped Idol comes;
Of Destiny the second son,
A sorry shade of number one

THE AUNTIES' SCRAP-BOOK

This nation cannot live on injustice! A house divided
against itself cannot stand, I say again and again.

Lincoln [6]

===

True Bonaparte in all but brain,
In heart as black, in hope more vain.
This survile Caliban of Fate
Rides throned upon the Ship of State,
(Monopoly's expensive float,
Modeled on the Federal boat).
And the chargers tried and stout
That drag the holy juggernaut,
They're of the famous Buckeye breed
Known by the general name of Greed.

Hail! stalwart son and Canton Hero! [7]
Thou Xerxes up to date, or Nero!
Thy vacuous face and vacant blinking
Show not the deep and devilish thinking
That makes thy mental puppets squirm
To figure out a second term
By geometric combinations
Of rotten politics and rations!

Hail! Jove with all the coward thunder!
Last in the fight, but first to plunder!
Thou sutler in the place of chief!
Thou magic word twixt thief and thief!
Thou traitor, when the Nation's heart
Stirred to espouse the victim's part,
Didst seek by every shameful wile
The noble purpose to beguile;
In vain--though not for long--for when
It came to soldiering the men,
Ye slaughtered more by base neglect
Then all the Spaniards could effect.

Whose God is their
belly and whose glory
is in their shame.
Phil. iii. 19

"To be weak is
miserable, doing or
suffering." Milton

THE AUNTIES' SCRAP-BOOK

No gentlemen, I have not asked for the nomination, and I will not now buy it with pledges. If I am nominated and elected, I shall not go into the presidency as the tool of this man or that man, or as the property of any factor or clique.   Lincoln
(Not the present incumbent at all at all.)

THE EMPEROR OF
THE PHILIPPINES!
The words of his
mouth were smoother
than butter but war
was in his heart,
Ps. lv. 21

Ye cannot serve
God and Mammon.
Matt. vi. 24

At last arose thy laggard star
Upon the rearward of the war,
The hour astrologers foretold
Thy safest to be firm and bold.
O then it was a charming sight,
After the impact of the fight,
To see thee rush with rage and might
Upon the tyrant lying prone
To pick his pockets quite alone.
Then with thy fingers at his throat
To make him deed to thee by note
The goods he didn't have; 'twas fine,
And quite in thy peculiar line.
Then thou still fired with martial
    gudgeon,
Didst seize the Despots' fallen
    bludgeon
To lay with sundry blows and whacks
On "new bought sullen people's" backs,
Forgetting "criminal aggression"
In zeal of Human Rights' Suppression.

As hounds that once have tasted gore
Race bellowing on the scent for more,
With nose to ground--so in thy noodle
Doth work the distant smell of boodle.

How slow thou wert to undertake
To raise thy finger for the sake
Of suffering Cubans, or to save
Them from starvation's cruel grave.
How wise thou wert, thou wily rat
To parley and prevaricate--

THE AUNTIES' SCRAP-BOOK

I am nothing, but truth is everything. I know I am right because I know that liberty is right, for Christ teaches it and Christ is God.

Lincoln

===

How piously thy deeds to fashion all
By laws more purely international
Respecting with minutest care
The oppressor's rights to a shade of hair.

Humanity could ne'er inspire
Thy lofty zeal like dirty hire.

For O, with what an altered mien
Ye turned upon the Philippine
As though to prove thy soul and brain
Together weighed but half a grain,
That justice counted not a pin,
Nor love of right, nor fear of sin,
Nor e'en the common manly pride,
The dread to wrong the weaker side--
When plunder was the enchanted word
To bid thee draw the assassin's sword.
Thou, who dost never bend the knee
But to invoke fresh infamy!
Thou sweating chattel slave to swine!
Who dost befoul the holy shrine
Of Liberty with murder! Thou,
What canting lies can save thee now,
Red handed as thou art, thy knife
Drinking the struggling patriot's life!
What shame can reach thy soddened heart
In shame, blood scarlet as thou art!
Who for a coral bead or rattle
'Gainst unarmed babes doth march to battle!
Calling with sanctimonious face

SENTIMENTAL NONSENSE.
Therefore, if thine enemy hunger, feed him, if he thirst, give him drink. Rom. xii. 20

If he ask for liberty, knock him on the head (McKinley's Interpretation)

Whoso sheddeth man's blood, by man shall his blood be shed. Gen. ix. 6

21

THE AUNTIES' SCRAP-BOOK.

My power is temporary and fleeting, yours is as eternal as the principle of liberty.
Cultivate and protect that sentiment, and your ambitious leaders will be reduced to the positions of servants instead of masters.   Lincoln.

Whatsoever a man soweth, that shall he also reap. Gal. vi. 8.

On God to sanction thy disgrace.
May He inflict on thee again
The curse of thine own cousin Cain!

So in thy leprosy accursed
Pass on--though bad, who'll call
    thee worst,
While 'neath thy waving pirate's pennant
Thou shippest rank Alger[8] first lieutenant,
While Hanna steers thy captain nervy,
And Eagan boards thy crew on scurvy,

Can there any good thing come out of Nazareth? John i. 46. Or the Capital at Washington?

And General Humpty Dumpty Shafter[9]
Provides them sauce of mirth and laughter.
(Thy duteous crew of toughs and thugs,
All chewing their Expansion Plugs,
Anointing with the rich solution
Thy copy of the Constitution.)
While 'twixt the decks thou'st shipped
    enough
Assorted "critters on the ho'f,"
"Bosses," such as would o'er weight
The strongest steel-ribbed Ship of State.
A carrion herd, the kind of meat
Ye sent the soldiers canned to eat--
As foul, though living--nay, so nasty,
To name it words have no capacity.
Platt, Croker, Elkins, Penrose, Quay[10]

Though thou shouldst bray a fool in a mortar, yet will his foolishness not depart from him. Prov. xxvii. 22.

Devour with greed thy Imperial Hay.[11]
While now and then a startling bray
Proclaims when Cabot Lodge[12] feels gay.

Who next appears they know by smell
The imps who hold the nose and yell--
Hailing great Alger, Limbo's chief,

22

THE AUNTIES' SCRAP-BOOK

All honor to Jefferson; to a man who in the concrete
pressure of a struggle for national independence by a single
people, had the coolness, forecast, and capacity, to introduce
into a merely revolutionary document an abstract truth,
applicable to all men and all times, and so to embalm it there
that to-day and in all coming days it shall be a rebuke and a
stumbling-block to the harbingers of reappearing tyranny and
oppression!   Lincoln
        A solar-plexus blow to imperialism!

In popping cans of rotten beef.
This darling of Beelzebub
Rides in a coffin-shaped tub
By Swift, Armour & Co. supplied,
In letters printed on the side.
Full pleased he looks, nor without cause
If pleasure means all hell's applause.
What noisome devils do for love,   A good tree cannot
He's caught the very odor of.   bring forth evil
He, in the civil war disgraced,   fruit, neither can a
In William's war is fitly placed,   corrupt tree bring
Where gifts of moral putrefaction   forth good fruit.
Procure a field of widest action.   Matt. vii. 18.
                                               Mr. McKinley's tree
Who'd view this hero's field of glory   bears Eagan and
In peaceful camps may read the story,   Alger, rotten beef,
Where blanch the bones of many a soldier   a war against freedom,
To swell the martial pride of Alger.   etc., etc. It must be
This gay dispenser of typhoid   a good tree.
And beef the very flies avoid,
Embalmed with all the chemist's skill,
By stomach ache guaranteed to kill--
His fame can hardly die at once
Till Nature can eclipse the dunce
With something even more sublime
From out the slimy ooze of Time.
Brave Alger's name must stand a mystery
Unique 'mid the pickle jars of history,
Enduring as a Pharoah's mummy
Deep in the future's "bulging tummy,"
And strange as though a drunken cabby

23

THE AUNTIES' SCRAP-BOOK

So I say in relation to the principle that all men are
created equal, let it be as nearly reached as we can. If we
cannot give freedom to every creature, let us do nothing that
will impose slavery upon any other creature.

Lincoln

PROPHECY FOR 1900
  For they have sown
the wind, and they
shall reap the whirl-
wind. Hosea viii. 7

Were buried in Westminster Abbey.
When Homer's fame is o'er and past
The scent of it is bound to last,
And scholars in the blank abyss
Of ages yet unborn to this
Turn back through volumes thick and musty
With weary eyes and fingers dusty,
When Alger's record is expected
They'll smell it and be disinfected.
And woe to him whose importunity
Should scorn deodorant immunity,
But turn, forewarned, in proud rebellion
Full on the conduct of the Hellion
In all its strength. It scarce needs
  telling
He'd suffer in his sense of smelling.

To-day amid the "epoch makers"
He blooms the prince of undertakers,
And every day and every hour
Contributes to the olfactory power
Of his accumulated curse
Of crimes or blunders, which e'er's
  worse.
His breezy infamy alike on land sports
Or floats o'er seas in sickened
  transports.
He lends to war its life and soul,
This rose in William's buttonhole.
Long may he last his Chief to cheer
And swell the Campaign fund next year.

Clad in the coat tails of humanity
What ape is this whose foul profanity
Makes imp and fallen angel blush

24

THE AUNTIES' SCRAP-BOOK

In those days our Declaration of Independence was held
sacred by all, and thought to include all; but now, to aid in
making the bondage of the negro universal and eternal it is
assailed and sneered at, and constructed and hawked at, and torn,
till if its framers could rise from their graves they could not
at all recognize it.   Lincoln

===

And spreads through Hell a frightened hush,
Who but the proselyte of Dagon,
Canned Carrion Commissary Eagan,
Heaping his mountainous abuse
In terms recondite and abstruse,
On General Miles,[13] while Alger giggles,
So much the joke his liver tickles.
Eagan,[14] McKinley's masterpiece
In excrement, the ambergrease
Corruption's mighty whale exudes,
Whose rare residuum includes
The Executive bouquet with some
Perfumes of Eagan quite as rum.

He journeys with appropriate pride
Behind his chief, his legs astride
A squirming maggot, huge and soft,
As though the beast had battened oft
On soldier food, the kind of ration
He said he'd make them eat, damnation
O'ertake them else,--so far the braggart
Mistook a soldier for a maggot.
Thus mounted with his thumb to nose
In joy derisive, on he goes
As merry as the bull of Bashan,
To contemplate his sweet vacation
Of six long years with pay and pension,
To make no secondary mention
Of all his joy in being laggard
In naught that best becomes a blackguard,
Or of his perfect satisfaction

Dagon was a fishy
God--Eagan is a god-
less fish.

Ambergrease, used
by perfumers to inten-
sify perfumes. Sup-
posed to be a disease
or exudition of
whales, because it is
found in them--see
Cruise of the
Cachalot, page 48.

25

Filipinos, let us be constant! Let us strengthen the bonds of
our union.

Aguinaldo

In winning his reward by action,
So easy for such ample hire,
As proving himself a dastard liar.
Though faith 'tis difficult as sin for me
To measure which is the deepest infamy,
Bearing gratuitous false witness
And poisoning troops with equal fitness,
Or the being worthy to receive
The bounty of the Executive.
Eagan, however that may be
Let this contribute to thy glee,--
The Hell of war is nothing to
The Hell of being fed by you.

Ah me! times change, and passing strange is
The moving pantomime of changes,
Nor can I swear they're growing properer
Since Dame Columbia took to opera,
In comic roles and scanty clothing
To chant, without apparent loathing,
But rather in a simpering manner,
The opera bouffe composed by Hanna.
Or with mock serious expression,
McKinley's hymn about aggression,
A noble piece, though out of date,
(I think it isn't sung of late).
It used to take the upper gallery.
And quite disarm their noisy raillery.

Times change, and with the shifting seasons
Try every garb excepting reason's,
And every language dead or live

26

. . If we do this, we shall not only have saved the Union but shall have so saved it as to make and to keep it forever worthy of saving. We shall have so saved it that the succeeding millions of free, happy people, the world over, shall raise up and call us blessed to the latest generations.

Lincoln

To prove that two and two make five,
That those who prate of truth have rabies,
And justice is only fit for babies
To cut their teeth on, and that might
Is always holier than right.
(Our "Teddy"[15] cut his ornamental
Magazine of frontal dental
Ivories by assiduous suckin'
Of his big toes and hence his luck in
Getting his army brogans stuck in
His mouth when'er his yap of Cerberus
Opens to howl for war perturberous.)

Times change, and the hopes of the heart are sere
As the leaves on the oak of yester year,
And the living springs of thought are as dust
In the heat of the Babylonian lust,
And the water of live is gall in the cup
And the right is down and the wrong is up,
And the host and the worthy bidden guest
The harpies drive from the waiting feast,
And only the clergy can stick it out
To gorge with the foul Imperial rout,--
To offer grace and pray and snivel
And pander God to the thankless Devil,
And cringe by Satan's chair and wait
Like dogs for bones from their master's plate.

Time's changes: may the Fates swift wing 'em
Till John D. Long[16] returns to Hingham,
Enriched with naval lore to float

27

Let us persist in our idea which is only the legitimate and
noble aspirations of a people, which is desirous at all cost to
preserve its national honor spotless and pure as crystal.
Aguinaldo [17]

On the deck of a side wheel Hingham boat;
Till Griggs[18] goes back to those he
rhymes with,
The herd he erst had merry times with,
Endeared by more than ties of blood,
The trusts that root in the Jersey mud.
Till even the Black Disgrace himself,
Is laid aside on the Canton shelf,
To sweetly dream while life declines
Of slaughter in the Philippines--
As an old hound, grown blind and toothless,
Delights to dream of carnage ruthless.
(A hound in the chase for spoils outworn,
A mangy derelict forlorn,
Left all unchained at last to snore
By the Grand Old Party's[19] kitchen door,
To snore, start up and snore again,
While in his weak, befuddled brain
He's hot upon the trail and hears
"On William" as the quarry nears.
And now the first in the belching pack,
He falls on the stricken quarries back,
And the warm blood slakes his hungry jaws
And the huntsmen shout in wild applause.
He wakes: 'was the scullion's passing
kick.)

"Christ is behind
the guns at Manila."
Eminent Divine.
Right for one
behind the
Filipinos' guns.

Times change, nor can they change too quick
Till they again bring in a season
When Liberty is not called Treason,
When murder's murder and the cross
Is not made villainy's stalking horse,
And the missionaries cease from rattling

28

We hold these truths to be self-evident, that all men are
created free and equal.

Declaration of Independence

The guns of the new apostle Gatling,
Whose very Christianizing breath
Cuts short all argument by death--
Giving the sacrament in lead
Like that in the Rev. Abbot's head.
Could Paul have seen with his own eyes
How six inch shells evangelize,
He surely would have finished preaching
And took to the modern way of teaching,
And had the heathen on the run
Armed with a Krag-Jorgensen gun.

Times change, but not till time reduces
Things to their elemental juices,
The Reverend "gents" whose race is 'twixt
A jackass' and a horse's mixed
Will other prove, I this a pity call,
Than wrong's best friends at moments critical;
As when to cite a recent savory
Sample they befriended slavery,
Or Britain more than a hundred years back,
As at this hour like mules with ears back
They approve the civilizing ravages
Of war more savage than the savages,--
Bespeaking Jesus Christ's endorsement--
Judas Iscariot's is of course meant.

Next comes in lovely Eagan's rear
A pageant suitable to cheer--
Nay move the Reverend ones to mirth
Whose happy dream is "war on earth,

29

We have never concealed our aspirations for independence,
and the fact that we will struggle on to obtain it, perhaps from
those who are now our enemies and to-morrow will be our allies,
as they were for the overthrowal of the power of Spain.

Aguinaldo

===

Ill will to men, to God the Glory,"
(The God of Babylonian story,
God of the Reverends Hoyt, the Herbivorous,
And Wise, from whom the Lord deliver us.)
'Tis Butcher Otis[20] and his men
Fresh from the Philippine slaughter pen.
Our Weyler who out Weylers Weyler,[21]
And viler if there is a viler,
Whose coward warfare naught respects,
Nor prisoners nor the female sex,
Old men, nor children, the base Sioux--
'Tis strange he doesn't scalp them too
As well as murder. Such fair trophies
Worked into covers for the "sofies"
And White House chairs would tend to assuage
Great "Rain-in-the-Face's" bloody rage,
And show the nations who inspect us
Near to the right way to respect us--
And give our "new and glorious place"
In history the last touch of grace.

Then, too, they'd do to patch the boots
Of Golden Calf on William's toots,
Or turned to napkins they'd be "winners"
At diplomatic White House dinners.
Or best of all the heathen skin
To th' knees of William's pants sewed in
Would help preserve his Sunday pair
And pad his joints with Malay hair.
Sure, God would answer William's wants
In such a pious pair of pants.

THE AUNTIES' SCRAP-BOOK

Filipinos! Delicate flower of the East, scarcely eight
months weaned from the breast of thy mother! Thou has dared to
brave a great and powerful nation such as is the United States,
after barely organizing and disciplining thy little army. Yet we
reply we will be slaves to none. . . .

Aguinaldo

Upon a load of dripping corses
Drawn by those long suffering horses,
"Benevolent assimilation,"
And "Holy Christian Civilization,"
The nimrod Otis takes his pleasure
Jovial and jocund beyond measure,
With an infanticidal booze on
Contracted in the Isle of Luzon.

The Imperial Rabbit Courser, loot he
And murder thinks is a warrior's duty.

To lend the crimson victor light
On either hand, a sickening sight,
Impaled on rows of sharpened sticks,
(One of the old Imperial tricks),
The Filipino babes and wives
Yield up in agony their lives,
Smeared and alight with burning tar
Dread holocaust--while echoes far
And near their piteous wails repeat,
Rocking the very judgment seat
Of God Almighty. Such sad wailing,
In Heaven never lacks availing.

Perched on a corpse by Otis' side,
Close as a loving groom to bride,
Sits the sweet murderer and looter,
Weyler, our brave Conquerer's tutor,
Whose pure and wise tuition we know's
Been bettered on the Filipinos,

It is wonderful how
our brilliant adminis-
tration faithfully
copies Spanish methods.
Manufactured news,
extermination of rebels
(more wholesale than
the Spaniards dreamed
of) and bombast about
"honor and
sovereignty." what
depth below this?

A sickening allegory,
but not overdrawn in
point of cruelty--see
soldiers' letters.

31

Let us readopt the Declaration of Independence, and the practices and policy which harmonize with it. Let North and South, let all Americans--let all lovers of liberty everywhere, join in the good and great work.

Lincoln

When ye therefore shall see the abomina-tion of desolation," Matt. xxiv. 15

And there shall be great tribulation, such as was not since the beginning of the world to this time, no nor ever shall be. Matt. xxiv. 21

HOPE FOR WHEATON AND THE TENNESSEE BOYS
But who shall offend one of these little ones, . . . it were better for him that a millstone were hanged about his neck, and that he were drowned in the depths of the Sea. Matt. xvii. 6.
Mr. Howells is reported to have said that he failed to see how anything good literary or otherwise could come of war, and he is right if he did. Perhaps he had just been reading the "Story of the Captains," or "How to make a mountain of a molehill I climbed in Cuba," by Col. Roosevelt, 20 vols.[24]
And except those days should be shortened, there should be no flesh saved. . . those days shall be shortened. Matt. xxiv. 22

Where precepts of extermination
Have found a tropic germination.
As witness General Wheaton's giving
Orders to leave no "nigger" living--
The shooting of wounded and of captured
Which soldiers write about enraptured
In letters home--a pleasant serial
To enrich the literature Imperial.
The pen is mightier than the sword,
As prove our volunteers abroad,
Who cause more slaughter here, tho' aliens,
Among the Imperial Bum-battalions,
By their epistolary scrawls,
Then there amid their bloody brawls--
Indifferently exterminators
There of patriots, here of traitors.
True, Howells[22] says that war's deficient
In making authors more proficient--
Our soldier boy who slays, then copies it
With pen and paper, proves the opposite.
Next follows at the Chieftain's back,
And trudging in his gory track--
The sad self-immolated Schurman,[23]
An erst while honest Dutch or German,
Who lent himself to be a "rooter"
For our Imperial Free-booter--
Serving upon the Philippine
Commission--worth about a bean,
Except to publish now and then,
'Mid foreign climes and new bought men,

32

Rather than make a war of conquest on this people I would anchor and sail out of the harbor. Admiral Dewey to H. Clay MacCauley.

===

ADMINISTRATION ALPHABET

He has been pulled off as we go to press--giving McKinley a more naked grandeur by his lack.

A is for Alger so sprightly and gay--
You can't blow him off and he won't fly
  away--
A--Adhesive Alger.

B is for Beef which Alger declares
"If some of it's rotten what of it, who
  cares?
B--Bilious Bad Beef.

C is for cans of the beef of the Trust.
So gaseous and putrid it's likely to "bust."
C--Cacaphonous Cans.

D is for Drivel--the Administration's
Simple receipt for Expansion orations.
D--Ditchwater Drivel.

E is for Egan--a word to refine
On nauseous and nasty and things in that
  line.
E--Elegant Egan.

F is for Fool, you have seen him before,
He hollers "Expansion!" and acts like a
  bore.
F--Fol-de-rol Cabot Lodge.

G for Guns which McKinley has sent
To teach Filipinos what Jesus Christ meant.
G--Gospel of Guns.

H is for Hanna or Hell, you may please
Yourself in your choice, they're alike as
  two peas.
H--Hell of a Hanna.

33

THE AUNTIES' SCRAP-BOOK

Is not that (the Philippine war) the statesmanship of the
great Master who limited not His mission or that of his Disciples
to His own chosen people, but proclaimed that His gospel should
be preached in all the world, unto all nations, that greatest
statesman of all times, Jesus Christ. John D. Long.
0 generation of vipers, how can ye being evils, speak good
things?"
Blessed are the merciful for they shall obtain mercy.
Matt.v.7

I is the Inkling the Public will get
That glory and Piracy land them in debt.
I--Insuperable Inkling.

J is for Jackass who thought he would speak
So he went to the Senate and brayed for a week.
J--Joyous Foraker.[25]

K is for king with a crown on his head--
If McKinley could have one he'd wear it
   in bed.
K--Kuss the old king.

L is to Let on the Canton Home Door.
It will not be there in a year or so more.
L--Lonely to Let.

M is for Muddle--for one that is jolly see
William McKinley his Philippine policy.
M--Mischievous Muddle.

N is for Not and it always applies
To the Administration when coupled with wise.
N--Negative Not.

0 stands for oppression which is the
   main stanchion
Of that dark delusion we nickname
   Expansion.
0--Obnoxious oppression.

P is for Patriot--not of the kind
Who gambles on Destiny going in blind.
P--Practical Patriot.

Q is for Quibble--the nearest to reason
The Administration can venture this
season.
Q--Quaint little Quibble.

If you offered McKinley
a $10 horse for $75
would he buy it and say
it was his destiny to
do so?
That is if it wasn't
Uncle Sam who had to
pay for it.

34

THE AUNTIES' SCRAP-BOOK

I leave you, hoping that the lamp of liberty will burn in
your bosom until there shall no longer be a doubt that all men
are created free and equal.   Lincoln

R is for Religion and Rapine and Ravage
Our civilization conveys to the savage.
R--Rampant Religion of Rapine and Ravage.

S is for Service--the kind that is civil
McKinley has sweetly consigned to the Devil.
S--Suffering Service.

T is for Traitor--one Smith says that Atkinson's
such, but he talks through his hat.
T--Terrible Traitor.

U is for undertaker, the sole friend in need
of soldiers when Egan has sent them their feed.
U--Useful Undertaker.

V is for virtue--just glance at our "Teddy."
He couldn't have more for he's got it already.
V--Virulent Virtue.

W is for whitewash--McKinley requires
From a Board of Enquiry which never enquires.
W--worthless old Whitewash.

X is for Xerxes--Imperial Monster!
Let him copy McKinly as much as he wants ter.
X--Excellent Xerxes.

Y is for Yarmouth whose bloaters are known,
We've some in the Senate as good as our own bloaters.
Y--Yearning for Yarmouth bloaters.

Z is for Zeus, the Imperial Breeder,
He turned goose like McKinley to chase a Mis Le(a)da(er).
Z--Zealous old Zeus.

NOTE--His Philippine Polly (see?)

35

TEXTS FOR IMPERIALISTS

Woe unto you Scribes and Pharisees! hypocrites . . . Ye
serpents, ye offspring of vipers, how shall ye escape the
judgment of Hell! Therefore behold I send unto you prophets and
wise men and scribes. Some of them shall ye kill and crucify, .
. . that upon you may come all the righteous blood shed on earth,
from the blood of Abel the righteous, and the blood of Zachariah,
son of Barachiah.   Matthew xxiii, 29-35

To save themselves and help the flag
The patriot trusts contributed
Some fifteen millions to the "Swag"
To be betimes distributed.

'Twas done: The voters bought or bribed
Or morally irrelevant--
A clean majority inscribed
For Hanna his White Elephant--

And down to Hell Mark wired along   The Lorelei was a
"We've won upon the 'moral lay,'   fabled maiden who sat
'Repudiation' was our song,   upon a rock by the
McKinley did the 'Lorelay.'   Rhine and sang seduc-
                                          tive songs in such a
"Start up the fires, make Hades howl,   manner that boatmen
We'll celebrate a tiny mite--   were bewitched by them
And tickle every sinner's soul   and allowed their boats
With brimstone mixed with dynamite.   to drift into a fatal
                                          whirlpool near by.
"And let the ministers devote   (See Mark Twain's
A sermon to Morality,   Tramp Abroad)
And by our glorious triumph note
Its uses in Rascality.

"That all the rising Imps may see
The value of hipocrisy,
And how to win a victory
As touching a democracy.

"Then turning to our busy past,
Expend a little gabble on
The way we did things, per contrast,
In Ninevah and Babylon.

TEXTS FOR IMPERIALISTS

No servant can serve two masters, for either he will hate
the one and love the other, or else he will hold to the one and
despise the other. Ye cannot serve God and Mammon.   Luke xvi. 13

"And then explain the various need,
To bring the lesson home at once,
That different times and races breed--
Though all roads lead to Rome at once.

"The wholesome homily expand
To signify how sin ever
May lure the freest folds to stand
At last with Impious Ninevah.

"Ah, those were times! 'Tis our devout
Desire to bring them in again,
And where a Nation grows a snout
'Tis ours the game to win again.

"The Golden Calf has paved the way,
And we have won the outer works--
The Citadel is in our pay,
To undermine the stouter works.

"Ay, soon their boasted Sphereborn Maid,
Their Liberty, we'll 'diddle' her--
She'll jig it like a jolly jade--
The Devil for her fiddler.

"Where sanctimonious Cant and Greed
The birds of kindred feather go,
We'll send a vulture of Hell's breed
And let 'em forth together go.

"He'll lead them to a little snare
We'd lay our valued all upon,
Baited with most consummate care
For Greed and Cant to fall upon.

37

TEXTS FOR IMPERIALISTS

The Scribes and Pharisees sit on Moses seat . . . . Yea they
bind heavy burdens grievous to be borne, and lay them on men's
shoulders; but they themselves will not move them with their
finger.   Matthew xxiii, 2-3-4

"And Greed will silently devour
The bait, with unctuosity
Will Cant her mouthing prayers forth pour
With sickening verbosity.

"And straight McKinley will reply
As being the vicegerent
Of God on Earth, by letting fly
Haphazard and belligerent.

"That War to Cant and Greed may add
Its rage to stir the muddle up,
And rendering all the people mad,
Their intellects quite fuddle up.

"The venal press will stand us in
With 'Glory' for an overword,
To waft us with our hungry Sin
Incontinently cloverward.

"'World Power,' 'Expansion,' 'Destiny,'
'Our Trust,' 'Our solemn Duty to
The World at Large,' the naked lie
Shall garnish with their beauty too.

"For, mark, not all the world nor all
The powers of Hell may deal ill or
Procure the Samson Nation's fall
As sure as lying Delilah.

"And such a feminine ally
In Sensual Prosperity,
Is ours to fell the giant by
With quietest celerity.

Let us not hamper the
fresh young life of the
Imperialist, as,
bursting the coccon of
the constitution, he
soars through the
Empyrean lighted
onward by the tinsel
stars of meretricious
catchwords. Let us not
recall to his mind that
yesterday he was only a
worm, a slug, like the
rest of us, either bald
or fuzzy; nor shorten
his delusive joy by any
loud or sudden noise.
"Day cometh when no
moth may flit."

38

TEXTS FOR IMPERIALISTS

Woe unto you Scribes and Pharisees, hypocrites, for ye are
like unto whited sepulchres which outwardly appear beautiful but
inwardly are full of dead men's bones and all uncleanness. Even
so ye also outwardly appear neighbors unto men, but inwardly ye
are full of hypocrisy and iniquity.

Matthew xxiii. 27-28

"Well, boys, goodby, we cannot miss
With Roosevelt to howl for us--
His 'strenuous Life' is worth the hiss
That netted the first soul for us.

"Fix up the Auditorium;
Next National Convention it
Is likely I shall hold at home,
I half forgot to mention it."

So Master Hanna's message went
To all the Hades officers--
The Imps scarce knowing what he meant
By his elated prophecies.

But we begin to see the trend
Of his extreme excursiveness.
As history begins to lend
A light on his conversiveness.

Of Cant he spoke of and of Greed
And War in each particular
We've all the evidence we need
Both ocular and auricular.

What act the second may reveal
In Hanna's high dramatical
Attempt, we're quite content to feel
At present's problematical.

TEXTS FOR IMPERIALISTS

And he said unto them ye are they that justify yourselves in the sight of men; but God knoweth your hearts, for that which is exalted among men is an abomination in the sight of God.

THE RHYMED ROOSEVELT--A STUMPING ODE

Tune: "I'm The Plumber!"

I'm a howling, thumping, growling,
   jumping,
Broadway cable car,
I'm a trolley on a down hill slope
With my fender up for war.
It's moil and strife and a "strenuous
   life"
And the smash and the grind of things,
And the jangling, wrangling, mangling,
   strangling
Joy that a battle brings,
And the shell's sweet hiss that is my
   bliss,
And that gives my spirit wings.

"Strenuous life" is one of Teddy's luminous catchwords. I've got a cat that leads a "strenuous life" I should judge every night. "I believe there should be a little less gun-powder and more diplomacy." Brig. Gen. Funston,[26] "Roosevelt of Philippines."

TO THE FARMERS:

Ho! there you mossbacks, farmers,
You cowards, I know you well,
Stop raising crops, you whisker-chops,
And go to raising hell!
With an axe and a hoe and a scythe, and
   a mow-
Ing machine and a fork and a flail,
And a twelve pound bar, you're fixed
   for war
On a very respectable scale:--
Stir up a row, no matter how,
Then lay for it tooth and nail.

REFRAIN

I'm a cut and thrusting bronco-busting,
Megaphone of Mars,
And its fire I breathe and I cut my
   teeth
On nails and wrought-iron bars.
I'd sit up all night to witness a fight

"I am almost a peace-at-any-price man. When life and property can be saved it is almost a crime not to follow that rule." Brig. Gen. Funston, "Roosevelt of Philippines."

TEXTS FOR IMPERIALISTS

Ye hypocrites, ye know how to interpret the face of the
earth and the heavens, but how is it ye know not how to interpret
this time? and why even of yourselves judge you not what is right?

Luke xii. 57-8

Between two roaches, I'm
A truceless, trucculent, Teddy the Terror,
And I'm in it every time
When a scrap is on with the Spanish Don,
And my stinger is out for Crime.

TO THE MECHANICS

Teddy has a
plenitude of
carefully per-
verted instincts,
combined with the
ethical resources
of a red-skin on
the warpath.

You men of the subtle hand and eye,
Of the hammer and sharp-edged tools,
Of the saw and wrench and horse and bench,
Leave making of things to fools!
'Tis better to hash and shiver and smash
And to gorge a terrible glee
On a riotous mass of shattered glass
And of broken machinery,
Than to meanly bend to tinker and mend
On the supple and coward knee!

REFRAIN

"I am a
Republican, but an
Anti-Expansionist."
Brig.-Gen. Funston,
"Roosevelt of
Philippines."

A whoop and a blow is all I know,
And a curse and a rain of lead
And the charge of horse and the weltering
   course
And the wound that is reeking red.
And I revel in the smoke and din
And the verve of the double-quick,
And the final set of the bayonet
And the yelp at the final stick.
And the spatter of brains upon the plains--
And the gore that is mushy and thick.

TEXTS FOR IMPERIALISTS

And the Pharisees who were lovers of money heard all these things, and they scoffed at him.   Luke xvi. 14

TO A HERD OF COWS

You peaceful, stupid, vacant group, I'd
Like to see you take
A little more delight in gore
For honor and glory's sake!
Quit chewing the cud and hustle for
   blood
With a jag of the ripping horn!
Get up and moo! swash round and strew
The earth with the standing corn,
Till the son of the soil shall curse
   his toil
And the hour he was born!

The Philippine seem
to be gifted with a
Roosevelt with a brain
attachment--couldn't
we trade ours for him
by throwing in a few
mules, to do the
thinking?

TO THE UNIVERSE

I'm a glaring, staring, raring, tearing,
Rudyard Kiplingite,[27]
I'm something great for a vertebrate,
And I'm toeing in for a fight.
I'm a war-cry squawking, tommy hawking,
Aboriginal Red Skin man.
What I can compass by way of a rumpus
Is Hell let loose on a first-class plan.
Boys, if you're ready, three cheers for "Teddy!"
I know him, he isn't a Sissy Anne!

(Tumultuous applause with a fire engine.)

THE ROMAN SPIRIT

   Curtius was a Roman youth who jumped into a hole in the Forum as a modest offering of "piety and valor" to appease the Gods and bribe them to shut it up, the hole. The hole closed up and Curtius was held in honorable memory every after.

TEXTS FOR IMPERIALISTS

It is easier for a camel to go through a needle's eye, than
for a rich man to enter the kingdom of heaven.   Matthew xix. 24

Mark Hanna is another Roman hailing from the classical
region around the western part of New York and Eastern Ohio.
Seeing that his party was about to sink beneath his weight of
"piety and valor" he recently made a loud proclamation of jumping
overboard, like a mordern Curtius. The only difference being
that Curt jumped to save his country from a nuisance, whereas
Mark was prompted by the desire to save his pet nuisance from his
country. Both acts were honorable in their degree, but Mark's
proved an improvement over Curt's in the sequel. Instead of
giving himself as food for sharks Mark jumped aboard a boat bound
for Europe, whence he may return in due time to save his nuisance
in its next hour of need--whereas Curt once gone was gone forever.
I wish they could have changed places!

> Though time may change the theatre bill
> A Roman is a Roman still.
> Beneath the costume of the showman,
> The Roman spirit makes the Roman.
>
> I have a little tale to tell,
> Which verifies this axiom well--
>
> Along ago, when folks got frisky
> On Roman punch instead of whiskey,--
> In simple times before the mixture,
> Of cocktails came to be a fixture,
> When Philosophs were doomed to think
> Unaided by fermented drink--
> When civilizing swigs found no room,
> An earthquake shook the Roman Forum.
> 'Twas such an unexampled spasm
> It left in the midst a gaping chasm,
> Like Teddy's or Vesuvius' crater
> And empty as an Expansion Prater,
> But deep,--in fact so deep my loose flesh
> To think of it contracts in gooseflesh.

TEXTS FOR IMPERIALISTS

And the Lord said unto him, do ye Pharisees cleanse the
outside of the cup and platter; but your inward part is full of
extortion and wickedness.   Luke xi. 39

No so the Populi Romani;
They wasted little time in Blarney,
But straight began from good positions,
To fill it up with politicians,
And what they termed their prize Hell Chokers,
As we would say their Platts and Crokers.

Their argument was good and sound
Enough to fill a hole in the ground,
Yet when this grateful task was finished
The size of the hole was not diminished.
"For why," the Elders reasoned well,
"The bottom opens into Hell,
And so these Politicians went
But homewards, so to say, Hell bent."

Now what is Rome without a forum,
Or Roman Senate without a quorum,
And how's the quorum going to meet
Without a forum under its feet?
The chasm must be filled, of course,
Or things would go from bad to worse,
But how? The question seemed belated
The more, the more it was debated.

Just then the Man of the Hour appeared,
A youth without the sign of a head.
He said he'd undertake the job soon,
And worked it out like our own Hobson,[28]
Much to the general satisfaction,
And then he cleared the decks for action.

TEXTS FOR IMPERIALISTS

Woe unto you Scribes and Pharisees, hypocrites! for you
compass sea and land to make one proselyte; and when he is become
so, ye make him two-fold more a son of hell then yourselves.
Matthew xxiii. 15

Says he, "The forum's cracked. I call
You Romans far from practical.
You have a great big hole on your hands,
You chuck in cats and empty cans
And politicians without ceasing,
And still the hole shows no decreasing.
You dreamed that you were filling it
With things you valued--aber nit.
The gods who made this darned abyss
Are not to be appeased like this.
They hold these offerings for a bluff,
They do not want your cast off stuff.

"Friends, Countrymen and Romans, what
Is the most valued thing you've got?"
The Roman populace ne'er wants a
Moment's thought to find an answer
To such a query--with one long
Strong breath, particularly strong,
The People shouted "Virtue and Piety!"
The noise was deafening and rioty,
Then all was still. The man of the hour
Drew himself up like a small tower
Of what they spoke of--"O," says he,
"By that of course you must mean me.

"To save the State, to save the Forum,
To save the Senate and the Quorum,
I, Curtius, consecrate mesulf
To jump in yon imposing gulf.
Now, then, bring out me hoss and shirt

THE AUNTIES' SCRAP-BOOK

Be just at home; then right your scroll
Of honor o'er the sea
And bid the broad Atlantic roll,
A Ferry of the Free.
(Read Pacific)   Emerson

Of mail, armor and shield," says Curt,
"I'll dress up for the part;--the fact is
I'd do it neater for some practice."--
"Your style's all right, my noble boy,"
The People shouted out with joy,
"Don't hesitate on that account,
But get your armor on and mount.
We swear you are our chiefest treasure,
'Tis strange we didn't know your measure
Before, and though we're sad to lose yer,
We love yer so we can't refuse yer.
But that's our sacrifice." At this
The girls turned on the Hobson Kiss,29
And thoroughly osculated Curt,--
He always was a little flirt.
Ah! Life is sweet and honey laden,
The kisses of the Roman maiden!
The tidal wave of snowy draperies,
Besieged him for the lips sweet raperies,
And still they came, and still though faint,
Brave Curtius proved a patient saint,
Three times he moved to mount his hack,
And thrice the maidens pulled him back,
For one more round. A sudden jealousness,
To witness their affectionate zealousness
Possessed the Populace.--"This yer Curt
Had better jump or he'll get hurt."
They muttered as they made a move
To give the engaging youth a shove.
Too late. Before the thing was wist of,
Brave Curtius was fairly kissed off

46

THE AUNTIES' SCRAP-BOOK

United States! The ages plead
Present and past in undersong,
Go put your creed into your deed
Nor speak with double tongue.

Emerson

===

The edge of the precipice. The abyss
Closed over him with a final kiss--
And so he fixed the crack in the Forum,
And gave the Senate room for a quorum.

Part II.

Now, then, the second half of my story,
Is not the less instinct with glory--
Though brief it is and not so tragic--
It has the histrionic magic
Of Curtius' feat, although the ending
Be not what one would call heartrending.

Instead of a chasm, fancy a boat,
Overloaded and barely afloat,
And ready to sink at the very next wave
Of the Popular Sea;--in the boat we have
Hanna to steer and the G.O.P.,
Packed in as closely as they can be.
McKinley has got a little toy gun,
With which he is banging away for fun,
And the rest of the crew, they holler and yell,
To see McKinley shoot so well.
And if anyone ventures, like Senator Hoar,[30]
To say that he doesn't, they raise a roar,
And call him a Tr-r-raitor for talking so.
He ought to catch hold and help 'em row.

McKinley has got the Constitution
Pinned to a barrel to try his fuse on,
He's laid a wager, that in the sequel,

For he that worketh high and wise
Nor pauses in his plan,
Will take the sun out of the skies
'Ere freedom out of man.

                                        Emerson

He can shoot out of it "Free and Equal."
The boat begins to take in water,--
Someone must jump and Alger oughter.
But Alger won't. The treacherous sea
Is as calm as a treacherous sea can be.
It isn't pleasant, it is so clear,
The fishes under the boat look queer
And shuddery, as though they waited
With great indifference for their fated
Food--Eagan, he tried to foison
Some of his beef off on 'em for poison.

The boat is sinking; McKinley's chemise
Is stuck up on oars to capture a breeze.
This kind of a picnic don't agree
With the members of the G.O.P.,
And many a valiant brow is wet
With dripping beads of anxious sweat.
Now, Hanna, you know, is in the stern,
It doesn't take him an age to learn
That an ocean steamer is coming that way
And would be upon 'em without delay.
So then he thinks this hour is nice
For some saved up self-sacrifice.
Says he, "My boys, unless I blunder
This boat of ours is going under,
Some one must jump. I consecrate
Myself, and gladly, to my fate--
I will, I'll jump." He waited here
For the rest of the crew to interfere

THE AUNTIES' SCRAP-BOOK

To found a great Empire for the sole purpose of raising up a
people of customers may at first sight appear a project fit only
for a nation of shop keepers. Adam Smith, Wealth of Nations,
Vol. II., Book. IV. Vide Gage's plan to sell bedsteads to
Filipinos and the "absurd" Smith's butter tub idea.

In vain. They thought it were a lark
To see the adipose agile Mark
At a game of hide and seek with a shark.
But good McKinley wiped his eye.
He said, "I'm sorry, I hope to die,
If ever we get to land, we'll set
A monument up for you, Mark, you bet,
It don't seem right." Here Hanna gave
His jeweled hand a majestic wave.
The Cabinet fainted and Griggsy cried,
While "the kingmaker" slid over the side
Just in time to catch a guy rope
That swung from the steamer bound for Europe.
Mark swung aboard and tossed his hat,
And hoped they "would weather it after that,"
And so the Roman spirit flared
In the heart of Hanna unimpaired.

TWO PRAYERS

"I saw a Tagal warrior lying quite still face upwards with a
bullet wound in his breast."   Newspaper

FACED to the stars he lies,
Silence to silence, deep to deep,
As he were following through the night
His own soul's re-awakened flight,
Far upward through the radiant skies,
To where the Eternal in Paradise,
Beyond the gates of human sleep,
Awaits it with the crown of light,
Pouring love out of His eyes,
Love and truth all souls to steep,
In endless glory, in endless might.
His glory, that is our shame;
His angel, that is our angel that was,
That freedom in whose pure behest,
He proudly bared his dusky breast,
To the ribald Yankee rifles aim,
She, the sweet Guardian of Fame,
No longer ours, beside the corse
Of the poor Tagalog doth rest,
Prayerfully breathing his humble name,
Amid the martyrs to her cause,
Her Legion, more than Emperors blest.
Tagalog, poor no more,
But only as saints and heroes be,
As martyrs purged of the body gross,
Poor but as Jesus upon the cross,
Poor with Eternity in store,
With endless truth for thy precious ore,
Poor, but we enjoy thy poverty
Thou gainest the soul with the body's loss,
We win but the husk, and slam the door
In the face of God. Thou, thou art free,
And we thy enslavers, the slaves to a mortal dross.

50

No. 2 The President went to church and joined in the singing.

There amid the congregation,
Shaven and smooth and gravely bland,
With appropriate sanctimony,
See the blood-stained murderers stand.

While the pious, sleek, obsequious,
Pulpit-pumper rattles through
With his verses from the Bible,
And the work he has to do.

Now they kneel; the name of Jesus
Saponaceously slips,
With meloduous intonations,
From the congregation's lips.

He, the monstrous malefactor,
Even without a twinge of shame,
Dares to call upon his Maker,
In the Prince of Peace's name.

And the Great Creator listens,
Quite intently to his snivel,
What can make the Great Creator
Pay attention to such drivel?

At the Master's side an angel
Is recording in a book.
This most edifying meekness,
With a beatific look.

All the prayer he neatly ledgers,
With a flourish of the pen.
And the flush of satisfaction,
While the seraphs sing "Amen."

What can ail the Great Creator?
He has lost His cheerful gladness,
And His countenance grows pallid,
With intensifying sadness.

All the Seraphs in a circle,
Trembling stand quite hushed and still,
While the Might Master thunders,
To the angel with the quill.

"Prayer is a breath, a passing vapor,
Deeds alone the truth denote,
By their fruitage ye shall know them,"
(Even God will sometimes quote).

51

"Underneath this canting prattle
Let the harvesting of sin,
Let the deeds of hell be graven
One by one, and counted in.

"Public honor prostituted
Faith betrayed and vows belied,
And the sluices of corruption
Hammered up and opened wide.

Write it in the tears of Freedom,
In the shambles crimson stain,
Mark the thousands basely butchered
For a preaccursed gain.

"Mark it with the point of iron,
In the book of adamant--
Murder, with the blacker shading
Of hypocrisy and cant."

* * * * * * * * * * * * * * * * *

Christ, the judge, meantime is welcoming
Even upon the Sabbath's day,
Flight of souls that come up shrieking
From about Manila Bay.

EXPLANATORY NOTES

[1]William Lloyd Garrison (1805-1879), famous Abolitionist; in favor of the immediate abolition of slavery; founder of the Liberator (1831), and of the American Anti-Slavery Society (1833).

[2]John Brown (1800-1859), considered the greatest of the white Abolitionists by black Americans; captured Harper's Ferry, Virginia in 1859 with the aim of overthrowing slavery. Taken prisoner with his men, among them several Negroes, and convicted of treason, hanged on December 2, 1859.

[3]Ralph Waldo Emerson (1803-1882), American transcendentalist essayist, poet, and philosopher.

[4]George Gordon Byron (1788-1824), British poet.

[5]Marcus Alanzo Hanna, known as Mark (1837-1904), Ohio businessman and politician, supported McKinley for Governor of Ohio and later for President of the United States in 1896 and 1900, raising large sums of money for him. Elected to U.S. Senate (1897-1904).

[6]Abraham Lincoln (1809-1865), sixteenth President of the United States; delivered his "House Divided" speech on June 16, 1858, before the state Republican convention at Springfield, Illinois.

[7]The reference is to William McKinley (1843-1901), twenty-fifth President of the United States and former Governor of Ohio.

[8]Russell Alexander Alger (1836-1907), Secretary of War in McKinley's cabinet, who resigned in 1899 after much criticism.

[9]William R. Shafter (1835-1906), commanding general in charge of the expeditionary force to Santiago de Cuba during the war with Spain. Notorious for his great weight. Severely criticized for his poor strategy. During the war with Spain, American soldiers were supplied with "embalmed beef" which made the meatpacking companies rich but the soldiers violently ill, and caused more than a few deaths.

[10]Thomas Collier Platt (1833-1910), powerful New York Republican leader, known as "Boss Platt."
   Richard Croker (1841-1922), Tammany Hall leader in New York City, known as "Boss Croker."
   Stephen Benton Elkins (1841-1911), U.S. Senator from West Virginia, and Republican boss of the state.
   Boies Penrose (1860-1921), U.S., Senator from Pennsylvania and Republican boss of the state after the death of Matthew Quay.
   Matthew Stanley Quay (1833-1904), U.S. Senator from and Republican boss of Pennsylvania.

[11]John Milton Hay (1838-1905), secretary to Abraham Lincoln, novelist, poet, and biographer of Lincoln; Ambassador to Great Britain, and U.S. Secretary of State under McKinley and Roosevelt (1898-1905), responsible for the Open Door Policy in China.

[12]Henry Cabot Lodge (1850-1924), U.S. Senator from Massachusetts, leading conservative Republican and expansionist.

[13]Nelson Appleton Miles (1839-1925), Major General of the United States Army who served in Cuba and Puerto Rico during the war against Spain.

[14]T. F. Eagan, Ohio politician close to McKinley.

[15]"Teddy" was Theodore Roosevelt (1858-1919), twenty-sixth President of the United States, organizer of the "Rough Riders," the first voluntary cavalry unit of the war against Spain. Served in Cuba as Colonel. Roosevelt was a leading imperialist.

[16]John Davis Long (1838-1915), Governor of Massachusetts and Congressman who was appointed Secretary of the Navy by President McKinly in 1897.

[17]Emilio Aguinaldo (1869-1964), Filipino leader; led a rebellion against Spain in 1896; exiled to Hong Kong; returned to the Philippines to work with the United States to defeat Spain, and then led an insurrection against the U.S. Army troops when the United States refused to grant independence to the Philippines. Established a republic at Malolos with himself as President in 1899. Captured by General Frederick Funston of the U.S. Army in 1901.

[18]John William Griggs (1849-1927), Republican Governor of New Jersey, appointed Attorney General in McKinley's cabinet in 1898.

[19]Better known by its abbreviation GOP. The nickname of the Republican Party.

[20]Elwell Stephen Otis (1838-1909), Major-General in command of the American VIII Army Corps, and later commander of the Department of the Pacific and military governor of the Philippines.

[21]Valeriano Weyler y Nicolau, Captain General of the island of Cuba after January, 1896, who introduced the infamous reconcentrado or reconcentration policy which established concentration camps for the Cuban people under such terrible conditions that it was to earn Weyler the name "Butcher."

[22]William Dean Howells (1837-1920), leading American novelist, editor, and critic; editor of the Atlantic Monthly; author of The Rise of Silas Lapham (1885), and many other novels, dramas, stories, etc.

[23]Jacob Gould Schurman (1854-1942), educator and diplomat, president of Cornell University and president of the first United States Philippine Commission.

[24]This is a thrust at Theodore Roosevelt's account of the Battle of San Juan Hill in his book The Rough Riders, published in 1899, and which Mr. Dooley (Peter Finley Dunne) satirized as Alone in Cuba.

[25]Joseph Benson Foraker (1846-1917), U.S. Senator from Ohio.

[26]Frederick Funston (1865-1917), U.S. general, helped suppress the Filipinos; hailed by the imperialists but condemned by anti-imperialists for the capture of Aguinaldo.

[27]Rudyard Kipling (1865-1936), British novelist, short-story writer, and poet, chiefly remembered for his celebration of British imperialism, his tales and poems of British soldiers in India and Burma, and his tales for children.

[28]Lt. Richmond Pearson Hobson was taken prisoner by the Spaniards after his attempt to trap Cervera's fleet inside Santiago harbor failed. But his action was made an heroic episode of the war in the press.

[29]When Lt. Richmond Pearson Hobson appeared in the United States after the war, he was kissed by a number of young women. From then on, wherever he went, he was mobbed by young women anxious to kiss Hobson.

[30]George Fisbie Hoar (1826-1904), U.S. Senator from Massachusetts, active in civil service reform, and a leader of the anti-imperialist movement.

3. ERNEST HOWARD CROSBY

OUR FOREIGN POLICY

The President (advancing to the footlights from the center
of a chorus of Cabinet Ministers and Senators):

> "When we told them we'd make them a nation
>   And free them in time,
> That we looked upon forced annexation
>   As aggression and crime,
> When we lured them by every assurance
>   To fight by our side,
> And flattered their pluck and endurance,
>   The fact is--"

Chorus (smiling):
> "Why, the fact is, we lied!"

The President:
> "Now we're one of the great Lying Powers.
>   In the days of our youth,
> When struggle and weakness were ours,
>   Then we dabbled in truth.
> But when we grew big like the others,
>   And, strong in our pride,
> Gave our word to our weak island-brothers,
>   The fact is--"

Chorus (chuckling):
> "Why, the fact is, we lied!"

The President:
> "We have joined the great circle of robbers
>   It was long, long ago

That we criticised grabbers and jobbers
And were honest and slow.
Now we're laughing from Maine down to Texas
At the idiots who cried:
'But you promised us not to annex us!'
For the fact is--"

Chorus (laughling):
"Why, the fact is, we lied!"

The President:
"Thus the Tsar swore to Riga and Finland
With a lie for an oath,
And then from the coast, away inland
He trampled on both.
Thus the nobles who govern Great Britain
Told lies on the Nile,
And canceled the pledge they had written
In falsehood and guile.

"And we, are we less than the British
Whose word is so glib?
He must be uncommonly skittish
Who shies at a fib!
Shall we yield to the masterful Russian
As he perjures his name?
It is hardly a thing for discussion--
We must play the same game.

"Thank the Lord, we are not sentimental!
It is dollars and trade
That governs the soul governmental--
That's the way we are made.
If we praise up the old declaration
On the Fourth of July,
And man's equal rights by creation,
The fact is--"

All Together (winking):
"Why, the fact is, we lie!"

Life reprinted in The Public, May 4, 1901

58

Selections from <u>Plain Talk in Psalm and Parable</u>

THE NEW FREEDOM

I

Americans, you once were free,--
  Free as the broad prairie and the forest profound,--
And then, after your Revolution, you led the world.
Your example fired France, and France set Europe aflame.
Without battalions or men of war you were in the van of the
  nations.
A mere handful, living in straggling hamlets along
  a thousand miles of narrow seaboard;
Without arms, you were invincible;
Without a fortress, you were invulnerable.
Your strength was your freedom.

II

Times change, and freedom changes with them,
For freedom must from age to age be born again.
The political liberty of Seventy-six, the equality before the
  law, of which you talk so much, is no longer the living
  ideal that it was;
It is now a fossil for antiquaries to toy with.
Will you play with it in the rear while the nations go marching
  on?

III

Think you to lead again by dint of armies and navies and coast
  defenses?
Not so is the world mastered.
Spread your frontiers, take Cuba and Hawaii, beguile Canada if
  you can, push on over the great Southern Hemisphere;
Will these lands be yours?
There is only one possession in them worth the capturing, and that
  is the hearts of men;
And these hearts can never be won by a nation of slaves.
Be free, and all mankind will flock to your standard.

IV

While you talk of freedom, do you not feel the fetters that are
  fastening on your limbs?
While you hurrah, are you unconscious of the burden which you are
  bearing?
Are you never weary of the endless task?
Can you still be cheered by the devilish dream of becoming
taskmasters in your turn?
Up, and to death with the tyrant!

59

Let there be no half measures; he must be torn from his insolent
    throne.
Show him no quarter; plunge the dagger in deep and again and
    again; let him welter in his blood.

V

There, at last you are rising. Where is the oppressor, do you cry?
You will not find him in the streets.
Look for him in your own souls, for the kingdom of hell is
    within you.
There reigns the greed for gold;
There it is that you are either trampling on your fellow-men or
    longing to be numbered with the tramplers;
There it is that your rebellion, your revolution must begin.

THE REGIMENT

I

The regiment is passing down the street to embark for the war.
The band is playing a stirring, swelling march.
The colonel rides alone, with the easy excellence and mastery of
    a perfect horseman on a perfect horse.
The rank and file march proudly by with eyes fixed before them.
There is conscious courage and self-sacrifice in their look.
Their bayonets are glancing in the sun.

II

The crowd on each side is carried away with enthusiasm, hurrahing,
    waving handkerchiefs and hats, and some even shedding
tears.
It is indeed a thrilling sight.
I stand at a window disapproving, and yet the excitement beats up
    against me and overwhelms me.
It is fine; it is grand; it is splendid!
I wave my handkerchief with the rest, and my eyes too become
    moist.

III

And yet I know what these men are advancing to.
They will slaughter other men as courageous and self-sacrificing
    as themselves, and against whom they have no grievance.
They will grasp others as lovable by the throat in a death
    struggle, and one life or the other will go out in hate.
They will fill a distant land with moanings and groanings and
    torments, with widows and orphans.
They will do all this and more, and yet I am forced unwillingly
    to feel that there is something magnificent in their
    spirit and carriage.

What baleful influence has thus mingled the good with the evil?
How come God and the devil to be thus inextricably intertwined?
Ah, it is the riddle of the age, to separate these contrary
        principles of life and death,
To stamp out all that is cruel and diabolical, without treading
        on the smallest atom of divine manliness and devotion.
Must we wait long for a heaven-born solution?
God forbid! but meanwhile I stand at my window, waving my
        handkerchief with shame and hesitation.

THE BLACK MAN'S BURDEN

Take up the black man's burden!
   Not his across the seas,
But his who grows your cotton,
   And sets your heart at ease,
When to the sodden rice fields
   Your children dare not go,
Nor brave the heat that singes like
   The foundry's fiery glow.

Take up the black man's burden!
   He helped to share your own
On many a scene by battle-clouds
   Portentously o'erblown;
On Wagner's[1] awful parapet,
   As late where Shafter's plan
Was for the boys to take the lead,
   He showed himself a man.

Take up the black man's burden!
   'T is heavy with the weight
Of old ancestral taint, the curse
   Of new-engendered hate;
The scorn of those who throw to him
   Their table's meanest crust--
Children of those who made him serve
   Their idleness and lust.

Take up the black man's burden!
   When you were out for votes,
His geese--they all were swans to you,
   And sheep were all his goats.
'T was "Pompey this" and "Pompey that,"
   And "Pompey, bless your heart!"
But it's "Devil take you, Pompey!" now
   You play the lion's part.

Take up the black man's burden!
   If you have got a brief

For all the suffering of the earth,
   To give them swift relief;
Don't let the millions here at home,
   Whose bonds you struck away,
Learn from your heedlessness to cry,
   "Give back the evil day!"

Take up the black man's burden!
   O black men, unto you
The summons is, when those forget
   Who should be kind and true!
Put not your trust in such as boast
   Straight hair and paler skin;
Their duty calls them otherwhere.
   Fight your own fight and--win.

Take up the black man's burden!
   Poor patient folk and tame--
The heritage of cursing,
   Of foolishness and blame.
Your task the task of earning,
   By many an evil pressed,
Warm, touched with human pity,
   The friendship of the best.

February 21, 1899

Ernest Crosby, Plain Talk in Psalm and Parable, Boston, 1899, pp. 58-60, 109-11, 115-17

WAR AND HELL

I

"War is hell," because it makes men devils.
    You and I, striving for a moment to squeeze or hack the
    life out of each other, are we not at once transformed into
    demons?
Hell is ever man's handiwork.

II

"British victory in the Soudan!
    The enemy clung obstinately to the trenches, and were
    bayonetted in them.
Nothing could have been finer than the behavior of the troops."
Nothing finer indeed!
White Christian soldiers, three thousand miles from home, in the
    pay of white Christian bond-holders, bayonetting black
    Mohammedans for defending their native land, and setting
    the example of bloodshed to brown Mohammedans whom they had
    already trained to slaughter!
Good God, is it too much to hope that the day may come when every
    sane man will shrink from running a bayonet into a
    fellow-creature as he would now shrink from torturing a
    baby?
We look back with pity, contempt, and detestation on the times of
    the rack and wheel and fagot--we, who are still in the tick
    of the Dark Ages ourselves!
A thousandfold better to be a true Mussulman dervish fighting for
    his home, than one of these Christian hypocrites
    emphasizing their barbarian butcheries with chaplains and
    crosses and Te Deums and every kind of shameless lie and
    blasphemy!

III

How they buzzed round the fires at Smithfield,
    The black, perverse, froward, reverend clergy!
(Like June beetles round the hall lamp),
Teaching the Gospel and knowing not the first word of it--
More cruel, revengeful, bloodthirsty than the ignorant mob they
        instructed--
Blind, malignant, pompous leaders of the blind!

And so to-day round the fires of war--the flash of artillery and
        glance of bayonets
(But at safe distance, impotent),
Again the dismal brood swarms--hysterical, smirking, grimacing--
Still as oblivious of all their Master taught,

Still going further than the thoughtless popular in their lust and
    frenzy,
Still impious, blasphemous, sacrilegious, profane--
Gloating like harpies over the nation's sins.

IV

Just a glimpse at the coast of England as we touch at Plymouth on
    our way up the Channel.
What are those red spots on the shore?
They are the red coats of soldiers breaking out like the blotches
    of scarlet fever all over the land.
Poor, sick England, what foul disease have you got in your blood?
Silly children may think as they look in the glass that the rash
    on their faces is pretty.
And so you English are silly children.
And you have inoculated my country too with your distemper.
America has caught it and is proud of it.
We pretend that we like to reel along with high temperature and
    drum-pulse beating loud.
A few years ago a man might travel from ocean to ocean without
    seeing a single epaulet; it was the glory of the land.
But now we are as sick as any of you.
The world is a great hospital of silly, sick nations, boasting of
    the number of their pestiferous pustules.

V

There is "great rejoicing at the nation's capital." So says the
    morning's paper.
The enemy's fleet has been annihilated.
Mothers are delighted because other mothers have lost sons just
    like their own;
Wives and daughters smile at the thought of new-made widows and
    orphans;
Strong men are full of glee because other strong men are either
    slain or doomed to rot alive in torments;
Small boys are delirious with pride and joy as they fancy
    themselves thrusting swords into soft flesh, and burning
    and laying waste such homes as they themselves inhabit;
Another capital is cast down with mourning and humiliation just
    in proportion as ours is raised up, and that is the very
    spice of our triumph.
How could we exult without having a fellow man to exult over?
Yesterday it was the thrill of grappling with him and hating him.
To-day we grind our heel into his face and despise him.
This is life--this is patriotism--this is rapture?
But we--what are we, men or devils? and our Christian capital--
    what is it but an outpost of hell?

VI

Who are you at Washington who presume to declare me the enemy of
    anybody or to declare any nation my enemy?
However great you may be, I altogether deny you authority to sow
    enmity and hatred in my soul.
I refuse to accept your ready-made enemies, and, if I did accept
    them, I should feel bound to love them, and, loving them,
    would you have me caress them with bombshells and bayonets?
When I want enemies, I reserve the right to manufacture them for
    myself.
If I am ever scoundrel enough to wish to kill, I will do my own
    killing on my own account and not hide myself behind your
    license.
Before God your commissions and warrants and enlistment rolls,
    relieving men of conscience and independence and manhood,
    are not worth the paper they are written on.
Away with all your superstitions of a statecraft worse than
    priestcraft!
Hypnotize fools and cowards if you will, but for my part, I choose
    to be a man.

VII

I am no patriot.
    I do not wish my countrymen to overrun the world.
I love the date-palm equally with the pine-tree, and each in its
    place.
I am as true a friend to the banana and orange as to the pear and
    apple.
I thank the genial breath of climate for making men different.
I am glad to know that, if my people succeed in spreading over the
    face of the earth, they will gradually differ from each
    other as they attune themselves to every degree of latitude
    and longitude.
Humanity is no air to be strummed on one note or upon one
    instrument
It is a symphony where every note and instrument has its part,
    and would be sadly missed.
I do not take the side of the cornet against the violin, for the
    cornet needs the violin.
I am no patriot.
I love my country too well to be a patriot.

VIII

I saw them take the blockhouse on the hill by storm.
First advancing slowly in the woods in groups, dodging from tree
    to tree and firing rapidly, the machine gun grinding out
    death with its sharp metallic rattle, while the smell of
    powder fills the air,
Now they rush into the open and up the steep slope.

Some of them fall. One I see plunge backward down the hill with
    his arms in the air; another stumbles forward up-hill on
    his face and elbows.
For an instant they waver; then up again they go.
Men spring up from the ground at the top of the hill and run away.
The assailants disappear for a moment in invisible trenches, and
    then I see them, too, running beyond.
There is a great hurrah; the flag comes down on the blockhouse
    and another goes up.
They dance about like children, shouting, throwing up their caps,
    and waving their swords and muskets in a delirium of joy.
I do not blame them. They have never felt such a thrill before.
Shall we deprive them of the most ecstatic moment of their
    lives?
Ecstasy with murder is better perhaps than the dull level of
    existence without.
It would do them no good to go without murder.
There is no good in going without things.
The good consists in having something better than the things you
    go without.
Oh, if they only knew that there is a higher ecstacy, a deeper
    thrill, an inexhaustible courage and contempt of death!
Then how quickly they would let pistol and bayonet drop harmless
    from their hands!

                                IX

Hail to the hero!
    Decked out in blue, red, and gilt, as in warpaint--
Rejoicing like a savage in a long head-feather and gold shoulder
    fringes--
Proud to commit with these adornments all the crimes for which he
    would be disgraced and punished as a felon without them--
Modestly bearing on his breast a star and ribbon which say, "I am
    a hero," as plainly as the beggar's placard says "I am
    blind"--
Followed by a brass band and bass drum, which screw up his
    courage at a pinch like the war dance and tom-tom of the
    Central African and red-skin--
Vain of his manliness in the field while indulging in effeminate
    quarreling over the honors, at the rate of a month's
    quarreling to a half-hour's fighting--
Admitting that he obeys orders without thinking, and thus
    proclaiming his complete abdication of conscience and
    intellect--
Rushing home from the fray to advertise himself in the magazines
    at a hundred dollars a page--
Hail to the hero!

O shade of Cervantes!
Come back and draw for us another Don Quixote.
Prick this bubble of militarism as you pricked that other bubble
    of knight-errantry.

66

The world yearns for your reappearing.
Come and depict the hero!

X

But, you say, there have been good wars.
Never, Never, Never!
As I look back at our "good" war--at the indelible bloody splash
upon our history--the four years' revel of hatred--the
crowded shambles of foiled Secession--
I see that it was all a pitiable error.
That which we fought for, the Union of haters by force, was a
wrong, misleading cause: the worship of bigness, the
measure of greatness by latitude and longitude.
A single town true enough to abhor slaughter as well as slavery
would have been better worth dying for than all that
tempestuous domain.
From the seed then sown grew up imperialism and militarism and
capitalism and a whole forest of stout, deep-rooted ills in
whose shadow we lead an unhealthy, stunted life to-day.
The incidental good--the freedom of the slaves, illusive,
unsubstantial freedom at best, freedom by law but not from
the heart--does it really quite balance the scales?

XI

Nay, violence can only degrade a noble cause.
Behold the French Revolution.
Wave of brotherly love, sweeping over feudal France
(When noblemen embraced coal-heavers and threw away their
privilege and rank),
Breath from heaven, inspiring a nation with new life,
What changed you into a frightful tempest, all hell raining and
thundering and lightening upon the defenseless earth?
Goddess of freedom and love, how were you transformed into the
fiend of bloodshed and hate?
Ah! they did not know, those Titanic lovers, that violence,
however employed, drives out all liberty and love in the
end.
Violence curdles the love that wields it into hatred, and
wherever it strikes, as from the drooping branch of a
banyan tree, spring up fresh shoots of hate.
Oh, if they had only known!
And we, when another such wave passes over the land, shall we
have learned?
Shall we know the truth better than they?

XII

Down with the tiger in each of us!
He has his proper place, no doubt, in the economy of
nature, but it is in the depth of our own private
bottomless pit.

67

There he growls and mutters as he chafes behind the bars.
There is only one safe course to pursue: lock him up firmly and
securely, and pay no heed to his subterranean roar.

XIII

What do they accomplish who take the sword?
Now and then they cut off the ear of a servant of the high
priest;
Quite as often they lose their own.
While they who say, "Put up thy sword into its place," tho they
die, yet succeed sometimes in changing the heart of the
world.

XIV

What is true peace but conscious strength?
What is war but conscious weakness seeking to give proof of
its strength?
Peace is a god, not a goddess, a man not a woman--
A brawny, bearded man of might, with nothing but the kindly look
in his eyes to distinguish him from the vulgar giant.
He can afford to smile at War, the headstrong boy, rushing,
red-faced, blundering, blustering, with impetuous arms,
hither and thither.
Peace has outgrown all that, for Peace is a man.

XV

The old, old dream of empire--
The dream of Alexander and Caesar, of Tamerlane and Genghis
Kahn--
The dream of subject peoples carrying out our sovereign will
through fear--
The dream of a universe forced to converge upon us--
The dream of pride and loftiness justified by strength of arms--
The dream of our arbitrary "Yea" overcoming all "Nays"
whatsoever--
The dream of a cold, stern, hated machine of an empire!

But there is a more enticing dream:
The dream of wise freedom made contagious--
The dream of gratitude rising from broken fetters--
The dream of coercion laid prostrate once for all--
The dream of nations in love with each other without a thought of
a common hatred or danger--
The dream of tyrants stripped of their tyrannies and oppressors
despoiled of their prey--
The dream of a warm, throbbing, one-hearted empire of brothers!

And will such a life be insipid when war has ceased forever?
Be not afraid.

Do lovers find life insipid?
Is there no hero-stuff in lovers?

XVI

I am a great inventor, did you but know it.
    I have new weapons and explosives and devices to substitute
    for your obsolete tactics and tools.
Mine are the battle-ships of righteousness and integrity--
The armor-plates of a quiet conscience and self-respect--
The impregnable conning-tower of divine manhood--
The Long Toms of persuasion--
The machine guns of influence and example--
The dum-dum bullets of pity and remorse--
The impervious cordon of sympathy--
The concentration camps of brotherhood--
The submarine craft of forgiveness--
The torpedo-boat-destroyer of love--
And behind them all the dynamite of truth!
I do not patent my inventions.
Take them. They are free to all the world.

XVII

I am a soldier too, and I have the battle of battles on my hands.
You little warriors who, while fighting each other, are yet at
    heart agreed, and see the same false life with the same
    distorted eyes,
I have to make war upon all of you combined, and upon the
    infernal War Spirit which inspires you in the bargain.

"REBELS"

You bought them from the Spanish king,
    You bought the men he stole;
You bought perchance a ghastlier thing--
    The Duke of Alva's soul!

"Freedom!" you cry, and train your gun
    Oh men who would be freed,
And in the name of Washington
    Achieve a Weyler's deed.

Boast of the benefits you spread,
    The faith of Christ you hold;
Then seize the very soil you tread
    And fill your arms with gold.

Go, prostitute your mother-tongue,
    And give the "rebel" name
To those who to their country clung,
    Preferring death to shame.

And call him "loyal," him who brags
    Of countrymen betrayed--
The patriot of the money-bags,
    The loyalist of trade.

Oh, for the good old Roman days
    Of robbers bold and true,
Who scorned to oil with pious phrase
    The deeds they dared to do--

The days before degenerate thieves
    Devised the coward lie
Of blessings that the enslaved receives
    Whose rights their arms deny!

I hate the oppressor's iron rod,
    I hate his murderous ships,
But most of all I hate, O God,
    The lie upon his lips!

Nay, if they still demand recruits
    To curse Manila Bay,
Be men; refuse to act like brutes
    And massacre and slay.

Or if you will persist to fight
    With all a soldier's pride,
Why, then be rebels for the right
    By Aguinaldo's side!

                THE MILITARY CREED

The American Admiral in command at Samoa was asked what he thought
of expansion. He is reported to have answered, "I do not think;
I obey orders."

        "Captain, what do you think," I asked,
            "Of the part your soldiers play?"
        The captain answered, "I do not think--
            I do not think--I obey."

        "Do you think you should shoot a patriot down
            And help a tyrant slay?"
        The captain answered, "I do not think--
            I do not think--I obey."

        "Do you think that your conscience was meant to die
            And you brains to rot away?"
        The captain answered, "I do not think--
            I do not think--I obey."

"Then if this is your soldier's code," I cried,
    "You're a mean, unmanly crew,
And with all your feathers and gilt and braid
    I am more of a man than you;

"For whatever my lot on earth may be,
    And whether I swim or skin,
I can say with pride, 'I do not obey--
    I do not obey--I think!

CUBA LIBRE

When we sailed from Tampa Bay
    (Cuba Libre!)
And our ships got under weigh
    "Cuba Libre!"
As we floated down the tide,
Crowding to the steamer's side,
You remember how we cried
    "Cuba Libre!"

When we spied the island shore
    (Cuba Libre!)
Then we shouted loud once more
    "Cuba Libre!"
As we sank Cervera's ships,
Where the southern sea-wall dips,
What again was on our lips?
    "Cuba Libre!"

These are foreign words, you know--
    "Cuba Libre!"--
That we used so long ago
    (Cuba Libre!)
And in all the time between
Such a lot of things we've seen,
We've forgotten what they mean--
    "Cuba Libre!"

Let us ask the President
    (Cuba Libre!)
What that bit of Spanish meant--
    "Cuba Libre!"
Ask the Senate, Root, and Hay[2]
What on earth we meant to say,
When we shouted night and day,
    "Cuba Libre!"

But alas! they will not speak
    (Cuba Libre!)
For their memories are weak
    (Cuba Libre!)

71

If you have a lexicon,
Borrowed from a Spanish don,
Send it down to Washington
(Cuba Libre!)

THE PIRATE FLAG

I had an ugly dream last night,
    And I was far away,
A-sailing on a man-of-war
    Far up Manila Bay.
And as I cast a glance aloft
    It made me stand aghast
To see a jet-black pirate flag
    A-flying from the mast.

And then around me fore and aft
    The guns began to roar.
And flames sprang up and soon enwrapped
    A village on the shore.
I took my glass and clearly saw
    Women and children run,
While soldiers in the palms behind
    Were potting them for fun.

Far to the left some dusky men
    Fought bravely on a knoll,
But, overcome at last, they raised
    A white rag on a pole;
Yet still the soldiers shot them down
    And I could almost hear
Their laughter as they seemed to shout,
    "No prisoners wanted here!"

Then when the last defender fell
    The men rushed in with glee,
And from each house they came with loads
    Of plunder sad to see;
And soon we sent a boat ashore--
    Blue-jackets and marines--
To get our share of loot and swag,
    And spoil the Philippines.

I turned and asked a sailor lad--
    For now they stood at ease--
What pirates we might chance to be
    Who plagued these summer seas.
"Oh, we're no pirates," he replied,
    "Don't asked me that again;
This is a ship of Uncle Sam
    And we are Dewey's men."

"But how is that?" I said once more;
    "Where are our stripes and stars?
And does that inky flag up there
    Belong to honest tars?"
"To tell the truth, it's rather queer,"
    Replied embarrassed Jack,
"But something in the climate here
    Has turned Old Glory black.

"We wash her in the briny sea
    And in the streams on land;
We scrub her with the best of soap,
    And rub her in the sand;
And all our Chinese laundrymen
    And all our laundry maids
Have tackled her, but still she looks
    Black as the ace of spades.

"There's something in the climate here
    That changes things around,
And what the reason of it is
    We none of us have found.
And so we don't know what to say,
    Or even what to think,
When people ask us what has made
    Old Glory black as ink."

Just then the boat came back from shore
    Well laden down with spoil--
With goods that told of many years
    Of Filipino toil;
And Jack ran off to get his part,
    Nor came he ever back,
And I awoke and never learned
    What turned Old Glory black.

THE REAL "WHITE MAN'S BURDEN"

With apologies to Rudyard Kipling

Take up the White Man's burden.
    Send forth you sturdy kin,
And load them down with Bibles
    And cannon-balls and gin.
Throw in a few diseases
    To spread the tropic climes,
For there the healthy niggers
    Are quite behind the times.

And don't forget the factories.
    On those benighted shores

They have no cheerful iron mills,
    Nor eke department stores.
They never work twelve hours a day,
    And live in strange content,
Altho they never have to pay
    A single sou of rent.

Take up the White Man's burden
    And teach the Philippines
What interest and taxes are
    And what a mortgage means.
Give them electrocution chairs,
    And prisons, too, galore,
And if they seem inclined to kick,
    Then spill their heathen gore.

They need our labor question, too,
    And politics and fraud--
We've made a pretty mess at home,
    Let's make a mess abroad.
And let us ever humbly pray
    The Lord of Hosts may deign
To stir our feeble memories
    Lest we forget--The Maine.[3]

Take up the White's Man's burden.
    To you who thus succeed
In civilizing savage hordes,
    They owe a debt, indeed;
Concessions, pensions, salaries,
    And privilege and right--
With outstretched hands you raised to bless
    Grab everything in sight.

Take up the White Man's burden.
    And if you write in verse,
Flatter your nation's vices
    And strive to make them worse.
Then learn that if with pious words
    You ornament each phrase,
In a world of canting hypocrites
    This kind of business pays.

THE PEACE CONGRESS

Around a long green table sat
    Ambassadors of peace,
To ponder for the Christian world
    How war and strife might cease;
And captains of the sea were there
    And captains of the land,

And with the tassels of their swords
    Played many an idle hand.

And some who had the morning's news
    Were reading there with zest
Of battles in the farthest East
    And battles in the West;
While at the door two sentries stood,
    With muskets at their side
And bayonets fixed, to show that peace
    Depends on war and pride.

The president then rang his bell,
    And up a bishop rose,
And prayed for all the kings and queens
    In most poetic prose.
His lips that every week had asked
    For victory in war,
Now prayed that in our time sweet Peace
    Might come for evermore.

Then suddenly the hall grew bright,
    The roof was rent in two,
And down from heaven an angel came
    To their astonished view;
The envoys looked aghast, the priest
    Muttered a faint "Amen!"
A stern voice answered, "I am Peace'
    What would you have, ye men?

"Why is it that you call me here
    From God's unsullied air--
Here, where the smell of blood corrupts
    The spirit of your prayer?
Here where you dare to name my name
    Holding a blood-stained sword?"
(The troubled counsellors now hid
    Their hilts beneath the board.)

"And who are these who guard the place?"
    (They slunk behind the door,
And two such frightened shamefaced men
    I never saw before.)
"What means these tawdry epaulets,
    And all this martial show?
The very pictures on the wall
    But tell of war and woe.

"Read me that journal lying there;
    Let its reports accuse."
The president then picked it up
    And read the morning's news;

And it was pitiful to hear
    His wretched, stammering tale,
And it was pitiful to see
    His trembling lips turn pale.

He read about the Philippines,
    Where prisoners are slain
By Yankee heroes while they curse
    The cruelty of Spain;
He read of pious Englishmen
    Who slaughter as they please
To boom Egyptian bonds, and stab
    The wounded Soudanese.

He read of Russian men-at-arms
    Who torture as they will
The gentle, peaceful Doukhobors
    Because they will not kill;
He read of mighty realms that rob
    Poor China of her soil,
And carve up Africa because
    The victor's is the spoil.

He read of Poland tyrannized,
    Of Ireland held by hate,
Of Finland cheated of her rights,
    And Kruger's tottering state,
Of Cuba and the Congo too,
    Samoa and far Tonquin--
The whole world made a hell of blood
    By governmental sin.

He ceased to read, and for a time
    An awful silence fell,
While all were waiting anxiously
    To hear what Peace might tell.
At last she spake, and, breathing fast
    With loud, indignant speech,
She thundered at the sorry crew
    With words that shook them each.

"And thus it is," she cried in scorn,
    "You and your masters deal;
You fill the world with pain and grief
    And grind it with your heel;
You build huge ships to murder men;
    You make the heart breed hate;
You make the earth breed dynamite--
    And then you call you great.

"You live by murder, hate and theft,
    And no one will pretend

Your masters have the least design
    To bring them to an end.
Ye hypocrites! who know full well
    That Peace can never reign
Until you cease from making war
    Nor take my name in vain.

"Begone, base slaves of despots base,
    And drop your idle task,
Or else the world will laugh, for now
    I've stripped you of your mask.
Go home, and tell your masters all
    What they well knew before:
That when at last Peace rules the earth,
    Then they will rule no more."

She stopped and forth she stretched her hand,
    And, at this sign of hers,
They fled, their swords between their legs
    Like a whipped pack of curs.

THE EPITAPH

Above his grave they raised a stone
    That towered toward the sky,
And on it they carved in shadows deep
    These words that held mine eye:

"Here lies a patriot soldier bold,
    Who at his country's call
With joy laid down his youthful life;
    Sweet is it thus to fall."

That night by the ghostly moonlit stone
    We saw an angel stand,
And he wiped that labored legend out
    With a sweep of his silver hand.

Then with a finger that seemed to glow
    Like a flame that was pale and blue
He traced a single white-hot word
    That scorched us through and through.

"Angel of Truth," we cried, aghast
    (How did we know his name?),
"What means upon our hero's tomb
    This word of burning shame?

"Was he a 'traitor' who fought so well
    Against his nation's foe--
A 'traitor,' who gave his life's red blood
    When his country bade it flow?"

77

"He was a traitor," like a bell
    Of silver Truth replied:
"Traitor to more than country's call
    Or patriot's loyal pride--

"Traitor to freedom when he sought
    To subjugate the free--
Traitor to love when, steeped in hate,
    He crossed the distant sea--

"Traitor to conscience when he stilled
    Its cry of pain within--
Nay, traitor to his country too
    For helping her to sin."

Back toward the stars the angel rose,
    And when he disappeared
We chiseled out that shameful word,
    Tho deep the stone was seared,

And once again we carved the lines
    Which told our hero's deed.
So deep and clear the words appear
    That he who runs may read.

And there they stay until this day
    To publish his renown.
For tho we feared the angel's wrath,
    He never again came down.

Ernest Crosby, Swords and Plowshares, New York and London, 1906,
pp. 11-23, 25-26, 28-35, 38-42, 48-49

EXPLANATORY NOTES

[1]The reference is to the battle of Fort Wagner during the Civil War.

[2]The reference is to the Platt Amendment, a series of clauses drawn up in the name of Senator Orville H. Platt of Connecticut, but in reality was the product of Elihu Root, Wall Street lawyer and Secretary of War. Root consulted with Secretary of State John Hay in formulating the Platt Amendment which, among other things, gave the United States the right to intervene militarily in Cuba when it felt it was necessary to do so. It was added to the Cuban Constitution in 1902 as a condition of the withdrawl of U.S. troops still occupying Cuba.

[3]On February 15, 1898, the battleship Maine, on a visit in the harbor of Havana, Cuba, was sunk by a huge explosion. Two hundred and sixty-four men and two officers were killed in the destruction of the ship. Although it has never been determined exactly who was responsible for the destruction of the Maine, the incident was used by the jingo "Yellow Press" to whip up public anger against Spain, charging that she was behind the explosion.

4. WILLIAM LLOYD GARRISON[1]

ONWARD, CHRISTIAN SOLDIER!

The Anglo-Saxon Christians, with Gatling gun and sword,
In serried ranks are pushing on the gospel of the Lord.
On Afric's soil they press the foe in war's terrific scenes,
And merrily the hunt goes on thoughout the Philippines.

What though the Boers are Christians' the Filipinos, too!
It is a Christian act to shoot a fellow-creature through:
The bombs with dynamite surcharged their deadly missles fling,
And gayly on their fatal work the dum-dum bullets sing.

The dead and mangled bodies, the wounded and the sick,
Are multiplied on every hand, on every field are thick.
"O gracious Lord," the prayer goes up, "to us give victory swift!"
The chaplains on opposing sides the same petitions lift.

The mahdis and the sirdars along the great Soudan
Are learning at the cannon's mouth the brotherhood of man;
The holy spirit guides aloft the shrieking shot and shell,
And Christian people shout with joy at thousands blown to hell.

The pulpits bless the victor arms and praise the bloody work,
As after an Armenian raid rejoiced the pious Turk.
The Christian press applauds the use of bayonet and knife;
For how can social order last without the strenuous life?

The outworn, threadbare precept, to lift the poor and weak,
The fallacy that this great earth is for the saintly meek,
Have both gone out of fashion: the world is for the strong;
That might shall be the Lord of right is now the Christian song.

The Jesus that we reverence is not the lowly man
Who trod in poverty and rags where Jordan's waters ran:
Our savior is an admiral upon the quarter-deck,
Or else a general uniformed, an army at his beck.

How natural that a change should come in nineteen hundred years,
And Bibles take a place behind the bullets and the beers!
We need a new Messiah to lead the latest way,
And gospel version well revised to show us how to prey.

Then onward, Christian soldier! through fields of crimson gore,
Behold the trade advantages beyond the open door!
The profits on our ledgers outweigh the heathen loss;
Set thou the glorious stars and stripes above the ancient cross!

TO OUR BETRAYED ALLIES

O men and brothers in Luzon,
    Through swamp and forest hunted down,
By brute invaders driven on
    From burning town to town,

Yield not to promptings of despair,
    Nor deem your base betrayal due
To the great people who are heir
    To Freedom's birthright true.

Themselves betrayed, their cause is yours!
    For every wrong on you that falls
On them tenfold its fury pours
    In measure that appals.

They have not spoken: the dread voice
    That your enslavment has decreed,
Springs from usurpers' lips, whose choice
    Was fixed by gold and greed.

Await the verdict yet to come
    With patient faith, however hard
It is to hope in silence dumb,
    And weary doubts discard.

Our fate to yours is iron-linked,
    On you depends our weal or woe;
Our liberty will be extinct
    With your own overthrow!

Meanwhile, within this guilty land
    The conflict deepens, conscience wakes:
The day of reckoning is at hand,
    The dawn of promise breaks!

THIRTEEN SONNETS

POEM

Since they who hold the "faculty divine,"
Bereft of vision or in abject thrall,
Use not their glorious gift at Freedom's call,
Accept this humbler verse, O country mine!
As in a fearful nightmare, where combine
The murderer's dagger and the victim's fall,
A sight to freeze the marrow and appall,
The dreamer paralyzed can make no sign,
So in the months of horror that have sped
With agonizing scenes of slaughter rife--
The nation lost in darkness, reason fled,
Unmindful of Oppression's threatening knife--
I, like the tortured dreamer on the bed,
Struggle to lift my warning cry for life.
June 1, 1899

WILLIAM McKINLEY

Whether as tool or tyrant, History's pen
Upon the nation's scroll of lasting shame
Shall pillory in letters black thy name,
Time can alone adjudge. To living men
With liberty aflame, no empty words
Can justify the slaughter of the brave,
Battling for freedom and a freeman's grave,
As fought Armenians 'gainst Turks and Kurds.
How in the future will this record read:
"Here lie the patriots of the Philippines,
Murdered to satisfy a nation's greed
By men whose rebel fathers, on the greens
Of Lexington and Concord, dared to bleed
And die for what to freemen freedom means"?
March 10, 1899

AGUINALDO

Thine, Aguinaldo, is the common fate
Of all who seek, in Freedom's holy cause,
Deliverance from foreign yokes and laws,
Against a foe of overwhelming weight.
Thou hast great compeers of an earlier date,
TOUSSAINT, BOZZARIS, KOSCIUSKO,[2] men
Misunderstood, maligned, defeated, then
Immortalized among the brave and great.
Take heart and comfort if thy soul be sad.
Not vain nor wasted thy heroic stand:

83

Thou hast unmasked a nation falsely clad
In altruistic garb, revealed a land
Blind to distinctions between good and bad,
And smiting Liberty with ruthless hand.
March 19, 1899

THE CHURCH RECREANT

The Easter lilies in their robes of white
Once more the alters of the church adorn,
To typify the resurrection morn
When from the tomb the Christ arose to light.
O Church! thyself entombed in darkest night,
With hollow worship of the man-child born
In Bethlehem's manger, cheerless and forlorn,
When shall thy resurrection greet the sight?
Should the great Nazarene once more appear
This Easter morning, and from pious lips
Defence of rapine and of murder hear,--
Pleas for foul deeds that Freedom's light eclipse,--
Straight would his burst of scorn false temples clear,
His words indignant scourge like scorpion whips!
April 2, 1899

ABASED

Much has I read upon the storied page
Of deadly conflicts on the battlefield,
Whose issue oft the fate of nations sealed,
For War's dread footsteps crimson every age.
And I have thrilled with horror at the rage
Of brothers who against each other wield
Destructive weapons, keen, but not more steeled
Than hearts which in embittered war engage.
What happiness to feel that our dear land,
Though self-baptized in blood for freedom's sake,
Abhorred unholy conquest and could stand
A high example for the world to take!
But now our ship of State, in pirate hand,
Incarnadines the water in its wake!
April 8, 1899

CONTRITION

Great Abdul Hamid, whose puissant might
Keeps not alone one empire at thy beck,
But Europe's mightiest monarchs holds in check,
Grant we may find acceptance in thy sight!
Assassin, despot, monster, Nature's blight,--
The millstone names we hung upon thy neck

Repentantly we lift, and now would deck
Thy swarthy brow with garlands snowy white.
The winds of "destiny and duty" sweep
With forceful impulse through the nation's heart,
Ideals reversing and convictions deep
Uprooting to destroy and rend apart.
Welcome, red slaughter and the flames that leap!
Hail, horrors born of war's relentless art!

April 10, 1899

TREASON

"Stop thief!" the thief himself, when hotly pressed,
Vociferates with lusty accents loud,
To mystify and turn aside the crowd,
That unobserved he may elude arrest.
So treason is most flagrantly confessed
By men of aspect virtuous and proud,
From whose false lips is loyalty avowed,
And "traitor" shouted to confuse the quest.
Mark well the accusers, though in reverend guise,
In cabinet or press or pulpit found,
Entrenched behind a bulwark made of lies,
They launch anathemas of empty sound.
The loyal heart authority defies
When that, disloyal, passes freedom's bound.

April 29, 1899

INVOCATION

If death be but the open door to light,
The entrance to a kingdom of the soul,
Where eyes from mount of vision may control
The outgrown world with a diviner sight,
O ye, who held the van in freedom's flight,
Reveal to us this troubled nation's goal!
Not more asunder north from southern pole
Than this dark present from your forecast bright.
When the great charter signed by Lincoln's pen
From out the land of bondage brought a race,
How little did ye dream that, later, men
Would dare this seal of promise to efface!
Has virtue vigor to uprise again,
Or sinks one more republic in disgrace?

April 30, 1899

AWAKENING

"Too far the nation has advanced to turn
On its imperial and predestined way:

85

Duty and destiny decree its sway
O'er conquered islands where the tropics burn.
Why with abstract ideals the mind concern,
When power and wealth the sacrifice repay?
Expedient counsel should the wise obey,
And grasp with might the things for which they yearn."
So speak Democracy's most deadly foes,
With voices confident and gloating eyes,
Forgetting conscience for a paltry prize
Which holds concealed incalculable woes.
"Triumph not, fools!" Imperilled Freedom's cries
Have roused the people from their drugged repose.
May 31, 1899

TO GEORGE S. BOUTWELL [3]

Not thine the sadness of an outlived fame,
Nor fate to lag superfluous on the stage:
Thou addest only strength to ripest age
And lustre to a lifelong honored name.
In a degenerate day when public shame
And private avarice stain the nation's page,
When sordid ends the growing youth engage,
Thy burning words are like a torch of flame.
New England glories in thy manhood rare,
Which, breaking party shackles, stands erect
And breathing deeply of diviner air,--
Enrolls thy name among the great elect.
Thy topmost boughs the richest leafage bear,
Thy latest fruit compels the world's respect.
Dec. 20, 1899

TO GEORGE FRISBIE HOAR

Amidst the voices of the market-place,
Drowning the public conscience with their din,
Defying righteousness, exalting sin,
Thy notes ring clear above the tumult base.
Thine the unflinching courage to outface
The clamorous worship of material gods,
Holding to noble aims, despite the odds
That menace justice and the human race.
Revived the great traditions of the State!
Otis and Adams[4] reincarnate speak;
Charles Sumner's[5] strength and Andrew's[6] fervid light
In thee are living and regenerate.
The downcast and oppressed thy counsel seek,
And upward gaze at thee on Freedom's height.
Jan.11, 1900

ETERNAL VIGILANCE THE PRICE

Men think because from bloody war and strife
Freedom emerges with triumphant feet,
Mounting the throne of Justice for her seat,
Her reign of glory holds a lasting life.
Never illusion with more danger rife!
Lulled to repose, for rest and sleep are sweet,
She dreams, while back, with stealthy footsteps fleet,
Oppression rushes with its murderous knife.
With Washington to guide, what need to guard?
Answer, thou civil war from slavery's womb!
With Lincoln in the firmament enstarred,
Has not the vanquished monster found its tomb?
Feigned its insensibility; unslain,
    Behold it rising to its prey again!
Jan. 26, 1900

THE DEVIL'S ADVOCATE

There never yet were wanting men of speech,
Persuasive and mellifluous, to give aid
To tyrants when, abandoned and betrayed,
Freedom for pity did the world beseech.
Then smooth and affluent phrases overreach
A feeble faith and conscience, and pervade
The press, the pulpits, and the marts of trade,
As the insidious tide pervades the beach.
But, when the music and the glamour cease,
Returning reason dissipates the spell,
And captive senses find a quick release.
Silenced the siren song of "All is well!"
The fancied picture of a reign of peace,
    Fading, reveals the warring strife of hell.
March 25, 1900

Liberty Poems, Boston, 1900, pp. 36-37, 42, 108-120

87

EXPLANATORY NOTES

[1]The poems in this section were published in Liberty Poems, but have been separated from that collection and appear here under the name of the poet.

William Lloyd Garrison was the son of the great Boston Abolitionist of the same name; a woolen trader in Boston and a leading anti-imperialist.

[2]Toussaint L'Ouverture (1743-1803), the Negro slave who led the uprising against French domination to establish what became in 1804, after his death in a French prison, the Republic of Haiti.

Marco Bozzari, Italian for Markos Botsaris (1788-1823), an important leader early in the Greek War of Independence, killed in a battle against Turkey for Greek independence.

Thaddeus Kosciusko (1746-1817), Polish hero who served with the American army during the War for Independence, and later led a rebellion for the liberation of Poland.

[3]George Sewall Boutwell (1818-1905), Secretary of the Treasury under President Grant; U.S. Senator from Massachusetts, and a leader of the anti-imperialist movement.

[4]James Otis (1725-1783), Revolutionary patriot in Massachusetts; author of The Rights of the British Colonies Asserted and Proved (1763), in which he upheld the natural rights of the colonists.

The reference to Adams is probably to Samuel Adams (1722-1803), Massachusetts Revolutionary patriot and a leading organizer of the Sons of Liberty.

[5]Charles Sumner (1811-1874), Leading anti-slavery U.S. Senator from Massachusetts, champion of equal rights for Black Americans, and opponent of American expansion, represented by the attempt of President Grant to annex San Domingo in 1871.

[6]John Albion Andrew (1818-1867), Anti-Slavery Civil War Governor of Massachusetts; helped organize the first all-Negro regiment, the Fifty-Fourth of Massachusetts.

5. Selections from LIBERTY POEMS[1]

AT THE GATES OF GOD.

"Vengence is mine, saith the Lord, I will requite."

With face upturned to Luzon's sky, with back to Luzon's sod,
The body lay; the indignant soul knocked at the gates of God;
And his prayer the Angel of Wrath upbare in haste to the throne
    of God.

"Justice! Do justice, white man's God! They slay us in thy name;
Thy love their cannon roar; thy truth they speak with tongues of
    flame;
And for light to read Christ's word aright, our pagan roof-trees
    flame.

"They came as friends from the Great White Chief and his people
    over sea.
'Spain fights for land and gold,' they said. 'We fight to make
    men free;
And our deed is born of a nation's creed, that God wills all men
free.'

"Then we clasped our hands with a traitor's hand, we had faith in
    a liar's faith.
They have kept their word as white men do, they have made us free
    of death;
And their deed is born of a nation's greed and its pact with Hell
    and Death!"

All Heaven stood silent. Each on each gazed with expectant eyes
Till the Angel of Pity bowed his head, and a murmur swelled:
    "Arise!"

And the shout from gates to throne rang out: "Lord God of
   vengeance, rise!"

And forth of the host came Love and Truth and knelt before the
   Throne.
"Lord, for Thy name they take in vain, make Thou this cause Thine
   own."
And the word from behind the veil was heard: "I make this cause
   Mine own."

But the Angel of Wrath, at that word appalled, fell prostrate in
   his place,
And prayed, "Have mercy, God," and wept, as he lay upon his face.
There is need for tears, when Wrath must plead, and Pity hide his
   face!

Let men and angels weep hot tears; but not for the lifeless clod,
And not for the soul untimely sent with a people's wrongs to God:
Be their grief for the soul of the Great White Chief when he
   stands at the gates of God!

                    Solomon Solia Cohen, in Springfield Republican

                        A PARABLE
              A Malay and a Hottentot
                 Were fighting on the plains,
              In most unruly fashion,
                 For very doubtful gains,
              When there came a Christian gentleman
                 Toward them through the rains.

              The Malay and the Hottentot
                 Were very, very bare.
              For dampness and malaria
                 They plainly didn't care.
              But the well-dressed Christian gentleman
                 Began to shake and swear.

              "I wish you wouldn't fight," said he,
                 "It's shocking and it's rude;
              But, since you will, I've brought to you
                 A basketful of food.
              I think the Malay needs it most:
                 I've brought it for his good."

              No thanks the Christian gentleman
                 From either party drew.
              They fought with angry vehemence,
                 And quite obscured his view.
              Said he at last, "Such wickedness
                 Will never, never do."

                            90

He loaded his revolver,
    This kind and goodly man,
And shot as straight and fired as fast
    As many Christians can;
And then he truly felt himself
    A good Samaritan.

"I've killed'em both," said he with pride;
    "Their pain is hard to see.
But men must suffer when it comes
    To such a point with me.
What I have done is all because
    Of my humanity."

The dying Hottentot looked up,
    The dying Malay, too.
The Christian gentleman was just
    Departing from their view.
He held what they were fighting for,
    And held it tightly, too.

"Oh shameful sight!" they cried aloud.
    "What could I do?" he said.
"Some one must take this property,
    For soon you will be dead.
I didn't wish to fight," said he:
    "Your deeds be on your head!"

"This is a noble war!" he cried.
    "I come to save the weak:
The oppressed are e'er my brethren."
    The Malay tried to speak.
"I wish," he said with emphasis;
    "I wish I had your cheek!"

M. A. L. L., in Boston *Evening Transcript*

IN THE TRENCHES

Fighting in a blazing sun, in thickets,
    With a grim foe who well knows how to fight;
Standing in the rain when all our pickets
    Are destitute, and clothes are "out of sight";
Firing from the trenches hot and sizzling,
    And standing where the water's to the knees;
Fighting when the rain is pouring, drizzling,
    And parched troops are dying for a breeze;
            This is Empire.

Our flag floats o'er trenches damp, ill-smelling,
    And reeking with the odors of the dead,

While far and near yellow men loud yelling
    With sword and torch make all the vista red;
Fighting with fever, and, O God! with Death,
    In hospitals beneath a tropic sun,
No woman's hand to soothe the latest breath,
    When, far from home, the soldier's work is done;
        This is Empire.

Facing death in rice-fields which are shambles,
    For yellow men who're fighting to be free;
Here, amid the cactus and the brambles,
    Old Glory seems ashamed across the sea;
Dying here before malarial breezes,
    That swamp across the camp-ground and the bay,
Bringing here the fever quick that siezes
    And lays the strong may low within a day;
        This is Empire.

Sleeping in the marshes where the fevers
    Prostrate the men in windrows at a breath,
Hearing words of those who would deceive us
    With promises that we are near the death;
Fighting when there's never hope of winning,
    With elements upon the other side;
And while Death and Pestilence sit grinning
    O'er flooded fields where gallant men have died;
        This is Empire.

Fighting niggers who themselves are fighting
    For the same cause our fathers fought to save;
Fighting in a way that is forever blighting
    The fairest heritage our fathers gave;
Fighting in a cause that is forever grabbing,
    The cause that is the old-time robber's still;
Fighting in a cause that's only stabbing
    The one we battled for at Bunker Hill;
        This is Empire.

Corporal John Mulcahey, in Boston Record

LITTLE BROWN BROTHER

Little Brown Brothers across the sea,
Running your race for liberty,
Here's to you.
We've been there ourselves.

Odd little Brown Men, like "jack-rabbits" you run.
Bank the Krag-Jorgenson: "Pick 'em off, it's great fun!"
Halt!
"Jack-rabbits," are they?
Well, even sparrows fall not unheeded.
Where's Christ?

Across the shame-stricken, sobbing sea
Comes a sad, stern voice from Galilee:
"As unto the least of my brethren,
So unto me.
Are there thorns in their feed in their race to be free?
There were thorns on my brow there at Calvary."
Spare us, O Christ, lest we crucify thee.

Halt! Who goes there?
Not jack-rabbits, not rebels, but Men
Fighting for life, liberty, homes.
Homes! Bamboo huts.
Well, homes are homes, brown stone or bamboo.
We've sung that and sworn it
By Paine's[2] sacred bones.

A Brown Man lies dead 'neath his own island sky:
A Brown Wife utters a strange wild cry.
The billowy deep brings the piteous sound.
Hearts are the same God's sweet world 'round.

O little Brown Child whose father lies low
Just when will your love and your loyalty flow
As dew from the daisies, as incense from roses,
To the Flag and the Nation that made you an orphan?

Little Brown Brothers across the blue sea,
Are your bare brown feet all bleeding and torn?
So were ours.
Valley Forge! Brandywine![3]
Where's Lafayette?[4]
There is blood on hot sands:
There was blood on sharp ice.
God made of one blood all nations of earth,
Brothers all.
Lord God of Nations, spare us Cain's mark.

Little Brown Brothers across the blue sea,
Battling so bravely for liberty,
Here's to you.
We've been there ourselves: and won.

Annie L. Diggs, 1899

IMPERIALISM

The robbers of the earth ride forth,
    East, West, and North and South,
The sword of Satan in their hand,
    And God's word in their mouth.
And woe to those whom they shall meet!
    And woe to those they seek!

The earth shall drink deep of their blood.
To heaven shall rise their shriek.

They take a people by the throat;
    "Stand and deliver!" say:
"We want your land, we want your wealth,
    We want your freedom aye;
And would ye, ingrates, dare deny
    These things we want to us,
Since we have come to Christianize
    And civilize ye thus?

"Lo, ye are weak and ignorant,
    While we are strong and great;
And so, in Christian charity,
    We've come to rule your State.
We've come to civilize ye, and
    We've come to teach ye pray.
Bow down, bow down, ye savages,
    Or else we needs must slay!"

And ever around the earth they ride
    To see what they may gain;
And ever the road they ride runs red
    With the blood of martyrs slain;
And ever God's name is on their lips,
    Whate'er the deed to be done;
And ever the psalm of the sabre rings
    With the gospel of the gun.

Vincent F. Howard, in Springfield Republican

THE VOICES OF THREE

A VOICE IN 1776:
    Daughter of Law and Liberty am I,
    Born while rebellion raged along the sky;
    The nations scorned till sudden on my knees
    I prayed, then shock and angry agonies!
    O God, the sword was ever at my breast.
    Year upon year I fainted, never rest
    Bade me despair not, nay! but sacrifice
    Stirred all my spirit. With a heart like ice
    Th' aggressor fought me. I could dare to die,
    So lived, the child of Law and Liberty.

A VOICE IN 1899:
    Daughter of Law and Liberty am I,
    Born while rebellion raged along the sky.
    She by whose aid I struggled to be free
    To my breast turns Excalibur; but he
    Wages no hearty war, though nations mock,

94

Though I am torn by passion, doubt, and shock.
Despair invites, but I withstand despair
With racial weakness in the strength of prayer.
Mother, O Liberty, thy help I seek!
Open her eyes who threatens me in dream
Or evil spell that makes her evil seem.
She knows not what she does. Awake her, then,
That the stern truth may come into her ken.
She cannot slay me, though I daily die.
She cannot quench the resolution high,
The indomitable will she cannot stir,--
A sight for Heaven, when light awakens her!

LIBERTY:
Columbia, arouse, awake, let shame
Burn in thy being for this antic blame
And boast of conflict. With a call divine
I call thee! Rise and solace--

THE FIRST VOICE (TO THE SECOND VOICE):
                                    Sister mine!

Chicago   G. Herbert Clarke

ABOVE THE HYMNS OF THE TE DEUMS PEALING.

Above the hymns of the Te Deums pealing,
          I hear a sigh;
Above the paeans and the psalms of triumph,
          A people's cry.

Above the cloud-veils of the incense rising
          Through countless naves,
Black drifts of cannon smoke, its breath defiling
          An east sea's waves.

Stronger than perfumes from the lilies' censers,
          The scent of blood,
Blown from those islands whose encarmined rivers
          The brown fields flood.

Beneath the pulsing of the organ's heart-throbs,
          A plaintive wail;
Behind the shoulders of the white-robed choir boys,
          Thin faces pale.

"Lo! He is risen!" chant the fresh young voices;
          Yea! far away!
So far, He cannot hear His weaker children
          Who mourn to-day!

95

Palms for the one, and ashes for the other,
            And homes of flame;
While men to freedom born tear from them freedom,
            In freedom's name.

Father of all! forgive Thy sons, the conquerors,
            Their blasphemy.
Father of all! pity Thy sons, the conquered,
            Who honor Thee.

Perchance, more truly, though they carve Thy semblance
            From wood and stone,
Than they whose songs of praise to-day rise proudly
            To Thy white Throne;

For neither shard nor sacrifice, given truly,
            Dost Thou abhor,
But prayer from hearts that plot their brother's bondage
            While lip adore.

                    Frances Bartlett, in Boston Evening Transcript

OUR NEW NATIONAL HYMN

We are marching on to glory with the Bible in our hands,
We are carrying the gospel to the lost in foreign lands;
We are marching on to glory, we are going forth to save
With the zeal of ancient pirate, with the prayer of modern knave;
We are robbing Christian churches in our missionary zeal,
And we carry Christ's own message in our shells and bloody steel.
By the light of burning roof-trees they may read the Word of Life,
In the mangled forms of children they may see the Christian
      strife.
We are healing with the Gatling, we are blessing with the sword;
For the Honor of the Nation and the Glory of the Lord.

Then march on, Christian soldiers! with sword and torch in hand,
And carry free salvation to each benighted land!
Go, preach God's Love and Justice with steel and shot and shell!
Go, preach a future Heaven and prove a present Hell!
Baptize with blood and fire, with every gun's hot breath
Teach them to love the Father, and make them free in Death;
Proclaim the newer gospel; the cannon giveth peace,
Christ rides upon the warship his army to increase.
So Bless them with the rifle and heal them with the sword,--
But the Honor of the Nation and the Glory of the Lord!

                    William G. Eggleston, in Sunday Republican

Of course, we folks air gwin ter praise
    The man thet worked the notion
Uv takin' ships, an' taouns, and forts,
    An' isluns uv the ocean;
But air there not some powerful risks
    Aour nation iz a-runnin'
Becorz aour nimble sailor man
    At warrin' wuz so cunnin'?

Thet wuz a gallant feat o' hiz,
    A proper smart proceedin':
It won fer us a elephant;
    But ken we dew ther feedin'?
An' is't aour mission in the worl'
    Tew go araoun' a-showin'
The annermuls an' snaix an' sich
    Thet other lan's are growin'?

An' if them isluns we ken keep
    Still, it is best tew hol' 'em,
Espeshurly ez sum will say
    Aour Dewey went an' stole 'em?
'Tware better far a-strengthenin' stakes
    Araoun' aour hum persesshuns
Thun takin' thet fer which, sum time,
    We'll hev ter make confessions.

An' 'tisn't things a nation hez
    Thet makes her less or greater;
But, fust, it's haou she got the truck,
    An', then, whut is their natur'.
When gunnin', 'tisn't orl the shots
    Thet caounts, but shot's thet's hittin';
An' nuther is it thet erlone,
    But whut's the burds they're gittin'.

An' then, ergin, its wrong tew shute
    The burds that's good at singin';
An', roamin' raoun', sum gunners find
    Whut's mighty peert at stingin'.
An' ain't them isluns an' their tribes
    But honnets tew the claspin'?
An' ain't there orlus stings tew thet
    Which greediness air graspin'?

"Tware thus uv ol', an' naou 'tis trew,
    The past an' present preachin'
Air givin' warnin's orl the time
    Thet's clear tew bimeby reachin',
A-tellin' thet there's orlus good
    Fer them in right ways keepin',

An' thet accordin's whut is sowed
    There's tares or wheat fer reapin'!

But rises sum tew adverkate
    The missionary notion
Uv Christianizin' tribes upon
    Them isluns uv the ocean.
Jess let 'em pruve their doctrine trew
    By startin' fer Manila;
An' leastways give besides their tork
    Their sanction by their siller!

In argerin' a pint, 'tis strange
    Haou pious sum folks dew be;
An' ain't there werk ernuff fer them
    In Portereek an' Kuby?
An' is this lan' so good thet they
    Vamoose eraoun' creation
Tew hunt fer foreign tribes tew save
    From heathern degredation?

When in aour kentry blacks abaoun'
    Whut never hern much preachin',
When yellar tribes hev sought this lan'
    Thet sorely need sum teachin',
When here the Injuns hardly fit
    The missionary notion,
Why hunt fer mission fields beyon'
    Ther Asheratic Ocean?

Ye know ye grabbed them Fillerpeans
    Tew make yewer kentry bigger,
An' soseter give yerselves a chance
    Before the worl' ter figger.
Ez turnin' hither commerce thet
    Shell bring the kentry millions,
Uv course, ye hope 'twill yield fer yew
    Sum insurdentul billions!

So, fellers, own up straight an' trew
    Thet ackshuns' pruve you're greedy,
An' don't preten' your objec' is
    Befriendin' uv ther needy,
Nor tell erbaout the isluns whare
    Your prairs an' teers air given
Fer edderkatin' ignorance
    An' fittin' souls for heaven!

Arila Greene, in Springfield Republican

EXPANSION

EPISTLE FROM AL. BEBE TO JOSH WHITCOMB

Josh Whitcomb, you should be ashamed
    To argue so agin' expandin'.
We want to grow. We can't be blamed
    For what the traders are demandin'.
This land of ours we like so well,
Just let it grow, and swell and swell!

Suppose George Washington did say
    That any great big standin' army
Will cost much more than it will pay,
    And very likely will prove harmy.
George lived about a hundred years ago;
There's lots of things he didn't seem to know.

Them words of Jefferson we cite
    From that old solemn Declaration,
'Bout men bein' born with equal rights,
    Was meant to have a reservation:
Else how could Tom, at his first chance,
Buy all that stuff he bought from France?

When Jim Monroe paid his respex
    To them there european kings,
Requestin' them just not to vex
    Republics on this side, and things,
He never thought this country'd go
Ang grab an archypellygo.

Abe Lincoln, he was always tellin'
    "Bout people rulin' for the people;
While he was even then compellin'
    Some people to respect some people.
Abe was so full of common people's cares,
He quite forgot to plan for millionaires.

Now, Josh, you know our navy men
    Have gobbled up the Fillypeens,
With folds, eight million, maybe ten;
    A mixeder lot you never seen.
Why can't we boss them for their good?
A handsome profit bein' understood!

Suppose them fellers begs for freedom?
    They hain't been taught to think like us:
They need our millionaires to lead 'em,
    Else they'll be overrun by trusts.
Folks that want liberty and light
Don't often get 'em 'less they fight.

Didn't our civil-service man,
  The president of the commission,
Lay out the very nicest plan
  To beat the schemin' politician?
"Send them your wisest men," said he:
Of course, he really meant, "Send me."

Now Gineral Shafter has a plan
  To rule them simple-hearted creeters,
And for a military man
  I think there's nothing could be neater:
Just kill five million, and thereafter
What's left will love us, says our Shafter.

Josh, kickin' ain't a bit of use:
  The mighty dollar runs this nation.
You'll only have to stand abuse
  And be alone 'ginst all creation,
If you keep talkin' 'bout what's right,
And don't remember cash is might.

Who does this talkin' 'bout what's right?
  Why, just some workin'men and cranks;
And who's for takin' all in sight?
  Men who have money in the banks!
Now, Josh, don't go repeatin' them there slanders
'Bout gover'ment contractors bein' all expanders!

What's that 'bout "Christ" and "feller-men,"
  And "doin' as ye would be done by"?
Times isn't now as they was then:
  We now need all that we can come by.
Don't you suppose Christ sometimes spoke in figgers?
And didn't mean by "men" half-breeds and niggers!

Feb. 24, 1899   W.A.B., in Springfield <u>Republican</u>

CHRIST IN THE PHILIPPINES

Outstretched he lay upon the gory sand,
His shattered rifle in his shattered hand,
His black face twisted with his dying pain,
His limbs contorted in their last fierce strain.
Deep midnight brooded o'er that battle-mound,
And o'er the mangled corpses strewn around;
While the thick palpitating tropic heat
In swelling waves on the rank foliage beat.

The invading banner of red, white, and blue
To this poor wretch no further wrong could do.
His naked breast had met the Mauser's flash,
The sabre's sweep, the Gatling's volleyed crash.

The home for which he bravely stood at bay
A smouldering heap of blackened ashes lay.
Children and wife were wastrels, scattered far,
Lost flotsam tossing on the waves of war.

And, lo! just ere the midnight hour was done,
Amid the trembling mist a halo shone.
A form majestic came, and stood above
The sombre field: two sad eyes beamed their love,
Two hands in which the nail-prints glistened red
Were spread in blessing o'er those dusky dead;
And then a fearful deed the shades behold
On that small hill, so like a skull in mold.

For Greed and Ignorance and Pride,
Cloaked in pretence, their real forms to hide,
Stole through the night and laid their eager grasp
On that pale king so passive in their clasp.
Thorns once again upon his brown appear.
A shadowy cross once more their hands uprear,
And there 'mid those poor souls for whom he died
The living Christ again was crucified!

                Arthur Mark Cummings, in Boston Evening Transcript

                    "BENEVOLENT ASSIMILATION "

What sacred call hath Freedom's chosen land
        With fire and sword to make ten thousand slaves;
        To teach the gospel of the Christ who saves,
By dragging prostrate foes with red right hand
Before his shrine? What mission to command
        That they do homage to a flag which waves
        In lawless conquest o'er their brothers' graves?
How shall these untaught pagans understand
        The learnéd subtleties of clerk and priest,
That chains can bind in Christian brotherhood,
        That those who love God most may spare men least,
That messages of love are writ in blood,
        That wars are needful, since we must increase
        The power of those who own the Prince of Peace?

                                        Oakes Burleigh

                    "OLD GLORY"--"NEW SHAME "

"The last week has been one of the bloodiest of the war since the
first day's fighting around Manila. Authentic reports, mostly
official, show a total of 378 Filipinos killed, 12 officers and
244 men captured, and many more wounded. The number wounded is
hardly guessable. Considering that the Filipinos entirely lack

                                101

hospital facilities, a great majority of the wounded will die. Probably the week's work finished 1,000 insurgents. The Americans' loss was 9 killed, 16 wounded. Two sergeants and one private were killed in ambushes while escorting provision trains."
Manila despatch, April 22, 1900

Are we wild wolves, then,
Gorged in our den?
Look to your flag, O Freedom's men!
'Tis filthy with mud
Soaked with innocent blood,
Loathed of the free and abhorred of God.

Shame on this lust
For the golden dust,
For "commerce" and "markets" in which fools trust!
Shame on these wars
Of Plutus and Mars--
Strips and Dollars, not Stripes and Stars!

Drunken and gory,
Damn not the proud story
That shines in each stripe and each star of "Old Glory"!
The great Declaration
That made us a NATION--
_____ but by vipers of this generation.

Shall cant, murder, greed,
Blacken Freedom's bright creed?
Look to it, men of Freedom's breed!
Wash clean your aim,
Wash your smirched name,
Wash from "Old GLory" the foul "New Shame"!

Cambridge, Mass, May 1, 1900   Francis Ellingwood Abbot

HYMN OF AMERICAN EXPANSION

After Walt Whitman

Camarados! Filipinos!
You who are struggling to be free, grip my hand in yours.
        I, too, have fought for freedom.
My emblem is the bird o'Freedom--the Eternal Hen.
Stick to me, Camarados; I will see you home.
I will free you from the chains of an outworn tyranny.
I, too, despise the effete hidalgo and his Old World despotism.
(Hard to the boom of our cannon! Good old Dewey!
What is that which protrudes above the blue wave of Manila Bay?
It is the funnel of a Spanish Frigate of an obsolete type.
Your foes and mine writhe in the grip of the sharks.
 Que en paz descansen!)

102

Yes, I am passionately addicted to peace, especially to peace won
      with war.
I will give peace to the conquered Don,--peace and dollars.
They shall take the tarnation dollars, and cede their colonies.
Vamos, Filipinos, I will not part with you; I will see you home.
(Have you read the fable of the horse and the stag?)
Vamos, Camarados, let me feel the grip of your hand in mine.
In the vista of the future I can see (but a great way off)
      a hazy possibility of independence for the Filipines.
Meanwhile, if you are not free, you are, at least, slaves of the
      free-born Yankee.
I have freed you from an outworn tyranny: now kiss the chains of
      a tyranny that is brand-new.
You have escaped from King Log: now make the best of President
      Stork.
Come, then, and join in the hymn of American Expansion.
Camarados! Filipinos!

Anonymous, London World.

TREASON, FOLLY, AND COWARDICE.

If this be treason,--to speak out
To save the land I love from shame;
To doubly hate a wrong that seeks
Alliance with her honored name;
To point the timely cure ere yet
The insidious poison does it work;
God make me worthy of the word,
Traitor I stand, with Edmund Burke.[6]

If this be folly,--to unsheathe
A stainless sword in freedom's fight,
That men of alien birth and blood
May grasp their own God-given right;
To count that good for others gained
Rich payment of the bloody debt,
Nor seek to garner selfish fruits;
Count me a fool, with Lafayette.

If this be cowardice,--to dread
The lust of conquest, greed of power,
The road the drunken empires old
Reeled downward to their fatal hour;
To fear to quit, for foreign strife,
The nobler work so well begun,
The paths where peace and honor join;
A coward I, with Washington.

O Nation, nurtured in the lap
    Of Liberty, her sacred cause

Still make thine own, the sovereign sway
    Of free-born men 'neath equal laws.

Dash not the down-trod millions' hope,
    Cheat not the waiting centuries' trust,
One people holding faith in Man,
    One State too great to be unjust!

For Freedom knows no here nor there,
    Her life is one in every part;
And tyrant stab, wherever dealt,
    Much reach, or soon or late, her heart.

Anonymous

UNFIT FOR FREEDOM.

Unfit for Freedom! 'Tis the word
That Israel from the Pharaoh heard;
Thus Philip of the Grecians spoke,
And Caesar of the Roman folk;
Thus Charles the First and George the Third,
And every fashioner of a yoke;
Thus Toombs and Davis[7] of their slaves,
Thus pious William of the braves
Of Cuba and Luzon. That lie
Is Tyranny's unchanging cry;
    "They are not fit!"

But who is fit to rule them? Say,
O slaves of Croker, Platt, and Quay!
Are ye, that meekly wear the chains,
Self-forged, of viler rule than Spain's?
Yours would but mean your Bosses' sway,
The rule of them that count their gains
In items of your freedom lost.
That freedom--won at what high cost
Of brave men's blood--you could not keep.
Of you shall History say, and weep;
    "They were not fit!"

Solomon Solis Cohen.

A PROTEST.

What, fair Columbia, has the end occurred?
    Has Freedom's cause been dealt the fatal blow?
And by thy hand? Why, from thy shores was heard
    The shout of liberty, ordained to go

Round the begirded earth; to link thy realm
    To every land with the great, breakless chain

104

Of human right; the foes of right to whelm
  With fear and rout on every hill and plain.

From the four winds the peoples, listening, bent
  To catch that joyful noise that bade them hope
That Freedom's blessings for them, too, were meant;
  And dost thou turn, and leave them still to grope?

You smote your tyrant with a hero's hand;
  You struck the shackles from your million slaves;
You drove the oppressor from fair Cuba's land,
  Abashed, and beaten back across the waves.

But now when, by your own example led,
  A people clamor for their native right,
Swelled with vain pride and greed that turns your head,
  You seek to crush them with tyrannic might,

Have you forgot your name; "Land of the Free"?
  Have you forgot, O proud and mighty State,
That all the legions of humanity
  Are waiting, "hanging, breathless, on your fate"?

Oh, high the mark thy founders set for thee;
  And just and noble was thy primal aim.
Wouldst thou prove equal to thy destiny?
  Refrain, then, from a course that makes thy shame.

Chicago, Oct. 7, 1899   Harry Blunt, in Chicago Public

VIVAT RESPUBLICA!

Undo the wrong!
Hear'st not the voice austere
Of Conscience vibrate through the deep
Where, in tense faith, the nation's heart abides?

Dare to renounce!
Think ye the nation brave
That striketh down, in fell emprise,
Zealots of freedom building Freedom's state?

Vow to retrieve!
Think ye the nation great
That spurns the prayer of wards distressed?
Hailed as deliv'rer, shows a virtue feigned?

What saith our law?
Where find ye grant or grace
In pact or code our land avows,
Empire's dark despot-sway to emulate?

105

Remember Rome!
Dread fate was hers, but just.
Mark Britain's bane, blood-guilt, greed-gain.
Men of America, wait ye prone for this?

Why tempt the curse
Brute Might and Mammon breed?
How strange that freemen court their thrall,
Mad to be minions under heathen gods!

Hear the crude plea:
The State must war to thrive,
And man, like Nature, kill to bless!
Is Christ forsaken? brotherhood forsworn?

The valiant life,
With nations as with men,
Will quell the vaunts of Lust and Pride,
Mount to self-conquest and reck naught of Fame.

"The die is cast!"
This! from the lords to be,
Ignored the people's Nay or Yea.
Hope of democracy, will ye bow or rule?

Republic, live!
True to thy creed, thou shalt.
But, if thy fairest virtues bleed,--
Bleed, and thou listless! Naught can stay thy fall.

William Tully Seeger, in Springfield _Republican_

New York, May 11, 1900

WHAT WOULD LINCOLN SAY?

Lines Written for the Anti-Trust Convention at
Chicago, Ill., Feb. 12, 1900.

Could Lincoln come again with mortal breath,
    And here among his people living stand,
His lips no longer sealed by silent death,
    His heart still hungry for his native land,
And could he voice some counsel, wise and kind,
    To teach his country in a doubtful day,
A light to guide the blind who lead the blind,
    What would the sage, immortal Lincoln say?

What would he say of men who spurn aside
    The high ideal on which our sires were bent,
The great seed-fact for which they fought and died,
    A government derived from free consent?

106

What would he say when all our strength and skill
        Are mustered forth to crush and shoot away
The self-same cause that hallowed Bunker Hill,
        What would the freedom-loving Lincoln say?

He held, with Washington, we should remain
        A land apart, a refuge for the free;
Nor be entangled in the warring train
        Of robber dynasties beyond the sea.
What would he say of compacts framed by stealth,
        Of whispered leagues to make the weak a prey,
Of Old World empires and our Commonwealth
        Yoked thus together,--what would Lincoln say?

He held that toil should have the highest place
        In all the land, East, West, and North and South,
Held that the sweat of no true toiler's face
        Should fall for bread to fill another's mouth.
Behond the reign of plutocratic greed!
        The few who rise, the many who decay.
The classes' surfeit and the masses' need,
        The wealth, the want; ah! what would Lincoln say?

What would he say? Speak out, O honored dust!
        Send forth an answer from thy patriot grave!
Shall you bright flag, our nation's hope and trust,
        Float once again above a cowering slave?
Is this Republic, reared in blood and tears,
        Doomed to decline and pass in shame away?
Speak out, thou Mentor of our better years,
        We wait to hear what Lincoln's tomb will say!

                                    Howard S. Taylor

EXPLANATORY NOTES

[1]Liberty Poems, Inspired by the Crisis of 1898-1900, an anthology of anti-imperialist verse, was published by the New England Anti-Imperialist League in Boston in 1900. A number of the 75 poems by 50 poets in the collection are published in the previous section on William Lloyd Garrison.

[2]Thomas Paine (1737-1809), a great American political liberal and radical; author of Common Sense (1776) which stirred the colonists to demand independence from England; the Crisis papers (1776), and The Rights of Man (1791-1792) in support of the French Revolution.

[3]The bitter winter of the stay of 11,000 men of George Washington's army after defeats at the Battles of Brandywine and Germantown was spent at Valley Forge, Pennsylvania. The heroism of the troops at Valley Forge during the winter of 1777-1778 became legendary.
   The Battle of Brandywine was fought on September 11, 1777 at Brandywine Creek in Pennsylvania. In the evening Washington withdrew his army to Chester, Pennsylvania with a loss of about 1,000 men.

[4]Marquis de Lafayette (1757-1834), French general and statesman who served as a major general in the Continental army during the War for Independence.

[5]The style of "Then Fillerpeans," appears to be modelled after The Bigelow Papers, the humorous poems written by James Russell Lowell in 1848, voicing anti-slavery opposition to the Mexican War then in progress.

[6]Edmund Burke (1729-1797), British statesman and orator; member of Parliament where he advocated liberal treatment of the American colonies in the speeches American Taxation (1774), and Conciliation with America (1775). Later became a leading Conservative and bitterly opposed the French Revolution.

[7]Robert Augustus Toombs (1810-1885), U.S. Senator from Georgia, strong supporter of slavery, and Secretary of State in the Confederate States of America after secession of the Southern states from the Union.
   Jefferson Davis (1808-1889), U.S. Senator from Mississippi, stronger defender of slavery, and President of the Confederate States of America.

108

6. MISCELLANEOUS POEMS

HOME BURDENS OF UNCLE SAM

For The Public

"Take up the white man's burden,"--
Yes, Uncle Same, oh, do!
But why seek other countries
Your burdens to renew?
Great questions here confront you.
Then, too, we have a past--
Don't pose as a reformer!
Why, nations look aghast!

"Take up the white man's burden,"--
But try to lift more true.
Recall the poor wild Indian
Whom ruthlessly we slew.
Ignoble was our treatment,
Ungenerously we dealt
With him and his hard burden,
'Tis known from belt to belt.

"Take up the white man's burden,"--
The negro, once our slave!
Boast lightly of his freedom,
This problem still is grave.
We scoff and shoot and lynch him,
And yet, because he's black,
We shove him out from office
And crowd him off the track.

"Take up the white man's burden,"--
Yes, one of them is sex.

Enslaved are your brave women,
No ballot, while you tax!
Your labors and your conflicts
Columbia's daughters share,
Yet still denied the franchise,
Quick give! be just! deal fair!

"Take up the white man's burden,"--
Start in with politics.
Clean out the rotten platform,
Made up of tricks and tricks,--
Our politics disgraceful,
In church and school and state.
We have no "ruling bosses,"
Oh, no! the country's great.

"Take up the white man's burden,"--
But, oh, if you are wise
You'll seek not "motes" far distant,
With "beams" in your own eyes.
Why fight the foreign despots,
Or Filipino isles?
Come, "scrap it" with "home tyrants!"
And politicians' wiles.

"Take up the white man's burden,"--
Right here in our own times.
Give justice, 'tis demanded
This side of distant climes.
Yes, take the white man's burden,
But take it here at home;
With self, oh, Samuel, wrestle,
And cease the seas to roam!

Syracuse, N.Y.   Anna Manning Comfort.
The Public, May 13, 1899.

AMERICA.

A refuge for the oppressed. Now, God be praised,
    Here they may live at peace. By her just laws
    All men are free and equal. No more wars
For greed of gold or land. . . .

Such was this country; but, within the hour,
    False creed of conquest, luring her to ill,
She is become an armed, imperial power,
    Crushing a weaker people to her will.
Let freedom's banner then to earth be hurled
And raise the despot's flag of the grim old world.

                                        Anonymous, (1899)

110

THE PHILIPPINE CONQUEST

It is the army of an empire and not of a republic.
Our soldiers in the Philippines
are not fighting for any principle.
They are not defending their homes.
They are not staying aggression.
They are not repelling an attack upon liberty.
There is no sentiment in the struggle.
There is no conscience in the fight.
It is of no consequence to our soldiers
whether they win or lose,
except as a matter of honor, advancement and money.
For these they are there to conquer,
as the Arabs were in Spain,
as Spain was in Peru and Mexico,
and as Great Britain is in South Africa.
To conquer for spoils not for themselves,
because they are only hired men,
but for the trusts at home--
as the Spanish regulars fought for gold
for the sovereign,
as the Englishman is fighting for the banks of London.

Edgar Lee Masters, The New Star Chamber, (1900)

HARRY WILMANS

After this volunteer speaks from his Spoon River grave
about the War of 1898, John Wasson, a Revolutionary War hero,
implies that the U.S. troops in the Philippines were like the
redcoates of 1775, while the natives defending their islands were
like the farmers of Lexington: "If Harry Wilmans who fought the
Filipinos / Is to have a flag on his grave / Take it from mine!"

I was just turned twenty-one,
And Henry Phipps, the Sunday-school superintendent,
Made a speech in Bindle's Opera House.
"The honor of the flag must be upheld," he said,
"Whether it be assailed by a barbarous tribe of Tagalogs
Or the greatest power in Europe."
And we cheered and cheered the speech and the flag he
    waved
As he spoke.
And I went to the war in spite of my father,
And followed the flag till I saw it raised
By our camp in a rice field near Manila,
And all of us cheered and cheered it.
But there were flies and poisonous things;

111

And there was the deadly water,
And the cruel heat,
And the sickening, putrid food;
And the smell of the trench just back of the tents
Where the soldiers went to empty themselves;
And there were the whores who followed us, full of
    syphilis. . .
And days of loathing and nights of fear
To the hour of the charge through the steaming swamp,
Following the flag,
Till I fell with a scream, shot through the guts.
Now there's a flag over me in Spoon River!
A flag! A flag!

Edgar Lee Masters, <u>Spoon River Anthology</u>, New York, 1915,
pp. 185-86

TAKE UP THE BLACK MAN'S BURDEN

Take up the Black Man's burden--
    "Send forth the best ye breed."
To judge with righteous judgment
    The Black Man's work and need.
To set down naught and malice,
    In hate or prejudice.
To tell the truth about him,
    To paint him as he is.

Take up the Black Man's burden,
    Ye of the bold and strong.
And might make right as only
    It does no weak race wrong;
When yours--his chances equal,
    Give him the fairest test.
Then, "Hands off" be your motto
    And he will do the rest.

Take up the Black Man's burden,
    Don't curse him in advance,
He can not lift a White Man's load
    Without a White Man's chance;
Shut out from mill and workshop
    from counting-room and store,
By caste and labor unions
    You close Industry's door.

Take up the Black Man's burden,
    Don't crush him with his load;
Nor heap it up in courses
    By scoff and jeers bestowed--
The haughty Anglo Saxon
    Was savage and untaught--

A thousand years of freedom
A Wonderous change has wrought.

Take up the Black Man's burden,
Black men of every clime.
What though your cross be heavy,
Your sun, but darkly shine,
Stoop with a freeman's ardor
Lift high a freeman's head,
Stand with a freeman's firmness,
March with a freeman's tread.

Take up the Black Man's burden,
"Send forth the best ye breed"
To serve as types of progress,
To teach, to pray, to pleed.
Let the glory of your people
Be the making of great men,
The lifting of the lowly,
To noble thought and aim.

Take up the Black Man's burden,
Black freeman stand alone,
If need be! Gird your armor,
For conflicts yet to come;
When weighed be not found wanting,
But find or make a way,
To honor, fame and fortune,
To God and destiny.

Kansas City, Mo., March 18, 1899   J. Dallas Bowser.
The Freeman, (Indianapolis), April 22, 1899

AGUINALDO

In Freedom's name, dare'st thou to stand
And lift against her chosen band
Who make to seize thy native land
Her sacred steel?
Rebel, stand back! by God's command,
Submit, and kneel!

What, thou, a savage, to invoke
From her quick hand a battle-stroke!
Would's thou by havoc so provoke
The conquering free?
Go, slope thy neck to wear the yoke
Of slavery.

Rebel! thou vile and wretched clod!
To rise upon thy native sod,
To claim the sweetest gift of God--
    The patriot's crown!
Know ye that freemen bear the rod
    To beat thee down.

Thy crime--the crime of those whose swords
Flash'd in the van of frantic hordes,
What time they rose to choke their lords
    For rights of men--
The crime that history oft records
    With bitter pen.

The crime of those whose stubborn skill
Made stout the crest of Bunker Hill;[1]
Who fought that day by Bannock's rill
    When England broke;
Of him who rushed his blood to spill
    On Austrian oak.

Traitor, to bear the path of those
Who twice in martial heat arose
And shook the world with freeman's blows
    To save their own--
The kindest friends, the noblest foes,
    That time has known.

Who conquer but to teach thee how
To bend thy neck to loom and plow,
To strain the sweat from wrinkled brow
    Of constant toil--
Who civilize, they care not how,
    So they may spoil.

Stand forth, thou form of Liberty!
Speak out, thou voice of History!
Where foulest wrong and wrath agree
    To spot thy page--
The worst of tyrants are the free,
    In every age.

And these who, striking in her name,
Beat down to earth thy living claim,
Shall write in blackest words the shame
    Of their foul act--
Look up! they cannot kill thy fame--
    Thou are a Fact.

A fact, like Wallace[2] and the few
Who flush'd her inmost soul and knew
The sources of the light she threw
    Against the storm--

Freedom, in thee, doth shape anew
Her dazzling form.

Thomas Fleming Day, Coast Seamen's Journal, May 24, 1899.

IMPERIALIST HYMN.

Lord, from far-western lands we come
To save these heathen for Thine own.
We bring them bayonets and rum,
We bring them death and woe and moan
Sweet fruits that Liberty has grown.

Thou who hast been our guide and guard
Half round the globe, be still our ark;
Bless Thou our guns, our faith reward,
Speed every bullet to its mark,
Till rebels all are stiff and stark.

Thou who are Peace smile on our war,
As erst Thou did on son of Nun;
The heathen break, their courage mar,
Hold up our hands till set of sun,
Till we can get them on the run.

Thou knowest Lord how deep our zeal
For heathen vile in darkness drear,
Who fight with bows, who will not kneel
Help us O lord, to make them fear.
And teach them how to drink our beer.

Chicago, Ill.   --Matthew Dix.
Appeal to Reason, April 14, 1900.

EXPLANATORY NOTES

[1]Battle of Bunker Hill was the first major engagement of the American Revolution. The Battle, fought on June 17, 1775, in Boston ended in a British defeat.

[2]Sir William Wallace (1270-1305), one of Scotland's greatest national heroes, leader of the Scottish resistance forces against the British.

CHAPTER II

SATIRE

1. GEORGE ADE

STORIES OF "BENEVOLENT ASSIMILATION"

I. THE MISSIONARY ARRIVES

The afternoon sun was impaled on the highest peak of the western range. Already the timbered slopes showed the penciling of long shadows. To the east, beyond the squared rice fields of rank and watery greenness, the river sparkled. Winding its way lazily and indirectly, it was here and there lost among the cool sedges of the low clumps of trees so that it seemed to be fragments of mirror, strewn lengthwise of the valley.

The Kakyak house crowned the first uplift in the grand ascent. It was a long, low house, holding refuge in a garden of trees. The walls were of bamboo stalks woven rudely around wooden uprights. A thatched roof, thick and cushion-like, overhung the frail rectangle. It seemed to overtop the house and crown it beyond proportion, like a man's hat dropped jokingly on a small boy.

In front of the house--that is, to the east of it--a mat of laced rushes had been unrolled within the slanting outlines of the shade. Francisco Kakyak, aged 20, was squatted on this mat, resting forward on a guitar, which he brushed with his right hand. His brother Patricio sat near him, his feet underneath him and his toes pointed backward, boy fashion. Patricio was only 8 years old and his part of the musical performance was to watch and listen. The brothers were remarkably alike. Each was a glossy olive as to color, and each wore a white cotton shirt, open at the breast, and loose lower garments of blue drilling gathered with a puckering belt at the waist. The white cotton shirt fell outside of the trousers. The legs and feet were bare.

Francisco Kakyak and Patricio Kakyak were sons of Mr. Bulolo Kakyak, independent Tagalo, who was squatted just outside the doorway with his back comfortably propped against the bamboo wall. Bulolo Kakyak was about five feet and four inches tall and weighed not more than 120 pounds. The brown of his skin had begun to show the coppery burnish of age and there were white

119

hairs in the light, sparse beard at each side of his chin. The
hair on his head, however, was coal-black, wiry and straight, like
that of his sons. His black eyes were pinched into a squint by
the rising cheekbones. The sons had the same kind of eyes. All
three of these male members of the Kakyak family had high heads
which were flattened behind. The faces were likewise flattened,
each nose being small and unobtrusive, so that the Kakyak head
was very much in the shape of a mandarin orange set on edge.

Bulolo Kakyak, father of the two on the mat, wore the same
boyish costume of unconfined shirt and flappy trousers. Beside
him lay a wide hat of braided straw. He had lighted a long cigar
of uneven rolling and was blowing the smoke upward, gazing at two
small and fleecy clouds, deserted in mid-sky.

While Francisco Kakyak caressed the taught strings of his
guitar and Patricio Kakyak knelt and listened and the father
contemplated the sky through the haze of his cigar smoke, another
member of the Kakyak family, on the end of the rug remote from
the two brothers, trickled white rice through her fingers and
blew away the dust and chaff. Eulalie Kakyak, or Miss Eulalie
Kakyak as she might now be termed, lately having become a ward of
the United States of America, was a doll of 18, as brown as a
coffee berry. She had small, squinty eyes, like those of her
father and brothers, and her hair was just as black and coarse as
theirs, but it was smoothed back from the forehead with feminine
care. Her flat nose had been varied by a watchful Providence into
an admirable pug, and the pug nose is never a blemish when worn by
a girl of 18.

One of Eulalie's shoulders was carelessly exposed above a
drooping white waist garment, which fitted loosely and was drawn
within the confines of a skirt--a blue and white plaid print
reaching somewhat below the knees. She was bare-legged and
barefooted, but the small pair of sandals on the ground near her
might have been hers.

Mrs. Kakyak was in the house, engaged with her domestic
duties. She was not much larger than her daughter, and she wore
the same style of cotton garments, so that when she came to the
doorway to speak to Eulalie, a stranger seeing her standing there
in her childish costume would have thought her a little girl who
had become wrinkled and work-worn years before her time.

"Is supper about ready, Luneta?" asked Mr. Bulolo Kakyak,
still gazing upward through the clouds of smoke.

"When it's ready I'll let you know," replied his wife, as
she turned away.

Mr. Kakyak made no rejoinder. He had been married for
twenty-three years.

Francisco sang softly, hovering over his guitar with his
head down. Patricio forgot the music and looked up through the
arching leaves of the palm trees, to where a bird with yellow
plumage was circling above its nest. Eulalie arose from the mat
with the bowl of rice in her arms and skillfully picked up the
sandals with her toes. She went into the house with a shuffling
walk. Bulolo Kakyak closed his eyes and feigned slumber. The
sun dropped its last shattered rim behind the mountain crest and

a curtain of shade was drawn swiftly across the valley. Inside
the house could be heard the low voices of Eulalie and her mother.
Francisco was singing a love song.

It was then that the missionary appeared.

Patricio was the first to hear him. The sound of hard sole
leather grating on the pebbles of the path was not usual, and
Patricio jumped up and looked down the slope toward the patch of
tobacco. He saw a man come from between two of the tufted palm
trees and begin the easy climb toward the house.

"Father!" exclaimed the boy, in a frightened whisper, "Look!
Some one is coming."

Mr. Kakyak opened his eyes and said: "Eh?" Francisco ceased
playing and straightened back from his guitar. The stranger,
ascending the hill rapidly, stood before them.

The missionary was quite unlike the missionary of fact or
fiction. The missionary of all established literature had side
whiskers and a long black coat. He carries a scriptural volume
in one hand. His countenance is mournful. He expects to be
cooked and eaten sooner or later.

The real missionary, who put his suitcase on the ground and
preceded his speech by three quick and scrutinizing glances at
the Kakyaks, was a tall young man with a red mustache, studious
gray eyes and a rather large and protuberant nose, denoting power
of penetration. He wore coat and trousers of soft gray cloth,
but no waistcoat. His trousers were supported by a yellow belt.
His shirt was of the neglige pattern and his cravat was a short
blue bow. He wore a straw hat.

"Good evening," he said, speaking briskly. "This is the
home of Mr. Bulolo Kakyak, I believe. Which is Mr. Kakyak?"

"That's my name," said Mr. Kakyak, staring hard at the
stranger.

"Well, Mr. Kakyak, permit me to introduce myself. My name
is Washington Conner and I am an agent, or a missionary you might
say, representing the United States of America. No doubt you and
the members of your family are aware of the fact that you are now
citizens of the biggest and grandest republic on earth. As a
matter of fact you're not exactly citizens, but you are under our
protecting care, and if you're not happy it's because you don't
know a good thing when you see it."

"We have had reports of the war from our neighbors further
up the valley," said Mr. Kakyak. "We knew that we were to be
governed by a country somewhere on the other side of the ocean,
but you are the first of these so-called Americans to come this
way. We have heard of your soldiers pursuing the insurgents----"

"Rebels," corrected the missionary.

"Well, let us say my countrymen--pursuing them and shooting
them, and we had hoped that no Americans would ever reach this
valley. You see that our crops have not been destroyed or our
houses burned----"

"The rebels did that," said the missionary.

"No matter who did it, it came with the war. I am afraid my
poor countrymen were happier under Spanish rule. The Spanish

fought the insur--the rebels, but they were poor shots and could not kill as many."

"If your countrymen are fighting the United States it is because they do not appreciate the blessings and advantages with which our government would endow this island," said Mr. Conner. "As soon as this war is over we are going to start in and civilize all those who haven't been killed. I may say that the rebel army is shattered and disorganized. More of our troops are on the way over to garrison the towns. This part of the island is already pacified. An abiding peace seems to be near at hand. Therefore, the government which I have the honor to represent thinks it is time to begin the great work of benevolent assimilation. I am here to explain to you the merits of the philanthropic plan for making all of you just as civilized as I am."

With that, he sat on the edge of his suitcase and outlined his scheme.

II. THE FAMILY DECIDES TO ASSIMILATE.

When Washington Conner, the missionary representing the United States of America, had seated himself in front of the Kakyak residence and started in to explain his plan for civilizing the Tagalos Mrs. Bulolo Kakyak and her daughter Eulalie heard the talking and came to the door.

The five members of the family listened with serious interest as Mr. Conner set forth to them in ready phrases the necessity of adopting the habits, the customs and the civilizing implements of North America.

"We are going to begin in this island a process of benevolent assimilation," said Mr. Conner.

"What is that?" asked Mr. Bulolo Kakyak.

"A benevolent person," said Mr. Conner, pulling reflectively at his red mustache, "a benevolent person is one who has the disposition to do good to others and make them happy. Assimilation refers to the act of bringing to a resemblance, likeness or identity. The plan of benevolent assimilation, for which I am the agent, contemplates the instruction of you islanders in all the details of our American civilization. We love you; therefore we are going to put before you certain examples and precepts to enable you to become similar to us. In the language of a popular song, 'Of course you can never be like us, but be as like us as you're able to be.'"

"But why should we try to be like you?" asked Mrs. Kakyak from her place in the doorway.

"Because we want you to," replied Mr. Conner. "These islands have fallen into our hands, or at any rate they will fall into our hands as soon as we get enough troops here to conquer all of them, and it occurs to us that we have been designated by a wide Providence to take charge of you simple-minded islanders and educate you. You are the white man's burden."

"We don't want to be," said Mr. Kakyak.

"Well, you are, just the same. You have been described to us as 'half devil and half child.'"

122

"He's not complimentary, to say the least," remarked Eulalie, with a frightened glance at her mother.

"I don't think we are as bad as all that," said Mr. Kakyak, reproachfully. "To be sure we live in a small house here, and we wear as few clothes as possible, but you must admit that we are peaceable and industrious. We work in the fields every day. On Sunday we go to mass. My two sons have attended the parish school and have learned to read and write. Eulalie can play on the harp. We are content with----"

"I know, I know," said Mr. Conner. "We understand that you Tagalos are a docile and industrious people, and there is no disposition on our part to underrate any of your domestic virtues, but we understand, also, that you are prone to be untruthful at times and that you frequently cheat in trading. In order to prepare myself for missionary work among the sullen people of this island I have read all the late books and magazine articles dealing with our new possessions, and there seems to be a general agreement that, although you are not illiterate, and although you are outwardly pious, still you will misrepresent and deceive under certain provocations."

"Are the people in your country honest and truthful?" asked Mr. Bulolo Kakyak.

Mr. Conner frowned slightly and then said, after a few moments of deliberation: "During political campaigns we may exaggerate, and in moments of excitement may draw the long bow--now and then. As far as honesty is concerned I will not deny that we sometimes gouge one another in horse trades; but, no matter what our lapses may be, we invariably prescribe honesty as the best policy for other people, particularly if they are dark people and live a long distance away. Another thing, there is a great difference between the barbaric lying and cheating of a primitive race of islanders and the judicious misrepresentation of a cautious and highly civilized race. Of all the people who have lived in North America, George Washington was the only one who never told a lie. At the same time, we now have our lying so systematized that a great many persons seem to be fully as truthful as George was. When you have been benevolently assimilated you may not be cured of lying, but you will lie so well that no one can catch you at it."

"That would be an advantage," said Mr. Kakyak, nodding his head.

"I can't see why the people in the United States, 10,000 miles away, are so much worried about our welfare," said Francisco, the 20-year-old-son. "They never heard of us until about a year ago, and now they're chasing us up every valley on the island, trying to----"

"Assimilate us," suggested the father.

"Yes, I suppose that's what they call it. For one, I don't want to be assimilated."

"If you know when you're well off you will take advantage of the instruction which I am about to offer you," said the missionary. "The United States is going to keep this island, and the philanthropic scheme of assimilation, which has been officially indorsed at the white house, is going to be inaugurated at once. Those who don't want to be assimilated had better take to the jungle. This isn't the first time that we've tried this benevolent assimilation. We've assimilated Indians, Mexicans and Chinamen, to say nothing of several millions of Negroes, and when any one of them hung back, I'll tell you, it went hard with him."

"I am a man of peace and I'll do almost anything to keep the soldiers out of this valley," said Mr. Kakyak. "We are ready to take lessons and do just as you say."

"Good!" exclaimed Mr. Conner. "I'll have my trunks moved up here the first thing in the morning and we'll begin work at once. I trust the results will be satisfactory. Probably you have no idea of how much you will have to learn before you can be classed as a civilized person. I am going to begin my task by telling you something about our great political parties. Do you realize, Mr. Kakyak, that as you are now a subject of the United States you must identify yourself with a party?"

"Must I, indeed?"

"Yes, sir, you and these other members of your interesting household must be either republicans or democrats.

"There are two parties, then?"

"There are two parties that stand a chance of winning. No civilized man of fair intelligence will belong to a party unless there's some show of winning out."

"What are you--a republican or a democrat?"

"I am now a republican," replied Mr. Conner. "That's how I got this job as missionary. If there should be a change of administration next year I might be induced to listen to reason and find much virtue in the democratic platform."

"I suppose it would be the part of wisdom to ally one's self with the party in power," said Mr. Kakyak, meditatively.

"First rate!" exclaimed the missionary, seizing him by the hand. "You have the instinct of a patriot. That is what we call in civilized speech 'getting into the band wagon.'"

"At the same time I would prefer not to make any choice until I have talked with you at some length. When do you wish to begin instruction?"

"To-morrow morning. I will lodge with you to-night if you have no objections."

"Certainly not. I will swing a hammock for you under the banana trees."

"You couldn't let me have a folding bed, could you?"

"We haven't any."

"Ah, that's so. You are not civilized as yet. Well, swing your hammock and I will turn in."

Darkness had settled upon the jungle of the mountainside and wide fields of the valley.

That night the stranger slept in the hammock under the palms. The Kakyak family talked of him in whispers before they retired. They were distrustful and apprehensive.

III. MR. KAKYAK DECIDES TO BE A REPUBLICAN

"Now Mr. Kakyak, we will begin the course of instruction by
telling you something about the great political parties," said
Mr. Washington Conner, the missionary from the United States of
America. He and Mr. Bulolo Kakyak, the Tagalo agriculturist,
were seated in the shade of the nipa hut.

"As I am now an American subject and have a proprietary
interest in American politics, I am naturally anxious to find out
what is what," said Mr. Kakyak, squatting into a comfortable
attitude.

"Have you made up your mind which you wish to be--a
republican or a democrat?" asked Mr. Conner.

"What is the difference between a republican and a
democrat?" asked the Filipino.

The missionary whittled fine shavings from a piece of split
bamboo and half closed his eyes as he meditated upon his reply.

"There are supposed to be certain live issues dividing the
two parties," said the missionary. "For instance, the republicans
are supposed to favor a high protective tariff--although not all
republicans are high protectionists and not all high
protectionists are republicans. The democrats are in favor of
free trade, a tariff for revenue only, a tariff for revenue
exclusively, a tariff for revenue with incidental protection and
a tariff affording protection to the products of democratic
states. The republicans are in favor of a gold standard, all
except the bi-metallists and the silver republicans. The
democrats are in favor of free silver, at a ratio of 16 to 1, or
any other ratio that will win, all except the gold democrats, who
are not in favor of any ratio at all. Each party is in favor of
civil-service reform when the other party tries to make a sweep
of the offices. Both parties are opposed to all trusts and
combinations of capital, as nearly as you can gather from late
platforms. Although the platforms for 1900 have not been framed,
I have every reason to believe that all republicans, except the
anti-expansionists will indorse President McKinley's plan of
colonial extension and benevolent assimilation, while all
democrats, except a large body of imperialists, will denounce the
campaign of conquest in these islands. And there you are!"

"That being the case," said the Tagalo, "I think I will take
to the woods."

"Nonsense," said the missionary. "You must make a choice."

"But I can't see that there's very much difference between
the two parties. You say that some democrats indorse nearly
everything in the republican platform and some republicans are
opposed to expansion, high protection and the gold standard. How
can they be republicans?"

"They are republicans because they vote the republican
ticket. A republican is one who votes the republican ticket. A
democrat is one who votes the democratic ticket."

"In your country how does a man make up his mind which
ticket to vote?"

125

"He usually follows the example of his father. That is always a safe and easy plan."

"But my father was neither a republican nor a democrat. He was a rebel."

"An insurgent patriot, you mean."

"You called them 'rebels' yesterday and warned me not to use the term 'insurgent' any more."

"Those of your countrymen who fought Spanish rule were insurgent patriots, as nearly as I could learn from reading the publications in my own country a year ago. Those who are now resisting American authority and trying to thwart our scheme of benevolent assimilation are disorderly rebels. There is a wide distinction between an insurgent patriot and a disorderly rebel and you want to get it clearly fixed in your mind."

"Whether insurgent or rebel, he did not give me a distinction in American politics and I fear I am not qualified to make a choice between the two parties you mention. At the same time, as I am now a subject of the United States, I suppose I ought to be something."

"By all means," said the missionary. "I can assure you that I well understand your hesitancy because there are no geographical predilections here in the island of Luzon. If you lived in Reading, Pa., you would have no trouble over coming to a decision. You would be a republican by instinct. Or, if you were a resident of Talladega, Ala., you would be a democrat, so as to get into society. But here in Luzon it is different, I will admit. Still, as you say, it is highly important that you should be something."

"Hold on! I have it!" exclaimed Mr. Kakyak. "You say that the issues have become rather cloudy and indefinite here of late and that there are varying beliefs in each party. Why wouldn't it be a good idea for me to hold aloof from both parties for awhile? By declining to ally myself permanently with either of these political organizations I could be free to act upon each issue independently, as it were. That is, I might support the republican ticket this year, and then next year, if the republican administration had made serious mistakes or nominated candidates of low intelligence and bad records, I could change around and vote the democrat ticket. By doing that I wouldn't bind myself to the democratic party forever, mind you. I would simply vote to give it a chance to correct temporary abuses of power."

"Great Scott!" gasped the missionary. "How did you ever get that perverted idea into your head? Do you know what you would be if you ever went to changing about like that?"

"Why--no," replied Mr. Kakyak, somewhat frightened at the missionary's manner.

"You'd be a mugwump."[1]

"A what?"

"A mugwump."

"That doesn't sound very nice."

"A mugwump is the most detestable of all creatures. All true partisans recoil from him as from a deadly adder. Little children hoot at him as he passes along the street with an umbrella under his arm. He is represented in the comic papers as

126

wearing side-whiskers and gum shoes. He cannot vote at primary elections. No mugwump may ever hope to get on the police force. He is the torment of the political prophet and the day-bogey of the campaign manager. You ought to read what the New York Tribune says about him. I implore you, Mr. Kakyak, not to make this supreme mistake at the very outset of your political career. Be a populist, be a prohibitionist, be anything that bears a party name, but don't be a mugwump. Once the brand of mugwump is put on you you are a political Jonah, to be mistrusted for all time. You won't be able to get a political job if you live to be 100 years old. If at any time you venture to address your fellow-citizens on any topic of public interest and claim a respectful consideration of your arguments some editorial writer will pick you up and say, 'This man is a mugwump,' and that will settle it! He won't have to strain himself to refute your arguments. You will be ruled out of the game of politics on your own damning record. No, Mr. Kakyak, be something. Those were the exact words that you used only a few moments ago. Be something! Be either a republican or a democrat, and after you have selected your party stick to it through thick and thin. If you happen to be a democrat and believe in protection and the gold standard you vote for free trade and 16 to 1, understand? It may go a little hard at the time, but after you get to be an old man and want to act as a delegate to something or other it will count largely in your favor if you can swell around political headquarters and say: 'I'm 69 years old, coming this fall, and I never voted anything but the straight ticket.' Then people will respect you. But whatever you do don't become known as a mugwump."

"Perhaps you are right," said Mr. Kakyak. "I am an unsophisticated Tagalo and you are wise with the experience of triumphant democracy. But I don't know which I ought to be. From what you say, I don't believe it makes much difference. I believe I'll toss a coin. Heads, I'm a republican; tails, I'm a democrat."

He pulled a copper coin from the loose pocket of his trousers and tossed it into the air.

"Heads!" ejaculated the missionary. "You are now a republican. Welcome to the grand old party. Remember that hereafter you indorse the administration."

Thus ended the first lesson.

IV. THE MISSIONARY RELENTS

On the morning of the second day after his arrival at the Kakyak home Washington Conner went back to the railway station, about four miles away, and brought up his heavy baggage. The large trunks filled a wagon, which was creakingly pulled by two downcast water buffaloes. When the wagon crawled the eminence through the avenue of palms and stopped in front of the Kakyak house the American missionary, who was straddling the topmost Saratoga, waved his hand at the Kakyak family and said: "My samples of civilization. Wait until you see what I have in these trunks."

"Do you need as many as that?" asked Mr. Bulolo Kakyak. "What in the world have you got in them?"

"You will learn in due time, Mr. Kakyak," said Conner. "I have in these trunks a great many articles that will give you some idea of the civilization which it is your duty to adopt. Mrs. Kakyak and Eulalie will be particularly interested in the contents of that black trunk with the brass knobs on it."

"My, but isn't it large!" said the daughter.

"If you are going to be a civilized young woman, Eulalie, you must make up your mind to carry several large trunks with you when you travel. You can usually measure a person's moral and intellectual worth by the amount of luggage that he takes with him when he goes on a trip. For instance, the English tourist, who is acknowledged to be the most civilized being on earth, usually carries several hatboxes, a bundle of sticks and a portable bathtub in addition to his trunks and Gladstone bags."

As the missionary was talking he clambered down from his high perch and gave a sign to the native driver to begin the unloading of the trunks. Mr. Kakyak and his son Francisco helped the driver, while Mr. Conner stood by and nervously gave directions. After the trunks had been tumbled to the ground they were dragged, one by one, into the house. Conner promised to unpack the black trunk with the brass knobs and reveal to Mrs. Kakyak and Eulalie the interesting objects at which he had hinted.

"Mr. Kakyak, you and the boys may go to your work in the fields if you wish," said Conner. "My instruction for to-day will concern only Mrs. Kakyak and Eulalie. I want to exhibit to them the wearing apparel of our great republic and give them some idea of the costumes that they will be expected to wear when they have been assimilated."

Mr. Kakyak and the boys departed down the hill. Eulalie looked up at the tall missionary and her eyes sparkled with anticipation.

"Are the garments worn in your country so much different from ours?" she asked.

"Oh, decidedly so; decidedly so," replied Conner with a smile of superior wisdom, although he was secretly charmed by her naive manner. "Why, Eulalie, you are now a young lady, old enough to have callers of an evening and seriously think, now and then, of matrimony; yet I find you bareheaded and barelegged. A young lady should never be barelegged except at the seashore. And your skirt, I am compelled to say, is outrageously short unless you intend to ride a bike."

"A bike?" inquired Mrs. Kakyak.

"Truly enough the island of Luzon is in a benighted state," said Conner, looking at Mrs. Kakyak and shaking his head. "Later on, Mrs. Kakyak, I will explain to you what a bike is. For the present I will confine my observations to the subject of wearing apparel. The criticism of Eulalie's costume will apply with equal force to the one which you are now wearing. In the United States it would not be considered just the thing for a lady of 40 to----"

"My age is 35," said Mrs. Kakyak, sharply, while Eulalie suppressed a smile.

"Well, of 35, then--I say it would hardly be considered the proper thing for her to appear in public places barelegged and with her garments hanging loosely about her person. And look at Eulalie there. Notice how carelessly she exposes one of her shoulders."

"I didn't know it was improper," said Eulalie in a shamed whisper, as she attempted to lift the loose folds of her waist over the little brown shoulder.

"It is improper, according to our idea," said Mr. Conner. "After you become civilized you may display both shoulders, but not one at a time. I say you may display both shoulders, but not at all times, understand?"

"Yes?" questioned Eulalie, greatly interested.

"You must never make a display of your bare shoulders except in the evening. That's one of the unchangeable laws of our higher civilization. If you were to appear in the morning in a costume which did not fully cover your shoulders you would be regarded as a shameless hussy and banished from polite circles for all time."

"But in the evening it is all right." said Eulalie with a puzzled frown.

"In the evening it is more than all right--it is the only correct thing to do."

"Why so?" asked Eulalie.

"Yes; why should there be any difference?" chimed in Mrs. Kakyak.

"There are reasons, ladies," said Conner, "but I am not sure that they would appeal to your primitive understanding. Please don't expect me to tell the reason for anything. Suffice to say that according to the American code of etiquette it is not proper for a young girl to roam about in broad daylight with one of her shoulders uncovered. She ought to wait until nightfall. Otherwise she will be talked about. I have a shirt waist in the black trunk and I will see that Eulalie wears it hereafter. In the meantime I want to show Mrs. Kakyak something."

He disappeared into the house and they heard him unlocking a trunk and rattling the trays. Presently he came out, beaming at them and carrying in his left hand a large object of indefinite shape, woven of rough straw, swathed in puckery ribbons of gay colors and surmounted by a supple feather of prodigious length.

"Look!" he exclaimed, holding it in front of Mrs. Kakyak.

"What is it?" she asked, wonderingly.

"A hat."

"A what?"

"A hat--hat."

"What is it for?"

"It is worn."

"Where?"

"In the United States of America."

"I mean on what part of the person."

"On the head--on top of the head."

"Merciful Luna!" gasped Mrs. Kakyak.

"Look at the feather," said Eulalie, laughing gayly. "Why the feather?"

129

"The feather has a certain value as a decorative effect," said Conner.

"Has it?"

"We think so in America," said Conner, rather stiffly, for he was not at all pleased by their open ridicule of his piece de resistance.

"Imagine any woman wearing that on top of her head!" said Mrs. Kakyak, and both she and her daughter laughed aloud.

Conner fairly lost his temper.

"Ladies, it ill becomes you to laugh at a work of art which has been indorsed by the discriminating taste of our great republic," he said. "After 2,000 years of progress and evolution our branch of the Caucasian race has decided that this hat is the ultimate of propriety and elegance as an article of adornment for women. Why do you presume to make fun of it? What do you know about styles? Whether you like it or not, Mrs. Kakyak, you will be expected to wear it."

"Never!" said Mrs. Kakyak, firmly.

"If you are to become one of us you must wear this kind of hat," said Conner, meeting her stubborn gaze. "Now, why are you so contrary? I have, waiting for you in the house, a complete costume, including a corset, and I am sure that after you have worn it for an hour you will never return to the simple garb of the Tagalos."

"What is it that you have?" asked Eulalie; "a cor--what?"

"A corset--a stiff jacket that you put around your body and then lace very tightly so as to make your waist appear smaller than it really is."

"Barbarous!" said Eulalie.

"It must be horribly uncomfortable," said Mrs. Kakyak.

"And I don't see the use of it," added Eulalie. "I don't want my waist to seem any smaller than it really is."

"Not now, but you will--as soon as you begin to imbibe the spirit of our civilization," said Conner. "Now, Eulalie, be a good girl. Put on the garments I have brought for you. You might as well yield gracefully. We are determined to carry out our philanthropic plan of assimilation, and that involves, first of all, the adoption of American wearing apparel. We want to establish a demand for millinery and tailor-made dresses over here, so that trade may follow the flag. Take your mother into the house, Eulalie, and help her to put on the various articles of apparel in that top tray. Put on the corset first of all."

"Come mother, we might as well do it," said Eulalie. "You heard father promise Mr. Conner that we would obey him in everything."

"If we must, I suppose we must," said Mrs. Kakyak, spitefully.

They went into the house.

After nearly a half-hour Mrs. Kakyak came forth. The huge hat toppled on her head. The frightful clamping of her waist seemed to cause pain, for her face bore an expression in which grief, humiliation, anger and apprehension were clearly evident. The waist, with its tight sleeves, clung to the corset in many a wrinkle. The skirt stood out flaringly. Mrs. Kakyak's bare feet showed underneath.

She stood awkwardly with her feet wide apart and her arms thrown into angles, like a jointed automaton.

"Oh, mother, you're a sight!" said Eulalie, who seemed undecided whether to laugh or cry.

"I--know it," said Mrs. Kakyak. "I can hardly breathe."

"You'll become accustomed to it in a little while," said the missionary, soothingly.

"I--don't want to," said Mrs. Kakyak, resentfully. "I'm going--to take--these things off."

"Now, Mrs. Kakyak!" began Conner as she retreated into the house, "remember----"

Eulalie laid her hand on his arm and stood before him.

"Please, Mr. Conner, don't be too hard on mother," she said, looking up at him with pleading in her dark eyes. "Please don't compel her to wear those ridiculous garments."

The missionary was embarrassed.

"Eulalie, I--I don't want to be harsh with you and your mother," he said, "but really, you know, you must learn to wear another sort of costume, now that you are subjects of the United States. The administration is very determined in regard to this matter of assimilation."

"Am I so hideous in this costume?" she asked, still with her hand on his arm.

Washington Conner looked down at the quizzical baby face, the tantalizing snub nose, the coils of glossy hair with the white flowers carelessly thrust into them, and the olive shoulder which lifted itself provokingly from the snowy waist. The landscape suddenly blurred and he feared that he would be unable to speak.

"I didn't say--I didn't mean that you were hideous," he replied, "I think you're nice."

"Then don't be so cross. Come, let us sit under the tree."

Gently she took him by the hand and Conner weakly yielded to her soft persuasions. He did no more missionary work that day, preferring to hear Eulalie sing Spanish love songs.

V.   THE SUMMER TRIP

"Where are you going this summer," asked Mr. Washington Conner as he sat at breakfast with the Kakyak family.

"Going?" repeated Mr. Bulolo Kakyak. "We won't go anywhere unless the soldiers come up the valley."

"You ought to go somewhere," said the American missionary, shaking his head. "If you can't go to the seashore you ought to go up on the mountain for awhile; or, if that is too much trouble, you might get a tent and an oil stove and go over and camp by the river for a couple of weeks. You see, in America, every family that can afford it goes away from home during the summer. If the men can't get away, the women, at least, are expected to be absent for a month or more,"

131

"Is it some sort of religious rite--some form of penance--this leaving home every summer?" asked Eulalie, who had received her childhood training in the mother church.

"Oh, no; nothing of the sort," replied Conner. "It is a social custom. It is one of the methods by which a family may demonstrate its possession of money and its sense of the conventional proprieties. Do you follow me?"

"I don't!" said Mrs. Kakyak, who was the forceful and outspoken member of the family. "You say that in the United States all people who can afford to do so close their houses in the summer and go out and live in lonely and remote places."

"Not at all! The places are not necessarily remote or lonely. There may be big summer hotels, with bands playing and a ball every night."

"But why do they go?" asked Mrs. Kakyak.

"Theoretically, because mind and body need rest after the wear of every-day work at home. Again, those who go away are supposed to escape the hot weather, although I do not urge this as a sufficient reason for the usual outing, because people have been known to suffer from heat at several summer hotels. The real reason for going somewhere every summer is this--if you don't go, people would say you were of no social consequence and couldn't afford the trip."

"I wouldn't care what people said," remarked Mrs. Kakyak.

"This indifference to the opinion of others is the common trait of savagery," said Conner. "As soon as you have become assimilated and have learned what is what, by contact with the sophisticated members of our great republic, your conduct will be governed almost entirely by the desire to avoid being criticised. I may say that the secret of the white man's civilization is this deference to the opinions of others. Don't give any one the chance to talk about you. Don't let other people know everything. Disguise your real feelings and so carry yourself that your outward bearing will compel respect."

"I call that hypocrisy," said Mr. Kakyak.

"Hypocrisy is a harsh term," said Conner, "Why not call it a diplomatic compromise with the convention of society? You will find, Mr. Kakyak, after you have been assimilated, that you will have to do a great many things that you don't want to do, in order to escape the disapproval of that impersonal but dangerous mentor, public opinion. For instance, we have had under discussion this morning the matter of going away for the summer. You can't understand why people should go away, arguing, no doubt, that most people can find in their own homes the best provision for comfort in any kind of weather. But when you come to understand that it is the custom for all prominent people to move from one place to another during the heated seasons, and that persons who do not move are necessarily not prominent, you will have a kindly feeling for the man who economizes all year so that his wife may live at a summer hotel for two months. Now that you are subjects of the United States and have expressed a willingness to accept our brand of civilization, I may as well warn you that if you desire to hold up your head in society you must make it a rule to go somewhere every summer. Otherwise you will find it rather embarrassing to meet a friend in the autumn and have him ask: 'Where did you go this summer?' Fancy being compelled to say: 'I didn't go anywhere. I remained at home.' Go somewhere, if only for a week, in order that you may escape humiliation."

"If you say we must go somewhere, I suppose we must," said Mr. Kakyak, somewhat ruefully, "but, so far as I'm concerned, I'd rather stay at home."

"It seems to me the sheerest nonsense, this thing of traipsing away somewhere when we ought to stay at home and keep cool," added his wife.

"Mrs. Kakyak, I am really disappointed in you," said Conner. "You seem determined to thwart all my plans for your betterment and uplifting. You persistently disobey me. Why are you not wearing your corset and shirt waist? Didn't I tell you to put them on every morning?"

"But I can't breathe with that dreadful thing compressing my body," she replied.

"Nonsense, nonsense!" said Conner, airily. "You can breathe. You must breathe. Thousands of women in my country wear them at all hours, and not only breathe, but actually take violent exercise, such as dancing and playing golf. I tell you in all seriousness, Mrs. Kakyak, that if you are to be a credit to the United States of America, which has done you the honor of adopting you, you must cease going barefooted and you must pay more attention to your shape."

Mrs. Kakyak was so awed by the missionary's professorial manner that she did not venture to continue the argument, but merely nodded in sullen assent. Eulalie had gone from the house, and Conner followed her. Without knowing it, he had taken to following Eulalie most of the time. She was in the scant shade of nipa, looking away across the rice swamps, and (horror upon horrors!) she was smoking a large cigar.

Conner was at her elbow before she saw him. Quickly she put the cigar behind her, and then looked up at him, doubtful and alarmed.

"Eulalie, of all things!" he said. "Smoking!"

"Ye-es," she faltered, timorously. "I somehow felt that you wouldn't approve of it, but in Luzon all the girls smoke."

"Approve of it? I should say not! What do you think Mr. McKinley would say if he knew that you were smoking a cigar this morning? And after all he's done to make you happy!"

"I'm sorry," she said.

"You have reason to be. It is a most disgusting habit--for women. One of our principal objects in taking possession of these islands was to cure the Tagalo ladies of the tobacco habit."

"Then the women in your country do not smoke?"

"Very few of them do."

"I suppose they are held in contempt and loathing?"

"Well, perhaps they should be, but many of them are very prominent society ladies, and it doesn't behoove any one to hold them in contempt and loathing."

133

"Well, why do you scold me for doing something that is done by prominent society ladies in your own country?"

"Oh, simple maid of Luzon! Can't you grasp the subtle distinction between smoking as a refined luxury and smoking as an elemental vice, or dissipation? Another thing. The ladies in my country smoke cigarettes instead of cigars, and they never smoke in public."

"Hereafter I will remain in the house while I am smoking," said Eulalie.

"That will be better," remarked the missionary. "There is another matter I want to call to your attention. I notice that you are given to the distressing habit of chewing the nuts and green leaves of the betel tree, thereby staining your lips and giving your breath a vegetable and peppery tang which I do not like when I sit alongside of you. Please stop chewing the betel, Eulalie. It is almost as bad as chewing tobacco. If you must chew something, chew gum."

"What is gum?"

"Is it possible that you never heard of chewing-gum? Truly, you are in need of a few civilizing influences. There is a stick of gum [taking one from his pocket]. It is a rubbery compound, sweetened and flavored."

"What do you do with it?"

"Put it in your mouth and chew it."

"Then do you swallow it."

"Certainly not."

"Just keep on chewing it?"

"That's all."

"You don't ex--that is, you're not supposed to----?"

"Decidedly not!"

Eulalie put the stick of gum into her mouth and chewed industriously.

"Do a great many people in your country chew gum?" she asked.

"Do they? Why, the manufacturers of chewing-gum have made their millions."

"My jaws ache," said Eulalie, "and I don't seem to be accomplishing anything."

"Keep at it," said Conner, with an encouraging smile. "All this comes under the head of assimilation.

VI. EULALIE AND THE STRANGER

Mr. Washington Conner, traveling representative of the civilization of the United States of America and advocate of the doctrine of benevolent assimilation, was somewhat of a puzzle to Miss Eulalie Kakyak of Luzon, and yet she discovered that she had a growing interest in the tall stranger. Perhaps his tallness had something to do with her growing interest. The young men of Luzon were hardly more than 5 feet in height and weighed about 120 pounds each. Mr. Conner straightened to within a half-inch of 6 feet and he must have weighed 170 pounds. Physically, at least, he was a superior being. Little girls usually have a feeling of awe in the presence of large men until they discover that they have a certain power which the large men cannot resist, and then the awe gives way to a coquettish sense of authority.

For the first day or two Eulalie had stood in fear of Mr. Conner. His comparative immensity of stature was appropriately supplemented by a rather heavy and rasping voice and a frowning manner. Furthermore, he was an American, and her countrymen had been at war with the Americans, therefore it was not strange that she regarded the missionary with distrust and doubted his motives. He had talked volubly in order to reassure the Kakyak family of the straightforwardness of his intentions, and yet he had not explained the situation to Eulalie's satisfaction.

Why were the Americans so anxious that the Tagalos should be "assimilated" and become like unto the people of the United States? Why should not the Tagalos be permitted to seek happiness in their own way, without the guidance or intervention of people living thousands of miles away? Why should Eulalie's father be dragged into the complications of American politics? Why should Eulalie's mother be compelled to wear a disfiguring hat, a torturesome corset and a stiff shirt waist when she preferred the loose garments of Luzon?

These and many other questions Eulalie had asked, and Mr. Conner had answered them, but Eulalie held that his answers were manifestly absurd. Mr. Conner said that the Kakyak family should do this, that or the other thing in such and such a way because it was the American way of doing that particular thing. He said that the Kakyak family had become American subjects as the result of a very adroit business deal with the Spanish government. The reason for allowing them to become American subjects whether they craved the honor or not was that, as American subjects, they could be played upon by certain influences which would result in their "assimilation." The government at Washington desired that the inhabitants of the Philippine islands should become gentle and temperate and humane and well-behaved, the same as all people in the United States. The Tagalos, of all the tribes, had resisted American authority, and sadly enough, as Mr. Conner put it, for they should have been the first to welcome it--because the Tagalos can read and write, they have schools and churches, they love good music and print their own books, they have a certain capacity for government and organization. Mr. Conner expressed regret that the Tagalos, a comparatively intelligent tribe, with at least the rudiments of what he termed "culture," had resisted the philanthropic efforts of the United States, while the sultan of Sulu, who was a polygamous bush-whacker, had shown much better judgment, for he had embraced the new civilization and become a shining advocate at a salary of $12,000 a year.

However, Mr. Conner was quite sure that sooner or later the Tagalos would be convinced of the error of their resistance and would partake of the blessings of northern civilization, only to become deeply attached to it when they had comprehended its full beauty.

The missionary had talked to Eulalie in the foregoing strain day after day, and yet the maiden was puzzled as to the merits of his case. She tried to believe that the tall stranger was sincere. Certainly he had the manner of sincerity, and yet she fancied at times that he was merely obeying orders and trying to bolster up a policy that did not fit at the joints. But she was very young and quite unsophisticated, and perhaps her judgment need not be projected into a controversy which belongs to statesmen and business promoters.

But, to repeat an earlier observation, if Eulalie was puzzled she was likewise interested. Had she not discovered that the stranger, great and gruff and dictatorial as he had seemed at the beginning, could be wound around her tiny brown finger? A week had passed since Conner had ordered, with military firmness, that she discard the short skirt and the insufficient waist of Luzon for the long skirt, the shirt waist and the feathered hat which he brought in the black trunk. Yet Eulalie still wore the short skirt; her bare shoulder still peeked baldly above the loose neckband of her waist; her head dress was still a cluster of white plumes, plucked fresh every morning from the moist boundaries of the ricefield.

Why had she dared to disobey? Because she knew how to cuddle and coax. The trick of the eyes was hers, because no girl needs to learn from a book. It was known in Luzon before any American landed on the island to show off his patented improvements on nature.

She knew how to put her hand on Washington Conner's sleeve and pout and whisper that he must not be cruel. Yes, Eulalie knew all these, although she had never attended a finishing school or lived at a summer hotel. And Washington Conner, although he knew many things (mostly facts) and had take a degree at an inland college, did not know how to resist these caressing blandishments, and there is no record of the fact that he wished to resist them.

All this was hardly to his credit. He had gone to Luzon to put into execution the serious plan of a very serious gentleman named McKinley, and he should not have been diverted from the straight path of his undertaking by any wayside glimpse of a little girl with a brown shoulder. He was a man with a mighty mission, and he had no business to while away his time with a snip of a maiden whom he could have picked up lightly and set on his knee. He could have done so, and he would have been glad to do so, doubtless, only that he was restrained by a sense of the proprieties. He had come to Luzon to pose as an example for the simple islanders, and of course knew that he ought not to begin by making bold with flirtatious young women. If he did such a thing the Tagalos might suspect that it was part of the American code of morals which he was striving to introduce.

He spent much of his time with Eulalie and they talked a great deal, but his conduct was at all times circumspect. Only, he had not changed her in the least. She was still Eulalie of Luzon and not Miss Kakyak of the United States of America.

With the other members of the family, Mr. Bulolo Kakyak and wife, Luneta, and the two sons, Francisco and Patricio, he felt that he was rather more successful. He had lectured to them

daily. He compelled Mrs. Kakyak to wear her corset for at least
an hour each day. Mr. Kakyak had begun the task of reading
political editorials. More than that, the missionary had induced
the family to take a summer vacation on the American plan and had
moved them over to the riverside, where they were uncomfortably
huddled under an improvised tent, made by lacing together several
mats.

On the first day of the camping out Eulalie and Washington
Conner were sitting on the river bank, intent on nothing and with
no desire for serious occupation.

"It's fearfully warm to-day," said the missionary.

"It must seem so to you, poor man," said Eulalie. "Why
don't you remove your coat?"

"Remove my coat? Dear me! No, thank you. You mustn't ask
a gentleman to remove his coat, Eulalie."

"Why not?"

"Well, in the United States it is not considered good form
for a gentleman to sit in the presence of a lady and not wear a
coat."

"But you are not in the United States now."

"No, but I must observe the etiquette of my own country."

"I don't see why."

"Because--well, it's the very point I've been trying to
impress on your family, Eulalie. We have decided upon certain
social customs and certain rules of conduct, and if we abandon
these what becomes of our much-vaunted civilization?"

"I don't care what becomes of it," replied Eulalie, with a
petulant little smile. She began to pick up small pebbles from
between the grass-blades and toss them out into the water.

There was a long pause, and then Eulalie asked again:
"Won't you please take off your coat?"

"Why do you insist?"

"Because I am sure you must be uncomfortable."

"I am, but as I have told you, a man in the United States
isn't permitted to be in his shirt sleeves while he is sitting
and talking to a young lady."

"But the United States is many thousands of miles away. Your
friends won't see you. I am the only one who will see you, and I
would prefer to have you comfortable. That's a very pretty shirt
you have on. Oh, pshaw! You're the stubbornest man I ever saw."

"I don't mean to be, Eulalie," he said, rather sheepishly, as
he arose and pulled off his coat, tossing it back into the soft
grass.

"There!" she exclaimed. "Now, I know you will feel better."
There was a light of triumph in her eyes.

As for Washington Conner, he felt as Adam or Samson or Marc
Antony must have felt at that moment when he realized that the
woman had the long leverage on the situation.

VII. THE SONGS OF A COUNTRY

Although the Kakyak family of the Tagalo tribe of the island
of Luzon did not show a ready disposition to take up with

American methods, put on American garments and adjust their daily life to a new code of American morals, it must be said for them that they were deeply interested in what the missionary had to say regarding America. Having become American subjects they naturally felt a curiosity as to the kind of government which had taken forcible possession of them. And as Mr. Conner had told them that they must become "assimilated" or take the consequences they wanted to know a great deal about the people of the United States, whom they were not supposed to imitate as closely as possible.

They were inquisitive. They asked many questions. They obtained a large amount of information. Yet such is the perverseness of human nature and so deeply set is all insular prejudice that these Tagalos were not being convinced that the American civilization was any more desirable than the kind they had known in the island of Luzon.

And here we may point out some remarkable facts. Every person in the world, unless he has an extra-judicial temperament and had traveled long distances in a fair-minded search for truth, judges the universe by the standards of his own half-acre. The salesman in a Broadway furnishing store haw-haws at the farm hand shuffling along the unaccustomed street. The proprietor of the country restaurant snickers at the city youth in white flannels who comes in to get a bite of lunch, and never for a moment questions his own general superiority over the young man from town. In Italy there are people who sleep eight in a room and never bathe and seem perpetually glossed with olive oil, who look out above their dusty casements and have an amused contempt for the American tourists tramping the streets below. If you would know the scalding truth about the British, ask a rural politician who has never stepped across a state line. And so the instances might be multiplied. The Kakyak family was just about as hide-bound and opinionated as the average family in the United States and that is why there was no willingness to admit that Mr. Conner as a type of man was nobler than any Tagalo who might be named. When the Kakyaks submitted to his authority they did so under protest, just as the colonial fathers fed the Hessian troops in order to placate the invader and not invite further calamity.

Because the family was so interested in America and asked so many questions, Conner was somewhat deceived as to the real situation. He forgot that the Kakyaks might be interested in learning of the peculiarities of a foreign tribe and still have no desire to adopt those peculiarities. All Americans like to read about those African kingdoms in which the belle of the village wears a ring in her nose and falls in love with the young man who can kill the largest game. Americans read of these savage customs and yet they are not impelled to adopt them. In America the village belle continues to wear the rings in her ears and she falls in love with the young man who draws the largest salary.

The reader will therefore understand that the Kakyak family might be willing and anxious to learn all about America and still have little inclination to be Americans. Something that happened while the family was camping out on the river bank may illustrate this point.

It was late in the afternoon and the family, according to custom, was squatted on the mats in the open air, listening to Eulalie and the guitar. Conner, the missionary, was seated flat on the ground with his back against a tree. Eulalie sang something from "Carmen." Conner did not recognize it.

"It's from 'Carmen,'" she said.

"Oh, indeed?" he said. "Grand opera! I remember now that before coming out here I read that you Tagalos are very good musicians--that you rather go in for high-class music."

"Oh, yes, we love music," replied Eulalie. "You will find either a harp or a guitar in every Tagalo house."

"That's rather in your favor," said Conner. "At least, it isn't to your discredit, but I'm inclined to believe that any nation that is too much given to music doesn't do very well in a business way. Music and moneymaking seldom go together. Very few musicians become wealthy. In America that is our principal objection to music. We think it's all right as a diversion for women, but an able-bodied man ought to be out doing something practical. Now if the Spaniards had spent less time playing the mandolin and more time at target practice we wouldn't have whipped them so easily."

"Ah, but music--it is such a comfort," said Eulalie. "It is the food of the soul."

"Oh, it's all right in its way," said Conner, as if he were conceding something.

"Have you ever heard our Filipino national hymn?" she asked.

"I don't see how the Filipinos can have a national hymn," said Conner, frowning. "We do not recognize the Filipinos as a nation. I suppose you refer to the piece of music written by one of the rebels and officiously termed the Filipino national hymn."

"That is what she means," said Mr. Bulolo Kakyak, with a warning shake of the head at his daughter. "She forgets that we have renounced allegiance to any Filipino government and are trying to be good American subjects. Hereafter, Eulalie, if you wish to sing any national hymn, you will sing the national hymn of the United States."

"But I don't know it," she said.

"Then I have no doubt that Mr. Conner will teach it to you. What is it like, Mr. Conner?"

"Well--you see, as a matter of fact we haven't any regular national hymn," he replied. "We have several patriotic songs that are quite popular--'America,' for one, but that is adapted from 'God Save the Queen' which is British. Then we have 'The Star-Spangled Banner,' 'Hail Columbia,' 'Yankee Doodle' and others, but not one of them has been formally adopted as a national hymn. I don't know why we've never agreed upon a national hymn. I suppose it's because we've been too busy."

"I think it very strange that the United States, which, you say, is the most powerful and progressive nation in the world, has no national hymn," said Mrs. Kakyak, with a suggestion of sarcasm.

139

"Come to think of it, I believe 'The Star-Spangled Banner' is our national hymn," said Conner. "Yes, I believe they do call it our national air."

"What is it like?" asked Francisco.

"I don't sing very well."

"I mean the words."

"Well, let me see. It begins 'Oh, say, can you see?' I'll try it.

"Oh, say, can you see, by the morn-er-by the dawn's early light. What so proudly we hailed at the starlight's last gleaming; Whose-eh--"

"And the--"

He stopped and shook his head. "I'm afraid I can't remember it," he said.

"Well, I'll declare," said Mrs. Kakyak. "There's a patriotic American doesn't know the words of his national song." She seemed rather pleased by his failure.

"I assure you that very few Americans know the words of that song," said Conner. "I remember we had a concert on the boat coming over, and there was only one American aboard who remembered all the words."

"Shameful!" remarked Eulalie.

"Oh, I don't know, Eulalie," said the missionary. "You must remember that music is not such an important factor in our life as it is among the Latins and all people of more southerly climes."

"When we are assimilated you are not going to deprive us of our music, are you?" asked Mr. Kakyak, as if alarmed.

"Bless you, no! We will permit you to retain your love of music, but we hope to induce you to take up American songs."

"Then you do have your own songs?" asked Eulalie.

"Why, I heard the American soldiers singing a song when they went through the valley below," interrupted Francisco. "It was the only song they seemed to know, and I thought it must be the national hymn. It was something about 'a hot time.'"

"Oh, I know that," said the missionary. "Yes indeed! That's the most popular song in America. Let me have the guitar, Eulalie. I'll see if I can't pick out the chords and sing it for you. I use to play a little when I was in college."

He plucked awkwardly at the strings until he found the semblance of an accompaniment, and then sung as follows, in a strained tenor:

"'When-you-hear-the bells go ding-a-ling-ling
All bow down and sweetly we will sing;
And when you hear that song
In the chorus all join in--
There'll be a hot time in the old town to-night!'"

The Kakyak family listened with quiet amazement.

"What a remarkable song!" exclaimed Eulalie.

"What does it mean?" asked little Patricio.

"Nothing in particular, but it is supposed to be enlivening," replied the missionary. "It is one of the many coon songs which are so immensely popular in my country. I suppose about three per cent of the population in the United States goes in for Wagner, Brahms, Tschaikowsky, Gounod, Verdi and Mascagni; but the other ninety-seven per cent likes the coon songs. You don't see anything else in the music-store windows. I'll sing one of them for you. It will give you some idea of what you must take up with, now that you are going to be like us." And he sung:

"'I guess I'll have to telegraph my baby;
    I need the money bad; indeed I do-o-o!
For Lucy am a very generous lady,
    And I can always touch her for a few.
I find the Western Union a convenience,
    No matter where I roam:
I'll telegraph my baby,
She'll send me ten or twenty, maybe;
    Then I won't have to walk back home."

"Isn't that the weirdest thing you ever heard?" asked Mrs. Kakyak, looking at her husband.

"Here's another that was spreading like wildfire about the time I sailed," said the missionary.

"'Hello, my baby! Hello, my honey!
Hello, my rag-time gal!
Send me a kiss by wire;
Honey, my heart's on fire!
If you refuse me, honey, you lose me;
    Then you'll be left alone.
Telephone and tell me I'm you own!'"

"These seem to be lullabys," said Eulalie. "They are addressed to a baby."

"In my country 'baby' is a term of endearment addressed by a young man to the object of his affections," said the missionary.

"It sounds rather mushy to me," said Mrs. Kakyak,

"Why do you call them coon songs?" asked Mr. Kakyak.

"Well, 'coon' is a familiar and slangy synonym for plantation negro, of whom we have several millions in our country. We get most of our songs in America from the illiterate type of country negro."

"But I should think that in the process of assimilation the negro would be compelled to take his songs from the white man," said Mr. Kakyak.

Mr. Conner hesitated a moment before explaining.

"The negro is not yet fully assimilated," he said. "It will take time."

"But you say you are imitating him," insisted Mr. Kakyak. "I thought that the darker race always took a secondary place and was dependent on the Caucasian, receiving instruction from him. That's what you have told us. Yet now you confess that you get your songs from the negro. Who was it said, 'Let me write the songs of a country and I care not who makes the laws'?"

"You do not understand," replied the missionary. "We may borrow our popular songs from the negro, but in the important matter of handling the dollars we are still on top, and will continue to remain there."

"Even when the negro has become assimilated?" asked Mr. Kakyak.

"Well, we are not going to assimilate him to that extent."
"Sing us another of the songs of your country," said Eulalie.
"I think they're awfully foolish, but they're rather interesting."
"I forgot to tell you that in acquiring the coon songs you
must also learn to do the cake walk," said the missionary.
"What in the world is a cake walk?" asked Mrs. Kakyak.
"It is a sort of friendly contest between several persons or
several couples to determine who or which can walk the most
gracefully. We vary the ordinary method of locomotion with a
great many eccentric steps and postures, and the results are
really surprising. I'm afraid you don't grasp my meaning. I'll
just give you an idea of what the cake walk is like."
He arose and extended his arms, looked upward at the sky and
walked to and fro in front of the Kakyak family, his body thrown
into a backward curve, his legs closed and unclosed like two
jacknives.
"What do you think of it?" he asked when he had stopped and
was wiping his moist brow.
The Kakyak family was convulsed with laughter. Eulalie had
put her head to the ground and was writhing in the giggles.
"Oh--Oh--Oh!" she shrieked. "Of all the idiotic things!"
"Do they really do that in your country?" asked Mr. Kakyak,
looking keenly at the missionary as if suspecting a joke.
"Of course."
"Well, well, well!"

VIII. AN UNRULY PUPIL

Mr. Washington Conner, the American missionary, almost
regretted having given Mr. Bulolo Kakyak the "School History of
the United States." The contents of this small volume by John
Bach McMaster started the Tagalo on an endless train of questions.
Some of these questions were very hard to answer, as will be set
forth hereafter. The main difficulty of framing answers to the
childlike interrogatories lay in the fact that Mr. Kakyak could
not grasp the fundamental truth that a white man is necessarily
superior in all particulars to a man with a brown covering.
Although the school history made trouble, no fair-minded
person will be forward enough to say that the book should have
been kept away from Mr. Kakyak. He had become subject to the
government of the United States of America, and it was not only
his right but his bounden duty to study the history of the
country to which he owed allegiance. Mr. Conner knew that the
administration wished to bring about the assimilation of the
Tagalos by kindly and educational methods, so he started Mr.
Kakyak on the volume.
The missionary had a second purpose in putting the head of
the family hard at work on a course of reading. While Mr. Kakyak
was intent on the history, Mr. Conner and Eulalie were left to
themselves. They were together most of the time, not because
they planned to be together, but because they could not
reasonably desire to be anywhere else. They spent a great many
half-idle hours rambling in the groves and across the upland near

142

the Kakyak house. Sometimes Mr. Conner lifted Eulalie over the high incumbrances of the pathway or set her on a shelving rock in front of him and marveled at the quantity of animal glee which this sprightly and squirming little maiden derived from their harmless adventures.

If Mr. Conner neglected his task as schoolmaster it was because he found the role of playmate more satisfying. Often enough Eulalie became the instructor, giving him the names of the gorgeous wild flowers which hemmed their sauntering journeys or addressing the stanch trees by their musical titles. The missionary was interested in the trees. He explained to the girl that the United States prized the island of Luzon very highly because of these hard woods, which in due time were to be made into furniture for the American markets.

"Eulalie, you won't recognize this valley after we've had it for a few years." he said to her one day. "We will have a railway line through here, saw-mills all along the river and probably a new town with trolley cars and a ball park."

"Oh, I hope not," said Eulalie. "It might help your countrymen to make money, but what would become of us?"

"Your family would become assimilated and work in one of our factories."

"I think we are happier in our present condition."

"The object of our modern civilization is not to make people happy, but to make them useful," replied Conner. "Of course, if people can be reasonably happy at the same time that they are making themselves useful, so much the better for them."

"But surely your countrymen will not cut down all these beautiful trees and leave this hillside covered with ugly stumps and tangled brush?" she asked.

The missionary explained to her that a mere sentimental preference for shade and foliage, or what some people term the aesthetic conscience, must never stand in the way of a manufacturing enterprise. The reason for this was that a manufacturing enterprise gave employment to many people and made them more useful than they could possibly be while living in an environment of unbroken fields and uncleared forests.

He said that a hustling American didn't permit his regard for scenery to interfere with plans for money-making. For instance, the landscapes throughout America were checkered with flamboyant bill-boards advertising patent medicines, bicycles and various makes of beer.

"And when the Americans have taken actual possession will we have these huge advertising signs all over the face of the mountain?" asked Eulalie, regretfully.

"Yes, wherever they can be seen from the train."

"Well, then, I hope they don't come very soon."

The missionary had given up trying to correct many of Eulalie's whimsical objections to the American way of doing things. Her bits of spiteful rejoinder amused rather than displeased, giving a continued zest to their talk.

Very few young men find abiding pleasure in the society of a young woman who is entirely docile and complaisant. The imperfections of a maiden--that is, the disproportion of physical features and the little cloudbursts of temper--give to her an individual charm. One who answered the specifications of a Greek model and professed only the angelic traits would be an intolerable bore. Her conduct would lack the element of surprise. Her companionship would never promise the pleasant irritation of conflict. The young man would know what to expect. There could be no quarreling and therefore no "making up," with its inevitable delights.

If Eulalie's nose had been straight and long, instead of pug; if she had looked down at the ground instead of looking up at Conner with a mischievous challenge lurking in her bright eyes; if she had shown a lamb-like obedience, instead of sly resistance; if she had adopted the conventional and starchy shirtwaist instead of continuing to wear the soft body garment which allowed her bare shoulder to protrude--in short, If she had not been Eulalie, it is possible that Mr. Washington Conner would have put her in the class with other members of the Kakyak family and kept resolutely at the work of benevolent assimilation. As it was, he found himself irresistibly inclined to follow her about and look at her, to pursue the soft crackle of her skirt through the narrow and winding pathways of the ascending woodland, to beam patronizingly at her naive inquiries and to admire that odd and elfish beauty which might have escaped the analysis of the critic, but which to him was overwhelmingly present.

In America he had sat in many rocking chairs on many verandas and talked to young women on numerous topics which did not interest him or the young women, and for some of these young women he had felt a suppressed admiration and a frightened longing, but never, never until he met Eulalie did he know what it was to compromise his dignity and almost refuse to feel any shame in it. Never, until he began to run wild with this kittenish and altogether impossible young creature of Luzon was he compelled to resist the impulse to take hold of hands and go romping. He held himself back from temptation by assuring himself that Eulalie was a child of nature and did not belong in the same social division with one who had been valedictorian at a presbyterian college. Yet, while mentally maintaining this attitude of superiority, his outward conduct proved that she could manage him.

When they roamed together she compelled him to lay aside his coat, although he had told her that a real gentleman must never remove his coat in the presence of a lady. Then she induced him to take off his choking collar and wear only a loose handkerchief about his neck, although he protested that to do such a thing was wretched form.

One day, when they came sauntering down the path on their return from an aimless expedition, the missionary had several wild flowers stuck in his auburn hair. They toppled above his head like an uneasy crown. Eulalie had put them there while he looked into her face only a few inches away, helpless with bliss, and begged her not to do it.

As they came toward the house he was smiling sheepishly, but the smile gave change to an expression of annoyance when Eulalie ran ahead and shrilly called to the family to come out and look at him. It was just the hoydenish act he might have expected of a young person who had never read the Ladies' Home Journal.

Here was an awkward situation for a dignified person, who pretended to be an exemplar. Mrs. Kakyak and little Patricio came through the doorway and were loud in their mirth. The missionary hastily pulled the flowers from his hair and had a blushing consciousness that Eulalie had taken tremendous liberties with him.

He was saved from any prolonged embarrassment by Mr. Kakyak, who was squatted in a characteristic attitude under one of the palm trees. Mr. Kakyak called to the missionary and said he wished to ask a few questions. The school history was open in front of him and he had been reading the appendix, which included the declaration of independence and the constitution of the United States, together with the various amendments thereto.

The questions propounded by Mr. Kakyak and the answers made by Mr. Conner are of sufficient importance to demand a separate chapter, dealing largely with the proposition that "governments derive their just power from the consent of the governed."

IX. TWO REBELLIONS

"I just wanted to ask you about a certain passage in the school history," said Mr. Kakyak, the Tagalo, addressing the American missionary.

Washington Conner--"Yes?"

Kakyak--"Here it is. (Reads.) 'We hold these truths to be self-evident; that all men are created equal; that they are endowed by their Creater with certain unalienable rights; that among these are life, liberty and the pursuit of happiness. That to secure these rights governments are instituted among men, deriving their just powers from the consent of the governed; that whenever any form of government becomes destructive of these ends it is the right of the people to alter or to abolish it--'"

Conner--"I remember the passage perfectly. You are reading from the second paragraph of the declaration of independence. What of it?"

Kakyak--"Well, do the people of your country still indorse the sentiments contained in that declaration?"

Conner--"I don't suppose we are legally bound by anything contained in the declaration of independence. In a general way, however, we still agree with what it says there."

Kakyak--"Do you still maintain that 'governments derive their just powers from the consent of the governed'?"

Conner--"Nothing contained in that declaration of independence applies to the Malay division of the human race. That declaration was prepared by white men."

Kakyak--"Then it should read: 'All men (except Malay) are created equal,' or perhaps 'all white men are created equal'?"

Conner--"For a great many years that passage was supposed to mean 'all white men,' just as you suggest. Stephen A. Douglas, an eminent statesman, maintained that the unalienable rights of life, liberty and the pursuit of happiness and the privileges of self-government belonged to the white man alone. Abraham Lincoln claimed that the word 'men' had a more general application and included negroes as well. We had a very bitter and destructive civil war in America, and after it was all over we reached the conclusion that the negro has the same unalienable rights as the white man. But we have never admitted that the Tagalo has these rights, if that's what you're driving at."

Kakyak--"I am simply seeking information--trying to find out the exact status of my countrymen. You see the Filipino insur-- rebels, I mean--have set up the claim that they have the same rights that the Americans claimed in 1776. They have organized a provisional government, just as the colonies did. They are fighting for--well, what they conceive to be their rights. In what respect are they different from the thirteen colonies that rebelled against Great Britain?"

Conner--"The situation here is entirely different. Our forefathers in America threw off the British yoke because they had been made the victims of a long train of abuses which you will find set forth in the declaration of independence in front of you--two whole pages. The Tagalos, on the other hand, are resisting a government which is to be wise, humane and just, with charity for all."

Kakyak--"How do we know this?"

Conner--"Because we tell you so."

Kakyak--"You say the thirteen colonies resisted British authority because they had been persecuted and unjustly taxed. Suppose that after they had issued this declaration of independence and founded a provisional government of their own Great Britain had relented and promised to correct all the abuses of which there had been complaint. Do you think the colonists would have been willing to go back and accept British rule?"

Conner--"Perhaps not, but--"

Kakyak--"Another question. I read in here that France helped the colonists in their war against Great Britain, the same as the Americans last year helped us in our revolt against the Spanish, here in this island. Now, suppose that before the British had been driven from the colonies Great Britain and France had made a treaty in which Great Britain, in consideration of a large sum of money, had transferred the colonies to France. Do you think the colonists would have accepted French rule simply because the French had been their friends during the war?"

Conner--"Your questions are preposterous, Mr. Kakyak. It is evident that you are trying to demonstrate that the present rebellion in this island bears some resemblance to the revolutionary uprising in America in 1776. You seem to forget that the colonial fathers were an intelligent, high-minded body of patriots, while the Tagalos are simple islanders who have a vague longing to govern themselves and mistake this longing for genuine patriotism."

Kakyak--"Whether it be patriotism or not, a great many of them have been willing to die for it. Your colonial fathers couldn't do more than that."

Conner--"Look here, Mr. Kakyak, do you realize that your conversation to-day borders very closely on treason?"

Kakyak--"Perhaps so. I have become rather inflamed from reading the declaration of independence."

Conner--"I can see that you still cling to the idea that the Tagalos ought to have a government of their own."

Kakyak--"I think they ought to be given a chance to govern themselves."

Conner--"But the Tagalos are only one tribe."

Kakyak--"We number one and a half millions. There were only three million colonists."

Conner--"But they were a different kind of people."

Kakyak--"They held slaves. We are too civilized to do that."

Conner--"Don't you see that it would be impossible, under prevailing conditions, to give you Tagalos a separate and independent government? You are only one of many tribes. Why, there are tribes right on this island that are ready and willing to accept American rule."

Kakyak--"Those are the bow men who live in the remote jungles. They do not have schools and churches and printing presses as we do, and so they have never been educated to a desire for liberty. I read in this history that when the colonists rebelled against the British the Indians who lived on the British possessions surrounding the thirteen colonies did not join in the rebellion or the revolution, but continued to be friendly with the British. If I am not mistaken they helped the British on more than one occasion, and massacred whole villages of the rebels--I mean the colonists. So, you see, the colonists did not have the sympathy of the savage tribes any more than we have. I'll admit that the Tagalos do not hold all the territory in Luzon, but they occupy all that part of the island which is civilized and under cultivation. As far as that's concerned, the thirteen colonies were only a little patch of North America. They occupied less than one-forth of the British holdings in North America, yet they presumed to found a government of their own without the consent or co-operation of the inhabitants of the Indian country and the province acquired from the French."

Conner--"I don't know what you hope to accomplish by all these parallels. Suppose you do satisfy yourself that your countrymen are real liberty-loving patriots, the same as our forefathers in America were, what are you going to do about it?"

Kakyak--"I don't know, I'm sure."

Conner--"Did you expect us to come over here and destroy the Spanish fleet and afterward pay out $20,000,000 for the mere satisfaction of permitting you people to govern yourselves?"

Kakyak--"That's what we thought."

Conner--"Then you have very elementary notions of business."

Kakyak--"Let me begin at the beginning and tell how and why we have been deceived."

Conner--"Mistaken, you mean."

Kakyak--"Perhaps that would be a better word. When your fleet under the command of Admiral Dewey came to Manila we were under the impression that the Americans had come to help us drive out the Spanish and set up a government of our own. That's what my people have been fighting for and praying for ever since I can remember. Some of my neighbors said: 'If the Americans come in here and defeat the Spanish they will take the island for themselves instead of letting us have a republic of our own." Then Aguinaldo and other leaders who had talked with the Americans assured us that the war against Spain was a war of humanity, that the Americans had gone into it because they believed in the rights of men and could no longer endure the spectacle of Spanish cruelties in Cuba. We were told that the Americans were willing to spend any amount of money to enforce justice and confer the blessings of liberty on a struggling people. We know that your countrymen were pledged to drive the Spanish out of Cuba and help the Cubans to establish a stable government of their own. We thought you would treat us the same as you have treated the Cubans."

Conner--"We didn't promise you a stable government of your own. We have never conceded that you had a right to govern yourselves. Evidently you have jumped at conclusions."

Kakyak--"But we heard such favorable reports of you that we believed you would give us a chance at self-government, even though you had made no specific promises. We thought that your conscience might help you to a conclusion."

Conner--"Do you realize that we have paid $20,000,000 for these islands? Do you expect a business nation to go to work and throw away any such sum of money? You may rest assured that we will keep these islands, especially since President Schurman has reported so favorably on the good qualities of the Tagalos.[2] I notice that he says in an interview that in two generations you Tagalos will be as far advanced, in all respects, as the Japanese."

Kakyak--"When we are as far advanced as the Japanese do you think we will still consent to be governed by a foreign power?"

Conner--"I don't like the terms you use. You talk of 'government' and 'foreign power' as if the United States intended to oppress you, instead of making you highly civilized through the workings of benevolent assimilation."

Kakyak--"Well, I wish I knew just what was going to become of us. After this war is over, Mr. Conner, after all the fighting rebels have been killed and peace has been restored, don't you think your countrymen will relent somewhat and decide to give us a chance to govern ourselves."

Conner--"I shouldn't like to hold out false hopes, Mr. Kakyak. I think I can best answer your question by reading a newspaper clipping which I have just received from the United States. It is an extract from a speech delivered by President McKinley at the Ocean Grove camp meeting. Here it is." (Reads)

"The flag does not mean one thing in the United States and another thing in Puerto Rico and the Philippines. There has been doubt expressed in some quarters as to the purpose of the government respecting the Philippines. I can see no harm in stating it in this presence. Peace first, then, with charity for all, an established government of law and order, protecting life and property and occupation, for the well being of the people, in which they will participate under the stars and stripes."

Kakyak--"What does it mean?"

Conner--"Well, a true statesman is always indefinite, but as nearly as I can figure it out it means, 'You don't get it.' Note the word 'occupation.' That means that we are going to remain."

Kakyak--"How about that word 'participation'?"

Conner--"'Participation' is a beautifully copious word. That's why Mr. McKinley used it. But it satisfied the people at the camp meeting, so you ought not to kick."

X. SPORTS AND PASTIMES

One morning when the American missionary returned from a stroll with Eulalie (they were in search of a certain gorgeous yellow flower which blooms within a few weeks after the close of the rainy season), he turned the corner of the Kakyak house and came upon a scene which aroused him to extreme indignation.

Francisco and Patricio, the two sons of Bulolo Kakyak, were squatted down facing each other, and each held a struggling gamecock. The lean and sinewy birds fought to free themselves. They stabbed the air in quick strokes with their pointed beaks, and the snappy little eyes glowed like beads of fire, so fierce was their hatred and so eager was the desire for battle.

Patricio, the smaller boy, had difficulty in restraining his bird, which squirmed and flung itself within the boy's chubby grasp.

On the ground were four copper coins. Washington Conner saw at a glance that the two sons were tantalizing and exciting the two gamecocks, preliminary to a death battle, and that the money on the ground represented a wager on the result.

To say that Washington Conner was indignantly horrified would be putting it very mildly. Before coming to the Philippines he had read that the Tagalos were given to the brutal pastime of cockfighting, but this was the first time he had happened upon the inhuman sport.

"Stop!" he commanded. "Don't you dare to set those birds to fighting! Release them at once."

"If we release them they will fight," said little Patricio, with a bad boy's grin. "We have to keep them tied up all the time or else they kill one another."

"Well, then, tie them up again. Whatever you do, don't let them fight. It seems to me that I arrived just in time to prevent a very degrading exhibition. How can you boys, who claim to possess some of the attributes of a civilized people, sit here and see two birds tear each other to pieces?"

Francisco, the elder son, had tucked his fighting bird back under his arm, and he regarded the missionary with sullen hatred, apparently inclined to disobey.

"The birds want to fight," said he. "They can't do anything else, and I don't see why we shouldn't have the fun of seeing them fight."

"Fun!" exclaimed Conner. "You call that fun? Why, in America we cannot find language strong enough to express our disapproval of such cruel and bloddy enjoyments."

"That's strange," remarked Francisco. "One of our neighbors who has been down to Manila to sell his produce says that the American soldiers crowd into the cockpits every day in order to see the birds fight."

"Doubtless they go there to study the sports of a half-civilized people and prepare themselves for reformatory work," said Conner. "Their presence at a cockfight need not indicate that they approve of such shocking exhibitions.

"But they bet on the result, too, or at least our neighbor says so. He says he never saw such betting."

"If any of our soldiers have been attending cockfights and betting on the results they have done so without the consent or the approval of the national administration," said the missionary. "The government at Washington is determined to abolish these barbarous sports and pastimes in the colonies--bull-fighting in Cuba, cock-fighting in the Philippines. We are a humane people and a people much given to the reformation of others, and it will be a great reward to our national conscience if we can induce you lowly tribes to give up gambling and the torture of dumb animals.

"I take it that in your country you do not gamble or torture dumb animals," said Francisco, in a manner which was almost sneering. It was evident that the information he had received of American doings in Manila had made him skeptical.

"There may be a little gambling in America, but as regards the torture of dumb creatures I can say, with pride, that our enlightened civilization has undertaken to protect domestic animals, and that any man who maltreats or tortures one of them is subject to prosecution in a court of law. Cock-fighting, for instance, is strictly forbidden. The only cockfights we have are conducted in secluded and out-of-the-way places.

"But you do have cockfights occasionally," asked Francisco, who seemed to find some comfort in the missionary's confession.

"Only at rate intervals," replied Conner. "Most of our sports and pastimes are rational and harmless."

"What are some of your sports?" asked Francisco. "If you are going to prevent cock-fighting I suppose we shall have to take up with some sort of amusement that is approved by your government."

"Oh, we have many games and sports at home," said Conner. "We have baseball, tennis, golf, croquet and so on. Also we have horse-racing. There is some gambling at our racetracks, I am sorry to say, but we do not approve of it. In fact, it is in direct violation of law, so we feel that we are not responsible for it."

"These are quiet sports, I suppose," said Francisco. "That is, I dare say that those who play them are in no danger of being hurt."

"Not in the games I have mentioned," replied Conner. "Tennis, golf and croquet are especially safe. I don't believe I ever heard of any one being hurt while playing croquet. We have other games that are quite rough; football, for instance. A great many of the young men who play that game are either killed or injured."

"I suppose it is very unpopular on that account," suggested Francisco.

"Well, I can't say that it is," replied Conner.

"At any rate it cannot be as that other game you mentioned, the one that was particularly free from brutality and the element of danger--croquet, I think you called it."

Conner had to laugh.

"I'll not try to deceive you," said the missionary. "In New York city I have seen 40,000 spectators at a football game. I doubt if more than eight spectators ever sat through a game of croquet. You must remember that we men of the north are better adapted for personal encounter and have more endurance than you little people of the warm climes. We are fond of sports which to you would seem rough and bearish. In fact, I am afraid that we have a decided preference for smashing and bruising games such as football and pugilism."

"What is pugilism?" asked Francisco.

"Pugilism is another name for prize-fighting; that is, fighting with the fists to win a certain prize, usually a sum of money. Two men face each other in a square which is inclosed by ropes, and at a given signal they begin striking at each other. Their hands are padded so as to protect the fists and permit the contestants to strike harder blows. They keep at it until one or the other is too exhausted to continue or receives a blow which disables him so that he cannot rise from the ground within ten seconds after he falls."

"I should think some one would be killed," said the smaller boy.

"Some one is killed now and then," replied the missionary. "I must admit that it is rough sport. Nearly every one in America is opposed to it, as a matter of public record. At the same time all of us seem more or less interested when there is to be an important contest. The newspapers have column after column about the fighters and their condition and the predictions made by their friends. The people read every line of it and want more. And you ought to see the crowds that assemble to hear the bulletins read on the night of a championship battle."

"But how can you induce men to stand up and take their chances of being pounded to pieces?" asked Francisco.

"The rewards are very large," replied the missionary. "As much as $30,000 has been offered in one prize. If a fighter becomes a champion he commands an immense salary as a stage attraction. You can have no idea of the popularity of a successful pugilist."

"Yet you say we are savage and only half-civilized because we permit chickens to fight," suggested Francisco.

151

"We are a rugged people and we enjoy rugged sport," said the missionary. "Furthermore, a man is a reasoning creature and when he goes into a fight he goes in of his own volition. It is better that a man should be bruised and pounded than that a dumb animal such as a bull or a gamecock should be killed to gratify a lust for pain and slaughter."

"I don't think so," said Francisco.

"Then we differ in our opinions. Mind you, I am not attempting to defend prize-fighting. A prizefight is a brutal and degrading spectacle. Everybody says so. It is forbidden by law in nearly every state in our union, and yet, somehow or other, we continue to have prizefights and the people continue to be feverishly interested in them, notwithstanding that we are the most humane and cultured people on earth. Now, that seems contradictory, doesn't it? The fact is, we do a great many things that people living far away in another climate and a different environment, and having peculiar hereditary traits, cannot rightly understand."

"That's what we think," replied Francisco. "We think the Americans cannot rightly understand the Tagalos."

"We understand everything," replied Conner. "Wait until I read you a few speeches from the Congressional Record."

XI. HOUSE DECORATION

"There is one thing I have had in mind ever since I arrived here, and that is the necessity of some attempt at decoration in this house," said the American missionary, speaking to Mrs. Kakyak. "This habitation of yours is little better than four walls."

"What changes would you suggest?" asked Mrs. Kakyak.

"I would suggest that you add many of the beautifying effects such as we have in America. In the first place I think you ought to build two or three bay windows on the outside and put on as many jig-saw scallops as you can find room for. That is what we usually do in America. As for the interior of your house, I am pained to observe that you have very few of the articles which are regarded as essential in my own country."

"We have everything that we really need," said Mrs. Kakyak. "Why should we clutter up the interior with a lot of decorative material? We are never in the house when it is possible to remain out of doors."

"We need many articles that do not cater directly to our physical wants or contribute to our comfort," said Mr. Conner. "Take a marble-top table with gilded legs, for instance. We cannot eat a marble-top table. We cannot recline upon it. We cannot put any heavy articles on top of it for fear of bending the legs. Yet a marble-top table is an essential in the average American household. Why? because it is a direct appeal to the aesthetic sense. The same may be said of the crayon portrait, such as you will find in nine-tenths of all the front rooms in America. A savage or a half-civilized person, such as you, would look at a crayon portrait and ask, 'Of what use is it?' The

152

drawing, for instance, may not resemble the person who was
supposed to be the subject, but the true aesthete does not care
for any such mean detail as accuracy. If the frame is ornate and
the whole effect of white and gilt and black drawing produces a
soothing effect on the nervous system, then the crayon portrait
has accomplished its full purpose. It has helped to make some one
happier. Therefore I urge you to hang some crayon portraits at
the earliest opportunity. You Tagalos are dreadfully behind the
age in the matter of house decoration. I don't remember to have
seen a crayon portrait since I landed on this island of Luzon."

"No, we haven't got that far along." said Mrs. Kakyak,
dolefully. "I suppose you have a great many things in your
country that we have never heard of."

"Undoubtedly," said Conner. "Now, if you will step into the
front room with me I will give you some idea of the changes that
ought to be made in order that you may approximate the American
standard of artistic taste."

She followed him into the second apartment of the bamboo
house, which was cool and empty, save for a grass hammock swung
diagonally from corner to corner.

"In the first place, you ought to have a Brussels carpet on
the floor," said Conner, pausing in the center of the room and
surveying its bareness with a frown of displeasure. "A few, a
very few, people in America now prefer hard, polished floors,
half-covered with rugs. But the vast majority hold that a parlor
should be carpeted with Brussels, bearing a design of green
vine-leaves and orange flowers. Then you ought to have some
plush furniture. Blue is a good color--a sofa and several
chairs. In the center of the room here, under a brass
chandelier, would be the marble-top table with the curved legs of
which I have already spoken. As it is a fragile piece of
furniture it would be better to put nothing on top of it except a
photograph album and a vase filled with artificial flowers. Over
at that side of the room (indicating) there should be a piano.
If not a piano, than a cottage organ, and if not a cottage organ,
a what-not bearing mineral specimens, sea-shells, birds' eggs,
with the original contents blown out, and any other articles such
as delight the eye. I forget to tell you that the plush
furniture should be liberally decorated with tidies."

"What are those?" asked Mrs. Kakyak.

"A tidy is something like a towel, except that it is
smaller, has perforations in it, and you are not supposed to dry
yourself with it. Tidies should be pinned on plush chairs or
balanced on top of them."

"I should think they would get twisted around or else be
pulling off all the time."

"They are something of a nuisance, but we must be prepared
to make sacrifices for the sake of Art. Did I speak to you about
the wall paper?"

"Not yet."

"Well, you should have wall paper on the walls, and in
addition to the crayon portraits I have suggested you ought to
hang a few oil paintings. They can be bought at any furniture

store in America. By way of variety, you might put a few posters on the wall. I brought several posters with me, just to give you some idea of our standard of taste in the graphic arts."

So saying, he went to the adjoining room and brought out a roll of heavy prints, from which he peeled a glaring representation of a long female thrown into an attitude of convulsion.

"What is it?" asked Mrs. Kakyak.

"It is a high art woman," replied the missionary. "You will begin to like this after you have mastered the crayon portrait and the low-priced oil painting."

"It doesn't resemble a woman or anything else that I can see," remarked Mrs. Kakyak.

"I have only to repeat that it will require time to educate you up to an appreciation of this sort of thing."

There was brief pause.

"If we were to go ahead and put all this decorative material into the front room I don't suppose we would use the apartment any oftener than we do now," said Mrs. Kakyak.

"Certainly not," said Conner. "In the ordinary American home the front room is a darkened sanctuary which no one must enter unless he has arrayed himself in his Sunday clothes. It is a holy of holies reserved for the sacred rites of funeral, marriage or the church sociable."

"What a strange people you are!" exclaimed Mrs. Kakyak. "I am sure that we shall never be able to copy all of your peculiarities."

"At least you can try," said the missionary. "I want you to promise me that at the very first opportunity you will have one of Mr. Kakyak's tintypes enlarged into a crayon portrait."

XII. SOCIAL CUSTOMS

"I don't remember that you and your mother have made any calls since I have been here," said the missionary one morning.

"I don't know what you mean," said Eulalie.

"Is it possible that here in the inland of Luzon the ladies are not given to the custom of going out on certain days to call at the homes of their acquaintances?"

"Of course, if we wish to see one of our friends and have a talk with her we go over to her house, but we never have any set time for such things."

"And you do not dress for it?"

"Why--no."

"Goodness me! Tell your mother to come out here. I might as well talk to both of you at the same time."

Eulalie stepped to the doorway and called aloud to her mother, who appeared in a few moments, wiping her wet hands on her skirt. She had been washing vegetables for the evening repast.

"Mother, there is something Mr. Conner wishes to say to you. It seems that if we are to become the same as the Americans we must set aside certain days for visiting."

"'Calling' is a better word," suggested the missionary. "What I mean is that you shall keep a list of the women friends who happen to strike at about your social level, and at least-- well, once a month, say--you must make the rounds and call on all of them. Then, on days when you are not going from house to house, you must remain at home, so that they may come and call on you."

Mrs. Kakyak shook her head wearily and murmured the Tagalo equivalent for "merciful Providence!" Then she said:

"It seems to me that this wonderful civilization, of which you are forever talking, consists of a huge assortment of ceremonies which are the outgrowth of artificial conditions and which are contrary to the natural instincts of any human being."

"Certainly," replied Conner. "The purpose of civilization is to repress and hold down the natural instincts, so that people may be governed by rule and precedent, rather than by whimsical inclinations. If a woman were governed by her inclination in the matter she would not take the trouble to attire herself in her best costumes and pay repeated attentions to people whom she disliked very much. But under the fixed rules governing social intercourse she compels herself to perform these unpleasant duties, and even pretends to enjoy them, and when a woman does that she cannot be further away from primitive conditions. When you have become thoroughly civilized, Mrs. Kakyak, you will know what it is to approach a woman whom you thoroughly detest, kiss her with feigned heartiness and beg of her to come and take tea with you at her first opportunity."

"And yet you say we are a treacherous and deceptive people because some of us who pretent to be amigos are really in sympathy with the rebel government," said Mrs. Kakyak, with a spiteful smile.

"I don't see any justice in that observation," said the missionary. "A tagalo who professes to be friendly to Americans while he is really in sympathy with his fighting countrymen is a traitor and is guilty of treason, and richly deserves the severe punishment which we are meting out to men of his kind whenever we can trap them in some overt act. But a woman who professes an affection for some one whom she despises is what we call, in the United States, 'gracious.'"

"That is your name for it, is it?" asked Mrs. Kakyak.

"Yes, ma'am," replied Conner. "Why, you couldn't expect people who were exchanging calls or attending social functions every week to make a practice of expressing their actual sentiments. If they did society wouldn't last two days. No matter how wretched they may be, it is 'Charmed,' 'Delighted,' 'Jolly time' and so on, and although no one believes any one else, the general effect of this 'graciousness' is to alleviate and somewhat reduce the suffering which is inseparable from a contact with refined society. Do you follow me?"

"Oh, I suppose so," said Mrs. Kakyak, wearily. "You suggest, then, do you, that I put in a lot of my time going around to see women who don't want to see me and for whom, I may say with emphasis, I don't care two straws."

"Sh-h! Sh-h-h! You will never make any headway in correct society if you talk in that manner. Let us say, rather, that I do advise you to take up the social obligations incumbent upon one in your station of life."

"That is, I am to call on every one I know and then on certain days I am to sit at home and permit them to come in and go through certain formalities of conversation with me? I should think it would be a dreadful bore to receive callers all afternoon."

"Oh, there is always a way of escape from these onerous social duties," said the missionary, with a knowing smile. "When the callers come you may find it to your advantage to be out or to be seriously indisposed and quite unequal to the task of receiving any one."

"Do you mean that we should go away from home in order to avoid meeting our friends?" asked Eulalie.

"And I do not see that it would be an advantage to be seriously indisposed," added Mrs. Kakyak.

"Your simplicity is refreshing," said Conner. "I do not mean that you need to go out or that you need to be really ill. But there is no great harm in having some one meet the callers at the door and give a plausible excuse for you. Don't think that the callers will be offended because of your failure to put in an appearance. They will leave their cards, and as soon as the door has closed they will depart in high satisfaction and probably say to themselves, 'Well, we've got that off our minds, and it didn't take much time either.' The two cards which the ladies left, with other cards which accumulate, are put into a receptacle in the hallway or the front room, so that any one who visits the house may look at these and become aware of the fact that you have a calling acquaintance with many important people."

"Did you ever the like, Eulalie?" asked Mrs. Kakyak, as she took hold of her daughter's hand. "I never dreamed that there were such strange customs anywhere in the world. What's more, I don't see that there is any sense in such proceedings. As I understand it, I go to various houses and call on women merely for the sake of putting in an appearance. I haven't any particular message to deliver and perhaps we have no mutual interests."

"So much the better," said Conner, nodding his head. "In that case the conversation is not apt to be prolonged and you can depart all the sooner. The shorter the call the more satisfactory it is, as a rule."

"Very well, then; we will assume that I hurry through and go back home. Next day some of these women come to see me. I do not crave their society. I dread the tedium of interchanging conventional remarks all afternoon, so I take refuge in my own apartment and send out word either that I am not at home or that I am suffering from--what?"

"Usually a nervous headache," said the missionary.

"Quite so. My callers are informed that I am suffering from a nervous headache. What am I doing, as a matter of fact?"

"You are in loose wrapper, reading the latest novel."

"This quality of deception does not come under the head of falsehood?"

"Certainly not, because no one is deceived. The lady who comes to your front door and who is told that you will be unable to see her because of a severe headache probably knows, or at least suspects, that you are propped up in a comfortable attitude in your own room reading a book. She isn't very angry. She knows how it is herself. Next time you go to her house and ring the bell you will doubtless hear that she is confined to her room with the same kind of headache."

"Well, admitting that there is no sin in telling such a falsehood----"

"Fibs, fibs," corrected Conner.

"Admitting that, why should I go around and encourage women to call on me if I don't want to see them when they come to repay the call? Why not keep away from those women whose society has no charm for me?"

"My dear Mrs. Kakyak, is it possible that any woman can be so deficient in social ambition? If you are to make any headway in your own circle; if you are to be known as a matroness and a club officer or get your name into print as a dictator in society, you must have a following, and the only way to have a following is to maintain a large calling list and pay strict attention to your social duties."

"I don't think I will ever have any ambition in that direction," she said, smiling at Eulalie.

"Perhaps you would prefer to be an old-fashioned woman, who stays at home as much as possible and concens heself principally with her family and her household duties. I wish to warn you that this type of woman is not very popular in America at present. If you will take my advice, now that you are about to be benevolently assimilated, you will try to make yourself a 'new woman,' as the term goes in America. You must learn to wear masculine garments, make public speeches and organize all sorts of clubs. What was your maiden name, Mrs. Kakyak?"

"Luneta Paranda."

"Then you should be known as Luneta Paranda-Kakyak, instead of Mrs. Bulalo Kakyak. The new woman doesn't allow her husband to overshadow her."

"Do you like the new woman?" asked Eulalie, softly, as she looked up at Washington Conner and smiled quizzically.

"I admire her very much as a fellow-worker in any philanthropic enterprise," said Conner. "Of course I don't believe I'd care to marry a new woman. It never occurred to me before, but I don't believe I would."

XIII. MR. CONNER MAKES A REPORT

Following is a copy of the report forwarded by Mr. Washington Conner after he had labored for a month with the Kakyak family of the island of Luzon:

"To the Bureau of Benevolent Assimilation, War Department, Washington, D. C., United States of America: I have the honor to

157

submit herewith my first report as special instructor and pioneer missionary in the department of benevolent assimilation.

"One month ago I arrived in the island of Luzon to begin the noble work of civilizing the Tagalos by example and precept. For experimental purposes I selected a family residing in a by-valley only a few miles from Manila. This is within the pacified district. The name of the family is Kakyak. The head of the family is Bulolo Kakyak, a well-to-do agriculturist, who seems kindly disposed toward American sovereignty, although he has a lingering desire that his country should be given a chance to govern itself. I have used all the arguments you so kindly forwarded to me. I have assured him that the Tagalos are a tribe, and not a nation, and that he will be happier as a colonial subject than as an independent citizen. Of late he pretends to accept my view of the situation, but I suspect that he is in secret sympathy with his countrymen who are still opposing our humane intentions. If this is the case I can well believe that the Tagalos are as treacherous and unreliable as they have been painted.

"Only the other day he said to me: 'Don't you think that a man who is ready to die for the right of self-government is entitled to a chance to govern himself?' This question might indicate an incendiary state of mind. I have told him that such sentiments were treasonable and un-American. He has promised to be more careful in the future.

"Mrs. Kakyak, wife of Bulolo, is a woman of shrewish temperament and all the spiteful prejudices of her sex. In spite of my best endeavors I cannot compel her to wear a corset more than an hour or two each day, and she positively refuses to appear in public wearing an American hat with a heroa feather in it. I have talked to her by the hour in regard to our social customs, home etiquette, household decoration, rules for entertaining, etc. She listens with slack patience and then declares that it is all a mess of foolishness. She is the most stubborn of my pupils, and I fear it will be a difficult job to assimilate her.

"There are three children. The daughter, Eulalie, is a remarkably bright and spirited young woman to whom I have been devoting a great deal of time. She evinces a decided interest in all the institutions and customs of our great republic, but when I explain them to her in detail she seems to be intensely amused. I attribute this lack of gravity to her extreme youth. It may be that with further labor I shall be able to convince her that she will be happier after she has embraced our complicated civilization.

"Of the two sons one is approaching manhood and the other is of tender years and is a pupil in the parish school. I regret to say that the entire family can read and write. Truly enough, 'a little learning is a dangerous thing.' The Kakyaks have obtained a smattering of information by reading, and they ask many troublesome questions when I try to convince them that the Tagalos should yield themselves willingly into our hands and trust implicitly in the piety of our intentions.

"For instance, Francisco, the elder son, asked me the other day if the American Indians had become completely 'assimilated.' I could not enter into a discussion of the Indian question with a mere youth, so I told him, in guarded language, that the Indians were not yet totally 'assimilated,' but would be in another generation or two.

"This question, propounded by the elder son, will give you some idea of what I have to contend with every day. I understand that in the islands south of here, where the natives can neither read nor write, the emissaries of our beloved country have no difficulty in making peace treaties.

"I understand also that the leaders of the Tagalo rebellion are educated men and that 70 percent of the members of the Filipino congress are university graduates. It is a deplorable and unexplainable fact that these educated men should not perceive the folly of wishing for an independent government.

"So long as the war for the suppression of the rebellion is being carried forward I fear that the work of benevolent assimilation will be sadly hindered. For some reason or other these Tagalos have an affection for their countrymen in arms, and it annoys and irritates them to hear every day or two of a few hundred of these misguided wrteches being shot down in the trenches. They are a simple-minded people, a people that are not capable of drawing just conclusions. Therefore they fail to understand that any Tagalo who takes up arms in support of an independent government deserves to be shot. They do not seem to take our view of the matter at all.

"There must be something essentially wrong with the reasoning faculties of these Tagalos. I find that 95 percent of them want to have a government of their own. We can no longer trust any of them. All the mayors we installed with such hopeful ceremony have gone over to the enemy. Now, as I have said before, while the natives are in this sullen and unreceptive mood it will be rather difficult to command their love and respect or carry forward the commendable plans for their 'benevolent assimilation.'

"I have attempted to soften the Kakyak family by appealing to the Christian sentiment of the members. You know the Tagalos are a very pious people and have a profound reverence for the scriptures. Therefore, when they have shown resentment at our military operations here in the island or have spoken with some show of bitterness over the death of a few male relatives I have quoted to them passages on the order of the following: 'Love your enemies,' 'Servants, be obedient to them that are your masters,' 'Pray for them which despitefully use you,' 'Unto him that smiteth thee on the one cheek offer also the other, and him that taketh away thy cloak forbid him not to take thy coat also.'

"Instead of being pacified by these injunctions they have retaliated by quoting to me 'And as ye would that men should do unto you, do ye also to them likewise.' I have explained to them that the golden rule cannot possibly be applied to the present situation in the Philippines, but what are you going to do with a stubborn people who have become inflamed by false hopes?

159

"In answer to their inquiries as to the privileges they will enjoy under American rule I have followed instructions and told them that they will be allowed to 'participate.' Then they have asked, 'To what extent will we participate?' My reply has been, 'You must leave that to us.' They have not been fully satisfied with this reply, but I can't think of anything else to say. If you can figure out a more diplomatic reply, please forward it to me at once.

"In conclusion I may say that the Kakyak family is not greatly changed from what it was when I arrived here, one month ago. This leads me to believe that the process of benevolent assimilation will be very slow. It may require a century or so to transform the Tagalos into good Americans. The quickest method would be to encourage immigration from the United States. If we could fill all parts of Luzon with Americans, intent on developing the resources of the island, the natives would naturally adopt our progressive methods as a measure of self-preservation. If they failed to do so, however, it wouldn't make so much difference, because with a sufficient number of enterprising Americans over here the Tagalos would not have much to do with the conduct of affairs. But I suppose Americans will be slow to immigrate in large numbers on account of the enervating climate. So that, after all, it may not be practicable to educate the Tagalos by contact. Perhaps it would be better to continue the policy of benevolent assimilation by cable. In this way we can avoid the climate.

"Now that I am here, I will continue my labors as instructor, but at this writing I cannot report with unqualified hopefulness.

"I am, very respectfully,

"WASHINGTON CONNER."

After the missionary had completed his report he read it over and said to himself: 'It isn't very definite, that's a fact. But then the situation isn't very definite, either."

XIV. MR. CONNER BEGINS TO DOUBT

One morning soon after Mr. Washington Conner forwarded his first formal report to the Bureau of Benevolent Assimilation a white man came out of the Kakyak house and stretched his arms lazily in the warm sunshine.

The man wore duck trousers, low shoes, a soft shirt of negligé pattern, and instead of a collar he had a handkerchief loosely knotted around his neck. On his head was a native straw hat, dished downward to shade the whole face. The face, by the way, was the face of Mr. Washington Conner, and it may be added that it needed a shave.

The missionary had intended to shave himself three days before, but every morning he awoke to a tropical languor and said: "Oh, well, tomorrow." Besides, the Kakyaks did not mind. What was the use of keeping up appearances if the appearances served no purpose? This was the question Conner asked himself. The act of shaving involved labor, and he was very glad to avoid it. In one hand Mr. Conner carried a cigar. He had been smoking

160

a great deal ever since the first week of his arrival. The climate seemed to encourage the use of tobacco.

In his other hand was a paper-covered novel. He had been trying for a week to get beyond the second chapter, but he was compelled to admit that he was becoming too lazy to read. The weather was not conducive to any kind of prolonged exertion. Now that the rainy season was well past, the sun shone with steady vigor and the heat was of midsummer fierceness.

Conner had held out for the proprieties as long as possible. Reluctantly at first he laid aside his coat and began to lounge in his shirt sleeves. Then the binding collar and the suffocating cravat were discarded, for the sake of comfort and because Eulalie had begged him not to be ridiculous.

He learned that white trousers and soft shirts were more sensible than woolen garments and a starched front.

His own straw hat with its rigid framework and preposterously small brim easily gave way to a native hat of light weaving which was not a burden to carry and was a better protection against the pitiless rays of the sun.

Conner's face and hands had taken on a deep tan. One day Eulalie put her little hand alongside of his and said, with an exclamation of delight, "Aha, you are getting to be as brown as I am. Another year and you will be a Tagalo."

She was so pleased at her own suggestion that Conner could not forget it. He had to admit that he had compromised on several points, and had permitted himself to be governed more or less by his environment.

Instead of inducing the simple islanders to adopt the American costume, he had permitted Eulalie to coax him into the slovenly habits of her people.

Mrs. Kakyak and Eulalie still managed to escape the civilizing corset, while the missionary himself, who had started out to be an examplar, practically had adopted the native dress. In fact, Washington Conner had a very striking resemblance to a Tagalo as he came out of the house that morning and drowsily regarded the landscape. The rudely-woven hat, the white nether garments and the loose shirt were of Luzon and not of Ohio.

Could it be possible that the great missionary, who had come to assimilate the Tagalos, was being assimilated by them? To answer this question would be to forecast the outcome of this slow narrative, but the reader has a right to his own opinion. It is a poor rule that will not work both ways.

If the national administration had appeared before Washington Conner all of a sudden, as he stood in front of the Kakyak house, there is no doubt that the administration would have been shocked and the missionary would have been ashamed. The administration in Washington supposed that Conner was wearing the garb of a college professor and was lecturing to the Tagalos for at least eight hours every day on the beauties of American civilization.

Conner realized this, and often said to himself: "I wish the administration would come down and try it for awhile."

It is very easy for a people living in a cool and bracing climate to outline the duties of their fellow-creatures who happen to be down nearer the equator. For at least a century the people of the northern states have been telling the people of the southern states: "Why don't you get up early and stay out late and develop your resources?" And the southern people have replied: "Why don't you trade climates with us?"

Washington Conner began to be of the opinion that probably there was some truth in the old theory that climate had a large influence on the habits of a people and of an individual. Before leaving the United States he had been full of high resolves and eager for work, and now that he was in the summering heat he had fallen in with the indolent habits of the Kakyaks and was ready to excuse himself for every neglect of duty. He remembered having read that many authors who are nominally industrious in a temperature of 50 degrees are little better than sluggards when they arrive in Italy, and that instead of holding to their work they lie in the shade and look up at the sky.

There was further analogy in his experience at home. He remembered how, every spring, he made large plans for the summer. He decided to go on long bicycle tours, tramp across two or three states, camp out for a month, or do something else equally positive and enterprising. Then when the long sultry days came and the trees stood motionless and the heatwaves trembled above the white pavements, he discovered that there was no fun in doing anything that called for heavy exertion, and all the elaborate plans were easily forgotten.

He reflected further that the late autumn back in Ohio was a season for overcoats, tippets and gloves, that there was a tingle in the air and that a smashing game of football was the favorite diversion of the season. To any one living in Ohio during the autumn months, with a good frosty air as a steady tonic, all labor seemed agreeable, no doubt. Mr. Conner told himself that if he were back in Ohio and thoroughly warmed by his morning portion of buckwheat cakes and coffee, nothing would seem more plausible and feasible than the scheme of benevolent assimilation. But inasmuch as he was in Luzon and not in Ohio, and inasmuch as the hot weather had taken all the Ohio starch out of him and the fruits of a month's labor were not manifest, it may be said, in all candor, that the missionary was beginning to have his doubts. It seemed to him that he could better understand why the soldiers who enlisted for service in the Philippines had been so anxious to return home, instead of remaining in the jungle to further the glorious work of assimilation.

The Americans did not seem to be happy in the Philippines and he doubted if the Filipinos would be happy in the United States. The two races were so different that now and then he wondered if the same kind of government was suited to both of them. He did not give expression to his doubts on this subject because that would have been treason, but he had doubts just the same.

And sometimes, the situation being so complex and puzzling, he feared that the policy of "benevolent assimilation" was not the way out of the difficulty. And sometimes when he fell to meditating on the subject he had to confess that, after all, he didn't exactly know what "benevolent assimilation" meant. He wondered if the administration knew. It didn't seem to him that these Filipinos could ever be induced to take up with the Ohio way of doing things. As far as that was concerned he hadn't been doing things in the Ohio way since arriving in Luzon. So he had to wonder who was being assimilated, anyway.

XV. EULALIE

There was a square envelope in the roll of mail which little Patricio brought from the station and delivered to Mr. Washington Conner, who was under a tree, as usual, smoking a cigar, as usual, and idly chatting with Eulalie, as usual.

The missionary first read several formal letters, some of them from department chiefs of the Bureau of Benevolent Assimilation, advising him how to go about it to convince the Tagalos that the road to happiness lay parallel with the path of meek submission.

Also, Mr. Conner tore the wrappers from several newspapers and glanced along the solid columns. He noticed that in several large cities tumultuous gatherings in hotel dining halls had applauded the sentiment that the Flag was the Symbol of Freedom. From this he gathered that the United States was still determined to confer the blessings of liberty on the Tagalos, no matter how many had to be piled in the trenches.

He read that Admiral Dewey had arrived in New York and had declared in no uncertain tone for and against the Tagalos. In one interview he said the Tagalos were more nearly capable of self-government than were the Cubans. The missionary took good care that Mr. Kakyak did not see this interview. He had been telling Mr. Kakyak that the congress of the United States had recognized the independence of Cuba and declared her worthy of a trial at self-government, because the Cubans were a superior race, who, by their close proximity to the United States and their free intercourse with Americans, had become partly assimilated! And now Admiral Dewey had said that the Cubans were inferior to the Tagalos. He knew very well that Mr. Kakyak would ask, "Why do you deny us the opportunity you have pledged to the Cubans?" and he was not sure that he could give a proper and convincing answer.

Mr. Conner was beginning to learn the Tagalos. A Tagalo is a very suspicious and exacting person. He prefers a definite assurance to a flight of oratory in regard to a star-spangled banner.

While Washington Conner was mediating lazily upon the difficulties of his position he uncovered the square envelope and opened his eyes a little wider. The envelope was a light blue and the address was in that tall and angular writing affected by the women of his native land.

Eulalie sat a few feet away gazing thoughtfully at the big missionary and hesitating to speak while he was intent on his mail. She observed the sudden change of expression when he saw the square envelope and with a woman's intuition she knew that the letter was not official.

When Conner split the envelope and withdrew the folded sheets, Eulalie caught the faint odor of perfume and her extremest suspicions were confirmed.

The missionary grinned as he read one page after another. It was a letter from a girl in his college town. She was that rare exception--a friend who does not allow time or distance to weaken an obligation. Nine years before she had promised Mr. Washington Conner, the senior valedictorian, that she would write to him occasionally, and she had kept her promise, although Conner had been woefully tardy in answering and his letters had been brief and colorless compared with her entertaining resume of affairs in and around the college.

This letter, coming to him unexpectedly on a hillside in Luzon, served two purposes. It helped to remind him that at one time he had been a college senior with a flapping frock coat and an abnormally high silk hat. Furthermore, it had the effect of arousing curiosity, not to say jealousy, in Miss Eulalie Kakyak.

"You seem pleased with your letter," she said, watching him keenly from under her long, downcast lashes.

"I--ah--yes!" he exclaimed, suddenly finding himself, for he had been 10,000 miles away, once more helping to plant the class ivy. "Oh, yes, it's a very interesting letter."

"Why did you smile?"

"When was that?"

"While you were reading the letter."

"Did I smile?"

"Yes, you smiled all the time."

"The letter is rather amusing."

"It is from a woman, isn't it?"

"Why do you think so?"

"Oh, well the color for one thing, then the perfume, but most of all the way you smiled."

"Yes, it's from a girl at home, one of my old school friends."

"Is she beautiful?"

Conner had to laugh aloud.

"No, Henrietta is not beautiful by any means," he replied. "She is a good soul, and one of the cleverest girls I ever knew, but she is far from being a beauty. She is what we call at home a good fellow. She used to chum with the men in the class, and we called her 'Hen' for short."

"How old is she?" asked Eulalie after a pause.

"I'll declare, you're taking an unusual interest in Henrietta. Let's see, how old is she? Not very old--about thirty."

"Thirty!"

"Yes--why, are you surprised?"

"But you spoke of her as girl."

"Oh, well, at home a girl is a girl until she marries."

"And do some girls wait until 30 before they marry?"

"It depends on what luck they have."

"But a woman is so old at thirty, I shouldn't think any one would marry an old woman."

"My dear child, it wouldn't be safe for you to use such language in several women's clubs that I happen to know about. Why, a woman at 30 is simply in full bloom. We don't speak of a woman as 'old' until she is past 50, and she doesn't speak of herself as being 'old' until she is past 70."

"Then you have in your country one thing I would like to possess. I would like to know the secret of preserving one's youth."

"I don't think there is any secret to it. It is all due to climate and heredity."

"The same as your peculiar civilization?" suggested Eulalie.

"Yes," said Conner, hesitatingly. "I understand, of course, that in this climate and under the conditions which have evolved your branch of the human family the women develop into full womenhood very early in life, and then------." He stopped.

"And then fade and wrinkle into old women almost as rapidly as they grew into beauty," said Eulalie. "There is no need of denying it. The woman who wrote you the letter is 30 years old, and yet you spoke of her as a girl. When I am 30 I will be thin and have bony arms and wrinkles, the same as mother has now. Isn't it horrible?"

"If you adopt our civilization you may learn how to conceal the marks of advancing age," said Conner.

"Now you tempt me for the first time. It is the dread of my life--the loss of my youth and to know that it should come so soon."

"Nonsense! You are merely a little girl."

"I arrived at the marrying age two years ago. Mother has chided me again and again for not marrying as soon as I had the chance."

"Oh, you had a chance, had you?" he inquired, in a startled tone. "Well, why did you refuse him?"

"Who said that I refused him?"

"OH!"

"You are very fortunate," she said, looking at him quizzically. "When you go back to your home you will marry some girl who will be just as pretty year after year, as when you married her. But if I marry, in ten short years I will be--ah, dreadful, an old woman."

Conner was nervously distressed by Eulalie's sad forecast. He tried to reassure her.

"I don't think you ought to worry about anything that is going to happen to you ten years after you are married," he said. "So far as my observation goes, a man doesn't judge his wife by her personal appearance after they have lived together for ten years. They are considerably past the honeymoon by that time."

"Ah, but you wouldn't marry a girl if you knew she would be old and ugly in a few years," said Eulalie, half in a questioning way.

"I might," said Conner, decisively, and Eulalie laughed.

XVI. TREACHERY

The night was warm and Washington Conner, finding himself oppressed and uneasy in the confined air of the chamber that had been assigned to him, stealthily made his way out of the Kakyak house. In the valley all was calm and moonlight. The whole soft landscape lay so motionless before him it seemed an artificial panorama.

At one corner of the house he found a matting, which he unrolled within the shadow, so that when he reclined he might not have the moonlight in his eyes. Being soothed by the cooler air of outdoors he dozed away and had slept, he did not know how long, when he became conscious of the sound of voices. He opened his eyes and slowly recalled himself to the situation. At first he had thought he was back in the boarding house at Washington. With the full awakening he remembered that he was in Luzon, lying on a mat just outside the Kakyak house.

Two people not far away were talking in low tones. He listened and recognized the voice of Eulalie. The other voice was strange to him. He rolled over quite slowly, so as to make no noise, and cautiously peeked around the corner of the house. He saw Eulalie standing beside a man who was only a few inches taller than herself. The man wore a broad straw hat which shaded his face. His loose coat was drawn in at the waist line by a heavy belt. The trousers were short and the man was barefooted. In his left hand he trailed a stocky rifle, which Conner knew to be a Mauser. There was a rebel soldier, and Eulalie was in conference with the enemy!

"Oh, Josefo, do you really think there will be more fighting?" she asked.

"More than ever before," he replied. "The Americans are landing at Manila by shiploads. We hear that soon there will be 60,000 here. We cannot stand against them. They will crowd us into the jungle and before another rainy season comes we may be crushed or scattered."

"Mr. Conner says you ought to stop fighting and trust to the Americans."

"If I dared to suggest surrender I would be court-martialed and shot. I must go with my company and fight to the end. Does he suspect that I come here?"

"Oh, I don't think so. We do all we can to make him believe we are friendly and submissive. He has been very kind to me."

"Yes, but he is our enemy, remember that."

"He says he is our friend."

"Yes, and I, when I put on my white suit and go down to the city, then I am a friend to the Americans, but as soon as fighting begins I must go with the Tagalos. You know that. Every man must follow his own flag, right or wrong. I learned that from the American soldiers at Manila. You know they have a saying in America: 'My country, may it always be right, but right or wrong, my country.' You may think the Americans all right, Eulalie, because Mr. Conner has been good to your family, but as long as the Americans are killing our people you must be loyal to the Filipino cause, no matter what your private convictions may be. We hear from Aguinaldo that in America there are some people who believe that the Tagalos should be given a chance to govern themselves, but all such people are told that it is treason to offer encouragement to an enemy. And so, even if you think we would be better off it we laid down our arms and submitted to foreign rule, you must not say so until the war is over."

"Yes, you are right," said Eulalie, taking hold of his hand. "Mr. Conner has told us that we must be as much like the Americans as possible. If the Americans are loyal to their government, then I suppose we must be loyal to ours, even if we do think that terrible mistakes are being made."

"If you feel that mistakes are being made, say nothing about them. No matter what Aguinaldo does, take it for granted that he is the essence of wisdom and remember that carping criticism may hamper his plans. If you hear evil reports as to his financial operations, don't believe them. Any statesman is liable to be misunderstood when he begins to dabble in business transactions."

"Before you came I was about ready to declare my allegiance to the new rulers," said Eulalie, thoughtfully, "but since you have spoken thus I can see that it is my duty to remain loyal to my own people and the flag they have raised, although I firmly believe that the Americans are kind and humane and would give us a liberal government."

"Never tell what you believe. Remember that you are now living under a republic--the Filipino Republic. In a republic one must accept the verdict of the majority without question or protest. An overwhelming majority of our tribe is opposed to any foreign rule, so our duty is clear. We must continue to fight."

"I know, but did you come here to tell me this?"

"No I came to-night because I feared the influence of this white man. I want you to go with me."

"Go with you?"

"Yes, your brother Francisco is going. Your father would go, too, but he is getting old, and, besides, it is better that he should stay here to protect his little farm and grow rice to feed our troops, if we can hold out for another crop. As soon as we join the regiment we will be married by a Spanish priest we are holding captive. You can be of use with the regiment, cooking for us and nursing the wounded."

Eulalie hesitated for a moment, and then she said, "Well, I will go."

Washington Conner listened in breathless horror to these revelations.

So the Kakyak household, in spite of his patient teachings, was still a hotbed of treason! And Eulalie, whom he had regarded as a playful and innocent child, had been under the malign influence of the rebels all the time, and was now going away with one Josefo. Josefo--what a name! Josefo--incarnation of all that he had taught her to shun and hate!

Never until that moment had he understood the diabolical treachery of the Tagalo mind. Now he began to perceive how and why these wiley and double-dealing people had been able to

167

deceive even Gen. Otis[3] and the peace commissioners. For two months these Kakyaks had smiled upon him and given apparent heed to his serious teachings, and now he learned that all the time they had been in active sympathy with their own countrymen. His brain fairly reeled at the mental contemplation of such infamy.

What was he to do? Eulalie and Francisco were about to join the rebels. Was it now his duty to prevent such a calamity?

Even as he watched the two from his sheltered hiding Francisco came out of the house and joined them. Josefo told Francisco that Eulalie had promised to go with them, and Francisco embraced his sister with great ardor. This action suggested a palpable duty to Josefo, who added a lingering kiss to his passionate embrace.

It may be needless to say that Washington Conner was infinitely distressed to see this beautiful little creature fondled by a bare-legged rebel.

Yet there were certain reasons why he should not cry a protest or make any attempt to frustrate the whole treasonable undertaking. In the first place, his instructions from the government had been to use kindly methods and not resort to force. He was present to inculcate certain morals and not to usurp the functions of the military.

In the second place, he was unarmed, whereas Josefo carried a Mauser rifle; therefore any attempt to interfere with Josefo's plans would have been ill-advised and possibly dangerous.

So he lay there in quiet, stunned and sick at heart, listening to Eulalie moving about so softly within the house, gathering her effects preparatory to the flight. Evidently she believed that Conner was still in his room and did not want him to be awakened. Then there was another purr of voices and Eulalie came out of the house, followed by her father and mother. The whole family was in the conspiracy. There could be no doubt of it.

The five walked a hundred yards or more and stopped for a final conference. Conner kept close to the wall and slipped back into his own room, where he gave himself up to bitter reflection.

On the steamer from Japan to 'Frisco Mr. Washington Conner, returning missionary, found an old college friend who had been traveling for pleasure.

The friend was interested in the new possessions.

"How about the Filipinos?" he asked, as they were taking their back-and-forth constitutional on the long deck the second day out.

"A very treacherous and unreliable people," replied Conner. "I labored hard with a family over there, but they deceived me all the time. They didn't want to be assimilated."

"So you gave it up?"

"I came away because I was disgusted with the situation. The daughter of the household, to whom I had given most of my time, skipped out with a rebel sweetheart one night. I didn't so much as know of his existence until the night of their departure. By George, do you know some of those girls are very attractive?"

"Oh, ho! That's why you gave up your mission, eh?"

"Not at all. You don't think I could have any serious regard for a brown girl, do you?"

"Why not, if you were going to further the cause of assimilation? It seems to me that if you had married her that would have been right in the line of your duty."

"Candidly, I will confess that when she went away with that oily scoundrel of a Josefo I was terribly cut up. It was preposterous and out of the question, I know, but I found great pleasure in her society. I thought she was artless and confiding. It seems that I was mistaken."

"I still infer that you gave up your whole undertaking because of one little Tagalo girl."

"No, I gave it up because I didn't want to be assimilated. I was wearing fewer clothes every week--gradually retrograding to the breech-clout. The indolence of the tropics got into my bones, and I didn't so much as attempt to get it out. I found the climate very enervating."

"Are the Filipinos capable of self-government?" asked the friend.

"Well, you know there isn't any country on earth that is ready to admit that any other country is capable of self-government. Besides, it's pretty hard to fix a standard of capacity. Now, I have known for years that the Mexicans are not capable of self-government, and yet Mexico manages to get along. All the students agree that our American cities have not shown a capacity for self-government and yet they do govern themselves after a fashion, assisted by the superior morals and intelligence of our state legislatures. I don't suppose that the best wisdom of Europe has ever come to an agreement that the people of the United States are fit to govern themselves, and yet we are pretty well satisfied with our condition. Inasmuch as it is customary to fix a high standard of intelligence and morals when judging of the capacity of some other country to administer its own government I suppose I am justified in saying that the Tagalos are not capable of self-government. Still, I would prefer not to give an explicit opinion until I land at 'Frisco and learn what are the present views of the administration."

"And the glorious work of benevolent assimilation?"

"That will be continued by the army. The army seems to have more influence with the native population."

THE END.

Chicago Record. July 8,15,22,29, August 5,12,19,26, September 2, 9,16,23,30, October 4,11,18, 1899.

[1] The "mugwumps: were reform Republicans who bolted the Republican Party after the nomination of James G. Blaine as Republican presidential candidate in 1884. At a conference the "mugwumps" denounced the convention's action and invited the Democrats to nominate an honest, independent candidate for whom independent citizens could vote. After Grover Cleveland's nomination by the Democratic party, the mugwumps endorsed him as a leading example of "political courage and honesty and of administrative reform" while simultaneously denouncing Blaine as a "representative of men, methods, and conduct which the public conscience condemns." "Mugwump" leaders included George Curtis, Carl Schurz, Henry Cabot Lodge, and Theodore Roosevelt.

[2] Jacob Gould Schurman (1854-1942), president of Cornell University, was president of the first United States Philippine Commission in 1899. Schurman favored granting the Philippines independence like that of Cuba under American Protection.

[3] Elwell Stephen Otis (1838-1909), was made major-general of volunteers on May 4, 1898, and ordered to the Philippines. In Manila he was placed in command of the VIII Army Corps, and then relieved General Wesley Merritt in command of the Department of the Pacific and as military governor of the Philippines.

2. PETER FINLEY DUNNE

"MR. DOOLEY" ON TERRITORIAL EXPANSION

"Well," said Mr. Dooley, "we've got 'em."

"Again?" said Mr. Hennessy, with a faint attempt at a joke.

"Niver mind," said Mr. Dooley. "We've got th' Ph'lippeens. Th' Spanyards withdrew to th' anti-room an' says wan' 'Let's get through.' Says another: 'I say so, too. If i et another dinner I'd bust. What do they want?' 'Th' Ph'lippeens.' 'Will they take thim?' 'We'll thry an' see.' An' they come out, an' says the chairman, Seynor Morte Rice, he says, 'Oh, crool an' avaricious foe,' he says, 'wretched vampires,' he says, 'that wud suck th' las' dhrop iv blood frim th' fallen form iv poor Spain,' he says. 'We have no other recoorse,' he says. 'We must surrinder to ye,' he says, 'th' brightest flower in th' diadam iv lovely but busted Hispynolio,' he says, 'th' Peril iv the Pass-ific is yours,' he says. 'Take it,' he says, 'anless,' he says, 'ye're such monsthers iv croolty that ye'd rayfuse,' he says. An' we've got th' Ph'lippeens,' Hinnissy' we've got thim th' way Casey got the bulldog--be th' teeth.

"What're we goin' to do with thim, says ye? That shows, Hinnissy, ye're a mugwump. A mugwump's a man that always wants to know what's goin't to happen nex' an' hopes it wont. What d'ye think we're going to do with thim? Sthring thim an' wear thim f'r beads? Hinnissy, if all th' people in this counthry was like th' likes iv ye, they'd be on'y enough iv ye to hold a rayform meeting' an' ye'd be livin' in a balloon off th' coast iv Maine, ye--ye dam'd Pilgrim father, ye!"

"I have a cousin that lives in Lynn," said Mr. Hennessy.

"What diff'rence does it make to you an' me what we do with th' Ph'lippeens annyhow?" Mr. Dooley went on, not heeding the interruption. 'I'm here an' th' Ph'lippeens are there, an' there's too much wather between us to make frinds. But I know what'll happen. 'Twill be, what has happened in this very town manny a time. They'se a sthretch iv prairie just outside th' city

171

limits an' nobody iv our kind wants to live there because it's too quite. But bimeby some people moves in frim Ohio an' builds a house or two an' th' aldherman frim this ward moves f'r to annix it to th' city. An' ivry ol' lady says: 'Haven't we growed enough? What's th' use iv takin' in more territory? Isn't our governmint bad enough as it is?' An' thin th' good Irish people moves in an' conquers th' savidge inhabitants, an' th' nex' ye know that prairie is blossoming like a rose garden an' has become a dimmycratic sthronghold. That's expansion.

"Th' throuble with you, Hinnissy, is ye think you an' Congressman Noonan can set down in th' back room with a piece of chalk an' ol' slate a' figure out what's going to happen, but ye can't. Ye can't figure it about ye'ersilf, an' how can ye figure it about th' Ph'lippeens, that ye niver see? As Hogan an' McKinley both says: 'Th' nation's in th' hands iv th' Lord, an'll give Him what assistance it can spare fr'm its other jooties,' Th' first thing to be done is to appint a sthrong ar'rmy iv officials that can' find annything f'r in this counthry. Th' committyman tol' me yesterdah that there was three hundhred applications f'r th' bridge whin Dorsey, that was there befure, passed over to th' other shure an' got th' job in th' planin' mill. An' ye think they'se no wan fit to conthrol a popylation iv naygurs. I tell ye, anny man that's sthrong enough to even think he can get a job tur'rnin' a bridge in this counthry has force enough to be king iv th' Ph'lippeens in wan year! 'Tis so.

"Well, some iv these la-ads'll be kilt an' some'll come home an' thin wan day a la'ad that's been bumped-agin in th' sthreet car'll sthretch himsilf an' say: 'Glory be, but this is a small counthry afther all,' an' he'll sail away an' he wont have anny job to eat off an' he'll have to make a living' be lickin' th' poor, benighted haythens that we've got to lift up, an' others like him'll go along afther him an' whin th' dimmycratic con-vintion meets Aguinaldo O'Brien an' Perforated Don Carlos Cassidy'll be contistin' which'll cast th' vote iv th' imperyal state iv Ph'lippeens f'r William J. Bryan, th' boy orator iv th' Plate.

"That's what'll happen, Hinnissy. 'Tis not th' la-ads th' govermint'll sind out, but th' la-ads that go out on their own hook, an' have to fight to eat. Be hivins, Hinnissy, they'll be great doin's down there whin wan iv thim opprissed an' tortured people that f'r hundherds iv years have been undher th' ir'n heel iv th' tyrant gets gay with a la-ad that's r-run a Bohemyan prim'ry in this counthry. 'Twill be like th' foolish German man that escaped from jail be jumpin' from th' roof onto a picket fence. We're a gr-reat civilizin' agent, Hinnissy, an' as Father Kelly says, 'so's th' steam roller. An' bein' a quiet man, I'd rather be behind thin in fr-ront whin th' sthreet has to be improved."

"'Twill cost a power iv money," said Mr. Hennessy, the prudent.

"Expand, ixpind," said Mr. Dooley. "That's a joke, an' I med it."

Chicago Journal reprinted in The Literary Digest, December 17, 1898

MR. DOOLEY IN PEACE AND IN WAR

ON THE PHILIPPINES

"I know what I'd do if I was Mack," said Mr. Hennessy. "I'd hist a flag over th' Ph'lippeens, an' I'd take in th' whole lot iv thim."

"An' yet," said Mr. Dooley, "tis not more thin two months since ye larned whether they were islands or canned goods. Ye'er back yard is so small that ye'er cow can't turn r-round without buttin' th' woodshet off th' premises, an' ye wudden't go out to th' stock yards without takin' out a policy on yer life. Suppose ye was stadin' at th' corner iv State Sthreet an' Archey R-road, wud ye know what car to take to get to th' Ph'lippeens? If your son Packy was to ask ye where th' Ph'lippeens is, cud ye give him anny good idea whether they wan in Rooshia or jus' west iv th' thracks?"

"Mebbe I cudden't," said Mr. Hennessy, haughtily, "but I'm f'r takin' thim in, anny-how."

"So might I be," said Mr. Dooley, "if I cut on'y get me mind on it. Wan iv the worst things about this here war is th' way it's makin' puzzles f'r our poor, tired heads. Whin I wint into it, I thought all I'd have to do was to set up here behind th' bar with a good tin-cint see-gar in me teeth, an' toss dinnymite bombs into th' hated city iv Havana. But look at me now. Th' war is still goin' on; an' ivry night, whin I'm countin' up the cash, I'm askin' mesilf will I annex Cubia or lave it to the Cubians? Will I take Porther Ricky or put it by? An' what shud I do with the Ph'lippeens? Oh, what shud I do with thim? I can't annex thim because I don't know where they ar-re. I can't let go iv thim because some wan else'll take thim if I do. They are eight thousan' iv them islands, with a popylation iv wan hundhred millyon naked savages; an' me bedroom's crowded now with me an' th' bed. How can I take thim in, an' how on earth am I goin' to cover th' nakedness iv them savages with me wan shoot iv clothes? An' yet 'twud break me heart to think iv givin' people I niver see or heerd tell iv back to other people I don't know. An', if I don't take thim, Schwartzmeister down th' street, that has half me thrade already, will grab thim sure.

"It ain't that I'm afraid iv not doin' th' r-right thing in th' end, Hinnissy. Some mornin' I'll wake up an' know jus' what to do, an' that I'll do. But 'tis th' annoyance in th' mane time. I've been r-readin' about th' counthry. 'Tis over beyand ye're left shoulder whin ye're facin' east. Jus' throw ye'er thumb back, an' ye have it as ac'rate as anny man in town. 'Tis farther thin Boohlgahrya an' not so far as Blewchoochoo. It's near Chiny, an' it's not so near; an', if a man was to bore a well through fr'm Goshen, Indianny, he might sthrike it, and thin again he might not. It's a poverty-sthricken counthry, full iv goold an' precious stones, where th' people can pick dinner off

173

th' threes an' ar-re starvin' because they have no stepladders. Th' inhabitants is mostly naygurs an' Chinnymen, peaceful, industhrus, an' law-abidin', but savage an' bloodthirsty in their methods. They wear no clothes except what they have on, an' each woman has five husbands an' each man has five wives. Th' r-rest goes into th' discard, th' same as here. Th' islands has been ownded be Spain since befure th' fire; an' she's threated thim so well they're now up in ar-rms again her, except a majority iv thim which is thurly loyal. Th' natives seldom fight, but whin they get mad at wan another they r-run-a-muck. Whin a man r-runs-a-muck, somehimes they hand him an' sometimes they discharge him an' hire a new motorman. Th' women ar-re beautiful, with languishin' black eyes, an' they smoke see-gars, but ar-re hurried an' incomplete in their dhress. I see a pitcher iv wan th' other day with nawthin' on her but a basket of cocoanuts an' a hoop-skirt. They're no prudes. We import juke, hemp, cigar wrappers, sugar, an' fairy tales fr'm th' Ph'lippeens, an' export six-inch shells an' th' like. Iv late th' Ph'lippeens has awaked to th' fact that they're behind th' times, an' has received much American amminition in their midst. They say th' Spanyards is all tore up about it.

"I larned all this fr'm th' papers, an' I know 'tis sthraight. An' yet, Hinnissy, I dinnaw what to do about th' Ph'lippeens. An' I' all alone in th' wurruld. Ivrybody else has made up his mind. Ye ask anny con-ducthor on Ar-rchy R-road, an' he'll tell ye. Ye can find out fr'm the papers; an', if ye really want to know, all ye have to do is to ask a prom'nent citizen who can mow all th' lawn he owns with a safety razor. But I don't know."

"Hang on to thim," said Mr. Hennessy, stoutly. "What we've got we must hold."

"Well," said Mr. Dooley, "if I was Mack, I'd lave it to George. I'd say: 'George,' I'd say, 'if ye're f'r hangin' on, hang on it is. If ye say, lave go, I dhrop thim.' 'Twas George won thim with th' shells, an' th' question's up to him."

"It looks to me," said Mr. Dooley, "as though me frind Mack'd got tired iv th' Sthrateejy Board, an' was goin' to lave th' war to th' men in black."

"How's that?" asked Mr. Hennessy, who has at best but a clouded view of public affairs.

"Well," said Mr. Dooley, "while th' sthrateejans have been wearin' out their jeans on cracker-boxes in Wash'n'ton, they'se been goin' on th' mos' deadly conflict iver heerd tell iv between th' pow'rful preachin' navies iv th' two counthries. Manila is nawthin' at all to th' scenes iv carnage an' slaughter, as Hogan says, that's been brought about be these desthroyers. Th' Spanyards fired th' openin' gun whin th' bishop iv Cades, a pow'rful turreted monitor (ol' style), attacked us with both for'ard guns, an' sint a storm iv brimstone an' hell into us. But th' victhry was not f'r long with th' hated Spanyard. He was answered be our whole fleet iv preachers. Thin he was jined be th' bishop iv Barsaloona an' th' bishop iv Mahdrid an' th' bishop iv Havana, all battle-ships iv th' first class, followed be a

fleet iv cruisers r-runnin' all th' way fr'm a full-ar-rmored
vicar gin'ral to a protected parish priest. To meet thim, we sint
th' bishop iv New York, th' bishop iv Philadelphia, th' bishop iv
Baltimore, an' th' bishop iv Chicago, accompanied be a flyin'
squadhron iv Methodists, three Presbyteryan monitors, a fleet iv
Baptist submarine desthroyers, an' a formidable array iv
Universalist an' Unitaryan torpedo boats, with a Jew r-ram.
Manetime th' bishop iv Manila had fired a solid prayer, weighin'
a ton, at San Francisco; an' a masked batthry iv Congregation-
alists replied, inflictin' severe damage. Our Atlantic fleet is
now sarchin' f'r th' inimy, an' the bishop iv New York is
blockadin' th' bishop iv Sandago de Cuba; an' they'se been an
exchange iv prayers between th' bishop iv Baltimore an' th'
bishop iv Havana without much damage.

"Th' Lord knows how it'll come out. First wan side prays
that th' wrath iv Hiven'll descind on th' other, an' thin th'
other side return th' compliment with inthrest. Th' Spanish
bishop says we're a lot iv murdherin', irreligious thieves, an'
ought to be swept fr'm th' face iv th' earth. We say his people
ar-re th' same, an' manny iv thim. He wishes Hivin to sink our
ships an' desthroy our men; an' we hope he'll injye th' same
gr-reat blessin'. We have a shade th' best iv him, f'r his
fleets ar-re all iv th' same class an' ol' style, an' we have
some iv th' most modhern prayin machines in the warruld; but he
prays har-rd, an' 'tis no aisy wurruk to silence him."

"What d'ye think about it?" asked Mr. Hennessy.

"Well," said Mr. Dooley, "I dinnaw jus' what to think iv
it. Me own idee is that war is not a matther iv prayers so much
as a matther iv punchin'; an' th' on'y place a prayer book stops
a bullet is in th' story books. 'Tis like what Father Kelly
said. Three weeks ago las' Sundah he met Hogan; an' Hogan,
wantin' to be smart, ast him if he'd offered up prayers f'r th'
success iv th' cause. 'Faith, I did not,' says th' good man. 'I
was in too much iv a hurry to get away.' 'What was th' matther?'
ast Hogan. 'I had me uniform to brush up an' me soord to
polish,' says Father Kelly. 'I am goin' with th' rig'mint
to-morrah,' he says; an' he says, 'If ye hear iv me waitin' to
pray,' he says, 'anny time they'se a call f'r me,' he says, 'to
be in a fight,' he says, 'ye may conclude,' he says, 'that I've
lost me mind, an' won't be back to me parish,' he says. 'Hogan,'
he says, 'I'll go into th' battle with a prayer book in wan hand
an' a soord in th' other,' he says; 'an,' if th' wurruk calls f'r
two hands, 'tis not th' soord I'll dhrop,' he says. 'Don't ye
believe in prayer?' says Hogan. 'I do,' says th' good man;
'but,' he says, 'a healthy person ought,' he says, 'to be
ashamed,' he says, 'to ask f'r help in a fight,' he says."

"That's th' way I look at it," said Mr. Hennessy. "When
'tis an aven thing in th' prayin', may th' best man win."

"Ye're r-right, Hinnissy," said Mr. Dooley, warmly. "Ye're
r-right. An' th' best man will win."

"Well," said Mr. Dooley, "I see be th' pa-apers that th' snow-white pigeon iv peace have tied up th' dogs iv war. It's all over now. All we've got to do is to arrest th' pathrites an' make th' reconcenthradios pay th' stamp tax, and' be r-ready f'r to take a punch at Germany or France or Rooshia or anny counthry on th' face iv th' globe.

"An' I'm glad iv it. This war, Hinnissy, has been a gr-reat sthrain on me. To think iv th' suffrin' I've endured! F'r weeks I lay awake at nights fearin' that th' Spanish ar-rmadillo'd lave the Cape Verde Islands, where it wasn't, an' take th' thrain out here, an' hur-rl death an' desthruction into me little store. Day be day th' pitiless exthries come out an' beat down on me. Ye hear iv Teddy Rosenfelt plungin' into ambus-cades an' Sicrity iv Wars; but d'ye hear iv Martin Dooley, th' man behind th' guns, four thousan' miles behind them, an' willin' to be further? They ar-re no bokays f're me. I'm what Hogan calls wan iv th' mute, ingloryous heroes iv th' war; an' not so dam mute, ayther. Some day, Hinnissy, justice'll be done me, an' th' likes iv me; an', whin th' story iv a gr-reat battle is written, they'll print th' kilt, th' wounded, th' missin', an' th' seryously disturbed. An' thim that have bore thimsilves well an' bravely an' paid th' taxes an' faced th' deadly newspa-apers without flinchin' 'll be advanced six pints an' given a chanst to tur-rn jack f'r th' game.

"But me wurruk ain't over jus' because Mack has inded th' war an' Teddy Rosenfelt is comin' home to bite th' Sicrety iv War. You an' me, Hinissy, has got to bring on this here Anglo-Saxon 'lieance. An Anglo-Saxon, Hinnissy, is a German that's forgot who was his parents. They're a lot iv thim in this counthry. There must be as manny as two in Boston: they'se wan up in Maine, an' another lives at Bogg's Ferry in New York State, an' dhrives a milk wagon. Mack is an Anglo-Saxon. His folds come fr'm th' County Armagh, an' their naytional Anglo-Saxon hymn is 'O'Donnell Aboo.' Teddy Rosenfelt is another Anglo-Saxon. An' I'm an Anglo-Saxon. I'm wan iv th' hottest Anglo-Saxons that iver come out iv Anglo-Saxony. Th' name iv Dooley has been th' proudest Anglo-Saxon name in th' County Roscommon f'r many years.

"Schwartzmeister is an Anglo-Saxon, but he doesn't know it, an' won't till some wan tells him. Pether Bowbeen down be th' Frinch church is formin' th' Circle Francaize Anglo-Saxon club, an' me ol' frind Dominigo that used to boss th' Ar-rchey R-road wagon whin Callaghan had th' sthreet conthract will march at th' head iv th' Dago Anglo-Saxons whin th' time comes. There ar-re twinty thousan' Rooshian Jews at a quarther a vote in th' Sivinth Ward; an', ar-rmed with rag hooks, they'd be a tur-r-ble thing f'r anny inimy iv th' Anglo-Saxon 'lieance to face. Th' Bohemians an' Pole Anglo-Saxons may be a little slow in wakin' up to what th' pa-apers calls our common hurtage, but ye may be sure they'll be all r-right whin they're called on. We've got together an Anglo-Saxon 'lieance in this wa-ard, an' we're goin' to ilict Sarsfield O'Brien, prisidint, Hugh O'Neill Darsey vice-prisidint, Robert Immitt Clancy sicrety, an' Wolfe Tone

Malone three-asurer. O'Brien'll be a good wan to have. He was
in the Fenian r-raid, an' his father carrid a pike in
forty-eight. An' he's in th' Clan. Besides, he has a sthrong
pull with th' Ancient Ordher iv Anglo-Saxon Hibernyans.

"I tell ye, whin th' Clan an' th' Sons iv Sweden an' th'
Banana Club an' th' Circle Francaize an' th' Pollacky Benivolent
Society an' th' Rooshian Sons of Dinnymite an' th' Benny Brith an'
th' Coffee Clutch that Schwartzmeister r-runs an' th' Turrnd'ye-
mind an' th' Holland society an' th' Afro-Americans an' th' other
Anglo-Saxons begin f'r to raise their Anglo-Saxon battlecry,
it'll be all day with th' eight or nine people in th' wurruld
that has th' misfortune iv not bein' brought up Anglo-Saxons."

"They'se goin' to be a debate on th' 'lieance at th'
ninety-eight picnic at Ogden's gr-rove," said Mr. Hennessy.

"P'r'aps," said Mr. Dooley, sweetly, "ye might like to borry
th' loan iv an ice-pick."

ON A LETTER FROM THE FRONT

Mr. Dooley looked important, but affected indifference, as
he mopped the bar. Mr. Hennessy, who had learned to study his
friend in order to escape disagreeable complications, patiently
waited for the philosopher to speak. Mr. Dooley rubbed the bar
to the end, tossed the cloth into a mysterious recess with
practised movement, moved a glass or two on the shelf, cleaned
his spectacles, and drew a letter from his pocket.

"Hm-m!" he said: "I have news fr'm th' fr-ront. Me nevvew,
Terry Donahue, has sint me a letther tellin' me all about it."

"How shud he know?" Mr. Hennessy asked.

"How shud he know, is it?" Mr. Dooley demanded warmly. "How
shudden't he know? Isn't he a sojer in th' ar-rmy? Isn't it him
that's down there in Sandago fightin' f'r th' honor iv th' flag,
while th' likes iv you is up here livin' like a prince, an' doin'
nawthin' all th' livelong day but shovel at th' rollin'-mills?
Who are ye f'r to criticize th' dayfinders iv our counthry who
ar-re lyin' in th' trinches, an' havin' th' clothes stole off
their backs be th' pathriotic Cubians,[2] I'd like to know? F'r
two pins, Hinnissy, you an' I'd quarrel."

"I didn't mean nawthin'," Mr. Hennessy apologized. "I
didn't know he was down there."

"Nayether did I," said Mr. Dooley. "But I informed mesilf.
I'll have no wan in this place speak again th' ar-rmy. Ye can
have ye'er say about Mack. He has a good job, an' 'tis r-right
an' proper f'r to baste him fr'm time to time. It shows ye'er in
good thrim, an' it don't hur-rt him. They'se no wan to stop his
pay. He goes up to th' cashier an' dhraws his forty-wan-sixty-six
jus' th' same whether he's sick or well, an' whether he's pulled
th' box reg-lar or has been playin' forty-fives in th' back room.
But whin ye come to castin' aspersions on th' ar'rmy, be hivens,
ye'll find that I can put me thumb on this showcase an' go over at
wan lep."

"I didn't say annything," said Mr. Hennessy. "I didn't know
about Terry."

"Iv coorse, ye didn't," said Mr. Dooley. "An' that's what I'm sayin'. Ye're here wallowin' in luxury, wheelin' pig ir'n fr'm morn till night; an' ye have no thought iv what's goin' on beyant. You an' Jawn D. Rockefeller an' Phil Ar-rmour an' Jay Pierpont Morgan an' th' r-rest iv ye is settin' back at home figurin' how ye can make some wan else pay ye'er taxes f'r ye. What is it to ye that me nevvew Terry is sleepin' in ditch wather an' atin' hard tacks an' coffee an' bein' r-robbed be leber Cubians, an' catchin' yellow fever without a chanst iv givin' it to e'er a Spanyard. Ye think more iv a stamp thin ye do iv ye'er counthry. Ye're like th' Sugar Thrust. F'r two cints ye'd refuse to support th' govermint. I know ye, ye bloated monno-polist."

"I'm no such thing," said Mr. Hennessy, hotly. "I've been a Dimmycrat f'r thirty year."

"Well, annyhow," said Mr. Dooley, "don't speak disrayspictful iv th' ar-rmy. Lave me r-reed you Terry's letter fr'm th' fr-ront. 'M--m: In th' trinches, two miles fr'm Sandago, with a land crab as big as a lobster crawlin' up me back be way iv Kingston, June 6, Dear Uncle Martin.' That's th' way it begins. 'Dear Uncle Martin: We are all well here, except him that is not, an' hope ye're injyin' th' same gr-reat blessin'. It's hotter down here thin Billy-be-dam'd. They'se a rollin'-mill near here jus' th' same as at home, but all th' hands is laid off on account iv bad times. They used ol'-fashioned wooden wheelbahrs an' fired with wood. I don't think they cud handle th' pig th' way we done, bein' small la-ads. Th' coke has to be hauled up in sacks be th' gang. Th' derrick hands got six a week, but hadn't anny union. Helpers got four twinty. Puddlers was well paid. I wint through th' plant befure we come up here, an' r-run a wagon up th' plank jus' to keep me hand in. Tell me friends that wan gang iv good la-ads fr'm th' r-road cud wurruk anny three iv th' gangs down here. Th' mills is owned be Rockefellar, so no more at prisint fr'm yer affecshunate nevvew, Peter Casey, who's writin' this f'r me.'"

"'Tis a good letter," said Mr. Hennessy. "I don't see how they cut get derrick hands f'r six a week."

"Me friend Jawn D. knows how," said Mr. Dooley.

ON OUR CUBAN ALLIES

"Well, sir," said Mr. Dooley, "dam thim Cubians! If I was Gin'ral Shafter, I'd back up th' wagon in front iv th' dure, an' I'd say to Gin'ral Garshy, I'd say, 'I want you'; an' I'd have thim all down at th' station an' dacently booked be th' desk sergeant befure th' fall iv night. Th' impydince iv thim!"

"What have they been doin'?" Mr. Hennessy asked.

"Failin' to undherstand our civilization," said Mr. Dooley. "Ye see, it was this way. This is th' way it was: Gin'ral Garshy with wan hundherd thousan' men's been fightin' bravely f'r two years f'r to liberyate Cubia. F'r two years he's been marchin' his sivinty-five thousan' men up an' down th' island, desthroyin' th' haughty Spanyard be th' millyons. Whin war was declared, he offered his own sarvice an' th' sarvices iv his ar-rmy iv fifty

thousan' men to th' United States; an' while waitin' f'r ships to
arrive, he marched at th' head iv his tin thousan' men down to
Sandago de Cuba an' captured a cigar facthry, which they soon
rayjooced to smokin' ruins. They was holdin' this position--
Gin'ral Garshy an' his gallant wan thousan' men--whin Gin'ral
Shafter arrived, there was Gin'ral Garshy with his gallant band
iv fifty Cubians, r-ready to eat at a minyit's notice.

"Gin'ral Shafter is a big, coorse, two-fisted man fr'm
Mitchigan, an', whin he see Gin'ral Garshy an' his twinty-five
gallant followers, "Fr-ront,' says he. 'This way,' he says,
'step lively,' he says, 'an' move some iv these things,' he
says. 'Sir,' says Gin'ral Garshy, 'd'ye take me f'r a dhray?' he
says. 'I'm a sojer,' he says, 'not a baggage car,' he says.
'I'm a Cubian pathrite, an' I'd lay down me life an' the lives iv
ivry wan iv th' eighteen brave men iv me devoted ar-rmy,' he
says; 'but I'll be dam'd if I carry a thrunk,' he says. 'I'll
fight whiniver 'tis cool,' he says, 'an' they ain't wan iv these
twelve men here that wudden't follow me to hell if they was awake
at th' time,' he says; 'but,' he says, 'if 'twas wurruk we were
lookin' f'r, we cud have found it long ago,' he says. 'They'se a
lot iv it in this counthry that nobody's usin',' he says. 'What
we want,' he says, 'is freedom,' he says; 'an', if ye think we
have been in th' woods dodgin' th' savage corryspondint f'r two
year,' he says, 'f'r th' sake iv r-rushin' yer laundhry home,' he
says, ''tis no wondher,' he says, 'that th' r-roads fr'm
Marinette to Kalamazoo is paved with goold bricks bought be th'
people iv ye're native State,' he says.

"So Shafter had to carry his own thrunk; an' well it was f'r
him that it wasn't Gin'ral Miles', the weather bein' hot. An'
Shafter was mad clear through; an', whin he took hold iv Sandago,
an' was sendin' out invitations, he scratched Garshy.[3] Garshy
took his gallant band iv six back to th' woods; an' there th'
three iv thim ar-re now, ar-rmed with forty r-rounds iv canned
lobster, an' ready to raysist to th' death. Him an' th' other
man has written to Gin'ral Shafter to tell him what they think iv
him, an' it don't take long."

"Well," said Mr. Hennessy, "I think Shafter done wrong. He
might've asked Garshy in f'r to see th' show, seein' that he's
been hangin' ar-round f'r a long time, doin' th' best he cud."

"It isn't that," explained Mr. Dooley. "Th' throuble is th'
Cubians don't undherstand our civilization. Over here freedom
means hard wurruk. What is th' ambition iv all iv us, Hinnissy?
'Tis ayether to hold our job or to get wan. We want wurruk. We
must have it. D'ye raymimber th' sign th' mob carrid in th'
procession las' year? 'Give us wurruk, or we perish,' it said.
They had their heads bate in be polismen because no
philan-thropist'd come along an' make thim shovel coal. Now, in
Cubia, whin th' mobs turns out, they carry a banner with the
wurruds, 'Give us nawthin' to do, or we perish.' Whin a Cubian
comes home at night with a happy smile on his face, he don't say
to his wife an' childher, 'Thank Gawd, I've got wurruk at last!'
He says, 'Thank Gawd, I've been fired.' An' th' childher go out,
and they say, 'Pah-pah has lost his job.' And Mrs. Cubian buys

179

hersilf a new bonnet; and where wanst they was sorrow an' despair all is happiness an' a cottage organ.

"Ye can't make people here undherstand that, an' ye can't make a Cubian undherstand that freedom means th' same thing as a pinitinchry sintince. Whin we thry to get him wurruk, he'll say: 'Why shud I? I haven't committed anny crime.' That's goin' to be th' throuble. Th' first thing we know we'll have another war in Cubia whin we begin disthributin' good jobs, twelve hours a day, wan sivinty-five. Th' Cubians ain't civilized in our way. I sometimes think I've got a touch iv Cubian blood in me own veins."

Peter Finley Dunne, Mr. Dooley in Peace and in War, Boston, 1899, pp. 44-67

Notes to Peter Finley Dunne

[1]Feninans were Irish-Americans, members of a secret organization founded in New York City in the mid-19th century, whose goal was the overthrow of British rule in Ireland.

[2]This reflects the changing attitude towards the Cubans after the war with Spain started when they were maligned in the American press as lazy men interested only in robbing American soldiers rather than the patriots they had been previously pictured. (See Philip S. Foner, The Spanish-Cuban-American War and the Birth of American Imperialism, 1898-1902 [New York, 1972] 2: 339-70.)

[3] Mr. Dooley is referring to the deterioration of relations that occurred between General William R. Shafter, in charge of the U.S. forces in the siege of Santiago de Cuba and General Calixto García, the Cuban revolutionary general who had played a leading role in battling the Spaniards since the outbreak of the Second War for Independence in 1895. Although the Cuban troops furnished valuable aid to the Americans in taking Santiago, General García was not permitted to participate in the surrender negotiations or to share in the control of the city after its surrender. In a letter to General Shafter, July 17, 1898, García expressed his bitterness over the American insult to the Cuban Revolution and resigned his position as commander-in-chief of the Cuban army. (For the details of the Shafter-García conflict, See Foner, op.cit., pp. 355-75.)

SELECTIONS FROM

MR. DOOLEY IN THE HEARTS OF HIS COUNTRYMEN

EXPANSION

"Whin we plant what Hogan calls th' starry banner iv Freedom
in th' Ph'lippeens," said Mr. Dooley, 'an' give th' sacred
blessin' iv liberty to the poor, downtrodden people iv thim
unfortunate isles,--dam thim!--we'll larn thim a lesson."
"Sure," said Mr. Hennessy, sadly, "we have a thing or two to
larn oursilves."
"But it isn't f'r thim to larn us," said Mr. Dooley. "'Tis
not f'r thim wretched an' degraded crathers, without a mind or a
shirt iv their own, f'r to give lessons in politeness an' liberty
to a nation that mannyfacthers more dhressed beef than anny other
imperyal nation in th' wurruld. We say to thim: 'Naygurs,' we
say, 'poor, dissolute, uncovered wretches,' says we, 'whin th'
crool hand iv Spain forged man'cles f'r ye'er limbs, as Hogan
says, who was it crossed th' say an' sthruck off th' comealongs?
We did,--by dad, we did. An' now, ye mis'rable, childish-minded
apes, we propose f'r to larn ye th' uses iv liberty. In ivry
city in this unfair land we will erect school-houses an' packin'
houses an' houses iv correction; an' we'll larn ye our langage,
because 'tis aisier to larn ye ours than to larn oursilves
yours. An' we'll give ye clothes, if ye pay f'r thim; an', if ye
don't, ye can go without. An', whin ye're hungry, ye can go to
th' morgue--we man th' resth'rant--an' ate a good square meal iv
ar-rmy beef. An' we'll sind th' gr-reat Gin'ral Eagan over f'r
to larn ye etiquette, an' Andhrew Carnegie to larn ye pathriteism
with blow-holes into it, an' Gin'ral Alger to larn ye to hould
onto a job; an', whin ye've become edycated an' have all th'
blessin's iv civilization that we don't want, that'll count ye
one. We can't give ye anny votes, because we haven't more thin
enough to go round now; but we'll threat ye th' way a father shud
threat his childher if we have to break ivry bone in ye're
bodies. So come to our ar-rms,' says we.
"But, glory ge, 'tis more like a rasslin' match than a
father's embrace. Up gets this little minkey iv an' Aggynaldoo,
an' says he, 'Not for us,' he says. 'We thank ye kindly; but we
believe,' he says, 'in pathronizin' home industhries,' he says.
'An,' he says, 'I have on hand,' he says, 'an' f'r sale,' he
says, 'a very superyor brand iv home-made liberty, like ye'er
mother used to make,' he says. ''Tis a long way fr'm ye'er plant
to here,' he says, 'an' be th' time a cargo iv liberty,' he says,
'got out here an' was handled be th' middlemen,' he says, 'it
might spoil,' he says. 'We don't want anny col' storage or
embalmed liberty,' he says. 'What we want an' what th' ol'
reliable house iv Aggynaldoo,' he says, 'supplies to th' thrade,'
he says, 'is fr-esh liberty r-right off th' far-rm,' he says. 'I
can't do annything with ye'er proposition,' he says. 'I can't
give up,' he says, 'th' rights f'r which f'r five years I've

183

fought an' bled ivry wan I cud reach,' he says. "Onless,' he
says, 'ye'd feel like buyin' out th' whole business,' he says.
'I'm a pathrite,' he says; 'but I'm no bigot,' he says.
    "An' there it stands, Hinnisy, with th' indulgent parent
kneelin' on th' stomach iv his adopted child, while a dillygation
fr'm Boston bastes him with an umbrella. There it stands, an'
how will it come out I dinnaw. I'm not much iv an expansionist
mesilf. F'r th' las' tin years I've been thryin' to decide
whether 'twud be good policy an' thrue to me thraditions to make
this here bar two or three feet longer, an manny's th' night I've
laid awake tryin' to puzzle it out. But i don't know what to do
with th' Ph'lippeens anny more thin I did las' summer, befure I
heerd tell iv thim. We can't give thim to anny wan without
makin' th' wan that gets thim feel th' way Doherty felt to Clancy
whin Clancy med a frindly call an' give Doherty's childher th'
measles. We can't sell thim, we can't ate thim, an' we can't
throw thim into th' alley whin no wan is lookin'. An' 'twud be a
disgrace f'r to lave befure we've pounded these frindless an'
ongrateful people into insinsibility. So I suppose, Hinnissy,
we'll have to stay an' do th' best we can, an' lave Andhrew
Carnegie secede fr'm th' Union. They'se wan consolation; an'
that is, if th' American people can govern thimsilves, they can
govern annything that walks."
    "An' what 'd ye do with Aggy--what-d'ye-call-him?" asked Mr.
Hennessy.
    "Well," Mr. Dooley replied, with brightening eyes, "I know
what they'd do with him in this ward. They'd give that pathrite
what he asks, an' thin they'd throw him down an' take it away
fr'm him."

A HERO WHO WORKED OVERTIME

    "Well, sir," said Mr. Dooley, "it looks now as if they was
nawthin' left f'r me young frind Aggynaldoo to do but time. Like
as not a year fr'm now he'll be in jail, like Napoleon, th'
impror iv th' Fr-rinch, was in his day, an' Mike, th' Burglar,
an' other pathrites. That's what comes iv bein' a pathrite too
long. 'Tis a good job, whin they'se nawthin' else to do; but
'tis not th' thing to wurruk overtime at. 'Tis a sort iv
out-iv-dure spoort that ye shud engage in durin' th' summer
vacation; but, whin a man carries it on durin' business hours,
people begin to get down on him, an' afther a while they're ready
to hang him to get him out iv th' way. As Hogan says, 'Th' las'
thing that happens to a pathrite he's a scoundhrel.'
    "Las' summer there wasn't a warmer pathrite annywhere in our
imperyal dominions thin this same Aggynaldoo. I was with him
mesilf. Says I: 'They'se a good coon,' I says. 'He'll help us
f'r to make th' Ph'lippeens indepindint on us f'r support,' I
says; 'an', whin th' blessin's iv civilization has been extinded
to his beloved counthry, an',' I says, 'they put up intarnal
rivinue offices an' post-offices,' I says, 'we'll give him a good
job as a letter-carrier,' I says, 'where he won't have annything
to do,' I says, 'but walk,' I says.

"An' so th' consul at Ding Dong, th' man that r-runs that end iv th' war, he says to Aggynaldoo: 'Go,' he says, 'where glory waits ye,' he says. 'Go an' sthrike a blow,' he says, 'f'r ye'er counthry,' he says. 'Go,' he says. 'I'll stay, but you go,' he says. 'They's nawthin' in stayin', an' ye might get hold iv a tyrannical watch or a pocket book down beyand,' he says. An' off wint th' brave pathrite to do his jooty. He done it, too. Whin Cousin George was pastin' th' former hated Castiles, who was it stood on th' shore shootin' his bow-an-arrow into th' sky but Aggynaldoo? Whin me frind Gin'ral Merritt was ladin' a gallant charge again blank catredges, who was it ranged his noble ar-rmy iv pathrites behind him f'r to see that no wan attackted him fr'm th' sea but Aggynaldoo? He was a good man thin,--a good noisy man.

"Th' throuble was he didn't know whin to knock off. He didn't hear th' wurruk bell callin' him to come in fr'm playin ball an' get down to business. Says me Cousin George: "Aggynaldoo, me buck,' he says, 'th' war is over,' he says, 'an' we've settled down to th' ol' game,' he says. 'They're no more heroes. All iv thim has gone to wurruk f'r th' magazines. They're no more pathrites,' he says. 'They've got jobs as gov'nors or ar-re lookin' f'r thim or annything else,' he says. 'All th' prom'nint saviors iv their counthry,' he says, 'but mesilf,' he says, 'is busy preparin' their definse,' he says. 'I have no definse,' he says; 'but I'm where they can't reach me,' he says. 'Th' spoort is all out iv th' job' an', if ye don't come in an' jine th' tilin masses iv wage-wurrukers,' he says, 'ye won't even have th' credit iv bein' licked in a gloryous victhry,' he says. 'So to th' woodpile with ye!' he says; 'fr ye can't go on cillybratin' th' Foorth iv July without bein' took up f'r disordherly conduct,' he says.

"An' Aggynaldoo doesn't undherstand it. An' he gathers his Archery Club ar-round him, an' says he: 'Fellow-pathrites,' he says, 'we've been betrayed,' he says. 'We've been sold out without,' he says, 'gettin' th' usual commission,' he says. 'We're still heroes,' he says; 'an' our pitchers is in th' pa-apers,' he says. 'Go in,' he says, 'an' sthrike a blow at th' gay deceivers,' he says. 'I'll sell ye'er lives dearly,' he says. An' th' Archery Club wint in. Th' pathrites wint up again a band iv Kansas sojers, that was wanst heroes befure they larned th' hay-foot-sthraw-foot, an' is now arnin' th' wages iv a good harvest hand all th' year ar-round, an' 'd rather fight than ate th' ar-rmy beef, an' ye know what happened. Some iv th' poor divvles iv heroes is liberated fr'm th' cares iv life; an' th' r-rest iv thim is up in threes, an' wishin' they was home, smokin' a good see-gar with mother.

"An' all this because Aggynaldoo didn't hear th' whistle blow. He thought th' boom was still on in th' hero business. If he'd come in, ye'd be hearin' that James Haitch Aggynaldoo'd been appointed foorth-class postmasther at Hootchey-Kootchey; but now th' nex' ye know iv him 'll be on th' blotther at th' polis station: 'James Haitch Aggynaldoo, alias Pompydoor Jim, charged

with carryin' concealed weepins an' raysistin' an officer.'
Pathriteism always dies when ye establish a polis foorce."

"Well," said Mr. Hennessy, "I'm kind iv sorry f'r th' la-ads
with th' bows an' arrows. Maybe they think they're pathrites."

"Divvle th' bit iv diff'rence it makes what they think, so
long as we don't think so," said Mr. Dooley. "It's what Father
Kelly calls a case iv mayhem et chew 'em. That's Latin,
Hennissy; an' it manes what's wan man's food is another man's
pizen."

"I think," said Mr. Dooley, "th' finest pothry in th'
wurruld is wrote be that frind iv young Hogan's, a man be th'
name iv Roodyard Kipling. I see he pomes in th' pa-aper,
Hinnissy; an' they're all right. They're all right, thim pomes.
They was wan about scraggin' Danny Deever that done me a wurruld
iv good. ҷhey was a la-ad I wanst knew be th' name iv Deever,
an' like as not he was th' same man. He owed me money. Thin
there was wan that I see mintioned in th' war news wanst in a
while, --th' less we f'rget, th' more we raymimber. That was a
hot pome an' a good wan. What I like about Kipling is that his
pomes is right off th' bat, like me con-versations with you, me
boy. He's a minyiteman, a r-ready pote that sleeps like th'
dhriver iv thruck 9, with his poetic pants in his boots beside
his bed, an' him r-ready to jump out an' slide down th' pole th'
minyit th' alarm sounds.

"He's not such a pote as Tim Scanlan, that hasn't done
annything since th' siege iv Lim'rick; an' that was too hundherd
year befure he was bor-rn. He's prisident iv th' Pome Supply
Company,--fr-resh pothry delivered ivry day at ye'er dure. Is
there an accident in a grain illyvator? Ye pick up ye'er mornin'
pa-aper, an' they'se a pome about it be Roodyard Kipling. Do ye
hear iv a manhole cover bein' blown up? Roodyard is there with
his r-ready pen. ''Tis written iv Cashum-Cadi an' th' book iv
th' gr-reat Gazelle that a manhole cover in anger is tin degrees
worse thin hell.' He writes in all dialects an' anny language,
plain an' fancy pothry, pothry f'r young an' old, pothry be
weight or linyar measuremint, pothry f'r small parties iv eight
or tin a specialty. What's the raysult, Hinnissy? Most potes I
despise. But Roodyard Kipling's pothry is aisy. Ye can skip
through it while ye're atin' breakfuss an' get a c'rrect idee iv
th' current news iv th' day,--who won th' futball game, how
Sharkey is thrainin' f'r th' fight, an' how manny votes th'
pro-hybitionist got f'r gov'nor iv th' State iv Texas. No col'
storage pothry f'r Kipling. Ivrything fr-resh an' up to date.
All lays laid this mornin'.

"Hogan was in to-day readin' Kipling's Fridah afthernoon
pome, an' 'tis a good pome. He calls it 'Th' Thruce iv th'
Bear.' This is th' way it happened: Roodyard Kipling had just
finished his mornin' batch iv pothry f'r th' home-thrade, an' had
et his dinner, an' was thinkin' iv r-runnin' out in th' counthry
f'r a breath iv fr-resh air, whin in come a tillygram sayin' that
th' Czar iv Rooshia had sint out a circular letther sayin'
ivrybody in th' wurrld ought to get together an' stop makin' war
an' live a quite an' dull life. Now Kipling don't like the

czar. Him an' th' czar fell out about something, an' they don't
speak. So says Roodyard Kipling to himsilf, he says: 'I'll take
a crack at that fellow,' he says. 'I'll do him up,' he says.
An' so he write a pome to show that th' czar's letter's not on
th' square. Kipling's like me, Hinnissy. When I want to say
annything lib-lous, I stick it on to me Uncle Mike. So be
Roodyard Kipling. He doesn't come r-right out, an' say, 'Nick,
ye're a liar!' but he tells about what th' czar done to a man he
knowed be th' name iv Muttons. Muttons, it seems, Hinnissy, was
wanst a hunter; an' he wint out to take a shot at th' czar, who
was dhressed up as a bear. Well, Muttons r-run him down, an' was
about to plug him, whin th' czar says, 'Hol' on,' he says,--'hol'
on there,' he says. 'Don't shoot,' he says. 'Let's talk this
over,' he says. An' Muttons, bein' a foolish man, waited till
th' czar come near him; an' thin th' czar feinted with his left,
an' put in a right hook an' pulled off Muttons's face. I tell ye
'tis so. He jus' hauled it off th' way ye'd haul off a porous
plasther,--raked off th' whole iv Muttons's fr-ront ilivation.
'I like ye'er face,' he says, an' took it. An' all this time,
an' 'twas fifty year ago, Muttons hasn't had a face to shave.
Ne'er a one. So he goes ar-round exhibitin' th' recent site, an'
warnin' people that, whin they ar-re shootin' bears, they must
see that their gun is kept loaded an' their face is nailed on
securely. If ye iver see a bear that looks like a man, shoot him
on th' spot, or, betther still, r-run up an alley. Ye must niver
lose that face, Hinnissy.

   "I showed th' pome to Father Kelly," continued Mr. Dooley.
   "What did he say?" asked Mr. Hennessy.
   "He said," Mr. Dooley replied, "that I cud write as good a
wan mesilf; an' he took th' stub iv a pencil, an' wrote this.
Lemme see-- Ah! here it is:--

   'Whin he shows as seekin' frindship with paws that're
        thrust in thine,
     That is th' time iv pearl, that is th' thruce iv th' line.

   'Collarless, coatless, hatless, askin' a dhrink at th' bar,
     Me Uncle Mike, the Fenyan, he tells it near and far,

   'Over an' over th' story: 'Beware iv th' gran' flimflam,
     There is no thruce with Gazabo, th' line that looks like
        a lamb.'

   "That's a good pome, too," said Mr. Dooley; "an' I'm goin'
to sind it to th' nex' meetin' iv th' Anglo-Saxon 'liance."

Peter Finley Dunne, Mr. Dooley in the Hearts of His Countrymen,
   Boston, 1899, pp. 3-17

3. AMBROSE BIERCE

A PROVISIONAL SETTLEMENT

McKinley, A President.   Sagasta, a Prime Minster.[1]
Aguinaldo, a Patriot.

SAGASTA--Senor Presidente, you are very good, and you will
find Spain is not unreasonable. I have instructed my peace
commissioners to concede quite a number of the demands that yours
will probably make.
McKINLEY--And the others?
SAG.--Why, of course, Senor, a demand that is not conceded
is refused.
McK.--But if my commissioners have the sorrow to insist?
SAG.--In that case Spain knows how to defend her honor.
McK.--How, for example?
SAG.--If need be, with the naked breasts of her sons!
McK.--My good friend, you err widely. The thing which there
may be a dispute about is not Spanish honor, but Spanish soil.
SAG.--In every square foot of which, Senor Porco--I mean
Presidente--Spanish honor is rooted.
McK.--Sir, I shall consult my Secretary of Agriculture as to
the desirability of annexing land which produced a crop like
that. But this is your day to be dull: can you really suppose
that in permitting you to have peace commissioners I expected
them to claim the right of dissent? However these matters may be
debated, there is but one deciding power--the will of the
American Executive.
SAG.--Senor, you forget. Supreme over all, there is God!
McK.--O, I don't know. He's not the only----
SAG.--Holy cats!
                              [Enter Aguinaldo.]
McK.--First of all, Senor Prime Minister, you must renouce
the island of Luzon, and----

AGUINALDO--Yes, Senor, that being the most important island of the group, and the one in which you have not now even a foothold, its renunciation will naturally precede that of the others, as my great and good ally is pleased to suggest. With regard to Luzon you have only to say, "We renounce"; I, "We accept."

McK.--Please have the goodness to hold your tongue.

AG.--With both hands, your Excellency.

McK.--Second, Senor, you must assure a liberal government to the other islands.

SAG.--With great pleasure, your Excellency; quite cheerfully.

McK.--Please do not wink. Third, there must be----

AG.--Excuse me; I was brought up a Spanish subject. What is a liberal government?

McK.--That is for Spain to decide.

AG.--I don't see what Spain will have to do with it.

McK.--My friend, you slumber--peaceful be thy dreams. Third, there must be complete separation of church and state.

SAG.--What! a Drabolocracy? You shock me!

McK.--Fourth, none of the islands, nor any part of them, is to be ceded to any foreign nation without the consent of the United States.

AG.--You understand, Senor--you hear that! Spain can never again acquire a square foot of these islands, not even by reconquest or a corrupt bargain with a recreant Filipino dictator, for she will again have to reckon with our powerful protectors, whom may the good God reward!

McK.--The trouble with you is, you talk too much. Fifth, the United States must have in the Philippines equal commercial privileges with Spain.

AG.--Equal? May I never again run amuck if they shall not have superior! Why, I have it in mind to issue a proclamation closing every port to the ships of Spain. As to the United States, commercial primacy is a small reward for their assistance in the closing scene of our successful rebellion.

SAG.--Of course, as you say, I shall have to accept whatever terms you have the great kindness to offer. As I understand your proposal, Spain retains all the islands but Luzon; that is to belong to the United States, and----

AG.--What!

SAG.--This worthy Oriental appears to be laboring under a misapprehension.

McK.--I know of nothing else that could make an Oriental labor.

AG.--Senores, the language of diplomacy is to me an unfamiliar tongue: I have imperfectly understood--pardon me. Is it indeed intended that the United States shall take Luzon and Spain take all else?

McK.--"Retain" is the word.

AG.--"Retain?" Why, that means to keep, to hold what is already possessed. What you gentlemen have in possession in this archipelago is the ground covered by the feet of your soldiers. Now, what right have you, Senor Presidente, to the island of Luzon? The right of conquest? You have not conquered it.

McK.--My dear fellow, you distress me. I conquered this gentleman, and he is going to be good enough to give me the island as a testimonial of his esteem.

AG.--But he doesn't own it. I had taken it away from him before you defeated him--all but the capital, and by arrangement with your man Dewey----

SAG.--Caram----!

AG.--I assisted to take that. Why, he supplied me with arms for the purpose!

SAG.--Arms with which I had had the unhapiness to supply him.

AG.--What is my reward? I am driven from the city which I assisted to conquer, and you take not only that but the entire island, which you had no hand in conquering.

SAG. (aside)--Faith! he'll conquer it before he gets it.

McK.--My friend, you are a Malay, with a slight infusion of Chinese, Hindu and Kanaka. Naturally, you cannot understand these high matters.

AG.--I understand this: We Filipinos rebelled against Spain to liberate our country from oppression. We wrested island after island, city after city, from her until Manila was virtually all that she had left. As we were about to deprive her of that and regain the independence which, through four hundred years of misrule, she had denied us we experienced a dire mischance. You quarreled with her because she denied independence to Cuba. Spanish dominion, which we had stabbed, was already dead, but you arrived just in time to kick the corpse while it was yet warm, and for this service you propose to administer upon the estate, keeping the most valuable part for your honesty. You will then revive the dead, buried and damned and reinstate him in possession of the remainder!

McK. (aside)--O, will I?

SAG.--Apparently, Senor Presidente, this worthy person is afflicted with a flow of language. (Aside) The Porco Americano has the habit of blushing.

McK. (to Sagasta)--Yes, the Filipino always has his tongue in his ear. (To Aguinaldo) Proceed with the address.

AG.--It is as if the French, having assisted your forefathers to independence, had kept Boston and all New England for themselves and restored the other colonies to Great Britain. If the Good Samaritan, arriving while the man fallen among thieves was still struggling with them, had assisted him to beat them off, had then taken his purse and delivered him to the theives again you would have had a Scriptural precedent.

SAG. (writing in a notebook)--"At a certain temperature the Porco Americano can sweat."

McK.--My great and good friend, you seem to have your climate with you, as well as your chin. I must beg you to abridge your oration against manifest destiny.

AG.--Destiny was a long time manifesting herself, but she had not been idle since. In the last four months you have torn up the three American political Holy Scriptures: Washington's Farewell Address, the Monroe Doctrine and the Declaration of Independence. You now stand upon the fragments of the last and

191

declare it an error that governments derive their just powers
from the consent of the governed. In Hawaii you are founding a
government on the consent of less than three per centum of the
governed.[2] In my country you propose to found one government
and restore another against the unanimous dissent of eight
millions of people whom you cheated into an alliance to that
end. You cajoled them into assisting at the cutting of their own
throats. Your only justification in making this war at all was
Spain's denial in Havana of the political principle which you now
repudiate in Honolulu and Manila. Senores, we shall resist both
the American and the Spanish occupation. You will be
allies--embrace!

[Exit Sagasta.]

McK.--My dear boy, you are unduly alarmed: the notion of
letting Spain keep those other islands is merely a Proposal
Retractable--in undiplomatic language, an offer with a string to
it.

AG.--And your plan of holding Luzon--after taking it?

McK.--Rest in peace: that is only what we call an Intention
Augmentable.

AG.--Ah, Senor, you make me so happy!

The Collected Works of Ambrose Bierce, New York and Washington,
1912, vol. XII, pp. 201-08.

EXPLANATORY NOTES

[1] Praxedas Mateo Sagasta became Prime Minister of Spain on October 4, 1897 and remained in power during the war with the United States.

[2] Over the protests of the vast majority of the islanders, the McKinley Administration pushed the annexation of Hawaii through Congress in the form of a joint resolution requiring only a majority vote rather than by treaty which would require a two-thirds vote in the Senate. The legislature of Hawaii sent a protest to Washington pointing out that the "joint resolution has not been passed upon by the people of Hawaii, nor by their representatives in Legislature assembled, and called upon the people of the United States "to refrain from further participation in the wrongful annexation of Hawaii." The petition was ignored, and Hawaii was annexed against the wishes of its people.

4. MARK TWAIN

TO THE PERSON SITTING IN DARKNESS

Christmas will dawn in the United States over a people full of hope and aspiration and good cheer. Such a condition means contentment and happiness. The carping grumbler who may here and there go forth will find few to listen to him. The majority will wonder what is the matter with him and pass on.--New York Tribune, on Christmas Eve. From The Sun, of New York:

The purpose of this article is not to describe the terrible offences against humanity committed in the name of Politics in some of the most notorious East Side districts. They could not be described, even verbally. But it is the intention to let the great mass of more or less careless citizens of this beautiful metropolis of the New World get some conception of the havoc and ruin wrought to man, woman and child in the most densely populated and least known section of the city. Name, date and place can be supplied to those of little faith--or to any man who feels himself aggrieved. It is a plain statement of record and observation, written without license and without garnish.

Imagine, if you can, a section of the city territory completely dominated by one man, without whose permission neither legitimate nor illegitimate business can be conducted; where illegitimate business is encouraged and legitimate business discouraged; where the respectable residents have to fasten their doors and windows summer nights and sit in their rooms with asphyxiating air and 100-degree temperature, rather than try to catch the faint whiff of breeze in their natural breathing places, the stoops of their homes; where naked women dance by night in the streets, and unsexed men prowl like vultures through the darkness on 'business' not only permitted but encouraged by the police; where the education of infants begins with the knowledge of prostitution and the training of little girls

is training in the arts of Phryne; where American girls
brought up with the refinements of American homes are
imported from small towns up-State, Massachusetts,
Connecticut and New Jersey, and kept as virtually prisoners
as if they were locked up behind jail bars until they have
lost all semblance of womanhood; where small boys are taught
to solicit for the women of disorderly houses; where there
is an organized society of young men whose sole business in
life is to corrupt young girls and turn them over to bawdy
houses; where men walking with their wives along the street
are openly insulted; where children that have adult diseases
are the chief patrons of the hospitals and dispensaries;
where it is the rule, rather than the exception, that
murder, rape, robbery, and theft go unpunished--in short
where the Premium of the most awful forms of Vice is the
Profit of the politicians.
The following news from China appeared in The Sun, of
New York, on Christmas Eve. The italics are mine:
     The Rev. Mr. Ament, of the American Board of Foreign
Missions, has returned from a trip which he made for the
purpose of collecting indemnities for damages done by
Boxers.[1] Everywhere he went he compelled the Chinese to
pay. He says that all his native Christians are now
provided for. He had 700 of them under his charge, and 300
were killed. He has collected 300 taels for each of these
murders, and has compelled full payment for all the property
belonging to Christians that was destroyed. He also
assessed fines amounting to THIRTEEN TIMES the amount of the
indemnity. This money will be used for the propagation of
the Gospel.
     Mr. Ament declares that the compensation he has collected
is moderate, when compared with the amount secured by the
Catholics, who demand, in addition to money, head for head.
They collected 500 taels for each murder of a Catholic. In
the Wenchiu country, 680 Catholics were killed, and for this
the European Catholics here demand 750,000 strings of cash
and 680 heads.
     In the course of a conversation, Mr. Ament referred to the
attitude of the missionaries toward the Chinese. He said:
     'I deny emphatically that the missionaries are
vindictive, that they generally looted, or that they have
done anything since the siege that the circumstances did not
demand. I criticise the Americans. The soft hand of the
Americans is not as good as the mailed fist of the Germans.
If you deal with the Chinese with a soft hand they will take
advantage of it.'
     The statement that the French Government will return the
loot taken by the French soldiers, is the source of the
greatest amusement here. The French soldiers were more
systematic looters than the Germans, and it is a fact that
to-day catholic Christians, carrying French flags and armed
with modern guns, are looting villages in the Province of
Chili.

By happy luck, we get all these glad tidings on Christmas
Eve--just in time to enable us to celebrate the day with proper
gaiety and enthusiasm. Our spirits soar, and we find we can even
make jokes: Taels I win, Heads you lose.
Our Reverend Ament is the right man in the right place.
What we want of our missionaries out there is, not that they
shall merely represent in their acts and persons the grace and
gentleness and charity and loving kindness of our religion, but
that they shall also represent the American spirit. The oldest
Americans are the Pawnees. Macallum's History says:

> When a white Boxer kills a Pawnee and destroys his
> property, the other Pawnees do not trouble to seek him out,
> they kill any white person that comes along; also, they make
> some white village pay deceased's heirs the full cash value
> of deceased, together with full cash value of the property
> destroyed; they also make the village pay, in addition,
> thirteen times the value of that property into a fund for the
> dissemination of the Pawnee religion, which they regard as
> the best of all religions for the softening and humanizing
> of the heart of man. It is their idea that it is only fair
> and right that the innocent should be made to suffer for the
> guilty, and that it is better that ninety and nine innocent
> should suffer than that one guilty person should escape.

Our Reverand Ament is justifiably jealous of those
enterprising Catholics, who not only get big money for each lost
convert, but get "head for head" besides. But he should soothe
himself with the reflection that the entirety of their exactions
are for their own pockets, whereas he, less selfishly, devotes
only 300 taels per head to that service, and gives the whole vast
thirteen repetitions of the property-indemnity to the service of
propagating the Gospel. His magnanimity has won him the approval
of his nation, and will get him a monument. Let him be content
with these rewards. We all hold him dear for manfully defending
his fellow missionaries from exaggerated charges which were
beginning to distress us, but which his testimony has so
considerably modified that we can now contemplate them without
noticeable pain. For now we know that, even before the siege,
the missionaries were not "generally" out looting, and that,
"since the siege," they have acted quite handsomely, except when
"circumstances" crowded them. I am arranging for the monument.
Subscriptions for it can be sent to the American Board; designs
for it can be sent to me. Designs must allegorically set forth
the Thirteen Reduplications of the Indemnity, and the Object for
which they were exacted; as Ornaments, the designs must exhibit
680 Heads, so disposed as to give a pleasing and pretty effect;
for the Catholics have done nicely, and are entitled to notice in
the monument. Mottoes may be suggested, if any shall be
discovered that will satisfactorily cover the ground.
Mr. Ament's financial feat of squeezing a thirteen-fold
indemnity out of the pauper peasants to square other people's
offenses, thus condemning them and their women and innocent
little children to inevitable starvation and lingering death, in
order that the blood-money so acquired might be "used for the

propagation of the Gospel," does not flutter my serenity; although
the act and the words taken together, concrete a blasphemy so
hideous and so colossal that, without doubt, its mate is not
findable in the history of this or of any other age. Yet, if a
layman had done that thing and justified it with those words, I
should have shuddered, I know. Or, if I had done the thing and
said the words myself--however, the thought is unthinkable,
irreverent as some imperfectly informed people think me.
Sometimes an ordained minister sets out to be blasphemous. When
this happens, the layman is out of the running; he stands no
chance.

We have Mr. Ament's impassioned assurance that the
missionaries are not "vindictive." Let us hope and pray that
they will never become so, but will remain in the almost morbidly
fair and just and gentle temper which is affording so much
satisfaction to their brother and champion to-day.

The following is from the New York Tribune of Christmas
Eve. It comes from that journal's Tokio correspondent. It has a
strange and impudent sound, but the Japanese are but partially
civilized as yet. When they become wholly civilized they will
not talk so:

> The missionary question, of course, occupies a foremost
> place in the discussion. It is not felt as essential that
> the Western Powers take cognizance of the sentiment here,
> that religious invasions of Oriental countries by powerful
> Western organizations are tantamount to filibustering
> expeditions, and should not only be discountenanced, but
> that stern measures should be adopted for their
> suppression. The feeling here is that the missionary
> organizations constitute a constant menace to peaceful
> international relations.

Shall we? That is, shall we go on conferring our
Civilization upon the peoples that sit in darkness, or shall we
give those poor things a rest? Shall we bang right ahead in our
old-time, loud, pious way, and commit the new century to the
game; or shall we sober up and sit down and think it over first?
Would it not be prudent to get our Civilization-tools together,
and see how much stock is left on hand in the way of Glass Beads
and Theology, and Maxim Guns and Hymn Books, and Trade-Gin and
Torches of Progress and Enlightenment (patent adjustable ones,
good to fire villages with, upon occasion), and balance the
books, and arrive at the profit and loss, so that we may
intelligently decide whether to continue the business or sell out
the property and start a new Civilization Scheme on the proceeds?

Extending the Blessings of Civilization to our Brother who
Sits in Darkness has been a good trade and has paid well, on the
whole; and there is money in it yet, if carefully worked--but not
enough, in my judgment, to make any considerable risk advisable.
The People that Sit in Darkness are getting to be too scarce--too
scarce and too shy. And such darkness as is now left is really
of but an indifferent quality, and not dark enough for the game.
The most of those People that Sit in Darkness have been furnished

with more light than was good for them or profitable for us. We have been injudicious.

The Blessings-of-Civilization Trust, wisely and cautiously administered, is a Daisy. There is more money in it, more territory, more sovereignty, and other kinds of emolument, than there is in any other game that is played. But Christendom has been playing it badly of late years, and must certainly suffer by it, in my opinion. She has been so eager to get every stake that appeared on the green cloth, that the People who Sit in Darkness have noticed it--they have noticed it, and have begun to show alarm. They have become suspicious of the Blessings of Civilization. More--they have begun to examine them. This is not well. The Blessings of Civilization are all right, and a good commercial property; there could not be a better, in a dim light. In the right kind of a light, and at a proper distance, with the goods a little out of focus, they furnish this desirable exhibit to the Gentlemen who Sit in Darkness:

LOVE,	LAW AND ORDER,
JUSTICE,	LIBERTY,
GENTLENESS,	EQUALITY,
CHRISTIANITY,	HONORABLE DEALING,
PROTECTION TO THE WEAK,	MERCY,
TEMPERANCE,	EDUCATION,

--and so on.

There. Is it good? Sir, it is pie. It will bring into camp any idiot that sits in darkness anywhere. But not if we adulterate it. It is proper to be emphatic upon that point. This brand is strictly for Export--apparently. Apparently. Privately and confidentially, it is nothing of the kind. Privately and confidentially, it is merely an outside cover, gay and pretty and attractive, displaying the special patterns of our Civilization which we reserve for Home Consumption, while inside the bale is the Actual Thing that the Customer Sitting in Darkness buys with his blood and tears and land and liberty. That Actual Thing is, indeed, Civilization, but it is only for Export. Is there a difference between the two brands? In some of the details, yes.

We all know that the Business is being ruined. The reason is not far to seek. It is because our Mr. McKinley, and Mr. Chamberlain,[2] and the Kaiser, and the Czar and the French have been exporting the Actual Thing with the outside cover left off. This is bad for the Game. It shows that these new players of it are not sufficiently acquainted with it.

It is a distress to look on and note the mismoves, they are so strange and so awkward. Mr. Chamberlain manufactures a war out of materials so inadequate and so fanciful that they make the boxes grieve and the gallery laugh, and he tries hard to persuade himself that it isn't purely a private raid for cash, but has a sort of dim, vague respectability about it somewhere, if he could only find the spot; and that, by and by, he can scour the flag clean again after he has finished dragging it through the mud, and make it shine and flash in the vault of heaven once more as it had shone and flashed there a thousand years in the world's respect until he laid his unfaithful hand upon it. It is bad play--bad. For it exposes the Actual Thing to Them that Sit in Darkness, and they say:

What! Christian against Christian? And only for money? Is this a case of magnanimity, forbearance, love, gentleness, mercy, protection of the weak--this strange and over-showy onslaught of an elephant upon a nest of field-mice, on the pretext that the mice had squeaked an insolence at him--conduct which 'no self-respecting government could allow to pass unavenged?' as Mr. Chamberlain said. Was that a good pretext in a small case, when it had not been a good pretext in a large one?--for only recently Russia had affronted the elephant three times and survived alive and unsmitten. Is this Civilization and Progress? Is it something better than we already possess? These harryings and burnings and desert-makings in the Transvaal--is this an improvement on our darkness? Is it, perhaps, possible that there are two kinds of Civilization--one for home consumption and one for the heathen market?

Then They that Sit in Darkness are troubled, and shake their heads; and they read this extract from a letter of a British private, recounting his exploits in one of Methuen's victories, some days before the affair of Magersfontein, and they are troubled again:

We tore up the hill and into the intrenchments, and the Boers saw we had them; so they dropped their guns and went down on their knees and put up their hands clasped, and begged for mercy. And we gave it them--with the long spoon.

The long spoon is the bayonet. See Lloyd's Weekly, London, of those days. The same number--and the same column--contained some quite unconscious satire in the form of shocked and bitter upbraidings of the Boers[3] for their brutalities and inhumanities!

Next, to our heavy damage, the Kaiser went to playing the game without first mastering it. He lost a couple of missionaires in a riot in Shantung, and in his account he made an overcharge for them. China had to pay a hundred thousand dollars apiece for them, in money; twelve miles of territory, containing several millions of inhabitants and worth twenty million dollars; and to build a monument, and also a Christian church; whereas the people of China could have been depended upon to remember the missionaries without the help of these expensive memorials. This was all bad play. Bad, because it would not, and could not, and will not now or ever, deceive the Person Sitting in Darkness. He knows that it was an overcharge. He knows that a missionary is like any other man: he is worth merely what you can supply his place for, and no more. He is useful, but so is a doctor, so is a sheriff, so is an editor; but a just Emperor does not charge warprices for such. A diligent, intelligent, but obscure missionary, and a diligent, intelligent country editor are worth much, and we know it; but they are not worth the earth. We esteem such an editor, and we are sorry to see him go; but, when he goes, we should consider twelve miles of territory, and a church, and a fortune, over-compensation for his loss. I mean,

if he was a Chinese editor, and we had to settle for him. It is
no proper figure for an editor or a missionary; one can get
shop-worn kings for less. It was bad play on the Kaiser's part.
It got this property, true; but it produced the Chinese revolt,
the indignant uprising of China's traduced patriots, the Boxers.
The results have been expensive to Germany, and to the other
Disseminators of Progress and the Blessings of Civilization.

The Kaiser's claim was paid, yet it was bad play, for it
could not fail to have an evil effect upon Persons Sitting in
Darkness in China. They would muse upon the event, and be likely
to say:

Civilization is gracious and beautiful, for such is its
reputation; but can we affort it? There are rich Chinamen,
perhaps they could afford it; but this tax is not laid upon
them, it is laid upon the peasants of Shantung; it is they
that must pay this mighty sum, and their wages are but four
cents a day. Is this a better civilization than ours, and
holier and higher and nobler? Is not this rapacity? Is not
this extortion? Would Germany charge America two hundred
thousand dollars for two missionaries, and shake the mailed
fist in her face, and send warships, and send soldiers, and
say: 'Seize twelve miles of territory, worth twenty
millions of dollars, as additional pay for the missionaries;
and make those peasants build a monument to the
missionaries, and a costly Christian church to remember them
by?' And later would Germany say to her soldiers: 'March
through America and slay, giving no quarter; make the German
face there, as has been our Hun-face here, a terror for a
thousand years; march through the Great Republic and slay,
slay, slay, carving a road for our offended religion through
its heart and bowels?' Would Germany do like to America, to
England, to France, to Russia? Or only to China the
helpless--imitating the elephant's assault upon the
field-mice? Had we better invest in this Civilization--this
Civilization which called Napoleon a buccaneer for carrying
off Venice's bronze horses, but which steals our ancient
astronomical instruments from our walls, and goes looting
like common bandits--that is, all the alien soldiers except
America's; and (Americans again excepted) storms frightened
villages and cables the result to glad journals at home
every day: 'Chinese losses, 450 killed; ours, one officer
and two men wounded. Shall proceed against neighboring
village to-morrow, where a massacre is reported.' Can we
afford Civilization?

And, next, Russia must go and play the game injudiciously.
She affronts England one or twice--with the Person Sitting in
Darkness observing and noting; by moral assistance of France and
Germany, she robs Japan of her hard-earned spoil, all swimming in
Chinese blood--Port Arthur--with the Person again observing and
noting; then she seizes Manchuria, raids its villages, and chokes
its great river with the swollen corpses of countless massacred
peasants--that astonished Person still observing and noting. And
perhaps he is saying to himself:

201

It is yet another Civilized Power, with its banner of the Prince of Peace in one hand and its loot-basket and its butcher-knife in the other. Is there no salvation for us but to adopt Civilization and lift ourselves down to its level?

And by and by comes America, and our Master of the Game plays it badly--plays it as Mr. Chamberlain was playing it in South Africa. It was a mistake to do that; also, it was one which was quite unlooked for in a Master who was playing it so well in Cuba. In Cuba, he was playing the usual and regular American game, and it was winning, for there is no way to beat it. The Master, contemplating Cuba, said:

Here is an oppressed and friendless little nation which is willing to fight to be free; we go partners, and put up the strength of seventy million sympathizers and the resources of the United States: play!

Nothing but Europe combined could call that hand: and Europe cannot combine on anything. There, in Cuba, he was following our great traditions in a way which made us very proud of him, and proud of the deep dissatisfaction which his play was provoking in Continental Europe. Moved by a high inspiration, he threw out those stirring words which proclaimed that forcible annexation would be "criminal aggression;" and in that utterance fired another "shot heard round the world." The memory of that fine saying will be outlived by the remembrance of no act of his but one--that he forgot it within the twelvemonth, and its honorable gospel along with it.

For, presently, came the Philippine temptation. It was strong; it was too strong, and he made that bad mistake: he played the European game, the Chamberlain game. It was a pity; it was a great pity, that error; that one grievous error, that irrevocable error. For it was the very place and time to play the American game again. And at no cost. Rich winnings to be gathered in, too; rich and permanent; indestructible; a fortune transmissible forever to the children of the flag. Not land, not money, not dominion--no, something worth many times more than that dross: our share, the spectacle of a nation of long harassed and persecuted slaves set free through our influence; our posterity's share, the golden memory of that fair deed. The game was in our hands. If it had been played according to the American rules, Dewey would have sailed away from Manila as soon as he had destroyed the Spanish fleet[4]--after putting up a sign on shore guaranteeing foreign property and life against damage by the Filipinos, and warning the Powers that interference with the emancipated patriots would be regarded as an act unfriendly to the United States. The Powers cannot combine, in even a bad cause, and the sign would not have been molested.

Dewey could have gone about his affairs elsewhere, and left the competent Filipino army to starve out the little Spanish garrison and send it home, and the Filipino citizens to set up the form of government they might prefer, and deal with the friars and their doubtful acquisitions according to Filipino ideas of fairness and justice--ideas which have since been tested

and found to be of as high an order as any that prevail in Europe
or America.

But we played the Chamberlain game, and lost the chance to
add another Cuba and another honorable deed to our good record.

The more we examine the mistake, the more clearly we
perceive that it is going to be bad for the Business. The Person
Sitting in Darkness is almost sure to say:

"There is something curious about this--curious and
unaccountable. There must be two Americas: one that set
the captive free, and one that takes a once-captive's new
freedom away from him, and picks a quarrel with him with
nothing to found it on; then kills him to get his land."

The truth is, the Person Sitting in Darkness is saying
things like that; and for the sake of the Business we must
persuade him to look at the Philippine matter in another and
healthier way. We must arrange his opinions for him. I believe
it can be done; for Mr. Chamberlain has arranged England's
opinion of the South African matter, and done it most cleverly
and successfully. He presented the facts--some of the facts--and
showed those confiding people what the facts meant. He did it
statistically, which is a good way. He used the formula:
"Twice 2 are 14, and 2 from 9 leaves 35." Figures are effective;
figures will convince the elect.

Now, my plan is a still bolder one than Mr. Chamberlain's,
though apparently a copy of it. Let us be franker than Mr.
Chamberlain; let us audaciously present the whole of the facts,
shirking none, then explain them according to Mr. Chamberlain's
formula. This daring truthfulness will astonish and dazzle the
Person Sitting in Darkness, and he will take the Explanation down
before his mental vision has had time to get back into focus.
Let us say to him:

Our case is simple. On the 1st of May, Dewey destroyed
the Spanish fleet. This left the Archipelago in the hands
of its proper and rightful owners, the Filipino nation.
Their army numbered 30,000 men, and they were competent to
whip out or starve out the little Spanish garrison; then the
people could set up a government of their own devising. Our
traditions required that Dewey should now set up his warning
sign, and go away. But the Master of the Game happened to
think of another plan--the European plan. He acted upon
it. This was, to send out an army--ostensibly to help the
native patriots put the finishing touch upon their long and
plucky struggle for independence, but really to take their
land away from them and keep it. That is, in the interest
of Progress and Civilization. The plan developed, stage by
stage, and quite satisfactorily. We entered into a military
alliance with the trusting Filipinos, and they hemmed in
Manila on the land side, and by their valuable help the
place, with its garrison of 8,000 or 10,000 Spaniards, was
captured--a thing which we could not have accomplished
unaided at that time. We got their help by--by ingenuity.
We knew they were fighting for their independence, and that

they had been at it for two years.[5] We knew they supposed
that we also were fighting in their worthy cause--just as we
had helped the Cubans fight for Cuban independence--and we
allowed them to go on thinking so. Until Manila was ours
and we could get along without them. Then we showed our
hand. Of course, they were surprised--that was natural;
surprised and disappointed; disappointed and grieved. To
them it looked un-American; uncharacteristic; foreign to our
established traditions. And this was natural, too; for we
were only playing the American Game in public--in private it
was the European. It was neatly done, very neatly, and it
bewildered them. They could not understand it; for we had
been so friendly--so affectionate, even--with those
simple-minded patriots! We, our own selves, had brought
back out of exile their leader, their hero, their hope,
their Washington--Aguinaldo; brought him in a warship, in
high honor, under the sacred shelter and hospitality of the
flag; brought him back and restored him to his people, and
got their moving and eloquent gratitude for it. Yes, we had
been so friendly to them, and had heartened them up in so
many ways! We had lent them guns and ammunition; advised
with them; exchanged pleasant courtesies with them; placed
our sick and wounded in their kindly care; entrusted our
Spanish prisoners to their humane and honest hands; fought
shoulder to shoulder with them against "the common enemy"
(our own phrase); praised their courage, praised their
gallantry, praised their mercifulness, praised their fine
and honorable conduct; borrowed their trenches, borrowed
strong positions which they had previously captured from the
Spaniard; petted them, lied to them--officially proclaiming
that our land and naval forces came to give them their
freedom and displace the bad Spanish Government--fooled
them, used them until we needed them no longer; then derided
the sucked orange and threw it away. We keep the positions
which we had beguiled them of; by and by, we moved a force
forward and overlapped patriot ground--a clever thought, for
we needed trouble, and this would produce it. A Filipino
soldier, crossing the ground, where no one had a right to
forbid him, was shot by our sentry. The badgered patriots
resented this with arms, without waiting to know whether
Aguinaldo, who was absent, would approve or not. Aguinaldo
did not approve; but that availed nothing. What we wanted,
in the interest of Progress and Civilization, was the
Archipelago, unencumbered by patriots struggling for
independence; and War was what we needed. We clinched our
opportunity. It is Mr. Chamberlain's case over again--at
least in its motive and intention; and we played the game as
adroitly as he played it himself.

At this point in our frank statement of fact to the Person
Sitting in Darkness, we should throw in a little trade-taffy
about the Blessings of Civilization--for a change, and for the
refreshment of his spirit--then go on with our tale:

204

We and the patriots having captured Manila, Spain's
ownership of the Archipelago and her sovereignty over it
were at an end--obliterated--annihilated--not a rag or shred
of either remaining behind. It was then that we conceived
the divinely humorous idea of buying both of these spectres
from Spain! [It is quite safe to confess this to the Person
Sitting in Darkness, since neither he nor any other sane
person will believe it.] In buying those ghosts for twenty
millions,[7] we also contracted to take care of the friars
and their accumulations. I think we also agreed to
propagate leprosy and smallpox, but as to this there is
doubt. But it is not important; persons afflicted with the
friars do not mind other diseases.

With our Treaty ratified, Manila subdued, and our Ghosts
secured, we had no further use for Aguinaldo and the owners
of the Archipelago. We forced a war, and we have been
hunting America's guest and ally through the woods and
swamps ever since.

At this point in the tale, it will be well to boast a little
of our war-work and our heroisms in the field, so as to make our
performance look as fine as England's in South Africa; but I
believe it will not be best to emphasize this too much. We must
be cautious. Of course, we must read the war-telegrams to the
Person, in order to keep up our frankness; but we can throw an
air of humorousness over them, and that will modify their grim
eloquence a little, and their rather indiscreet exhibitions of
gory exultation. Before reading to him the following display
heads of the dispatches of November 18, 1900, it will be well to
practice on them in private first, so as to get the right tang of
lightness and gaiety into them:

"ADMINISTRATION WEARY OF PROTRACTED HOSTILITIES!"
"REAL WAR AHEAD FOR FILIPINO REBELS!"*
"WILL SHOW NO MERCY!"
"KITCHENER'S PLAN ADOPTED!"

Kitchener knows how to handle disagreeable people who are
fighting for their homes and their liberties, and we must let on
that we are merely imitating Kitchener,[8] and have no national
interest in the matter, further than to get ourselves admired by
the Great Family of Nations, in which august company our Master
of the Game has bought a place for us in the back row.

Of course, we must not venture to ignore our General
MacArthur's reports--oh, why do they keep on printing those
embarrassing things?--we must drop them trippingly from the
tongue and take the chances:

During the last ten months our losses have been 268
killed and 750 wounded; Filipino loss, three thousand two
hundred and twenty-seven killed, and 694 wounded.

---

*"Rebels!" Mumble that funny word--don't let the Person
catch it distincctly.

205

We must stand ready to grab the Person Sitting in Darkness, for he will swoon away at this confession, saying: "Good God, those 'niggers' spare their wounded, and the Americans massacre theirs!"

We must bring him to, and coax him and coddle him, and assure him that the ways of Providence are best, and that it would not become us to find fault with them; and then, to show him that we are only imitators, not originators, we must read the following passage from the letter of an American soldier-lad in the Philippines to his mother, published in Public Opinion, of Decorah, Iowa, describing the finish of a victorious battle:

WE NEVER LEFT ONE ALIVE. IF ONE WAS WOUNDED, WE WOULD RUN OUR BAYONETS THROUGH HIM.

Having now laid all the historical facts before the Person Sitting in Darkness, we should bring him to again, and explain them to him. We should say to him:

They look doubtful, but in reality they are not. There have been lies; yes, but they were told in a good cause. We have been treacherous; but that was only in order that real good might come out of apparent evil. True, we have crushed a deceived and confiding people; we have turned against the weak and the friendless who trusted us; we have stamped out a just and intelligent and well-ordered republic; we have stabbed an ally in the back and slapped the face of a guest; we have bought a Shadow from an enemy that hadn't it to sell; we have robbed a trusting friend of his land and his liberty; we have invited our clean young men to shoulder a discredited musket and do bandit's work under a flag which bandits have been accustomed to fear, not to follow; we have debauched America's honor and blackened her face before the world; but each detail was for the best. We know this. The Head of every State and Sovereignty in Christendom and ninety per cent. of every legislative body in Christendom, including our Congress and our fifty State Legislatures, are members not only of the church, but also of the Blessings-of-Civilization Trust. This world-girdling accumulation of trained morals, high principles, and justice, cannot do an unright thing, an unfair thing, an ungenerous thing, an unclean thing. It knows what it is about. Give yourself no uneasiness; it is all right.

Now then, that will convince the Person. You will see. It will restore the Business. Also, it will elect the Master of the Game to the vacant place in the Trinity of our national gods; and there on their high thrones the Three will sit, age after age, in the people's sight, each bearing the Emblem of his service: Washington, the Sword of the Liberator; Lincoln, the Slave's Broken Chains; the Master, the Chains Repaired.

It will give the Business a splendid new start. You will see.

Everything is prosperous, now; everything is just as we should wish it. We have got the Archipelago, and we shall never give it up. Also, we have every reason to hope that we shall have an opportunity before very long to slip out of our

Congressional contract with Cuba and give her something better in the place of it.[9] It is a rich country, and many of us are already beginning to see that the contract was a sentimental mistake. But now--right now--is the best time to do some profitable rehabilitating work--work that will set us up and make us comfortable, and discourage gossip. We cannot conceal from ourselves that, privately, we are a little troubled about our uniform. It is one of our prides; it is acquainted with honor; it is familiar with great deeds and noble; we love it, we revere it; and so this errand it is on makes us uneasy. And our flag--another pride of ours, our chiefest! We have worshipped it so; and when we have seen it in far lands--glimpsing it unexpectedly in that strange sky, waving its welcome and benediction to us--we have caught our breath, and uncovered our heads, and couldn't speak for a moment, for the thought of what it was to us and the great ideals it stood for. Indeed, we must do something about these things; we must not have the flag out there, and the uniform. They are not needed there; we can manage in some other way. England manages, as regards the uniform, and so can we. We have to send soldiers--we can't get out of that--but we can disguise them. It is the way England does in South Africa. Even Mr. Chamberlain himself takes pride in England's honorable uniform, and makes the army down there wear an ugly and odious and appropriate disguise, of yellow stuff such as quarantine flags are made of, and which are hoisted to warn the healthy away from unclean disease and repulsive death. This cloth is called khaki. We could adopt it. It is light, comfortable, grotesque, and deceives the enemy, for he cannot conceive of a soldier being concealed in it.

And as for a flag for the Philippine Province, it is easily managed. We can have a special one--our States do it: we can have just our usual flag, with the white stripes painted black and the stars replaced by the skull and cross-bones.

And we do not need that Civil Commission out there. Having no powers, it has to invent them, and that kind of work cannot be effectively done by just anybody; an expert is required. Mr. Croker can be spared. We do not want the United States represented there, but only the Game.

By help of these suggested amendments, Progress and Civilization in that country can have a boom, and it will take in the Persons who are Sitting in Darkness, and we can resume Business at the old stand.

North American Review, vol. CLXXII, February, 1901, pp. 161-76.

TO MY MISSIONARY CRITICS.

I have received many newspaper cuttings; also letters from several clergymen; also a note from the Rev. Dr. Judson Smith, Corresponding Secretary of the American Board of Foreign Missions--all of a like tenor; all saying, substantially, what is said in the cutting here copied:

"AN APOLOGY DUE FROM MR. CLEMENS.

The evidence of the past day or two should induce Mark Twain to make for the amen corner and formulate a prompt apology for his scathing attack on the Rev. Dr. Ament, the veteran Chinese missionary. The assault was based on a Pekin dispatch to the New York Sun, which said that Dr. Ament had collected from the Chinese in various places damages thirteen times in excess of actual losses. So Mark Twain charged Mr. Ament with bullyragging, extortion and things. A Pekin dispatch to the Sun yesterday, however, explains that the amount collected was not thirteen times the damage sustained, but one-third in excess of the indemnities, and that the blunder was due to a cable error in transmission. The 1-3d got converted into 13. Yesterday the Rev. Judson Smith, Secretary of the American Board, received a dispatch from Dr. Ament, calling attention to the cable blunder, and declaring that all the collections which he made were approved by the Chinese officials. The fractional amount that was collected in excess of actual losses, he explains, is being used for the support of widows and orphans.

So collapses completely--and convulsively--Mark Twain's sensational and ugly bombardment of a missionary whose character and services should have exempted him from such an assault.

From the charge the underpinning has been knocked out. To Dr. Ament Mr. Clemens has done an injustice which is gross but unintentional. If Mark Twain is the man we take him to be he won't be long in filing a retraction, plus an apology.

I have no prejudice against apologies. I trust I shall never withhold one when it is due; I trust I shall never even have a disposition to do so. These letters and newspaper paragraphs are entitled to my best attention; respect for their writers and for the humane feeling which has prompted their utterances requires this of me. It may be barely possible that, if these requests for an apology had reached me before the 20th of February, I might have had a sort of qualified chance to apologize; but on that day appeared the two little cablegrams referred to in the newspaper cutting copied above--one from the Rev. Dr. Smith to the Rev. Dr. Ament, the other from Dr. Ament to Dr. Smith--and my small chance died then. In my opinion, these cablegrams ought to have been suppressed, for it seems clear that they give Dr. Ament's case entirely away. Still, that is only an opinion, and may be a mistake. It will be best to examine the case from the beginning, by the light of the documents connected with it.

EXHIBIT A.

This dispatch from Mr. Chamberlain,* chief of the Sun's correspondence staff in Pekin. It appeared in the Sun last Christmas Eve, and in referring to it hereafter I will call it the "C. E. dispatch" for short:

The Rev. Mr. Ament, of the American Board of Foreign Missions, has returned from a trip which he made for the purpose of collecting indemnities for damages done by Boxers. Everywhere he went he compelled the Chinese to pay. He says that all his native Christians are now provided for. He had 700 of them under his charge, and 300 were killed. He has collected 300 taels for each of these murders, and has compelled full payment for all the property belonging to Christians that was destroyed. He also assessed fines amounting to thirteen times** the amount of the indemnity. This money will be used for the propagation of the Gospel.

Mr. Ament declares that the compensation he has collected is moderate, when compared with the amount secured by the Catholics, who demand, in addition to money, head for head. They collected 500 taels for each murder of a Catholic. In the Wen-Chiu country, 680 Catholics were killed, and for this the European Catholics here demand 750,000 strings of cash and 680 heads.

In the course of a conversation, Mr. Ament referred to the attitude of the missionaries toward the Chinese. He said:

'I deny emphatically that the missionaries are vindictive, that they generally looted, or that they have done anything since the siege that the circumstances did not demand. I criticise the Americans. The soft hand of the Americans is not as good as the mailed fist of the Germans. If you deal with the Chinese with a soft hand they will take advantage of it.'

In an article addressed "To the Person Sitting in Darkness," published in the NORTH AMERICAN REVIEW for February, I made some comments upon this C. E. dispatch.

In an Open Letter to me, from the Rev. Dr. Smith, published in the Tribune of February 15th, doubt is case upon the authenticity of the dispatch.

Up to the 20th of February, this doubt was an important factor in the case: Dr. Ament's brief cablegram, published on that date, took the importance all out of it.

In the Open Letter, Dr. Smith quotes this passage from a letter from Dr. Ament, dated November 13th. The italics are mine:

This time I proposed to settle affairs without the aid of soldiers or legations.

This cannot mean two things, but only one: that, previously, he had collected by armed force.

---

*Testimony of the manager of the Sun.

**Cable error. For "thirteen times" read "one-third." This correction was made by Dr. Ament in his brief cablegram published Feb. 20, above referred to.

210

Also, in the Open Letter, Dr. Smith quotes some praises of Dr. Ament and the Rev. Mr. Tewksbury, furnished by the Ref. Dr. Sheffield, and says:

Dr. Sheffield is not accustomed to speak thus of thieves, or extortioners, or braggarts.

What can he mean by those vigorous expressions? Can he mean that the first two would be applicable to a missionary who should collect from B, with the "aid of soldiers," indemnities possibly due by A, and upon occasion go out looting?

EXHIBIT B

Testimony of George Lynch (endorsed as entirely trustworthy by the Tribune and the Herald), war correspondent in the Cuban and South African wars, and in the march upon Pekin for the rescue of the legations. The italics are mine:

When the soldiers were prohibited from looting, no such prohibitions seemed to operate with the missionaires. For instance, the Rev. Mr. Tweksbury held a great sale of looted goods, which lasted several days.

A day or two after the relief, when looking for a place to sleep in, I met the Rev. Mr. Ament, of the American Board of Foreign Missions. He told me he was going to take possession of the house of a wealthy Chinaman who was an old enemy of his, as he had interfered much in the past with his missionary labors in Pekin. A couple of days afterward he did so, and held a great sale of his enemy's effects. I bought a sable cloak at it for $125, and a couple of statues of Buddah. As the stock became depleted it was replenished by the efforts of his converts, who were ransacking the houses in the neighborhood.--N.Y. Herald, Feb. 18.

It is Dr. Smith, not I, who has suggested that persons who act in this way are "thieves and extortioners."

EXHIBIT C

Sir Robert Hart, in the Fortnightly Review for January, 1901. This witness has been for many years the most prominent and important Englishman in China, and bears an irreproachable reputation for moderation, fairness and truth-speaking. In closing a description of the revolting scenes which followed the occupation of Pekin, when the Christian armies (with the proud exception of the American soldiery, let us be thankful for that,) gave themselves up to a ruthless orgy of robbery and spoliation, he says (the italics are mine):

And even some missionaries took such a leading part in 'spoiling the Egyptians' for the greater glory of God that a bystander was heard to say: 'For a century to come Chinese converts will consider looting and vengeance Christian virtues.'

It is Dr. Smith, not I, who has suggested that persons who act in this way are "thieves and extortioners." According to Mr. Lynch and Mr. Martin (another war correspondent), Dr. Ament helped to spoil several of those Egyptians. Mr. Martin took a photograph of the scene. It was reproduced in the Herald. I have it.

211

EXHIBIT D

In a brief reply to Dr. Smith's Open Letter to me, I said
this in the Tribune. I am italicizing several words--for a
purpose:

Whenever he (Dr. Smith) can produce from the Rev. Mr. Ament
an assertion that the Sun's character-blasting dispatch was
not authorized by him, and whenever Dr. Smith can buttress
Mr. Ament's disclaimer with a confession from
Mr. Chamberlain, the head of the Laffan News Service in
China, that that dispatch was a false invention and
unauthorized, the case against Mr. Ament will fall at once
to the ground.

EXHIBIT E

Brief cablegrams, referred to above, which passed between
Dr. Smith and Dr. Ament, and were published on February 20th:

Ament, Peking: Reported December 24 your collecting
thirteen times actual losses; using for propagating the
Gospel. Are these statements true? Cable specific answer.
                                                    SMITH.
Statement untrue. Collected 1-3 for church expenses,
additional actual damages; now supporting widows and
orphans. Publication thirteen times blunder cable. All
collections received approval Chinese officials, who are
urging further settlements same line.   AMENT.

Only two questions are asked; "specific" answers required;
no perilous wanderings among the other details of the unhappy
dispatch desired.

EXHIBIT F

Letter from Dr. Smith to me, dated March 8th. The italics
are mine; they tag inaccuracies of statement:

Permit me to call your attention to the marked paragraphs in
the inclosed papers, and to ask you to note their relation
to the two conditions named in your letter to the New York
Tribune of February 15th.
The first is Dr. Ament's denial of the truth of the dispatch
in the New York 'Sun' of December 24th, on which your
criticisms of him in the NORTH AMERICAN REVIEW of February
were founded. The second is a correction by the 'Sun's'
special correspondent in Peking of the dispatch printed in
the Sun of December 24th.
Since, as you state in your letter to the Tribune, 'the case
against Mr. Ament would fall to the ground' if Mr. Ament
denied the truth of the Sun's first dispatch, and if the
Sun's news agency in Peking also declared that dispatch
false, and these two conditions have thus been fulfilled, I
am sure that upon having these facts brought to your
attention you will gladly withdraw the criticisms that were
founded on a 'cable blunder.'

I think Dr. Smith ought to read me more carefully; then he
would not make so many mistakes. Within the narrow space of two
paragraphs, totaling eleven lines, he has scored nine departures

from fact out of a possible 9 1/2. Now, is that parliamentary? I do not treat him like that. Whenever I quote him, I am particular not to do him the least wrong, or make him say anything he did not say.

(1.) Mr. Ament doesn't "deny the truth of the C. E. dispatch;" he merely changes one of its phrases, without materially changing the meaning, and (immaterially) corrects a cable blunder (which correction I accept). He was asked to question about the other four-fifths of the C. E. dispatch. (2.) I said nothing about "special" correspondents; I named the right and responsible man--Mr. Chamberlain. The "correction" referred to is a repetition of the one I have just accepted, which (immaterially) changes "thirteen times" to "one-third" extra-tax. (3.) I did not say anything about "the Sun's news agency;" I said "Chamberlain." I have every confidence in Mr. Chamberlain, but I am not personally acquainted with the others. (4.) Once more--Mr. Ament did't "deny the truth" of the C. E. dispatch, but merely made unimportant emendations of a couple of its many details. (5.) I did not say "if Mr. Ament denied the truth" of the C. E. dispatch: I said, if he would assert that the dispatch was not "authorized' by him. For example, I did not suppose that the charge that the Catholic missionaries wanted 680 Chinamen beheaded was true; but I did want to know if Dr. Ament personally authorized that statement and the others, as coming from his lips. Another detail: one of my conditions was that Mr. Chamberlain must not stop with confessing that the C. E. was a "false invention," he must also confess that it was "unauthorized." Dr. Smith has left out that large detail. (6.) The Sun's news agency did not "declare the C. E. dispatch false," but confined itself to correcting one unimportant detail of its long list--the change of "13 times" to "one-third" extra. (7.) The "two conditions" have not "been fulfilled"--far from it. (8.) Those details labeled "facts" are only fancies. (9.) Finally, my criticisms were by no means confined to that detail of the C. E. dispatch which we now accept as having been a "cable blunder."

Setting to one side these nine departures from fact, I find that what is left of the eleven lines is straight and true. I am not blaming Dr. Smith for these discrepancies--it would not be right, it would not be fair. I make the proper allowances. He has not been a journalist, as I have been-a trade wherein a person is brought to book by the rest of the press so often for divergencies that, by and by, he gets to be almost morbidly afraid to indulge in them. It is so with me. I always have the disposition to tell what is not so; I was born with it; we all have it. But I try not to do it now, because I have found out that it is unsafe. But with the Doctor of course it is different.

EXHIBIT G

I wanted to get at the whole of the facts as regards the C. E. dispatch, and so I wrote to China for them, when I found that the Board was not going to do it. But I am not allowed to wait. It seemed quite within the possibilities that a full detail of the facts might furnish me a chance to make an apology to Mr. Ament--a chance which, I give you my word, I would have honestly used, and not abused. But it is no matter. If the Board is not troubled about the bulk of that lurid dispatch, why should I be? I answered the apology-urging letters of several clergymen with the information that I had written to China for the details, and said I thought it was the only sure way of getting into a position to do fair and full justice to all concerned; but a couple of them replied that it was not a matter that could wait. That is to say, groping your way out of a jungle in the dark with guesses and conjectures is better than a straight march out in the sunlight of fact. It seems a curious idea.

However, those two clergymen were in a large measure right--from their point of view and the Board's; which is, putting it in the form of a couple of questions:

1. Did Dr. Ament collect the assessed damages and thirteen times over? The answer is: He did not. He collected only a third over.

2. Did he apply the third to the "propagation of the Gospel?" The answer is this correction: He applied it to "church expenses." Part or all of the outlay, it appears, goes to "supporting widows and orphans." It may be that church expenses and supporting widows and orphans are not part of the machinery for propagating the Gospel. I supposed they were, but it isn't any matter; I prefer this phrasing; it is not so blunt as the other.

In the opinion of the two clergymen and of the Board, these two points are the only important ones in the whole C. E. dispatch.

I accept that. Therefore let us throw out the rest of the dispatch as being no longer a part of Dr. Ament's case.

EXHIBIT H

The two clergymen and the Board are quite content with Dr. Ament's answers upon the two points.

Upon the first point of the two, my own viewpoint may be indicated by a question:

Did Dr. Ament collect from B, (whether by compulsion or simple demand), even so much as a penny in payment for murders or depredations, without knowing, beyond question, that B, and not another, committed the murders or the depredations?

Or, in other words:

Did Dr. Ament ever, by chance or through ignorance, make the innocent pay the debts of the guilty?

In the article entitled "To the Person Sitting in Darkness," I put foward that point in a paragraph taken from Macallum's (imaginary) "History":

When a white Boxer kills a Pawnee and destroys his property, the other Pawnees do not trouble to seek him out, they kill any white person that comes along; also, they make some white village pay deceased's heirs the full cash value of deceased, together with full cash value of the property destroyed; they also make the village pay, in addition,

thirteen times* the value of that property into a fund for
the dissemination of the Pawnee religion, which they regard
as the best of all religions for the softening and
humanizing of the heart of man. It is their idea that it is
only fair and right that the innocent should be made to
suffer for the guilty, and that it is better that ninety and
nine innocent should suffer than that one guilty person
should escape.

We all know that Dr. Ament did not bring suspected persons
into a duly organized court and try them by just and fair
Christian and civilized methods, but proclaimed his "conditions,"
and collected damages from the innocent and the guilty alike,
without any court proceedings at all.** That he himself, and not
the villagers, made the "conditions," we learn from his letter of
November 13th, already quoted from--the one in which he remarked
that, upon that occasion, he brought no soldiers with him. The
italics are mine:

After our conditions were known many villagers came of their
own accord and brought their money with them.

Not all, but "many." The Board really believes that those
hunted and harried paupers out there were not only willing to
strip themselves to pay Boxer damages, whether they owed them or
not, but were sentimentally eager to do it. Mr. Ament says, in
his letter: "The villagers were extremely grateful because I
brought no foreign soldiers, and were glad to settle on the terms
proposed." Some of those people know more about theology than
they do about human nature. I do not remember encountering even
a Christian who was "glad" to pay money he did not owe; and as
for a Chinaman doing it, why, dear me, the thing is unthinkable.
We have all seen Chinamen, many Chinamen, but not that kind. It
is a new kind: an invention of the Board--and "soldiers."

CONCERNING THE COLLECTIONS

What was the "one-third extra"? Money due? No. Was it a
theft, then? Putting aside the "one-third extra," what was the
remainder of the exacted indemnity, if collected from persons not
known to owe it, and without Christian and civilized forms of
procedure? Was it theft, was it robbery? In America it would be
that; in Christian Europe it would be that. I have great
confidence in Dr. Smith's judgment concerning this detail, and he

----

*For "thirteen times" read "one-third."--M. T.

**In civilized countries, if a mob destroy property in a
town, the damage is paid out of the town treasury, and no tax-
payer suffers a disproportionate share of the burden; the mayor is
not privileged to distribute the burden according to his private
notions, sparing himself and his friends, and fleecing persons he
holds a spite against--as in the Orient--and the citizen who is
too poor to be a tax-payer pays no part of the fine at all.

calls it "theft and extortion"--even in China; for he was talking
about the "thirteen times" at the time that he gave it that strong
name.* It is his idea that, when you make guilty and innocent
villagers pay the appraised damages, and then make them pay
thirteen times that, besides, the thirteen stand for "theft and
extortion."

Then what does one-third extra stand for? Will he give that
one-third a name? Is it Modified Theft and Extortion? Is that
it? The girl who was rebuked for having borne an illegitimate
child, excused herself by saying, "But it is such a little one."

When the "thirteen-times-extra" was alleged, it stood for
theft and extortion, in Dr. Smith's eyes, and he was shocked.
But when Dr. Ament showed that he had taken only a third extra,
instead of thirteen-fold, Dr. Smith was relieved, content,
happy. I declare I cannot imagine why. That editor--quoted at
the head of this article--was happy about it, too. I cannot
think why. He thought I ought to "make for the amen corner and
formulate a prompt apology." To whom, and for what? It is too
deep for me.

To Dr. Smith, the "thirteen-fold-extra" clearly stood for
"theft and extortion," and he was right, distinctly right,
indisputably right. He manifestly thinks that when it got scaled
away down to a mere "one-third," a little thing like that was
something other than "theft and extortion." Why? Only the Board
knows! I will try to explain this difficult problem, so that the
Board can get an idea of it. If a pauper owes me a dollar, and I
catch him unprotected and make him pay me fourteen dollars,
thirteen of it is "theft and extortion"; if I make him pay only a
dollar and thirty-three and a third cents, the thirty-three and a
third cents are "theft and extortion" just the same. I will put
it in another way, still simpler. If a man owes me one dog--any
kind of a dog, the breed is of no consequence--and I---- But let
it go; the Board would never understand it. It can't understand
these involved and difficult things.

But if the Board could understand, then I could furnish some
more instruction--which is this. The one-third, obtained by
"theft and extortion," is tainted money, and cannot be purified
even by defraying "church expenses" and "supporting widows and
orphans" with it. It has to be restored to the people it was
taken from.

---

*In his Open Letter, Dr. Smith cites Dr. Ament's letter of
November 13th, which contains an account of Dr. Ament's
collecting-tour; then Dr. Smith makes this comment: "Nothing is
said of securing 'thirteen times' the amount of the losses."
Further down, Dr. Smith quotes praises of Dr. Ament and his work
(from a letter of the Rev. Dr. Sheffield), and adds this
comment: "Dr. Sheffield is not accustomed to speak thus in
praise of thieves, or extortioners, or braggarts." The reference
is to the "thirteen-times" extra-tax.

Also, there is another view of these things. By our
Christian code of morals and law, the whole $1.33 1-3, if taken
from a man not formally proven to have committed the damage the
dollar represents, is "theft and extortion." It cannot be
honestly used for any purpose at all. It must be handed back to
the man it was taken from.

Is there no way, then, to justify these thefts and
extortions and make them clean and fair and honorable? Yes,
there is. It can be done; it has been done; it continues to be
done--by revising the Ten Commandments and bringing them down to
date: for use in pagan lands. For example:

Thou shall not steal--except when it is the custom of the
country.

This way out is recognized and approved by all the best
authorities, including the Board. I will cite witnesses.

The newspaper cutting, above: "Dr. Ament declares that all
the collections which he made were approved by the Chinese
officials." The editor is satisfied.

Dr. Ament's cable to Dr. Smith: "All collections received
approval Chinese officials." Dr. Ament is satisfied.

Letters from eight clergymen--all to the same effect:
Dr. Ament merely did as the Chinese do. So they are satisfied.

Mr. Ward, of the Independent.

The Rev. Dr. Washington Gladden.

I have mislaid the letters of these gentlemen and cannot
quote their words, but they are of the satisfied.

The Rev. Dr. Smith, in His Open Letter, published in the
Tribune: "The whole procedure (Dr. Ament's), is in accordance
with a custom among the Chinese, of holding a village responsible
for wrongs suffered in that village, and especially making the
head man of the village accountable for wrongs committed there."
Dr. Smith is satisfied. Which means that the Board is satisfied.

The "head man"! Why, then, this poor rascal, innocent or
guilty, must pay the whole bill, if he cannot squeeze it out of
his poor-devil neighbors. But, indeed, he can be depended upon
to try, even to the skinning them of their last brass farthing,
their last rag of clothing, their last ounce of food. He can be
depended upon to get the indemnity out of them, though it cost
stripes and blows, blood, tears and flesh.

THE TALE OF THE KING AND HIS TREASURER

How strange and remote and romantic and Oriental and
Arabian-Nighty it all seems--and is. It brings back the old
forgotten tales, and we hear the King say to his Treasurer:

"Bring me 30,000 gold tomauns."

"Allah preserve us, Sire! the treasury is empty."

"Do you hear? Bring the money--in ten days. Else, send me
your head in a basket."

"I hear and obey."

The Treasurer summons the head men of a hundred villages,
and says to one:

"Bring me a hundred gold tomauns." To another, "Bring me five hundred;" to another, "Bring a thousand. In ten days. Your head is the forfeit."

"Your slaves kiss your feet! Ah, high and mighty lord, be merciful to our hard pressed villagers: they are poor, they are naked, they starve; oh, these impossible sums! even the half----"

"Go! Grind it out of them, crush it out of them, turn the blood of the fathers, the tears of the mothers, the milk of the babes to money--or take the consequences. Have you heard?"

"His will be done, Who is the Fount of love and mercy and compassion, Who layeth this heavy burden upon us by the hand of His anointed servants--blessed be His holy Name! The father shall bleed, the mother shall faint for hunger, the babe shall perish at the dry breast. The chosen of God have commended: it shall be as they say."

I am not meaning to object to the substitution of pagan customs for Christian, here and there and now and then, when the Christian ones are inconvenient. No; I like it and admire it. I do it myself. And I admire the alertness of the Board in watching out for chances to trade Board morals for Chinese morals, and get the best of the swap; for I cannot endure those people, they are yellow, and I have never considered yellow becoming. I have always been like the Board--perfectly well meaning, but destitute of the Moral Sense. Now, one of the main reasons why it is so hard to make the Board understand that there is no moral difference between a big filch and a little filch, but only a legal one, is that vacancy in its make-up. Morally, there are no degrees in stealing. The Commandment merely says, "Thou shalt not steal," and stops there. It doesn't recognize any difference between stealing a third and stealing thirteenfold. If I could think of a way to put it before the Board in such a plain and--

THE WATERMELONS

I have it, now. Many years ago, when I was studying for the gallows, I had a dear comrade, a youth who was not in my line, but still a thoroughly good fellow, though devious. He was preparing to qualify for a place on the Board, for there was going to be a vacancy by superannuation in about five years. This was down South, in the slavery days. It was the nature of the negro then, as now, to steal watermelons.[10] They stole three of the melons of an adoptive brother of mine, the only good ones he had. I suspected three of a neighbor's negroes, but there was no proof: and, besides, the watermelons in those negroes' private patches were all green and small, and not up to indemnity standard. But in the private patches of three other negroes there was a number of competent melons. I consulted with my comrade, the understudy of the Board. He said that if I would approve his arrangements, he would arrange. I said, "Consider me the Board; I approve:arrange." So he took a gun, and went and collected three large melons for my brother-on-the-half-shell, and one over. I was greatly pleased, and asked:

"Who gets the extra one?"

"Widows and orphans."

"A good idea, too. Why didn't you take thirteen?"

"It would have been wrong; a crime, in fact--Theft and Extortion."

"What is the one-third extra--the odd melon--the same?"

It caused him to reflect. But there was no result.

The justice of the peace was a stern man. On the trial, he found fault with the scheme, and required us to explain upon what we based our strange conduct--as he called it. The understudy said:

"On the custom of the niggers. They all do it."

The justice forgot his dignity, and descended to scarcasm:

"Custom of the niggers! Are our morals so inadequate that we have to borrow of niggers?" Then he said to the jury: "Three melons were owing; they were collected from persons not proven to owe them; this is theft. They were collected by compulsion; this is extortion. A melon was added--for the widows and orphans. It was owed by no one. It is another theft, another extortion. Return it whence it came, with the others. It is not permissible, here, to apply to any object goods dishonestly obtained--not even to the feeding of widows and orphans, for that would be to put a shame upon charity and dishonor it."

He said it in open court, before everybody, and to me it did not seem very kind.

A clergyman, in a letter to me, reminds me, with a touch of reproach, that "many of the missionaries are good men, kindhearted, earnest, devoted to their work." Certainly they are. No one is disputing it. Instead of "many," he could have said "almost all," and still said the truth, no doubt. I know many missionaries; I have met them all about the globe, and have known only one or two who could not fill that bill and answer to that description. "Almost all" comes near to being a proportion and a description applicable also to lawyers, authors, editors, merchants, manufacturers--in fact to most guilds and vocations. Without a doubt, Dr. Ament did what he believed to be right, and I concede that when a man is doing what he believes to be right, there is argument on his side. I differ with Dr. Ament, but that is only because he got his training from the Board and I got mine outside. Neither of us is responsible, altogether.

RECAPITULATION

But there is no need to sum up. Mr. Ament has acknowledged the "one-third extra"--no other witness is necessary. The Rev. Dr. Smith has carefully considered the act and labeled it with a stern name, and his verdict seems to have no flaw in it. The morals of the act are Chinese, but are approved by the Board, and by some of the clergy and some of the newspapers, as being a valuable improvement upon Christian ones--which leaves me with a closed mouth, though with a pain in my heart.

IS THE AMERICAN BOARD ON TRIAL?

Do I think that Dr. Ament and certain of his fellow missionaries are as bad as their conduct? No, I do not. They are the product of their training; and now that I understand the whole case, and where they got their ideals, and that they are merely subordinates and subject to authority, I comprehend that they are rather accessories than principals, and that their acts only show faulty heads curiously trained, not bad hearts.

Mainly, as it seems to me, it is the American Board that is on trial. And again, it is a case of the head, not of the heart. That it has a heart which has never harbored an evil intention, no one will deny, no one will question; the Board's history can silence any challenge on that score. The Board's heart is not in court: it is its head that is on trial.

It is a sufficiently strange head. Its ways baffle comprehension; its ideas are like no one else's; its methods are novelties to the practical world; its judgments are surprises. When one thinks it is going to speak and must speak, it is silent; when one thinks it ought to be silent and must be silent, it speaks. Put your finger where you think it ought to be, it is not there; put it where you think it ought not to be, there you find it.

When its servant in China seemed to be charging himself with amazing things, in a reputable journal,--in a dispatch which was copied into many other papers--the Board was as silent about it as any dead man could have been who was informed that his house was burning over his head. An exchange of cablegrams could have enabled it, within two days, to prove to the world--possibly-- that the damaging dispatch had not proceeded from the mouth of its servant; yet it sat silent and asked no questions about the matter.

It was silent during thirty-eight days. Then the dispatch came into prominence again. It chanced that I was the occasion of it. A break in the stillness followed. In what form? An exchange of cablegrams, resulting in proof that the damaging dispatch had not been authorized? No, in the form of an Open Letter by the Corresponding Secretary of the American Board, the Rev. Dr. Smith, in which it was argued that Dr. Ament could not have said and done the things set forth in the dispatch.

Surely, this was bad politics. A repudiating telegram would have been worth more than a library of argument.

An extension of the silence would have been better than the Open Letter, I think. I thought so at the time. It seemed to me that mistakes enough had been made and harm enough done. I thought it questionable policy to publish the Letter, for I "did not think it likely that Dr. Ament would disown the dispatch," and I telegraphed that the the Rev. Dr. Smith. Personally, I had nothing against Dr. Ament, and that is my attitude yet.

Once more it was a good time for an extension of the silence. But no; the Board has its own ways, and one of them is to do the unwise thing, when occasion offers. After having waited fifty-six days, it cabled to Dr. Ament. No one can divine why it did so then, instead of fifty-six days earlier.* It got a fatal reply--and was not aware of it. That was the curious confession about the "one-third extra"; its application, not to the "propagation of the Gospel," but only to "church expenses,"

220

support of widows and orphans; and, on top of this confession, that other strange one revealing the dizzying fact that our missionaries, who went to China to teach Christian morals and justice, had adopted pagan morals and justice in their place. That cablegram was dynamite.

It seems odd that the Board did not see that that revelation made the case far worse than it was before; for there was a saving doubt, before--a doubt which was a Gibraltar for strength, and should have been carefully left undisturbed. Why did the Board allow that revelation to get into print? Why did the Board not suppress it and keep still? But no; in the Board's opinion, this was once more the time for speech. Hence Dr. Smith's latest letter to me, suggesting that I speak also--a letter which is a good enough letter, barring its nine defects, but is another evidence that the Board's head is not as good as its heart.

A missionary is a man who is pretty nearly all heart, else he would not be in a calling which requires of him such large sacrifices of one kind and another. He is made up of faith, zeal, courage, sentiment, emotion, enthusiasm; and so he is a mixture of poet, devotee and knight-errant. He exiles himself from home and friends and the scenes and associations that are dearest to him; patiently endures discomforts, privations, discouragements; goes with good pluck into dangers which he knows may cost him his life; and when he must suffer death, willingly makes that supreme sacrifice for his cause.

Sometimes the head-piece of that kind of a man can be of an inferior sort, and errors of judgment can result--as we have seen. Then, for his protection, as it seems to me, he ought to have at his back a Board able to know a blunder when it sees one, and prompt to bring him back upon his right course when he strays from it. That is to say, I think the captain of a ship ought to understand navigation. Whether he does or not, he will have to take a captain's share of the blame, if the crew bring the vessel to grief.

*The cablegram went on the day (Feb. 18) that Mr. George Lynch's account of the looting was published. See "EXHIBIT B." It seems a pity it did not inquire about the looting and get it denied.

North American Review, vol. CLXXII, April 1901, pp. 520-34.

A DEFENCE OF GENERAL FUNSTON

I.

February 22. To-day is the great Birth-Day; and it was observed so widely in the earth that differences in longitudinal time made curious work with some of the cabled testimonies of respect paid to the sublime name which the date calls up in our minds; for, although they were all being offered at about the same hour, several of them were yesterday to us and several were to-morrow.

There was a reference in the papers to General Funston.

Neither Washington nor Funston was made in a day. It took a long time to accumulate the materials. In each case, the basis or moral skeleton of the man was inborn disposition--a thing which is as permanent as rock, and never undergoes any actual and genuine change between cradle and grave. In each case, the moral flesh-bulk (that is to say, character) was built and shaped around the skeleton by training, association and circumstances. Given a crooked-disposition skeleton, no power nor influence in the earth can mould a permanently shapely form around it. Training, association and circumstances can truss it, and brace it, and prop it, and strain it, and crowd it into an artificial shapeliness that can endure till the end, deceiving not only the spectator but the man himself. But there is nothing there but artificiality, and if at any time the props and trusses chance to be removed, the form will collapse into its proper and native crookedness.

Washington did not create the basic skeleton (disposition) that was in him; it was born there, and the merit of its perfection was not his. It--and only It--moved him to seek and prefer associations which were contenting to Its spirit; to welcome influences which pleased It and satisfied It; and to repel or be indifferent to influences which were not to Its taste. Moment by moment, day by day, year by year, It stood in the ceaseless sweep of minute influences, automatically arresting and retaining, like a magnet of mercury, all dust-particles of gold that came; and, with automatic scorn, repelling certain dust-particles of trash, and with as automatic indifference, allowing the rest of that base kinship to go by unnoticed. It had a native affinity for all influences fine and great, and gave them hospitable welcome and permanent shelter; It had a native aversion for all influences, mean and gross, and passed them on. It chose Its subject's associations for him; It chose his influences for him; It chose his ideals for him; and, out of Its patiently gathered materials, It built and shaped his golden character.

And we give him the credit!

We give God credit and praise for being all-wise and all-powerful; but that is quite another matter. No exterior contributor, no birth-commission, conferred these possessions upon Him; He did it Himself. But Washington's disposition was born in him, he did not create It; It was the architect of his character; his character was the architect of his achievements.

If my disposition had been born in him and his in me, the map of history would have been changed. It is our privilege to admire the splendor of the sun, and the beauty of the rainbow, and the character of Washington; but there is no occasion to praise them for these qualities, since they did not create the course whence the qualities sprang--the sun's fires, the light upon the falling rain-drops, the sane and clean and benignant disposition born to the Father of his Country.

Is there a value, then, in having a Washington, since we may not concede to him personal merit for what he was and did? Necessarily, there is a value--a value so immense that it defies all estimate. Acceptable outside influences were the materials out of which Washington's native disposition built Washington's character and fitted him for his achievements. Suppose there hadn't been any. Suppose he had been born and reared in a pirate's cave; the acceptable materials would have been lacking, the Washingtonian character would not have been built.

Fortunately for us and for the world and for future ages and peoples, he was born where the sort of influences and associations acceptable to his disposition were findable; where the building of his character at its best and highest was possible, and where the accident of favorable circumstances was present to furnish it a conspicuous field for the full exercise and exhibition of its commanding capabilities.

Did Washington's great value, then, lie in what he accomplished? No; that was only a minor value. His major value, his vast value, his immeasurable value to us and to the world and to future ages and peoples, lies in his permanent and sky-reaching conspicuousness as an influence.

We are made, brick by brick, of influences, patiently built up around the framework of our born dispositions. It is the sole process of construction; there is no other. Every man and woman and child is an influence; a daily and hourly influence which never ceases from work, and never ceases from affecting for good or evil the characters about it--some contributing gold-dust, some contributing trash-dust, but in either case helping on the building, and never stopping to rest. The shoemaker helps to build his two-dozen associates; the pickpocket helps to build his four dozen associates; the village clergyman helps to build his five hundred associates; the renowned bank-robber's name and fame help to build his hundred associates and three thousand persons who he has never seen; the renowned philanthropist's labors and the benevolent millionaire's gifts move to kindly works and generous outlays of money a hundred thousand persons whom they have never met and never will meet; and to the building of the character of every individual thus moved these movers have added a brick. The unprincipled newspaper adds a baseness to a million decaying character-fabrics every day; the high-principled newspaper adds a daily betterment to the character-fabric of another million. The swiftly-enriched wrecker and robber of railway systems lowers the commercial morals of a whole nation for three generations. A Washington, standing upon the world's utmost summit, eternally visible, eternally clothed in light, a

serene, inspiring, heartening example and admonition, is an
influence which raises the level of character in all receptive
men and peoples, alien and domestic; and the term of its gracious
work is not measurable by fleeting generations, but only by the
lingering march of the centuries.

Washington was more and greater than the father of a nation,
he was the Father of its Patriotism--patriotism at its loftiest
and best; and so powerful was the influence which he left behind
him, that that golden patriotism remained undimmed and unsullied
for a hundred years, lacking one; and so fundamentally right-
hearted are our people by grace of that long and ennobling
teaching, that to-day, already, they are facing back for home
they are laying aside their foreign-born and foreign-bred
imported patriotism and resuming that which Washington gave to
their fathers, which is American and the only American--which
lasted ninety-nine years and is good for a million more. Doubt--
doubt that we did right by the Filipinos--is rising steadily
higher and higher in the nation's breast; conviction will follow
doubt. The nation will speak; its will is law; there is no other
soverign on this soil; and in that day we shall right such
unfairnesses as we have done. We shall let go our obsequious
hold on the rear-skirts of the sceptred land-thieves of Europe,
and be what we were before, a real World Power, and the chiefest
of them all, by right of the only clean hands in Christendom, the
only hands guiltless of the sordid plunder of any helpless
people's stolen liberties, hands recleansed in the patriotism of
Washington, and once more fit to touch the hem of the revered
Shade's garment and stand in its presence unashamed. It was
Washington's influence that made Lincoln and all other real
patriots the Republic has known; it was Washington's influence
that made the soldiers who saved the Union; and that influence
will save us always, and bring us back to the fold when we stray.

And so, when a Washington is given us, or a Lincoln, or a
Grant,[11] what should we do? Knowing, as we do, that a conspicuous
influence for good is worth more than a billion obscure ones,
without doubt the logic of it is that we should highly value it,
and make a vestal flame of it, and keep it briskly burning in
every way we can--in the nursery, in the school, in the college,
in the pulpit, in the newspaper--even in Congress, if such a
thing were possible.

The proper inborn disposition was required to start a
Washington; the acceptable influences and circumstances and a
large field were required to develop and complete him. The same
with Funston.

II.

"The War was over"--end of 1900. A month later the mountain
refuge of the defeated and hunted, and now powerless but yet not
hopeless, Filipino chief was discovered.[12] His army was gone,
his Republic extinguished, his ablest statesman deported, his
generals all in their graves or prisoners of war. The memory of
his worthy dream had entered upon a historic life, to be an
inspiration to less unfortunate patriots in other centuries; the

225

dream itself was dead beyond resurrection, though he culd not believe it.

Now came his capture. An admiring author* shall tell us about it. His account can be trusted, for it is correctly synopsized from General Funston's own voluntary confession made by him at the time. The italics are mine.

"It was not until February, 1901, that his actual hiding-place was discovered. The clew was in the shape of a letter from Aguinaldo commanding his cousin, Baldormero Aguinaldo, to send him four hundred armed men, the bearer to act as a guide to the same. The order was in cipher, but among other effects captured at various times a copy of the Insurgent cipher was found. THe Insurgent courier was convinced of the error of his ways (though by exactly what means, history does not reveal), and offered to lead the way to Aguinaldo's place of hiding. Here was an opportunity that suggested an adventure equal to anything in penny-awful fiction. It was just the kind of a dare-devil exploit that appealed to the romantic Funston. It was something out of the ordinary for a brigadier-general to leave his command and turn into a scout, but Funston was irresistible. He formulated a scheme and asked General MacArthur's permission. It was impossible to refuse the daring adventurer, the hero of the Rio Grande, anything; so Funston set to work, imitating the peculiar handwriting of Lacuna, the Insurgent officer to whom Aguinaldo's communication referred. Some little time previous to the capture of the Tagalog courier, several of Lucuna's letters were found, together with Aguinaldo's cipher code. Having perfected Lacuna's signature, Funston wrote two letters on February 24 and 28, acknowledging Aguinaldo's communication, and informing him that he (Lacuna) was sending him a few of the best soldiers in his command. Added to this neat forgery General Funston dictated a letter which was written by an ex-Insurgent attached to his command, telling Aguinaldo that the relief force had surprised and captured a detachment of Americans, taking five prisoners whom they were bringing to him because of their importance. This ruse was employed to explain the presence of the five Americans: General Funston, Captain Hazzard, Captain Newton, Lieutenant Hazzard, and General Funston's aide, Lieutenant Kitchell, who were to accompany the expedition.

"Seventy-eight Macabebes, hereditary enemies of the Tagalogs, were chosen by Funston to form the body of the command. These fearless and hardy natives fell into the scheme with a vengeance. Three Tagalogs and one Spaniard were also invited. The Macabebes were fitted out in cast-off Insurgent uniforms, and the Americans donned field-worn uniforms of privates. Three days' ration were provided, and each man was given a rifle. The 'Vicksburg'

* "Aguinaldo." By Edwin Wildman. Lothrop Publishing Co., Boston.

226

was chosen to take the daring impostors to some spot on the east coast near Palanan, where Aguinaldo was in hiding. Arriving off the coast at Casignan, some distance from the Insurgent-hidden capital, the party was landed. Three Macabebes, who spoke Talalog fluently, were sent into the town to notify the natives that they were bringing additional forces and important American prisoners to Aguinaldo, and request of the local authorities guides and assistance. The Insurgent president readily consented, and the little party, after refreshing themselves and exhibiting their prisoners, started over the ninety-mile trail to Palanan, a mountain retreat on the coast of the Isabella province. Over the stony declivities and through the thick jungle, across bridgeless streams and up narrow passes, the footsore and bone-racked adventurers tramped, until their food was exhausted and they were too weak to move, though but eight miles from Aguinaldo's rendezvous.

"A messenger was sent forward to inform Aguinaldo of their position and to beg for food. The rebel chieftain promptly replied by dispatching rice and a letter to the officer in command, instructing him to treat the American prisoners well, but to leave them outside the town. What better condition could the ingenious Funston have himself dictated?

On the 23d of March the party reached Palanan. Aguinaldo sent out eleven men to take charge of the American prisoners, but Funston and his associates succeeded in dodging them and scattering themselves in the jungle until they passed on to meet the Americans whom the Insurgents were notified were left behind.

"Immediately joining his command, Funston ordered his little band of dare-devils to march boldly into the town and present themselves to Aguinaldo. At the Insurgent headquarters they were received by Aguinaldo's bodyguard, dressed in blue drill uniforms and white hats, drawn up in military form. The spokesman so completely hoodwinked Aguinaldo that he did not suspect the ruse. In the meantime the Macabebes maneuvered around into advantageous positions, directed by the Spaniard, until all were in readiness. Then he shouted, 'Macabebes, now is your turn!' whereupon they emptied their rifles into Aguinaldo's bodyguard. . . .

"The Americans joined in the skirmish, and two of Aguinaldo's staff were wounded, but escaped, the treasurer of the revolutionary government surrendering. The rest of the Filipino officers got away. Aguinaldo accepted his capture with resignation, though greatly in fear of the vengeance of the Macabebes. But General Funston's assurance of his personal safety set his mind easy on that point, and he calmed down and discussed the situation. He was greatly cast down at his capture, and asserted that by no other means would he have been taken alive,--an admission which added all the more to Funston's achievement, for Aguinaldo's was a difficult and desperate case, and demanded extraordinary methods."

Some of the customs of war are not pleasant to the civilian; but ages upon ages of training have reconciled us to them as being justifiable, and we accept them and make no demur, even when they give us an extra twinge. Every detail of Funston's scheme--but one--has been employed in war in the past and stands acquitted of blame by history. By the custom of war, it is permissible, in the interest of an enterprise like the one under consideration, for a Brigadier-General (if he be of the sort that can so choose) to persuade or bribe a courier to betray his trust; to remove the badges of his honorable rank and disguise himself; to lie, to practice treachery, to forge; to associate with himself persons properly fitted by training and instinct for the work; to accept of courteous welcome, and assassinate the welcomers while their hands are still warm from the friendly handshake.

By the custom of war, all these things are innocent, none of them is blameworthy, all of them are justifiable; none of them is new, all of them have been done before, although not by a Brigadier-General. But there is one detail which is new, absolutely new. It has never been resorted to before in any age of the world, in any country, among any people, savage or civilized. It was the one meant by Aguinaldo when he said that "by no other means" would he have been taken alive. When a man is exhausted by hunger to the point where he is "too weak to move," he has a right to make supplication to his enemy to save his failing life; but if he take so much as one taste of that food--which is holy, by the precept of all ages and all nations--he is barred from lifting his hand against that enemy for that time.

It was left to a Brigadier-General of Volunteers in the American army to put shame upon a custom which even the degraded Spanish friars had respected. We promoted him for it.

Our unsuspecting President was in the act of taking his murderer by the hand when the man shot his down. The amazed world dwelt upon that damning fact, brooded over it, discussed it, blushed for it, said it put a blot and a shame upon our race. Yet, bad as he was, he had not--dying of starvation-- begged food of the President to strengthen his failing forces for his treacherous work; he did not proceed against the life of a benefactor who had just saved his own.

April 14. I have been absent several weeks in the West Indies; I will now resume this Defence.

It seems to me that General Funston's appreciation of the Capture needs editing. It seems to me that, in his after-dinner speeches, he spreads out the heroisms of it--I say it with deference, and subject to correction--with an almost too generous hand. He is a brave man; his dearest enemy will cordially grant him that credit. For his sake it is a pity that somewhat of that quality was not needed in the episode under consideration; that he would have furnished it, no one doubts. But, by his own showing, he ran but one danger--that of starving. He and his party were well disguised, in dishonored uniforms, American and

228

Insurgent; they greatly outnumbered Aguinaldo's guard;* by his
forgeries and falsehoods he had lulled suspicion to sleep; his
coming was expected, his way was prepared; his course was through
a solitude, unfriendly interruption was unlikely; his party were
well armed; they would catch their prey with welcoming smiles in
their faces, and with hospitable hands extended for the friendly
shake--nothing would be necessary but to shoot these people
down. That is what they did. It was hospitality repaid in a
brand-new, up-to-date, Modern Civilization fashion, and would be
admired by many.

"The spokesman so completely hoodwinked Aguinaldo that he
did not suspect the ruse. In the meantime, the Macabebes
maneuvred around into advantageous positions, directed by
the Spaniard, until all were in readiness; then he shouted,
'Macabebes, now is your turn!' whereupon they emptied their
rifles into Aguinaldo bodyguard."--From Wildman's book,
already quoted.

The utter completeness of the surprise, the total absence of
suspicion which had been secured by the forgeries and falsehoods,
is best brought out in Funston's humorous account of the episode
in one of his rollicking speeches--the one he thought the
President said he wanted to see republished; though it turned out
that this was only a dream. Dream of a reporter, the General
says:

"The Macabebes fired on those men and two fell dead; the
others retreated, firing as they ran, and I might say here
that they retreated with such great alacrity and enthusiasm
that they dropped eighteen rifles and a thousand rounds of
ammunition.

"Sigismondo rushed back into the house, pulled his
revolver, and told the insurgent officers to surrender.
They all threw up their hands except Villia, Aguinaldo's
chief of staff; he had on one of those newfangled Mauser
revolvers and he wanted to try it. But before he had the
Mauser out of its scabbard he was shot twice; Sigismondo was
a pretty fair marksman himself.

"Alambra was shot in the face. He jumped out of the
window; the house, by-the-way, stood on the bank of the
river. he went out of the window and went clear down into
the river, the water being twenty-five feet below the bank.
He escaped, swam across the river and got away, and
surrendered five months afterwards.

"Villia, shot in the shoulder, followed him out of the
window and into the river, but the Macabebes saw him and ran
down to the river bank, and they waded in and fished him
out, and kicked him all the way up the bank, and asked him
how he liked it." (Laughter.)

While it is true that the Dare Devils were not in danger
upon this occasion, they were in awful peril at one time; in
peril of a death so awful that swift extinction by bullet, by the

*Eighty-nine to forty-eight.--Funston's Lotos Club
Confession.

axe, by the sword, by the rope, by drowning, by fire, is a kindly mercy contrasted with it; a death so awful that it holds its place unchallenged as the supremest of human agonies--death by starvation. Aguinaldo saved them from that.

These being the facts, we come now to the question, Is Funston to blame? I think not. And for that reason I think too much is being made of this matter. He did not make his own disposition, It was born with him. It chose his ideals for him, he did not choose them. It chose the kind of society It liked, the kind of comrades It preferred, and imposed them upon him, rejecting the other kinds; he could not help this; It admired everything that Washington did not admire, and hospitably received and coddled everything that Washington would have turned out of doors--but It, and It only, was to blame, not Funston; his It took as naturally to moral slag as Washington's took to moral gold, but only It was to blame, not Funston. Its moral sense, if It had any, was color-blind, but this was no fault of Funston's, and he is not chargeable with the results; It had a native predilection for unsavory conduct, but it would be in the last degree unfair to hold Funston to blame for the outcome of his infirmity; as clearly unfair as it would be to blame his because his conscience leaked out through one of his pores when he was little--a thing which he could not help, and he couldn't have raised it, anyway; It was able to say to an enemy, "Have pity on me, I am starving; I am too weak to move, give me food; I am your friend, I am your fellow-patriot, your fellow-Filipino, and am fighting for our dear country's liberties, like you--have pity, give me food, save my life, there is no other help!" and It was able to refresh and restore Its marionette with food, and then shoot down the giver of it while his hand was stretched out in welcome--like the President's. Yet if blame there was, and guilt, and treachery, and baseness, they are not Funston's, but only Its; It has the noble gift of humor, and can make a banquet almost die with laughter when it has a funny incident to tell about; this one will bear reading again--and over and over again, in fact:

"The Macabebes fired on those men and two fell dead; the others retreated, firing as they ran, and I might say here that they retreated with such great alacrity and enthusiasm that they dropped eighteen rifles and a thousand rounds of ammunition.

"Sigismondo rushed back into the house, pulled his revolver, and told the insurgent officers to surrender. They all threw up their hands except Villia, Aguinaldo's chief of staff; he had on one of those newfangled Mauser revolvers and he wanted to try it. But before he had the Mauser out of its scabbard he was shot twice; Sigismondo was a pretty fair marksman himself.

"Alambra was shot in the face. He jumped out of the window; the house, by-the-way, stood on the bank of the river. He went out of the window and went clear down into the river, the water being twenty-five feet below the bank.

He escaped, swam across the river and got away, and surrendered five months afterwards.

"Villia, shot in the shoulder, followed him out of the window and into the river, but the Macabebes saw him and ran down to the river bank, and they waded in and fished him out, and kicked him all the way up the bank, and asked him how he liked it." (Laughter.)

(This was a wounded man.) But it is only It that is speaking, not Funston. With youthful glee It can see sink down in death the simple creatures who had answered Its fainting prayer for food, and without remorse It can note the reproachful look in their dimming eyes; but in fairness we must remember that this is only It, not Funston; by proxy; in the person of Its born servant, It can do Its strange work; and practice Its ingratitudes and amazing treacheries, while wearing the uniform of the American soldier, and marching under the authority of the American flag. And It--not Funston--comes home now, to teach us children what Patriotism is! Surely It ought to know.

It is plain to me, and I think it ought to be plain to all, that Funston is not in any way to blame for the things he has done, does, thinks, and says.

Now, then, we have Funston; he has happened, and is on our hands. The question is, what are we going to do about it, how are we going to meet the emergency? We have seen what happened in Washington's case: he became a colossal example, an example to the whole world, and for all time--because his name and deeds went everywhere, and inspired, as they still inspire, and will always inspire, admiration, and compel emulation. Then the thing for the world to do in the present case is to turn the gilt front of Funston's evil notoriety to the rear, and expose the back aspect of it, the right and black aspect of it, to the youth of the land; otherwise he will become an example and a boy-admiration, and will most sorrowfully and grotesquely bring his breed of Patriotism into competition with Washington's. This competition has already begun, in fact. Some may not believe it, but it is nevertheless true, that there are now public-school teachers and superintendents who are holding up Funston as a model hero and Patriot in the schools.

If this Funstonian boom continues, Funstonism will presently affect the army. In fact, this has already happened. There are weak-headed and weak-principled officers in all armies, and these are always ready to imitate successful notoriety-breeding methods, let them be good or bad. The fact that Funston has achieved notoriety by paralyzing the universe with a fresh and hideous idea, is sufficient for this kind--they will call that hand if they can, and go it one better when the chance offers. Funston's example has bred many imitators, and many ghastly additions to our history: the torturing of Filipinos by the awful "watercure," for instance, to make them confess--what? Truth? Or lies? How can one know which it is they are telling? For under unendurable pain a man confesses anything that is required of him, true or false, and his evidence is worthless. Yet upon such evidence American officers have actually--but you know about those atrocities which the War Office has been hiding a year or two; and about General Smith's now world-celebrated order of massacre--thus summarized by the press from Major Waller's testimony:

"Kill and burn--this is no time to take prisoners--the more you kill and burn, the better--Kill all above the age of ten--make Samar a howling wilderness!"

You see what Funston's example has produced, just in this little while--even before he produced the example. It has advanced our Civilization ever so far--fully as far as Europe advanced it in China. Also, no doubt, it was Funston's example that made us (and England) copy Weyler's reconcentrado horror after the pair of us, with our Sunday-school smirk on, and our goody-goody noses upturned toward heaven, had been calling him a "fiend." And the fearful earthquake out there in Krakatoa that destroyed the island and killed two million people-- No that could not have been Funston's example; I remember now he was not born then.

However, for all these things I blame only his It, not him. In conclusion, I have defended him as well as I could, and indeed I have found it quite easy, and have removed prejudice from his and rehabilitated him in the public esteem and regard, I think. I was not able to do anything for his It, It being out of my jurisdiction, and out of Funston's and everybody's. As I have shown, Funston is not to blame for his fearful deed; and, if I tried, I might also show that he is not to blame for our still holding in bondage the man he captured by unlawful means, and who is not any more rightfully our prisoner and spoil than he would be if he were stolen money. He is entitled to his freedom. If he were a king of a Great Power, or an ex-president of our republic, instead of an ex-president of a destroyed and abolished little republic, Civilization (with a large C) would criticise and complain until he got it.

P.S. April 16. The President is speaking up, this morning, just as this goes to the printer, and there is no uncertain sound about the note. It is the speech and spirit of a President of a people, not of a party, and we all like it, Traitors and all. I think I may speak for the other Traitors, for I am sure they feel as I do about it. I will explain that we get our title from the Funstonian Patriots--free of charge. They are always doing us little compliments like that; they are just born flatters, those boys.

M.T.

North American Review, vol. CLXXIV, May, 1902, pp. 613-24.

KING LEOPOLD'S SOLILOQUY

[Throws down pamphlets which he has been reading. Excitedly combs his flowing spread of whiskers with his fingers; pounds the table with his fists; lets off brisk volleys of unsanctified language at brief intervals, repentantly drooping his head, between volleys, and kissing the Louis XI crucifix hanging from his neck, accompanying the kisses with mumbled apologies; presently rises, flushed and perspiring, and walks the floor, gesticulating]

-- --!! -- --!! If I had them by the throat? [Hastily kisses the crucifix, and mumbles] In these twenty years I have spent millions to keep the press of the two hemispheres quiet, and still these leaks keep on occurring. I have spent other millions on religion and art, and what do I get for it? Nothing. Not a compliment. These generosities are studiedly ignored, in print. In print I get nothing but slanders--and slanders again--and still slanders, and slanders on top of slanders! Grant them true, what of it? They are slanders all the same, when uttered against a king.

Miscreants--they are telling everything! Oh, everything: how I went pilgriming among the Powers in tears, with my mouth full of Bible and my pelt oozing piety at every pore, and implored them to place the vast and rich and populous Congo Free State in trust in my hands as their agent, so that I might root out slavery and stop the slave raids, and lift up those twenty-five millions of gentle and harmless blacks out of darkness into light, the light of our blessed Redeemer, the light that streams from his holy Word, the light that makes glorious our noble civilization--lift them up and dry their tears and fill their bruised hearts with joy and gratitude--lift them up and make them comprehend that they were no longer outcasts and forsaken, but our very brothers in Christ; how America and thirteen great European states wept in sympathy with me, and were persuaded; how their representatives met in convention in Berlin and made me Head Foreman and Superintendent of the Congo State, and drafted out my powers and limitations, carefully guarding the persons and liberties and properties of the natives against hurt and harm; forbidding whisky traffic and gun traffic; providing courts of justice; making commerce free and fetterless to the merchants and traders of all nations, and welcoming and safeguarding all missionaries of all creeds and denominations. They have told how I planned and prepared my establishment and selected my horde of officials--"pals" and "pimps" of mine, "unspeakable Belgians" every one--and hoisted my flag, and "took in" a President of the United States, and got him to be the first to recognize it and salute it.[13] Oh, well, let them blackguard me if they like; it is a deep satisfaction to me to remember that I was a shade too smart for that nation that thinks itself so smart. Yes, I certainly did bunco a Yankee--as those people phrase it. Pirate flag? Let them call it so--perhaps it is so. All the same, they were the first to salute it.

These meddlesome American missionaries! these frank British consuls! these blabbing Belgian-born traitor officials!--those tiresome parrots are always talking, always telling. They have told how for twenty years I have ruled the Congo State not as a trustee of the Powers, an agent, a subordinate, a foreman, but as a sovereign--sovereign over a fruitful domain four times as large as the German Empire--sovereign absolute, irresponsible, above all law; trampling the Berlin-made Congo charter under foot; barring out all foreign traders but myself; restricting commerce to myself, through concessionaries who are my creatures and confederates; seizing and holding the State as my personal property, the whole of its vast revenues as my private "swag"--mine, solely mine--claiming and holding its millions of people as my private property, my serfs, my slaves; their labor mine, with or without wage; the food they raise not their property but mine; the rubber, the ivory and all the other riches of the land mine--mine solely--and gathered for me by the men, the women and the little children under compulsion of lash and bullet, fire, starvation, mutilation and the halter.

These pests!--it is as I say, they have kept back nothing! They have revealed these and yet other details which shame should have kept them silent about, since they were exposures of a king, a sacred personage and immune from reproach, by right of his selection and appointment to his great office by God himself; a king whose acts cannot be criticized without blasphemy, since God has observed them from the beginning and has manifested no dissatisfaction with them, no shown disapproval of them, nor hampered no interrupted them in any way. By this sign I recognize his approval of what I have done; his cordial and glad approval, I am sure I may say.

Blest, crowned, beatified with this great reward, this golden reward, this unspeakably precious reward, why should I care for men's cursings and revilings of me? [With a sudden outburst of feeling] May they roast a million aeons in -- [Catches his breath and effusively kisses the crucifix; sorrowfully murmurs, "I shall get myself damned yet, with these indiscretions of speech."]

Yes, they go on telling everything, these chatterers! They tell how I levy incredibly burdensome taxes upon the natives--taxes which are a pure theft; taxes which they must satisfy by gathering rubber under hard and constantly harder conditions, and by raising and furnishing food supplies gratis--and it all comes out that, when they fall short of their tasks through hunger, sickness, despair, and ceaseless and exhausting labor without rest, and forsake their homes and flee to the woods to escape punishment, my black soldiers, drawn from unfriendly tribes, and instigated and directed by my Belgians, hunt them down and butcher them and burn their villages--reserving some of the girls. They tell it all: how I am wiping a nation of friendless creatures out of existence by every form of murder, for my private pocket's sake, and how every shilling I get costs a rape, a mutilation or a life. But they never say, although they know it, that I have labored in the cause of religion at the same time and all the time, and have sent missionaries there (of a "convenient stripe," as they phrase it), to teach them the error of their ways and bring them to Him who is all mercy and love, and who is the sleepless guardian and friend of all who suffer. They tell only what is against me, they will not tell what is in my favor.

They tell how England required of me a Commission of Inquiry into Congo atrocities, and how, to quiet that meddling country, with its disagreeable Congo Reform Association, made up of earls and bishops and John Morleys and university grandees and other dudes, more interested in other people's business than in their own. I appointed it. Did it stop their mouths? No, they merely pointed out that it was a commission composed wholly of my "Congo butchers," "the very men whose acts were to be inquired into." They said it was equivalent to appointing a commission of wolves to inquire into depredations committed upon a sheepfold. <u>Nothing</u> can satisfy a cursed Englishman!*

And were the fault-finders frank with my private character? They could not be more so if I were a plebeian, a peasant, a mechanic. They remind the world that from the earliest days my house has been chapel and brothel combined, and both industries working full time; that I practiced cruelties upon my queen and my daughters, and supplemented them with daily shame and humiliations; that, when my queen lay in the happy refuge of her coffin, and a daughter implored me on her knees to let her look for the last time upon her mother's face, I refused; and that, three years ago, not being satisfied with the stolen spoils of a whole alien nation, I robbed my own child of her property and appeared by proxy in court, a spectacle to the civilized world, to defend the act and complete the crime. It is as I have said: they are unfair, unjust; they will resurrect and give new currency to such things as those, or to any other things that count against me, but they will not mention any act of mine that is in my favor. I have spent more money on art than any other monarch of my time, and they know it. Do they speak of it, do

---

*This visit had a more fortunate result than was anticipated. One member of the commission was a leading Congo official, another an official of the government in Belgium, the third a Swiss jurist. It was feared that the work of the Commission would not be more genuine than that of innumerable so-called "investigations" by local officials. But it appears that the Commission was met by a very avalanche of awful testimony. One who was present at a public hearing writes: "Men of stone would be moved by the stories that are being unfolded as the Commission probes into the awful history of rubber collection." It is evident the commissioners were moved. Of their report and its bearing upon the international issue presented by the conceded conditions in the Congo State, something is said on a supplementary page of this pamphlet. Certain reforms were ordered by the Commission of Inquiry in the one section visited, but the latest word is that after its departure conditions were soon worse than before its coming.--M.T.

they tell about it? No, they do not. They prefer to work up
what they call "ghastly statistics" into offensive kindergarten
object lessions, whose purpose is to make sentimental people
shudder, and prejudice them against me. They remark that "if the
innocent blood shed in the Congo State by King Leopold were put
in buckets and the buckets placed side by side, the line would
stretch 2,000 miles; if the skeletons of his ten millions of
starved and butchered dead could rise up and march in single
file, it would take them seven months and four days to pass a
given point; if compacted together in a body, they would occupy
more ground than St. Louis covers, World's Fair and all; if they
should all clap their bony hands at once, the grisly crash would
be heart at a distance of--" Damnation, it makes me tired! And
they do similar miracles with the money I have distilled from
that blood and put into my pocket. They pile it into Egyptian
pyramids; they carpet Saharas with it; they spread it across the
sky, and the shadow it casts makes twilight in the earth. And
the tears I have caused, the hearts I have broken--oh, nothing
can persuade them to let them alone!
    [Meditative pause] Well . . . no matter, I did beat the
Yankees, anyway! there's comfort in that.
    [Reads with mocking smile, the President's Order of
Recognition of April 22, 1884]
        . . . the government of the United States announces it
    sympathy with and approval of the humane and benevolent
    purposes of (my Congo scheme), and will order the officers
    of the United States, both on land and sea, to recognize its
    flag as the flag of a friendly government.
    Possibly the Yankees would like to take that back, now, but
they will find that my agents are not over there in America for
nothing. But there is no danger; neither nations nor governments
can afford to confess a blunder.
    [With a contented smile, begins to read from "Report by Rev.
W. M. Morrison, American missionary in the Congo Free State"]
        I furnish herewith some of the many atrocious incidents
    which have come under my own personal observation; they
    reveal the organized system of plunder and outrage which has
    been perpetrated and is now being carried on in that
    unfortunate country by King Leopold of Belgium. I say King
    Leopold, because he and he alone is now responsible, since
    he is the absolute sovereign. He styles himself such. When
    our government in 1884 laid the foundation of the Congo Free
    State, by recognizing its flag, little did it know that this
    concern, parading under the guise of philanthropy--was
    really King Leopold of Belgium, one of the shrewdest, most
    heartless and most conscienceless rulers that ever sat on a
    throne. This is apart from his known corrupt morals, which
    have made his name and his family a byword in two
    continents. Our government would most certainly not have
    recognized that flag had it known that it was really King
    Leopold individually who was asking for recognition; had it
    known that it was setting up in the heart of Africa an
    absolute monarchy; had it known that, having put down

African slavery in our own country at great cost of blood and money, it was establishing a worse form of slavery right in Africa.

[With evil joy] Yes, I certainly was a shade too clever for the Yankees. It hurts; it gravels them. They can't get over it! Puts a shame upon them in another way, too, and a graver way; for they never can rid their records of the reproachful fact that their vain Republic, self-appointed Champion and Promoter of the Liberties of the World, is the only democracy in history that has lent its power and influence to the establishing of an absolute monarchy!

[Contemplating, with an unfriendly eye, a stately pile of pamphlets] Blister the meddlesome missionaries! They write tons of these things. They seem to be always around, always spying, always eye-witnessing the happenings; and everything they see they commit to paper. They are always prowling from place to place; the natives consider them their only friends; they go to them with their sorrows; they show them their scars and their wounds, inflicted by my soldier police; they hold up the stumps of their arms and lament because their hands have been chopped off, as punishment for not bringing in enough rubber, and as proof to be laid before my officers that the required punishment was well and truly carried out. One of these missionaries saw eighty-one of these hands drying over a fire for transmission to my officials--and of course he must go and set it down and print it. They travel and travel, they spy and spy! And nothing is too trivial for them to print.

[Takes up a pamphlet. Reads a passage from Report of a "Journey made in July, August and September, 1903, by Rev. A. E. Scrivener, a British missionary"]

. . . . Soon we began talking, and without any encouragement on my part the natives began the tales I had become so accustomed to. They were living in peace and quietness when the white men came in from the lake with all sorts of requests to do this and that, and they thought it meant slavery. So they attempted to keep the white men out of their country but without avail. The rifles were too much for them. So they submitted and made up their minds to do the best they could under the altered circumstances. First came the command to build houses for the soldiers, and this was done without a murmur. Then they had to feed the soldiers and all the men and women--hangers on--who accompanied them. Then they were told to bring in rubber. This was quite a new thing for them to do. There was rubber in the forest several days away from their home, but that is was worth anything was news to them. A small reward was offered and a rush was made for the rubber. 'What strange white men, to give us cloth and beads for the sap of a wild vine.' They rejoiced in what they thought their good fortune. But soon the reward was reduced until at last they were told to bring in the rubber for nothing. To this they tried to demur; but to their great surprise several were shot by the soldiers, and the rest were told, with many curses and blows, to go at once or more would be killed. Terrified, they began to prepare their food for the fortnight's absence from the village which the collection of rubber entailed. The soldiers discovered them sitting about. 'What, not gone yet?' Bang! bang! bang! and down fell one and another, dead, in the midst of wives and companions. There is a terrible wail and an attempt made to prepare the dead for burial, but this is not allowed. All must go at once to the forest. Without food? Yes, without food. And off the poor wretches had to go without even their tinder boxes to make fires. Many died in the forests of hunger and exposure, and still more from the rifles of the ferocious soldiers in charge of the post. In spite of all their efforts the amount fell off and more and more were killed. I was shown around the place, and the sites of former big chiefs' settlements were pointed out. A careful estimate made the population of, say, seven years ago, to be 2,000 people in and about the post, within a radius of, say, a quarter of a mile. All told, they would not muster 200 now, and there is so much sadness and gloom about them that they are fast decreasing.

We stayed there all day on Monday and had many talks with the people. On the Sunday some of the boys had told me of some bones which they had seen, so on the Monday I asked to be shown these bones. Lying about on the grass, within a few yards of the house I was occupying, were numbers of human skulls, bones, in some cases complete skeletons. I counted thirty-six skulls, and saw many sets of bones from which the skulls were missing. I called one of the men and asked the meaning of it. 'When the rubber palaver began,' said he, 'the soldiers shot so many we grew tired of burying, and very often we were not allowed to bury; and so just dragged the bodies out into the grass and left them. There are hundreds all around if you would like to see them.' But I had seen more than enough, and was sickened by the stories that came from men and women alike of the awful time they had passed through. The Bulgarian atrocities might be considered as mildness itself when compared with what was done here. How the people submitted I don't know, and even now I wonder as I think of their patience. That some of them managed to run away is some cause for thankfulness. I stayed there two days and the one thing that impressed itself upon me was the collection of rubber. I saw long files of men come in, as at Bongo, with their little baskets under their arms; saw them paid their milk tin full of salt, and the two yards of calico flung to the headmen; saw their trembling timidity, and in fact a great deal that all went to prove the state of terrorism that exists and the virtual slavery in which the people are held.

That is their way; they spy and spy, and run into print with every foolish trifle. And that British consul, Mr. Casement, is just like them. He gets hold of a diary which had been kept by

238

one of my government officers, and although it is a private diary and intended for no eye but its owner's, Mr. Casement is so lacking in delicacy and refinement as to print passages from it. [Reads a passage from the diary]

Each time the corporal goes out to get rubber, cartridges are given him. He must bring back all not used, and for every one used he must bring back a right hand. M. P. told me that sometimes they shot a cartridge at an animal in hunting; they then cut off a hand from a living man. As to the extent to which this is carried on, he informed me that in six months the State on the Mambogo River had used 6,000 cartridges, which means that 6,000 people are killed or mutilated. It means more than 6,000 . . . for the people have told me repeatedly that the soldiers kill the children with the butt of their guns.

When the subtle consul thinks silence will be more effective than words, he employs it. Here he leaves it to be recognized that a thousand killings and mutilations a month is a large output for so small a region as the Mambogo River concession, silently indicating the dimensions of it by accompanying his report with a map of the prodigious Congo State, in which there is not room for so small an object as that river. That silence is intended to say, "If it is a thousand a month in this little corner, imagine the output of the whole vast State!" A gentleman would not descend to these furtivenesses.

Now as to the mutilations. You can't head off a Congo critic and make him stay headed-off; he dodges, and straightway comes back at you from another direction. They are full of slippery arts. When the mutilations (severing hands, unsexing men, etc.) began to stir Europe, we hit upon the idea of excusing them with a retort which we judged would knock them dizzy on that subject for good and all, and leave them nothing more to say; to wit, we boldly laid the custom on the natives, and said we did not invent it, but only followed it. Did it knock them dizzy? did it shut their mouths? Not for an hour. They dodged, and came straight back at us with the remark that "if a Christian king can perceive a saving moral difference between inventing bloody barbarities, and imitating them from savages, for charity's sake let him get what comfort he can out of his confession!"

It is most amazing, the way that that consul acts--that spy, that busy-body. [Takes up pamphlet "Treatment of Women and Children in the Congo State; what Mr. Casement Saw in 1903"]

Hardly two years ago! Intruding that date upon the public was a piece of cold malice. It is intended to weaken the force of my press syndicate's assurances to the public that my severities in the Congo ceased, and ceased utterly, years and years ago. This man is fond of trifles--revels in them, gloats over them, pets them, fondles them, sets them all down. One doesn't need to drowse through his monotonous reports to see that; the mere sub-headings of its chapters prove it. [Reads]

Two hundred and forty persons, men, women and children, compelled to supply government with one ton of carefully

prepared foodstuffs per week, receiving in remuneration, all
told, the princely sum of 15s 10d.!
Very well, it was liberal. It was not much short of a penny
a week for each nigger. It suits this consul to belittle it, yet
he knows very well that I could have had both the food and the
labor for nothing. I can prove it by a thousand instances.
[Reads]

Expedition against a village behindhand in its
(compulsory) supplies; result, slaughter of sixteen persons;
among them three women and a boy of five years. Ten carried
off, to be prisoners till ransomed; among them a child, who
died during the march.
But he is careful not to explain that we are obliged to
resort to ransom to collect debts, where the people have nothing
to pay with. Families that escape to the woods sell some of
their members into slavery and thus provide the ransom. He knows
that I would stop this if I could find a less objectionable way
to collect their debts. . . . Mm--here is some more of the
consul's delicacy! He reports a conversation he had with some
natives:

Q. How do you know it was the white men themselves who
ordered these cruel things to be done to you? These things
must have been done without the white man's knowledge by the
black soldiers.

A. These white men told their soldiers: "You only kill
women; you cannot kill men. You must prove that you kill
men." So then the soldiers when they killed us (here he
stopped and hesitated and then pointing to . . . he said:)
then they . . . and took them to the white men, who said:
'It is true, you have killed men."

Q. You say this is true? Were many of you so treated
after being shot?

All [shouting out]: Nkoto! Nkoto! (Very many! Very Many!)
There was no doubt that these people were not inventing.
Their vehemence, their flashing eyes, their excitement, were
not simulated.
Of course the critic had to divulge that; he has no
self-respect. All his kind reproach me, although they know quite
well that I took no pleasure in punishing the men in that
particular way, but only did it as a warning to other
delinquents. Ordinary punishments are no good with ignorant
savages; they make no impression.
[Reads more sub-heads]

Devastated region; population reduced from 40,000 to
8,000.
He does not take the trouble to say how it happened. He is
fertile in concealments. He hopes his readers and his Congo
reformers, of the Lord-Aberdeen-Norbury-John-Morley-Sir-Gilbert-
Parker stripe, will think they were all killed. They were not.
The great majority of them escaped. They fled to the bush with
their families because of the rubber raids, and it was there they
died of hunger. Could we help that?

240

One of my sorrowing critics observes: "Other Christian rulers tax their people, but furnish schools, courts of law, roads, light, water and protection to life and limb in return; King Leopold taxes his stolen nation, but provides nothing in return but hunger, terror, grief, shame, captivity, mutilation and massacre." That is their style! I furnish "nothing": I send the gospel to the survivors; these censure-mongers know it, but they would rather have their tongues cut out than mention it. I have several times required my raiders to give the dying an opportunity to kiss the sacred emblem; and if they obeyed me I have without doubt been the humble means of saving many souls. None of my traducers have had the fairness to mention this; but let it pass; there is One who has not overlooked it, and that is my solace, that is my consolation.

[Puts down the Report, takes up a pamphlet, glances along the middle of it.]
This is where the "death-trap" comes in. Meddlesome missionary spying around--Rev. W. H. Sheppard. Talks with a black raider of mine after a raid; cozens him into giving away some particulars. The raider remarks:

"I demanded 30 slaves from this side of the stream and 30 from the other side; 2 points of ivory, 2500 balls of rubber, 13 goats, 10 fowls and 6 dogs, some corn chumy, etc."

"How did the fight come up?" I asked.

"I sent for all their chiefs, sub-chiefs, men and women, to come on a certain day, saying that I was going to finish all the palaver. When they entered these small gates (the walls being made of fences brought from other villages, the high native ones) I demanded all my pay or I would kill them; so they refused to pay me, and I ordered the fence to be closed so they couldn't run away; then we killed them here inside the fence. The panels of the fence fell down and some escaped."

"How many did you kill?" I asked.

"We killed plenty, will you see some of them?"

That was just what I wanted.

He said: "I think we have killed between eighty and ninety, and those in the other villages I don't know, I did not go out but sent my people."

He and I walked out on the plain just near the camp. There were three dead bodies with the flesh carved off from the waist down.

"Why are they carved so, only leaving the bones?" I asked.

"My people ate them," he answered promptly. He then explained, "The men who have young children do not eat people, but all the rest ate them."

On the left was a big man, shot in the back and without a head. (All corpses were nude.)

"Where is the man's head?" I asked.

"Oh, they made a bowl of the forehead to rub up tobacco and diamba in."

We continued to walk and examine until late in the

241

afternoon, and counted forty-one bodies. The rest had been eaten up by the people.

On returning to the camp, we crossed a young woman, shot in the back of the head, one hand was cut away. I asked why, and Mulunba N'Cusa explained that they always cut off the right hand to give to the State on their return.

"Can you not show me some of the hands?" I asked.

So he conducted us to a framework of sticks, under which was burning a slow fire, and there they were, the right hands--I counted eighty-one in all.

There were not less then sixty women (Bena Pianga) prisoners. I saw them.

We say that we have as fully as possible investigated the whole outrage, and find it was a plan previously made to get all the stuff possible and to catch and kill the poor people in the death-trap.

Another detail, as we see!--cannibalism. They report cases of it with a most offensive frequency. My traducers do not forget to remark that, inasmuch as I am absolute and with a word can prevent in the Congo anything I choose to prevent, then whatsoever is done there by my permission is my act, my personal act; that I do it; that the hand of my agent is as truly my hand as if it were attached to my own arm; and so they picture me in my robes of state, with my crown on my head, munching human flesh, saying grace, mumbling thanks to Him from whom all good things come. Dear, dear, when the soft-hearts get hold of a thing like that missionary's contribution they completely lose their tranquillity over it. They speak profanely and reproach Heaven for allowing such a fiend to live. Meaning me. They think it irregular. They go shuddering around, brooding over the reduction of that Congo population from 25,000,000 to 15,000,000 in the twenty years of my administration; then they burst out and call me "the King with Ten Million Murders on his Soul." They call me a "record." The most of them do not stop with charging merely the 10,000,000 against me. No, they reflect that but for me the population, by natural increase, would now be 30,000,000, so they charge another 5,000,000 against me and make my total death-harvest 15,000,000. They remark that the man who killed the goose that laid the golden egg was responsible for the eggs she would subsequently have laid if she had been let alone. Oh, yes, they call me a "record." They remark that twice in a generation, in India, the Great Famine destroys 2,000,000 out of a population of 320,000,000, and the whole world holds up its hands in pity and horror; then they fall to wondering where the world would find room for its emotions if I had a chance to trade places with the Great Famine for twenty years! The idea fires their fancy, and they go on and imagine the Famine coming in state at the end of the twenty years and prostrating itself before me, saying: "Teach me, Lord, I perceive that I am but an apprentice." And next they imagine Death coming, with his scythe and hour-glass, and begging me to marry his daughter and reorganize his plant and run the business. For the whole world,

you see! By this time their diseased minds are under full steam,
and they get down their books and expand their labors, with me
for text. They hunt through all biography for my match, working
Atilla, Torquemada, Ghengis Khan, Ivan the Terrible, and the rest
of that crowd for all they are worth, and evilly exulting when
they cannot find it. Then they examine the historical earthquakes
and cyclones and blizzards and cataclysms and volcanic eruptions:
verdict, none of them "in it" with me. At last they do really
hit it (as they think), and they close their labors with
conceding--reluctantly--that I have one match in history, but
only one--the Flood. This is intemperate.

But they are always that, when they think of me. They can
no more keep quiet when my name is mentioned than can a glass of
water control its feelings with a seidlitz powder in its bowels.
The bizarre things they can imagine, with me for an inspiration!
One Englishman offers to give me the odds of three to one and bet
me anything I like, up to 20,000 guineas, that for 2,000,000
years I am going to be the most conspicuous foreigner in hell.
The man is so beside himself with anger that he does not perceive
that the idea is foolish. Foolish and unbusinesslike: you see,
there could be no winner; both of us would be losers, on account
of the loss of interest on the stakes; at four or five per cent.
compounded, this would amount to--I do not know how much,
exactly, but, by the time the term was up and the bet payable, a
person could buy hell itself with the accumulation.

Another madman wants to construct a memorial for the
perpetuation of my name, out of my 15,000,000 skulls and
skeletons, and is full of vindictive enthusiasm over his strange
project. He has it all ciphered out and drawn to scale. Out of
the skulls he will build a combined monument and mausoleum to me
which shall exactly duplicate the Great Pyramid of Cheops, whose
base covers thirteen acres, and whose apex is 451 feet above
ground. He desires to stuff me and stand me up in the sky on
that apex, robed and crowned, with my "pirate flag" in one hand
and a butcher-knife and pendant handcuffs in the other. He will
build the pyramid in the centre of a depopulated tract, a
brooding solitude covered with weeds and the mouldering ruins of
burned villages, where the spirits of the starved and murdered
dead will voice their laments forever in the whispers of the
wandering winds. Radiating from the pyramid, like the spokes of
a wheel, there are to be forty grand avenues of approach, each
thirty-five miles long, and each fenced on both sides by skulless
skeletons standing a yard and a half apart and festooned together
in line by short chains stretching from wrist to wrist and
attached to tried and true old handcuffs stamped with my private
trade-mark, a crucifix and butcher-knife crossed, with motto, "By
this sign we prosper"; each osseous fence to consist of 200,000
skeletons on a side, which is 400,000 to each avenue. It is
remarked with satisfaction that it aggregates three or four
thousand miles (single-ranked) of skeletons--15,000,000 all told--
and would stretch across America from New York to San Francisco.
It is remarked further, in the hopeful tone of a railroad company
forecasting showy extensions of its mileage, that my output is

500,000 corpses a year when my plant is running full time, and
that therefore if I am spared ten years longer there will be
fresh skulls enough to add 175 feet to the pyramid, making it by
a long way the loftiest architectural construction on the earth,
and fresh skeletons enough to continue the transcontinental file
(on piles) a thousand miles into the Pacific. The cost of
gathering the materials from my "widely scattered and innumerable
private graveyards," and transporting them, and building the
monument and the radiating grand avenues, is duly ciphered out,
running into an aggregate of millions of guineas, and then--why
then, (-- !! -- !!) this idiot asks me to furnish the money!
[Sudden and effusive application of the crucifix] He reminds me
that my yearly income from the Congo is millions of guineas, and
that only 5,000,000 would be required for his enterprise. Every
day wild attempts are made upon my purse; they do not affect me,
they cost me not a thought. But this one--this one troubles me,
makes me nervous; for there is no telling what an unhinged
creature like this may think of next. . . . If he should think
of Carnegie--but I must banish that thought out of my mind! it
worries my days; it troubles my sleep. That way lies madness.
[After a pause] There is no other way--I have got to buy Carnegie.
        [Harassed and muttering, walks the floor a while, then takes
to the Consul's chapter-headings again. Reads]
        Government starved a woman's children to death and killed
her sons.
        Butchery of women and children.
        The native has been converted into a being without
ambition because without hope.
        Women chained by the neck by rubber sentries.
        Women refuse to bear children because, with a baby to
carry, they cannot well run away and hide from the soldiers.
        Statement of a child: "I, my mother, my grandmother and
my sister, we ran away into the bush. A great number of our
people were killed by the soldiers. . . . After that they
saw a little bit of my mother's head, and the soldiers ran
quickly to where we were and caught my grandmother, my
mother, my sister and another little one younger than us.
Each wanted my mother for a wife, and argued about it, so
they finally decided to kill her. They shot her through the
stomach with a gun and she fell, and when I saw that I cried
very much, because they killed my grandmother and mother and
I was left alone. I saw it all done!"
        It has a sort of pitiful sound, although they are only
blacks. It carries me back and back into the past, to when my
children were little, and would fly--to the bush, so to speak--
when they saw me coming. . . .
        [Resumes the reading of chapter-headings of the Consul's
report]
        They put a knife through a child's stomach.
        They cut off the hands and brought them to C. D. (white
officer) and spread them out in a row for him to see. They
left them lying there, because the white man had seen them,
so they did not need to take them to P.

Captured children left in the bush to die, by the soldiers.

Friends came to ransom a captured girl; but sentry refused, saying the white man wanted her because she was young.

Extract from a native girl's testimony:

"On our way the soldiers saw a little child, and when they went to kill it the child laughed, so the soldier took the butt of his gun and struck the child with it and then cut off its head. One day they killed my half-sister and cut off her head, hands and feet, because she had bangles on. Then they caught another sister, and sold her to the W. W. people and now she is a slave there."

The little child laughed! [A long pause. Musing] That innocent creature. Somehow--I wish it had not laughed.

[Reads]

Mutilated children.

Government encouragement of inter-tribal slave-traffic. The monstrous fines levied upon villages tardy in their supplies of foodstuffs compel the natives to sell their fellows--and children--to other tribes in order to meet the fine.

A father and mother forced to sell their boy.

Widow forced to sell her little girl.

[Irritated] Hand the monotonous grumbler, what would he have me do! Let a widow off merely because she is a widow? He knows quite well that there is nothing much left, now, but widows. I have nothing against widows, as a class, but business is business, and I've got to live, haven't I, even if it does cause inconvenience to somebody here and there?

[Reads]

Men intimidated by the torture of their wives and daughters. (To make the men furnish rubber and supplies and so get their captured women released from chains and detention.) The sentry explained to me that he caught the women and brought them in (chained together neck to neck) by direction of his employer.

An agent explained that he was forced to catch women in preference to men, as then the men brought in supplies quicker; but he did not explain how the children deprived of their parents obtained their own food supplies.

A file of 15 (captured) women.

Allowing women and children to die of starvation in prison.

[Musing] Death from hunger. A lingering, long misery that must be. Days and days, and still days and days, the forces of the body failing, dribbling away, little by little--yes, it must be the hardest death of all. And to see food carried by, every day, and you can have none of it! Of course the little children cry for it, and that wrings the mother's heart. . . .

[A sigh] Ah, well, it cannot be helped; circumstances make this discipline necessary.

[Reads]

245

The crucifying of sixty women!

How stupid, how tactless! Christendom's goose flesh will
rise with horror at the news. "Profanation of the sacred
emblem!" That is what Christendom will shout. Yes, Christendom
will buzz. It can hear me charged with half a million murders a
year for twenty years and keep its composure, but to profane the
Symbol is quite another matter. It will regard this as serious.
It will wake up and want to look into my record. Buzz? Indeed
it will; I seem to hear the distant hum already. . . . It was
wrong to crucify the women, clearly wrong, manifestly wrong, I
can see it now, myself, and am sorry it happened, sincerely sorry.
I believe it would have answered just as well to skin them. . . .
[With a sigh] But none of us thought of that; one cannot think of
everything; and after all it is but human to err.

It will make a stir, no doubt, these crucifixions. Persons
will begin to ask once more, as now and then in times past, how I
can hope to win and keep the respect of the human race if I
continue to give up my life to murder and pillage. [Scornfully]
When have they heard me say I wanted the respect of the human
race? Do they confuse me with the common herd? do they forget
that I am a king? What king has valued the respect of the human
race? I mean deep down in his private heart. If they would
reflect, they would know that it is impossible that a king should
value the respect of the human race. He stands upon an eminence
and looks out over the world and sees multitudes of meek human
things worshipping the persons, and submitting to the oppressions
and exactions, of a dozen human things who are in no way better
or finer than themselves--made on just their own pattern, in
fact, and out of the same quality of mud. When it talks, it is a
race of whales; but a king knows it for a race of tadpoles. Its
history gives it away. If men were really men, how could a Czar
be possible? and how could I be possible? But we are possible;
we are quite safe; and with God's help we shall continue the
business at the old stand. It will be found that the race will
put up with us, in its docile immemorial way. It may pull a wry
face now and then, and make large talk, but it will stay on its
knees all the same.

Making large talk is one of its specialities. It works
itself up, and froths at the mouth, and just when you think it is
going to throw a brick--it heaves a poem! Lord, what a race it
is!

A CZAR - 1905

A pasteboard autocrat; a despot out of date;
   A fading planet in the glare of day;
   A flickering candle in the bright sun's ray,
Burnt to the socket; fruit left too late,
   High on a blighted bough, ripe till it's rotten.

By God forsaken and by time forgotten,
Watching the crumbling edges of his lands,
   A spineless god to whom dumb millions pray,
   From Finland in the West to far Cathay,

Lord of a frost-bound continent he stands,
   Her seeming ruin his dim mind appalls,
And in the frozen stupor of his sleep
   He hears dull thunders, pealing as she falls,
And mighty fragments dropping in the deep.*

It is fine, one is obliged to concede it; it is a great
picture, and impressive. The mongrel handles his pen well.
Still, with opportunity, I would cruciflay him. . . . "A
spineless god." It is the Czar to a dot--a god, and spineless; a
royal invertebrate, poor lad; soft-hearted and out of place. "A
spineless god to whom dumb millions pray." Remorselessly correct;
concise, too, compact--the soul and spirit of the human race
compressed into half a sentence. On their knees--140,000,000.
On their knees to a little tin diety. Massed together, they
would stretch away, and away, and away, across the plains, fading
and dimming and failing in a measureless perspective--why, even
the telescope's vision could not reach to the final frontier of
that continental spread of human servility. Now why should a
king value the respect of the human race? It is quite
unreasonable to expect it. A curious race, certainly! It finds
fault with me and with my occupations, and forgets that neither
of us could exist an hour without its sanction. It is our
confederate and all-powerful protector. It is our bulwark, our
friend, our fortress. For this it has our gratitude, our deep
and honest gratitude--but not our respect. Let it snivel and
fret and grumble if it likes; that is all right; we do not mind
that.
   [Turns over leaves of a scrapbook, pausing now and then to
read a clipping and make a comment]
The poets--how they do hunt that poor Czar! French, Germans,
English, Americans--they all have a bark at him. The finest and
capablest of the pack, and the fiercest, are Swilburne (English,
I think), and a pair of Americans, Thomas Bailey Eldridge and
Colonel Richard Waterson Gilder, of the sentimental periodical
called Century Magazine and Louisville Courier-Journal. They
certainly have uttered some very strong yelps. I can't seem to
find them--I must have mislaid them. . . . If a poet's bite were
as terrible as his bark, why dear me--but it isn't. A wise king
minds neither of them; but the poet doesn't know it. It's a case
of little dog and lightning express. When the Czar goes
thundering by, the poet skips out and rages alongside for a
little distance, then returns to his kennel wagging his head with
satisfaction, and thinks he has inflicted a memorial scare,
whereas nothing has really happened--the Czar didn't know he was
around. They never bark at me; I wonder why that is. I suppose
my Corruption-Department buys them. That must be it, for
certainly I ought to inspire a bark or two; I'm rather choice
material, I should say. Why--here is a yelp at me.

*B. H. Nadal, in New York Times.

[Mumbling a poem]
. . . What gives thee holy right to murder hope
And water ignorance with human blood?

From what high universe-dividing power
Draw'st thou thy wondrous, ripe brutality?

O horrible . . . Thou God who seest these things
Help us to blot this terror from the earth.

. . . No, I see it is To the Czar,* after all. But there
are those who would say it fits me--and rather snugly, too.
"Ripe brutality." They would say the Czar's isn't ripe yet, but
that mine is; and not merely ripe but rotten. Nothing could keep
them from saying that; they would think it smart. "This terror."
Let the Czar keep that name; I am supplied. This long time I have
been "the monster"; that was their favorite--the monster of crime.
But now I have a new one. They have found a fossil Dinosaur
fifty-seven feet long and sixteen feet high, and set it up in the
museum in New York and labeled it "Leopold II." But it is no
matter, one does not look for manners in a republic. Um . . .
that reminds me; I have never been caricatured. Could it be that
the corsairs of the pencil could not find an offensive symbol
that was big enough and ugly enough to do my reputation justice?
[After reflection] There is no other way--I will buy the
Dinosaur. And suppress it.
　　[Rests himself with some more chapter-headings. Reads]
More mutilation of children. (Hands cut off.)
Testimony of American Missionaries.
Evidence of British Missionaires.
　　It is all the same old thing--tedious repetitions and
duplications of shop-worn episodes; mutilations, murders,
massacres, and so on, and so on, till one gets drowsy over it.
Mr. Morel intrudes at this point, and contributes a comment which
he could just as well have kept to himself--and throws in some
italics, of course; these people can never get along without
italics:
　　　　It is one heartrending story of human misery from
　　　　beginning to end, and it is all recent.
Meaning 1904 and 1905. I do not see how a person can act
so. This Morel is a king's subject, and reverence for monarchy
should have restrained him from reflecting upon me with that
exposure. This Morel is a reformer; a Congo reformer. That
sizes him up. He publishes a sheet in Liverpool called The West
African Mail, which is supported by the voluntary contributions
of the sap-headed and the soft-hearted; and every week it steams
and reeks and festers with up-to-date "Congo atrocities" of the
sort detailed in this pile of pamphlets here. I will suppress
it. I suppressed a Congo atrocity book there, after it was
actually in print; it should not be difficult for me to suppress
a newspaper.

*Louise Morgan Sill, in Harper's Weekly.

248

[Studies some photographs of mutilated Negroes, throws them down. Sighs]
The kodak has been a sore calamity to us. The most powerful enemy indeed. In the early years we had no trouble in getting the press to "expose" the tales of the mutilations as slanders, lies, inventions of busy-body American missionaries and exasperated foreigners who found the "open door" of the Berlin-Congo charter closed against them when they innocently went out there to trade; and by the press's help we got the Christian nations everywhere to turn an irritated and unbelieving ear to those tales and say hard things about the tellers of them. Yes, all things went harmoniously and pleasantly in those days, and I was looked up to as the benefactor of a down-trodden and friendless people. Then all of a sudden came the crash! That is to say, the incorruptible kodak--and all the harmony went to hell! The only witness I have encountered in my long experience that I couldn't bribe. Every Yankee missionary and every interrupted trader sent home and got one; and now--oh, well, the pictures get sneaked around everywhere, in spite of all we can do to ferret them out and suppress them. Ten thousand pulpits and ten thousand presses are saying the good word for me all the time and placidly and convincingly denying the mutilations. Then the trivial little kodak, that a child can carry in its pocket, get up, uttering never a word, and knocks them dumb!
. . . . What is this fragment?
[Reads]
But enough of trying to tally off his crimes! His list is interminable, we should never get to the end of it. His awful shadow lies across his Congo Free State, and under it an unoffending nation of 15,000,000 is withering away and swiftly succumbing of their miseries. It is a land of graves; it is The Land of Graves; it is the Congo Free Graveyard. It is a majestic thought: that is, this ghastliest episode in all human history is the work of one man alone; one solitary man; just a single individual-- Leopold, King of the Belgians. He is personally and solely responsible for all the myriad crimes that have blackened the history of the Congo State. He is sole master there; he is absolute. He could have prevented the crimes by his mere command; he could stop them today with a word. He withholds the word. For his pocket's sake.
It seem strange to see a king destroying a nation and laying waste a country for mere sordid money's sake, and solely and only for that. Lust of conquest is royal; kings have always exercised that stately vice; we are used to it, by old habit we condone it, perceiving a certain dignity in it; but lust of money--lust of shillings--lust of nickels-- lust of dirty coin, not for the nation's enrichment but for the king's alone--this is new. It distinctly revolts us, we cannot seem to reconcile ourselves to it, we resent it, we despise it, we say it is shabby, unkingly, out of character. Being democrats we ought to jeer and jest, we ought to

rejoice to see the purple dragged in the dirt, but--well, account for it as we may, we don't. We see this awful king, this pitiless and blood-drenched king, this money-crazy king towering toward the sky in a world-solitude of sordid crime, unfellowed and apart from the human race, sole butcher for personal gain findable in all his caste, ancient or modern, pagan or Christian, proper and legitimate target for the scorn of the lowest and the highest, and the execrations of all who hold in cold esteem the oppressor and the coward; and--well, it is a mystery, but we do not wish to look; for he is a king, and it hurts us, it troubles us, by ancient and inherited instinct it shames us to see a king degraded to this aspect, and we shrink from hearing the particulars of how it happened. We shudder and turn away when we come upon them in print.

Why, certainly--THAT IS MY PROTECTION. And you will continue to do it. I know the human race.

Mark Twain, King Leopold's Soliloquy: A Defense of His Rule, Boston, 1905.

[1]The "Boxers" were members of a secret society in China, "The Righteous Harmony Fists," but since they kept in training by gymnastics, they were called "Boxers." Their goal was to eject all foreigners from their country. In 1900, they started the "Boxer Rebellion" to achieve this goal; occupied Peking and attacked the foreign legations. They were brutally suppressed by foreign armies, and the Chinese government was forced to pay damages for the assult on foreigners.

[2]Joseph Chamberlain (1836-1914), British politician and architect of the imperialist policies carried out by the British government around the beginning of the twentieth century. Chamberlain was secretary of state for the colonies in the Conservative government from 1895 to 1903.

[3]Boers were the South Africans of Dutch descent, who founded the South African Republic. In the South African War (1899-1902), the Boers of the South African Republic waged war against the British Empire. The Boers eventually surrendered in 1902, thus ending the independent existence of the Boer republics, but the racist policies of the Boers towards blacks in South Africa both continued and intensified.

[4]George Dewey (1837-1917), U.S. naval officer who was in Hong Kong when he received news of war with Spain; sailed for Manila in the Philippines, and destroyed the Spanish squadron in the Battle of Manila Bay, August 13, 1898.

[5]The Philippines had long been the scene of unrest and dissatisfaction with Spanish rule, and in 1896, inspired by the writings of Dr. José P. Rizal and other Filipino intellectuals, the Filipinos arose in rebellion against Spanish tyranny. On November 11, 1896, insurgent general Emilio Aguinaldo engaged General Ramon Blanco and forced him to withdraw, and the victory further fanned the flames of revolt.

[6]Immediately after the battle in Manila Bay, Dewey had suggested that the Filipino chief, Emilio Aguinaldo, might be able to render valuable services in the war against Spanish forces on the island. Aguinaldo and his men assumed a strong offensive after the fall of Manila, placing large parts of the island under the effective rule of the Filipinos. While U.S. officials publically praised the Filipinos, Navy Secretary Long, alarmed by this development, privately cautioned Dewey to be careful in his relations with the Filipinos lest they get the idea that the United States favored independence for the island after Spanish rule was overthrown. (Navy Department Annual Report, 1898, Appendix, p. 101.)

[7]In the Treaty of Paris ending the war between the United States and Spain, the Philippine Islands were transferred to the United States for the consideration of $20,000,000.

[8]Herbert Kitchener (1850-1916), British field marshall, was commander in chief of the British forces in the South African War. During the last 18 months of the war, he combatted guerrila resistance by such methods as burning Boer farms and herding Boer women and children into concentration camps.

[9]Instead of real independence, the United States forced Cuba to accept the Platt Amendment which reduced her to the status of a semi-colony.

[10]In their narratives after they escaped from slavery, many former slaves emphasized that stealing was a way of getting for themselves what they believed they were entitled to since it was their labor which had produced the products.

[11]Ulysses Simpson Grant (1822-1835), eighteenth President of the United States; formerly commander of all the armies of the United States during the Civil War. As President, Grant's administration was marked by corruption, and it is strange that Twain linked him with Washington and Lincoln.

[12]The reference is to the capture of Emilo Aguinaldo by General Frederick Funston.

[13]Twain is in error here. While the United States had been part of the group that had drawn up the Berlin Act, President Grover Cleveland had withheld it from Senate ratification.

CHAPTER III

FICTION

1. WILLIAM DEAN HOWELLS

EDITHA

The air was thick with the war feeling, like the electricity
of a storm which had not yet burst. Editha sat looking out into
the hot spring afternoon, with her lips parted, and panting with
the intensity of the question whether she could let him go. She
had decided that she could not let him stay, when she saw him at
the end of the still leafless avenue, making slowly up towards
the house, with his head down and his figure relaxed. She ran
impatiently out on the veranda, to the edge of the steps, and
imperatively demanded greater haste of him with her will before
she called him aloud to him: "George!"

He had quickened his pace in mystical response to her
mystical urgence, before he could have heard her; now he looked
up and answered, "Well?"

"Oh, how united we are!" she exulted, and then she swooped
down the steps to him, "What is it?" she cried.

"It's war," he said. and he pulled her up to him and kissed
her.

She kissed him back intensely, but irrelevantly, as to their
passion, and uttered from deep in her throat. "How glorious!"

"It's war," he repeated, without consenting to her sense of
it; and she did not know just what to think at first. She never
knew what to think of him; that made his mystery, his charm. All
through their courtship, which was contemporaneous with the
growth of the war feeling, she had been puzzled by his want of
seriousness about it. He seemed to despise it even more than he
abhorred it. She could have understood his abhorring any sort of
bloodshed; that would have been a survival of his old life when
he thought he would be a minister, and before he changed and took
up the law. But making light of a cause so high and noble seemed
to show a want of earnestness at the core of his being. Not but
that she felt herself able to cope with a congenital defect of
that sort, and make his love for her save him from himself. Now
perhaps the miracle was already wrought in him. In the presence
of the tremendous fact that he announced, all triviality seemed

to have gone out of him; she began to feel that. He sank down on
the top step, and wiped his forehead with his handkerchief, while
she poured out upon him her question of the origin and
authenticity of his news.

All the while, in her duplex emotioning, she was aware that
now at the very beginning she must put a guard upon herself
against urging him, by any word or act, to take the part that her
whole soul willed him to take, for the completion of her ideal of
him. He was very nearly perfect as he was, and he must be
allowed to perfect himself. But he was peculiar, and he might
very well be reasoned out of his peculiarity. Before her
reasoning went her emotioning: her nature pulling upon his
nature, her womanhood upon his manhood, without her knowing the
means she was using to the end she was willing. She had always
supposed that the man who won her would have done something to
win her; she did not know what, but something. George Gearson
had simply asked her for her love, on the way home from a
concert, and she gave her love to him, without, as it were,
thinking. But now, it flashed upon her, if he could do something
worthy to have won her--be a hero, her hero--it would be even
better than if he had done it before asking her; it would be
grander. Besides, she had believed in the war from the beginning.

"But don't you see, dearest," she said, "that it wouldn't
have come to this if it hadn't been in the order of Providence?
And I call any war glorious that is for the liberation of people
who have been struggling for years against the cruelest
oppression. Don't you think so, too?"

"I suppose so," he returned, languidly. "But war! Is it
glorious to break the peace of the world?"

"That ignoble peace! It was no peace at all, with that
crime and shame at our very gates." She was conscious of
parroting the current phrases of the newspapers, but it was no
time to pick and choose her words. She must sacrifice anything
to the high ideal she had for him, and after a good deal of rapid
argument she ended with the climax: "But now it doesn't matter
about the how or why. Since the war has come, all that is gone.
There are no two sides any more. There is nothing now but our
country."

He sat with his eyes closed and his head leant back against
the veranda, and he remarked, with a vague smile, as if musing
aloud, "Our country--right or wrong."

"Yes, right or wrong!" she returned, fervidly. "I'll go and
get you some lemonade." She rose rustling, and whisked away;
when she came back with two tall glasses of clouded liquid on a
tray, and the ice clucking in them, he still sat as she had left
him, and she said, as if there had been no interruption: "But
there is no question of wrong in this case. I call it a sacred
war. A war for liberty and humanity, if ever there was one. And
I know you will see it just as I do, yet."

He took half the lemonade at a gulp, and he answered as he
set the glass down: "I know you always have the highest ideal.
When I differ from you I ought to doubt myself."

A generous sob rose in Editha's throat for the humility of a man, so very nearly perfect, who was willing to put himself below her.

Besides, she felt, more subliminally, that he was never so near slipping through her fingers as when he took that meek way.

"You shall not say that! Only, for once I happen to be right." She seized his hand in her two hands, and poured her soul from her eyes into his. "Don't you think so?" she entreated him.

He released his hand and drank the rest of his lemonade, and she added, "Have mine, too," but he shook his head in answering, "I've no business to think so, unless I act so, too."

Her heart stopped a beat before it pulsed on with leaps that she felt in her neck. She had noticed that strange thing in men: they seemed to feel bound to do what they believed, and not think a thing was finished when they said it, as girls did. She knew what was in his mind, but she pretended not, and she said, "Oh, I am not sure," and then faltered.

He went on as if to himself, without apparently heeding her: "There's only one way of proving one's faith in a thing like this."

She could not say that she understood, but she did understand.

He went on again. "If I believed--if I felt as you do about this war-- Do you wish me to feel as you do?"

Now she was really not sure; so she said: "George, I don't know what you mean."

He seemed to muse away from her as before. "There is a sort of fascination in it. I suppose that at the bottom of his heart every man would like at times to have his courage tested, to see how he would act."

"How can you talk in that gastly way?"

"It is rather morbid. Still, that's what it comes to, unless you're swept away by ambition or driven by conviction. I haven't the conviction or the ambition, and the other thing is what it comes to with me. I ought to have been a preacher, after all; then I couldn't be asked it of myself, as I must, now I'm a lawyer. And you believe it's a holy war, Editha?" he suddenly addressed her. "Oh, I know you do! But you wish me to believe so, too?"

She hardly knew whether he was mocking or not, in the ironical way he always had with her plainer mind. But the only thing was to be outspoken with him.

"George, I wish you to believe whatever you think is true, at any and every cost. If I've tried to talk you into anything, I take it all back."

"Oh, I know that, Editha. I know how sincere you are, and how-- I wish I had your undoubting spirit! I'll think it over; I'd like to believe as you do. But I don't, now; I don't, indeed. It isn't this war alone; though this seems peculiarly wanton and needless; but it's every war--so stupid; it makes me sick. Why shouldn't this thing have been settled reasonably?"

"Because," she said, very throatily again, "God meant it to be war."

"You think it was God? Yes, I suppose that is what people will say."

"Do you suppose it would have been war if God hadn't meant it?"

"I don't know. Sometimes it seems as if God had put this world into men's keeping to work it as they pleased."

"Now, George, that is blasphemy."

"Well, I won't blaspheme. I'll try to believe in your pocket Providence," he said, and then he rose to go.

"Why don't you stay to dinner?" Dinner at Balcom's Works was at one o'clock.

"I'll come back to supper, if you'll let me. Perhaps I shall bring you a convert."

"Well, you may come back, on that condition."

"All right. If I don't come, you'll understand."

He went away without kissing her, and she felt it a suspension of their engagement. It all interested her intensely; she was undergoing a tremendous experience, and she was being equal to it. While she stood looking after him, her mother came out through one of the long windows onto the veranda, with a catlike softness and vagueness.

"Why didn't he stay to dinner?"

"Because--because--war has been declared," Editha pronounced, without turning.

Her mother said, "Oh, my!" and then said nothing more until she had sat down in one of the large Shaker chairs and rocked herself for some time. Then she closed whatever tacit passage of thought there had been in her mind with the spoken words: "Well, I hope he won't go."

"And I hope he will," the girl said, and confronted her mother with a stormy exaltation that would have frightened any creature less unimpressionable than a cat.

Her mother rocked herself again for an interval of cogitation. What she arrived at in speech was: "Well, I guess you've done a wicked thing, Editha Balcom."

The girl said, as she passed indoors through the same window her mother had come out by: "I haven't done anything--yet."

In her room, she put together all her letters and gifts from Gearson, down to the withered petals of the first flower he had offered, with that timidity of his veiled in that irony of his. In the heart of the packet she enshrined her engagement ring which she had restored to the pretty box he had brought it her in. Then she sat down, if not calmly yet strongly, and wrote:

"George:--I understood when you left me. But I think we had better emphasize your meaning that if we cannot be one in everything we had better be one in nothing. So I am sending these things for your keeping till you have made up your mind.

"I shall always love you, and therefore I shall never marry any one else. But the man I marry must love his country first of all, and be able to say to me,

"'I could not love thee, dear, so much,
      Loved I not honor more.'

"There is not honor above America with me.   In this great
hour there is no other honor.
      "Your heart will make my words clear to you. I had never
expected to say so much, but it has come upon me that I must say
the utmost.   Editha "

      She thought she had worded her letter well, worded it in a
way that could not be bettered; all had been implied and nothing
expressed.
      She had it ready to send with the packet she had tied with
red, white, and blue ribbon, when it occurred to her that she was
not just to him, that she was not giving him a fair chance. He
had said he would go and think it over, and she was not waiting.
She was pushing, threatening, compelling. That was not a woman's
part. She must leave him free, free, free. She could not accept
for her country or herself a forced sacrifice.
      In writing her letter she had satisfied the impulse from
which it sprang; she could well afford to wait till he had
thought it over. She put the packet and the letter by, and
rested serene in the consciousness of having done what was laid
upon her by her love itself to do, and yet used patience, mercy,
justice.
      She had her reward. Gearson did not come to tea, but she
had given him till morning, when, late at night there came up
from the village the sound of a fife and drum, with a tumult of
voices, in shouting, singing, and laughing. The noise drew
nearer and nearer; it reached the street end of the avenue; there
it silenced itself, and one voice, the voice she knew best, rose
over the silence. It fell; the air was filled with cheers; the
fife and drum struck up, with the shouting, singing, and laughing
again, but now retreating; and a single figure came hurrying up
the avenue.
      She ran down to meet her lover and clung to him. He was
very gay, and he put his arm round her with a boisterous laugh.
"Well, you must call me Captain now; or Cap, if you prefer;
that's what the boys call me. Yes, we've had a meeting at the
town-hall, and everybody has volunteered; and they selected me
for captain, and I'm going to the war, the big war, the glorious
war, the holy war ordained by the pocket Providence that blesses
butchery. Come along; let's tell the whole family about it.
Call them from their downy beds, father, mother, Aunt Hitty, and
all the folks!"
      But when they mounted the veranda steps he did not wait for
a larger audience; he poured the story out upon Editha alone.
      "There was a lot of speaking, and then some of the fools set
up a shout for me. It was all going one way, and I thought it
would be a good joke to sprinkle a little cold water on them.
But you can't do that with a crowd that adores you. The first
thing I knew I was sprinkling hell-fire on them. 'Cry havoc, and
let slip the dogs of war.' That was the style. Now that it had

come to the fight, there were no two parties; there was one country, and the thing was to fight to a finish as quick as possible. I suggested volunteering then and there, and I wrote my name first of all on the roster. Then they elected me--that's all. I wish I had some ice-water."

She left him walking up and down the veranda, while she ran for the ice-pitcher and a goblet, and when she came back he was still walking up and down, shouting the story he had told her to her father and mother, who had come out more sketchily dressed than they commonly were by day. He drank goblet after goblet of the ice-water without noticing who was giving it, and kept on talking, and laughing through his talk wildly. "It's astonishing," he said, "how well the worse reason looks when you try to make it appear the better. Why, I believe I was the first convert to the war in that crowd to-night! I never thought I should like to kill a man; but now I shouldn't care; and the smokeless powder lets you see the man drop that you kill. It's all for the country! What a thing it is to have a country that can't be wrong, but if it is, is right, anyway!"

Editha had a great, vital thought, an inspiration. She set down the ice-pitcher on the veranda floor, and ran up-stairs and got the letter she had written him. When at last he noisily bade her father and mother, "Well, good-night. I forgot I woke you up; I sha'n't want any sleep myself," she followed him down the avenue to the gate. There, after the whirling words that seemed to fly away from her thoughts and refuse to serve them, she made a last effort to solemnize the moment that seemed so crazy, and pressed the letter she had written upon him.

"What's this?" he said. "Want me to mail it?"

"No, no. It's for you. I wrote it after you went this morning. Keep it--keep it--and read it sometime--" She thought, and then her inspiration came: "Read it if ever you doubt what you've done, or fear that I regret your having done it. Read it after you've started."

They strained each other in embraces that seemed as ineffective as their words, and he kissed her face with quick, hot breaths that were so unlike him, that made her feel as if she had lost her old lover and found a stranger in his place. The stranger said: "What a gorgeous flower you are, with your red hair, and your blue eyes that look black now, and your face with the color painted out by the white moonshine! Let me hold you under the chin, to see whether I love blood, you tiger-lily!" Then he laughed Gearson's laugh, and released her, scared and giddy. Within her wilfulness she had been frightened by a sense of subtler force in him, and mystically mastered as she had never been before.

She ran all the way back to the house, and mounted the steps panting. Her mother and father were talking of the great affair. Her mother said: "Wa'n't Mr Gearson in rather of an excited state of mind? Didn't you think he acted curious?"

"Well, not for a man who'd just been elected captain and had set 'em up for the whole of Company A," her father chuckled back.

"What in the world do you mean, Mr. Balcom? Oh! There's Editha!" She offered to follow the girl indoors.

"Don't come, mother!" Edith called, vanishing.

Mrs. Balcom remained to reproach her husband. "I don't see much of anything to laugh at."

"Well, it's catching. Caught it from Gearson. I guess it won't be much of a war, and I guess Gearson don't think so, either. The other fellows will back down as soon as they see we mean it. I wouldn't lose any sleep over it. I'm going back to bed, myself."

Gearson came again next afternoon, looking pale and rather sick, but quite himself, even to his languid irony. "I guess I'd better tell you, Editha, that I consecrated myself to your god of battles last night by pouring too many libations to him down my own throat. But I'm all right now. One has to carry off the excitement, somehow."

"Promise me," she commanded, "that you'll never touch it again!"

"What! Not let the cannikin clink? Not let the soldier drink? Well, I promise."

"You don't belong to yourself now; you don't even belong to me. You belong to your country, and you have a sacred charge to keep yourself strong and well for your country's sake. I have been thinking, thinking all night and all day long."

"You look as if you had been crying a little, too," he said, with his queer smile.

"That's all past. I've been thinking, and worshipping you. Don't you suppose I know all that you've been through, to come to this? I've followed you every step from your old theories and opinions."

"Well, you've had a long row to hoe."

"And I know you've done this from the highest motives--"

"Oh, there won't be much pettifogging to do till this cruel war is--"

"And you haven't simply done it for my sake. I couldn't respect you if you had."

"Well, then we'll say I haven't. A man that hasn't got his own respect intact wants the respect of all the other people he can corner. But we won't go into that. I'm in for the thing now, and we've got to face our future. My idea is that this isn't going to be a very protracted struggle; we shall just scare the enemy to death before it comes to a fight at all. But we must provide for contingencies, Editha. If anything happens to me--"

"Oh, George!" She clung to him, sobbing.

"I don't want you to feel foolishly bound to my memory. I should hate that, wherever I happened to be."

"I am yours, for time and eternity--time and eternity." She liked the words; they satisfied her famine for phrases.

"Well, say eternity; that's all right; but time's another thing; and I'm talking about time. But there is something! My mother! If anything happens--"

She winced, and he laughed. "You're not the bold soldier-girl of yesterday!" Then he sobered. "If anything happens, I want you to help my mother out. She won't like my doing this thing. She brought me up to think war a fool thing as well as a bad thing. My father was in the Civil War; all through it; lost his arm in it." She thrilled with the sense of the arm round her; what if that should be lost? He laughed as if divining her: "Oh, it doesn't run in the family, as far as I know!" Then he added gravely: "He came home with misgivings about war, and they grew on him. I guess he and mother agreed between them that I was to be brought up in his final mind about it; but that was before my time. I only knew him from my mother's report of him and his opinions; I don't know whether they were hers first; but they were hers last. This will be a blow to her. I shall have to write and tell her--"

He stopped, and she asked: "Would you like me to write, too, George?"

"I don't believe that would do. No, I'll do the writing. She'll understand a little if I say that I thought the way to minimize it was to make war on the largest possible scale at once--that I felt I must have been helping on the war somehow if I hadn't helped keep it from coming, and I knew I hadn't; when it came, I had no right to stay out of it."

Whether his sophistries satisfied him or not, they satisfied her. She clung to his breast, and whispered, with closed eyes and quivering lips: "Yes, yes, yes!"

"But if anything should happen, you might go to her and see what you could do for her. You know? It's rather far off; she can't leave her chair--"

"Oh, I'll go, if it's the ends of the earth! But nothing will happen! Nothing can! I--"

She felt her lifted with his rising, and Gearson was saying, with his arm still round her, to her father: "Well, we're off at once, Mr. Balcom. We're to be formally accepted at the capital, and then bunched up with the rest somehow, and sent into camp somewhere, and got to the front as soon as possible. We all want to be in the van, of course; we're the first company to report to the Governor. I came to tell Editha, but I hadn't got round to it."

She saw him again for a moment at the capital, in the station; just before the train started southward with his regiment. He looked well, in his uniform, and very soldierly, but somehow girlish, too, with his clean-shaven face and slim figure. The manly eyes and the strong voice satisfied her, and his preoccupation with some unexpected details of duty flattered her. Other girls were weeping and bemoaning themselves, but she felt a sort of noble distinction in the abstraction, the almost unconsciousness, with which they parted. Only at the last moment he said: "Don't forget my mother. It mayn't be such a walk-over as I supposed," and he laughed at the notion.

He waved his hand to her as the train moved off--she knew it among a score of hands that were waved to other girls from the

platform of the car, for it held a letter which she knew was
hers. Then he went inside the car to read it, doubtless, and she
did not see him again. But she felt safe for him through the
strength of what she called her love. What she called her God,
always speaking the name in a deep voice and with the implication
of a mutual understanding, would watch over him and keep him and
bring him back to her. If with an empty sleeve, then he should
have three arms instead of two, for both of hers should be his
for life. She did not see, though, why she should always be
thinking of the arm his father had lost.

There were not many letters from him, but they were such as
she could have wished, and she put her whole strength into making
hers such as she imagined he could have wished, glorifying and
supporting him. She wrote to his mother glorifying him as their
hero, but the brief answer she got was merely to the effect that
Mrs. Gearson was not well enough to write herself, and thanking
her for her letter by the hand of someone who called herself "Yrs
truly, Mrs. W. J. Andrews."

Editha determined not to be hurt, but to write again quite
as if the answer had been all she expected. Before it seemed as
if she could have written, there came news of the first skirmish,
and in the list of the killed, which was telegraphed as a trifling
loss on our side, was Gearson's name. There was a frantic time
of trying to make out that it might be, must be, some other
Gearson; but the name and the company and the regiment and the
State were too definitely given.

Then there was a lapse into depths out of which it seemed as
if she never could rise again; then a lift into clouds far above
all grief, black clouds, that blotted out the sun, but where she
soared with him, with George--George! She had the fever that she
expected of herself, but she did not die in it; she was not even
delirious, and it did not last long. When she was well enough to
leave her bed, her one thought was of George's mother, of his
strangely worded wish that she should go to her and see what she
could do for her. In the exaltation of the duty laid upon her--it
buoyed her up instead of burdening her--she rapidly recovered.

Her father went with her on the long railroad journey from
northern New York to western Iowa; he had business out at
Davenport, and he said he could just as well go then as any other
time; and he went with her to the little country town where
George's mother lived in a little house on the edge of the
illimitable cornfields, under trees pushed to a top of the
rolling prairie. George's father had settled there after the
Civil War, as so many other old soldiers had done; but they were
Eastern people, and Editha fancied touches of the East in the
June rose overhanging the front door, and the garden with early
summer flowers stretching from the gate of the paling fence.

It was very low inside the house, and so dim, with the closed
blinds, that they could scarcely see one another: Editha tall
and black in her crapes which filled the air with the smell of
their dyes; her father standing decorously apart with his hat on
his forearm, as at funerals; a woman rested in a deep arm-chair,
and the woman who had let the strangers in stood behind the chair.

The seated woman turned her head round and up, and asked the woman behind her chair: "Who did you say?"

Editha, if she had done what she expected of herself, would have gone down on her knees at the feet of the seated figure and said, "I am George's Editha," for answer.

But instead of her own voice she heard that other woman's voice, saying: "Well, I don't know as I did get the name just right. I guess I'll have to make a little more light in here," and she went and pushed two of the shutters ajar.

Then Editha's father said, in his public will-now-address-a-few-remarks tone: "My name is Balcom, ma'am--Junius H. Balcom, of Balcom's Works, New York; my daughter--"

"Oh!" the seated woman broke in, with a powerful voice, the voice that always surprised Editha from Gearson's slender frame. "Let me see you. Stand round where the light can strike on your face," and Editha dumbly obeyed. "So, you're Editha Balcom," she sighed.

"Yes," Editha said, more like a culprit than a comforter.

"What did you come for?" Mrs. Gearson asked.

Editha's face quivered and her knees shook. "I came--because--because George--" She could go no further.

"Yes," the mother said, "he told me he had asked you to come if he got killed. You didn't expect that, I suppose, when you sent him."

"I would rather have died myself than done it!" Editha said, with more truth in her deep voice than she ordinarily found in it. "I tried to leave him free--"

"Yes, that letter of yours, that came back with his other things, left him free."

Editha saw now where George's irony came from.

"It was not to be read before--unless--until-- I told him so," she faltered.

"Of course, he wouldn't read a letter of yours, under the circumstances, till he thought you wanted him to. Been sick?" the woman abruptly demanded.

"Very sick," Editha said, with self-pity.

"Daughter's life," her father interposed, "was almost despaired of, at one time."

Mrs. Gearson gave him no heed. "I suppose you would have been glad to die, such a brave person as you! I don't believe he was glad to die. He was always a timid boy, that way; he was afraid of a good many things; but if he was afraid he did what he made up his mind to. I suppose he made up his mind to go, but I knew what it cost him by what it cost me when I heard of it. I had been through one war before. When you sent him you didn't expect he would get killed."

The voice seemed to compassionate Editha, and it was time. "No," she huskily murmured.

"No, girls don't; women don't, when they give their men up to their country. They think they'll come marching back, somehow, just as gay as they went, or if it's an empty sleeve, or even an empty pantaloon, it's all the more glory, and they're so much the prouder of them, poor things!"

264

The tears began to run down Editha's face; she had not wept till then; but it was now such a relief to be understood that the tears came.

"No, you didn't expect him to get killed," Mrs. Gearson repeated, in a voice which was startlingly like George's again. "You just expected him to kill some one else, some of those foreigners, that weren't there because they had any say about it, but because they had to be there, poor wretches--conscripts, or whatever they call 'em. You thought it would be all right for my George, your George, to kill the sons of those miserable mothers and the husbands of those girls that you would never see the faces of." The woman lifted her powerful voice in a psalmlike note. "I thank my God he didn't live to do it! I thank my God they killed him first, and that he ain't livin' with their blood on his hands!" She dropped her eyes, which she had raised with her voice, and glared at Editha. "What you got that black on for?" She lifted herself by her powerful arms so high that her helpless body seemed to hang limp its full length. "Take it off, take it off, before I tear it from your back!"

The lady who was passing the summer near Balcom's Works was sketching Editha's beauty, which lent itself wonderfully to the effects of a colorist. It had come to that confidence which is rather apt to grow between artist and sitter, and Editha had told her everything.

"To think of your having such a tragedy in your life!" the lady said. She added: "I suppose there are people who feel that way about war. But when you consider the good this war has done--how much it has done for the country! I can't understand such people, for my part. And when you had come all the way out there to console her--got up out of a sick-bed! Well!"

"I think," Editha said, magnanimously, "she wasn't quite in her right mind; and so did papa."

"Yes," the lady said, looking at Editha's lips in nature and then at her lips in art, and giving an empirical touch to them in the picture. "But how dreadful of her! How perfectly--excuse me--how vulgar!"

A light broke upon Editha in the darkness which she felt had been without a gleam of brightness for weeks and months. The mystery that had bewildered her was solved by the word; and from that moment she rose from grovelling in shame and self-pity, and began to live again in the ideal.

Harper's Monthly 110(January, 1905): 214-25, and reprinted in Between the Dark and the Daylight, New York, 1907, pp. 127-143

2. ERNEST HOWARD CROSBY

CAPTAIN JINKS, HERO

A Bombshell

"Bless my soul! I nearly forgot," exclaimed Colonel Jinks, as he came back into the store. "To-morrow is Sam's birthday and I promised Ma to bring him home something for a present. Have you got anything for a boy six years old?"

"Let me see," answered the young woman behind the counter, turning round and looking at an upper shelf. "Why, yes; there's just the thing. It's a box of lead soldiers. I've never seen anything like them before"--and she reached up and pulled down a large cardboard box. "Just see," she added as she opened it. "The officers have swords that come off, and the guns come off the men's shoulders; and look at the--"

"Never mind," interrupted the colonel. "I'm in a hurry. That'll do very well. How much is it?"

And two minutes later he went out of the store with the box in his hand and got into his buggy, and was soon driving through the streets of Homeville on his way to his farm.

No one had ever asked Colonel Jinks where he had obtained his title. In fact, he had never put the question to himself. It was an integral part of his person, and as little open to challenge as his hand or his foot. There are favored regions of the world's surface where colonels, like poets, are born, not made, and good fortune had placed the colonel's birthplace in one of them. For the benefit of those of my readers who may be prejudiced against war, and in justice to the colonel, it should be stated that the only military thing about him was his title. He was a mild-mannered man with a long thin black beard and a slight stoop, and his experience with firearms was confined to the occasional shooting of depredatory crows, squirrels, and rats with an ancient fowling-piece. Still there is magic in a name. And who knows but that the subtle influence of the title of colonel may have unconsciously guided the searching eyes of the

267

young saleswoman among the Noah's arks and farmyards to the box of lead soldiers?

The lad for whom the present was intended was a happy farmer's boy, an only child, for whom the farm was the whole world and who looked upon the horses and cows as his fellows. His little red head was constantly to be seen bobbing about in the barnyard among the sheep and calves, or almost under the horses' feet. The chickens and sparrows and swallows were his playmates, and they seemed to have no fear of him. The black colt with its thick legs and ruffled mane ran behind its gray dam to hide from every one else, but it let Sam pat it without flinching. The first new-hatched chicken which had been given to him for his very own turned out to be a rooster, and when he found that it had to be taken from him and beheaded he was quite inconsolable and refused absolutely to feast upon his former friend. But with this tenderness of disposition Sam had inherited another still stronger trait, and this was a deep respect for authority, and such elements of revolt as revealed themselves in his grief over his rooster were soon stifled in his little heart. He bowed submissively before the powers that be. From the time when he first lisped he had called his parents "Colonel Jinks" and "Mrs. Jinks." His mother had succeeded with great difficulty in substituting the term "Ma" for herself, but she could not make him address his father as anything but "Colonel," and after a time his father grew to like it. No one knew how Sam had acquired the habit; it was simply the expression of an inherently respectful nature. He reverenced his father and loved his father's profession of farmer. His earliest pleasure was to hold the reins and drive "like Colonel Jinks," and his earliest ambition was to become a teamster, that part of the farm work having peculiar attractions for him.

In the afternoon on which we were introduced to the Colonel, Sam was watching on the veranda for his father's return, and was quick to spy the parcel under his arm, and many were the wild guesses he made as to its contents. The Colonel left it carelessly upon the hall table, and Sam could easily have peeped into it, but he would as soon have thought of cutting off his hand.

"What's in that box in the hall, Colonel Jinks?" he asked in an embarrassed voice at supper, as he fingered the edge of the tablecloth and looked blushingly at his plate.

"Oh, that?" replied his father with a wink--"that's a bombshell." And a bombshell indeed it proved to be for the Jinks family.

The box was put upon a table in the room in which little Sam slept with his parents, and he was told that he could have it in the morning. He was a long time going to sleep that night, trying to imagine the contents of the mysterious box. Not until he had quite made up his mind that it was a farmyard did he finally drop off. At the first break of day Sam was out of bed. With bare feet he walked on tiptoe across the cold bare floor and seized the precious box. He lifted the lid at one corner and put in his hand and felt what was there, and tried to guess what it could be. Perhaps it was a Noah's Ark; but no, if those were people there were too many of them. He would have to give it up. He took off the cover and looked in. It was not a farmyard, at any rate, and the corners of his mouth became tremulous from disappointment. No they were soldiers. But what did he want of soldiers? He had heard of such things, but they had never been anything in his life. He had never seen a real soldier nor heard of a toy-soldier before, and he did not quite know what they were for. He crept back to bed crestfallen, his present in his arms. Sitting up in bed he began to investigate the contents of the box. It was a complete infantry batallion, and beautiful soldiers they were. Their coats were red, their trousers blue, and they wore white helmets and carried muskets with bayonets fixed. Sam began to feel reconciled. He turned the box upside-down and emptied the soldiers upon the counterpane. Then he noticed that they were not all alike. There were some officers, who carried swords instead of rifles. He began to look for them and single them out, when his eye was caught by a magnificent white leaden plume issuing from the helmet of one of them. He picked up this soldier, and the sight of him filled him with delight. He was taller and broader than the rest, his air was more martial--there was something inspiring in the way in which he held his sword. His golden epaulets were a miracle of splendor, but it was the plume, the great white plume, that held the boy enthralled. A ray of light from the morning sun, reflected by the window of the stable, found its way through a chink in the blind and fell just upon this plume. The effect was electric. Sam was fascinated, and he continued to hold the lead soldier so that the dazzling light should fall on it, gazing upon it in an ecstasy.

Sam spent that entire day in the company of his new soldiers,--nothing could drag him away from them. He made his father show him how they should march and form themselves and fight. He drew them up in hollow squares facing outward and in hollow squares facing inward, in column of fours and in line of battle, in double rank and single rank.

"What are the bayonets for, Colonel Jinks?"

"To stick into bad people, Sam."

"And have the bad people bayonets, too?"

"Yes, Sam."

"Do they stick their bayonets into good people?"

"Oh, I suppose so. Do stop bothering me. If I'd known you'd ask so many questions, I'd never have got you the soldiers."

His parents thought that a few days would exhaust the boy's devotion to his new toys, but it was not so. He deserted the barnyard for the lead soldiers. They were placed on a chair by his bed at night, and he could not sleep unless his right hand grasped the white-plumed colonel. The smell of the fresh paint as it peeled off on his little fingers clung to his memory through life as the most delicious of odors. He would tease his father to play with the soldiers with him. He would divide the force in two, and one side would defend a fort of blocks and books while the other assaulted. In these games Sam always insisted in having the plumed colonel on his side. Once when Sam's colonel had succeeded in capturing a particularly impregnable fortress on top of an unabridged dictionary his father remarked casually:

"He's quite a hero, isn't he, Sam?"

"A what?" said Sam.

"A hero."

"What is a hero, Colonel Jinks?" And his father explained to him what a hero was, giving several examples from history and fiction. The word took the boy's fancy at once. From that day forward the officer was colonel no longer, he was a "hero," or rather, "the hero." Sam now began to save his pennies for other soldiers, and to beg for more and more as successive birthdays and Christmases came round. He played at soldiers himself, too, coaxing the less warlike children of the neighborhood to join him. But his enthusiasm always left them behind, and they tired much sooner than he did of the sport. He persuaded his mother to make him a uniform something like that of the lead soldiers, and the stores of Homeville were ransacked for drums, swords, and belts and toy-guns. He would stand on guard for hours at the barn-yard gate, saluting in the most solemn manner whoever passed, even if it was only a sparrow. The only interest in animals which survived his change of heart was that which he now took in horses as chargers. He would ride the farm-horses bare-back to the trough, holding the halter in one hand and a tin sword in the other with the air of a field marshal. When strangers tapped him on the cheek and asked him--as is want of strangers--"What are you going to be, my boy, when you grow up?" he answered no longer, as he used to do, "A driver, sir," but now invariably, "A hero."

It so happened some two or three years after Sam's mind had begun to follow the paths of warfare that his father and mother took him one day to an anniversary celebration of the Methodist Church at Homeville, and a special parade of the newly organized "John Wesley Boys' Brigade" of the church was one of the features of the occasion. If Mrs. Jinks had anticipated this, she would doubtless have left Sam at home, for she knew that he was already quite sufficiently inclined toward things military; but even she could not help enjoying the boy's unmeasured delight at this, his first experience of militarism in the flesh. The parade was indeed a pretty sight. There were perhaps fifty boys in line, ranging from six to eighteen years of age. Their gray uniforms were quite new and the gilt letters "J.W.B.B." on their caps shone brightly. They marched along with their miniature muskets and fixed bayonets, their chubby, kissable faces all a-smile, as they sang, "Onward, Christian Soldiers," with words adapted by their pastor:

> "Onward, Christian soldiers,
> 'Gainst the heathen crew!
> In the name of Jesus
> Let us run them through

By a curious coincidence their captain had a white feather in his cap, suggesting at a considerable distance the plume of the leaden "hero." Sam was overcome with joy. He pulled the "hero" from his pocket (he always carried it about with him) and compared the two warriors. The "hero" was still unique, incomparable, but Sam realized that he was an ideal which might be lived up to, not an impossible dream, not the denizen of an inaccessible heaven. From that day he bent his little energies to the task of removing his family to Homeville.

It is not so much strength as perseverance which moves the world. Colonel Jinks had laid up a competence and had always intended to retire, when he could afford it, to the market town. Among other things, the school facilities would be much better in town than in the country. Mrs. Jinks in a moment of folly took the side of the boy, and, whatever may have been the controlling and predominating cause, the fact is that, when Sam had attained the age of twelve, the Colonel sold the farm and bought one of the best houses in Homeville. Sam at once became a member of the John Wesley Brigade and showed an aptitude for soldiering truly amazing. Before he was fourteen he was captain, and wore, himself, the coveted white feather, and his military duties became the absorbing interest of his life. He thought and spoke of nothing else, and he was universally known in the town as "Captain Jinks," which was often abbreviated to "Cap." No one ever passed boyhood and youth in such congenial surroundings and with such complete satisfaction as "Cap" Jinks of the John Wesley Boy's Brigade.

CHAPTER II

East Point

But our relation to our environments will change, however much pleased we may be with them, and "Cap" Jinks found himself gradually growing too old for his brigade. The younger boys and their parents began to complain that he was unreasonably standing in the way of their promotion, and a fiery mustache gave signs to the world that he was now something more than a boy. Still he could not bring himself to relinquish the uniform and the white plume. A life without military trimmings was not to be thought of, and there was no militia at Homeville. Consequently he remained in the Boys' Brigade as long as he could. When at last he saw that he must resign--he was now two-and-twenty--he felt that there was only one course open to him, and that was to join the army; and he broached this plan to his parents. His mother did not like the idea of giving up her only son to such a profession, but Colonel Jinks took kindly to the suggestion. It would bring a little real militarism into the family and give a kind of ex post facto justification to his ancient title. "Sam, my boy," said he, "you're a chip of the old block. You'll keep up the family tradition and be a colonel like me. I will write to your Uncle George about it to-morrow. He'll get you an appointment to East Point without any trouble. Sam, I'm proud of you."

Uncle George Jinks, the only brother of the Colonel, was a member of Congress from a distant district, who had a good deal of influence with the Administration. The Colonel wrote to him asking for the cadetship and rehearsing at length the young captain's unusual qualifications and his military enthusiasm. A week later he received the answer. His brother informed him that the request could not have come at a more opportune moment, as he had a vacancy to fill and had been on the point of calling a public examination of young men in his district for the purpose of selecting a candidate; but in view of the evident fitness of his nephew, he would alter his plans and offer him the place without further ceremony. He wished only that Sam would do credit to the name of Jinks.

It was on a beautiful day in June that "Cap" Jinks bade farewell to Homeville. The family came out in front of the house, keeping back their tears as best they could at this the first parting; but Sam, tho he loved them well, had no room in his heart for regret. There was a vision of glory beckoning him on which obliterated all other feelings. The Boy's Brigade was drawn up at the side of the road and presented arms as he drove by, and he saw in this the promise of greater things. As he sat on the back seat of the wagon by himself behind the driver, he took from his pocket the old original "hero," the lead officer of his boyhood, and gazed at it smiling. "Now I am to be a real hero," he thought, "and all the world will repeat the name of Sam Jinks and read about his exploits. He put the toy carefully back in his breast pocket. It had become the talisman of his life and the symbol of his ambitions.

The long railway journey to East Point was full of interest to the young traveler, who had never been away from home before. His mind was full of military things, but he saw no uniforms, no arms, no fortifications anywhere. How could people live in such a careless, unnatural fashion? He blushed with shame as he thought to himself that a foreigner might apparently journey through the country from one end to the other without knowing that there was such a thing as a soldier in the land. What a travesty this was on civilization! How baseless the proud boasts of national greatness when only an insignificant and almost invisible few paid any attention to the claims of military glory! The outlook was indeed dismal, but Sam was no pessimist. Obstacles were in his dictionary "things to be removed." "I shall have a hand in changing all this," he muttered aloud. "When I come home a conquering general with the grateful country at my feet, these wretched toilers in the field and at the desk will have learned that there is a nobler activity, and uniforms will spring up like flowers before the sun." Where Sam acquired his command of the English language and his poetic sensibility it would be difficult to say. It is enough to know that these faculties endeavored, not without success, to keep pace with his growing ambition for glory.

Sam's first weeks at East Point were among the happiest in his life. Here, at any rate, military affairs were in the ascendant. His ideal of a country was simply an East Point infinitely enlarged. His neat gray uniform seemed already to transform him into a hero. When he thought of the great soldiers

who had been educated at this very place, he felt a proud spirit
swelling in his bosom. One night in a lonely part of the parade-
ground he solemnly knelt down and kissed the sod. The military
cemetery aroused his enthusiasm, and the captured cannon, the
names of battles inscribed here and there on the rocks, and the
portraits of generals in the mess-hall, all in turn fascinated
him. As a new arrival he was treated with scant courtesy and
drilled very hard, but he did not care. Tho his squad-fellows
were almost overcome with fatigue, he was always sorry when the
drill came to an end. He never had enough of marching and
counter-marching, of shouldering and ordering arms. Even the
"setting-up" exercises filled him with joy. When cavalry drills
began he was still more in his element. His old teamster days
now stood him in good stead. In a week he could do anything with
a horse,--he understood the horse, and the horse trusted him.
When he first emerged from the riding-school on horseback in a
squadron and took part in a drill on the great parade-ground, he
was prouder than ever before. He went through it in a delirium,
feeling like a composite photograph of Washington and Napoleon.
When the big flag went up in the morning to the top of the
towering flag-staff, Sam's spirits went up with it, and they
floated there, vibrating, hovering, all day; but when the flag
came down at night, Sam did not come down. He was always up,
living an ecstatic dream-life in the seventh heaven.

One night as Sam lay in his tent dreaming that he had just
won the battle of Waterloo, he heard a voice close to his ears.

"Jinks!"

"Yes, sir."

"Here is an order for you to report at once up in the woods
at old Fort Hut. The password is 'Old Gory'; say that, and the
sentinel will let you out of camp. Go along and report to the
colonel at once."

"What is it?" cried Sam. "Is it an attack?"

"Very likely," said the voice. "Now wake up your snoring
friend there, for he's got to go too. What's his name?"

"Cleary," answered Sam, and he proceeded gently to awaken
his tent-mate and break the news to him that the enemy was
advancing. It was not easy to rouse the young man, but finally
they both succeeded in dressing in the dark, and hastened away
between the tents across the most remote sentry beat. They were
duly challenged, whispered the countersign, and in a few moments
were climbing the rough and thickly wooded hill to the fort.

"I wonder who the enemy is," said Sam.

"Enemy? Nonsense," replied Cleary. "They're going to haze
us."

"Haze us? Good heavens!" said Sam. He had heard of hazing
before, but he had been living in such a realm of imagination for
the past weeks that the gossip had never really reached his
consciousness, and now that he was confronted with the reality he
hardly knew how to face it.

"Yes," said Cleary, "they're going to haze us, and I wonder
why I ever came to this rotten place anyhow."

"Don't, don't say that," cried Sam. "You were at Hale University for a year or two, weren't you? Did they do any hazing there?"

"Not a bit. They stopped it all long ago. The professors there say it isn't manly."

"That can't be true," said Sam, "or they wouldn't do it here. But why has it kept up here when they've stopped it at all the universities?"

"I don't know," said Cleary, "but perhaps it's wearing uniforms. I feel sort of different in a uniform from out of it, don't you?"

"Of course I do," exclaimed Sam. "I feel as if I were walking on air and rising into another plane of being."

"Well--ye-es--perhaps, but I didn't mean that exactly," answered Cleary. "But somehow I feel more like hitting a fellow over the head when I'm in uniform than when I'm not, don't you?"

"I hadn't thought of that," said Sam, "but I really think I do. Do you think they'll hit us over the head?"

"There's no telling. There's Captain Clark of the first class and Saunders of the third who are running the hazing just now, they say, and they're pretty tough chaps."

"Is that Captain Clark with the squeaky voice?" asked Sam.

"Yes, he spoiled it taking tabasco sauce when he was hazed three years ago. They say it took all the mucous membrane off his epiglottis."

There was silence for a time.

"Saunders is that fellow with the crooked nose, isn't he?" asked Sam.

"Yes; when they hazed him last year they made him stand with his nose in the crack of a door until they came back, and they forgot they had left him, and somebody shut the door on his nose by mistake. But he's an awfully plucky chap. He just went on standing there as if nothing happened."

"Splendid, wasn't it?" cried Sam, beginning to see the heroic possibilities of hazing. "Do you suppose that they have always hazed here?"

"Yes, of course."

"And that General German and General Meriden and all the rest were hazed here just like this?"

"Yes, to be sure."

Sam felt his spirits soaring again.

"Then I wouldn't miss it for anything," said he. "It has always been done and by the greatest men, and it must be the right thing to do. Just think of it. Meriden has walked up this very hill like you and me to be hazed!" There was exultation in his tone.

"Well, I only hope Meriden looked forward to it with greater joy than I do," said Cleary, with a dry laugh. "But here we are."

Before them under the ruined walls of the old redoubt called Fort Hut, stood a small group of cadets, indistinctly lighted by several moving dark-lanterns. While they were still twenty yards away, two men sprang out from behind a tree, grasped them by the arms, tied their elbows behind them, and, leading them off through

274

the woods for a short distance, bound them to a tree out of sight
of the rest, and left them there with strict injunctions not to
move. It never entered into the head of either of the prisoners
that they might disobey this order, and they waited patiently for
events to take their course. As far as they could make out by
listening, some others of their classmates were already undergoing
the ordeal of hazing. They could hear water splashing, suppressed
screams and groans, and continual whispering. The light of the
lanterns flickered through the trees, now and then illuminating
the topmost branches. Presently a man came and sat down near
them, and said:

"Don't get impatient. We're nearly ready for you." It was
the voice of one of their two captors.

"May I ask you a question, sir?" said Sam.

"Blaze away," responded the man.

"Was General Gramp hazed at this same place, do you know?"

"Yes," said the man. "In this very same place. And while
he was waiting he sat on that very log over there."

Sam peered with awe into the darkness.

"May I--do you think I might--just sit on it, too?" asked
Sam.

"Certainly," said the cadet affably, untying the rope from
the tree and leading Sam over to the log, where he tied him again.

Sam sat down reverently.

"How well preserved the log is," said Sam.

"Yes," said the guard; "of course they wouldn't let it decay.
It's a sort of historical monument. They overhaul it every
year. Anyway it's ironwood."

Sam thought to himself that perhaps some day the log might
be noted as the spot where the great General Jinks sat while
awaiting his hazing, and tears of joy rolled softly down over his
freckles. He was still lost in this emotion when steps were
heard approaching and the lantern-light drew nearer.

"Come, Smith, bring the prisoners in," said the same voice
that had waked Sam in his tent. He looked at the speaker and
recognized the tall, hatchet-faced, crooked-nosed Saunders. Two
or three cadets unfastened Sam and Cleary, still, however,
leaving their arms bound behind them, and brought them to the
open place under the wall where Sam had first seen them. Sam now
saw nothing; walking in the steps of Generals Gramp and German,
he felt the ecstasy of a Christian martyr. He would not have
exchanged his lot with any one in the world. Cleary, however,
who possessed a rather mundane spirit, took in the scene. Twenty
or thirty cadets were either standing or seated on the ground
round a circle which was illuminated by several dark-lanterns
placed upon the ground. In the center of the circle were a tub
of water, some boards and pieces of rope, and two large baskets
whose contents were concealed by a cloth.

"Come, boys," squeaked Captain Clark, a short, thickset
fellow who looked much older than the others and who spoke in a
peculiar cracked voice. "Come, let's begin by bracing them up."

"Bracing" was a process adopted for the purpose of making
the patient assume the position of a soldier, only very much

275

exaggerated--a position which after a few minutes becomes almost
intolerable. Cleary and Sam were promptly taken and tied back to
back to an upright stake which had escaped their observation.
They were tied at the ankle, knee, waist, under the arms, and at
the chin and forehead. By tightening these ropes as desired and
placing pieces of wood in between, against the back, the hazers
made each victim stand with the chest pushed preternaturally
forward and the chin and abdomen drawn preternaturally back.
Cleary found this position irksome from the start, and soon
decidedly painful, but Sam was proof against it. In fact, he had
been practising just this position for eight or ten years, and it
now came to him naturally. Clearly soon showed marks of
discomfort. It was a warm night, and the sweat began to stand
out on his forehead. As far as he was concerned the hazing was
already a success, but Sam evidently needed something more.
     "Here, give me the tabasco bottle," whispered Clark to Smith.
As the latter brought the article from one of the baskets,
Same said to him in a low voice,
     "Did General Gramp take it out of that same bottle?"
     "Yes," said Smith; "strange to say, it's the very same one,
and all through his life afterward he took tabasco three times a
day."
     Sam rolled his eyes painfully to catch a glimpse of the
historic bottle. Clark took it and applied it to Sam's lips. It
was red-hot stuff, and the whole audience rose to watch its
effect upon the victim at the stake. Sam swallowed it as if it
had been lemonade. In fact, he was only aware of the honor that
he was receiving. He had only enough earthly consciousness left
to notice that one of the cadets in the crowd was photographing
him with a kodak, and accordingly he did not even wink.
     "By Jove, he's lined with tin," ejaculated Saunders, whose
deflected nose gave him a sinister expression. "You ought to
have had his plumbing, Clark."
     "Shut up and mind your own business," said Clark. "Come,
let's give him the tub. This won't do. That other chap's happy
enough where he is."
     Sam was untied again and led forward to the middle of the
ring, the faithful Smith still keeping close to him.
     "Is that an old tub?" whispered Sam, still standing stiffly
as if his body had permanently taken the "braced" shape.
     "I should say so. All the generals were ducked in it.
Kneel down there and look in. Do you see that round dent in the
middle? That's were General Meriden bumped his head in it. He
never did things by halves."
     Sam did as he was told, and he felt that he was in a proper
attitude upon his knees at such a shrine. To him it was holy
water.
     "Now, Jinks," squeaked Clark.
     "Yes, sir," answered Sam.
     "Stand on your head now in that tub, and be quick about it."
     Sam fixed his mind upon General Meriden in the same
circumstances, drew in his breath, and endeavored to stand on his
head in a foot of water, holding on to the rim of the tub with

his hands. His legs waved irresolutely in the air with no apparent unity of motive, and bubbles gurgled about his neck and shoulders.

"Grab his legs!" shouted Clark.

Two cadets obeyed the order, and Clark took out his watch to time the ordeal. The instants that passed seemed like an age.

"Isn't time up?" whispered Saunders.

"Shut up, you fool, haven't I got my watch open?" replied Clark. "But, good heavens!" he added, "take him out--I believe my watch has stopped." And he shook it and put it to his ear.

Sam was hauled out and laid on the grass, but he was entirely unconscious. His tormentors were thoroughly scared. Fortunately they had all gone through a course of "first aid to the injured," and they immediately took the proper precautions, holding him up by the feet until the water ran out of his mouth and nose, and then rolling him on the tub and manipulating his arms. At last some faint indications of breathing set in, and they concluded to carry him down to his tent. Using two boards as a stretcher, six of them acted as bearers, and the procession moved toward the camp. Cleary would have been forgotten, had he not asked them to untie him, which they did, and he followed behind, walking most stiffly. As they neared the camp the party separated. Two of the strongest took Sam, whose mind was wandering, to his tent, and Clark made Cleary come and spend the night with him, lest anxiety at Sam's condition might impel him to report the matter to the authorities. How they all got to their tents in safety, and how the password happened to be known to all of them, we must leave it to the officers in command at East Point to explain. Sam was dropped upon his bunk without much consideration. The two cadets waited long enough to make sure that he was breathing, and then they decamped.

"It's really a shame," said Smith to Saunders, who tented with him, before he turned over to sleep; "it's really a shame to leave that fellow there without a doctor, but we'd all get bounced if it got out."

CHAPTER III

Love and Combat

At reveille the next morning, as the roll was called in the company street, Private Jinks did not answer to his name. They found him in his tent delirious and in a high fever. His pillow was a puddle of water. It was necessary to have him taken to the hospital, and before long he was duly installed there in a small separate room. The captain of his company instituted an inquiry into the causes of his illness and reported that he had undoubtedly fainted away and thrown water over himself to bring himself to. The surgeon in charge of the hospital thereupon certified that this was the case, and in this way bygones officially became bygones. It was late in the afternoon before Sam recovered consciousness. A negro soldier, who had been

detailed to act as hospital orderly, was adjusting his
bed-clothes, and Sam opened his eyes.

"Gettin' better, Massa Jinks?" said the man, smiling his
good will.

"Company Jinks, all present and accounted for," cried Sam,
saluting as if he were a first sergeant on parade.

"You're here in de hospital, Massa," said the man, who was
known as Mose; "you ain't on parade sure."

Sam looked round inquiringly.

"Is this the hospital?" he asked. "Why am I in the
hospital?"

"You've been hurtin' yourself somehow," answered Mose with a
low chuckle. "There's lots of fourth-class men hurts themselves.
But you'll be all right in a week."

"In a week!" exclaimed Sam. "But I can't skip drills and
everything for a week!"

"Now, don't you worry, Massa Jinks. You're pretty lucky.
We've had some men here hurted themselves that had to go home for
good, and some of 'em, two or three, never got well, and died.
But bless you, you'll soon be all right. Doctor said so."

Sam had to get what consolation he could from this. His
memory began to come back, and he recalled the beginning of the
hazing.

"Is Cadet Cleary in the hospital?" he asked.

"No, sah."

"Won't you try to get word to him to come and see me here,
if he can?"

"Yes, Massa, I'll try. But they won't always let 'em come.
Maybe they'll let him Sunday afternoon."

Sure enough, Cleary succeeded in getting permission to pay
Sam a call on Sunday.

"Well, old man, I've got to thank you for letting me out of
a lot of trouble," he cried as he clasped Sam's hand and sat down
by the bedside.

"Did they duck you, too?" asked Sam. "You must be stronger
than I am. It's a shame I couldn't stand it."

"No. When they'd nearly killed you they let me off. Don't
you be ashamed of anything. They kept you in there five
minutes--I'm not sure it wasn't ten. If you weren't half a fish,
you'd never have come to, that's all there is of that. And after
you'd drunk all that tabasco, too!"

"Is my voice quite right?" asked Sam.

"Yes, thank fortune, there's no danger of your squeaking
like Captain Clark."

Sam sighed.

"And is my nose quite straight?"

"Yes, of course; why shouldn't it be?"

Sam sighed again.

"I'm afraid," he said, "that no one will know that I've been
hazed."

He was silent for a few minutes. Then a smile came over his
face.

"Wasn't it grand," he went on, "to think that we were following in the steps of all the great generals of the century! When I put my head into the tub and felt my legs waving in the air, I thought of General Meriden striking his head so manfully against the bottom, and I thanked heaven that I was suffering for my country. I tried to bump my head hard too, and it does ache just a little; but I'm afraid it won't show."

He felt his head with his hand and looked inquiringly at Cleary, but his friend's face gave him no encouragement, and he made no answer.

"I think I saw somebody taking a snapshot of me up there," said Sam. "Do you think I can get a print of it? I wish you'd see if you can get one for me."

"It's not so easy," said Cleary. "He was a third-class man, and of course we are not allowed to speak to him. They've just divided us fourth-class men up among the rest to do chores for them. My boss is Captain Clark, and he's the only upper-class man I can speak to, and he would knock me down if I asked him about it. You'd better try yourself when you come out."

"Who am I assigned to?" asked Sam.

"To Cadet Smith, and he's a much easier man. You're in luck. But my time's up. Good-by," and Cleary hurried away.

Sam Jinks left the hospital just one week after his admission. He might have stayed a day or two longer, but he insisted that he was well enough and prevailed upon the doctor to let him go. He set to work at once with great energy to make up for lost time and to learn all that had been taught in the week in the way of drilling. The morning after his release, when guard-mounting was over, Cleary told him that Cadet Smith wished to speak to him, and Sam went at once to report to him.

"Jinks," said Smith, when Sam had approached and saluted, "I am going down that path there to the right. Wait till I am out of sight and then follow me down. I don't want any one to see us together."

"All right, sir," said Sam.

When Smith had duly disappeared, Sam followed him and found him awaiting him in a secluded spot by the river. Sam saluted again as he came up to him.

"I suppose you understand, Jinks, that none of us upper-class men can afford to be seen talking to you fourth-class beasts?"

"Yes, sir."

"Of course, it wouldn't do. Don't look at me that way, Jinks. When an upper-class man is polite enough to speak to you, you should look down, and not into his face."

Sam dropped his eyes.

"Now, Jinks, I wanted to tell you that you've been assigned to me to do such work as I want done. I'm going to treat you well, because you seem to be a pretty decent fellow for a beast."

"Thank you, sir," said Sam.

"Yes, you seem disposed to behave as you should, and I don't want to have trouble with you. All you'll have to do is to see that my boots are blacked every night, keep my shirts and clothes in order, take my things to the wash, clean out my tent, and be somewhere near so that you can come when I call you; do you understand?"

"Yes, sir."

"Oh, then, of course, you must make my bed, and bring water to me, and keep my equipments clean. If there's anything else, I'll tell you. If you don't do everything I tell you, I'll report it to the class committee and you'll have to fight, do you understand?"

"Yes, sir."

"That will do, Jinks; you may go."

"I beg your pardon, sir. May I ask you a question?"

"What?" shouted Smith. "Do you mean to speak to me without being spoken to?"

"I know it's very wrong, sir," said Sam, "but there's something I want very much, and I don't know how else to get it."

"Well, I'll forgive you this time, because I'm an easy-going fellow. If it had been anybody else but me, you'd have got your first fight. What is it? Out with it."

"Please, sir, when I was haz--I mean exercised the other night, I saw somebody taking photographs of it. Do you think I could get copies of them?"

"What do you want them for?" asked Smith suspiciously.

"I'd like to have something to remember it by," said Sam. "I want to be able to show that I did just what Generals Gramp and German did."

Smith smiled. "All right," he replied. "I'll get them for you if I can, and I'll expect you to work all the better for me. Now go."

"Oh, thank you, sir--thank you!" cried Sam; and he went.

That night he and Cleary talked over the situation in whispers as they lay in their bunks.

"I don't like this business at all," said Cleary. "I didn't come to East Point to black boots and make beds. It's a fraud, that's what it is."

"Please don't say that," said Sam. "They've always done it, haven't they?"

"I suppose so."

"Then it must be right. Do you think General Meriden would have done it if it had been wrong? We must learn obedience, mustn't we? That's a soldier's first duty. We must obey, and how could we learn to obey better than by being regular servants?"

"And how about obeying the rules of the post that forbid the whole business, hazing and all?" asked Cleary.

Sam was nonplussed for a moment.

"I'm not a good hand at logic," he said. "Perhaps you can argue me down, but I _feel_ that it's all right. I wouldn't miss this special duty business for anything. It will make me a better soldier and officer."

"Sam," said Cleary, who had now got intimate enough with him to use his Christian name,--"Sam, you were just built for this place, but I'll be hanged if I was."

280

The summer hastened on to its close, and the first- and
third-class men had a continual round of social joys. The hotel
on the post was full of pretty girls who doted on uniforms, and
there were hops, and balls, and flirtations galore. The "beasts"
of the fourth class were shut out from this paradise, but they
could not help seeing it, and Sam used his eyes with the rest of
them. He had never before seen even at a distance such elegance
and luxury. The young women especially, in their gay summer
gowns, drew his attention away sometimes even from military
affairs. There was a weak spot in his make-up of which he had
never before been aware. There was one young woman in particular
who caught his eye, a vision of dark hair and black eyes which
lived on in his imagination when it had vanished from his
external sight. Sam actually fancied that the young woman looked
at him with approving eyes, and he was emboldened to look back.
It was impossible for social intercourse between a young lady in
society and a fourth-class "beast" to go further than this, and
at this point their relations stood, but Sam was sure that the
maiden liked his looks. It so happened that her most devoted
admirer was none other than Cadet Saunders, who was continually
hovering about her. Sam was devoured with jealousy. In his low
estate he was even unable to find out her name for a long time.
He could not speak to upper-class men, and his classmates knew
nothing of the gay world above them. However, he discovered at
last that she was a Miss Hunter from the West. His informant was
a waiter at the hotel whom he waylaid on his way out one night,
for cadets were forbidden to enter the hotel.

"I suppose she has her father and mother with her?" Sam
suggested.

"Oh, no, sir. She's all alone. She's been here all alone
every summer this six years."

"That's strange," said Sam. "Hasn't she a protector?"

"Oh, yes! she has protectors enough. You see, she's always
engaged."

"Engaged!" exclaimed the unhappy youth. "How long has she
been engaged, and to whom?"

"Why, this time she's only been engaged two weeks," said the
waiter, "and it's Cadet Saunders she's engaged to; but don't
worry, sir, it's an old story. She's been engaged to a different
man every summer for six years, and at first she generally had
two men a summer. She began with officers of the first class,
two in a year; then she fell off to one in a season; then she
dropped to third class; and now she has Mr. Saunders because his
nose isn't just right, sir, if I may say so."

Sam hardly knew what to think. The news of her engagement
had plunged him into despair, but the information that engagement
was with her a temporary matter was decidedly welcome; and even
if it were couched in language that could hardly be called
flattering, still he was glad to hear it. Sam thanked the waiter
and gave him a silver coin which he could ill spare from his
pay, but he was satisfied that he had got his money's worth.

Sam ruminated deep and long over this hardwrung gossip. He
could not believe that the object of his dreams was no longer in

her first girlhood. There was some mistake. Then it was absurd
to suppose that she was reduced to the acceptance of inferior
third-class men. How could a waiter understand the charms of
Saunders' historical nose? Evidently she had selected him from
the whole corps on account of his exploits as an object of
hazing. Sam almost wished that Saunders' nose was a blemish, for
it would help his chances, but candor obliged him to admit that
it was, on the contrary, one of his rival's strong points, and he
sighed once again to think that he bore no marks on his own
person of the hazing ordeal. All that Sam could do now was to
wait. He recognized the fact that no girl with self-respect
would speak to a "beast," and he determined to be patient until
in another twelve-month he should have become a full-fledged
third-class man himself. The other engagements had proved
ephemeral, why not that with Saunders? Fortunately this new
sentiment of Sam's did not interfere with his military work.
Instead of that it inspired him with new fervor, and he now
strove to be a perfect soldier not only for its own sake, but for
her sake too.

Meanwhile Saunders began to imagine that Sam looked at his
fiancée a little too frequently and long, and he determined to
punish him for it. How was this to be done? In his deportment
toward the upper-class men Sam was absolutely perfect, and had
begun to win golden opinions from instructors and cadets alike.
He always did more than was required of him, and did it better
than was expected. He treated all upper-class men with profound
respect, and he did it without effort because it came natural to
him. He never ventured to look them in the eye, and he blushed
and stammered when they addressed him. Saunders tried to find a
flaw in his behavior so that he might have the matter taken up by
the class committee, but there was no flaw to be found.
Self-respect prevented him from giving the real reason, his
jealousy; besides, it was out of the question to drag in the name
of a lady.

One day Saunders, Captain Clark, Smith, and some other
cadets were discussing the matter of fourth-class discipline, and
the merits of some recent fights which had been ordered between
fourth-class men and their seniors for the purpose of punishing
the former, when Saunders tried skillfully to lead the
conversation round to the case of Sam Jinks.

"There are some fellows in the fourth class that need a
little taking down, don't you think so?" he asked.

"If there are, take them down," said Clark laconically.
"Who do you mean?"

"Why, there's that Jinks fellow, for instance. He struts
about as if he were a major-general."

"He is pretty well set up, that's a fact," said Smith, "but
you can't object to that. I must say he does his work for me up
to the handle. Look at that for a shine"; and he exhibited one
of his boots to the crowd.

"I wonder if he can fight?" said Saunders, changing his
tactics. "He's a well-built chap, and I'd like to see what he

can do. How can we get him to fight if we can't haul him up for misbehaving?"

"It's easy enough, if he's a gentleman," answered Clark, who was a recognized authority in matters of etiquette.

"How?" asked Saunders.

"Why, all you've got to do is to insult him and then he'll have to fight."

"How would you insult him?" asked Saunders eagerly.

"The best way," said Clark sententiously, "is to call him a hog in public, and then, if he is a gentleman, he will be ready to fight."

"I'll do it," said Saunders. "I'm dying to see that fellow fight. Of course, I don't care to fight him. We can get Starkie to do that, I suppose."

"Yes," said Clark. "We'll select somebody that can handle him and teach him his place, depend on that."

Saunders set out at once to carry out the program. As soon as he found Jinks in a group of fourth-class men, he went up to him, and cried in a loud voice,

"Jinks, you're a hog."

"Yes, sir," said Sam, saluting respectfully.

"Do you hear what I say? you're a wretched hog."

"Yes, sir."

"You're a hog, and if you're a gentleman you'll be ready to fight if you're asked to."

"Yes, sir," responded Sam, as Saunders turned on his heel and walked away. Somehow Clark's plan did not seem to have worked to perfection, but it must be all right, and he hastened to report the affair to his class committee, who promptly determined that cadet Jinks must fight, and that their classmate Starkie be requested to represent them in the encounter. Starkie weighed at least thirty pounds more than Sam, was considerably taller, had several inches longer reach of arm, and was a practised boxer. Sam had never boxed in his life. These facts seemed to the committee only to enhance the interesting character of the affair.

"We're much obliged to you, Saunders," said the chairman. "You've done just right to call our attention to the matter. These beasts must be taught their place. The only manly way to settle it is by having Starkie fight him. You have acted like a gentleman and a soldier.

The fight was arranged for a Saturday afternoon on the familiar hazing-ground near the old fort. Sam selected Cleary and another classmate for his seconds, and Starkie chose Saunders and Smith.

"Jinks," said Smith in a moment of unwonted affability, "you've got a chance now to distinguish yourself. I'll see that you get fair play. Of course, you'll have to fight to a finish, but you must take your medicine like a man."

"Did General Gramp ever have to fight here?" asked Sam, touching his cap.

"Of course," said Smith, "and on that very ground, too. You don't seem to have read much history."

283

The prospect of the fight gave Sam intense joy. His sense
of glory seemed to obliterate all anticipation of pain. This was
his first opportunity to become a real hero. When he was hazed
he only had to suffer; now, on the other hand, he was called upon
to act. He got Cleary to show him some of the simplest rules of
boxing, and he practised what little he could during the three
intervening days. He was quite determined to knock Starkie out
or die in the attempt.

At four o'clock on the day indicated a crowd of first- and
third-class men were collected to see the great event. No
fourth-class men were allowed to attend except the two seconds.
A ring was formed; Captain Clark was chosen as referee; and the
two combatants, stripped to the waist, put on their hard gloves
and entered the ring. Starkie eyed his antagonist critically,
while Sam with a heavenly smile on his face did not focus his
eyes at all, but seemed to be dreaming far away. When the word
was given, however, he dashed in and made some desperate lunges
at Starkie. It was easy to see in a moment that Sam could do
nothing. He could not even reach his opponent, his arms were so
much shorter. If Starkie held one of his arms out stiffly, Sam
could not get near him and was entirely at his mercy. The
third-class man consequently set himself leisurely to work at the
task of punishing the unfortunate Jinks. Two or three blows
about the face and jaw which started the blood in profusion ended
the first round. Sam did not recognize the inevitable result of
the fight, and was anxious to begin again. He did not seem to
feel any pain from the blows. Two or three rounds had the same
result, and Sam became weaker and weaker. At last he could only
go into the ring and receive punishment without making an effort
to avert it, but he did not flinch.

"Did you ever see such a chap?" said Smith to Saunders.
"Let's call the thing off."

"Nonsense," said the latter. "Wait till he's knocked
insensible"; and the rest of the spectators expressed their
agreement with him.

Just then a sound of marching was heard, and a company of
cadets were seen coming up the hill in command of an army officer.

"Hullo, Clark," whispered Smith. "Stop the fight. Here
comes old Blair, and he may report us."

"Not much," said Clark. "He'll mind his own business."

The company approached within a few yards of the ring.

"Eyes right!" shouted Captain Blair, and every man in the
company turned his eyes away from the assembled crowd, and Blair
himself stared into the woods on the other side of the path. The
company had almost passed out of sight when Blair's voice was
heard again.

"Front!" and the danger of detection had blown over.

After this faint interruption, Sam was brought up once more,
pale and bloody, and hardly able to stand. Yet he smiled through
the blood. Starkie stood off and gave him his coup de grace, a
full blow in the solar plexus, which doubled him up quite
unconscious on the ground. Clark declared the fight finished,
and the crowd broke up hastily, leaving Cleary and his associate

284

to get Sam away as best they could. They had a pail of water,
sponges and towels, and they bathed his face; and after half an
hour's work were rewarded by having him open his eyes. In
another half-hour he was able to stand, and supporting him on
each side, they led him slowly down to the hospital.

"What's the matter?" said the doctor as they entered the
office. "Oh! I see. You found him lying bleeding up by Fort
Hut, didn't you?"

Yes, sir," said Cleary.

"He must have fallen down and hit his head against a stone,
don't you think so?"

"Yes, sir."

"That's a dangerous place; the pine-needles make it very
slippery," said the doctor, as he entered the case in his
records. "Here, Mose, put Cadet Jinks to bed."

This time Sam was laid up for two weeks, but he felt amply
repaid for this loss of time by a visit from no less a person
than Cadet Smith.

"Mind you never tell any one I came here," said Smith, "and
treat me just the same when you come out as you did before; but I
wanted to tell you you're a brick. I never saw a man stand up to
a dressing the way you did, and that's the truth."

Tears of joy rolled down Sam's damaged face.

"I've brought you those photographs of the hazing, too,"
said Smith with a laugh. And he produced two small prints from
his pocket. Sam took them with trembling hands and gazed at them
with rapture. One of them represented Cleary and Jinks tied to
the stake, apparently about to be burned to death, and Sam was
delighted to see the ultra-perfect position which he had
assumed. The other photograph had been taken the moment after
Sam's immersion in the tub. He could see his hands clutching the
rim, while his legs were widely separated in the air.

"It might be General Meriden as well as me," he cried
joyously. "Nobody could tell the difference."

"That's so," said Smith.

"I shall always carry them next to my heart," said Sam.
"How can I thank you enough? I am sorry that I can't black your
boots this week."

"Oh! never mind," said Smith magnanimously, looking down at
his feet. "Cleary does them pretty well. You'll be out before
long."

When Sam was discharged from the hospital the cadet corps
had struck camp and gone into barracks for the year. The summer
maidens, too, had fled, and East Point soon settled down to the
monotony of winter work. Every cadet looked forward already to
the next summer: the first class to graduation; the second to
the glories of first-class supremacy in camp and ballroom; the
third class to their two months' furlough as second-class men;
but the fourth class had happier anticipations than any of the
rest, for they were to be transformed in June from "beasts" into
men, into real third-class cadets, with all the rights and
privileges of human beings. Sam's dream was also irradiated with
the hope of winning the affections of the fair Miss Hunter, to

285

whom he had never addressed a word, but of whose interest he felt
assured. He did not know where the assurance came from, but he
had little fear of Saunders now. Next summer Saunders would be
away on leave, anyhow. Sam knew, if no one else did, that he had
actually fought for the hand of Miss Hunter; and, tho he had been
defeated, had not Smith admitted that his defeat was a practical
victory? He felt that he had won Miss Hunter's hand in mortal
combat, and he dismissed from his mind all doubt on the subject.

CHAPTER IV

War and Business

Marian Hunter was, as we have already surmised, a lady of
experience. She was possessed, as is not uncommonly the case
with young ladies at East Point, of an uncontrollable passion for
things military. Manhood and brass buttons were with her
interconvertible terms, and the idea of uniting her young life to
a plain civilian seemed to her nothing less than shocking. The
pleasures of her first two or three summers at East Point and of
her first half-dozen engagements had partaken of the bliss of
heaven. The engagements had never been broken off, they had
simply dissolved one into the other, and she had felt herself
rising from step to step in happiness. Naturally her conquests
filled her with a supreme confidence in her charms. She was not
especially fickle by nature, but she discovered that a
first-class cadet, particularly if he was an officer and had
black feathers in his full-dress hat, was far more attractive to
think of than a supernumerary second lieutenant assigned to duty
in some Western garrison. Gradually, however, she found herself
less certain of winning whom she would. The competition of young
girls some two or three years her junior became threatening. She
was obliged to give up cadet officers for privates, and then
first-class privates for third-class privates, as the hotel
waiter had explained to Sam. At the time of Sam's arrival at the
Point she was having more difficulty than ever before, and she
became thoroughly frightened. She took up with Saunders because
he alone came her way, but the engagement was a poor makeshift,
and she could not get up any enthusiasm over it. She could
hardly pretend to be in love with him, and she felt conscious
that she had a foolish prejudice in favor of straight noses.
What was she to do? If she was to marry at all in the army--and
how could she marry anywhere else?--she must soon make up her
mind. Her experience now stood her in good stead. Had she not
seen these very first-class cadet officers only three years
before as mere despised "beasts," doing all kinds of drudgery for
their oppressors? Had she not seen her fiancé, Saunders,
himself, a short twelvemonth ago, with nose intact, slinking like
a pariah about the post? She had learned the lesson which the
younger girls had yet to learn, that from these unpromising
chrysalises the most gorgeous butterflies emerge, and like a wise
woman she began to study the fourth class. Sam stood out from
his fellows, not indeed as supremely handsome, altho he was not

bad-looking, but rather as the soldier par excellence of his class. Marian was an expert in judging the points of a soldier, and she saw at once that he was the coming man. She could not make his acquaintance or speak to him, but she could smile and thus lay the foundations of success for next year. It would be easy thus to reach the heart of a lonely "beast." And she smiled to a purpose, and it was that smile that won the untried affections of Sam Jinks.

When June at last came and the new fourth-class men began to arrive, Sam felt a new lift surge into his soul. For a year he had been duly meek and humble, for such it behooved a fourth-class man to be. Now, however, he began to entertain a measureless pride, such being the proper frame of mind of a man in the upper classes. He watched the hotel sedulously to learn when Miss Hunter made her appearance. One morning he saw her, and she smiled more distinctly than ever. He knew that his felicity was only a short way off. He must wait two weeks until the graduation ball and the departure of the old first class; then he could undertake to supplant the absent Saunders, who probably knew the history of Miss Hunter and was not unprepared for his fate.

Meanwhile great events had occurred, and thrown East Point into a state of excitement. The country was at war. Congress had determined to free the downtrodden inhabitants of the Cubapine Islands from the tyranny of the ancient Castalian monarchy. A call for volunteers had been issued, and the graduating cadets were to be hurried to the seat of war. During this agitation news arrived of a great naval victory. The mighty Castalian fleet had been annihilated with great loss of life, while the conquerors had not lost a man and had scarcely interrupted their breakfast in order to secure this crushing triumph. It was in the midst of such reports as these that the susceptible hearts of Sam Jinks and Marian Hunter came together. The graduating class had gone, and Sam had for two days been a full third-class man. For the first time he had occupied the front rank at dress-parade, and seen clearly the officer in command, the adjutant flitting about magnificently, the band parading up and down and turning itself inside out around the towering drum-major, the line of spectators behind, the bright faces and gay parasols, and among them the black eyes of Marian looking unmistakably at him. When at the end of the parade the company officers marched up to salute and the companies were dismissed, Sam saw a member of the new first class talking to her. He was now on an equality with all the cadets, and he boldly advanced and asked for an introduction. At last he had her hand in his, and as he pressed it rather harder than the occasion warranted, he felt his pressure returned. Sam's fate was sealed. He made no formal proposal, it was unnecessary. The engagement was a thing taken for granted. It was a novel experience for Marian as well as for Sam, as now for the first time she meant business. It is impossible in cold ink to reproduce the ecstasies of those many hours on Flirtation Walk, during which Sam opened his heart. For the first time in his life he had found a person as deeply interested in military matters as he was, and as much in love with military glory. He told her his whole history, including the lead soldiers and the Boys' Brigade. He laid bare to her his ambition to be a perfect soldier--a hero. He told her how disappointed he was to find no other cadet so completely wrapped up in his profession as he was, and how in her alone he had now realized his ideal not only of womanhood, but also of appreciation of the soldier's career. He rehearsed the thrilling experiences of hazing, and went over the fight in detail and told her how Saunders had brought it about.

"The horrid wretch!" she exclaimed, throwing her arms about his neck and kissing him. "I'm so glad they didn't break your nose."

"Are you really?" he asked, and as he read the truth in her eyes a weight was rolled from his soul.

He showed her the little lead officer with the plume, which he always carried as a mascot in his breast-pocket, and also the two hazing photographs which kept it company. She was delighted with them all.

"Oh! you will be a hero," she cried. "I am sure of it, and what a time we shall have of it, you dear thing!"

With his spare time thus occupied Sam did not see much of Cleary, who now shared another tent. One afternoon late in September he was on the way to the gate of the hotel grounds where he was accustomed to wait until Miss Hunter came out and joined him, when Cleary called him aside.

"Sam," he said, "I've got something of importance to say to you. Can't you come with me now?"

"Can't," said Sam. "Miss Hunter's waiting for me."

"Well, then, beg off to-morrow afternoon. I must have a talk with you."

"All right," answered Sam reluctantly. "If I must, I must, I suppose."

The next day found Sam and Cleary walking alone in the woods engaged in deep conversation.

"Sam, what would you say to going to the war?" asked Cleary.

"I'd give anything to go!" exclaimed Sam.

"You wouldn't want to stay on account of that girl of yours?"

"No, indeed; she would be first to want me to go."

"Then why don't you go?"

"How can I?" said Sam. "We've got three more years here. That ties us down for that time, and by the time that's over the war will be over too."

"That's what I think, and I'm sick of this place anyhow. I'm going to resign."

"Resign!" cried Sam. "Resign and give up your career!"

"Not altogether, old man. Don't get so excited. What's the use of staying here? We'll get sent off to some out-of-the-way post when we graduate, and perhaps we'll get to be captains before our hair is white, and perhaps we shan't; and then if a war breaks out we'll have volunteers young enough to be our sons made brigadiers over our heads. Aren't they doing it every day?

I'm not going to waste my life that way. I want to go to the war now, and I mean to go as a newspaper correspondent."

"Oh, Cleary!" exclaimed Sam reproachfully.

"Tut, tut, Sam. You're not up to date. We've got no field-marshals in our army and the newspaper correspondents take their place. Their names are better known than the generals, and they advertise each other and get a big share of the glory; and then they can always decently step aside when they've got enough. They needn't stay on the fighting-line, and that's a consideration. No, I'm sick of ordinary soldiering, but I'm willing to be a field-marshal. My father has an interest in the Metropolitan Daily Lyre, and I've written to him for an appointment as correspondent in the Cubapines. What I've learned here will help me a lot. But I want you to go with me."

"Me? Go with you? Do you think I'd be a newspaper correspondent?"

"No, of course not. It never entered my head. But why don't you get a commission in the volunteers from your uncle? He can get just what he wants, and they're talking of him for Secretary of War. All you've got to do is to resign here and apply for a commission as colonel. Then you'll probably land as a major, or a captain at any rate. By the time the war is over, you'll be a general, if I know you, and then you can be appointed captain in the regular army on retiring from the volunteers, when our class is just graduating. You're just made for a successful soldier. You've got the ambition and the courage, and you've got just the brains for a soldier. You don't want to remain a lieutenant until you are fifty, do you?"

There was great force in Cleary's argument, and Sam knew it. East Pointers were scandalized at the manner in which outsiders were jumped into important commands in the field, and when engagements took place the volunteers came in for all the praise, while the regulars who did almost all the work were hardly mentioned.

"I'll think it over," said Sam. "I'll speak to Marian about it. It's very kind of you to think of me."

"Not a bit," said Cleary. "I'm looking out for myself. If you go as a major and I go as correspondent, I'll just freeze to you and make a hero of you whether you will or not. I'll make your fortune, and you'll make mine. I'll see that you get a chance, and I know that you'll take it if you get it. You're just cut out for it. Now get permission from the young woman and we'll call it a go."

The following afternoon Sam walked over the same ground, but this time it was Marian who accompanied him. She was enthusiastic over Cleary's proposition.

"Just think of it! You'll come back a hero and a general, and I don't know what not, and we'll get married, and the President will come to the wedding; and then we'll have our wedding tour up here, and the corps will turn out and fire a salute, and we'll be the biggest people at East Point. Won't it be splendid?"

"Perhaps, dear, I'll never come back at all. Who knows? I may get killed."

"Oh, Sam! if you did, how proud I'd be of it. I'd wear black for a whole year, and they'd put up a monument to you over there in the cemetery and have a grand funeral, and I'd be in the first carriage, and the flag would be draped, and the band would play the funeral march. Oh, dear! how grand it would be, and how all the girls would envy me!"

Tears came to her eyes as she spoke.

"Just think of being the fiancée of a hero who died for his country! Oh, Sam, Sam!"

Sam took her in his arms.

"You're my own brave soldier's wife," he said. "I'd be almost ready to die for you, but if I don't, I'll come back and marry you. I'll write to uncle for a commission to-night, and ask his advice about resigning here either now or later. It hardly seems true that I may really go to a real war." And his tears fell and mingled with hers.

Sam's uncle fell in readily with Cleary's scheme. He was a politician and a man of the world, and he saw what an advantage it would be for his nephew to seek promotion in the volunteers, and how much a close friend among the war correspondents could help him. Furthermore, he had heard of Sam's excellent record at East Point and was disposed to lend him what aid could be derived from his influence with the Administration. When Sam's father learned that his brother approved of the project, he offered no objection, and a few weeks after Cleary had broached the subject, both of the young men sent in their resignations, and these were accepted. Cleary left at once for the metropolis to perfect his plans, while Sam remained for a few days at the Point to bid farewell to his betrothed. His uncle had at once sent in his name to the War Department as a candidate for colonel of volunteers with letters of recommendation from the most influential men at the Capital. While Sam was still at East Point he saw in the daily paper that his name had been sent in to the Senate as captain of volunteers with a long list of others, and almost immediately he received a telegram from his uncle announcing his confirmation without question. On the same morning came a letter from Cleary telling him to come at once to town and make the final arrangements before receiving orders to join his regiment. We shall draw a veil over the last interview between Sam and Marian. She was proficient in the art of saying farewell, and nothing was lacking on this occasion to contribute to its romantic effect. They parted in tears, but they were tears of hope and joy.

Cleary met Sam at the station in the city and took him to a modest hotel.

"It's going to be bigger than I thought," he said, as they sat down together for a good talk in the hotel lobby, after Sam had made himself at home in his room. "I'm going to run a whole combination. I've got in with a man who's a real genius. His name's Jonas. He represents the brewer's trust, and he's going out to start saloons with chattel mortgages on the fixtures.

It's a big thing by itself. But then besides that he's got orders to apply for street-railroad franchises wherever he can get them, and he is going to start agencies to sell typewriters and bicycles and some patent medicines, and I don't know what else. You see he wanted to represent the Consolidated Press as a sort of business agent, and The Daily Lyre belongs to the Consolidated, and that's the way I came across him. The fact is he represents pretty much all the capital in the country. It's a big combination. I'll boom him and you, and you'll help us, and then we can get in on the ground floor with him in anything we like. It's a good outlook isn't it, hey? Have you got your commission yet?"

"No," said Sam, "not yet. My uncle wants me to come and spend a few days with him at Slowburgh to make my acquaintance, and the commission will go there. I'm to be in the 200th Volunteer Infantry. I don't quite understand all your plans, but I hope I'll get a chance at real fighting for our country, and I should like to be a great soldier. You know that, Cleary."

"Yes, old man, I know it, and you will be, if courage and newspapers can do it. I'm sorry you didn't get a colonelcy, but captain isn't bad, and we'll skip you up to general in no time. You've always wanted to be a hero, haven't you? Well, the first chance I get I'll nickname you 'Hero' Jinks, and it'll stick, I'll answer for it!"

"Oh! thank you," said Sam.

"Now, good-by. I'll come in for you tomorrow and take you in to see our war editor. He's a daisy. So long."

When on the morrow Sam was ushered into the den of the war editor, he was surprised to see what a shabby room it was. The great man was sitting at a desk which was almost hidden under piles of papers, letters, telegrams, and memoranda. The chairs in the room were equally encumbered, and he had to empty the contents of two of them on the floor before Sam and Cleary could sit down.

"Ah, Captain Jinks, glad to see you!" he said.

Sam beamed with delight. It was the first time that he had heard his new title--a title, in fact, to which he had as yet no right.

"I suppose Mr. Cleary has explained to you," the editor continued, "what our designs are. Editing isn't what it used to be. It has become a very complicated business. In old times we took the news as it came along, and that was all that was expected of us; but if we tried that way of doing things now, we'd have to shut up shop in a week. When we need news nowadays we simply make it. I don't mean that we invent news--that doesn't pay in the long run; people learn your game and you lose in the end. No, I mean that we create the events that make the news. We were running short of news last year, that's the whole truth of it; and so we got up this war. It's been a complete success. We've quadrupled our circulation, and it's doubling every month. We're well ahead of the other papers because it's known as our war, and of course we are expected to know more about it than anybody else."

"But I thought the war was to free the oppressed Cubapinos--an outburst of popular sympathy with the downtrodden sufferers from Castalian misrule," interposed Sam, flushing. "That's the reason why I applied for a commission, and I am ready to pour out my last drop of blood for my country."

"Of course you are, my dear captain; of course you are. And your ideas of the cause of the war, as a military man, are quite correct. Indeed, if you will read my editorial of yesterday you will see the same ideas developed at some length."

He pressed an electric button on his desk, and a clerk entered.

"Get me a copy of yesterday's paper."

In a moment it was brought; the editor opened it, marked an article with a dash of his blue pencil, and handed it to Sam.

"There," said he, "put that in your pocket and read it. I am sure that you will agree with every word of it. Your understanding of the situation does great credit to your insight. That is, if I may use the term, the esoteric side of the question. It is only on the external and material side that it is really a Daily Lyre's war. There's really no contradiction, none at all, as you see."

"Oh! none at all," said Sam, with a sigh of relief. "I never quite understood it before, and you make it all so clear!"

"Now you will be prepared by what I have said to comprehend that it's just in this line of creating the news beforehand that we want to make use of you, and at the same time it will be the making of you, do you see?"

"Not quite," said Sam. "How do you mean?"

"Why, we understand that you're a most promising military man and that you intend to distinguish yourself. Suppose you do, what good will it do, if nobody ever hears of it? Doesn't your idea of heroism include a certain degree of appreciation?"

"Yes."

"Of publicity, I may say?"

Sam nodded assent.

"Or even in plain newspaper talk, of advertising?"

"I shouldn't quite like to be advertised," said Sam uneasily.

"That's a rather blunt word, I confess; but when you do some fine exploit, you wouldn't mind seeing it printed in full in the papers that the people at home read, would you?"

"No-o-o, not exactly; but then I should only want you to tell the truth about it."

"Of course; I know that, but there are lots of ways of telling the truth. We might put it in at the bottom of an inside page and give only a stick to it, or we might let it have the whole first page here, with your portrait at the top and headlines like that"; and he showed him a title in letters six inches long. "You'd prefer that, wouldn't you?"

"I'm afraid I would," said Sam.

"Well, if you didn't you'd be a blamed fool, that's all I've got to say, and we wouldn't care to bother about you."

292

"I'm sure it's very good of you to take me up," said Sam.
"Why do you select me instead of one of the great generals at the
front?"

"Why, don't you see? You wouldn't make a practical
newspaper man. The people are half tired of the names of the
generals already. They want some new names. It's our business
to provide them. Then all the other newspapers are on the track
of the generals. We must have a little hero of our own. When
General Laughter or General Notice do anything, all the press of
the country have got hold of them. They've got their photographs
in every possible attitude and their biographies down to the last
detail, and pictures of their birthplaces and of their families
and ancestors, and all the rest of it. We simply can't get ahead
of them, and people are beginning to think that it's not our war
after all. When we begin to boom you, they'll find out that
we've got a mortgage on it yet. We'll have the stuff all ready
here to fire off, and no one else will have a word. It'll be the
greatest beat yet, unless Mr. Cleary is mistaken in you and you
are not going to distinguish yourself."

"I don't think he is mistaken," said Sam solemnly. "I do
intend to distinguish myself if I get the chance."

"And we'll see that you have the chance. It's a big game
we're playing, but we hold the cards and we don't often lose.
You're not the only card, to be sure. We've got a lot of men at
the front now representing us. Several of our correspondents
have made a hit already, and some of them have made themselves
more famous than the generals! Ha, ha! Our head editor is going
out next month, and of course we'll see to it that he does
wonders. Hullo! there's Jonas now. Why, this is a lucky
meeting. Here, Jonas. You know Cleary. Mr. Jonas, Captain
Jinks. I'll be blessed if here isn't the whole combination."

Mr. Jonas, who had come into the room unannounced, and
perched himself on the corner of a table, was a rather short man
with a brown beard and eye-glasses, and wore his hat on the back
of his head.

"Well, Jonas, how are things going?" asked the editor.

"A 1. Couldn't be better. I've just been down at
Skinners'--"

"Skinner & Company, one of the biggest financial houses in
the street," the editor explained to Sam.

"And they've agreed to go the whole job. First of all,
it'll be chiefly trade. I showed them the contracts for boots
and hats for the army, and they were tickled to death. They'll
let us have as much as we want on them. I didn't have the
embalmed-beef contract with me--it smells too bad to carry round
in my pocket, hee-hee!--but I explained it to them, and it's even
better. They're quite satisfied."

"And how is the beer business going?"

"Oh! that's a success already. Look at this item," and he
pulled a newspaper from his pocket and showed it to the editor.

"One hundred more saloons in Havilla than there were at this
time last year! Can that be possible?" ejaculated the latter.

"Yes, and I'm behind fifty-eight of them. That agent I sent out ahead is a jewel."

"Have you been up at the Bible Society?"

"Yes, and I've got special terms on a hundred thousand Testaments in Castalian and the native languages. That will awaken interest, you see, and then we'll follow it up with five hundred thousand in English, and it will do no end of good in pushing the language. It will be made the official language soon, anyway. What a blessing it will be to those poor creatures who speak languages that nobody can understand!"

"How is the rifle deal coming out?"

"Only so-so. The Government will take about three-quarters of the lot. The rest we'll have to unload on the Cubapinos."

"What!" exclaimed Sam, "aren't they fighting against us now?"

"Oh! we don't sell them direct of course," added Jonas, "but we can't alter the laws of trade, can we? And they require that things get into the hands of the people who'll pay the most for them, hey?"

"Naturally," said the editor. "Captain Jinks has not studied political economy. It's all a matter of supply and demand."

"I'm ashamed to say I haven't," said Sam. "It must be very interesting, and I'm much obliged to you for telling me about it."

"I suppose it's too early to do anything definite about concessions for trolleys and gas and electric-lighting plants," said the editor.

"Not a bit of it. That's what I went to see Skinner about to-day. I'm sounding some of the chief natives already, and our people there are all right. Skinner's lawyers are at work at the charters, and I'll take them out with me. We can put them through as soon as we annex the islands."

"But we promised not to annex them!" cried Sam.

The editor and Jonas looked knowingly at each other.

"The captain is not a diplomatist, you see," said the former. "As for that matter, a soldier oughtn't to be. You understand, Captain, that all promises are made subject to the proviso that we are able to carry them out."

"Certainly."

"Now it's perfectly clear that we can never fulfill this promise. It is our destiny to stay there. It would be flying in the face of Providence and doing the greatest injury to the natives to abandon them. They would fly at each other's throats the moment we left them alone."

"They haven't flown at each other's throats where we have left them alone," mused Sam aloud.

"I didn't say they had, but that they would," explained the editor.

"Oh! I see," said Sam, and he relapsed into silence.

"Talking of electric lights," continued Jonas, "I've got a book here full of all sorts of electric things that we'll have to introduce there. There's the electrocution chair; look at that design. They garrote people in the most barbarous manner out there now. We'll civilize them, if we get a chance!"

294

"Perhaps they won't have the money to buy all your things," remarked Cleary, who had been a silent and interested spectator of the interview.

"Yes," said Jonas, "we may have trouble with the poorest tribes. We must make them want things, that's all. The best way to begin is to tax them. I've got a plan ready for a hut-tax of five dollars a year. That's little enough, I should think, but some of them never see money and they'll have to work to get it. That will make them work the coal and iron-mines. Skinner has his eye on these, too. When the natives once begin to earn money, they'll soon want more and then they'll spend it on us."

"But the Government there will be too poor to take up great public expenditures for a long time yet," said Cleary.

"Don't be too sure of that. They haven't even got a national debt. That's one of the first things we'll provide for. They're a most primitive people. Just think of their existing up to the present time without a national debt! They're mere savages."

"Well," said Cleary, rising, "I think we've taken enough of your valuable time and we must be off."

"Wait a moment," said the editor. "Have you explained all that I told you to the captain?"

"Not yet," answered Cleary, "but I'll do it now on the way to his hotel. He is going to leave town to-day, and he may be ordered to sail any day now. I will try to go on the same ship with him."

"Perhaps I can manage it, too," said Jonas, as he shook hands with the two friends, "if I can finish up all these arrangements. I must be on the ground there as soon as I can."

As Sam and Cleary left the room the editor and Jonas settled down to a confidential conversation, and there were smiles upon their lips as they began talking.

CHAPTER V

Slowburgh

While Sam accepted the explanations of the editor and Jonas as expressions of wisdom from men who had had a far wider experience than his, he had some faint misgivings as to some of the business enterprises in which his new friends were embarked, and he hinted as much to Cleary.

"Some of those things do sound rather strange," answered Cleary, as they walked away, "but you must look at the world in a broad way. Is our civilization better than that of the Cubapinos?"

"Undoubtedly."

"Well, then, we must be conferring a favor upon them by giving it to them. We can't slice it up and give them only the plums. That would be ridiculous. They must take us for better and worse. In fact, I think we should be guilty of hypocrisy if we pretended to be better than we are. Suppose we gave them a better civilization than we've got, shouldn't we be open to the charge of misrepresentation?"

"That's true," said Sam. "I didn't think of that.

"Yes," Cleary went on; "at first I had some doubts about that saloon business particularly, but the more you think of it, the more you see that it's our duty to introduce them there. It's all a part of our civilization."

"So it is," said Sam. "And then people have always done things that way, haven't they?"

"Yes, of course they have."

"Then it must be all right. What right have we to criticize the doings of people so much wiser than we are? I think you are quite right. As a correspondent you ought to be satisfied that you are doing the right thing. To me as a soldier it's a matter of no importance anyway, because a soldier only does what he's told, but you as a civilian have to think, I suppose, and I'm glad you're satisfied and can make such a conclusive case of it. What was it that the editor wanted you to tell me?"

"Oh! yes. I came near forgetting. You see what a lot they're going to do for us; now we must help them all we can. They want you to leave behind with them all the material about yourself that you can get together. You must get photographed at Slowburgh in a lot of different positions, and in your cadet uniform and your volunteer rig when you get it. Then you must let them have all your earlier photos if you can. 'Hero Jinks as an infant in arms,' 'Hero Jinks in his baby-carriage,' 'Hero Jinks as a schoolboy'--what a fine series it would make! You know what I mean. Then you must write your biography and your opinions about things in general, and give the addresses of all your friends and relations so that they can all be interviewed when the time comes. You'll do it, won't you? It's the up-to-date way of doing things, and it's the only way to be a military success."

"If it's the proper way of doing things I'll do it," said Sam.

"That's a good fellow! I'll send you a list of questions to answer and coach you as well as I can. I'm dying to get off and have this thing started. Isn't Jonas great? He's got just my ideas, only bigger. You see, he explained to me that in this country trusts have grown up with great difficulty, and it was hard work to establish the benefits which they produce for the public. They were fought at every step. But in the Cubapines we have a clean field, and by getting the Government monopoly whenever we want it, we can found one big trust and do ever so much good. I half wish I were a Cubapino, they're going to be benefited so, and without doing anything to deserve it either. Some people are born lucky."

"I can't quite follow all these business plans," said Sam. "My head isn't trained to it; but I'm glad we're going to do good there, and if I can do something great to bring it about, it will give me real happiness."

"It will, old man, it will. I"m sure of it," cried Cleary, as he took his leave of Sam in front of the hotel. "Let me know

what steamer you're going by as soon as you get orders, and I'll
try to manage it to get a passage on her too. They often carry
newspaper men on our transports.

On the following day Sam went to visit his uncle at
Slowburgh, a small sea-port of some four thousand inhabitants
lying several miles away from the railroad. The journey in the
train occupied six hours or more, and Sam spent the time in
learning the Castalian language in a handbook he had bought in
town. He had already taken lessons in the language at East Point
and was beginning to be fairly proficient. He alighted at the
nearest station to Slowburgh and entered the rather shabby
omnibus which was standing waiting. Sam felt lonely. There was
nothing military about the station and no uniform in sight. He
no longer wore a uniform himself, and the landscape was painfully
civilian. Finally the horses started and the 'bus moved slowly
up the road. Sam was impatient. His fellow countrymen were
risking their lives thousands of miles away, and here he was,
creeping along a country road in the disguise of a private
citizen, far away from the post of duty and danger. He looked
with disgust at the plowmen in the fields busily engaged in
preparing the soil for next year's grain.

"What a mean, poor-spirited lot," he thought. "Here they
are, following their wretched plows without a thought of the
brave soldiers who are defending their country and themselves so
many leagues away. It is the soldier, suffering from hunger and
fever and falling on the battlefield in the agony of death, who
makes it possible for these fellows to spend their days in
pleasant exercise in the fields. The soldier bears civilization
on his back, he supports all the rest, he is the pedestal which
bears without complaint the civilian as an idle ornament. The
soldier, in short, is the real man, the only perfect product of
creation."

And his heart was filled with thankfulness that he had
selected the career of a soldier and that there never could be
any doubt of his usefulness to the world. The only other
occupants of the omnibus were two men--one of them a commercial
traveler, and the other an aged resident of Slowburgh who had
been at the county town for the day, as Sam gathered from their
conversation.

"I don't suppose that the war has caused much excitement at
Slowburgh?" asked Sam at last, introducing the subject uppermost
in his mind.

"It ain't jest what it was when I went to the war," said the
old man; "but there is a deal o' talk about it, and all the young
men are wanting to go."

"Are they?" cried Sam, in delight. "And did you serve in
the war? How very interesting! Did you offer your life for your
country without hope of reward?"

"That's just what I did, young man, and if you doubt it,
here's my pension that I drew to-day in town, twelve dollars a
month, and they've paid it now these thirty-four years."

"That's a pretty soft thing," said the commercial man.
"Better'n selling fountain-pens in the backwoods."

"A soft thing!" cried the old man, "I ought to have twice as much. There's Abe Tucker gets fifteen dollars because he caught cold on picket duty, and I get a beggarly twelve."

"Were you severely wounded?" asked Sam.

"Well, no-o-o, not exactly, tho I might just as well 'a' been. I was down bad with the measles. This is an ongrateful country. Here it is only thirty-five years after the war, and they're only paying a hundred and forty millions a year to only a million pensioners. It's a beggarly shame!"

"Were there that many men in the war?" asked the traveler.

"Pretty near it, I reckon. But p'r'aps in thirty-five years there'd be a natural increase. Think of it, a million men throwing away their lives for a nothing like that! I jest tell our young fellers that they'd better stay at home. Why, we've had to fight for what we've got. You wouldn't think it, but we've had to pass around the hat, and shove it hard under the nose of Congress, too, just as if we were beggars and frauds, and as if we hadn't sacrificed everything for our country!"

"It's an outrage," cried Sam sympathetically. "But I hope you won't keep the young men from going. I'm going soon, and perhaps the country will be more generous in future."

"Take my advice, young man, and whenever anything happens to you while you're away, take down the names of the witnesses and keep their affidavits. Then you'll be all ready to get your pension as soon as you come back. It took me three years to straighten out mine. Then I got the back pay, of course, but I ought to have had it before. I've got a claim in now for eight dollars more a month running all the way back. It amounts to over three thousand dollars, and I ought to have it."

"Was that for the measles, too?" asked the stranger.

The old man glared at his interrogator, but did not deign to reply.

"Our Congressman, old Jinks, has my claim," he said, turning to Sam. "But he doesn't seem to be able to do anything with it."

"He's my uncle," said Sam, fearing that he might hear something against his worthy relative.

"So you're George Jinks' nephew, are you? Are you goin' to be a captain? Do tell! I read about it in the Slowburgh Herald last week. I'm real glad to see you. You're the first officer I've seen in ten years except the recruiting officer last week."

"Did they have a recruiting officer here, in Slowburgh?" asked Sam.

"Yes, they did, and there was thirteen fellers wanted to go, but he only took five of 'em, and they hain't gone yet. The rest was too short or too fat or too thin or something."

"Didn't any more men want to go than that?"

"No," said the old man. "They all want to wear soldier-clothes, but they don't all want to go fighting. They've got up a militia battalion for them now, and 'most everybody in town's got a uniform. I hadn't seen a uniform in the county before in I don't know how long--except firemen, I should say."

"I'm so glad they've got them now," cried Sam. "Doesn't it improve the looks of the place? It's so much more homelike and-d-d glorious, don't you think so?"

The old man had no opportunity to reply, as the 'bus now drew up at the front door of the principal hotel. The commercial traveler got out first and went into the house; the old man followed, and turning to Sam as he passed him, he said with a glance at the vanishing stranger:

"He's a copperhead, that feller."

He went on toward the bar-room door, but called back as he went:

"If you get lonesome over at Jinks', come in here in the evening. Ask for me; my name's Reddy."

Sam did not get out of the omnibus, but told the driver to take him to Congressman Jinks'; and on they went, first to the right and then to the left along the wide and gently winding streets, which would have been well shaded with maples if the yellow leaves had not already begun to fall. They drove in at last through a gate in a wooden fence and round a semi-circular lawn to the front of a comfortable frame house, and in a few moments he was received with open arms by his relations.

Congressman Jinks was a widower and had several children, all of whom, however, were away at school except his eldest daughter, a young lady of Sam's age, and his youngest, a girl of seven. The former, Mary, was a tall damsel with fair hair and a decidedly attractive manner. Mr. Jinks reminded Sam of his father with the added elegancies of many years' life at the Capital.

"Well, Samuel, I am glad to see you at last. We know all about you, and we're expecting great things from you," he cried out in a hearty voice. Sam felt at home at once.

"Come, Mary, show your cousin his room. Here, give me your grip. Yes, you must let me carry it. Now get ready for supper as soon as you can. It's all ready whenever you are."

After supper they all sat round a wood fire, for it was a little chilly in the evening now. Mr. Jinks had his little girl in his lap, and they talked over family history and the events of the day. Sam asked who Mr. Reddy was whom he had met in the train.

"Oh! you mean old Reddy. Was he drunk? No? That's odd."

"He'd been away for the day drawing his pension," said Sam.

"Of course," said Mr. Jinks. "I might have known it. That is his one sober day in the month. He sobers up to go to town, but he'll make up for lost time to-night. That twelve dollars will last just a week, and it all goes into the bar-room till. He's been that way ever since I was a boy, tho they say he was a steady enough young fellow before he went to the war. It's a curious coincidence, but there are two or three old rum-soaked war veterans like that hanging round every tavern in the country, and I'd like to know how much pension money goes that way. It's a great system tho, that pension system. I see something of it in Whoppington when I'm attending Congress. It distributes the money of the country and circulates it among the people. I like

299

to see the amount increase every year. It's a healthy sign. I'm
trying to get some more for Reddy. It helps the county just that
much. Swan, the hotel man, spends it here. I believe in
protecting home industries and fostering our home market. I wish
you could have heard my speech on the war-tax bill--it covered
that point. My, how this war is costing, tho! A million dollars
a day! But it's well worth it. The more money we spend and the
higher the taxes, the more circulation there is. You ought to
see how things are booming at Whoppington. I'm sorry you
couldn't come to see me there, but I had to be here this week
looking after election matters in my district. In Whoppington
all the hotels are full of contractors and men looking for
commissions in the army, and promoters and investors, all with an
eye to the Cubapines. You can just see how the war has brought
prosperity!"

"I should have liked to see Whoppington very much," said
Sam, "but I suppose I must wait till I come back. It must be
very different from other cities. You must feel there as if you
were at the center of things--at the very mainspring of all our
life, I mean."

"You've hit the nail on the head," said his uncle.
"Whoppington holds up all the rest of the country. There is the
Government that makes everything go. There's no business there
to speak of; no manufacturers, no agriculture in the country
round--nothing to distract your attention but the power of the
Administration that lies behind all the rest. Just think what
this country would be without Whoppington! Just imagine the
capital city sinking into the ground and what would we all do?
Even here at Slowburgh what would be left for us?"

"Wouldn't we have breakfast to-morrow morning, papa?" asked
the little girl in his lap.

"Er-er-well, perhaps we might have breakfast----"

"Wouldn't we have clothes, papa?"

"Perhaps we might have--but no, we couldn't either; it's the
tariff that gives us our clothes by keeping all foreign clothes
out of the country, and then we shouldn't have er-er----"

"It would upset the post-office," suggested Sam, coming to
the rescue.

"Yes, to be sure, that is what I meant. It would cause a
serious delay in the mails, that's certain."

"And then there would be no soldiers," added Sam.

"Of course. How stupid of me to overlook that. How would
you like to see no soldiers in the street?"

"I shouldn't like it at all, papa."

"Yes, my dear boy," he proceeded, turning to Sam, "I would
not want to have it repeated in my district, but I confess that I
am always homesick for Whoppington when I am here. That's the
real world there. There's the State Department where they manage
all the foreign affairs of the world. What could we do without
foreign affairs? And the Agricultural Department. How could we
get in our crops without it? And the Labor Department. Every
man who does a day's work depends on the Labor Department for his
living, we may say. And the----"

300

"The War Department," said Sam.

"Yes, the War Department. We depend on that for our wars. Perhaps at first that does not seem to be so useful, but----"

"Oh! but, Uncle George, surely it is the most useful of all. What could we do without wars. Just fancy a country without wars!"

"I don't know but you're right, Sam."

"And then the Treasury Department depends a good deal on the War Department," said Sam, in triumph, "for without the War Department and the army it wouldn't have any pensions to pay."

"That's so."

"Papa," said Mary Jinks, who had modestly taken no part in a conversation whose wisdom was clearly beyond her comprehension-- "papa, why didn't everybody go to the war like Mr. Reddy, and then they'd all have pensions and nobody'd have to work."

"It's their own fault if they didn't," answered her father; "and if some people are overworked they have only their own selves to thank for it. I have no patience with the complaints of these socialists and anarchists that the poor are getting poorer and the number of unemployed increasing. In a country with pensions and war taxes and a tariff there's no excuse for poverty at all."

"Yes," said Sam, "they could all enlist if they wanted to."

The following day was spent in driving about the country. Mr. Jinks was obliged to visit the various centers in his Congressional district, and he took Sam with him on one of these expeditions. The country was beautiful in the clear, cold autumn air. The mountains stood out blue on the horizon, and the trees were brilliant with red and yellow leaves. Sam, however, had no eyes for these things. He was eager to hear about the militia company, and was pleased to see several pairs of military trousers, altho they were made to do duty with civilian coats. Such for him were the incidents of the day. After supper in the evening he bethought him of old Reddy's invitation to the hotel bar-room, and thinking that he might learn more about the local military situation there, he excused himself and hied him thither. He found the room crowded with the wiseacres of the place, the Bohemian, drinking element perhaps predominating. The room was so full of smoke that, as Sam entered, he could hardly distinguish its contents, but he saw a confused mass of men in wooden arm-chairs tipped at every conceivable angle, surrounding a tall round stove which was heated white hot. The room was intensely warm and apparently totally wanting in ventilation.

"Here's my friend, Captain Jinks," said a husky voice which Sam recognized as that of old Reddy. "Here, take this chair near the fire."

Sam accepted the offered chair, altho he would have preferred a situation a little less torrid.

"Gentlemen, this is Captain Jinks," said the old man, determined to get all the credit he could from his acquaintance with Sam. "Captain, this is my friend, Mr. Jackson."

Mr. Jackson was a tall, thin, narrow-chested man with no shoulders, a rounded back, and a gray, tobacco-stained mustache.

His face was covered with pimples, and a huge quid of tobacco was concealed under his cheek. He was sitting on a chair tipped back rather beyond the danger-point, and his feet rested on the rim which projected from the stove half-way up. He made no effort to rise, but slowly extended a grimy, clammy hand which Sam pressed with some hesitation.

"Glad to make your acquaintance, Captain," he drawled in a half-cracked voice that suggested damaged lungs and vocal organs. "Shake hands with Mr. Tucker."

Mr. Tucker, a little, old, red-faced man on the other side of the stove, advanced and went through the ceremony suggested.

"We were just a-talking about them Cubapinos," explained Reddy. "The idee of them fellers a-pitching into us after all we've done for 'em. It's outrageous. They're only monkeys anyway, and they ought to be shot, every mother's son on 'em. Haven't we freed 'em from the cruel Castalians that they've been hating so for three hundred years?"

"They seem to be hating us pretty well just now," said a man in the corner, whose voice sounded familiar to Sam. He turned and recognized the commercial traveler of the day before.

"They're welcome to hate us," answered Jackson, "and when it comes to a matter of hating I shouldn't think much of us if we couldn't make 'em hate us as much in a year as the Castalians could in three hundred. They're a blamed slow lot and we ain't. That's all there is of it. What do you think, Captain?

"I fear," said Sam, "that they don't quite understand the great blessings we're conferring on them."

"What blessings?" asked the drummer.

"Why," said Sam, "liberty and independence--no, I don't mean independence exactly, but liberty and freedom."

"Then why don't we leave them alone instead of fighting them?"

"What an idee!" exclaimed Tucker. "They don't know what liberty is, and we must teach 'em if we have to blow their brains out."

"You're too hard on 'em, Tucker," drawled Mr. Jackson. "We mustn't expect so much from pore savages who live in a country so hot that they can't progress like we do." Here Mr. Jackson took off his hat and wiped the beads of perspiration from his brow with a red bandanna handkerchief. "Don't expect too much from cannibals that have their brains half roasted by the tropical sun."

"That's a fact!" said some one in the throng.

"Yes," said Jackson, crossing his legs on a level well above his head, "them pore critters need our civilization, that's what they need," and he dexterously squirted a mouthful of tobacco juice on the white-hot stove, where it sizzled and gradually evaporated. "We must make real men of 'em. We must give 'em our strength and vigor and intelligence. They're a dirty lot of lazy beggars, that's the long and short of it, and we must turn 'em into gentlemen like us!"

A general murmur of approval followed this outburst.

302

"I hear," said Sam, anxious to get some definite information as to the warriors of the town, "I hear that several Slowburghers are going to the war."

"Yes," said Tucker, while Jackson after his effort settled down into a semi-comatose state, "six of our boys are a-going. There's Davy Black, he drives the fastest horse in these parts, and Tom Slade. Where is Tom? He's generally here. They'll miss him here at the hotel, and Jim Thomson who used to be bartender over at Bloodgood's, and the two Thatchers--they're cousins--that makes five."

"The village ought to be glad they are going to represent her at the front," said Sam.

"From all I can hear," said the commercial man, "I think they are."

"Naturally," cried Sam, "it will reflect great glory on the place. You ought to be proud of them."

"It'll help the insurance business here," said a young man who had not yet spoken.

"How is that?" asked Sam. "I don't exactly see."

"Well, it's this way. You see I'm in the insurance business and I can't write a policy on a barn in this township, there's been so many burned; and while I don't want to say nothing against anybody, we think maybe they won't burn so much when the Thatchers clear out."

"Nothin' ain't ever been proved against 'em," said Tucker.

"That's true," said the young man, "but perhaps there might have been if they'd stayed. They say that Squire Jones was going to have Josh Thatchers arrested next week for his barn, but he's agreed to let up if he'd go to the Cubapines. Maybe that isn't true, but they say so."

"I venture to say that it is a mistake," said Sam, who had been much pained by the conversation. "Young men who are so patriotic in the hour of need must be men of high character."

"Maybe they are and maybe they aren't," replied the insurance agent, "but old Mrs. Crane told me she was going to buy chickens again next week for her chicken-yard. There was so many stolen last year that she gave up keeping them, but next week she's beginning again, and next week the Thatchers are going away. It's a coincidence, anyhow."

"Oh, boys will be boys," said Reddy. "When they get a good pension they'll be just as respectable as you or me. Here comes Tom Slade now, and Josh Thatcher, too."

The door had opened, and through the smoke Sam described two young men, one a slight wiry fellow, the other a large, broad-shouldered, fair-haired man with a dull expression of the eye.

"Who says 'drinks all around'?" cried the former. "Everybody's blowing us off now."

"Here," said Jackson, waking up, "I'll do it, hanged if I don't. You fellows are a-going' to civilize the Cubapines, and you deserve all the liquor you can carry.

He got up and approached the bar and the crowd followed him, and soon every one was supplied with some kind of beverage.

303

"Here's to Thatcher and Slade! May they represent Slowburgh honorably in the Cubapines and show 'em what Slowburghers are like," said Jackson, elevating his iced cocktail.

The health was heartily drunk.

"And here is to that distinguished officer, Captain Jinks. Long may he wave!" cried old Reddy.

"Speech, speech!" exclaimed the convivial crowd.

"Gentlemen," responded Sam, "I am a soldier and not an orator, but I am proud to have my name coupled with those of your honored fellow townsmen. It is a sign of the greatness of our country that men of just the same character are in all quarters of this mighty republic answering their country's call. Soon we shall have the very pick of our youth collected on the shores of these ungrateful islanders who have turned against their best friends, and these misguided people will see for themselves the fruits of our civilization as we see it, in the persons of our soldiers. Permit me in responding to your flattering toast to propose the names of Mr. Reddy and Mr. Tucker as representatives of an older generation of patriots whose example we are happy to have before us for our guidance."

This, Sam's first speech, was received with great applause, and then Josh Thatcher proposed three cheers for Captain Jinks, which were given with a will. The only perverse spirit was that of the commercial traveler, who had sat in the corner reading an old copy of the Slowburgh Herald, and now on hearing the cheers, took a candle and went upstairs to bed.

"That man's no good," said Reddy with a shake of his head. While the whole company were expressing their concurrence with this sentiment, Sam bade them good-night and took his leave.

CHAPTER VI

Off For The Cubapines

By the next morning's mail Sam's commission arrived, and with it orders to report at once at the city of St. Kisco, whence a transport was about to sail on a date which gave Sam hardly time to catch it. He must hurry at once to town and get his new uniforms for which he had been fitted the week before, and then proceed by the fastest trains on the long journey to the distant port without even paying his parents a farewell visit. He found Cleary busily engaged in making his final arrangements, and persuaded him to cut them short and travel with him. Sam had hardly time to take breath from the moment of his departure from Slowburgh to the evening on which he and Cleary at last sat down in their sleeping-car. His friend heaved a deep sigh.

"Well, here we are actually off and I haven't got anything to do for a change. This is what I call comfort.

"Yes," said Sam, "but I wish we were in the Cubapines. This inaction is terrible while so much is at stake. It's a consolation to know that I am going to help to save the country, but it is tantalizing to wait so long. Then in your own way you're going to help the country too," he added, thinking that he might seem to Cleary to be monopolizing the honors.

"I'll help it by helping you," laughed Cleary. "I've got another contract for you. You see the magazines are worth working. They handle the news after the newspapers are through with it, and they don't interfere with each other. So I got permission to tackle them from The Lyre, and I saw the editor of Scribblers' Magazine yesterday and it's a go, if things come out as I expect."

"What do you mean?" asked Sam.

"Why, you are to write articles for them, a regular series, and the price is to be fixed on a sliding scale according to your celebrity at the time of each publication. It won't be less than a hundred dollars a page, and may run up to a thousand. It wouldn't be fair to fix the price ahead. If the articles run say six months, the last article might be worth ten times as much as the first."

"Yes, it might be better written," said Sam.

"Oh, I don't mean that. But your name might be more of an ad. by that time."

"I've never written anything to print in my life," said Sam, "and I'm not sure I can."

"That doesn't make any difference. I'll write them for you. You might be too modest anyhow. I can't think of a good name for the series. It ought to be 'The Autobiography of a Hero,' or 'A Modern Washington in the Cubapines,' or something like that. What do you think?"

"I'm sure I don't know," said Sam. "I must leave that to you. They sound to me rather too flattering, but if you are sure that is the way those things are always done, I won't make any objection. You might ask Mr. Jonas. Where is he?

"He's going on next week. He's the greatest fellow I ever saw. Everything he touches turns to gold. He's got his grip on everything in sight on those blessed islands already. He's scarcely started, and he could sell out his interests there for a cold million to-day. It's going to be a big company to grab everything. He's called it the 'Benevolent Assimilation Company, Limited'; rather a good name, I think, tho perhaps 'Unlimited' would be nearer the truth."

"Yes," said Sam. "It shows our true purposes. I hope the Cubapinos will rejoice when they hear the name."

"Perhaps they won't. There's no counting on those people. I'm sick of them before I've seen them. I'm just going to tell what a lot of skins they are when I begin writing for The Lyre. By the way, did you have your photographs taken at Slowburgh?"

"No," said Sam, "I forgot all about it, but I can write home about the old ones, and I've got one in cadet uniform taken at East Point."

"Well, we mustn't forget to have you taken at St. Kisco, and we can mail the photos to The Lyre, but you must be careful not to overlook a thing like that again. The people will want to know what the hero who saved the country looked like."

305

"Even if I don't do anything very wonderful," said Sam, "and I hope I shall, I shall be taking part in a great work, and doing my share of civilizing and Christianizing a barbarous country. They have no conception of our civilized and refined manners, of the sway of law and order, of all our civilized customs, the result of centuries of improvement and effort."

Cleary picked up a newspaper to read.

"What's that other newspaper lying there?" asked Sam.

"That's The Evening Star; do you want it?" and he handed it to him.

"Good Lord! what's that frightful picture?" said Cleary, as Sam opened the paper. "Oh, I see; it's that lynching yesterday. Why, it's from a snap-shot; that's what I call enterprise! There's the darkey tied to the stake, and the flames are just up to his waist. My! how he squirms. It's fearful, isn't it? And look at the crowd! There are small boys bringing wood, and women and girls looking on, and, upon my word, a baby in arms, too! I know that square very well. I've often been there. That't the First Presbyterian Church there behind the stake. Rather a handsome building," and Cleary turned back to his own paper, while Sam settled down in his corner to read how the leading citizens gathered bones and charred flesh as mememtoes and took them home to their children. No one could have guessed what he was reading from his expression, for his face spoke of nothing but a guileless conscience and a contented heart.

One day at St. Kisco gave just time enough for the photographs, and most of the day was devoted to them. Sam was taken in twenty poses--in the act of leading his troops in a breach, giving the order to fire, charging bayonets himself with a musket supposed to have been taken from a dead foe, standing with his arms folded and his cap pulled over his eyes in the trenches, and waving his cap on a bastion in the moment of triumph. Cleary lay down so that his friend might be pictured with his foot upon his prostrate form. The photographer was one who made a specialty of such work, and was connected with a cinematograph company.

"If you have good luck sir, and become famous," he said, "as your friend thinks you will, we'll fight your battles over again over there in the vacant lot; and then we'll work these in, and you'll soon be in every variety show in the country."

"But I may be mounted on horseback," said Sam.

"That's so," said Cleary. "Can't you get a horse somewhere and take him on that?"

"We never do that, sir. Here's a saddle. Just sit on it across this chair, and when the time comes we'll work it in all right. We'll have a real horse over in the lot." And thus Sam was taken straddling a chair.

They left orders to send copies of the photographs to Homeville, Slowburgh, and to Miss Hunter who was still at East Point, and the remainder to The Lyre. That very evening they boarded the transport and at daybreak sailed away over the great ocean. The ship was filled by various drafts for different regiments and men-of-war. Sam's regiment was already at the seat

306

of war, but there were several captains and lieutenants assigned
to it on board, as well as thirty or forty men. Sam felt
entirely comfortable again for the first time since his
resignation at East Point. He was in his element, the military
world, once more. Everything was ruled by drum, fife, and
bugle. He found the same feeling of intense patriotism again,
which civilians can not quite attain to, however they may make
the attempt. The relations between some of the officers seemed
to Sam somewhat strange. The highest naval officer on board, a
captain, was not on speaking terms with the highest army officer,
a brigadier-general of volunteers. This breach apparently set
the fashion, for all the way down, through both arms of the
service, there were jealousies and quarrels. There was one great
subject of dispute, the respective merits of the two admirals who
had overcome the Castalian fleet at Havilla. Some ascribed the
victory to the one and some to the other, but to take one side
was to put an end to all friendships on the other.

"See here, Sam," said Cleary, not long after they had been
out of sight of land, "who are you for, Admiral Hercules or
Admiral Slewey? We can't keep on the fence, that's evident, and
if we get down on different sides we can't be friends, and that
might upset all our plans, not to speak of the Benevolent
Assimilation Trust."

"The fact is," said Sam, "that I don't know anything about
it. They're both admirals, and they both must be right."

"Nobody knows anything about it, but we must make up our
minds all the same. My idea is that Hercules is going to come
out ahead; and as long as one seems as good as the other in other
respects, I move that we go for Hercules."

"Very well," said Sam, "if you say so. He was in command,
anyway, and more likely to be right."

So Sam and Cleary allied themselves with the Hercules party,
which was in the majority. They became quite intimate with the
naval officers who belonged to this faction, and saw more of them
than of the army men. Sam was much interested in learning about
the profession which kept alive at sea the same traditions which
the army preserved on land. For the first few days of the voyage
the rolling of the ship made him feel a little sick, and he
concealed his failings as well as he could and kept to himself;
but he proved to be on the whole a good sailor. He was
particularly pleased to learn that on a man-of-war the captain
takes his meals alone, and that only on invitation can an
inferior officer sit down at table with him. This appealed to
him as an admirable way of maintaining discipline and respect.
The fact that all the naval men he met had their arms and bodies
more or less tattooed also aroused his admiration. He inquired
of the common soldiers if they ever indulged in the same artistic
luxury, and found out to his delight that a few of them did.

"It's strange," he remarked to Cleary, "that tattooing is
universal in the navy and comparatively rare in the army. I
rather think the habit must have been common to both services,
and somehow we have nearly lost it. It's a fine thing. It marks

a man with noble symbols and mottoes, and commits him to an honorable life, indelibly I may say."

"It's a little like branding a mule," said Cleary.

"Yes," said Sam; "the brand shows who owns the mule, and the tattooing shows a man belongs to his country."

"And if he's shipwrecked and hasn't any picture-books or newspapers with him, he can find all he wants on his own skin," said Cleary.

"Joke as you please, I think it's a patriotic custom."

"Why don't you get tattooed then?" asked Cleary.

"Do you think there's anybody on board can do it?" cried Sam enthusiastically.

"Of course. Any of those blue-jackets can tell you whom to go to."

Sam was off before Cleary had finished his sentence. Sure enough, he found a boatswain who was renowned as an artist, and without further parley he delivered himself into his hands. Cleary was consulted on the choice of designs, and the result was pronounced by all the connoisseurs on board--and there were many--to be a masterpiece. On his chest was a huge spread-eagle with a bunch of arrows, bayonets, and lightening-flashes in his claws. Cannon belched forth on each side, and the whole was flanked by a sailor on one side and a soldier on the other. His arms were tattooed with various small designs of crossed swords, flags, mottoes, the title of his regiment, and other such devices. The boatswain now thought that his task was complete, but Sam insisted on having his back decorated as well, altho this was rather unusual. The general stock of subjects had been exhausted, and Cleary suggested that a representation of Sam himself, striking off the fetters of a Cubapino, would be most appropriate. After discussing a number of other suggestions offered by various friends, this one was finally adopted and successfully carried out. The operation was not altogether painless and produced a good deal of irritation of the skin, but it served to pass Sam's time and allay his impatience to be in the field, and Cleary became so much interested that he consented to allow the artist to tattoo a few modest designs of cannon and crossed bayonets on his own arms. Sam's comparatively high rank among officers who were, many of them, his juniors in rank but his seniors in years, might have made his position at first a difficult one had it not been for his entire single-mindedness and loyalty to his country. If the powers that be had made him a captain, it was right that he should be a captain. He obeyed implicitly in taking his seat near the head of the table, as he would have obeyed if he had been ordered to the foot, and he expected others to accept what came from above as he did.

One afternoon a report sprang up that land was in sight, and soon every eye was strained in one direction. Sam's eyesight was particularly good, and he was one of the first to detect the white gleam of a lighthouse. Soon the coast-line was distinct, and it was learned that they would arrive on the next day. By daybreak Sam was on deck, studying as well as he could this new land of heroism and adventure. Cleary joined him later, and the

308

two friends watched the strange tropical shore with its palm-groves and occasional villages, and a range of mountains beyond. A bay opened before them, and the ship turned in, passing near an old fortification.

"This is just where our fleet went in," said Cleary, examining a folding map which he held in his hand. "They passed along there single file," and he pointed out the passage.

"Wasn't it glorious! Just think of sailing straight on, no matter how many torpedoes there were!" exclaimed Sam.

"They knew blamed well there weren't any torpedoes," answered Cleary.

"How could they have known? They hadn't ever been here before? There might perfectly well have been a lot of them directly under them."

"Yes," said Cleary, "they might have grown up from the bottom of the sea. All sorts of queer things grow here. There might have been a sort of coral torpedoes."

"Cleary, you're getting more and more cynical every day. I wish you'd be more reasonable. What's the matter with you?"

"It must be the newspaper business. And then you see I don't wear a uniform either. That makes a lot of difference."

In another hour they passed the scene of the great naval battle. They could just distinguish the hulks of the wrecks well in shore.

"And there's Havilla!" cried Cleary.

And Havilla it was. They entered the great Oriental port with its crowded shipping. Small native boats were darting about between merchantmen and men-of-war. The low native houses, the fine buildings of the Castalian city, the palms, the Eastern costumes--all made a scene not to be forgotten. An officer of the 200th Volunteer Infantry came on board before the steamer had come to her moorings, with orders for Captain Jinks to report at once at their headquarters in one of the public buildings of the city. A lieutenant was left in charge of the 200th's detail, and Sam hastened ashore in a native boat and Cleary went with him. They had no difficulty in finding their way, and Sam was soon reporting to his chief, Colonel Booth, an elderly captain of the regular army, who had been placed at the head of this volunteer regiment. The colonel received him rather gruffly, and turned him over to one of his captains, telling him they would be quartered together. The colonel was inclined to pay no attention to Cleary, but when the latter mentioned the Benevolent Assimilation Company, Limited, he suddenly changed his tone and expressed great delight at meeting him. Sam and Cleary went off together with the captain, whose name was Foster, to visit the lodgings assigned by the colonel. They were in a building near by, which had been used as barracks by the Castalian army. A number of rooms had been fitted up for the use of officers, and Sam and Foster were to occupy one of these, an arrangement which promised to be most comfortable. Five companies of their regiment were quartered in the same building.

Cleary asked Foster's advise as to lodgings for himself, and Foster took him off with him to find a place, while Sam was left to unpack his luggage which had just arrived from the ship. They agreed to meet again in the same room at nine o'clock in the evening.

It was somewhat after the hour fixed that the three men came together. Foster brought out a bottle of whisky from a cupboard and put it on the table by the water-jug, and then offered cigars. Sam had never smoked before, but he felt that a soldier ought to smoke, and he accepted the weed, and soon they were all seated, smoking and drinking, and engaged in a lively conversation. Foster had been in the Cubapines since the arrival of the first troops, and it was a treat for both of his interlocutors to hear all the news at first hand from a participant in the events.

"How were things when you got here?" asked Cleary.

"Well, it was like this," answered Foster. "Nothing had happened then except the destruction of the fleet. Our fleet commanded the water of course, and the niggers had closed up round the city on land. The Castalians didn't have anything but the city, and when we came we wanted to take the city."

"Was Gomaldo in command of the Cubapino army then?" asked Sam.

"Yes, he has been from the beginning. He's a bad lot."

"How is that?" asked Cleary.

"Why, he has interfered with us all along as much as he could, just as if we didn't own the place."

"That's just what I thought," said Cleary. "The copperheads at home say we treated him as an ally, but of course that's rubbish."

"Of course," said Foster, "we never treated him as an ally. We only brought him here and made use of him, supplying him with some arms and letting him take charge of some of our prisoners. We couldn't tell him that we intended to keep the islands, because we were using him and couldn't get on without him. He's an ignorant fellow and hasn't the first idea of the behavior of an officer and a gentleman."

"Well, how did you take Havilla?" asked Sam.

"Oh, it was this way. The Castalians couldn't hold out because these monkeys had the place so tight that they couldn't get any provisions in. So they sent secret word to us that they would let us in on a certain day if we would keep the natives out. We agreed to this, of course. Then the Castalian general said that we must have some kind of a battle or he would be afraid to go home, and we cooked up a nice little battle. When the men got into it, however, it turned out to be quite a skirmish, and a number were killed on both sides. Then they surrendered and we went in and put a guard at the gates, and wouldn't let the niggers in. You wouldn't believe it, but they actually kicked at it. They're an unreasonable, sulky lot of beggers.

"Then what happened after that?" asked Sam.

"Oh, after that we sent the Castalians home and the Cubapinos moved back their lines a little, and we agreed to a sort of neurtal zone and a line beyond which we weren't to go."

310

"What was it that started the fighting between us and them?" said Sam.

"It's a little mixed up. I was at the theater that night, and in the middle of the play we heard firing, and all of us rushed off and found everything in motion, and it grew into a regular fight. We made them move back, and before long the firing ceased. I tried to find out the next day how it began. The fact is, the day before, General Notice had ordered the 68th to move forward about half a mile, and they did so. The Cubapinos objected and insisted on crossing the new picket-line. That evening an officer of theirs walked across it and was shot by the sentinel. That started it."

"Was the regiment moved across the line fixed on their side of the neutral zone?" said Cleary.

"Oh, yes. But that was all right. Don't we own the whole place? And the regiment was only obeying orders."

"I wonder why the general gave the orders?" asked Cleary, musing as he looked into the smoke which he was puffing forth.

"They say it was because he had what he called 'overmastering political reasons.' That is, there was the army bill up in Congress and it had to go through, and he was given the tip that some fighting would help it, and he took the hint. It was good statesmanship and generalship, too. All subordinate things must bend to the great general interests of the country. It was a good move, for it settled the business. Gomaldo sent in the next day and tried to patch up a truce, but Notice wouldn't see his messengers. He told them they must surrender unconditionally. It was fine, soldierly conduct. He's a brick."

"What has he gone home for?" asked Sam.

"Why, he'd conquered them. Why shouldn't he go home? They're giving him a grand reception at home, and I'm glad to see it."

"But he says that he has pacified the islands and brought the war to a close!"

"So he did, in the military sense. He couldn't tell that the scamps wouldn't submit at once. It wasn't his fault that they showed such unreasonable bitterness and obstinacy."

"How much territory do we hold now?" said Sam.

"We've got the city and a strip along the bay where the fleet is; about five miles back, I should say. But it's hardly safe to wander off far at night."

"What's going to happen next?" asked Cleary. "I want to send home some news to The Lyre as soon as I can, and I want my friend Jinks here to have a chance to distinguish himself--and you too," he added hastily.

"We'll probably get to work by next week, the way things look now. General Laughter is rather slow, but he means business. Gomaldo is getting a big army together, and we may have to take the offensive to get ahead of him. Now I suppose we ought to turn in. How would you like to take a look at Havilla to-morrow and see the place where the naval battle was? We can get off duty in the afternoon. All right, let's meet at regimental headquarters at three."

311

Cleary bade them good-night, and Sam, who was beginning to feel uncomfortable effects from his cigar, was quite ready to go to bed.

Sam's morning was occupied in familiarizing himself with the regimental routine in barracks. The building enclosed a large court which was used for drills and guard-mounting parade, and he did not have occasion to leave it until he went to join his friends at headquarters. Promptly at three o'clock the three men sallied forth. Sam was struck with the magnificence of the principal buildings, including the palace and the cathedral.

"It's a fine city, isn't it?" he said.

"Yes, and the women are not bad-looking," said Cleary.

"The people don't quite look like savages," said Sam.

"You can't judge of them by these," said Foster. "Wait till you meet some negritos in the country."

"How large a part of the population are they?" said Sam.

"About one-fortieth, I think, but where principle is involved you can't go by numbers."

"Of course not," was Sam's reply. "What building is that," he added, "with our flag over it and the nicely dressed young women in the windows?"

"That?" said Foster, laughing; "oh, that's the Young Ladies' Home. We have to license the place. It's the only way to keep the army in condition. Why, we've got about fifty per cent infected now."

"Really?" cried Sam. "How our poor fellows are called upon to suffer for these ungrateful Cubapinos! Still they can feel that they are suffering for their country, too. That's a consolation."

"There's more consolation than that," said Foster, "for we're spreading the thing like wildfire among the natives. We'll come out ahead."

"I wish, tho, that they wouldn't fly Old Gory over the house," said Sam.

"There was some talk of taking it down, but you see it's the policy of the Administration never to haul down the flag when it has once been raised. It presents rather a problem, you see."

"It may wear out in time," said Sam, "altho it looks painfully new. What will they do then."

"I confess I don't know," said Foster. "They'll cross the bridge when they reach it."

"A good many of the shop signs are in English already," remarked Sam. "That's a good beginning."

"Yes," said Cleary. "But they seem to be almost all saloons, that's queer."

"So they are," said Sam.

"There are some pretty good ones, too," said Foster. "Just stop in here for a moment and take a drink."

They entered a drinking-place and found a bar planned on the familiar lines of home.

"Look at this list of our drinks," said Foster proudly. "Count 'em; there are eighty-two."

Sam examined the list, which was printed and framed and hanging on the wall, and they each took a glass of beer, standing. There were about a dozen men in the place, most of them soldiers.

"Do they do a big business in these places?" asked Sam.

"You'll think so when you see the drunken soldiers in the streets in the evening," answered Foster. "We're planting our institutions here, I tell you."

"Not only saloons," said Sam. "There's the post-office, for instance."

"They had a post-office before," said Cleary.

"But ours is surely better," rejoined Sam.

"It's better than it was," said Foster, "now that they've put the new postmaster in jail. They say he's bagged $75,000."

"It's a good example of the way we treat embezzlers," cried Sam. "It ought to be a lesson to these Cubapinos. He'll be sent home to be tried. They ought to do that with every one caught robbing the mails in any way."

"I'm afraid if they did the force would be pretty well crippled," said Foster.

"Then there's the custom house," said Sam. "They must be delighted to get rid of those Castalian swindlers."

"A merchant here told me," said Foster, "that they have to pay just as often now, but that they have to pay bigger sums."

"Of course," cried Cleary, "you wouldn't expect our people to bother with the little bribes the Castalians are after. We live on a larger scale. It will do these natives good to open their eyes to a real nation. I'm sorry any of them steal, but if they do, let 'em take a lot and be done with it."

"We must remember that these people are only civilians," said Sam. "What can we expect of them?"

"Our commissary and quartermaster departments aren't much better, tho," said Foster. "Somebody's getting rich, to judge from the prices we pay and the stuff we get. The meat stinks, and the boots are made with glue instead of stitches and nails."

"Then they must have been appointed from civil life," cried Sam.

"Come, Sam," said Cleary, "I'm a civilian now, and I'm not going to have you crow over us. How about Captain Peters, who was the pet of Whoppington and cleaned out the Deer Harbor fund?"

Sam walked on in silence.

"See here," said Foster, "I'm tired of going on foot. Let's take a cab. Here, you fellow!"

A two-wheeled wagon with an awning, drawn by a small, shaggy horse, drew up before them.

"There's a gentleman in it," said Sam. "We must wait for another."

"Nonsense!" cried Foster in a loud voice. "You evidently are a new arrival. It's only one of those monkeys. Here you, sir, get out of that!"

The native expostulated a little, shrugged his shoulders, and did as he was told, and the three men got in.

"I'm afraid he didn't like it," said Sam.

"Didn't like it? What of it?" said Foster. "Whatever we do in uniform is official business, and we've got to impress these fellows with our power and make them respect us."

They drove now through some narrow streets, past various native cafés half open to the air, where the habitués were beginning to collect, through a picturesque gate in the old city wall, and out on the Boulevard, which was now filled with people driving and walking. It was a gay scene, and reminded Cleary of some of the cities of the Mediterranean which he had visited.

"They're not quite as much like Apaches as I expected," said Sam, and neither of his friends ventured to respond.

"We haven't got time to go out to where the ships are sunk," said Foster, "but if we drive up that hill and get out and walk up a little farther we can see them in the distance. I've got my glasses with me."

In a few minutes they were at this point of vantage in a sort of unfrequented public park, and the three men took turns in looking at the distant wrecks through the captain's field-glass.

"It was a great victory, wasn't it?" said Sam.

"Well, perhaps it was," answered Foster; "but the fact is, that those old boats could hardly float and their guns couldn't reach our ships. We just took our time and blew them up and set them on fire, and the crews were roasted or drowned, that was all there was of it. I don't think much of naval men anyway, to tell the truth. They don't compare with the army. They're always running their ships aground if there's any ground to run into."

"Anyhow, if it had been a strong fleet we'd have wiped it out just the same, wouldn't we?" said Sam.

"Undoubtedly," said Foster. "It's a pity, tho, that the fight didn't test our naval armaments better. It didn't prove anything. If we'd only used our torpedo-boats, and they'd got out their torpedo-boat destroyers, and then we'd had some torpedo-boat-destroyer destroyers, and----"

"Yes," interrupted Cleary, "it is a pity."

"But it wasn't Admiral Hercules's fault," said Sam. "His glory ought to be just as great."

"Hercules! Hercules!" shouted Foster. "What had Hercules to do with it? He's a first-class fraud. It was Slewey who won the battle. You don't mean to tell me that you are Hercules men?"

Sam and Cleary tried in vain to explain their position, but Foster would not listen to them. The breach evidently was irreparable. He magnanimously turned over the cab to them, and went back to the city in another vehicle.

"Well, this is strange," said Sam. "I liked everything about Captain Foster, but I don't understand this."

"Oh, you will tho, old man," said Cleary. "I've found out this morning that it's the same thing all through the army and navy here. They're hardly any of them on speaking terms. If it isn't one thing it's another. It's the Whoppington fashion, that's all. The general of the army won't speak to the adjutant-general there, and they're always smuggling bills into Congress to retire each other, and that spirit runs all the way down through both services. I'm a civilian now, and I can see

314

with a little perspective. I don't know why military people are always squabbling like the women in an old ladies' home. No other professions do; it's queer. It's getting to be better to lose a battle than to win it, for then you don't have to fight for a year or two to find out who won it."

Sam entered a feeble protest against Cleary's criticisms, and the two relapsed into silence.

"Who did win that naval victory anyhow?" said Sam at last.

"That's just what I'd like to know," responded Cleary. "One of the admirals admits he wasn't there, and, if we are to believe the naval people, the other one spent most of his time dodging around the smokestack. But I think they're a little too hard on him; I can't imagine why. I hear they're going to establish a permanent court at Whoppington to determine who wins victories in future. It's not a bad idea. My own view is that the battle won itself, and I shouldn't be surprised if that was the way with most battles. It would be fun to run a war without admirals and generals and see how it would come out. I don't believe there'd be much difference. At any rate it looks so, if what the navy says is true, and one of the admirals was away and the other playing tag on the forward deck of the Philadelphia. Rum name for a battle-ship, the Brotherly Love, isn't it?"

To this Sam made no answer.

On arriving at the barracks he succeeded in having a separate room assigned to him, and thenceforth he and Foster were strangers.

CHAPTER VII

The Battle of San Diego

During the next few days there was much activity in the army. It was clear that there was an expedition in preparation. All sorts of rumors were floating about, but it was impossible to verify any of them. Some said that Gomaldo was advancing with a large army; others, that he had surrendered and that the army was about to take peaceable possession of the islands. Meanwhile Sam's position in the 200th Infantry was most unpleasant. Foster was a popular man in the regiment, and he had set all the officers against him. It was unfortunately a Slewey regiment, and it was too late for Sam to change sides--a thing which he was quite ready to do. He made up his mind never to mention the two admirals again, and regretted that he had named them once too often. He complained to Cleary.

"I'm afraid," he said, "that there's no chance of my doing anything. The colonel will see to it that I am out of the way if there's anything to do. I might as well have stayed at East Point."

"Brace up, old man! I've got an idea," said Cleary. "I'll fix you all right. Just you wait till to-morrow or the day after."

The next day in the afternoon Sam received an order to report at once at the headquarters of General Laughter. He hastened to obey, and was ushered into the presence of that distinguished officer in the palace. It was an impressive sight that met his eyes. The general was believed to weigh some three hundred pounds, but he looked as if he weighed nearer five hundred. He was dressed in a white duck suit with brass buttons, the jacket unbuttoned in front and showing his underclothes. He was suffering a good deal from the heat, and fanning himself incessantly. Several members of his staff were busied talking with visitors or writing at desks, but the chief was doing nothing. He was seated in a superb arm-chair with his back to a pier-glass.

"Ah! captain," he said. "I'm glad to see you. Have a whisky and soda? I've assigned you to duty on my staff. Report here again to-morrow at ten and have your things moved over to the palace. Major Stroud will show you your quarters, captain!"

Major Stroud advanced and shook hands with Sam. He was every inch a soldier in appearance, but old enough to be a retired field-marshal. The three indulged in whiskies and soda, and Sam took his leave after a brief formal conversation. He found Cleary waiting for him in the street.

"How on earth did you do it?" cried Sam.

"It's the B. A. C. L.," said Cleary.

"The what!"

"The Benevolent Assimilation Company, Limited. What do you suppose? With The Daily Lyre thrown in too."

"Oh! thank you, thank you, my dear, dear friend," ejaculated Sam, with tears in his eyes. "I was beginning to think that my whole life was a failure, and here I am just in the very best place in the world. I won't disappoint you, I won't disappoint you!"

In the few days at the barracks of the 200th Infantry, Sam had learned something of regimental work, and now he applied himself assiduously to the study of the business of the headquarters of a general in command in the field, for the army was practically in the field. At first it all seemed to him to be a maze quite without a plan, and he hoped that in time he would begin to see the outline of a system. But the more he observed the less system he saw. Everything that could be postponed was postponed. Responsibility was shifted from one staff officer to another. No one was held accountable for anything, and general confusion seemed to reign. The place was besieged with contractors and agents, and the staff was nearly worried to death. The general was always very busy--fanning himself--and the days went on.

One morning a fellow member of the staff, a young lieutenant whom he scarcely knew, called Sam aside and asked him for a half-hour's conference. They went off together into a deserted room, and the lieutenant began the conversation in a whisper.

"See here, Captain," said he, "we're looking for a patriotic fellow who cares more for his country than his own reputation. We understand that you're just the man."

"I hope so," said Sam, delighted at the prospect of an opportunity to distinguish himself.

316

"It's a rather delicate matter," continued the lieutenant, "and I must say it's rather a compliment to you to be selected for the job. The fact is, that Captain Jones is in trouble. He's about $3,000 short in his accounts."

"How did that happen?" asked Sam.

"Oh, that's not the point. I don't see that it makes any difference. But we've got to get him out of the scrape. The honor of the army is at stake. Civilians don't understand us. They don't appreciate our standards of honor. And if this thing gets out they'll charge us with all kinds of things. We've got to raise $3,000. That's all there is of it."

"Good heavens! how can we?" cried Sam. "I've hardly got anything left of my pay, but I can give, say $25, on the next pay-day."

"We're not going to pass the hat around. That would be beneath the dignity of the army. What we want you to do is this--and, indeed, we have settled it that you should do it. You are to go to-morrow afternoon to Banks & Company, the army contractors, and have a confidential talk with Banks. Tell him you must have $3,000 at once. Here's a letter of introduction to him. He will see that you represent the people that run things here. Tell him that his contracts will probably be preferred to Short & Co.'s, and tell him that for the future we shan't inspect his things as closely as we have in the past. You needn't go into particulars. He will understand. It's an ordinary business matter."

"I don't quite like the idea," said Sam, ruminating. "Why don't yo go yourself?"

"My dear Captain, I'm only a lieutenant. It requires a man of higher rank to do such an important piece of work. You're a new man on the staff, and we wanted to pay you an honor and give you a chance to show your patriotism. You will be saving the reputation and character of the army."

"Oh, thank you!" exclaimed Sam. "Are you sure that it's always done in just this way?"

"Always. It's an ordinary matter of business arrangement, as I've already told you."

"Then it must be all right, I suppose," said Sam.

"But it's not only that. It's a noble act to protect the character of a brother officer."

"So it is, so it is," said Sam. "I'll do it. I'll call and see him about it to-morrow afternoon."

"Hello!" shouted another officer, coming into the room. "Have you seen the orders? There's to be a conference of brigade and regimental commanders here to-night, and all staff officers are invited to attend. That means business."

Sam was overjoyed at the news, and the three men hastened to the headquarters' room to discuss it with their fellow officers.

Sam was present at the conference as a matter of course, and he watched the proceedings with the greatest interest. A map was stretched out on a magnificent gilt table in the middle of the room in which Sam had first seen the general, and most of the officers bend over it studying it. The general sat back in his arm-chair with his fan and asked everybody's advice, and no one appeared to have any advice to give.

"The fact is this, gentlemen," he said at last, "we've got to do something, and the question is, what to do. Burton," said he to his assistant adjutant-general," show them the plan that we've worked out."

Burton was one of the officers who were poring over the map, and he began to explain a general advance in the direction of the enemy. He pointed out the position which they were now supposed to occupy, some ten miles away.

"We ought to move out our lines to-morrow," he explained, "within, say, three or four miles of theirs. The regiments will keep the same order that they're in here at Havilla. We can't make the final arrangements until we get there. We may stay there a day or two to entrench ourselves, and then move on them at daybreak some day within a week."

"That's the plan, gentlemen," said the general. "What do you think of it?" and he began to question all the general and field officers present beginning with the youngest, and none of them had any suggestion to offer.

"Then it's understood that we start for this line here to-morrow morning at seven," said Burton.

They all assented.

"Now, boys, let's have some whisky," said the general, and the conference resolved itself into a committee of the whole.

Early in the morning the troops began to move forward. Sam, who acted as aide-de-camp, was sent out from headquarters once or twice to urge the various colonels to make haste, but there seemed to be no special orders as to the details of the movement. The regiments went as best they could and selected their own roads, finally choosing the positions that seemed most desirable to their commanders, who took care not to leave too great an interval between regiments. The men were set to work at once at putting up the tents and making entrenchments. It was some time after midday when the general and his staff finally left the headquarters in the city. Sam came downstairs with Major Stroud to mount his horse, and was surprised to see a landau with two horses drawn up at the door.

"Who's that for?" he cried.

"For the general," answered Major Stroud quietly.

"For the general! Why on earth doesn't he ride a horse?"

"There isn't a horse in the place that can carry him. He tried one when he first came here. He mounted it on a step-ladder, and the beast came down on his knees on the stone pavement and had to be shot. He hasn't tried it since."

After waiting on the street for a long time Sam had the privilege of seeing the general emerge from the palace and enter his carriage. He was perspiring and fanning as usual, but carried no whisky and soda. The staff officers, of whom there were a dozen or more, mounted and followed the carriage. Sam rode next to Stroud. There was much confusion in the roads which they traveled--wagons laden with tents and provisions and hospital stores, camp-followers of all descriptions, and some

318

belated soldiers besides. The general, however, had the right of way, and they proceeded with reasonable speed. They passed through native villages, rows of one- and two-story thatched houses on each side, with wooden palisades in front of them, well shaded by low but spreading palms. They passed large sugar refineries, built by the Castalians, and churches and convents. They passed rice-fields, some covered with water and others more or less dry, which sturdy peasants were busy harrowing with buffaloes. On the road they saw many two-wheeled carts drawn by single buffaloes, the man standing in the cart as he drove. At last they came to a halt on rising ground at the edge of a piece of woodland, and Colonel Burton, the adjutant-general, rode up beside the general's carriage and dismounted, and the two began to study the map again. After a long discussion the procession moved on again and finally stopped at the crest of a ridge, where the general alighted and soon selected a place for his tent. An hour had passed before the tents and baggage arrived, but notwithstanding the delay the tents were pitched and supper ready by sundown, and Sam found himself actually in the field on the eve of a battle. The eve, however, was somewhat prolonged. Several days passed, and Sam was kept pretty busy in riding to the various brigade and regimental headquarters and finding out how things were progressing: what was the state of the trenches, and what news there was from the enemy. Scouting parties were sent out, but their reports were kept secret, and Sam was left in the dark. There was a native village about half a mile to the rear, and the inhabitants were all friendly. Sam stopped there occasionally for a drink of water, and became acquainted with the keeper of the café, who was particularly amicable and fond of conversation. Cleary was on the lookout for accommodations in the neighborhood, and Sam introduced him to this native, Senor Garcia, who provided him with a room. One evening Sam was sitting with Cleary in the café when Garcia, as was his custom, joined them, and they began to talk in the Castalian language.

"We are glad you people are coming to rule our islands," said Garcia; "that is, those of us who know your history, because we know that you are a great people and love freedom."

"I am pleased to hear it," said Sam. "Cleary, I was sure that all the sensible natives would feel that way."

"You believe in liberty, equality, fraternity?"

"Of course we do," said Cleary.

"Yes," said Sam, "if you understand those words properly. Now liberty doesn't interfere with obedience. Our whole army here is built up on the idea of obedience. We've all got liberty, of course, but----"

"Liberty to do what?" asked Garcia innocently.

"Why, liberty to--well, to--yes, liberty to do as we're ordered," said Sam.

"Ah! I see," said Garcia. "And then you have equality."

"Yes," said Sam, "in a general way we have. But that doesn't prevent people from differing in rank. Now there's the general, he's my superior, and I'm the superior of the lieutenants, and we're all superior to the privates. We have

regular schools at home to teach us not to misunderstand the kind
of equality we believe in. There's one at East Point for the
army. This gentleman and I were educated there. We weren't
allowed even to look at our superiors. There's another
institution like it for the navy. And then every man-of-war and
every army garrison is a sort of college to spread these ideas
about rank. A captain of a ship can't even let his officers dine
with him too often. It's a fine system and it prevents us from
making any mistakes about what equality means."

"And then fraternity?" asked Garcia.

"Oh, that's just the same," said Cleary. "At East Point we
got a blow in the jaw if we showed the wrong kind of fraternity
to our betters."

"It's a wonderful system," said Garcia. "But I have heard
some of your people explain liberty, equality, fraternity a
little differently."

"They must have been civilians," said Sam. "The army and
navy represent all that is best in our country, and the people at
large do not understand the army and navy. Luckily for you, the
islands will be in charge of the army. There won't be any
mistake about the kind of liberty and equality we give you."

"I am so grateful," said Garcia, rolling up his eyes.

"Yes, Cleary," said Sam. "The people at home don't
understand us. Did you see that there's a bill in Congress to
allow men in the ranks, mere non-commissioned officers, to apply
for commissions? If they pass it, it will be the end of the
army. Just think of a sergeant becoming one of us! Oh, I
forgot, you aren't an officer, but you must know how I feel!"

Cleary expressed his sympathy, and Sam bade him and his host
good-night. On his way back through a path in the jungle he
thought he heard a light step behind him, but when he looked back
he could see nothing. When he arrived at the headquarters' tent
he found all the higher officers of the army there, and Stroud
whispered to him that they had heard that Gomaldo would take the
offensive the next morning, and that consequently a general
advance was ordered for daybreak in order that they might
forestall him. The general was rather taken by surprise and his
final plans were not ready, but it was arranged that at four
o'clock each regiment should advance, and that orders containing
further details would be sent to them by six o'clock at the
latest. Burton remained in the general's tent to perfect the
orders, and Sam went to the tent which he occupied with Major
Stroud to enjoy a few hours' sleep.

"I'm afraid we're not quite ready," said Sam.

"No army ever is," replied Stoud laconically.

"I wish the general were a little livelier and quicker,"
said Sam, blushing at his own blasphemy.

"And thinner?" said Stroud, smiling, as he twisted his white
mustache and smoothed his imperial. "Oh, he'll do very well.
He's a good solid point to rally around and fall back on, and
then we always know where to find him, for he can't get away very
far if he tries."

320

At half-past three in the morning the officers of the staff were called by a native servant and began to make their preparations. They breakfasted as best they could on coffee without sugar or cream, and some stale bread, with an egg apiece, and whisky. Sam felt unaccountably sleepy, and he thought that all the rest looked sleepy too. It was five o'clock before Burton had the orders ready for the various subordinate commanders, telling each of them in which direction to advance. The plan had been mapped out the night before, but the orders had to be copied and corrected. At last he came out and distributed them to Stroud, Sam, and several other officers--two orders to each, yawning painfully as he handed them out.

"I don't think I slept a wink last night," he said.

The two commands to which Sam's orders were directed were stationed on the extreme right of the army. He made a rough tracing of that part of the map and set out at once on a wiry little native pony. For some distance he followed the high-road, but then was obliged to turn into a branch road which led through the woods, and which soon became a mere wood-path. Before long he heard firing in front of him, and soon he recognized the sound of whistling bullets above his head. He found himself ducking his head involuntarily, and almost for the first time in his life he was conscious of being afraid. This was a surprise to him, as his thoughts during the night whenever he had been awake had been full of pleasant anticipations.

The path suddenly came out into an open rolling country, and Sam pulled up his horse, dismounted, and hiding behind some underbrush, took a look at the situation. There was a Gatling-gun, worked by a young officer and five men, a few hundred yards to the right at the edge of the woods. Beyond to the front he could see a line of troops firing at the enemy from behind a wall. Of the Cubapinos he could see nothing but the smoke of their guns and muskets here and there. Shells were falling in another part of the field, but nowhere near him. Bullets were flying thick through the air, and he heard them hissing constantly. As he looked he saw one of the Gatling crew fall over, doubled up in a heap. Sam moved along in the wood nearer to this gun, so that he might ask where he could find the brigade commander. As he approached he heard the lieutenant say:

"Dam those sharp-shooters. They've got our range now. With this damned smokeless powder they can pick us all off. Clark, bring some of that artificial smoke stuff here."

The soldier obeyed, and in a few moments a dense smoke rose above them, covering the whole neighborhood.

"What a wonderful thing these inventions are!" thought Sam, as he tied his horse to a tree and advanced crouching toward the battery. The lieutenant pointed out to him the position of the brigadier-general, some distance back on the right under cover of the jungle, and told him of a path that would take him there. Sam was not slow to follow his directions, for just then a shell exploded close by. He soon found the general surrounded by his staff on a partially wooded hill, from which, however, they could command the field with their glasses. Bullets were flying about

them, and an occasional shell sailed over their heads, but the
general seemed perfectly at home. He took the orders, opened
them and read them.

"That's strange," said he. "Last night I understood that I
was to make for that pass between the hills there on the left,
and now I'm ordered to take the first turning to the right. I
don't understand it. Do you know anything about it?"

"No, sir."

"Well, he must have changed his mind. Or else it was a
bluff to keep his plans from leaking out. Tell the general that
I will carry out his orders at once."

Sam inquired of the members of the staff where he would be
likely to find the 43d Volunteers, to whose colonel his other
orders were directed, but they had no information, except that in
the morning that regiment had been stationed farther over on the
right. Sam started out again, guiding himself as best he could
by a compass which he had in his pocket. He selected the paths
which seemed most promising, but the jungle between was
impenetrable on horseback. The firing on the extreme right
seemed to be farther in the rear, and he made his way in that
direction. Again he came out at the edge of the woods, and to
his surprise saw a battalion of the enemy at a short distance
from him. He turned his horse, stuck his spurs into him, and
went back along the path to the rear at a full run, while a
shower of bullets fell around him. He still kept on working to
the right in the direction of the firing which he heard in front
of him. At last in a hollow of the jungle he came upon a Red
Cross station, one of those advance temporary relief posts where
the wounded who are too much injured to be taken at once to the
rear are treated. Twenty or thirty men were lying in a row, some
of them on their coats, others on the bare ground. Two surgeons
were doing what they could in the line of first aid to the
injured, binding up arms and legs, dressing wounds, and trying to
stop the flow of blood from arteries. Two soldiers were lifting
a wounded man on a stretcher so that he might be carried to the
rear, and he was groaning with agony. Every one of the patients
was blotched in one place or another with blood, and some of them
were lying in pools of the crimson fluid. Sam felt a little sick
at his stomach. Two men came in with another stretcher, bringing
a wounded man from the front. The man gave a convulsive start as
they set him down.

"A bullet's just hit him in the head," said one of the men.
"I'm glad it wasn't me."

One of the doctors looked at the wounded man.

"He's dead," he said. "Damn you, what do you mean by
bringing dead men here?"

The two bearers took up their load again and dropped it out
of sight in the bushes. Sam did not like to interrupt the
doctors, who were overtasked, so he dismounted and tried to find
a wounded man well enough to answer his questions. One man at
the end of the row looked less pale than the rest, and he asked
him where he could find the 43d.

"That's my regiment, sir," he replied, as a twig, cut off by a bullet, fell on his face. "You'd better lie down here, sir; you'll be shot if you don't A lot of the wounded have been hit here again."

Sam sat down by his side.

"Our regiment is over that way," he said, pointing in the direction of the firing. "I don't know where the colonel is. We haven't seen him for hours. The lieutenant-colonel is down with fever. I think the major's in command. You ought to find him at the front. We've been falling back, and the firing sounds nearer than it did. I'm afraid the enemy will catch us here."

Sam did not wait to hear anything further, but, leaving his horse tied to a tree, he ran toward the front. He found many soldiers skulking along the path, and they directed him to the major. He discovered him sitting on the ground behind a stone wall.

"Here, major, are your orders. I understand you're in command."

"Not much," said the major. "The colonel's in command. You'd better find him."

"Where is he?"

"I'm sure I don't know. I haven't seen him since six o'clock."

"But this is your regiment, isn't it?"

"Well, yes. It's part of it."

Just then a young captain came running up from the front, and cried out to his major:

"Major, we're having a hard time of it there. Won't you come up and take charge? I'm afraid they'll force us back."

"No," said the major, "I won't. I'm going back there to that last village. It's a much better place to defend. Besides I'm not feeling well. You fellows can stay here if you like. I shan't order the regiment back, but I'll go back and get ready for them there. We ought to have trenches there, you know," and he got up and walked rapidly off down the road. The captain turned to Sam.

"I beg your pardon, captain," said he, "but what are we to do? Our officers have given out, and we're a new regiment and haven't any experience. Won't you take command?"

Sam was by no means satisfied in his mind that he would behave much better than the major, but here was an opportunity that he could not afford to lose.

"I'll see what I can do," said he. "Let's see what the orders are."

He opened the document and saw that it was a direction to keep on to the front until they arrived before the town of San Diego, which they were to assault and capture.

"Show me where your men are," said Sam. "Who have you got there?"

"We've got our own regiment, the 43d, and six or eight companies of the 72d--I don't know where they came from; and then there's a battery, and perhaps some others."

They hastened along the road together, urging the stragglers to join them, which many of them did. The way became more and more encumbered with men, and the bullets came thicker. Sam was thoroughly scared. He could feel his legs waver at the knee, and it seemed as if a giant had grasped him by the spine. They passed several musicians of the band.

"Start up a tune!" cried Sam. "Play something and follow us." At the same time he instinctively thrust his hand into his breast pocket and felt for his traveling Lares and Penates, namely, his tin soldier, his photographs of East Point, one of Marian, and her last letter. Meanwhile the band began to play and the bass-drummer wielded his huge drumstick with all his might. Sam began to feel happier, and so did the men about him. One of the musicians suddenly fell, struck dead by a bullet, and just then a shell burst over them and two or three men went down. With one accord the soldiers began to curse and swear in the most frightful manner and to insist on speedy vengeance. Sam was surprised to find himself enjoying the oaths. They just expressed his feelings, and he hurried on to the edge of the woods. In front of them they saw a line of their own men lying on the ground behind stones and logs, shooting at the enemy, whose line could be distinguished hardly more than a third of a mile away.

"They're nearer than they were," whispered the captain. "We must push them back or they'll have us. The men on the firing line are getting scared."

"We must scare them behind more than the enemy does in front," said Sam, drawing his revolver. "Here you, sir, get back into your place."

A man in the ranks, who was beginning to creep back, saw the revolver and dropped back in his position with an oath.

"Forward!" cried Sam, now thoroughly in the spirit of the occasion. "Come up to the front, all of you, and extend our line there to the right. Lie down and take careful aim with every shot."

The men did as they were told, and Sam took up his position behind the line with the captain, both of them standing in a perfect gale of bullets, while all the rest were lying down.

"Lie down," said Sam to the captain. "You've no business to risk your life like that."

"How about yours, sir?" said the captain, as he obeyed.

"I'll take care of myself, if you'll be good enough to let me," answered Sam.

The presence of a staff officer gave new courage to the men, and their marksmanship began to have effect on the enemy, who were seen to be gradually falling back. Sam took this opportunity to move his line forward, and he sent a lieutenant to direct the battery to cover his men when they should charge on the enemy's line. He moved his line forward in this way successively three or four times, and the troops were now thoroughly encouraged, and some of them even asked to be allowed to charge. Sam, however, postponed this final act as long as he could. It was not until he saw the captain whom he had met in the woods mangled and

324

instantly killed by a piece of shell that he became so angry that he could restrain himself no longer. He gave the order to fix bayonets, and with a yell the men rose from their lairs and rushed over the intervening ground to the enemy's position. The Cubapinos did not wait for them, but turned and ran precipitously. Sam and his men followed them for at least a mile, while they made a stand again.

"They're in the trenches now that they were in this morning," explained a lieutenant.

Here the same tactics were renewed, and in another half-hour Sam ordered his men to charge again. This time the enemy waited longer, and many of the attacking party fell, but before they reached the trenches the Cubapinos took flight, and Sam saw his soldiers bayonet the last two or three of them in the back. There were a good many dead in the trenches, all of them shot through the head. It was a proud moment for Sam when he stood on the edge of the trench and planted Old Gory there while the men cheered. A wounded Cubapino lay just before him, and one of the soldiers kicked him in the head and killed him. Sam noticed it, and was a little startled to find that it seemed all right to him.

"I've half a mind to kick th next wounded man I see," he thought. "It must be rather good sport"; but he did not do it.

The rest of the fight was in the nature of a procession. They pursued the flying Cubapinos as fast as they could, but were unable to come up with them. In a native village through which they passed, Sam asked an old man, who had been too weak to get away, how far off San Diego was, and learned that it was five miles away to the left. He could not understand this, but still kept on in that direction. As they left the village it burst into flames, for the last soldiers had set it on fire. Sam thought of the old man perishing in his hut, and it seemed to him a fine thing and quite natural. On their way they came across other bodies of troops who joined them, and it so happened that no one came forward of superior rank to Sam, and consequently he retained the command. Before they came in sight of San Diego he had quite a brigade under him. He halted them in front of the town and sent out a scouting party. There was no sound of firing now except in the distance. In an hour the scouting party came back and reported that the place had been vacated by the enemy, who for some reason had been seized by a panic. Sam ordered the advance to be resumed, and late in the afternoon found himself in possession of San Diego. He began to take measures at once to fortify the place, when the brigadier-general whom he had seen in the morning marched in with his brigade and took over the command from him, congratulating him on his success, which was already the talk of the army. Sam turned over the command to him with much grace and dignity, and, borrowing a horse, set off for the old headquarters which he had left in the morning, for he learned that, altho the enemy were completely defeated and scattered, still the general would not move his headquarters forward to the front till the following day.

The general received him with great cordiality.

325

"Everything turned out just as I planned it," he said, "but, Captain, you helped us out at a critical point there on the right. I shall mention you in despatches. You may depend on being promoted and given a good post. You ought to have a regiment at least."

Sam was taking his supper when Cleary came in, hot and grimy.

"Well, you're a great fellow," he said, "to get away from me the way you did this morning. But didn't I tell you, you were the stuff? Why, you won the battle. Do you know that you turned their left flank?"

"To tell the truth, I didn't know it." said Sam.

"Well, you did."

"But the general planned everything." said Sam.

"Yes," said Cleary, "but I'll tell you more about that. I'm doing some detective work, and I'll have something to tell you in a day or two. But I wish I'd been with you. I had my kodak all ready. However, they can make up the pictures at home. How's this for headlines?" and he took some notes from his pocket. "'Great Victory at San Diego. Captain Jinks Turns Defeat into Victory. Hailed as Hero Jinks by the Army. General Laughter's Plans Carried Out through the Young Hero's Co-operation.' What do you think of that? We'll put the part about the general in small caps, because he's not quite solid with the trust. I'm not going to write up anybody but you and the Mounted Mustangs; those are my orders."

"How did the Mustangs make out?" asked Sam. "They were way off on the left, and I haven't heard anything about them."

"They did very decently," said Cleary, "considering they were never under fire before. They kept up pretty well with the regulars, and fortunately they had a regular regiment on each side. They really did well."

"Did they make any fine cavalry charges?" inquired Sam.

"Calvary charges! Bless your heart, they didn't have any horses, and it's lucky they didn't. They had their hands full without having to manage any horses!"

CHAPTER VIII

Among The Moritos

On the following day headquarters were moved into San Diego. Sam was lodged in the town hall with the general, and Cleary got rooms close by. There were rumors of renewed activity on the part of the Cubapino, but it was thought that their resistance for the future would be of a guerrilla nature. There was, however, one savage tribe to the north which had terroized a large district of country, and the general decided that it must be subdued. Sam heard of this plan, but did not know whether he would be sent on the expedition or not, and urged Cleary to use his influence so that he might be one of the party.

"I'll manage it for you, old man," said Cleary, two or three days after the battle. "I've got the general in a tight place, and all I've got to do is to let him know it and he'll do whatever I want."

"What do you mean?"

"Why, he had about as much to do with the San Diego fight as the man in the moon."

"What?"

"Well, I'll tell you the story. I've run down every clue and here it is. You see somehow Colonel Burton got the orders mixed up that morning and addressed every one of them to the wrong general."

"Is it possible?" exclaimed Sam. "That explains why they couldn't understand the orders there in the Third Brigade, and why I took all day to find San Diego. I wonder if it's true. Why on earth didn't Gomaldo win then? It must have been a close call."

"It's plain enough why he didn't win," said Cleary. "That chap Garcia was one of his spies, and a clever one too. He got all he could out of you and me, but that wasn't much. Then he had the native servant of the general in his pay. As soon as you left on the night before the battle he cleared out too, and he got a statement from the native servant of all the general intended to do. He got the news to Gomaldo by midnight, and before sunrise the Cubapino forces were ready to meet each of our columns when they advanced. They had ambushes prepared for each of them. If the orders had gone out straight we'd have been cleaned out, that's my opinion. But you see, they all went wrong and the columns advanced along different roads, and poor Gomaldo's plans all went to pot. I believe he had Garcia hanged for deceiving him. You haven't seen the general's servant since the battle, have you?"

"Now that you speak of it, I don't think I have," said Sam. "But he's a great general all the same, don't you think so?"

"Of course," answered Cleary.

"I wonder if all battles are won like that?" said Sam.

"I half think they are," said his friend. "And then the generals smile and say, 'I told you so.'"

"Cleary," said Sam, "I want you to answer me one question honestly."

"Out with it."

"Did I have much to do with winning that battle or not?"

"To tell the honest truth, Sam, between me and you, I don't know whether you did or not. But The Lyre will say that you did, and that will settle it for history."

Sam sighed and made no other reply.

The expedition against the Moritos started out a week later. It consisted of two regiments, one of colored men under a certain Colonel James, the other of white volunteers, with a brigadier-general in command. Sam was assigned to the command of the volunteer regiment with the temporary rank of major, its colonel having been wounded at the battle of San Diego. For a whole day they marched northward unmolested, and encamped at night in a valley in the mountains with a small native village as headquarters. There had been little incident during the day.

327

They had burned several villages and driven off a good many cattle for meat. Sam was surprised to see how handsome the furniture was in the little thatched cottages of the people, perched as they were on posts several feet high. It was a feast day, and the whole population had been in the streets in their best clothes. The soldiers snatched the jewels of the women and chased the men away, and then looted the houses, destroying what they could not take, and finally setting them on fire.

"It's better so," said Sam to his adjutant. "Make war as bad as possible and people will keep the peace. We are the real peace-makers."

He heard shouts and cries as he passed through the villages, and had reason to think that the soldiers were not contented with mere looting, but he did not inquire. He took his supper with the general at his headquarters. Colonel James and Cleary ate with them, for Cleary was still true to his friend's fortunes and determined to follow him everywhere. After an evening of smoking and chatting, Sam, Cleary, and Colonel James bade the general good-night and started for their quarters, which lay in the same direction. It was a gorgeous moonlight night, such a night as only the tropics can produce, and they sauntered slowly along the mountain road, enjoying the scene.

"There is a question that I have been wanting to ask you, Colonel," said Sam to Colonel James as they walked on together. "What do you think of darkies as soldiers? I have never seen much of them, and as you have a negro regiment, you must know all about it."

"Well, the truth is, Major," responded the colonel, "I wouldn't have my opinion get out for a good deal, but I'll tell you in confidence. They are much better soldiers than white men, that's the long and short of it."

"How can you explain that? It's most surprising!" cried Sam.

"Well, they're more impressible, for one thing. You can work them up into any kind of passion you want to. Then they're more submissive to discipline; they're used to being ordered about and kicked and cuffed, and they don't mind it. Besides, they're accustomed from their low social position to be subordinate to superiors, and rather expect it than not. They are all poor, too, and used to poor food and ragged clothes and no comforts, and of course they don't complain of what they get from us."

"You mean," said Cleary, "that the lower a man is in the scale of society the better soldier he makes."

"Well," answered the colonel, "I hadn't ever put it just in that light, but that's about the size of it. These darkies are great hands at carrying concealed weapons too. If it isn't a razor it's something else, and if there's a row going on they will get mixed up in it, but they're none the worse as soldiers for that."

"Let's go up to that point there and take the moonlight view before we turn in," suggested Cleary.

The others agreed, and they began to climb a path leading up to the right. It was much more of a climb than they had expected, and when they had become quite blown they sat down to recover their breath.

"I think we'd better go back," said Colonel James. "We may lose our way, and it isn't safe here. The Moritos are known to be thick in these mountains, and they might find us."

"Oh, let's go a little farther," said Cleary, and they set out to climb again.

"The path seems to stop here," said Sam, who was in the lead. "This must be the top, but I don't see any place for a view. Perhaps we'd better go back."

Cleary did not repeat his objection, and they began to retrace their steps. For some time they went on in silence.

"The path begins to go up-hill here," said Cleary, who now led. "I don't understand this. We didn't go down-hill at all."

"I think we did for a short distance," answered Sam.

They went on, still ascending.

"There doesn't seem to be any path here," said Cleary. "Do you see it?"

His companions were obliged to admit that they did not.

"We'd better call for help," said Sam, and the three men began to shout at the top of their voices, but there was no reply. An hour must have elapsed while they were engaged in calling, and their voices became husky, but all in vain.

"Hist!" said Cleary at last. "I think I hear some one coming. I heard the branches move. They have sent out for us, thank fortune! I didn't like the idea of sleeping out here and making the acquaintance of snakes and catching fevers."

The words were hardly out of his mouth when three shadowy figures sprang out of the bushes and grasped each of the three men from behind, holding their elbows back so that they could not use their arms, and in a moment a veritable swarm of long-haired, half-clad Moritos were upon them, pinioning them and emptying their pockets and belts. It was quite useless to make any resistance, the attack had been too sudden and unexpected. Cleary cried out once, but they made him understand that, if he did it again, they would stab him with one of their long knives. When the captives were securely bound, the captors began to discuss the situation in their own language, which was the only language they understood. There was evidently some difference of opinion, but after a few minutes they came to some kind of agreement. The legs of the prisoners were unbound, and they were made to march through the jungle, each one with two guards behind him, who pricked him with their lances if he did not move fast enough. Their only other arms seemed to be bows and arrows. The march was a very weary one, and through a wild, mountainous country which would have been impassable for men who did not know it thoroughly. Occasionally they seemed to be following obscure paths, but as often there was no sign of a track, and the thick, tropical vegetation made progress difficult. For an hour or two they climbed up the half-dry bed of a mountain torrent, and more than once they were ankle deep in swampy ground. The Moritos passed through the jungle with the agility and noiselessness of cats, but the three white men floundered along as best they

could. Their captors uttered never a word and would not allow
them to speak.

The sun was just rising over a wilderness of mountains when
they came to a small clearing in the woods, apparently upon a
plateau near the top of a mountain. In this clearing there were
a number of isolated trees, in each one of which, at about twenty
feet above the ground, was a native hut, looking like a huge
bird's nest. A small crowd of natives, including women and
children, ran toward them shouting, and now for the first time
the men of the returning party began to talk too. Some of them
tied the legs of their prisoners again and sat them down on the
ground, while the others rehearsed the history of their exploit.
It was a curious scene to witness. The men as well as the women
wore their long, coarse hair loose to the waist. Some of the men
had feathers stuck in their hair, and all of them were
grotesquely tattooed.

"I wonder if they're cannibals?" said Cleary, for there
seemed to be opportunity now for conversation.

"I don't think there are any in this part of the country,"
said Colonel James. "Here comes our breakfast anyway."

All the inhabitants of the village had been inspecting the
captives with great interest, especially the women and children.
Two women now came running from the group of tree-houses with
platters of meat, and the crowd opened to let them approach.

"Don't ask what it is," said Cleary, as he gulped down his
rations.

"I can't eat it!" cried Sam.

"Oh, you must, or you'll offend them," said Colonel James.

And they completed their repast with wry faces. When they
had finished, one of the warriors, whom they had noticed before
on account of his comparative height and the magnificence of his
decorations, came up to them and addressed them, to their great
surprise, in Castalian. He explained to them that he was the
famous savage chief, Carlos, who as head of the Moritos ruled the
entire region, and that they were prisoners of war; that he had
learned Castalian as a boy from a missionary in the mountains
when the land was at peace; and that a palaver would be held on
the following day, to which the heads of the neighboring villages
would be invited, to determine what to do with them. He showed
special interest in Sam's red hair and mustache, and smoothed
them and pulled them, asking him if they had been dyed. When he
was informed that they were not, he was filled with admiration
and called up his favorites to examine this wonder of nature.
Sam had noticed that from the moment of his arrival he had been
the object of admiration of the women, and this fact was now
accounted for.

The three prisoners had no reason to complain of their
treatment during the day. A guard was set upon them, but the
ropes by which they were tied were loosened, and they were
allowed from time to time to walk about. Most of the morning
they passed in much-needed sleep. In the afternoon Carlos
visited them again with some of his men, and set to work to
satisfy his curiosity as to their country, translating their

330

answers to his friends. His Castalian was very bad, but so was
that of his captives; yet they succeeded in making themselves
understood without difficulty.

"Do you have houses as high as those?" he asked, pointing to
the human nests in the trees.

"Yes, indeed," said Cleary. "Near my home there is a house
nearly a quarter of a mile long and twice as high as that tree,
and nine hundred people live in it."

There were murmurs of astonishment as this information was
translated.

"What is that great house for?" asked the chief.

"It's a lunatic asylum."

"What is that."

"A house for lunatics to live in."

"But what is a lunatic?"

Cleary tried in vain to explain what a lunatic was. The
Moritos had never seen one.

"We have plenty of such houses at home," said Sam, "and we
have had to double their size in ten years to hold the lunatics;
they are splendid buildings. There was one not very far from the
college where my friend and I were educated. But some of our
prisons are even larger than our lunatic asylums."

"What is a prison," asked Carlos.

"Oh," said Sam, "don't you understand that either? It's a
house in which we lock up criminals--I mean men who kill or rob
us."

"Oh, I see," replied Carlos. "You mean your enemies whom
you take prisoner in battle."

"No, I don't. I mean our own fellow citizens who murder and
steal."

"Do you mean that you sometimes kill each other and steal
from each other, your own tribe?"

"Yes," said Sam. "Of course people who do so are bad men,
but there are some such among us."

A great discussion arose among the natives after hearing
this.

"What do they say?" asked Colonel James in Castalian.

"They say," said the chief, "that they can not believe this,
as they have never heard of members of the same tribe hurting
each other."

"We do all we can to prevent it," said Sam. "In our cities
we have policemen to keep order; that is, we have soldiers
stationed in the streets to frighten the bad men."

"Do you have soldiers in the streets of your towns to keep
you from killing each other!" exclaimed the chief, in
astonishment. "Who ever heard of such a thing? I do not
understand it," and, altho Sam repeated the information in every
conceivable way permitted by his limited vocabulary, he was
unable successfully to convey the idea.

"It is strange how uncivilized they are," he said to his
friends.

"Do you live on bananas in your country?" asked Carlos.

"No; we eat them sometimes, but we live on grain and meat," said Sam.

"You must have to work very hard to get it."

"Yes, we do, sometimes twelve hours a day."

"How frightful! And is there enough for all to eat?"

"Not always."

"And are your people happy when they work so hard and are sometimes hungry?"

"Not always," said Sam. "Sometimes people are so unhappy that they commit suicide."

"What?"

"I mean they kill themselves."

There was now another heated discussion.

"What do they say?" asked Colonel James.

"They say that they did not know it was possible for people to kill themselves. I did not know it either. It is very strange."

"What limited intelligences they have!" exclaimed Sam.

"They say," continued Carlos, in a somewhat embarrassed manner, "that if you are condemned to death, they wish one of you would kill himself, so that they can see how it is done."

"There's a chance for you, Sam," said Cleary, but Sam did not seem to see the joke.

"I am very sorry," said Carlos, seating himself nearer to Sam, "I am very sorry that we may have to kill you, for I like you; but what can we do? It is a rule of our tribe to kill prisoners of war."

"I really don't see what they can do, if that is the case," said Sam in English. "If that is their law, and they have always done it, of course from their point of view it is their military duty. I don't see any way out of it? Do you?"

"It wouldn't break my heart if they failed to do their duty in this case," said Cleary. "For heaven's sake, don't tell him what you think. Let's keep him feeling agreeable by our conversation. He's fallen in love with you, Sam. Perhaps he'll give you to one of his daughers and she may marry you or eat you, whichever she pleases."

"I wish you wouldn't joke about these things," said Sam. "It's a serious piece of business. There's no glory in being tomahawked here in the mountains."

"And I haven't got my kodak with me either," said Cleary.

"What made you come into my country?" asked Carlos. "Did you not know how powerful I am? And what have I ever done against you?"

"We came because we were ordered to," said Sam.

"And do you do what you are ordered to, whether you approve of it or not?"

"Of course we do."

"That is very strange," said Carlos. "We never obey anybody unless we want to and think he is doing the right thing. I tell my men here what I want to do, and if they agree to it they obey me, but if they don't I give it up. But you do things that you think are wrong and foolish because you are ordered to. It is very strange!"

"We are military men," said Sam. "It requires centuries of civilization to understand us."

"How do you kill your prisoners?" asked Carlos.

"We don't kill them," answered Sam.

"I don't know about that, Sam," said Cleary in English. "We didn't take many prisoners at San Diego."

"That's a fact," answered Sam, in the same language. "We didn't take many. I never thought of that."

"Don't tell him, tho," added Cleary.

"But when you soldiers have to execute an enemy for any reason, how do you do it?"

"We shoot them with rifles," said Sam.

"Is that all?"

"No; we make them dig their graves first," interposed Cleary. "That's a hint to him," he whispered. "It's better than the stew-pot."

"Dig their graves first!" exclaimed the chief, and he turned to his men and explained the matter to them. They were evidently delighted.

"What are they saying?" asked James again.

"They say that that is a grand idea, and that they will adopt it. They think civilization is a great thing, and they want to be civilized," said Carlos.

"There, I knew they weren't cannibals!" said the colonel.

There was silence for several minutes, and Carlos smoothed Sam's locks with his hand.

"We must entertain him," said Cleary. "Say something, Sam, or he'll get down on us."

"Say something yourself," said Sam, who was thoroughly vexed at his friend's ill-timed flippancy.

"Does your tribe live in these mountains and nowhere else?" asked Cleary.

"Oh, no. We have brothers everywhere. They are in all the islands, and all over the world."

"You tell them by your language, I suppose."

"No, some of them do not speak our language. That makes no difference. We tell our brothers in other ways."

"How?" said Cleary.

"There are four marks of the true Morito," said the chief. "Their young men are initiated by torture. That is one mark. Then their chief men wear feathers on their heads. That is the second. And the third mark is that they are tattooed, as I am," and he pointed to the strange figures on his naked chest; "and the fourth is that they all use the sacred tom-tom when they dance."

"Sam," said Cleary, "have you got those East Point photographs in your pocket?"

"Yes," said Sam, thrusting his hand into his bosom.

Cleary rolled over to Carlos as well as his ropes would allow, threw his arms about his neck, and cried out in Castalian, "Oh, my brother, my long-lost brother!"

333

There was a general commotion. The savages drew their knives, and for a moment there seemed to be danger for the prisoners.

"What on earth are you trying to do, Mr. Cleary?" exclaimed Colonel James. "It seems to me that your pleasantries are in very doubtful taste while our lives are in the balance."

Cleary made no answer, but went on crying, "Oh, my brothers, my long-lost brothers!"

"What do you mean?" ejaculated Carlos, in a rage. "I will give you one minute in which to explain, and then your head will fall."

"We are your brothers. We are Moritos. We are your people from a distant island, and you never knew it!"

"Is this true?" asked the chief, looking at Sam and the colonel.

"Swear to it," whispered Cleary.

"We swear that it is true," replied the two officers.

"Then prove it, or you shall all three die tonight. I am not to be trifled with. Proceed."

"Senor," said Cleary, "you have said that you recognize Morito young men by the fact that they have passed through the torture. We have passed through the torture. My friend will show you the pictures taken of both of us when we were about to be burned at the stake, and also one of himself passing through the ordeal of water. Sam, show him the photos."

Sam took the two pictures from his pocket and handed them to Cleary, who held them in his hand while Carlos peered over his shoulder.

"You see here," he said, "that we are tied to the stake. You may recognize our features. You see the expression of pain on our faces. These men standing around are our elder brothers who initiated us. It was done by night in a sacred grove where our ancestors have indulged in these rites for many ages. That wall is part of a ruin of a temple to the god of war."

Carlos evidently was impressed. He took the dim print, with its fitful lantern-light effects, and studied it, comparing the faces with those of his prisoners. Then he showed it to his followers, and they all spoke together.

"They say," said their chief at last, "that they believe you speak the truth. But how do we know that the old man was initiated too?"

"He is an old man," said Cleary. "He had a picture like this in his pocket when he was young. We all carry them with us as long as they hold together. But they will wear out. You may see that this one is wearing out already."

"That is true," assented the chief. "But your picture proves against you as well as for you. You have no feathers in your heads there, and you are wearing none now," and he proudly straightened up those on his head.

"In our country we have not many feathers as you have here," answered Cleary. "The birds do not come often to that land, it is so cold. Only our greatest men wear feathers. When we reach home and grow old and wise and valiant, perhaps we shall all have feathers. This old warrior of ours has feathers at home, but he does not carry them on journeys. My young friend and I are yet too young. We have a picture of our old friend here with his feathers."

"Good heavens!" exclaimed Sam. "What are you driving at. We'll be worse off than ever now."

"Just you let me manage this affair," said Cleary. "Give me that photo of the dress-parade at East Point that you showed me last week."

Sam did as he was told. It represented the dress-parade at sunset, the companies drawn up in line at parade-rest and the band in full blast going through its evolutions in the foreground, with a peculiarly magnificent drum-major in bear-skin hat and plumes at the head, swinging a gorgeous baton.

Cleary exhibited it to Carlos.

"There is our elderly friend," said he, indicating the drum-major. "He is leading the national war-dance of our people. There is the tom-tom," he added triumphantly, pointing at the bass-drum, which was fortunately presented in full relief.

Carlos was taken aback, and he made a guttural exclamation of surprise.

"Do you dress like that when you are at home?" he asked of Colonel James.

"I do," replied the colonel majestically.

"Then I bow down before you," said the chief, kneeling down and touching the ground with his forehead three times. "But," he added, as he rose to his feet, "you have not yet proved that we are brothers. Where are your tattoo-marks? Look at mine!"

"Sam, strip," whispered Cleary, and Sam tore off his coat and shirt, displaying the masterpieces of the artistic boatswain. A cry of admiration went up from the assembled savages. Carlos rushed at him, threw his arms about his neck, and rubbed his nose violently against his.

"For heaven's sake, save me, Cleary!" cried Sam. "My nose will be worse than Saunder's, and Marian is prejudiced against damaged noses."

Cleary thought it best not to interfere, and finally the chief grew tired of this exercise. He hardly paid any attention while Cleary showed the modest tattoo-marks on his arms, and Colonel James exhibited equally insignificant symbols on his, for he, too, had been tattooed in his youth. He was too much engrossed in Sam's red hair and his variegated cuticle.

"Here is the picture of the water-ordeal which you forgot to look at," said Cleary, as he collected the photographs. "This is my friend again with his head in the water and his legs stretched out in supplication to the god of the temple."

Carlos looked at it in ecstasy.

"Oh, my brothers!" he cried. "To think that I should not have known you! You torture each other just as we do. You are tattooed just as we are! You have bigger feathers and bigger dances and bigger tom-toms. You are bigger savages than we are! Come, let us feast together."

The repast was soon prepared in the center of the clearing. The prisoners, now unbound, washed and happy, were seated in the place of honor on each side of the chief. A huge pot of miscellaneous food was set down in the midst, and they all began to eat with their fingers, the chief picking out the tid-bits for his guests and putting them in their mouths. They were so much delighted with the results of the day's work that they ate heartily and asked no questions. When the meal was over, Cleary turned to the chief and thanked him in a little oration, which was received with great favor.

"We have found our brothers," he said in conclusion, "and you have found yours. You believe us now when we say that we have come to bless you and not to injure you. We will not take your land. We will generously give you part of it for yourselves. You see how we all love you, the aged warrior and the red-headed chief as well as I. Why will you not come with us when we set out on our journey to our great chief, or why, at any rate, will you not send your chiefs with us, to tell him that you have received us all as brothers and that we shall always be friends and allies?"

Carlos translated this speech sentence by sentence. Cleary was a good speaker, and they were impressed by his style as well as by his argument. They palavered together for some time; then Carlos arose and addressed his guests, but particularly Sam, whom he considered as the leader.

"Brothers," he said, "we are indeed brothers by the torture, tattoo, tom-tom, and top-feather. We did not know who you were, we did not understand you. We wished to be left in peace. We did not want to have the Castalians come here and rob us. We did not want their beads and their brandy. We wanted to be let alone. But you are our brothers. You are greater savages than we are. Why should we not go with you? The chiefs of our other villages are coming to-morrow at sunrise. I will conduct you back to your great chief with them, and we shall all rejoice together."

It was now nearly dark. Carlos apologized for not having accommodation for his guests in his tree-hut, but provided comfortable blankets on the ground and had a fire built for them in a secluded place near the village. The three men were soon sleeping peacefully, and they did not awake until the sun had already risen.

CHAPTER IX

On Duty at Havilla

When they awoke they heard the noise of voices in the village and hastened thither. The chiefs had already arrived and were exchanging greetings with Carlos and the other residents. Breakfast was prepared by the women on the same ground where they had dined, and by eight o'clock the expedition started, composed of some thirty warriors, several of whom were laden with presents in the shape of baskets and native cloth. When they neared the headquarters of the little invading army, the three white men went ahead and informed the sentinels that it was a peaceful embassy which followed them.

"You must leave me to tell the story of our exploit," Cleary had said, and his friends were so well satisfied with his record as a talker that they assented.

"General," said Cleary, as they entered his hut in the village, "we are bringing in all the chiefs of the Moritos. They are ready to lay down their arms and accept any terms. We have sworn friendship to them."

"How on earth have you managed it?" said the general.

"It is chiefly due to Captain Jinks, or, I should say, Major Jinks. They were about to kill us when, by the sheer force of his glance and his powers of speech, he actually cowed them, and they submitted to him."

"I have heard of taming wild beasts that way," said the general, "but I never quite believed it."

When the chiefs arrived they embraced every soldier they saw and showed every sign of joy. The general ordered a feast to be spread for them and addressed them in English. They did not understand a word of this harangue, but seemed most affected. When they heard that the great general of all was at San Diego, only a day's march away, they insisted on going thither, and the next day the brigade marched back again, leaving a small garrison behind. The army at San Diego could hardly believe its eyes when at sundown the expedition returned, having fully accomplished its object without firing a shot and accompanied by a band of Moritos. When Cleary's version of the exploit became known, Sam was openly acclaimed as a hero and the favorite of the army. General Laughter complimented him again, and again mentioned him in dispatches. A week later his promotion to be major of volunteers, for meritorious conduct in the field of San Diego, was announced by cable, and again after a few days he was made a colonel. Sam's cup was full.

"Sam," said Cleary one day, "I believe in your luck. You'll be President some of these days. All the time we were up in the mountains I knew it would come out all right because we had you along."

Meanwhile the chiefs had tendered their presents to General Laughter and had drunk plentiful libations of whisky and soda with him. They spent a week of festivity in the town and then returned, having agreed to all that was asked of them by their "brothers."

The rainy season now set in, and operations in the field became difficult. Furthermore, the general had decided that the war was at an end, and officially it was so considered. Some troops were left at San Diego, but the headquarters were removed again to Havilla, and Sam was back with the staff. He found himself received as a great man. His two exploits had made him the most famous officer in the army, even more so than the general in command. Soon after his return to the city one of the civil commissioners, who had been sent out by the Administration, gave a large dinner in his honor at the palace. The chief

337

officers and civil officials were among the guests, as well as
two or three native merchants who had remained loyal to the
invading army for financial and commercial reasons and had not
joined the rebels, who composed nine-tenths of the population.
These merchants were generally known in the army as the
"patriots," and were treated with much consideration by the civil
commissioners.

After dinner the host proposed a toast to Sam and accompanied
it with a patriotic speech which thrilled the hearts of his
audience. He pointed to the national flag which was festooned
upon the wall.

"Look at Old Gory!" he cried. "What does she stand for?
For the rights of the oppressed all over the earth, for freedom
and equal rights, for----"

There was a sound of boisterous laughter in the next room.
A young officer ran forward and whispered to the orator, "Be
careful; some of those captured rebel officers are shut up in
there, and perhaps they can overhear you. Be careful what you
say. Some of them speak English." The commissioner hemmed and
hawed and tried to recover himself.

"What does the dear old flag stand for?" he repeated. "For
liber-- No--for-r-r---- Well, 'pon my word, what does she stand
for?"

"For the army and navy," whispered a neighbor.

"Yes," he thundered. "Yes, the flag stands for the army and
navy, for our officers and men, for our men-of-war and artillery,
for our cavalry and infantry, that's what she stands for!"

This was received with great applause, and the speaker smiled
with satisfaction. Then gradually his expression became sad.

"I am sorry to say," he said,--"I am ashamed as a citizen of
our great land to be obliged to admit, that there are at home a
few craven-hearted, mean-spirited men--shall I call them men?
No, nor even women--there are creatures, I say, who disapprove of
our glorious deeds, who spurn the flag and the noble principles
for which it stands and to which I have alluded, who say that we
have no business to take away land which belongs to other people,
and that we have not the right to slaughter rebels and traitors
in our midst. I appeal to the patriotic Cubapinos at this board,
if we are not introducing a higher and nobler civilization into
these islands."

The native gentlemen bowed assent.

"Have we not given them a better language than their own?
Have we not established our enlightened institutions? For
instance, let me cite the custom house. We have the collector
here with us--and the post-office. The postmaster is----"

"Sh-sh-sh!" whispered the prompter again. "He's in jail."

"I mean the assistant postmaster is also with us. And there
are our other institutions, the ----"

"There's going to be a prize-fight to-night." cried a young
lieutenant who had taken too much wine, at the foot of the
table. "Dandy Sullivan against Joe Corker."

This interruption was too much for the commissioner, who was
quite unable to resume the thread of his remarks for several

moments. The guests in the mean time moved uneasily in their
seats, for most of them were anxious to be off to see the fight.
    "Those who carp against us at home," continued the speaker,
trying in vain to find some graceful way of coming to a close,
"those who dishonor the flag are the men who pretend to be filled
with humanity and to desire the welfare of mankind. They pretend
to object to bloodshed. They are mere sentimentalists. They are
not practical men. They do not understand our destiny, nor the
Consititution, nor progress, nor civilization, nor glory, nor
honor, nor the dear old flag, God bless her. They are
sentimentalists. They have no sense of humor."
    Here the audience applauded loudly, altho the speaker had
not intended to have them applaud just there. It occurred to him
that he might just as well stop at this point, and he sat down,
not altogether satisfied, however, with his peroration and vexed
to think that he had forgotten Sam altogether. The party broke
up without delay, and Sam walked off with Cleary, who had been
present, to see the prize-fight.
    "The commissioner isn't much of a talker, is he?" said
Cleary. "That was a bad break about the postmaster. I hear
they've arrested Captain Jones for embezzlement too."
    "Good heavens!" cried Sam, "what an outrage!" And he told
Cleary of his narrow escape from complicity in the matter, and
how the military operations had prevented him from calling on the
contractors. "Civilians don't understand these things," he
added. "They oughtn't to send them out here. They don't
understand things."
    "No. They haven't been brought up on tabasco sauce. What
can you expect of them?"
    They soon arrived at the Alhambra Theater at which the fight
was to take place, and found it in progress. A large crowd was
collected, consisting of soldiers and natives in equal
proportions. The last round was just finishing, and Joe Corker
was in the act of knocking his opponent out. The audience was
shouting with glee and excitement, the cheers being mixed with
hisses and cries of "Fake, fake!"
    "I know Corker," said Cleary. "Come, I'll introduce you."
    They pushed forward through the crowd, and were soon in a
room behind the stage, where Corker was being rubbed and washed
down by his assistants. Sam looked at the great man and felt
rather small and insignificant. "Here's a kind of civilian who
is not inferior to army men," he thought. "Perhaps he is even
superior." He would not have said this aloud, but he thought it.
    "How de do, Joe?" said Cleary, shaking hands. "That was a
great fight. You knocked him out clean. Here's my friend,
Colonel Jinks, the hero of San Diego and the pacifier of the
Moritos."
    Corker nodded condescendingly.
    "We enjoyed the fight very much," said Sam, not altogether
at his ease. "It reminded me of my own experience at East Point."
    "It was a good fight," said Corker, "and a damned fair one
too. I'd like to punch the heads of those fellers who cried
'fake.' It was as fair as fair could be, and Dandy and me was as

339

evenly matched as two peas. I always believe in takin' a feller of your size, and I did."

"That wasn't the way at East Point," said Cleary. "They didn't take fellows of their size there."

"That's against our rules anyway," said Corker.

"It must be a civilian rule," said Sam, beginning to feel his superiority again. "The military rule as we were taught it at East Point was to take a smaller man if you could, and you see, the army does just the same thing. We tackled Castalia and then the Cubapines, and they weren't of our size. We don't fight the powerful countries."

"That's queer," said Corker, drinking a lemonade.

"It's perfectly right," said Sam. "When a man's in the right, and of course we always are, if he fights a man of his size or one bigger than he is, he gives the wrong a chance of winning, and that is clearly immoral. If he takes a weaker man he makes the truth sure of success. And it's just the same way with nations."

Corker did not seem to be much interested by this disquisition, and Cleary dragged his friend away after they had respectfully bade the pugilist good-night. A crowd of soldiers was waiting outside to see Corker get into his carriage. They paid no attention whatever to Sam and Cleary.

"When it comes to real glory a prize-fighter beats a colonel all hollow," said Cleary, and they parted for the night.

Sam was retained on the general staff and assigned to the important post of censor of the press. His duties were most engrossing, for not only were the proofs of all the local newspapers submitted to him, but also all other printed matter. One day a large number of handbills were confiscated at a printer's and brought in for his inspection. He was very busy and asked his native private secretary to look them over for him. In a half-hour he came to him with a translation of the document.

"What does it say?" cried Sam. "I have no time to read it through."

"It says that governments are made to preserve liberty, and that they get their only authority from the free will of the people who are ruled by them," answered the clerk.

"That's clearly seditious," said Sam. "There must be some plot at the bottom of it. Have the whole edition burned and have the printer locked up."

A few days later a newspaper was brought to him announcing that the Moritos had massacred the garrison stationed among them, that the whole province of San Diego was in revolt, and that the regiment there would probably have to fall back on Havilla. Sam was much scandalized, and sent at once for the native editor.

"What does this mean?" said he.

"Pardon, my colonel," said the little man apologetically, "this is a newspaper and this is news. I am sure it is true."

"That is the civilian conception of news," said Sam, with disdain. "Officially this is not true. We have instructions, as you have often been told, not to allow anything to be printed

that can injure the Administration at Whoppington. Any one can
see how this would injure it, and news that can injure it is,
from the military point of view, untrue. General Notice is
making a tour of the country at home, receiving ovations
everywhere on account of the complete subjugation of the
islands. What effect will such news have upon his reception? Is
it a proper way to treat a general who has deserved well of his
country?"

"But," interposed the editor, "don't the people know that
you are continually sending out more troops?"

"The people do not mind a little thing like that," said
Sam. "When an officer and a gentleman says the war is over, they
believe it, and they show their gratitude by voting money to send
new regiments. Your action in printing this stuff is most
disloyal. I will send one of my assistants around to your office
with you to see that this edition is destroyed, and if you repeat
the offense you will be deported."

The unfortunate man retired, shrugging his shoulders. As he
went out Cleary came running in with a copy of the paper.

"Oh! you've got a copy of that, have you?" said Sam. "It's
an outrage to print such things, isn't it?"

"I'm afraid it's true," said Cleary.

"What difference does that make?" exclaimed Sam. "It's the
business of an army to conquer a country. We've done it twice,
and we can do it as often as we like again."

"Hear, hear!" cried Cleary. "You're becoming more and more
of a soldier as you get promoted. You have the true military
instinct, I see. Of course it makes no difference who holds the
country, but I'm a little disappointed in the Moritos. As for
San Diego, Colonel Booth of your old regiment is in command, and
I half think he didn't back up the Morito garrison out of
jealousy toward you. He wanted to have the Morito country go
back, so as to belittle our exploit. But we'll get even with
him. I've seen the cable-censor, and not a word about it will go
home. I have just sent a despatch saying that the whole island
is entirely in our hands and that the natives are swearing
allegiance by thousands."

"That's right," said Sam. "It's really a kindness to the
people at home, for if they think it's true it makes them just as
happy as if it were true, and I think it's positively cruel to
worry them unnecessarily."

"To be sure," said Cleary. "And if it does get out, we'll
throw all the blame on the Secretary of War and his embalmed
beef. They say he's writing a book to show that a diet of
mummies is the best for fighting men--and so the quarrels go on.
By the way, I just stopped a piece of news that might have
interested you. Do you know that you have suppressed the
Declaration of Independence?"

"Nonsense. I haven't seen a copy of it in two years."

"Well, here's a despatch that I got away from the
cable-office just in time. It would have gone in another ten
minutes. Here it is."

341

Sam took the paper and read an account of the printing by a native committee of fifty thousand copies of the Declaration in Castalian, and its immediate suppression by Colonel Jinks, the censor.

"It's a downright lie," cried Sam. "I'll call my native secretary and inquire into this," and he rang his bell.

"See here, what does this mean?" he asked the clerk who hurried in.

The man thought a minute.

"I do not know the Declaration of Independence," he said, "but perhaps that paper I translated for you the other day had something to do with it. I have not a copy here."

"Were they burned."

"Not yet, sir. They were siezed, and are in our dépot."

"Come, said Sam to Cleary, "let's go over there and look at it. It's a half-mile walk and it will do me good."

"How are things at San Diego?" asked Sam, as they walked along together. "You've been out there, haven't you?"

"Yes. We'll have to come in. The Cubapinos have got a force together at a town farther down the river and are threatening us there. We got pretty near them and mined under a convent they were in, and blew up a lot of them, but it didn't do them much harm, for a lot of recruits came in just afterward from the mountains. That convent was born to be blown up, it seems, for some Castalian anarchists had a plot to blow it up some years ago, and came near doing it, too. We made use of their tunnels, which the monks were too lazy to have filled up. The anarchist plot was found out, and they garroted a dozen of them."

"What inhuman brutes those anarchists are!" cried Sam. "Think of their trying to blow up a whole houseful of people! I wish we could take some one of the smaller islands and put all the anarchists of the world there and let them live out their precious theories. Just think what a hell it would be! What infernal engines of hatred and destruction they would construct, if they were left to themselves--machines charged with dynamite and bristling with all sorts of explosive contrivances!"

"Something like a battle-ship," suggested Cleary.

"Don't talk nonsense!" exclaimed Sam. "Only Castalian fiends would try to destroy law and order and upset the peaceable course of society in such a way. Do you suppose that any of our people at home would do such a thing?"

"None, outside of the artillery," answered Cleary. "Well, at any rate, our blowing up of the convent didn't do much good. There was some talk of putting poison in the river to dispose of them, but of course we couldn't do that."

"Of course not," said Sam. "That would be barbarous and against all military precedents. The rules of war don't allow it."

"They're rather queer, those rules," answered his friend. "I should like my enemies to take notice that I prefer being poisoned to being blown up with bombshells. In some respects they don't pay much attention to the rules, either. They don't take prisoners much nowadays. Most of the despatches now read,

342

'fifty natives killed,' but they say nothing of wounded or prisoners."

"We're fighting savages, we must remember that," said Sam.

"Then we've got a way of trying our pistols and rifles on natives working in the fields; it's rather novel, to say the least. I saw one man in the 73d try his new revolver on a native rowing a boat on the river, and over the fellow toppled and the boat drifted down-stream. The men all applauded, and even the officers laughed."

"Boys will be boys," said Sam, smiling. "They're good shots, at any rate."

"They are that. There were some darkies plowing up there just this side of San Diego, and some of our fellows picked them off as neatly as you please. It must have been eight hundred yards if it was a foot. But somehow I don't quite like it."

"War is war," said Sam, using a phrase which presumably has a rational meaning, as it is so often employed by reasonable people. "It doesn't pay to be squeamish. The squeamish men don't make good soldiers. I've seen enough to learn that. They hesitate to obey orders, if they don't like them."

As he said this they passed a small crowd of boys in the street. They were trying to make two dogs fight, but the dogs refused to do so, and the boys were beating them and urging them on.

"What stupid brutes they are," said Sam. "They're badly trained."

"They haven't had a military education," responded Cleary. "But I almost forgot to ask you, have you seen the papers from home this morning? They're all full of you and your greatness. Here are two or three," and he took them from his pocket.

Sam opened them and gazed at them entranced. There was page upon page of his exploits, portraits of all kinds, biographies, anecdotes, interviews, headlines, everything that his wildest dreams had imagined, only grander and more glorious. There was nothing to be seen but the words "Captain Jinks" from one end of the papers to the other.

"They've even got a song about you," said Cleary. "Here it is:

> "'I'm Captain Jinks of the horse-marines.
> I feed my horse on corn and beans.
> Of course it's quite beyond my means,
> Tho a captain in the army!"

"I don't altogether like it," said Sam. "What are the horse-marines? I don't believe there are any."

"Oh, that doesn't make any difference. It seems it's an old song that was all the go long before our time, and your name has revived it. It will advertise you splendidly. The whole thing is a grand piece of work for The Lyre. Jonas has been congratulating me on it. He'd come and tell you so, but he doesn't want to be seen with you. You've censured out everything I've asked you to for him, and he doesn't want people to know about his pull. That's the reason why he's never called on you. But he says it's the best newspaper job he ever heard of. I tell you we're a great combination, you and I. Perhaps I'll write a book and call it, 'With Jinks at Havilla.' Rather an original title, isn't it? But I'm afraid that all this talk at home will not make you very popular with the officers here, who knew you when you were only a captain. What would you say to being transferred to Porsslania? They want new men for our army there, and I've half a mind to go too for a change and act as the Lyre's correspondent there. They'll do anything I ask them now."

"I'd like it very much," said Sam. "I'm tired of this literary business. But here we are. This is our dépot."

The two men entered the long low building in which confiscated property was stored. A soldier who was acting as watchman showed them where the circulars were piled. Cleary took one and glanced over it.

As sure as fate, it's the Declaration of Independence!" he laughed.

Sam took up a copy and looked at it too.

"I believe it is," he said. "I didn't half look at it the other day. I'm ever so much obliged to you for telling me and stopping the telegram. But between you and me, the circular ought to be suppressed anyway. What business have these people to talk about equal rights and the consent of the governed? The men who wrote the Declaration--Jeffries and the rest--were mere civilians and these ideas are purely civilian. Come, let's have them burned at once," and he called up two or three soldiers, and in a few minutes the circulars formed a mass of glowing ashes in the courtyard.

CHAPTER X

A Great Military Exploit

One day while Sam was still waiting for Cleary to carry out his designs, his secretary told him that a sergeant wished to see him, and Sam directed him to shown him into his office. The man was a rather sinister-looking individual, and his speech betrayed his Anglian origin.

"Colonel," said he, after the door was closed and they were alone, "I'm only a sergeant promoted from the ranks, but I'm not just an ordinary common soldier. I know a thing or two, and I've got a plan and I thought perhaps you would be glad to 'ear of it. I'ave the 'abit of observing things, and most soldiers don't. Why, bless me, you can march them into a country and out again, and with their eyes front, they don't see a bloomin' thing. They're trained to see nothin'. They're good for nothin' but to do as they're bid. I used to be in the army in the old country, and once at Baldershot I saw Lord Bullsley come along on horseback and stop two soldiers carryin'a soup-pail.

"'Give me a taste of that,' says he, and one of them runs off and gets a ladle and gives him a taste. He spits it out and makes a face and shouts:

"'Good heavens! man, you don't call that stuff soup, do you?'

344

"'No, sir,' says the man. 'It's dish-water that we was a-hemptyin'.' That's the soldier all over again. He 'adn't sense enough to tell him beforehand."

"I don't see, sergeant, what that has to do with me," said Sam curtly.

"Well, sir, perhaps it hasn't. But I only wanted to say that I ain't that kind of a man. I sees and thinks for myself. Now I 'ear that they've got a letter captured from Gomaldo askin' General Baluna for reenforcements, and that they've got some letters from Baluna too, and know his handwritin'. I only wanted to say that I used to be a writin'-master and that I can copy any writin' goin' or any signature either, so you can't tell them apart. Now why couldn't we forge an answer from Baluna to Gomaldo and send the first reenforcements ourselves? He wants a 'undred men at a time. And then we could capture Gomaldo as easy as can be. We could find him in the mountains. I know a lot of these natives 'ere who would go with us if we paid them well."

"We should have to dress them up in the native uniform," said Sam. "I don't know whether that would be quite honorable."

The sergeant smiled knowlingly, but said nothing.

"Do you think we could get native officers to do such a thing?" Sam asked.

"Oh, yes! Plenty of them. I know one or two. At first they wouldn't like it. But give them money enough and commissions in our army, and they'd do it."

"How different they are from us!" mused Sam. "Nobody in our army, officer or man, could ever be approached in that way."

"It seems to me I've read somewhere of one of our principal generals--Maledict Donald, wasn't it?"

Sam thought best not to hear this.

"But we would have to send some of our own officers on such an expedition," he said. "We couldn't disguise them as natives."

"That wouldn't be necessary. They can go as if they were prisoners--you and two or three others you could pick out. I'd like to go too. And then I'd expect good pay if the thing went through, and a commission as lieutenant."

"There'd be no trouble about that," answered Sam. "I'll think it over, and perhaps consult the general about it and let you know by to-morrow.

"Very good, sir. I'm Sergeant Keene of the 5th Company, 39th Infantry."

As the sergeant went out Cleary came in, and Sam laid the matter before him.

"I know that fellow by sight," said Cleary. "They say he's served several terms for forgery and counterfeiting. I don't like his looks. That's a great scheme tho, if it does seem a little like bunco-steering. It's all right in war perhaps."

"Yes," said Sam. "We have a higher standard of honor than civilians. I'll go and see the general about it now."

After some consultant the general approved the plan and authorized Sam to carry it out. The latter set Keene to work at once at forging a letter from Baluna acknowledging receipt of the orders for reenforcements and informing Gomaldo that he was sending him the first company of one hundred troops. Meanwhile he selected three officers of the Regular Army to accompany him besides Keene, and through the latter approached three native officers who had been captured at San Diego. One of these was a close confidential friend of Gomaldo's, but Keene succeeded after much persuasion in winning them all over. It was an easier task to make up a company of native privates, who readily followed their officers when a small payment on account had been given to each man.

"I don't quite like the job," Sam confessed to Cleary, "but the general says it's all right and so it must be."

At last the expedition started out. All the natives were dressed in the native uniform, and the five white men were clad as privates in the invading army and held as prisoners. After passing the outposts near San Diego they turned toward the south in the direction of the mountains where Gomaldo's captured letter had been dated. They were received with rejoicings in each native village as soon as they showed the forged letter of Baluna and exhibited their white prisoners. The villagers showed much interest in the latter, but treated them kindly, expressing their pity for them and offering them food. They had no difficulty in obtaining exact directions as to Gomaldo's situation, but found that it lay in the midst of an uninhabited district where it was impossible to obtain supplies, the village where he had established his headquarters being the only one within many miles. They scraped together what food they could in the shape of rice, Indian corn, and dried beef, and set out on the last stage of their journey. There had been heavy rains recently, and the mountain paths were almost impassable. There were swift rivers to cross, precipices to climb, and jungles to penetrate. The heat was intense, and the men began to suffer from it. The advance was very slow, and soon the provisions gave out. It began to seem probable that the whole expedition would perish in the mountains. Sam called a council of war, and, at Keene's suggestion, picked out the two most vigorous privates, who went ahead bearing the alleged Baluna letter and another from Gomaldo's renegade friend, who was nominally in command, asking for speedy succor. The two ambassadors were well schooled in what they should say, and were promised a large sum of money if they succeeded.

For two long days the party waited entirely without food, and they were just beginning to despair, when the two men returned with a dozen carriers sent by Gomaldo bringing an ample supply of bread and meat. He also delivered a letter in which the native general congratulated his friend on his success in leading the reenforcements and in capturing the prisoners, and gave express instructions that the latter should be treated with all consideration. The carriers were commanded by a native lieutenant, who insisted that the prisoners should share equally with the native troops, and saw to it personally that Sam and his friends were served. His kindness cut Sam to the heart. After a few hours' delay the expedition set out again, and on the following day it reached the mountain village where Gomaldo had established himself.

Gomaldo's body-guard, composed of fifty troops neatly dressed in white uniforms, were drawn up to receive them, and the whole population greeted them with joy. Gomaldo himself stood on the veranda of his house, and, after saluting the expedition, invited the native officers who were to betray him in to dinner. At this moment Keene whispered to Sam and the latter signaled to the native officer, Gomaldo's treacherous friend who was in charge of him, and this man gave an order in a low voice, whereupon the whole expedition discharged their rifles, and half-a-dozen of the body-guard fell to the ground. In the mean time two of the native officers threw their arms round Gomaldo and took him prisoner, and his partizans were seized with a panic. Sam took command of his men, who outnumbered the loyal natives, and in a few minutes he had unchallenged control of the post without losing a single man, killed or wounded. Gomaldo was intensely excited and upbraided Sam bitterly when taken before him, but upon being promised good treatment he became more tractable. Sam gave orders that the villagers should bury the dead, among whom he regretted to see the body of the native lieutenant who had brought him food when they were starving; and then, after a rest of several hours, the expedition set out on the return journey, Gomaldo and his men accompanying it as prisoners.

The news of the capture preceded the party, and when, after a march of several days, they arrived at Havilla, Sam was received as a conquering hero by the army. Cleary took the first opportunity to grasp his hand.

"Is it really a great and noble act?" Sam whispered. "I suppose it is, for everybody says so, but somehow it has left a bad taste in my mouth, and I can't bear the sight of that fellow Keene."

"Never mind," said Cleary. "You won't have to see him long. We're going to Porsslania in a fortnight, you and I, and you'll have a chance to turn the world upside down there."

CHAPTER XI

A Dinner Party At Gin-Sin

During the past months great events had taken place in the ancient empire of Porsslania. Many years earlier the various churches had sent missionaries to that benighted land to reclaim its inhabitants from barbarism and heathenism. These emissaries were not received with the enthusiastic gratitude which they deserved, and some of the Porsslanese had the impudence to assert that they were a civilized people when their new teachers had been naked savages. They proved their barbarism, however, by indulging in the most unreasonable prejudices against a foreign religion, and when cornered in argument they would say to the missionaries, "How would you like us to convert your people to our religion?" an answer so illogical that it demonstrates either

347

their bad faith or the low development of their intellects. The missionaries of some of the sects, by the help of their governments, gradually obtained a good deal of land and at the same time a certain degree of civil jurisdiction. The foreign governments, wishing to bless the natives with temporal as well as celestial advantages, followed up the missionary pioneers with traders in cheap goods, rum, opium, and fire-arms, and finally endeavored to introduce their own machinery and factory system, which had already at home raised all the laboring classes to affluence, put an end to poverty, and realized the dream of the prophets of old. The Porsslanese resolutely resisted all these benevolent enterprises and doggedly expressed their preference for their ancient customs. In order to overcome this unreasonable opposition and assure the welfare of the people, the various Powers from time to time seized the great ports of the Empire. The fertile diplomacy of the courts found sufficient ground for this. Most frequently the pretext was an attack upon a missionary or even a case of cold-blooded murder, and it became a proverb among the Porsslanese that it takes a province to bury a missionary. Finally, all the harbors of the Empire were in the hands of foreigners, who used this advantageous position to confer blessings thick and fast upon the reluctant population, who richly deserved, as a punishment, to be left to themselves. At last a revolutionary party sprang up among this deluded people, claiming that their own Government was showing too much favor to foreign religions and foreign machines. The Government did not put down this revolt. Some said that it did not have the power and that the provinces were practically independent of the central authority. Others whispered that the Imperial Court secretly favored the rebels. However this may be, the Fencers, as the rebels were called from their skill with the native sword, succeeded without much difficulty in getting possession of the imperial city and imprisoning the foreign embassies and legations in the enclosure of the Anglian Embassy. The Imperial Court meanwhile fled to a distant city and left the entire control of the situation in the hands of the Fencers. The peril of the legations was extreme. They were cut off completey from the coast, which was many miles distant, and the foreign newspaper correspondents amused themselves by sending detailed accounts of the manner in which they had been tortured and murdered. The principal men among the Porsslanese assured the Powers that the legations were safe, but they were not believed. A great expedition was organized in which all the great Powers took a part. The forts near the sea were stormed and taken. The intermediate city of Gin-Sin was besieged and finally fell, and the forces advanced to the gates of the Capital. Before long they succeeded in taking possession of the great city. The Fencers fled in confusion, and at least two-thirds of the population fled with them, fearing the vengeance of the foreigners. The legations were saved, after one ambassador had been shot by an assassin. The city was divided into districts, each of which was turned over to the safe-keeping of one of the foreign armies, and the object of the expedition had been

348

accomplished. In the mean time many foreign residents, including many missionaries in various parts of the Empire, had been murdered, the inhabitants not recognizing the obvious fact that they and their countrymen were their best friends.

Affairs had reached this position when orders came to Havilla for Colonel Jinks to proceed to join the army in Porsslania, where he would be placed in command of a regiment. His fidus Achates, Cleary, had also received permission from his journal to accompany him, and the two set sail on a transport which carried details of troops. It is true that these troops could ill be spared from the Cubapines, as the country was still in the hands of the natives with the exception of here and there a strip of the seacoast, and there was much illness among the troops, many being down with fever and worse diseases. But it was necessary for the Government to make as good a showing in Porsslania as the other Powers, and the reenforcements had to go.

It was on a hot summer day that Sam and Cleary looked over the rail of the transport as they watched the troops come on board. It was a remarkable scene, for a crowd of native women were on the shore, weeping and arguing with the men and preventing them from getting into the boats.

"Who on earth are they?" asked Sam.

"It's a pretty mean practical joke," said Cleary. "That regiment has been up in the interior, and they've all had wives up there. They buy them for five dollars apiece. And the Governor of the province there, a friendly native, has sent more than a hundred of the women down here, to get rid of them, I suppose, and now the poor things want to come along with their young men. Some of them have got babies, do you see?"

After a long and noisy delay the captain of the transport, assisted by the officers of the regiment in question, persuaded the women to stay behind, giving a few coppers to each and making the most reckless and unabashed promises of return. The steamer then weighed anchor and was soon passing the sunken Castalian fleet.

"The Court at Whoppington has just allowed prize-money to the officers and men for sinking those ships," said Cleary. "They didn't get as much as they wanted, but it's a good round sum."

"I'm glad they will get some remuneration for their hard work," said Sam.

"Do you see that native sloop over there?" said Cleary. "She's a pirate boat we caught down in the archipelago. She had sunk a merchant vessel loaded with opium or something of the kin, very valuable. They'd got her in shallow water and had killed some of the crew, and the rest swam ashore, and they were dividing up the swag when they were caught. They would have had I don't know how many dollars apiece. They were all hanged."

"Serves them right," said Sam. "We must put down piracy. Good-by, Havilla," he added, waving his hat toward the capital. "It makes me feel happy to think that I have actually ended the war by capturing Gomaldo."

349

"Not much!" cried Cleary. "Didn't you hear the news this morning? The Cubapinos are twice as active as ever. They're rising everywhere."

Not many days later, and after an uneventful voyage, the transport sailed into the mouth of the Hai-Po River and came to anchor off the ruins of the Porsslanese forts. Colonel Jinks had orders to proceed at once to Gin-Sin, and he left with Cleary on a river steamer. They were struck by the utter desolation of the country. There were no signs of life, but here and there the smoking ruins of a town showed where human beings had been. They noticed something floating in the water with a swarm of flies hovering over it.

"Good heavens! it's a corpse," said Cleary. "It's a native. That's a handsome silk jacket, and it doesn't look like a soldier's either. Look at that vulture. It's sweeping down on it."

The vulture circled round in the air, coming close to the body, but did not touch it.

"It has had enough to eat already," said an Anglian passenger who was standing near them. "Did you ever see such a fat bird? You'll see plenty of bodies before long. Do you observe those vultures ahead there? You'll find floating bodies wherever they are."

"I suppose they are the bodies of soldiers," said Sam.

"No, indeed, not all of them by any means. These Porsslanese must be stamped out like vipers. I'm thankful to say most of the armies are doing their duty. They don't give any quarter to native soldiers, and they despatch the wounded too. That's the only way to treat them, and they don't feel pain the way we do. In fact, they rather like it. The Tutonians are setting a good example; they shoot their prisoners. I saw them shoot about seventy. They tied them together four by four by their pigtails and then shot them. It's best, tho, to avoid taking prisoners; that's what most of them do."

"But you say these bodies are not all soldiers," said Cleary.

"No, of course not. You see the Mosconians kill any natives they please. Then those who are out at night are killed as a matter of course, and those who won't work for the soldiers naturally have to be put out of the way. It's the only way to enforce discipline. Look at these bodies now."

Corpses were now coming down the river one after another. Each had its attendant swarm of flies, and vultures soared in flocks in the air. The river was yellow with mud, and the air oppressively hot and heavy. Now and then a whiff of putrid air was blown across the deck. The three men watched the bodies drifting past, brainless skulls, eyeless sockets, floating along many of them as if they were swimming on their backs. "It is really a fine example of the power of civilization," said the stranger. "I don't approve of everything that has been done, by any means. Some of the armies have treated women rather badly, but no English-speaking soldiers have done that. In fact, your army has hardly been up to average in effectiveness. You and the Japs have been culpably lenient, if you will permit me to say so."

350

"We are only just starting out on our career as a military nation," said Sam. "You must not expect too much of us at first. We'll soon get our hand in. As for the Japs, why they're heathen. They can hardly be expected to behave like Christians. But we were afraid that the war was over and that we should find nothing to do."

"The war over! What an absurdity! I have lived in Porsslania for over thirty years and I ought to know something about it by now. There's an army of at least forty thousand Fencers over there to the northwest and another twenty-five thousand in the northeast. The Tutonians are the only people who understand it. Their first regiments have just arrived, and they are going to do something. They say the Emperor is coming himself, and he will put an end to this state of affairs. He is not a man to stand rebellion. All we can say is that we have made a good beginning. We have laid the whole province waste, and it will be a long time before they forget it."

The journey was hot and tedious; the desolated shore, the corpses and vultures, and an occasional junk with square-rigged sails and high poop were the only things upon which to fix the eye. When at last our travelers arrived at the city of Gin-Sin, Sam learned that his regiment had proceeded to the Capital and was in camp there, and it would be impossible for him to leave until the following day. He stopped with Cleary at the principal hotel. The city was in a semi-ruined condition, but life was already beginning to assume its ordinary course. The narrow streets, hung with banners and lanterns and cabalistic signs, were full of people. Barbers and scribes were plying their trades in the open air, and war was not always in sight. Sam's reputation had preceded him, and he had scarcely gone to his room when he received an invitation from a leading Anglian merchant to dine with him that evening. Cleary was anxious to go too, and it so happened that he had letters of introduction to the gentleman in question. He made his call at once and was duly invited.

There were a dozen or more guests at dinner, all of them men. Indeed, there were few white women left at Gin-Sin. With the exception of Sam and Cleary all the guests were Anglians. There was the consul-general, a little man with a gray beard, a tall, bald-headed, gray-mustached major-general in command of the anglian forces at Gin-Sin, two distinguished missionaires of many years' experience, several junior officers of the army, and a merchant or two. When dinner was announced they all went in, each taking precedence according to his station. Sam knew nothing of such matters, and was loath to advance until his host forced him to. He found a card with his name on it at the second cover on the right from his host. On his right was the card of a young captain. The place on his left and immediately on the right of the host bore no card, and the consul-general and the major-general both made for it. The former got there first, but the military man, who was twice his size, came into violent collision with him, pushed him away and captured the seat, while the consul-general was obliged to retreat and take the seat on the left of his host. The whole party pretended very hard to have noticed nothing unusual.

"Rather odd performance, eh?" whispered the captain to Sam. "You see how it is. Old Folsom says he take precedence because he represents the Crown, but the general says that's all rot, for the consul's only a commercial agent and a K.C.Q.X. Now the general is a G.C.Q.X., and he says that gives him precedence. Nobody can settle it, and so they have to fight it out every time they meet."

"I see," said Sam. "I don't know anything about such things, but I should think that the general was clearly in the right. He could hardly afford to let the army be over-ridden."

"Quite so," said the captain. "I don't suppose you know these people," he added.

"Not one of them, except my friend, Mr. Cleary. We only arrived to-day."

"The general is a good deal of a fellow," said the captain. "I was with him in Egypt and afterward in South Africa."

"Were you, indeed?" cried Sam. "Do tell me all about those wars. They were such great affairs."

"Yes, they were. Not much like this business here. Nothing could stop us in the Sudan, and when we dug up the Mahdi and threw his body away there was nothing left of the rebellion. I believe the best way to settle things here would be to dig up somebody--Confusus, for instance. If there's anything of that kind to be done our army could do it in style."

"It must be a very effective means of subjugating people," said Sam.

"Yes, and would you believe it? the natives objected to it. They asked us what we would think of it if they dug up our Queen. Just think of it! The impudent niggers! As if there was any similarity in the two cases."

"Outrageous," said Sam.

"And even at home and in Parliament, when our general was sitting in the gallery hearing them discuss how much money they would give him, some of the members protested against our digging the old fraud up. It was a handsome thing for the general to go there and face them down."

"It showed great tact, and I may say--delicacy," said Sam.

"Yes, indeed," said the captain. "That's his strong point."

"But I suppose that the war in South Africa was even greater," said Sam.

"Rather. Why we captured four thousand of those Boers with only forty thousand men. No wonder all Anglia went wild over it. Lord Bobbets went home and they gave him everything they could think of in the way of honors. It was a fitting tribute."

"The war is quite over there now, isn't it?" asked Sam.

"Yes," answered the captain, somewhat drily. "And so is yours in the Cubapines, I understand."

"Yes," said Sam. "I think the Cubapine war and the South African war are about equally over."

"Do you see that lieutenant there between your friend and the parson?"

352

"Yes."

"He got the Victorious Cross in South Africa. He saved a sergeant's life under fire. You see his cross?"

"How interesting!" said Sam. "He must be a hero."

"That chap with the mustache at the bottom of the table really did more once. He saved three men from drowning in a shipwreak in the Yellow Sea. He's got a medal for it."

"Why doesn't he wear it, too?" asked Sam.

"Civilians never do," said the captain. "It would look rather odd, wouldn't it, for him to wear a life-saving medal? You may be sure he keeps it locked up somewhere and never talks about it."

"It is strange that civilians should be so far behind military men in using their opportunities," said Sam.

"That old fellow with the long beard is Cope, the inventor of the Cope gun. He's a wonder. He was out here in the employ of the Porsslanese Government. Most of their artillery was designed by him. What a useful man he has been to his country! First he invented a projectile that could go through any steel plate then known, and all the navies had to build new steel-clad ships on a new principle that he had invented to prevent his projectiles from piercing them. Then what does he do, but invent a new projectile that could go through that, and they had to order new guns for it and build new ships to withstand it. He's done that four times. And he's got a rifle now that will penetrate almost anything. If you put two hundred Porsslanese of the same height in a row it would go through all their heads at five hundred yards. I hope they'll try the experiment before this affair is over."

The major-general had by this time exhausted all possible subjects of conversation with his host and sat silent, and Sam felt obliged to turn his attention to him, and was soon engaged in relating his experiences in the Cubapines. Meanwhile Cleary had been conversing with the brave young lieutenant at his side and the reverend gentleman beyond him. They had been discussing the slaughter of the Porsslanese, the lieutenant sitting back from the table while his neighbors talked across him.

"I confess," said the Rev. Mr. Parker, "that I am not quite satisfied with our position here. This wholesale killing of non-combatants is revolting to me. Surely it can not be Christian."

"I have some doubts about it too," said the young man. "I don't mind hitting a man that hits back. I didn't object to the pig-sticking in South Africa, and I believe that man-hunting is the best of all sports; but this killing of people who don't resist, and even smile in a sickly way while you do it and almost thank you--it really does go against me."

"Yes," said Cleary, "perhaps there is something in that."

"Oh, my dear young friend!" cried the clergyman, turning toward the lieutenant, "you don't know what joy it gives me to hear you say that. I have spoken in this way again and again, and you are the first man I have met who agrees with me. Won't you let your fellow officers know what you think? It will come

353

with so much more force from a military man, and one of your
standing as a V.C. Won't you now tell this company that you
think we are going too far?"

"Really, Doctor," said the young man, blushing, "really, I
think you exaggerate my importance. I wouldn't do any good.
Perhaps I have said a little more to you than I really meant.
This champagne has gone to my head a little."

"Just repeat what you said to us. I will get the attention
of the table."

"No, Doctor, for God's sake don't!" cried the lieutenant,
laying his right hand on the missionary's arm awhile he toyed
with his cross with the other. "To tell you the truth, I haven't
the courage to say it. They would think I was crazy. I would be
put in Coventry. I have no business to make suggestions when a
general's present."

Mr. Parker sighed and did not return to the subject.

After dinner Sam was introduced to Canon Gleed, another
missionary, who seemed to be on very good terms with himself, and
stood rubbing his hands with a benignant smile.

"These are great days, Colonel Jinks," he said. "Great
days, indeed, for foreign missions. What would St. John have
said on the island of Patmos if he could have cabled for
half-a-dozen armies and half-a-dozen fleets, and got them too?
He would have made short work of his jailers. As he looks down
upon us to-night, how his soul must rejoice! The Master told us
to go into all nations, and we are going to go if it takes a
million troops to send us and keep us there. You are going on to
the Capital to-morrow? You will meet a true saint of the Lord
there, your own fellow countryman, the Ref. Dr. Amen. He is a
true member of the Church Militant. Give him my regards when you
see him."

"I see there is another clergyman here," said Sam, looking
at Mr. Parker.

"Yes, and I must say I am surprised to see him. Let me warn
you, Colonel. He is, I fear, altogether heterodox. I don't know
what kind of Christianity he teaches, but he has actually kept on
good terms with the Porsslanese near his mission throughout all
these events. He is disloyal to our flag, there can be no
question of it, and he openly critizes the actions of our
governments. He should not be received in society. He ought to
be sent home--but, hist! some one is going to sing."

It was the young lieutenant who had seated himself at the
piano and was clearing his throat as he ran his hands over the
keys. Then he began to sing in a rather feeble voice:

"Let the French sip his cognac in his caffy,
Let the Cossack gulp his kvass and usquebaugh;
Let the Prussian grenadier
Swill his dinkle-doonkle beer,
And the Yankee suck his cocktail through a straw,
Through a straw,
And the Yankee suck his cocktail through a straw.

354

"Let the Ghoorka drink his pugaree and pukka,
Let the Hollander imbibe old schnapps galore.
    Tommy Atkins is the chap
    Who has broached a better tap,
For he takes his 'arf-and-'arf in blood and gore,
    Blood and gore,
For he takes his 'arf-and-'arf in blood and gore.

"When at 'ome he may content himself with whisky,
But if once he lands upon a foreign snore--
    On the Nile or Irrawady--
    He forgets his native toddy,
And he takes his 'arf-and-'arf in blood and gore,
    Blood and gore,
And he takes his 'arf-and-'arf in blood and gore.

"He's a connoisseur of every foreign vintage,
From the claret of the fat and juicy Boer
    To the thicker nigger brand
    That he spills upon the sand,
When he draws his 'arf-and-'arf in blood and gore,
    Blood and gore,
When he draws his 'arf-and-'arf in blood and gore.

"Fine, isn't it!" exclaimed Sam's neighbor, the captain, who
was standing by him, as they all joined in hearty applause. "I
tell you Bludyard Stripling ought to be our poet laureate. He's
the laureate of the Empire, at any rate. Why, a song like that
binds a nation together. You haven't any poet like that, have
you?"

"No-o," answered Sam, thinking in shame of Shortfellow,
Slowell, and Pittier. "I'm afraid all our poets are old women
and don't understand us soldiers."

"Stripling understands everything," said the captain. "He
never makes a mistake. He is a universal genius."

"I don't think we ever drink cocktails with a straw,"
ventured Sam.

"Oh, yes, you must. He never makes a mistake. You may be
sure that, before he wrote that, he drank each one of those
drinks, one after another."

"Quite likely," whispered Cleary to Sam, as he came up on
the other side."

"I wish I could hear it sung in Lunnon," said the captain.
"A chorus of duchesses are singing it at one of the biggest
music-halls every evening, and then they pass round their
coronets, lined with velvet, you know, and take up a collection
of I don't know how many thousand pounds for the wounded in South
Africa. It stirs my blood every time I hear it sung."

The party broke up at a late hour, and Sam and Cleary walked
back together to the hotel.

"Interesting, wasn't it?" said Cleary.

"Yes," said Sam.

"Canon is a good title for that parson, isn't it? He's a fighter. They ought to promote him. 'Bombshell Gleed' would sound better than 'Canon Gleed,'" said Cleary.

"'M," said Sam.

"And that old general looked rather queer in that red and gilt bob-tailed Eton jacket," said Cleary.

"Yes, rather."

"Convenient for spanking, I suppose."

"The captain next to me told me a lot about Bobbets," said Sam. "Wasn't he nearly kidnapped in South Africa?"

"Yes; that comes of sending generals away from home who only weigh ninety-five pounds. We hadn't any such trouble with Laughter. They'd have had to kidnap him with a derrick."

"I never thought of that," said Sam. "Perhaps that's the real reason they selected him. I shouldn't wonder."

"Of course it was," responded Cleary.

"What sort of chap was the one with the V.C. next to you?" asked Sam.

"A fine fellow," said Cleary. "But it does seem queer, when you think of it, to wear a cross like that, that says 'I'm a hero,' just as plain as the beggar's placard says, 'I am blind.'"

"I don't see why," said Sam.

"On the whole I think that a placard would be better," said Cleary. "Everybody would be sure to understand it. 'I performed such and such an heroic action on such and such a day, signed John Smith.' Print it in big letters and then stand around graciously so that people could read it through when they wanted to. I'll get the idea patented when I get home."

"It's a pity we don't give more attention to decorations at home," said Sam. "But I don't quite like the placard idea."

CHAPTER XII

The Great White Temple

On the following morning the two friends started on their journey up the river toward the Imperial City. They went on a barge filled with soldiers, some of them their own troops who had arrived earlier the same morning. The barge was drawn by ropes pulled by natives, who walked and ran along the banks of the river. It was a day of ever-increasing horrors. All the desolation which they had remarked the day previous was reproduced and accentuated, and as they were so much nearer to the bank, and occasionally took walks on shore, they saw it all more clearly. Sam was much interested in the foreign troops. Their uniforms looked strange and uncouth.

"What funny pill-boxes those are that those Anglian soldiers have stuck to the side of their heads," he said, pointing to two men at Gin-Sin before they set sail.

"Yes," answered Cleary. "They'll put on their helmets when the sun gets higher. They do look queer, tho. Perhaps they think our fellows look queer too."

"I never thought of that," said Sam. "Perhaps they do," and he looked at his fellow-countrymen who were preparing to embark,

endeavoring to judge of their appearance as if ne had never seen
them before. He scrutinized carefully their slouch hats creased
in four quarters, their loose, dark-blue jackets, generally
unbuttoned, and their easy-going movements.

"Perhaps they do look queer," he said at last. "I never
thought of that."

The river was more full of corpses than ever, and there were
many to be seen on the shore, all of them of natives. Children
were playing and bathing in the snallows, oblivious of the dead
around them. Dogs prowled about, sleek and contented, and
usually sniffing only at the cadavers, for their appetites were
already sated. At one place they saw a father and son lying hand
in hand wnere they had been shot wnile imploring mercy. A dog
was quietly eating the leg of the boy. The natives who pulled
the boat along with great difficulty under the not sun were drawn
from all classes, some of them coolies accustomed to hard work,
others evidently of the leisure classes who could hardly keep up
with the rest. Soldiers were acting as task-masters, and they
whipped the men who did not pull with sufficient strength. Now
and then a man would try to escape by running, but such deserters
were invariably brought down by a bullet in the back. More than
once one of the men would fall as they waded along, and be swept
off by the current. None of them seemed to know now to swim, but
no one paid any attention to their fate. Parties were sent out
to bring in other natives to take the place of those who gave
out. One of the men thus brought in was paralyzed on one side
and carried a crutch. The soldiers made sport of him, snatched
the crutch from him, and made him pull as best he could with the
rest. Sam, Cleary, and an Anglian officer wno had served through
tne whole war took a long walk together back from the river
during tne nalt at noon. They entered a deserted house, with
gables and a tiled roof, which by cnance had not been burned.
Tne house had been looted, and such of its contents as were too
large to carry away were lying broken to bits about the floor. A
nasty smell came from an inner room, and they looked in and saw
the whole family--father, mother, and tnree daughters--lying dead
in a row on the floor. A bloody knife was in the hand of tne man.

"They probably committed suicide when they saw the soldiers
coming," said the Anglian, whose name was Major Brown. "They
often do that, and they do quite right. When they don't, the
soldiers, and even the officers sometimes, do wnat tney will witn
the women and then bayonet them afterward. Our people draw the
line at that, and so do yours."

"We certainly conduct war most humanely," said Sam.

They heard a groan from another room, and opening tne door
saw an old woman lying in a pool of blood, quite unconscious.

"I'll put her out of ner misery," said the major, ana he
drew his revolver and shot her through the head.

The journey was a very slow one and occupied three days,
altho tne natives were kept at work as long as they could stand
it, on one day actually tugging at the ropes for twenty-one
nours. At last, however, the Imperial City was reached, and our
two travelers disembarked and, taking a donkey-cart, gave

357

directions to carry them to the quarter assigned to their own
army. Here as everywhere desolation reigned. A string of laden
camels showed, however, that trade was beginning to reassert
itself. They drove past miles of burned houses, through the
massive city walls and beyond, until they saw the welcome signs
of a camp over which Old Gory waved supreme. Sam was received
with much cordiality by the commandant, General Taffy, and
assigned to the command of the 27th Volunteer Infantry. The
general was a man well known throughout the army for his courage
and ability, but notwithstanding this Sam took a strong prejudice
against him, for he seemed to be half-hearted in his work and to
disapprove of the prevailing policy of pacification by fire and
sword. Sam ascribed this feebleness to the fact that he had been
originally appointed to the army from civil life, and that he had
not enjoyed the benefits of an East Point education.

As soon as Sam was installed in his new quarters, in the
colonel's tent of his regiment, he started out with Cleary to see
the great city and examine the scene of the late siege. They
found the Jap quarter the most populous. The inhabitants who had
fled had returned, and the streets were taking on their normal
aspect. Near the boundary of this district they saw a house with
a placard in the Jap language, and asked an Anglian soldier who
was passing what it meant.

"That's one of the Jap placards to show that the natives who
live there are good people who have given no offense," said he.

"Let's go in and pay them a call," said Cleary.

They entered, and passing into a back room found a woman
nursing a man who had evidently been recently shot in the side.
She shrank from them with terror as they entered, and made no
answer to their request for information. As they passed out they
met a young native coming in, and they asked him what it meant.

"Some Frank soldiers shot him because he could not give them
money. It had all been stolen already," said the lad in pigeon
English.

"But the placard says they are loyal people," said Cleary.

"What difference does that make to them?" was the reply.

Farther on in a lonely part of the town they heard cries
issuing from the upper window of a house. They were the cries of
women, mingled with oaths of men in the Frank language. Suddenly
two women jumped out of the window, one after the other, and fell
in a bruised mass in the street. Sam and Cleary approached them
and saw that they had received a mortal hurt. They were ladies,
handsomely dressed. The first impulse of Sam and Cleary was to
take charge of them, but seeing two natives approach, they called
their attention to the case and walked away.

"I suppose it's best not to get mixed up with the affairs of
the other armies," said Sam.

The quarter assigned to the Tutonians they were surprised to
find quite deserted by the inhabitants.

"I tell you, those Tutonians know their business," said
Sam. "They won't stand any fooling. Just see how they have
established peace! We have a lot to learn from them."

They saw a crowd collected in one place.

"What is it?" asked Sam of a soldier.

"They're going to shoot thirty of these damned coolies for jostling soldiers in the street," he answered.

Sam regretted that they had no time to wait and see the execution.

As they reentered their own quarter they saw a number of carts loaded down with all sorts of valuable household effects driven along. They asked one of the native drivers what they were doing, and he replied in pigeon English that they were collecting loot for the Rev. Dr. Amen. Farther on some of their own soldiers were conducting an auction of handsome vases and carved ornaments. Sam watched the sale for a few minutes, and bought in one or two beautiful objects for a song for Marian.

"Where did they get all this stuff?" he asked of a lieutenant.

"Oh, anywhere. Some of it from the houses of foreign residents even. But we don't understand the game as well as old Amen. He's a corker. He's grabbed the house of one of his old native enemies here, an awfully rich chap, and sold him out, and now he's got his converts cleaning out a whole ward. He's collected a big fine for every convert killed and so much extra for every dollar stolen, and he's going to use it all for the propagation of the Gospel. He's as good as a Tutonian, he is."

"I'm glad we have such a man to represent our faith," said Sam.

"He's pretty hard on General Taffy, tho," said the lieutenant. "He says we ought to have the Tutonian mailed fist. Taffy is much too soft, he things."

Sam bit his lips. He could not criticize his superior officer before a subaltern, but he was tempted to.

On reaching headquarters Sam found that he was to take charge of a punitive expedition in the North, whose chief object was to be the destruction of native temples, for the purpose of giving the inhabitants a lesson. He was to have command of his own regiment, two companies of cavalry, and a field-battery. They were to set out in two days. He spent the intermediate time in completing the preparations, which had been well under way before his arrival, and in studying the map. No one knew how much opposition he might expect.

It was early in the morning on a hot summer day that the expedition left the Capital. Sam was mounted on a fine bay stallion, and felt that he was entirely in his element.

"What camp is that over there on the left?" he asked his orderly.

"That's the Anglian camp, sir."

"Are you sure. I can't see their colors. They must have moved their camp."

"Yes, sir, I'm sure. I passed near there last night and I saw half-a-dozen of the men blacking their officers' boots and singing 'Britons, Britons, never will be slaves!' It must be a tough job too, sir, for everybody's boots are covered with blood. The gutters are running with it."

"I wish we had them with us to-day," said Sam. "They have done such a lot of burning in South Africa that they could show us the best way."

"Yes, sir. But then temple-burning is finer work than burning farmhouses, sir."

"That is true," said Sam.

Before night they had visited three deserted towns and burned down the temple in each with its accompanying pagoda. There is something in the hearts of men that responds to great conflagrations, and the whole force soon got into the spirit of it and burned everything they came across. Sam enjoyed himself to the full. His only regret was that there was no enemy to overcome. They camped out at night and continued the same work for several days, all the natives fleeing as soon as they came in sight. At last they reached the famous white temple of Pu-Sing, which was the chief object of religious devotion in the whole province. This was to be absolutely destroyed, notwithstanding its great artistic beauty, and then they were to return to the city in triumph. As they drew near to the building two or three shots were fired from it, and one soldier was wounded in the arm. The usual cursing began, and the men were restive to get at the Porsslanese garrison. Sam ordered the infantry to fire a volley, and then, as the return fire was feeble, he ordered the squadron of cavalry to charge, leading it himself. The natives turned and fled as soon as they saw them coming, and the cavalry, skirting the enclosure of the temple, followed them beyond and cut them down without mercy.

"Give them hell!" cried Sam. "Exterminate the vermin!" and he swore, quite naturally under the circumstances, like a trooper.

Some of the natives fell on their knees and begged for quarter, but it was of no use. Every one was killed. They numbered about two hundred in all. When the horsemen returned to the temple they found the infantry already at work at the task of looting it. Everything of value that could be carried was taken out, and the larger statues and vases were broken to pieces. Then the woodwork was cut away and piled up for firewood, and finally the whole pile set on fire. In all this work the leader was a sergeant of infantry who seemed to have a natural talent for it. Sam had noticed him before at the burning of the other temples, but now he showed himself more conspicuously capable. As the work of piling inflammable material against the walls of polished marble, inlaid with ivory, was nearing completion, Sam sent for this man so that he might thank and congratulate him. The soldier came up, his hands black with charcoal and his face smudged as well.

"You've done well, sergeant," said Sam. "I will mention you to the general when we return."

"Thank you, sir," said the man, and his voice sounded strangely familiar. Sam peered into his face. He had certainly seen it before.

"What is your name, sergeant?"

"Thatcher, sir."

360

"Why, of course, you're Thatcher--Josh Thatcher of Slowburgh.
Don't you remember that night at the hotel when we had a drink
together? Don't you remember Captain Jinks?"

"Yes, sir, but I didn't know you was he--a colonel, too,
sir," said the man, as Sam shook his hand warmly.

"I'm glad to see that you're doing credit to your town,"
said Sam.

"They'll be surprised to hear it at home, sir," said
Thatcher. "They was always down on me. They never gave me a
chance. Here they all speaks to me like you do, sir. Why, Dr.
Amen slapped me on the back and called me a fine fellow when I
brought him in a big load of stuff. I got it from houses of
people I didn't even know, and he said I was a good fellow. At
Slowburgh I took a chicken now and then, and only from somebody
who'd done me some mean trick, and they said I was a thief. Once
or twice I burned a barn there just for fun, and never anybody's
barn that wasn't down on me and rich enough to stand it, and they
said I was a criminal. And as for women, if they ever seed me
with one, they all said I was dissolute and a disgrace to the
place, and here I have ten times more of 'em than I want, and
everybody says it's all right, and they made me a corporal and
sergeant, and the generals talked to me like I was somebody, and
I swear as much as I like. I never shot anybody at home. I
suppose they'd have strung me up if I had, and here I just pepper
any pigtail I like. They called me a criminal at Slowburgh, just
think of that! I say that criminals are just soldiers who ain't
got a job--who ain't had any chance at all, I says. I wasn't
ever judged right, I wasn't."

There were tears in Thatcher's eyes as he ended this speech.

"You're a fine chap," said Sam. "I'll tell all about you
when you get home. This war has been the making of you. How are
the other Slowburgh boys?"

"They're all right, except my cousin Tom. He's down sick
with something. He's run about a little too much. He always was
a-sparking. He never knowed how to take care of himself. Jim
Thomson was wounded once, but he's all right now. We've all had
fever, but that's over too. But the fire's spreading, sir; we'd
better get out of this."

As he spoke a heavy charred beam fell just in front of him,
and the end of it came down with its full weight on Sam's leg,
snapping the bone in two near the ankle. The foot lay at right
angles, and the bone protruded. Several soldiers lifted the log
and Thatcher drew Sam out, and they bore him in haste out of the
building. He was laid on the ground quite unconscious, at some
distance from the temple, while the flames roared and leaped
toward heaven, wrapping the graceful, lofty nine-story pagoda in
their folds. It was in a beautiful garden that he lay, near a
pool filled with lotus flowers and at the end of a rustic
bridge. The air was heavy with the perfume of lilies. A surgeon
was called, and before long he was able to put the foot in place,
but only after sawing off a large piece of bone. A cart was
obtained, Sam was laid in it, a bottle of whisky was poured down
his throat, and the journey to the city began. The patient on

361

coming to himself experienced no pain. The liquor he had taken made him feel supremely happy. He was in an ecstasy of exultation, and would have liked to embrace all mankind. But gradually this feeling wore off and his leg began to pain him, at first slightly, then more and more until it became excruciating. The road was almost impassable, and every jolt caused him agony. For twelve hours he underwent these tortures until he reached the camp in the city, and was at once transferred to a temporary hospital which had been improvised in a public building. Here he lay for many weeks, suffering much, but gradually regaining the use of his leg. He was in charge of a particularly efficient woman doctor from home who had volunteered to serve with the Red Cross Society. Sam felt most grateful to her for her care, but he strongly disapproved of her attitude to things military. She seemed to have a contempt for the whole military establishment, insisted on calling him "young man," altho he was a colonel, usually addressed lieutenants as "boys," and laughed at uniforms, salutes, and ceremonies of all kinds.

"Men are the silliest things in the world," she said one day. "Do you suppose women would have a War Department that spent a lot of money on bomb-shells to blow people up and then a lot more on Red Cross Societies to piece them together again? Why, we would just leave the soldiers at home, and save all the money, and it would be just the same in the end."

"Not the kind of women I know," said Sam, thinking of Marian.

"I mean my kind of woman," said the doctor. "Do you think we'd sell guns and rifles to the Porsslanese and teach them how to use them, and then go to work and fight them after having armed them?" And she laughed a merry laugh.

"And do you think we'd pay men to invent all sorts of infernal machines like the Barnes torpedo, and then have our big ships blown up by them in time of peace. That is what brought on the whole Castalian and Cubapine war. The idea of praising a man like Barnes! He's been a curse to the world."

"It was really a blessing," said Sam. "It has spread civilization and Christianity all over."

"Well, that's one way of doing it," said she. "But when there are more women like me we'll take things out of the hands of you silly men and run them ourselves. Now, young man, you've talked enough. Turn over and go to sleep."

Cleary called on his friend almost every day and kept him informed. He sent home glowing accounts of Sam as the conqueror of the Great White Temple, and described his sufferings for his country with artistic skill. He also began work on the series of articles which Sam was expected to write for Scribblers' Magazine. His gossip about the events in the various camps entertained Sam very much, altho he was often irritated as well. In his capacity of correspondent Cleary saw and knew everything.

"Sam," said he one day, as the invalid was sitting up in an easy-chair at the window--"Sam, it's so long since I was at East Point that I'm becoming more and more of a civilian. You army people begin to amuse me. There's always something funny about you. The Tutonians are the funniest of all. The little red-cheeked officers with their blond mustaches turned up to their eyes are too funny to live. You feel like kissing them and sending them to bed. And the airs they put on! One of their soldiers happened to elbow a lieutenant the other day, and the chap ran him through with his sword, and no one called him to account. The officers justle and browbeat any civilian who will submit to it, and they try to get him into a duel, but I believe they're a cowardly lot at bottom. No man of real courage would bluster all over the place so."

"I admire their discipline," said Sam.

"And then there's the Franks. They're not quite so conceited, but they're awfully touchy. I think the mustaches measure conceit. The Tutonians' stick up straight, the Franks' stick right out at each side waxed to a point, and ours droop downward."

Sam began to twist his mustache upward, but it would not stay.

"I was in to see a Frank military trial the other day," said Cleary. "It was the most comical thing. There were three big generals on the court. I mean big in rank. They were about four feet high in size, and they kept looking at their mustaches in hand-glasses and combing their hair with pocket-combs. They were trying one of their lieutenants for having sold some secret military plans to a Tutonian attaché. Now the joke of it is that military attachés are appointed just for the purpose of buying secrets, and everybody knows it. They're licensed to do it. And then when they do just what they're licensed for, everybody makes a fuss. Well, the secrets were sold; there wasn't the slightest reason for thinking this lieutenant had sold them, but they had to punish somebody. They say they drew his name from a box. They had three officers to testify against him, and they were the stupidest liars I ever saw. They just blundered from beginning to end, and the president of the court helped them out and told them what to say, and corrected them. The third man said nothing at all except, 'Yes, my general; yes, my general.' Then they called the witnesses for the accused, and two officers stepped forward, when a couple of orderlies grabbed each of them, stuffed a gag into their mouths, and carried them out, while the court looked the other way, and the crowd shouted, 'Long live the army!' The court adjourned on account of the 'contumacy of the witnesses for the defense.' I went in again the next morning, and they announced that both the witnesses had committed suicide. Then the president took a judgment out of his pocket which I had seen him fingering all the first day, and read it off just as it had been written before the trial began, condemning the poor devil to twenty years' imprisonment. I never saw such a farce. Everybody shouted for the army, and the little generals kissed each other and cried, and they had a great time of it. And the president made a speech in which he said that they had saved the army and consequently the country too, and that honor and glory and the fatherland had been redeemed. They've all been promoted and decorated since. They're a queer lot, those Frank officers."

"We ought not to be too quick in judging foreigners," said
Sam. "Their methods may seem strange to us, but we are not
competent to critize tnem. Let each army judge for itself."
    "As a matter of fact," said Cleary, "every army is down on
tne others. If you believe what they say about eacn other
they're a pretty bad lot. They all say that the Mosconians are
barbarians, and they call tne Tutonians thugs. The rest of them
call the Franks woman hunters, and they all call us and the
Anglians auctioneers and looters and shopkeepers and drunkards,
and we're known as temple-burners and vandals too."
    "What an outrage!" ejaculated Sam.
    "The Anglians are more like us, but they've got a few old
generals and tnen a lot of small boys, and nothing much between.
I should think tne generals would feel like schoolmasters. I
told one of tneir officers that, and he said it was better than
having second lieutenants seventy-five years old as we do. We're
loving each other a lot just now, the Anglians and us, but one of
our naval officers let on to me that they were dying to have a
war witn them. You see, since South Africa nobody's afraid of
them except the Porsslanese, and they don't read the papers. And
how the Anglians despise the Franks! Why, we were discussing
lying in war at a lunch-party, and one of their generals was
there, a ratner dense sort of a machine of a man. They had been
saying tnat lying was an essential part of war, and that an
officer must be a good liar and able to deceive the enemy well,
as well as a good fighter, and tne coversation drifted off into
tne question of lying in general. Somebody asked the general if
he would say he was a Tutonian to save his life. 'Of course,' he
answered. 'But would you say you were a Frank under the same
circumstances?' asked some one else. 'Certainly not,' he said.
Everybody roared, but he didn't see any joke, and looked as grave
as an owl all the rest of the afternoon. Then the commanders are
all so jealous of eacn other. They are spying on each other and
putting sticks in each other's wheels. Officers are queer
people. There's only one profession that can compete with them
for feline amenities, and that is the actress profession."
    "Cleary," said Sam, "I let you talk this way for old
acquaintance's sake, but I wouldn't take it from any one else."
    "Fiddlestick! You know I'm right. The Anglian officers
like to hint at the frauds in our quartermaster's department at
Havilla, but I shut tnem up by asking how much their officers
made off tne norses tney bought for South Africa in Hungary.
Tnen tney shut up like a clasp-knife. Officers talk a lot about
tneir 'brotner officers' and you'd think they loved each other a
lot, but I find tney're all glad so many were killed in Soutn
Africa because it gives them a lot of promotion. I tell you the
officers of all the armies like to nave a good list of dead
officers after each battle, if they are only their superiors in
rank. I've been picking up all I can among the different
soldiers, and learning a lot. I was just talking to a lot of
Anglian soldiers now. They were sharpening sabers and bayonets
on grindstones. One of the older ones was telling me how they
used to flog in the army. They had a regular parade, and the

364

drummers used to lay on the lash, while a doctor watched so that they shouldn't go too far. Sometimes the young subalterns who were in command would faint away at the sight.

"'But it was so manly, sir,' the fellow said to me. 'The army isn't what it was. But the other armies keep it up still, and we still birch youngsters in the navy so we needn't despair of the world.'"

"When will the campaign be over?" asked Sam.

"There's no telling. All the armies are afraid to leave, for fear the ones that are left will get some advantage from the Porsslanese Government. They're a high old lot of allies. It's a queer business. But the missionaries are as queer as any of them. You ought to have heard old Amen last Sunday. How he whooped things up! He took his text from the Gospel of St. Loot, I think! He was trying to stir up Taffy to be more severe. Amen ought to be a soldier. Our minister plenipotentiary isn't a backward chap either. I went through the Imperial palace with him and his party the other day, and they pretty nearly cleaned it out, just for souvenirs, you know. He didn't take anything himself, as far as I could see; but his women, bless my soul, they filled their pockets with jade and ivory and what-not. There were some foreign looters in there at the same time, great swells too, and they just smashed the plate-glass over the cabinets and filled their pockets and their arms too. One old Porsslanese official was standing there, a high mandarin of some sort, and he had an emerald necklace around his neck. Some diplomat or other walked up to him and quietly took it off, and the old man didn't stir, but the tears were rolling down his cheeks."

"He had no right to complain," said Sam. "We clearly have the right to the contents of a conquered city by the rules of war."

"Perhaps. But there are some curious war rules. Some of the armies shoot all natives in soldiers' uniforms because they are soldiers, and then they shoot all natives who resist them in civil dress, because they are not soldiers and have no right to fight. I suppose they ought to go about naked. They used to kill their prisoners with the butt-end of their rifles, but that breaks the rifles, and now they generally use the bayonet."

"Here are some newspapers," said he on another occasion. "You've been made a brigadier for capturing Comaldo. Isn't that great? But they will call you 'Captain Jinks' at home, no matter what your rank is. The papers say so. The song has made it stick."

"I'm sorry for that," said Sam. "It would be pleasanter to be called 'General.'"

"It's all the same," said Cleary. "Wasn't Napoleon called the Little Corporal? It's really more distinguished."

"Perhaps it is," said Sam contentedly.

"Some of the papers criticize us a little too," added Cleary. "They say we are acting brutally here and in the Cubapines. Of course only a few say it, but their number is increasing."

365

"They make themselves ridiculous," said Sam. "They don't see how ludicrous their suggestions are that we should actually retire and let these countries relapse into barbarism. As that fellow said at Havilla, they have no sense of humor."

"And yet," retorted Cleary, "our greatest humorists, Mark Swain, Mr. Tooley, and the best cartoonists, and our only really humorous paper, Knife, are on that side."

"But they are only humorists," cried Sam, "mere professional jokers. You can't expect serious sense from them. They are mere buffoons. The serious people here, such as Dr. Amen, are with us to a man."

"I saw old Amen get caught the other day," said Cleary. "I was interviewing the colonel of the 15th, and in came Amen and began talking about the Porsslanese--what barbarians they were, no religion, no belief, no faith. Why, the idea of self-sacrifice was utterly unknown to them! Just then in came a young officer and said, 'Colonel, the son of that old native we're going to shoot this afternoon for looting, is bothering us and says he wants to be shot instead of his father. What shall we do with him?' Amen said good-day and cleared out. By the way, the colonel of the 15th is in a hole just now. He was shut up in the legations, you know, and all the women there were down on him because he wouldn't make the sentries salute them when the men were dead tired with watching. They are charging him with cowardice. There'll never be an end of this backbiting. It's almost as sickening as the throat-cutting and stabbing. I confess I'm getting sick of it all. When you see a private shoot an old native for not blacking his boots, when the poor fellow was trying to understand him and couldn't, and smiling as best he could, it's rather tough; and I've seen twenty babies as I've seen one lying in the streets with a bayonet hole in them. They have executions every day in one camp or another. I saw one coolie, who had been working fourteen hours at a stretch loading carts, shot down because he hadn't the strength to go on."

"I'm afraid the heat is telling on you, Cleary," said Sam. "This is all sickly sentimentality. War is war. The trouble with you is that there has been no regular campaign on to occupy your attention. This lying about doing nothing is a bad thing for everybody. Wait till the Tutonian Emperor comes out and we'll have something to do."

"He won't find any enemy to fight," said Cleary.

"Trust him for that," replied Sam. "He's every inch a soldier, and he'll find the way to make war, depend upon it. He's a religious man too, and he will back up the missionaries better than we've done."

"Yes. Amen thinks the world of him. Amen ought to have been a Tutonian soldier. He says the best imagery of religion comes from war. I told him I had an article written about a fight which said that our men 'fought like demons' and 'yelled like fiends,' and I would change it to read that they fought like seraphs and yelled like cherubim, but he didn't think it was funny."

CHAPTER XIII

The War-Lord

As soon as Sam was well enough to be moved the doctors sent
him down to the coast, and Cleary, who had been up and down the
river several times in the course of his newspaper work, went
with him. Sam still felt feeble, and altho he could walk without
a crutch, he now had a decided limp which was sure to be
permanent. They arrived at the port a few days before the
expected arrival of the Emperor, and the whole place was
overflowing with excitement. The Emperor, who had never seen a
skirmish, was notwithstanding considered the greatest general of
his time, and he was coming now to prove it before the world and
incidentally to wreak vengeance upon a people, one of whom had
killed his ambassador. The town was profusely decorated, the
Tutonian garrison was increased, and Count von Balderdash, the
commander-in-chief, himself took command. Six fleets were drawn
up in the wide bay to await the coming of the war-lord. It was
announced that he would make his entry at night, and that the
hour of arrival had been timed for a dark moonless night. This
was asserted to be for the better display of fireworks. Finally,
one morning the Tutonian fleet of four or five large vessels was
sighted in the distance. They steamed slowly up and down in the
distance until night fell, and then, as their colored electric
light, outlining the masts and funnels, became distinct in the
darkness, they began to approach. Each of the awaiting fleets
was distinguished with particular-colored lights, and they had
taken their position at a considerable distance from the shore,
leaving a passage near the ruined forts for the Emperor. Sam and
Cleary found a good lookout on a dismantled bastion, and saw the
whole parade. As the leading vessel came near the first fleet
the latter saluted with its guns. Suddenly the lights on the
advancing ship were extinguished, and a strong flash-light was
thrown from above upon the forward deck. There in bold relief
stood a single figure, brilliantly illuminated by the light.
Cleary and Sam turned their field-glasses upon it.
    "By Jove! it's the Emperor," cried Cleary. "He's got on his
admiral's uniform, and now he's passing his own fleet that
Balderdash brought with him."
    They looked at the striking scene for some minutes, and the
crowds on the wharves and shores murmured with surprise.
    "Bless my soul! he has disappeared," said Cleary again.
    Sure enough, he had suddenly passed out of sight, and as
suddenly the flash-light went out and the lights on the masts
reappeared. In another moment these lights were extinguished,
and the flash-light revealed a form standing in the same place in
a theatrical attitude with raised sword and uplifted face.
    "I believe it's he again," said Cleary. "He must have a
trap-door. He's got on another uniform. I think it's a Frank
admiral's uniform. There go the Frank guns. He's passing their
fleet."
    "Yes, it is a Frank naval uniform," said a foreign officer
near them, as he scrutinized the deck with his glasses.

Before each of the fleets the same maneuvre was carried out. As their guns fired, the Emperor would disappear for a few moments, and in an incalculably short time he would appear again in the uniform of an admiral of the fleet in question. When he had passed the last fleet he disappeared once more, and came back in sight clad in the white and silver armor of a general officer of his own army, with helmet and plume. The flash-light now changed colors through the whole gamut of the rainbow, and the Emperor knelt in the attitude of Columbus discovering America.

Sam was immensely impressed.

"Oh, Cleary!" he said, "if we only had an Emperor."

"The President is doing his best," said Cleary. "Don't blame him."

"Oh, but what can he do? Why haven't we some one like that to embody the ideal of the State, to picture us to ourselves, to realize our aspirations?"

As he said this a strange noise arose from the crowd near the landing-stage where the Emperor was about to alight. The far greater part of this crowd was composed of natives, and they had been entirely taken aback by the exhibition. They were just beginning to understand it, and as the war-lord moved about the deck followed by the glare of the flash-light, and again struck an attitude before descending into the gig which was to take him ashore, some one of the Porsslanese in the crowd laughed. His neighbor laughed too, then another and then another, until the whole native multitude was laughing. The laugh rippled along the shore through the long stretch of natives collected there like the swells from a passing steamer. It seemed to extend back from the shore through the whole town, and, tho it was undoubtedly fancy, Sam thought he heard it spreading, like the rings from a stone thrown into the water, over the entire land. The foreigners stood aghast. The Porsslanese are not a laughing people. They had never been known to laugh before except in the most feeble manner. The events of the past year had not been especially humorous, and the coming of the great war-lord was far from being a laughing matter. Yet with the perversity of heathen they had selected this impressive occasion for showing their incurable barbarism and bad taste. Sam fairly shuddered.

"It's a sacrilege," he cried. "I believe that nothing short of extermination will reclaim this unhappy land. They are calling down the vengeance of heaven upon them."

They walked back to town with the foreign officer.

"He's a wonderful man, the Emperor," said he, in indifferent English. "How quickly he changed his clothes, and what a complement it was!"

"A sort of lightning-change artist," said Cleary. "He could make his fortune at a continuous performance."

In the dark Sam blushed for his friend, but fortunately their companion did not understand the allusion.

"You should have seen him when he visited our Queen," he said. "She came to meet him in the uniform of a Tutonian hussar, breeches and all. You can imagine how he was touched by it. That very afternoon he called upon her dressed in the costume of

one of our royal princesses with a long satin train. It made him
wonderfully popular. Our Queen responded at once by making his
infant daughters colonels of several of our regiments. One of
them is colonel of mine," he added proudly.

"What would you do if you went to war with Tutonia, and one
of the kids should order you to shoot on your own army?" asked
Cleary. "It might be embarrassing."

But the foreigner did not understand this either.

"And to think that these Porsslanese dogs have received him
with laughter!" said he.

At eleven o'clock on the same evening the Emperor was
closeted with his aged field-marshal, von Balderdash, in a
handsomely furnished sitting-room. A Turk's head had been set up
in the middle of the room, and His Majesty, dressed in the
uniform of a cavalry general, was engaged in making passes at it
with a saber. He had already taken a ride on horseback with his
staff. The field-marshal stood wearily leaning against the wall
at the side of a desk piled up with papers.

"We have avenged the death of our ambassador," Balderdash
was saying. "We have sent out five punitive expeditions in all.
Our quarter of the imperial city shows the power of arms more
completely than any other. We have set the highest standard, and
our army is the admiration of all."

The count watched the face of his master as he spoke, but
there was no sign of satisfaction in it. The Emperor was out of
humor.

"We have not done enough," he said. "If we had, those
pagans would not have ventured to laugh--yes, actually to
laugh--in our imperial presence. Balderdash, you have not done
your duty. I shall take command myself at once. We must have a
real punitive expedition, and not one of your imitations. If
they want war, let them have it."

"We can not have war, Your Majesty, without an enemy, and we
can find no enemy. All their armed men are killed or have fled,
and the rest of the population run away from us as soon as we
appear."

"Count," said the Emperor sternly, "do you remember your
oath to our person? Do you know your duties as a field-marshal?"

"I think so, Your Majesty."

"Is it not your duty to provide every requisite for war at
my command?"

"Yes, Your Majesty."

"Then I depend upon you to provide an enemy. What military
requisite is more important? Remember the fate of Fismark, and
do your duty. We must have war. That is what I have come here
for, and I do not propose to be disappointed. We must have a
punitive expedition at once. What are my engagements for
to-morrow?"

"Your Majesty's mustache artist is coming at 5:30," replied
the count, looking at a memorandum. "Breakfast at 6--inspection
of infantry at 6:30--naval maneuvres at 8--reception of our
officers at 10:30--reception of foreign officers at 11:30--

reception of civilians at 12--luncheon at 12:30--photographer
from 1 to 3. We have made no appointments after 3, Your Majesty."
    "Then put down the punitive expedition for 3:15," said the
war lord, twisting his mustache in front of his eyes. "I propose
to have this whole nation kow-tow before me in unison before I
leave their miserable land. Take the necessary measures at once
for the ceremony. Now I am going to call out the whole garrison
and see if they are kept in readiness. You may go, and send me
an aide-de-camp. You understand that you must find me an enemy
on whom I can wreak vengeance for all these wrongs."
    "I understand, Your Majesty," said the count, bending low
before him. "I accept this Gospel of Your Majesty's most blessed
Person," and he took his leave.
    The expedition did not start promptly at 3:15, for
unexpected complications arose. The other powers wanted to send
out punitive expeditions too, and they sought to have it
established that the Porsslanese laugh was directed against all
the fleets as well as against the Emperor. A judicious
distribution of decorations persuaded all the armies to drop this
pretension except the Anglian, and it was finally arranged that
the Tutonian and Anglian armies should cooperate and take the
field together under the Emperor's immediate command. A week had
elapsed before this force was prepared, but it finally started
out, General Fawlorn commanding the Anglian contingent.
    Sam, who was still only convalescent and who had been
assigned some duties connected with forwarding despatches which
left him a great deal of leisure, looked with envious eyes upon
the departing host. He had never seen anything like the
magnificence of the uniforms of the Emperor's staff. He envied
them their gilt and stars, and he envied them the prospect of
winning the great battles which Balderdash had promised them.
They marched at once upon a fortified town in which a large force
of Fencers were reported to be established. They besieged it for
six days according to all the rules of the Tutonian manual, and
finally entered it with great precautions, and found it
absolutely empty. At one village a regiment of Anglian Asiatics
cut to pieces a hundred natives were were alleged to be Fencers,
but it transpired afterward that none of them were armed.
Balderdash was frightened half to death, expecting his imperial
master to protest against the lack of opposition, but, strange to
say, he took it very well and delivered orations on all occasions
extolling the prowess of his troops in putting to flight the
hordes of a vast empire. This campaign lasted a month, and the
expedition finally returned to the port and was received with all
the marks of glory that Tutonian officialism could command. The
Emperor at once cabled to several kings and all his relations
that Providence had graciously preserved him in the midst of
great dangers and brought his enterprise to a successful
termination.
    "They may be great soldiers," said Cleary one day to Sam,
"but they don't understand the newspaper business. The Emperor
has a natural talent for advertising, but it hasn't been properly
cultivated. They oughtn't to have let it leak out that there

370

wasn't even a battle. Why, Taffy says he could go from one end
of the Empire to the other with a squadron of cavalry! As for
me, I shouldn't mind trying it without the cavalry. When they
did kill any people, it was like killing pheasants at one of his
famous battues. I wonder he wasn't photographed in the middle of
a pile of them, the way he is when he goes shooting at home.
Perhaps he'll get up some sport here in a big hen-coop. I'll
suggest it to Balderdash."

Sam refused to think ill of the great war-lord, and embraced
every opportunity to see him. He had been formally presented to
him at a reception of officers, but there was a crowd present,
and Sam did not expect him to recognize him again. On one
occasion Sam happened to be standing in the street when the
Emperor, accompanied by some of his officers, came past on foot.
Sam stood on one side and saluted. To his surprise the Emperor
stopped and beckoned to him. Sam came forward, bowing, blushing,
and stammering.

"I am glad to see an officer of your country here, General,"
said His Majesty. "May I ask your name? Ah, Jinks! I have
heard your name before. What do you think of expansion, General?"

"I beg Your Majesty's pardon," said Sam, "but I do not
think. I obey orders."

The Emperor gave an exclamation of surprise and delight.

"Hear that, gentlemen," said he in his own language, turning
to his officers. "He does not think; he obeys orders! There is
a model for you. There is a motto for you to learn. God has
given you an Emperor to think for you. Our friend here, with
only a President to fall back on, has perceived the truth that a
soldier must not think. He thinks at his peril. General," he
added in English, "you have given my army a lesson to-day which
they will never forget. It will give me pleasure to decorate you
with the Green Cockatoo, third class."

Sam began to stammer something.

"Oh, yes, I remember. Your Government does not allow you to
receive it. If that restriction is ever removed, let me be
informed," and the Emperor passed on, while Sam determined to
write to his uncle and have this miserable civilian law changed.
It so happened that there was a great dearth of news at this
time, and Cleary made the most of this episode. It did almost as
much to make General Jinks famous as anything that he had done
before, and he was widely advertised at home as the officer who
had astounded the Emperor by his wisdom and given a lesson to the
finest army in the world.

"Sam, your luck never gives out," said Cleary. "They'll
make you a major-general, I expect, now."

"I should rather like to have the thanks of Congress,"
answered Sam, as if that were a mere bagatelle. This
conversation occurred in a restaurant. A young officer was
sitting alone at the next table, and he gave his order to the
waiter in a high, penetrating voice.

"Bless my soul! if that isn't Clark," cried Cleary. "See,
he's a second lieutenant still. Let's ask him over to our table."

"Go ahead," said Sam, "but don't say anything about East Point."

Cleary invited him over as a fellow countryman, and the three men dined together, never once saying anything to denote that they had met before. Whether Clark noticed that Cleary was rather persistent in offering him the red pepper for every course, it was impossible to determine.

It was generally supposed that the Emperor had done all that could be done in Porsslania, but those who believed this, knew little of the resources of the first soldier of Christendom. Even Count von Balderdash was ignorant of the card which his master had determined to play in view of all mankind.

"Balderdash," said he one night, as the poor count sat trying to repress his yawns and longing for bed,--"Balderdash, we have shown the heathen here what we can do. We have exacted vengeance from them. Now I wish to show to the civilized world, and especially to their armies here, that we have the best army, the best discipline, the greatest power on earth, and the bravest Christians in our ranks. I have not told you yet what I propose to do, but the time has come to go ahead with it. In our vessel, the Eagle, which we brought with us, there are confined thirty persons convicted at home of the frightful crime of lese-majesty, a crime which shows that the criminal is atheistic, anarchistic, and unfit to live. I had them selected among those who have near relations here in the army. They all have either sons, brothers, or fathers enlisted here. Of course at home our wretched parliamentary system would make it inadvisable to have them executed. Here there is no such difficulty. You have often heard me at the annual swearing in of recruits tell them that they are now my children and must do what I say, even if I should order them to shoot down their own parents. I wish to show the world that this is so, and that my soldiers believe it and will act upon it. Such an army will inspire terror indeed. Most of the prisoners are men, but I have included among them two or three of the most abandoned women, who have been imprisoned for criticizing my sacred person. You approve of my plan?"

"I approve of all that Your Majesty ever suggests."

"Of course it makes no difference whether you do or not, but I wish you to have the prisoners brought ashore. You must seek out their relatives among the troops, but do not let them know why. Then fix the execution for some day next week, and have a general parade of all the troops on that occasion.

The Emperor's secret was well kept, and, except that a special parade was to be held, no one knew what the object was. A glittering array of soldiers met the war-lord's eyes when he entered the public square where the army was drawn up. In pursuance of his orders the enlisted men who were related to the prisoners were alined in front of the center with a captain in command of them. The Emperor directed his horse to the spot and addressed the whole army, applying his remarks particularly, however, to the detail immediately before him.

"My children," said he, "when you took the oath of allegiance as my soldiers you became members of my family, and it

became your solemn duty to do my bidding, whatever that bidding
might be. My word became for you the Word of God. You gave your
consciences into my keeping, knowing that God had commissioned me
to relieve you of that responsibility. From that moment it was
your aim to become perfect soldiers, with your minds and
consciences deposited in my hands for safe-keeping. From that
day forth you no longer had minds nor consciences--your whole
duty was summed up in the obligation to obey orders. That is the
soldier's only duty. And I know, my children, that you are
perfect soldiers and that you stand ever ready to do that duty.
Soldiers in other armies may occasionally forget their calling
and indulge in the forbidden fruits of reason and conscience, but
the Tutonian soldier never! We all know this. For us no proof
is necessary. But I wish to demonstrate the fact to the world.
I have brought over with me across the sea certain of your
relations who have been guilty of the unparalleled crime of
lese-majesty. I have determined that they deserve death, and
that you shall carry out the execution. I have so arranged it
that each of the condemned shall be shot by his nearest relation,
be it father, son, or brother. You will show the world that you
are ready, nay, proud to carry out these my commands. I
congratulate you on being selected for this noble and patriotic
task. You are now before the footlights at the center of the
world's stage. Remember that the eyes of all mankind are upon
you and that you are my children. Field-marshal, carry out my
orders!"

Count von Balderdash gave some orders in an undertone; the
troops opened on the left, and disclosed a row of prisoners,
including several women, standing bound and blindfolded against a
wall, each one at a distance of several yards from his neighbor.
The captain ordered the detail into position, gave the necessary
orders to load, aim, and fire, and the condemned men and women
fell to the ground, each one pierced by the bullet of his or her
near relation.

The great concourse, composed largely of soldiers of the
various foreign armies (for most of them had now been withdrawn
from the Capital and Gin-Sin), looked on with wonder at this
spectacle. Sam, who was standing with the inventor Cope, scanned
the faces of the executioners with care, and was unable to detect
the slightest sign of emotion in them. They had not been
prepared in the least for the ordeal; they did not even know that
their relations had been brought from home, and yet they did
their duty as soldiers without changing the stolid expression of
their faces.

"Wonderful, wonderful!" he said to Cope. "These are indeed
perfect soldiers. Why, they move like clockwork, like marvelous
machines. And what a remarkable man the Emperor is--without
question the first soldier of his time and of all time. Was
there ever anything like it?"

"Never," answered the inventor.

Sam walked back to his lodgings alone. He wished to think,
and purposely avoided company. He did not notice the soldiers in
the streets, nor the natives in their round, pointed straw hats.

He ran into a man carrying water in two buckets hung from the ends of a pole balanced on his shoulders, and nearly upset his load. He started back and collided with a native woman with a baby tied to her back. When he reached his house, he sat down in an easy-chair in his bedroom and thought and thought and thought. For some hours his mind was filled with unmixed admiration for the Emperor and his army. He felt like an artist who had just seen a new masterpiece that surpassed all the achievements of the ages, or a musician who had listened to a new symphony that summed up and transcended all that had every gone before. Again and again he pictured to himself the great war-lord in his helmet and white plume, explaining so eloquently and admirably the duties of a soldier, and then his soldiers obeying his orders as if their service were a religion to them, as indeed it was. It grew dark, but Sam did not heed the darkness. Dinner-time came and went, but he was in a region far above such vulgar bodily needs.

"Oh, if we only had an emperor," he thought,--"and such an emperor! Why was I not born a Tutonian?"

This was an unpatriotic thought, and Sam was ashamed of it. Yet it was true, he would gladly have found himself one of His Majesty's subjects and a member of his incomparable army. Then he recalled his memorable interview with the Emperor, and rejoiced in the remembrance that he had deserved and received his commendation. He tried to imagine how it would feel to be one of his officers, or even one of his privates. If he had been selected as one of the squad to show the perfection of their discipline, how gladly he would have taken his place in line with the rest! He would have obeyed without flinching, he was sure of it. He put himself in the place of one of the squad. He is ordered to take his position opposite one of the condemned. He looks and sees that it is his Uncle George. Would he obey the order to shoot? Most certainly. The musket goes off and his uncle falls. He goes through the list of his friends and relations. He does not quite like to shoot the girls, but he does it. It is his duty. His commander-in-chief, who represents his Creator, has ordered it. He can rely implicitly on his wisdom. Then he thinks of Cleary. Yes, he would shoot Cleary down without hesitation. And then comes the turn of his father and mother. He has no trouble with the former, for he is sure that his father as a man must understand his feelings, and he sees a smile of approval on his face as he, too, falls prostrate. With his mother it is more difficult. There had not been much sympathy between them in recent years, yet he recalled his early boyhood on the farm, and it went against him to aim his piece at her. But after all it was his duty, and with an inaudible sigh he pulled the trigger. It was done. No one could have noticed his reluctance. It was quite likely that some of the soldiers that afternoon felt as much compunction as that. But as Sam went over all this long list of tests and passed them successfully, he felt, almost unconsciously, that he was coming to a precipice. His sense of happiness had left him, and he began to dread the end of his cogitations. There was a trial in

store that he was afraid of facing. In order to postpone it he
went over all his friends and relations again, and added mere
acquaintances to the list. He busied himself in this way for an
hour or two, but at last the final question forced itself upon
him and insisted upon an answer. Would he be willing to shoot
Marian under orders? It was with misgivings that he began to
imagine this episode. As before, he marched to his place and
lifted his rifle to aim. He sees before him the figure which had
been haunting his dreams ever since he left East Point. She is
bound; a handkerchief is tied over her eyes, but he sees the
mouth and longs to kiss it. He has a strong impulse to run
forward and throw his arms around her. The command "Fire!" is
given, but--he does not shoot. He can not. He has disobeyed
orders! He, the man whose one aim in life has been to become a
perfect soldier, who only just now was considering himself fit to
be a soldier of the war-lord, had disobeyed orders; he had shown
himself a mutineer, a deserter, a traitor; he had lost his
patriotism and loyalty; he had dishonored the flag; he had
trampled under foot all the gods that he had worshiped now for
many years. He had flatly broken the only code of morals that he
knew--he was a coward, a hypocrite, a mere civilian, masquerading
in the uniform of an officer! Sam buried his face in his hands
and the tears trickled down through his fingers. Then he sprang
up and walked to an fro for a long time. At last he took
Marian's photograph from his pocket and put it on his
dressing-table. He must be a man. He must hold true to his
faith. He screwed up his courage and went through the forms of
the afternoon in his room dimly lighted by lanterns in the
street. He stood up in the line before the Emperor, and again
listened to his inspiring speech. Now he felt sure that he would
not fail. He placed himself opposite the photograph when the
order was given. He raised an imaginary gun and aimed with
assurance--but just then his eye fell upon the face which he
could barely distinguish. He saw Marian again as she had been
when he bade her farewell. True, she was as much a believer in
the military scheme of life as he was, but he knew by instinct
that she would draw the line somewhere. She was not created to
be a martyr to her faith. The order "Fire!" came, but Sam,
instead of obeying, threw down his musket and ran forward, seized
the photograph and kissed it. He looked up, half expecting to
see a crowd of spectators eying him with derision. He cast
himself upon his bed with his clothes on and tossed about for a
long time, until at last sleep came to his relief.

When he awoke in the morning the sun had long been up. In
the first moments of waking and before he opened his eyes, he
could not recall what it was that was troubling him. Suddenly
the whole situation came back to him, tenfold clearer than
before. He saw at once beyond all possibility of contradiction
that he could not shoot Marian, no matter who ordered him to do
it; that for him the ideal of a perfect soldier was altogether
unattainable, and that he was obliged to admit to himself that
his entire life was a failure. The public might praise and

acclaim him, but he was essentially a fraud and could never secure his own approval.

CHAPTER XIV

Home Again

When Sam got up and began to undress to take his bath, his head swam so that he was obliged to lie down again. He tried again two or three times, but always with the same result, and finally he rang for a servant and sent for an army surgeon. The doctor came at once, took his temperature with a thermometer, and, after examining him, pronounced that he had a bad attack of fever, probably typhoid. He advised him to go to the hospital, and before noon Sam found himself comfortably installed in a hospital bed, screened off by a movable partition from a ward of fever patients. The doctor's surmise proved to be correct, and for weeks he was dangerously ill, much of the time being delirious. He suffered once or twice also from relapses, and showed very little recuperative force when the fever finally left him. Meanwhile he was very low-spirited. The idea preyed upon his mind that he was no soldier and could never be one, and he felt that the resulting depression had a great deal to do with his protracted illness. Cleary was assiduous in his attentions, but, intimate as they were, Sam could never bring himself to confess his culpable weakness to him. As he became convalescent he had other visitors, and among them Mr. Cope, the inventor of explosives and artillery.

"I am at work at a great invention which I shall owe partly to you and partly to the Emperor," said he on one occasion. "Do you remember that at that execution the Emperor said that the perfect soldier has no conscience or reason?" Sam winced. "And then you called my attention to the fact that the men performed their part like machines. That set me thinking. I am always on the lookout for suggestions, and there was one ready-made. Do you see? Why shouldn't a machine be made to take the place of a soldier? A great idea, isn't it? Now you see we've already done something in that line. A torpedo is simply an iron soldier that swims under water and needs no breath, and does as he is told. Think how absurd it is in battle to have a field-battery come up under fire at a gallop! They swing round, unlimber, load, and fire, then harness again, swing round again, and off they are. Meanwhile perhaps half the men and horses have been killed. Wouldn't it be better to have the whole battery a machine, instead of only the guns? The general could stay behind out of range, as he does to-day, and direct the whole thing with an electric battery and a telescope. It is not a difficult matter when you once accept the principle, and the principle can be extended to cavalry and infantry just as well. It will be a great thing for the nations that are best at mechanics, and that means you and us."

"I don't see," said Sam, "now you can get on without the courage of brave men."

376

"Courage! Why, what is more courageous than a piece of steel? It wouldn't be easy to frighten it. And it is just so with all soldierly qualities. Do you want obedience? What is more obedient than a machine? I suppose you admit that a human soldier may disobey orders sometimes."

"Perhaps," said Sam, blushing uneasily.

"You may be sure that a steel soldier won't unless he is disabled, and a human soldier may be disabled too. Then the Emperor said a soldier should not reason. There's no danger of a steel soldier trying that.

"'Theirs not to reason why,
    Theirs but to do and die.'

Why, the Light Brigade at Balaklava won't be in it with them. And it's just the same with regard to conscience. A piece of steel has no conscience. What we want is a machine soldier. A soldier must be obedient, and he must be without fear, conscience, or a mind of his own. In all these respects a machine can surpass a man. Why, you yourself, in praising those Tutonian soldiers, said that they went like clockwork. That's the highest military praise possible."

Sam was much disturbed by this conversation. Mr. Cope went on to tell how his Government had spent 23,000 to fire a single shot and test one of his new projectiles, but Sam was not interested. Then the inventor began to rally him about the lack of interest of soldiers in the inventions which they used.

"If you had had to depend on yourselves for inventions," he said, "you would still be fighting with cross-bows, or perhaps more likely with your teeth and finger-nails. No soldier ever invented anything. We inventors are the real military men."

At last Sam's unconscious tormentor took his departure, and the invalid rang for the hospital orderly so that he might tell him not to let him in again. To his surprise a new orderly appeared, a negro whose face was strangely familiar.

"What is it, sah?" he said.

"Is that you, Mose?" cried Sam. "Why, it's almost as good as being at home again."

"Bress my soul, Massa Jinks--I mean General, have you been a-hurtin' yourself again?" and the man chuckled to himself till his whole body shook. Under Mose's care Sam made more rapid progress and soon was able to go out in a sedan-chair, borne by three men, like a mandarin. The winter passed away and spring was about to set in. There was no prospect of active service in Porsslania, the Powers being unable to agree upon any policy. The Emperor had already gone home, and the various armies were much reduced in strength. Cleary had been ordered to return by his newspaper, and had taken passage in a passenger steamer for the first of May.

"Why can't you come with me?" he said to Sam. "You're entitled to a leave of absence, and when you get to Whoppington you can apply for some other berth."

Sam followed this wise advice and obtained a furlough of three months, and on the day fixed for sailing they embarked for home.

377

Sam was still an invalid, but the voyage did him a great
deal of good, and before they had been a week at sea he began to
look quite like his old self. There were few passengers who
interested him, but he became acquainted with one man of note, a
Porsslanese literatus, who was attached to the legation at
Whoppington, and sat on the other side of the captain of the
steamer at meals. This gentleman, who bore the name of Chung Tu,
was greatly interested in military matters and listened to Sam's
accounts by the hour. The night before their arrival at St.
Kisco, the regular dinner was, as usual, converted into a
banquet, and a band was improvised for the occasion. At the
close of dinner the martial hymns of all nations were played,
ending with "Yankee Doodle." It was impossible to resist the
impulse to laugh as this national jig brought up the rear, and
Sam was much displeased that the foreigners on board, and there
were many, should have laughed at his country. When he went up
on deck he found Cleary conversing with Chung Tu, and he placed
his steamer-chair beside theirs and joined the conversation.

"It's a great pity," said he, "that we have such a national
air as 'Yankee Doodle.' It holds us up to ridicule."

"Do you think so?" answered Chung Tu, who spoke English
perfectly. "That depends upon the point of view. You see you
take the military point of view. We Porsslanese are not a
military nation. We do not think much of armies. We do not try
to spread our territory by force, and we never encroach on our
neighbors' land, altho we are really overcrowded. Perhaps that
is the reason people dislike us. We are not much of an empire
either. We have very little central authority, and only a
handful of officials. We have free speech, and even the Emperor
can be freely criticized without fear. We have no conscription,
and no one need carry a passport, as they have to in some
countries. We are almost a democracy. We have no exclusive
hereditary rank. Any one may become a mandarin if he learns
enough to deserve it. We only wanted to be left alone without
armies, and we did not want to buy guns and ships. That is all.
We are almost a democracy, and that is the reason that I have
always studied your history with care. I have studied your state
papers and your hymns. I have made a special study of them, and
I have come to the opposite conclusion from you as to 'Yankee
Doodle.' It seems to me to be the work of a great poet and
prophet."

"What do you mean?" asked Sam.

"Let us consider it seriously," said Chung Tu. "Have you a
copy of it?"

"No," said Sam, laughing.

"Then please repeat it for us, and I will right it down."

Sam began to recite, but he found it difficult to keep his
face straight:

> "'Yankee Doodle went to town,
> Riding on a pony.
> He stuck a feather in his crown
> And called him macaroni.'"

378

"That is not my version," said the attaché, pulling a piece
of paper from the pocket of his silk jacket. "Here is mine," and
he read it solemnly and with emphasis:
              "'Yankee Doodle came to town,
               A-riding on a pony.
               He stuck a feather in his cap
               And called it macaroni.'"
Which reading is correct?" he asked of Cleary.
    "I'm sure I don't know," said Cleary, laughing.
    "How careless you are of your country's literature! In
Porsslania we would carefully guard the sayings of our ancestors
and preserve them from alteration. You have what you call the
'higher criticism.' You should direct it to the correction of
this most important poem. I have studied the matter as carefully
and accurately as a foreigner can, and I am satisfied that my
version is the most authentic. Come now, let us study it. Take
the first two lines:
              'Yankee Doodle came to town,
               A-riding on a pony.'
There is nothing difficult in that. You may say that the name is
a strange one, and I admit that 'Doodle' is a curious surname,
but 'Yang Kee' is a perfectly reasonable one from a Porsslanese
point of view, and leads me to suppose that the wisdom contained
in this poem came originally from our wise men. Perhaps the name
is put there as an indication of the fact. However, let us
accept the name. The hero came to town riding on a pony. That
was a very sensible thing to do. Remember that those lines were
written long before the discovery of railways or tram-cars or
bicycles or automobiles. You may say that he might have taken a
carriage or one of your buggies, but you forget that the roads
were exceedingly bad in those days, as bad as our roads near the
Imperial City, and it would have been dangerous perhaps to
attempt they journey in a vehicle of any kind. In riding to town
on a pony, then, he was acting like a rational man. But let us
read the rest of the verse:
              "'He stuck a feather in his cap
               And called it macaroni.'
For some reason or other which is not revealed, he puts a feather
in his cap, and immediately he begins to act irrationally and to
use language so absurd that the reading itself has become
doubtful. What is the meaning of this? A man whose conduct has
always been reasonable and unexceptionable, suddenly adopts the
language of a lunatic. What does it mean? You have sung this
verse for a century and more, and you have never taken the
trouble to seek for the meaning."
    Sam and Cleary did not attempt to defend their neglect.
    "It is clear to me," proceeded the philosopher, "it is very
clear to me that it is an allegory. What is the feather which he
puts in his cap? It is the most conspicuous feature of the
military uniform, the plume, the pompon, which marks all kinds of
military dress-hats. When he speaks of his hero as having
assumed the feather, he means that he has donned the uniform of a
soldier. He has come to town, in other words, to enlist. Then

379

behold the transformation! He begins at once to act
irrationally. The whole epic paints in never-fading colors the
disastrous effect upon the intellect of putting on
soldier-clothes. You will pardon me, my friends, if I speak thus
plainly, but I must open to you the hidden wisdom of your own
country."

Sam smiled. The idea of taking offense at any nonsense
which an ignorant pagan should say was quite beneath him.

"But that is not all. The style of the language and of the
music is most noteworthy. It is highly comical, and its object
evidently is to provoke a laugh, and at dinner this evening we
saw that its object was attained. All the other martial hymns to
which we listened were grave, ponderous compositions from which
the element of humor was rigidly excluded. It was left for the
author of 'Yang Kee' to uncover the ludicrous character of
militarism--he has virtually committed your nation to it. He was
a genius of marvelous insight. He saw clearly then what but few
of your fellow citizens are even now aware of, that there is
nothing more comical than a soldier. I am convinced that he was
a Porsslanese who had the good fortune to sow in your literature
the seed of truth. You think that as a nation you have a sense
of humor. I have studied your humorous literature. You laugh at
mothers-in-law and messenger-boys and domestic servants, and many
other objects which are altogether serious and have no element of
humor in them, and at the same time you are blind to the most
absurd of spectacles, the man who dresses up in feathers and gold
lace and thinks it is honorable to do nothing for years but wait
for a pretext to kill somebody," and Chung Tu leaned back in his
chair and smiled.

"It is we who have the sense of humor," he added. "When our
common people laughed at the Emperor in his uniforms, they showed
the same sound sense that appears in 'Yang Kee.' I thank you, my
dear friends, for listening to me so kindly and without anger,
but I hope to preach these ideas to your people, and as I take my
text from your national hymn, they must listen to me. Then there
is another common expression among you which shows, as so many
proverbs do, the fundamental truth. When a story is incredible
you say 'Tell that to the marines,' signifying that only a marine
would be stupid enough to believe it. Now what is a marine? As
the Anglian poet says, he is 'soldier and sailor too,' in other
words, he epitomizes the army and navy. It is the military man
who is foolish enough to believe anything and who keeps alive the
most absurd superstitions and customs. The ancient Greeks cast a
side-light on this truth, for their word for private soldier was
'idiot.' And on account of this strange stupidity of soldiers,
things that would be disgraceful in private life become glorious
in war. Their one virtue is obedience, unqualified by any of the
balancing virtues, and they wear liveries to show that they are
servile. And then the foolish things they try to do! You are
familiar with the Peace Conference--generals and admirals
spending weeks in uniform with swords at their sides to determine
how to stop fighting, as if there were anything to do but to
stop! I believe they had the grace to turn the war pictures in

380

the conference room to the wall. But fancy sending butchers to a
conference in the interests of vegetarianism! Of course nothing
was done or could be done there. And tne Emperor in nis uniform,
drunk with militarism, wanted us--all our nation--wanted me--to
kow-tow before him as if he were a god! But he did not get what
he wanted from us. His own people may grovel before him, but we
will not. Oh, these soldiers, these soldiers! You look down on
your hangmen and butchers. We look down on our men-butchers, the
soldiers, in the same way. We have soldiers just as you have
police, but it is a low calling with us, and most people would be
ashamed to have a soldier in the family. Pardon me, my dear
sirs. Perhaps I have spoken too plainly. I mean nothing
personal, but when I think of these wars, I can not control my
tongue. Good-night."

So saying, the attaché gathered up his robes and went below.
"Queer chap," said Sam. "He must be crazy."
"We've treated them rather badly, tho," said Cleary. "I'm
glad Taffy hasn't had any executions, but our minister and all
the rest have been insisting on executions of their big people,
and no one talks of executing any of ours, altho they have
suffered ten times as much as we have."
"You forget how the affair began," said Sam. "Suppose the
Porsslanese had sent us missionaries to teach us their religion,
and these missionaries had gradually got possession of land and
also some local power of governing, and then we had ruthlessly
murdered some of them and they had seized all our ports for the
purpose of benefiting us, do you suppose that we would have risen
like those miserable Fencers and massacred anybody? It is
inconceivable. They have the strangest aversion to foreigners
too."
"Some of them haven't," said Clearly. "Cnung Tu is a
friendly old soul, if he is cracked. He says he believes the
Powers have been turned loose on his country to punish them for
having invented gunpowder. He laughs at Cope's inventions. He
says his people set the fashion, and then wisely stopped when
they found that such inventions did more harm than good. I think
they have a right to complain of us. Why, there's one of our
soldiers in the steerage with seventeen of their pigtails with
the scalps still fastened to them as trophies! Old Chung says
our ribbons and decorations are the equivalent of the scalps
dangling at a savage's belt. I didn't tell him we had the
genuine article. But, come, you had better turn in. You'll have
a hard day to-morrow. I've advertised your coming for all I was
worth, and if they don't give you a send-off at St. Kisco, it
isn't my fault. I'm glad you're well enough to stand it."
"I'm not as well as I look," said Sam. "I've lost all my
nerve. I'm even worrying a little about all my loot in those
cases in the hold. It sometimes seems that I oughtn't to have
taken it."
"What!" cried Cleary. "Well, you are getting squeamish!
After all the fellows you've killed or had killed, I shouldn't
mind an ornament or two."

"Killing is a soldier's main business," said Sam. "Oh, well, I suppose looting is, too. I won't think anything more about it. Good-night."

While Sam and his friend were conversing on deck, another conversation which was to have a portentous effect upon the former's destiny was taking place in the upper corridor of the Peckham Young Ladies' Seminary at St. Kisco.

"He's perfectly lovely," said a young lady, standing barefoot before her door in her night-dress to a group of young ladies similarly attired. "I've got his photograph. And I'm not just going to stand still and see him pass. It's all very well to have the school drawn up in line on the wharf--that's better than nothing--but I want something more, and I'm going to have it."

"What will you do, Sally?" they all cried.

"I'm going to kiss him--there!" said she.

"Oh, Sally!"

"Yes, I will too."

"I believe she will if she says so," said one of the girls. "She won't stop at anything. Well, Sally Watson, if you kiss him, I will to."

"And I!" And I!" exclaimed the others; but at that moment a step was heard on the stairs, and the Peckham young ladies sought their beds and pretended very hard to be asleep, altho their hearts were thumping against their ribs at the mere thought of their daring resolution.

It was ten o'clock the next morning that the steamer came alongside the wharf. The city was in gala dress and flags waved everywhere. The day was observed almost as a holiday, and many schools permitted their pupils to take part in the procession which awaited the arrival of Captain Jinks, as Sam was now commonly known in his native land. A reception was arranged for him at the City Hall, and the Mayor came down to the steamer in a carriage with four horses to escort him thither. From the deck Sam could see a banner stretched across the street, on which was an inscription to the "Hero of San Diego, the Subduer of the Moritos, the Capturer of Gomaldo, the Conqueror of the Great White Temple, and the Friend and Instructor of the Emperor." A few months before, Sam would have enjoyed this display without alloy, but now his health was really shattered, and in the bottom of his heart he felt that he was unworthy of it all, for he was not the perfect soldier he had believed he was, and under his uniform beat the heart of a vulgar civilian. His military instincts had their limit; his obedience could only be relied upon under certain circumstanes. He was a mere amateur, and had no claim to rank as a military hero at all.

A swarm of reporters settled down upon General Jinks as soon as they could get on board, insisting upon having his opinion as to the growth of the city since he had seen it, the superiority of its climate to that of any part of the world, and the beauty of its women. Sam answered all these questions satisfactorily, and surrendered himself to the committee of citizens who had come on deck to welcome him. His luggage was passed without delay by

the Custom House officials, and he was conducted down the wharf
toward the carriage which awaited him. With true chivalry young
ladies' schools had been given the best positions on the wharf,
and Sam soon found himself passing through the double row of
pretty girls. He could hear such remarks as this:
"Isn't he good-looking!"
"What a lovely uniform!"
"Hasn't he got a fascinating limp!"
"How pale he is!"
"He does look just like a hero."
Sam flushed slightly at these comments, but suddenly, before
he had time to collect his thoughts, a slight form sprang forward
from the left and an inviting face presented itself to his, and
with the words, "May I, please?" a hearty kiss was planted on his
lips. Sam had no time to decline, if he had wished to. A murmur
of surprise and delight arose from the crowd, and in another
moment another damsel rushed upon him, and then another and
another. Before long he was the center of a throng of elbowing
young ladies of all kinds, fair, plain, and indifferent, all bent
upon giving him a kiss. Sam had indeed lost his nerve; for the
first time in his life he capitulated absolutely and let the
attacking party work its sweet will. It was with great
difficulty that he was rescued by the reception committee and
finally seated next to the Mayor in the landau.
"What a lot of cab-drivers you have there on the wharf!"
said Sam to the Mayor, after their first greetings. "I never saw
so many. Hear them crying out to the passengers coming ashore!"
"They're not cab-drivers," he answered. "They're pension
agents. They're not crying 'Want a cab?' but 'Want a pension?'"
"So they are," said Sam. "What is that tune the young
ladies are beginning to sing?"
"Don't you know?" said the Mayor, laughing. "It's 'Captain
Jinks.' You'll know it well enough before you are here long.
Listen."
Sam listened and heard sung for the first time lines that
were to be imprinted upon his tympanum until they became a
torture:

> "I'm Captain Jinks of the Cubapines,
> The pink of human war-machines,
> Who teaches emperors, kings, and queens
> The way to run an army."

The news of the kissing reached the City Hall before the
procession, and when he alighted there Sam had to kiss an immense
number of women who were determined not to be outdone by their
sisters at the wharf, while the whole crowd sang "Captain Jinks"
in a frenzy of enthusiasm. The reception accorded to Sam at
St. Kisco was so elaborate, and the arrangements made to do him
honor were so extended, that he was obliged to stay there for
several days. Meanwhile the news of his arrival and of his
gallantry in kissing his countrywomen, young and old, spread all
over the land and took hold of the popular imagination.

383

Invitations to visit various cities on his way across the
Continent began to come in, and everywhere Sam was acclaimed as
the hero and idol of the people.
"It's great, it's great, old man!" cried Cleary. "Why, that
kissing business is worth a dozen victories! The people here say
that no general or admiral has had such a send-off in St. Kisco.
Look at to-day's papers! Thirteen places have petitioned to have
their post-offices named after you. There will be Jinksvilles
and Jinkstowns everywhere, and one is called Samjinks. Then
they're naming their babies after you like wildfire. Samuela is
becoming a common girl's name, and one chap has called his girl
Samjinksina. All the girls are practising the Jinks limp, too.
I saw one huge picture of you painted on the dead side of a
house. It was an ad. of the 'Captain Jinks 5-cent Cigar.'
That's the limit of a man's ambition, I should say. And now
they're beginning to nominate you for President. I'm going to
try to work that up. I'm sending a despatch to The Lyre this
morning. If they take it up, we can put it through. The
Republicrats hold their convention at St. Lewis next month, and
they've been looking around for a military candidate, and you're
just the thing. Every woman in the country will be for you.
They won't dare to put up a candidate against you. You'll just
have a walk-over. That song, 'Captain Jinks,' will do it alone.
Everybody is singing it."
"I thought I was too young," said Sam. "Isn't there an age
limit?"
"Not a bit of it. They abolished that when they amended the
Constitution and made the President's term six years, and made
him ineligible for reelection."
"I'd rather have a military position," said Sam. "I'd
rather be general of the army. But I've lost my nerve--I'm not
well; and perhaps it's just as well that I should take a civilian
position."
"Civilian position! Nonsense! The President is
commander-in-chief of the army and navy, and the marines, too,
for that matter."
"But he hasn't a uniform," said Sam sorrowfully. "And as for
all this kissing, I'm sick of it. It tires me to death, and I
don't know what Marian will think of it. I've written to explain
that I can't help it, but she will see the reports first in the
papers and she may not like it at all."
"Oh, she's a sensible woman," said Cleary. "She will
understand a political and military necessity. She won't mind."

CHAPTER XV
Politics

But Marian did mind, and for once Cleary was mistaken. She
was delighted at the prominence which Sam had achieved, and saw
him mentioned as a candidate for President with pride and
gratification, but she did not see how that excused his
promiscuous osculation of the female population of the country,
and she determined that it should cease. She wrote to him

frequently and decidedly on the subject, and he reported her
protests to Cleary, who absolutely refused to allow them.

"It won't do," said he, as they discussed the subject at a
hotel in a small city on their line of progress. "This kissing
is your strong point. The Lyre is backing you up on the strength
of it. So is the Benevolent Assimilation Trust, Limited. In
every city and town the girls have turned out, and you've
captured them hands down. If you stop now it will upset the
whole business. The Convention delegates are coming out for you
by the dozen. Our committee is working it up so that it will be
nearly unanimous. There won't be another serious candidate, and
I doubt if they put anybody up against you when you're
nominated. You're as good as President now, but you must go on
kissing. That's all there is of it."

Sam wrote to Marian rehearsing these arguments, and he got
Cleary to write too, but the letters had no effect. At last he
received a telegram from her announcing her intention of meeting
him at St. Lewis. She reached that city before him and was
present at the station when he arrived, altho he did not know it,
and from a good point of vantage she saw him kissing the young
ladies of that city by wholesale to an accompaniment of "Captain
Jinks." It was more than she could stand, and when she joined
her fiancé at the hotel the meeting was very different from the
one he had so often pictured to himself. It was a stormy scene,
intermixed with tender episodes, but she gave it as her ultimatum
that the kissing must cease forthwith, and, in order to give a
good reason for it, she insisted that they be married at once.
Sam was willing to take this course, and Cleary was called into
their counsels. At first he bitterly opposed the project, but
Marian's blandishments finally succeeded, and she gained him as
an ally. He was sent as an emissary to the campaign committee
and presented the case as strongly as he could for her. The
proposition really seemed most plausible. Could anything help
the chances of a candidate more than his marriage to a handsome
young woman? The committee had doubts on the subject and waited
in person on Miss Hunter, but she persuaded them as she had
persuaded Cleary, and furthermore convinced them that whether
they were persuaded or not the marriage would take place. Marian
determined to fix the hour for the next day. She pledged the
committee to secrecy, and no word of the proposed wedding got
into the papers. At noon a clergyman was called into the hotel,
and in Sam's private sittingroom the pair were married with
Cleary and a few of the members of the committee as witnesses.
Almost before the ceremony was over they could hear the newsboys
crying out the tidings of the event.

"It's out of the question to talk about a wedding-tour,"
said Sam, after the ceremony. "I can't walk in the streets alone
without being mobbed, and with Marian we could not keep the
clothes on our backs. Just hear them singing 'Captain Jinks'
now!"

"Mark my words, dear," said his wife. "You will see when we
get the papers tomorrow with the news of our marriage, that it

has made you more popular than ever. Now send out word to the reports that you will not do any more public kissing."

In obedience to these orders Cleary, acting as go-between, conveyed the information as gently as he could to the representatives of the press, that as a married man General Jinks expected to be spared the ordeal of embracing all the young ladies of the country.

No one was prepared for the striking effect which this news, coupled with that of the marriage, had upon the newspapers and their readers. The first papers which Sam and his wife saw on the following morning were those of St. Lewis. They expressed sorrow at the fact that Captain Jinks had taken such a resolution when only a handful of the fair women of St. Lewis had had the opportunity of saluting him. Were they less beautiful and attractive than the ladies of St. Kisco who had kissed him to their hearts' content? Marian was visibly annoyed when she saw these articles, but she advised her husband to wait till they received the papers from other cities. These journals came, but, alas! they went rapidly from bad to worse. The Eastern papers with scarcely an exception took up the strain of those of St. Lewis. Why did Captain Jinks discriminate against the women of the East? He had kissed the whole West. Probably he had also kissed all the women of the Cubapines and Porsslania. It was only the women of the East that he could not find heart to salute in the same way. Here was a hero indeed, who insulted one-half of his own nation! It might have been expected that the Western press would have come to Sam's support, but they did not. They accused him of gross deception in not announcing that he had been from the first engaged to be married. Their young women had been fraudulently induced to kiss lips which had already been monopolized, but which they had been led to believe to be as free as the air of heaven. Black indeed must be the soul of a man who could stoop to such deception! As the days went on the public became more excited and the attacks more ferocious. It was rumored that his fiancée had married him against his will, that she was a virago and a termagant. Would the country be contented to see the Executive Mansion ruled by petticoats, and by those of a hussy at that? What sort of a hero was the man who could be ordered about by a woman and could not call his soul his own? Then they began to overhaul his record. Was he really the hero of San Diego? Was it not the mistakes of Gomaldo which caused his defeat? Was it not true that the boasted subjugation of the Moritos was brought about by the superstitious fear of the savages inspired by the figures tattooed on the captain's body? And the capture of Gomaldo, was it anything but a green-goods game on a large scale? What, too, was the burning of the great White Temple but an act of vandalism? And as for the friendship and praise of the Emperor, who was the Emperor, anyway, but an effete product of an exhausted civilization? Then had not Captain Jinks opposed the promotion of men from the ranks? What sort of a democrat was this? Sam felt these thrusts keenly. He had had no idea of the fickleness of the people, and it was hard to believe that in a single day they had ceased to adore him and

begun to revile him; and yet such was the case. Marian was also
overcome with mortification, and she heaped reproaches upon him
for their forlorn condition. Cleary proved himself to be a
stanch friend.

"It's too bad, old man," he said. "It'll blow over, but
you'll have to withdraw a while for repairs. The bottom had
dropped out of your boom, and of course you can't be a candidate
for President. Let's go quietly home. I'll go along with you.
The Lyre has had to drop you for the time. Scribblers' has sent
back the first article I wrote for you, and they say your name
has lost its commercial value. I've seen Jonas. He's here to
make sure of a friendly candidate, and he says you're out of the
question. He's doing well, I tell you. I asked him how it paid
to run a war for half a million a day and get a trade in return
of a few millions a year? 'It's the people pay for the war and
we get the trade,' said he. He'd like to have you President to
help them along, but he says it won't be possible. It's a
shame. You'd have run so well, if--. Your platform of 'Old
Gory, the Army and Navy,' would have swept everything before it.
But never mind. We'll try it again some day. I suppose your
luck couldn't hold out forever."

"Thanks, my dear Cleary," said Sam, grasping his hand.
"You've been a true friend. I don't think it makes much
difference. I am a sick man, and I must go home as soon as I
can."

CHAPTER XVI

The End

Sam was indeed a sick man, and the journey to the East
proved to be a severe strain upon him. Cleary saw that it would
be unwise to let him travel alone with his wife, and accordingly
he accompanied him to Slowburgh, which was on the way to
Homeville. They arrived in the afternoon, and Sam could hardly
walk to the carriage which awaited him. He was put to bed as
soon as he reached his uncle's house, and on the advice of his
uncle's doctor they sent at once to the county town for a trained
nurse to take charge of him, for it was out of the question for
him to travel farther. There was no train which Cleary could
conveniently take that evening to the metropolis, and he accepted
the urgent invitation of Congressman Jinks to spend the night.
It so happened that it was a gala day for Slowburgh. Four of her
soldier sons had returned a few days before from Porsslania and
the Cubapines, and this day had been set aside for a great
celebration and a mass-meeting at the Methodist church to welcome
them. The procession was to take place early in the evening, and
after supper Cleary went out alone to watch the proceedings,
leaving his friend to the care of his relatives. He took his
place on the curbstone of the principal street and was soon
conversing with his neighbors on each side, one of whom was our
old friend, Mr. Reddy, and the other the young insurance agent
whose acquaintance Sam had made at the hotel.

387

"It's going to be a great show," said the former. "I wish I was spry enough to parade too. It's going to be splendid, but it won't come up to the time we had when I came back from the war. They've kept them four boys drunk three days for nothing, but we was drunk a month."

"They've sobered them down for this evening, I believe," said the young man.

"They've done their best," said Reddy, "and I think they'll go through with it all right. It's a great time for them, but they'll have their pension days all the rest of their lives to remind them of it, four times a year."

"Who are going to take part in the procession?" asked Cleary.

"They're going to have all the military companies and patriotic societies of these parts," answered Reddy, "and then the firemen too of course; but they won't amount to much, for most of them are in the societies, and they'd rather turn out in them."

"What societies are there?" said Cleary.

"Oh, there's the Grandsons of the Revolution and the Genuine Grandsons of the Revolution, and the Daughters of Revolutionary Camp-Followers and the Genuine Daughters, and then the Male Descendants of Second Cousins of Heroes, and the Genuine Male Descendants, and the Connections by Marriage of Colonial Tax-Collectors, and then the Genuine Connections, and a lot of others I can't remember."

"The names seem to go in pairs," said Cleary.

"Well, you see, they always have a fight about something in these military societies, and then they split, and the party that splits away always takes the same name and puts 'Genuine' in front of it. That's the way it is."

"I suppose these societies do a lot of good, don't they?" asked Cleary. "These splits and quarrels remind me of the army. They must spread the military spirit among the people."

"Yes, they do," said the young man. "It's what they call esprit de corps. If fighting is military, they fight and no mistake, and the women fight more than the men. I don't know how many lawsuits they've had. Half of them won't speak to the other half. But they're all united on one thing, I can tell you, and that is in wanting to put down the Cubapinos."

"That they are," cried Reddy. "That's why they call 'em 'Patriotic Societies.' It was our ancestors as fought for freedom that they made the societies for. Our ancestors were patriotic and fought for freedom oncet, and now we're going to be patriotic and stick by the government just like they did."

"Yes, they fought for freedom, that's true. And what are the Cubapinos fighting for?" asked the young man.

"Oh, shucks!" cried Reddy. "I ain't a-going to argher with you. What were we talking about? Oh, yes. We were saying that them societies fight together. They do fight a good deal, that's a fact, and there's no end of trouble in our militia battalion too. They all want to be captain, and they don't get on somehow as well as the fire companies. But still it's a fine thing to see all this military spirit. I didn't see a uniform for years,

and now you can't hire a man to dig a ditch who hasn't got a
stripe on one leg of his trousers at any rate. Girls like
soldiers, I tell you, and they like pensions too. I've just got
married myself. My wife is seventeen. Now I've drawed my
pension for nearly forty years, and she'll draw it for sixty more
if she has any luck; that'll make over a hundred. That's
something like. Why, if one of these fellows is twenty now and
marries a girl of seventeen when he's ninety, and she lives till
she's ninety, they can keep drawing money for a hundred and fifty
years, and no mistake. It's better than a savings bank. Here
they come!"

The procession had formed round the corner at the other end
of the main street, and now the band began to play, and the
column could be seen advancing. First the band passed with an
escort of small boys running along in the gutter on either side.
Then came two carriages containing the heroes, two in each. They
held themselves stiffly and took off their hats, and no one would
have supposed that they had drunk too much if the fact had not
been universally understood by the public. Behind them came a
line of other carriages in which were seated the magnates of the
town, including the office-holders and the prominent business
men. They all had that self-important air which is inseparable
from such shows and which denotes that the individual is feeling
either like a great man or a fool. Then came the militia
battalion, a rather shamefaced lot of young men who seemed to be
painfully aware that they were not at all real heroes like the
soldiers in the carriages, but merely make-believe imitations.
The patriotic societies followed, genuine and non-genuine,
resplendent in "insignia," sashes, and badges.

"There's my wife, she's a G.C.M.C.T.C.," said Reddy proudly,
pointing out a very plain young woman with gold spectacles. "And
here come the Genuine Ancesters of Future Veterans. See that old
woman there on the other side? She made all the fuss. You see
when anybody wants to get into a society and finds they can't get
in they go off and start another. And some people that hadn't
any tax collectors or connections or anything, they just got up
the 'Ancestors of Future Veterans,' and everybody in town wanted
to get into that. And old Miss Blunt there, she wanted to come
in too, and she's over seventy, and they said she couldn't be an
ancestor nohow, and she said she could and she would, and they
voted forty-one to forty against her, and the forty went off and
founded the Genuine Ancestors, and they're twice as big as the
other now. Hear 'em applaud?"

The old lady walked along with a martial tread, and was
loudly cheered as she passed.

"Now we'd better get into the church if we want seats," said
the young man, and Cleary followed him, leaving the ancient
warrior behind. The church was very crowded and very hot, and
Cleary had to sit on a step of the platform, but it was an
exhibition of patriotism worth beholding. The band played with
great gusto, and the whole audience was at the highest pitch of
excitement. The chairman made an address, and Josh Thatcher
responded in a few words for himself and his three companions.

389

Then flowers were presented to them, and a little girl recited the "Charge of the Light Brigade," but the main feature of the program was the oration of Dr. Taylor, the pastor of the church. He was famed as an orator not only in his denomination and in the county but in the National Order of Total Abstinence, of which he was a leading light. In his address he welcomed the four heroes back to their hearths and firesides. He thanked them for having conquered so many lands and spread the blessings of civilization and Christianity to the ends of the earth.

"We have been told, my friends, by wicked and unpatriotic scoffers, that these wars have stirred up the passions of our people, that there are more lynchings and deeds of violence than ever before, and that negro soldiers returning from the war have shot down citizens from car-windows. I have even been told that its effect is to be seen in the attempts of worthy citizens, including a distinguished judge, to have the whipping-post reestablished in our midst. I can only say for myself that such traitors and traducers should be the first victims of the whipping-post. (Cheers.) So far from crime having increased since the departure of these young heroes, I can testify that there has been a marked decrease in our community. Since they left, not a single barn has been burned, not a chicken stolen. My friend, Mrs. Crane, informs me that she keeps more chickens than ever before, and that she has not missed one in over a year. I am also told that during the absence of these young men the amount of liquor drunk in our town has sensibly diminished. The war then has been a blessing to us and to our nation."

During these remarks Josh Thatcher, who was sitting in the front row, gave sundry digs in the ribs to his cousin Tom, and they both laughed aloud.

"We welcome our heroes back," continued the orator. "We open our arms to them. All that we have is theirs. We applaud their manly courage and Christian self-sacrifice. We shall never, never forget their services, and we shall recite their noble deeds to our children and to our children's children."

The meeting broke up with three cheers and a tiger for each of the four heroes. For an hour later the crowds stood in the street talking over the great events of the day, each of the young veterans forming the center of an admiring group, Tom Thatcher being surrounded by a bevy of pretty girls who seemed to find nothing objectionable in his pimpled face and hoarse voice. Cleary stood for a long time watching them and talking with the insurance man.

"It's their night," said the latter, "but it won't last long. We know them too well. When the barns begin to burn again, folks'll all know what it means. I wish they'd keep a war going a long way off forever for these fellows. It would be a good riddance. And that's all talk of old Taylor's anyway. He won't take them to his heart, not by a great deal. I heard Dave Black ask him for a job to-day, and he wants a man too, and he said, 'What--an ex-soldier? Not much!' The words were out of his mouth before he knew what he'd said. He's a slick one."

When Cleary returned to Mr. Jinks' house, he found Sam much worse, and the gravest fears were entertained as to his recovery. In the morning he was a little easier, and Cleary was able to have a little talk with him before he left. Sam had been told by the doctor that his condition was serious, and he had no desire to get well.

"You must brace up, old man," said Cleary cheerily. "I'll come back in a few days and we'll lay out our plans for the future. You're the finest soldier that ever lived, and I haven't done with you yet."

"Don't say that, don't say that!" cried Sam. "I'm no soldier at all. I wanted to be a perfect soldier, and I can't. It's that that's breaking my heart. I don't mind the nomination for President nor anything else in comparison. My poor wife! Why did I let her marry a coward like me? I can't tell you now, but if I'm alive when you come here again I'll tell you all."

"Nonsense, old man," said Cleary. "You've got the fever on you again. It's in your blood. When it gets out, you'll be all right."

It was with tears in his eyes that Cleary bade his friend good-by, for he could see that he was a very sick man. It was impossible, however, for him to remain longer, and as Sam's wife and cousin were there to nurse him, and his father and mother had been telegraphed for, he felt that there was no necessity for him to remain.

After the lapse of three weeks Cleary received the sad news that Sam had shown unmistakable signs of insanity and had been removed to an insane asylum. His father wrote that while his insanity was of a mild form, the doctors thought it best for him to be placed in an institution where he could receive the most scientific treatment. Six months later Cleary, who was now one of the editors of the Lyre, went on a sad pilgrimage to see his friend. The asylum was several hours away from the metropolis beyond East Point, and was none other than the great building which they had described to the chief of the Moritos. Cleary took a carriage at the station and drove to his destination, and at last arrived at the huge edifice in the midst of its wide domain. He went into the reception-room and explained his errand. After a while a young doctor came to him, and told him that he could have an interview with Captain Jinks at once, and offered to act as his guide. It was a long walk through corridors and passages and up winding stairs to Sam's apartment, and Cleary questioned the doctor as they went.

"Captain Jinks is a dear fellow," said the doctor in response to his inquiries. "We are all fond of him. At first he was a little intractable and denied our right to direct him, but now that we've got it all down on a military basis, he will do anything we tell him. I believe he would walk out of the window if I ordered him too. But I have to put on a military coat to make him obey. We keep one on purpose. As soon as he sees it on anybody he's as obedient as a child. He's such a perfect gentleman, too. It's a very sad case. Here's his room."

The doctor knocked.

"Who goes there?" cried a husky voice, which Cleary hardly recognized as Sam's.

"A friend," answered the doctor.

"Advance, friend, and give the countersign," said the same voice.

"Old Gory!" cried the doctor, with most unmilitary emphasis, and he opened the door and they entered.

Cleary saw what seemed to be the shadow of Sam, pale, haggard, and emaciated, sitting in a shabby undress uniform before a large deal table. Upon the table was a most elaborate arrangement of books and blocks of wood, apparently representing fortifications, which were manned by a dilapidated set of lead soldiers--the earliest treasures of Sam's boyhood, which had been sent to him from home at his request. Sam did not lift his eyes from the table, and moved the men about with his hand as if he were playing a game of chess.

"Here is a friend of yours to see you, Captain," said the doctor.

Sam slowly raised his head and looked at Cleary for some time without recognizing him. Gradually a faint smile made its appearance.

"I know you," he said in the same strained voice. "I know you. You're----"

"Cleary," said Cleary.

"Cleary? Cleary? Let me see. Why, to be sure, you're Cleary." And he rose from his chair unsteadily and took the hand that Cleary offered him.

"How are you, old man? I'm so glad to see you again," said Cleary.

"And so am I," said Sam, who now seemed to be almost his old self again. "Sit down."

Cleary drew up a chair to the table, while the doctor retired and shut the door.

"How are you getting on?" said Cleary. "You're going to get well soon, aren't you?"

"I am well now," said Sam. "I was awfully ill, I know that, but it all came from my mind. I think I told you that. My heart was breaking because I couldn't be a perfect soldier. I had to face the question and grapple with it. It was an awful experience; I can't bear to speak of it or even think of it. But I won. I'm a perfect soldier now! I can do anything with my men here, and I will obey any order I receive, I don't care what it is."

As he spoke of his experience a pained expression came over his face, but he looked proud and almost happy when he announced the result of the conflict.

"They say I'm a lunatic, I know they do," he continued, looking round to see that no one else was present, and lowering his voice to a whisper. "They say I'm a lunatic, but I'm not. When they say I'm a lunatic they mean I'm a perfect soldier--a complete soldier. And they call those fine fellows lead soldiers! Lunatics and lead soldiers indeed! Well, suppose we are! I tell you an army of lead soldiers with a lunatic at the

392

head would be the best army in the world. We do what we're told, and we're not afraid of anything."

Sam stopped talking at this juncture and went on for some time in silence maneuvering his troops. Finally he picked up the colonel with the white plume, and a ray of light from the afternoon sun fell upon it, and he held it before him, gazing upon it entranced. The door opened, and the doctor entered.

"I fear you must go now, Mr. Cleary. He can't stand much excitement. He's quiet now. Just come out with me without saying anything," and Cleary followed him out of the room, while Sam sat motionless with his eyes fixed on his talisman.

"He sits like that for hours," said the doctor. "It's a kind of hypnotism, I think, which we don't quite understand yet. I am writing up the case for The Medical Gazette. It's a peculiar kind of insanity, this preoccupation with uniforms and soldiers, and the readiness to do anything a man in regimentals tells him to."

"It's rather more common, perhaps, out of asylums than in them," muttered Cleary, but the doctor did not hear him. "Do you think he will ever recover, doctor?" he continued.

The doctor shook his head ominously.

"And will he live to old age in this condition?"

"He might, if there were nothing else the matter with him, but there is, and perhaps it's a fortunate thing. He's got a new disease called filariasis, a sort of low fever that he picked up in the Cubapines or Porsslania. There's a good deal of it among the soldiers who have come back. We have a lot of lunatics from the army here and several of them have this new fever too. It wouldn't kill him alone either, but the two things together will surely carry him off. He will hardly live another half-year."

"I suppose his family is looking out for him?" said Cleary.

"His mother visits him pretty regularly, and his father comes sometimes," said the doctor, "but I think his wife has only been here twice. And she's living at East Point, too, only an hour or two away. She's a born flirt, and I think she's tired of him. I'm told that one of this year's graduates there, a fellow named Saunders, is paying attention to her, and when the poor captain dies, I doubt if she remains long a widow."

"Then I suppose there is nothing I can do for the dear old chap?" asked Cleary, with tears in his eyes, as he took his leave of the doctor at the door of the building.

"Nothing at all, my dear sir. He has everything he wants, and in fact he wants nothing but his lead soldiers. He won't even let us give him a new set of them. And he has all the liberty he wants on the grounds here, and he can walk or even take a drive if he wishes to, for he is perfectly harmless."

"Perfectly harmless!" repeated Cleary to himself, as he got into his carriage. "What an idea! A perfectly harmless soldier!"

THE END

3. RAYMOND L. BRIDGMAN
EXTRACTS FROM LOYAL TRAITORS

A Story of Friendship for the Filipinos

"Fear not them that kill the body and after that
have no more that they can do "

Farewell, adored fatherland! Our Eden lost, farewell!
 Farewell, O sun's loved region, pearl of the Eastern sea!
Gladly I die for thy dear sake: yea, thou knowest well
Were my sad life more radiant far than mortal tongue could tell,
 Yet would I give it gladly, joyously for thee.

On bloodstained fields of battle, fast-locked in madd'ning strife,
 Thy sons have dying blest thee, untouched by doubt or fear.
No matter wreaths of laurel; no mater where our life
Ebbs out, on scaffold, or in combat, or under torturer's knife,
 We welcome Death, if for our hearths, or for our country dear

--Dr. José Rizal[1]
(Written just before he was executed)

Not long before the time for landing he asked to have
Wheelwright visit him, and when he came said that he wished to
have a talk with him.

"What is it about, Douglass?" asked Wheelwright;--"the topic
we have discussed before?"

"Yes, but in a more practical way. Since I've been lying
here I've been thinking a great deal about what I ought to do for
the Filipinos. I know how you feel about what we are doing to
them. Now, I have just been pretty near death, Mr. Wheelwright,
and things seem different to me from what they ever did before.
It seems to me as if it does not make so much difference how soon
I die, provided I do some good in the world. Suppose I stay here
on this boat and work as long as I live, or do something else of
the same sort? What does it amount to? My mother was a slave,
and I know something of the wrongs of our race. I know that her
body was all covered with scars from the terrible bites of the
bloodhounds which pursued her when she tried to run away to
freedom. I know what the Emancipation Proclamation meant to the
Negro race. I believe that I have some idea of what freedom and
liberty and duty mean. Now we are trying to conquer the
Filipinos. As nearly as I can understand it, they have just as
much right to their freedom as we have to ours. If the black
people have a right to their liberty, if there is such a thing as
human rights anyway, I don't see why the Filipinos have not a
right to themselves. We can't get any right to them by buying
them or by conquering them. But I am ashamed to say that there
are two regiments of Negroes in the United States army who have
gone over to help the white men conquer these brown men, killing
them because they are fighting for their liberty and independence.
Perhaps I may be wrong, but I believe I am right, and it seems to
me that my duty calls me to go over and fight with the Filipinos
and help them to get their independence."

Wheelwright had sat in silence during this rather long
speech of his companion, but in his heart, with every word, there
had been growing a great, burning admiration for the black man
lying before him. Douglass was one of the most intelligent
Negroes Wheelwright had ever met, and by patient study had freed
himself from many of the crudenesses of his race and was in fact
a student and thinker of no mean proportions.

"You know how I feel about the policy of our government,
Douglass," said Wheelwright, after a moment. "You know that I
believe practically as you do in the matter. But what makes you
think that it would be right for you to go over there and fight
against our own soldiers?"

"Mr. Wheelwright, we are doing wrong to them, and somebody
must pay the penalty of it. The Filipinos are right, and no man
can make it right for us to kill them for defending their native
land. I believe I can help them. It would encourage them if
only one American, and he even a black man, came out to help
them. I could stand the climate. I could learn their language.
I could help them in a great many ways. I am going to get well
from this hurt, and it seems to me as if my life could not be
spent better than in helping these much abused people to their

liberty and their rights. I am ready to die for them, if necessary. My life could not be spent better."

"Now, Douglass," said Wheelwright, "let me tell you that this idea of yours is one not wholly foreign to myself. The same question has come up in my mind: if I believe that the Filipinos are right, why should I not help them? If our government is striking down the rights of men, why should not I, as a free man and bound to do my duty to uphold the cause of freedom, oppose my country by every means in my power? That is the question which comes up to me frequently. I much more than half believe that you are right in your wish--in your purpose to go to them."

"Think it over more, Mr. Wheelwright. Perhaps you will come to think altogether as I do, and we will go out together."

"Certainly I will think it over; and I want you to see my friend George Brown, one of the very best men there are in Boston, and talk over your plan with him. Perhaps he will approve it. Or, perhaps he will convince you that it is your duty to stay here and do what you can to get your fellow black men to stand up for the cause of the Filipinos in this country, and so help to change the purpose of the Republican party and of the Administration. If you are to go, he will be able to help you on your way to the Philippines. At any rate, I want you to meet him, for what he says will be well worth hearing."

As soon as possible after the boat reached Boston, Wheelwright arranged a meeting for Brown, Douglass, and himself; a meeting which was of the highest personal consequences to each of them and which might prove to have national significance.

CHAPTER XI

Brown, Douglass, and Wheelwright enter the Filipino Service

The meeting was in Brown's office, one evening, when they would be in no danger of callers. Thus they could discuss the great question of patriotic duty without interruption.

"What better place in Boston could there be for a talk on justice and international loyalty?" remarked Douglass, with the quick sentiment of his race. "As I turned in from the street I noticed that this is the Equitable Building!"

"Yes," said Brown, "these offices were my father's before me. It was the name of the building that drew him to it. And in fact, the word well characterizes his life, his idea in the practice of his profession, and his highest ambition for his son. May his son never disappoint him!"

Wheelwright had already told Brown about Douglass's purpose, and had added that he himself was so deeply impressed by the soundness and unselfishness of Douglass's views that the question had been forced upon him whether he ought not to accompany the black man into the service of the Filipino Republic.

At Brown's request Douglass again went over the principal reasons by which he had come to his conclusion. He stated again his belief that his life ought to be spent in positive service to the cause of human liberty as a personal and race tribute and

requital to the memory of Abraham Lincoln, whose Proclamation
freed his mother, and to the spirit of human liberty which makes
all men free under government of the people, by the people, and
for the people; a government which cannot tolerate colonies, and
in which there must be the harmonious assimilation of all the
people who share the government. He set forth his conviction
that duty to country may involve a higher standard than support
of any Administration; that it may at times demand armed
resistance to an Administration, in order to preserve the true
spirit and forms of liberty; the danger to the United States if
it should permanently adopt the policy of conquest; his positive
belief that the Filipinos were thoroughly right in their moral
and political position, and that the United States was without
legal or moral justification for its war against them. These and
other arguments involving his personal duty to help the weaker
party fighting for its rights against the nation of which he was
a part, and to whose unjust course he seemed to become a party
unless he made this personal protest, he set forth intelligently
and with enthusiasm.
    The disclosures made a deep impression upon the mind of
George Brown. Sympathizing as he did, completely, in Douglass's
opposition to the Philippine policy of the Administration, and
sharing his horror of the awful and inhuman means by which the
United States sought to crush the brave patriots into subjection,
demanding unconditional surrender on penalty of death before any
assurance whatever would be given regarding their status under
the government of the United States, Brown nevertheless had not
yet thought of carrying his opposition to the point of personally
helping the Filipinos in arms against the United States forces.
But the more he thought about it, the more he realized the
strength of Douglass' position, and he knew enough of human
nature and of the terrible course of human history to realize
that sometimes only the utmost personal sacrifice is equal to an
emergency.
    Brown had no doubt of the moral soundness of Douglass's
argument. He recognized that there is a higher allegiance than
to the government or to the nation of which one is a citizen.
First of all he put personal loyalty to his Maker, with all the
right and justice which are inherent in infinite perfection, and
saw through the fallacy of those who say that it is treason to
oppose "the Administration." But he wanted further time in which
to consider the matter; and so, after an hour's further
conversation, they postponed any conclusion until the following
evening.

    "Brown," said Wheelwright, twenty-four hours later, when
they resumed their discussion of the pressing personal question;
"the more I think of this matter, the clearer I am about it. I
believe that Douglass is right and that I shall go out with him."
    "Don't let us influence you against your judgment and
ꞁnscience, Mr. Brown," said Douglass. "But I don't see how we
    do differently. I have made up my mind, and I am ready to be
    ꞁiced for liberty and for the Republic of the United States,

398

if necessary, even if I am found fighting against its present mistaken and ruinous policy."

"My good friend," replied Brown, "I shall try to follow my conscience and my judgment at all times. I only want to be sure that I am right; to be certain that I can stand before the bar of God and say that I have done the best I could, no matter what my fellow-men may think of me and no matter what the consequences may be to myself. If duty demands that I fight against the Administration, I shall not hesitate."

"How can you come to any other conclusion than ours?" asked Wheelwright, with sudden friendly vehemence.

"I cannot!" replied Brown. "I cannot, as I see the facts and my duty. We three men are without ties which hold us here by any plausible pretense of duty stronger than the call of duty to go to the aid of the Filipinos. I have come to the conclusion that I ought to go with you."

"Thank the Lord!" ejaculated Douglass.

"God bless you," said Wheelwright.

"And after all, it is no sudden fancy," replied Brown, "nor any spasm of conscience. Since you were here last night, I have gone over this matter most carefully; but you know that I have been in full accord with you on the main question all the time, and for a long period. We have no moral right to the Philippine Islands, and, ultimately, moral rights must decide this contest. It makes no difference whatever as to the standing of the case in international law. We must do right to the Filipinos as men equal with us in the human race. International law is only the recognition by the Great Powers of accomplished facts, as far as national existence is concerned. Because Spain was recognized as the owner of the Philippines, that gave her no moral right over the people there. And even if she once had a right, the Filipinos had thrown off their yoke. The accident that international law, moving at a snail's pace, had not kept up with the accomplished facts does not alter the facts. The United States could not buy a title from Spain, because Spain did not own the islands. She had been ousted by the Filipinos, by force, from every place but Manila, and a Filipino Republic had been established with working Constitution and full authority of law."

"The Administration might argue that the United States owns the Philippines by conquest," interposed Wheelwright.

"The United States cannot claim the Philippines by conquest," replied the lawyer, "because a war of conquest has no possible moral ground to rest on. We cannot justify our course 'because it will be for the good of mankind,' for there is no possible moral ground for conquering people, slaughtering them incidentally by tens of thousands, in order to spread civilization. We cannot justify our course on the ground that our motives are good, for the rights of the Filipinos to self-government, so long as they are not the enemies of mankind, are not in the slightest degree dependent upon our intentions toward them. I may have good intentions toward a beggar in the street, but that does not justify me in killing him if he does not like to submit to my intentions."

399

"But the beggar in this case is unable to resist. There is where the Administration has the advantage."

"The Administration does not dare, and never will dare, to give the beggar a chance to be heard. It dare not appeal to reason or to justice. Furthermore, the policy is totally wrong and dangerous from the point of view of the peace and prosperity of the United States. If we keep the Philippines, we must admit them to a share in our government, or hold them as a colony forever. We cannot do the latter, for our government is not adapted to it, and we have no right to hold them in subjection. Assimilation on an equality, or complete national independence, are the only alternatives. But if we admit Filipinos to our Senate and House of Representatives on equal terms with the members from the present States, then we are no longer governed by ourselves; we are goverened to some extent by the Filipinos. They would vote upon questions affecting our entire policy regarding our present territory. In close questions, matters which concern the States would often be settled, very likely, by the Filipino contingent; and close votes are usual in progressive policies when new ideas are making their way against natural conservatism. The United States would thus be in part governed, I say, by the Filipinos, and the Philippine Islands would be in part governed by the Congress of the present States of the Union. Such an arrangement would bring endless wrongs and injustice. Each people ought to be independent of the other, and their right relation will be found only under a body of international law which recognizes the rights of the small and large nations equally."

"However you have reached your decision," said Wheelwright, "I am mightily glad you believe it is your duty to go."

"As to my duty," replied Brown, "it is clear that our government is totally wrong, on moral grounds and on grounds of policy. We ought to change our course. We are carrying out our mistaken policy through the blood of a people weaker than ourselves who are absolutely right by any standard of morals and human rights which is recognized in this Republic. That we may be true to the spirit of the United States, then, the question is what we ought to do. Our government at the present hour is hostile to the basic principles on which it stands. Our duty is first to God and his truth before it can be to any interpretation of men, no matter how largely they are in a majority and no matter how sincere may be their benevolent intentions."

"Then we must ----?"

The interrogation was begun, but in the intensity of his emotion Wheelwright was unable to finish.

"Yes," assented Brown, deliberately but with a painful tension of voice that spoke the secret hurt in his soul that such a course seemed necessary--that such a course seemed the only way open to a man who saw things as he saw them; "yes,--we must ꞁpose the government."

For fully a minute the three men sat in silence, looking at ꞁther. Not one of them stirred. A mail-wagon rattled out ꞁ driveway under the post-office opposite; the clock in

400

the high tower in the neighboring Square struck ten; even the sputtering of the electric light on the corner near-by was plainly audible.

Then Brown went on.

"We must oppose the government. Now, how can we best do this? Most of our fellow citizens who sympathize with us at all in this matter believe that they ought to work to change public opinion. That is vitally important and I will not criticise them. But it is also possible that we may do more by strengthening the Filipinos to hold out for their rights. If they can keep the field indefinitely, as the Boers promise to do, resisting by arms our effort to conquer them, it may help to bring our people to see their side of the case. They are now suffering and enduring death as bravely as did our Revolutionary forefathers. They have the right stuff in them for a nation. If they can hold on till a change in the Administration, our people may get over their land-hunger a trifle; they may see that the trade of China is not worth the blood of these men and the tears of these widows and orphans. Therefore, we are doing right to help the Filipinos prolong the contest."

"But many people might say," suggested Wheelwright, "that it would be wrong to help perpetuate needless slaughter."

"There is not a particle of force in any such argument as that," rejoined Brown. "These people have the right to determine in what manner they will fight for their liberties. If they believe that it is better to submit, and to agitate by peaceful means, then that is their privilege, though it can never make it right for us to force them to submit. But if they choose to die for their independence, that, too, is not only their privilege, but their right, and we cannot condemn them if they prefer death to loss of national independence. 'Liberty or death' is a true American motto, and no man who has a spark of sense or of appreciation of what true Americanism is, or of what true liberty is, can criticise a man for dying for his nation's cause, even if it seems absolutely hopeless. If they want to die rather than live, they have the right to make the choice, and, in dying, to inflict as much injury as possible upon their oppressors."

No one favored enough to see this group of three men and overhear their talk would have held for a moment that it was any light conversation in which they were engaged. They sat in painful earnestness, close to each other in their tremendous absorption in the great theme, drops of sweat on their faces. On the black skin of Douglass the perspiration, gleaming in the office lights, shone red.

"Now," added Brown, with intense force, "I believe that our duty to our country requires us to face death for the cause of the Filipinos, just as much as it required our fathers to face death for the Union in the Civil War. I have made up my mind! I am ready to go! I will go with you, and we will give our lives to the cause of human liberty and to maintaining the principles of the Republic of the United States,--to which I shall always be loyal, whether or not I fight under the national flag."

Thus the three patriots reached their decision.

401

As they rose from their seats, still gazing into each other's faces in the intensity of their holy purpose, the eyes of Brown and Wheelwright met in awe as they saw on the dark forehead of Douglass the perspiration shining in the reflected incandescent electric lights like a red dew of prophecy. Instinctively they felt that it was prophecy, and in the hearts of both there was a weight of woe for their comrade which mingled with the joy of their divine hope, yet which could not quench it.

And for themselves as well as for Douglass--! Were the chances not equal for all three?

As they were going down the stairs, Wheelwright, walking one step behind, laid his hand on Brown's shoulder. When he reached the foot he said:

"You spoke last night of your father, George. Of course you have thought of the stigma there will be upon your name,--a stigma in which he must share. In the eyes of the multitude our course is nothing less than that of-- is nothing less than enduring shame. I was going to say 'of traitors' but the word traitor sticks in my throat."

They stepped into Milk Street, and Brown waved his hand upward across the front of the building they had just left.

"You see this massive granit pile," he said. "In stateliness and strength my father's character is like unto it. He knows all--I have told him; and while he would prefer that I should remain in Boston--for he is old now, and if I go away we may never see each other again--he yet says I must be my own judge of duty. That the probable stigma will not cause him to blanch you will be confident when I tell you that, although he some time ago ceased to come to the office, he will in my absence return to these chambers and endeavor to hold my business together. How is that for a young old man of eighty? But what of yourself and the 'stigma,' and what of Douglass?"

"Bless your brotherly heart!" cried Douglass. "For me and for all my race what stigma can be added to the one condemning fact that we are black! In this great free land what have I to-day, and what have the seven millions of people like unto me? In the South, after nearly forty years of emancipation, we have still the Jim Crow car, the torch at our hearth-stone if we are prosperous, the quick execution without trial if we err; and in the North we have any position we can secure--if it be menial enough: the place of a deck-hand, of a janitor or bell-boy, of a coachman or waiter. Is there any stigma to be added? But with you the case is different, and you should consider the matter fully. In the eyes of your fellows and in the eyes of the law you will indeed be traitors, and no sticking of the word in Wheelwright's throat may prevent a noose from encircling it."

"I myself much prefer the word 'loyalist' to the word 'traitor,'" remarked Brown smiling. "And in truth to-day in this ˄nd only those like unto us are loyalists, for we are loyal to principles on which the nation was founded, while the ˄ty have forsaken those principles."

"Yes," said Wheelwright, "we are the loyalists! Yet, even if no physical harm come to us, will it be otherwise than with a sneer that the majority will affirm of us, 'Three "loyalists" against eighty millions of destructionists!'"

Brown answered simply:

"It must needs be that the sneer cometh, but woe is unto him from whom it comes--the woe of a pitiful ignorance of right, an ignorance none the less pitiful if unconscious, and doubly, nay, a hundred fold pitiful if it be perverse."

Walking up Milk Street arm in arm, the three men paused for a moment in front of the birthplace of Franklin,[2] the ambassador of freedom. In the flicker of the street lights the gilt bust of the great statesman and deprecator of war seemed to smile down upon them from its elevated niche. Reaching Washington Street, the walls and steeple of the Old South meeting-house echoed to their midnight tread as it had echoed to the tread of freedom-lovers in '76.

Their decision reached, the next course of the trio was to carry that decision, without delay, into action. No one of them required a long time for preparation. It was easy for Douglass and Wheelwright to sever their connection with the steamship company. Brown's legal business was to be in the hands of his father.

There was one most important matter for Brown, however, before he sailed for London. His love for Faith Fessenden still burned as brightly as it did when he had faced his fate before and made the worst of it; and he could not leave the country, perhaps never to return, without telling her why he went, doing what he could to justify his course to her, and, if possible, laying for himself some foundation for at least a bit of hope for the indefinite future. She had continued friendly and frank. They had occasionally talked over the Philippine question, for Brown was so intensely interested that he could not refrain from it, and he had always found in her a most willing listener.

"Do you really think that you ought to risk your life for the Filipinos," she now asked him, when he called to tell her of his purpose.

"It is not only for the Filipinos, but for my own country also," he answered. "Both causes focus in the same point, and patriotism compels me to go, just as much as does my sense of duty to the people whom our government is treating so unjustly. Americans must atone for the wrongs done by Americans, and those who are willing must suffer for those who are unwilling to go to that extreme."

"But why can you not work here to change public sentiment, and accomplish your purpose in that way?"

"Because that is not enough. Without help the poor Filipinos are likely to be crowded to the wall and lose all power of resistance. It is of the untmost consequence for them to preserve a form of government and the semblance of an army, no matter if the government must frequently change its seat in order to escape capture, nor if the army must run more than it fights. They must keep their boat's head to the wind."

"Well, George, I believe that men should do their duty to their country and to mankind. Our mothers in the Revolution and in the Civil War suffered much that the men might fight for country. But,--George, I shall be very, very sorry to have you go,"

"Why shall you be sorry, and not rather pleased, that one of your friends gives himself to his country and to mankind?"

"Because I can't help it!"

"I shall be sorrier than I can say, Faith, to go where I cannot see you or hear of you,--and possibly you might not be sorry to hear about me! I hope that sometime I shall come home leaving a Filipino Republic behind me!"

"I also hope so, George; and be sure that while you are there I shall do what I can here to promote the Filipino cause and the cause of true American principles, for I too believe that they are one!"

"I admire this spirit in you Faith. I did not expect you to go quite so far. More than ever I must ask you to let me tell you that I still feel toward you just as I have felt all the time! I can't go away without saying so. Don't blame me!"

"Oh, George, I am very sorry for you! Why don't you give me up!"

"Because I can't. You are my life. But I will not pain you. You are very good to think as you do about my going and I am glad you approve my purpose. Good-bye."

He took both her hands in his, and this time she did not withdraw them.

"Good-bye, George. I hope you will succeed, and surely I hope that you will come home safe and sound. I shall want very, very much to see you."

"Good-bye again."

"Good-bye."

The trip to London was without marked incident. Thence the three volunteers for the Filipino service went to Paris and made the acquaintance of Agonçillo, the Filipino representative there. They told him of their journey and convinced him of their sincerity and reliability. By Brown's suggestion, Agonçillo sent word at once to the Filipino Junta in Hong Kong, telling them of the little band. He also gave Brown and his friends information about the Filipinos in Hong Kong, where to find them, and how to get in communication with Manila.

In the outward passage by steam across the Indian Ocean and around to Hong Kong, the earnest trio were necessarily exposed to the perils of wind and wave; but on the whole it may be said that they experienced only the familiar and commonplace incidents of 'n easy voyage. During the trip Wheelwright utilized his Spanish the best possible degree in instructing Brown and Douglass in 'anguage which they must use in order to make their services 've in the Philippines.

On reaching Hong Kong they had no difficulty in finding the Junta. By general consent they remained there several weeks, perfecting their Spanish and acquiring especially the vocabulary most in use among the Filipinos, and developing their plans of assistance.

Brown's prominent contention was that, somehow or other, there must be kept up at least a nucleus of a Filipino government, with a military organization, about which the people might rally, to which they would be glad to contribute, and which as representative of the Filipino people could communicate with American officers, demanding recognition even if the Americans refused the recognition desired. Such a representative of national honor in arms and in government was needed as should be able to show that, even after years of trial, it had never been crushed out of existence.

So they learned and studied and planned. They ascertained also who would meet them in Manila, and whom they could depend upon in helping to raise the government to the highest possible activity and strength.

CHAPTER XII

In Which American Sacrifice Strives to Promote
Filipino Nationality

It was about New Year's, 1900, that the three companions set
foot on the Philippine islands at Manila. Their unselfish
purpose had decreased no whit--indeed, it had grown to more and
more as they came nearer and nearer to the land where purpose was
to be transformed into action. Their plans had now taken a
somewhat definite shape, conditioned upon the co-operation of the
Filipino leaders. Fully convinced that some form of Filipino
government must be maintained, and finding these views shared by
the Junta at Hong Kong, a path of immediate procedure was mapped
out. A member of the Junta had gone over on a preceding vessel
to prepare the Filipino leaders for their new American
supporters, and to give a general idea of what plans they might
present, though these involved no material departure from the
ideas already held by the most far-seeing patriots at Manila and
elsewhere on the islands.

Manila was reached without incident and no time was lost in
making the needless acquaintance of Americans there, either in
civil or military life . . .

Just then came the sharp report of a rifle in the forest, at
a little distance in the rear of the fortifications. In an
instant others and still others followed. Then came the running
forms of Filipinos who has been furthest from the camp in that
direction.

"Wheelwright, we are attacked," said Brown. "Get your men
in shape instantly."

Wheelwright stepped forward quickly toward the running men
and soon had them facing the attack, sheltering themselves behind
trees and making some show of returning the American fire. Brown
ran toward the main body of Filipinos, shouted to the commanding
officer that the Americans were on them, and ran back to the scene
of action. Douglass had been not far from Brown and Wheelwright
when the firing began and he hurried forward to give his support.

The Filipino officer ordered his men promptly into action,
and under cover of the trees they resisted the onset of the
Americans for a few minutes. Brown made his way near to
Wheelwright, and steadied him as he rallied the brave Filipinos
against the impetuous onset of the Americans, who showed equal
gallantry in action.

As they were blazing away from behind trees, making a heroic
resistance to the attack, Wheelwright noticed that Brown was not
effective as usual, and chaffed him about it.

"Brown, what is the matter with you? You don't seem to be
much but standing around."

"To tell the truth, Wheelwright, I don't feel like killing
this morning."

you are not doing it. I suppose it is that girl in

406

"In my heart, you mean."

"In your eyes, I believe, so you can't see the sights of your rifle."

"I'll see them when the fighting gets hotter, if it does. I don't call this much of a skirmish."

The firing became hotter, but Brown seemed to mind it very little, though he was on the alert and ready for any emergency. Right in the midst of a patter of bullets he called to his friend:

"Wheelwright."

"Well, crazy loon, what is it?"

"This is heaven."

"You'll be in heaven in good earnest, in the spirit, and your body on the ground with a hole in it, if you are not more careful; and the rest of us will be there, too, if we don't drive back these fellows. Fire away, Brown."

"Anything you say to help you, but there is no need of being worried. Take it easy and shoot straight. The little brown men are doing bravely."

"So they are, and you ought to give them a hand."

"All right, here goes."

And Brown blazed away toward the steadily advancing Americans.

"My God, captain, this is hell!" cried out a little Filipino, running back from his too close encounter with American rifles, where he had seen comrades falling around him and had got a puff or two close to his head.

"Little man, come here," said Brown firmly. "Step behind this tree. Load your rifle again. Steady, little fellow. We will give them a good turn yet."

The Filipino rallied, and was immediately facing toward the enemy, as brave as any on the other side.

But the American advance was too strong. They drove forward with a force. Brown was crowded back toward the fortification. Wheelwright was shot through the knee and put out of the fighting. Douglass and some of his Filipino supporters were separated from the main body. Soon the Americans caught sight of the machine gun which the Filipinos had not yet had opportunity to bring into action. Rushing forward, the attacking troops shot down the men who were trying to bring it to bear in the needed quarter, captured it, and scattered the nucleus of Filipinos who were vainly trying to protect this most important part of their fortification.

With this, the direct onslaught of the battle was over. The surprise by the Americans had been successful.

Douglass and the men with him were pursued and nearly surrounded. The American troops came near enough to distinguish, between the trees, that a Negro was leading the Filipinos, and cries of "Kill the black nigger!" rang through the forest.

Douglass fought coolly and determinedly--he was not fighting for himself, but for a great cause, and he needed and could afford calmness. The Filipinos kept close to him, sheltering themselves by the trees and firing with no bad skill upon their foes, while still the cry, "Kill the black nigger!" sprang with increasing menace from the lips of men infuriated as they saw their comrades now and then falling around them from the shots of the despised Filipinos who were Douglass's companions.

In the forest the retreating men had an advantage, and it seemed as if Douglass and the Filipinos with him were to escape from the American fire without further loss. Suddenly, however, they were obliged to cross an open space entirely void of cover. Immediately, they were exposed to their pursuers, and with a shout of triumph fire was again opened upon them.

Two Filipinos fell dead. Several of the party, Douglass himself among them, turning to face their foes, were wounded and dropped helpless to the ground. Devotion to the foreigner in their service instantly inspired some of Douglass's comrades, at the risk of their lives, to try to help the wounded man to cover, with the hope that he might be concealed in the undergrowth and escape with his life. This devotion meant death to several of the would-be rescuers. American fire quickly stretched upon the ground all but two of the little handful of self-sacrificing brown men, and these two then ran for the woods.

Hot with the combat and pursuit, the Americans rushed forward into the space where lay the wounded.

"Ho! ho! Here's that infernal nigger!" shouted one, as he came upon Douglass.

"Good enough for him, damn him! Can't we start a fire? Let's roast him!" exclaimed the next man who rushed up.

"Look here, you black devil," demanded a third, as a group wearing the uniform of the United States army now gathered around the prostrate man. "Who are you?"

"I am an American citizen" was Douglass's firm reply.

"That's all right! And you're a dirty nigger! You know what the white folks would do with you if they had you at home, and I guess nigger-ashes are just as good fertilizer in Luzon as they are in Mississippi. Come on, boys, rush him over to the bushes. Let's have some fun roasting the damned traitor."

"No! I say No! We won't be so low down as that," spoke up one who seemed to be looked up to by the others of the group. "Just finish him with your pig-stickers, or with a bullet, along with his Filipino 'friends' here. I won't consent to any roasting."

"Well, all right, old boy, if you say so. Bullet it is."

Then, turning to Douglass while his companions inhumanly dispatched the wounded Filipinos, the soldier cried out: "Come, coon! Short prayers! Your time's come! American niggers who fight for yellow Filipinos and against white American soldiers get no mercy here."

"My prayers were all said long ago," replied Douglass ꜟutly, without flinching, though with growing weakness from the ds which had first brought him down. Then suddenly his face ᵃnsfigured before them as by a great inspiration and --by an exalted sense of triumph and the coming of eternal "I never expected to see this glorious hour," he said. ꞏoes for the same cause as Abraham Lincoln's!"

408

"Hang Abe Lincoln!" was the soldier's reply, and a bullet from his rifle through the heart of Douglass sealed the martyrdom of the American patriot to the cause of human liberty.

Just as Douglass's slayer lowered his rifle, "Crack," came a report from the edge of the woods to which the two escaped Filipinos had fled, and the murderer fell dead in his tracks. The friends of Douglass were still trying to be true to him!

Once more the Americans took up the pursuit, while the nimble, fertile-minded, and faithful Filipinos made a circuit back to the field, recovered the martyred Negro's body, and bore it away to be specially honored by decent burial.

Such was the end of Washington Douglass, the child of a slave mother in a free land, a patriot who died to save the children of another free land from oppression. And died not in vain. There are those yet alive in the island of Luzon who never hear his name without a deep throb of gratitude, who tell his deeds to their children, and who while they live will never forget the zeal of this martyrdom for their cause.

On the main field of battle the wounded Wheelwright had been left in the hands of the Americans. Brown, with the surviving Filipinos, retreated further into the forest until the Americans ceased to follow. It was an unfortunate day for the patriots, and the loss of their stronghold was a disaster to their prestige. The consequences, moreover, to both of the white Americans who were fighting on the side of the Filipinos were little short of being as serious as to Douglass and the others who had fallen under the American fire, and who went to make up the total, as stated in the official report, of 118 Filipinos killed and eleven wounded.

EXPLANATORY NOTES

[1]José Rizal (1861-1896), Philippine patriot, physician, and man of letters whose whole life was devoted to the achievement of an end to Spanish oppression. He founded the Liga Filipina on July 3, 1892, and his two novels inspired the Filipinos to fight for freedom. From 1892 until shortly before his execution by the Spaniards for treason at Bagumbayan, Manila on December 30, 1896, Dr. Rizal lived in exile.

[2]Benjamin Franklin (1706-1790), printer, author, inventor, statesman, diplomat, and scientist, was born in Milk Street, Boston on January 17, 1706.

INDEX

413

413

Schurz, Carl, 170
Seeger, William Tully, 105-06
Senator North, xiv, xlvi
Shafter, William R., 53, 181
Shaw, Robert Gould, xvi-xvii, 11
Sho-Gun, The, lx
Sinclair, Upton, xliii, lxiv
Single tax, xxiii-xxiv
Slave narratives, 252
Smith, Judson S., 209, 210, 212, 215-17
Social Democratic Party, xvi
Socialist Labor Party, xvi
Socialists, xvi, xxiv
Spanish-American War, xxvii-xxviii, xxix, xxx, xxxii, xxxiii, xxxvii, xliii, xlvi, 53, 183
Spirit of the Service, The, xlvi
Spoon River Anthology, lvi
Springfield Republican, xv
Stanley, Henry, xxxix
Stedman, Edmund, xviii
Steffens, Lincoln, xiv
Stephens, Leslie, lxii
"Stories of Benevolent Assimilation," xxviii-xxix, 119-69
Stratemeyer, Edward, xlvii, lxv
"Stupendous Procession, The," xxxvii-xxxviii
Sultan of Sulu, The, lx
Sumner, Charles, 86-88
Swords of Ploughshares, xxvi, liii-liv, 63-78

"Take up the Black Man's Burden," 112-13
Taylor, Howard S., 106-07
"Them Fillerpeans," 97-98
"Thirteen Sonnets," 83-87
Tolstoy, Leo, xxiv, lxiv, liii
Tompkins, C. Berkeley, lvix
"To My Missionary Critics," xxxvii, 209-11
Toombs, Robert Augustus, 104, 108
"To Our Betrayed Allies," 82

"To the Person Sitting in Darkness," xxxiii-xxxv, lxii, 195-207
Treason, anti-imperialists accused of, lx-lxii
"Treason, Folly, and Cowardice," 103-04
Treaty of Paris, xxx
Twain, Mark, xiv, xxxvii, xxvii-xliii, 195-250
Twichell, Joseph, xxxix, xxxii

United States-Filipino War, xxxiv-xxxv, xxxvii, xxxix, xliii, li-liv, 101-02, 223-32
United States imperialism, lv
"United States of Lyncherdom, The," xxxvii
United States Philippine Commission, 55

Valley Forge, 108
Villard, Oswald Garrison, xviii
"Voices of Three, The," 94-95

Wallace, William, 116
"War and Hell," 63-71
Warner, Charles Dudley, xiv
"War Prayer, The," lxiii
Washington, George, 103, 108, 191, 223-24, 225-26, 231, 252
Washington Anti-Imperialist League, xxxv
"Water-cure," xxxix, 231
Welch, Richard E., Jr., lxii
Weyler y Nicolau Valeriano, xxii, 54
"What Would Lincoln Say?" 106-07
"White Man's Burden," xxiii-xxiv, lviv, 73-74, 112-13
Whitman, Walt, xxvi, li, 102
Whittier, John Greenleaf, xxxii, 11
Wilcox, Ella Wheeler, xv-xvi, lvii
Winslow, Erving, xxxv
Women, discrimination against, 109-10

415